God, Our Righteousness

By
Fidelis A. Olafusi, Kss

ii

Acknowledgement

Thanks to God who in His mysterious ways has made great provision for man, using various means.

The contribution of my daughter, Dr Pauline Olukemi Akinrinola, MD ("Doctor A"), herself a pediatrician, pastor, author and entrepreneur, to the production and publication of this book cannot be overstated. It would be due recognition to say that without her assistance and that of her publishing outfit, Lighthousebooks.com this work might not have seen the light of day. Such was the extent to which she facilitated the project. It pleased God to bless me mightily through her and her brothers.

I owe an incredible debt of gratitude to the following faith support groups – The Catholic Community in the Lagos Archdiocese –St. Jude Catholic Church Mafoluku and St. John the evangelist Catholic church Shogunle; Our Lady of Loreto, Catholic Parish, Foxfiled and Ave Maria, Parker, both in the Archdiocese of Deriver, Colorado (USA);to the Liturgy of Hours, the United States Conference of Catholic Bishops(usccb.org) and indeed, the electronic resource house, Laudate, for their inexhaustible resources.

What can I say other than 'thank you!' to the 'You Version' electronic free Bible resources platform – (perhaps over a score different versions are on their portal). I am equally grateful to the Bible Gateway for access to its similar resources on their free e-platform. Please you all have become honorary partners of this work, thank you.

Special thanks go to my spiritual mentors – His Eminence, Cardinal Olubunmi Okogie, Emeritus Archbishop of Lagos Archdiocese; and his successor, His Grace Most Revd. Alfred Adewale-Martins, Rev Fathers. Patrick Laffey (SMA) (late); Justus Pokrzewinski (OP), Nick Ugwu (OP), A. Abiodun Ademoye (OP), Rev. Father Edward, Father David Blue-Jacket, Father Al Leur (RIP) of the Presentation Ministry, Ohio;

Lay Colleagues in the Association of Papal Knights and Medalists, the Association of Sacred Heart of Jesus and Immaculate Heart of Mary, the Lagos Archdiocesan Laity council, St. Patrick's society, St. Augustine's society, the Divine Mercy Apostolate, the Catholic men organization, etc. Surely, there are many more names deserving to be mentioned but for space constraint. I owe a debt of gratitude, to you all. I am grateful also to Late Pa. Makinde, Mr. Augustine Olaniyan and wife, Augustina; Sir Iwuchukwu, Kcss, Messrs Louis Nwanze, Bernard Okonkwo, Raphael Ajakaiye, Lucky Okiya.

With deep respect, I acknowledge the contribution of the field Marshals in Pentecostal evangelism in Nigeria – Pastor Adejare Adeboye of the Redeemed Christian Church of God (RCCG), Archbishop Okonkwo of the Redeemed Christian Mission (TREM), Rev. Dr Kumuyi of the Deeper Life Bible Ministry, the Apostolic Church, the Christ Apostolic Church, Methodist Church, Baptist Church, Anglican Church (Nigerian Communion), Dr. Abriara, Pastor Oshofa's The Celestial Church of Christ, Pastor Wilson Badejo of the Four Square Christian Church,

Rev Dr. Ezekiel, Rev Dr. Olukoya of the Mountain of Fire Ministries, Dr Oyedepo's Living Church Ministries, Pastor Chris Oyakhilome's Christ Embassy, The Seventh Day Adventist Mission, The Salvation Army, The Church of the Lord (Aladura), Faith Tabernacle, Prophet extraordinary and solace for the afflicted (of blessed memory) Temitope Joshua of The Synagogue Church of all Nations.

I respect your assiduity. Don't rest on your oars; "let them be one." It can start from your indefatigable self or from your church or from us here in Nigeria, May God's will be done!

It is my hope that this work will prove to be the needed impetus for all to cooperate more than ever before not least in our profession of the faith but in much more.

Thanks to my secretarial staff: Mrs Toyin Musa, Miss Maryam Olarewaju, Miss Adejoke Adesanwo, Mr Olamilekan Adeleye, Miss Miskiyah Idris, among others. Thank you all.
God, Our Righteousness (Jer 33:15 NKJV)

Dedication

To the One who is able to keep us from stumbling and to present us unblemished and exultant in the presence of His glory; to the only God, our Saviour through Jesus Christ, our Lord.
Be glory, praise, worship, obedience, thanksgiving and love for ever and ever. Amen.
To the Universal Church – that you may emerge united, docile to the Lord and a refuge of last resort against the Anti-Christ.

Contents

Preface

How do we pass through this big, wide world successfully and fulfilled? And how do we handle our interactions with fellow creatures in a way that fulfils our expectation of justice and fairness?

"More tortuous than anything else is the human heart, beyond remedy; who can understand it?" (Jer 17: 9 NABRE)

God, our righteousness (Jer 33: 15 NKJV)

All understanding as to what is right or wrong comes wholly from the Lord, the Creator of our earth with its array of plant-, animal- and human life. That this creation has endured for so long is a tribute to the unfailing wisdom with which it had been created.

Culture, freedom and Christianity

We may have grown used to our system of government and justice dispensation, perhaps enthusing in it as dependable, and thinking that it has fared so well without tying it to the apron strings of religion, or bringing God into it, and, therefore, that it might as well stay that way. History, however, sees the matter differently:

"With the collapse of the Roman Empire, Christianity became the standard bearer of Western civilization."

"Intellectual life, dominated by the Roman Catholic Church culminated in … scholasticism…" (which preceded the Renaissance Age.)

Columbia Electronic Encyclopaedia © 2013 by Farlex

"The only force capable of providing a basis for social unity was the Roman Catholic Church."

"Christian values pervaded scholarship and literature…"

Encyclopaedia Britannica Western culture owes a lot to Christianity. After the fall of the West Roman Empire, Europe became one huge church state randomly referred to as

1

Christendom, jointly administered by the Church (the sacerdotium) and the secular princes (the imperium). Our democracy and the freedom we enjoy today took their modern root from that period.

People feel this way out of religious antipathy or aloofness.

Undeniably, there are disturbing issues associated with the practice of religion: people feel unease with the religious chauvinists who appropriate God to themselves as if He is the chief of their tribe or a permanent ally of some sort suggesting a partisan god! Others see religion in terms of glossolalia or the frenzy of a people whose emotions are being manipulated. Others shun religion because of religionists who package it in the garb of the superstitious and the unscientific. Who will not be disgusted by the fact that the so-called respectable religions cannot agree among themselves on basic issues like who the personality of God is? He is depicted as different objects or persons by the different religions. These are just a few of the stuff that are disturbing to the well-intentioned. Sometimes, the sects within the mainstream complicate the picture by their fanaticism, as they can't see eye to eye with their fellow adherents. Can anything be right about these things?

"The first kind of indifference in human society is indifference to God, which then leads to indifference to one's neighbour and to the environment… We have come to think that we are the source and creator of ourselves, our lives and society."

"…indifference leads to self-absorption and a lack of commitment."

Pope Francis: "Overcome indifference and win peace."
Message: 49th World Day of Peace, Jan 1, 2016.

But we defeat ourselves when we choose to throw away the baby with the bath water. The Lord God is real and by Christian understanding, is the Creator of all; He deals with all in justice and mercy.

Human beings' idea of justice is innately jaundiced; wholly centred on himself, upon his personal good, frequently to the utter exclusion of what is good to other persons. Ultimately, the actuation of self-will in all matters and the imposition of one's preferences or judgment on others is the 'right thing' to do, barring that no one else has the capability to thwart or smash it. What is 'just', therefore, is determined by the victory of violence over equity. Who dare stand in the way of the strongest man in the community?

Divine justice, on the other hand, is based on goodness, mercy and compassion; on strict avoidance of partiality – neither the strong nor the weak is favoured; and is definitely averse to the use of violence.

The Christian faith teaches obedience to God (1 Thes 4: 1)

"The Christian faith is not a pastime, and church is not one club among others, or even of a similar or even of a different sort."[2]

"If morality, as we have seen, is not the enslavement of man but his liberation, then, the Christian faith is the advance post of his freedom."

[2]: Pope Emeritus Benedict XVI (Daily Meditations)

Faith and Truth

"Faith has to do with truth…"[1]

([1]: Pope Emeritus, Benedict XVI: Daily Meditations)

Jesus says, "I am the way, the truth and the life…" (Jn 14: 6 NKJV)

Paul decries the worship of an unknown God (Acts 17: 23).

"The hope of Christianity – the outlook of faith – ultimately rests quite simply on the fact that faith tells the truth. The outlook of faith is the outlook of the truth that may be obscured and trampled upon but can never perish."

Pope Emeritus Benedict XVI. op cit

Faith, like knowledge of the physical sciences ought to grow.

Surely, faith, is knowledge-based, it ought to grow organically with time, just as is happening with the physical sciences and technology. Growth in faith could only mean, in this context, new truths about God unveiled, or deeper insights gained into old truths.

Some religious people, by claiming to know everything there is to be known about a truth (which they hardly understand), thereby gullibly foreclose further inquiry that could have led to deeper illumination or higher clarity. We could err, it seems to me, for then, perhaps inadvertently, we forsake further insights that are possible. What are they hiding, or what do they stand to gain – turning all of us into dummies? That is not the way we treat the physical sciences; hence progress is made steadily on that flank. Why should our understanding be static? Truth is sacrosanct, it requires no external defender! That time is long past when religion maintained a secrecy affinity with voodoo.

This predilectiongives rise to the resurgence of dissenters – revisionists, sects, denominations – in the mainstream religions and outright heretics.

The religions and their sects are each deaf to one another so that consensus, and therefore the truth, cannot emerge: sectionalism stays. Why should two people of faith, fired by the same impetus find themselves in so much disagreement that they can no longer walk together? With whom will they then parley, with people with uncritical minds? The pious are denied the Spirit-led leadership they need, and the flock is made to flounder. Observers laugh at us; agnostics vaunt that religion is the opium of the naïve!

Clearly, we should dismantle all impediments against objective research and scholarship in theology.

We are challenged by the existence of inexplicable phenomena that we call "mysteries". These are grey spots in our understanding, even anomalies, that require elucidation.

It is equally unsettling the way adherents of the various religions postulate conflicting and sometimes incoherent expletives, doctrines and dogmas claiming absolute certainty over unproven fundamental issues of faith. No distinction is made between innocuous propositions or hypotheses and truisms, axioms and dictums. Let us subject these to dispassionate probe; gather the facts together and throw them open. How beneficial it would be for our faith if all can agree on these fundamental truths. It is not too late for all who genuinely profess the faith (monotheism) to develop an appetite for ferreting out the truth. "Let them be one!"

"My people perish for lack of knowledge" (Hos 4: 6)

"It is love I ask of you, and the knowledge of God, not sacrifice." (Hos 6: 6)

That true religion is not a fetish or a farce – a commercially packaged superstition or a charadc – is addressed in this first volume of this work. Those intent on making money by manipulating people's susceptibilities should quit or be eased out of Christianity (Jesus paid for our redemption with His precious blood!).

Religious pluralities and the truth

"I believe, in order to **understand**; and I understand, the better to **believe**."

St Augustine of Hippo (354-430 AD)

Very regrettably, society has not been able to agree on who the Lord Creator is! Due to widespread deception and demonic manipulation beliefs are so variegated. Even among monotheists there are significant divergences in their beliefs. It is the Devil who is stirring the confusion and who benefits by this chaos. He fakes some things God has made to deceive and mislead men, causing them to stumble. There is no reason why we should permit this state of affairs to continue forever! Public servants have long recognized the duty to protect the public from the nefarious activities of miscreants and fraudsters. The body of Christ should take a cue.

It is in the interest of the world to identify the truth; for truth to emerge. We can then strip other so-called 'religions', of the religious toga. They are private personal past-times of those who indulge in them. We would thus restrict our reverence to the true and only God.

We should all admit that fact and stop glorifying deception or fables. Every human society deserves to know the truth about the Creator, who the Lord God is. And leaders of men have a responsibility here; an obligation to deploy public resources to illumine the truth concerning the reality of the Deity who created us. Why spend billions of dollars to probe the solar system, a few stars among several, when God Himself has been manifesting Himself to mankind? All we need do is to follow His lead.

If there is no deceit in us, should we not all come together – considering our common objective to make God known and obeyed?

"Sing to the Lord, all you lands
Announce His salvation, day after day
Tell His glory among the nations
Among all people, His wondrous deeds
For great is the Lord and highly to be praised
Awesome is He, beyond all the gods." (Ps 96: 1-4 NABRE)

Let us tolerate for now, these other practices until we arrive at a convergence in our perception of the truth – for the sake of peaceful co-existence. There is no need to bring nationalism into this; all these conflicting theologies simply can't be all right! For purposes of a dispassionate examination, we may hold that they all may be wrong! All who hold the view that religion has a place in the affairs of men ought to cooperate in this heroic assignment to ferret the truth that does not change complexion at the crossing of national and ethnic borders. There should be no place for religious laissez faire. It is a curse and an expensive foolishness to entertain. But this is no plea for bigotry or state clamp down on freedom of opinion, of expression or of association. That may well be the precursor of dictatorship or the intolerance of dissenting opinions. That would be courting fanaticism, resentment, violence, death and wickedness. Rather, it is a plea against the rejection of rationalism.

You will observe that we liberally employ analogies, syntheses, comparisons, inferences and deductions in this book.

The limitation of the rational process

Of course, these logical processes can be faulted because, if a fact or an assumption escapesnotice or is not explicitly stated in an analysis, or the context of a discussion is ignored, the conclusion may be different. Still, accord or the discovery of the truth, is fostered by this procedure.

Religious Issues of grave concern

Besides the concern for the absence of accord among the major world religions over the most rudimentary concepts about God, it is equally disheartening that our knowledge of God has not progressed beyond what it was 2000 years ago! We are no longer using today, the rudimentary form of utensils used just five hundred years ago! But imagine an adult who died one hundred years ago resurrecting into his former native place, how bewildered he would be because of the technological changes that had taken place. But not so for our knowledge of God, It would seem that religious appurtenances have taken over as the ultimate object of worship. Our theology is no longer directed at knowing God. Rather, we multiply the liturgy, multiply sects and multiply denominations to give ourselves the illusion that all is well – operating a religion of all comers – where everybody does whatever he pleases!

All religions should lead us to a knowledge or revelation of God. Mankind should be anxious to live up to the duty of responding to His love or whatever expectation He has for us. We are co-sojourners on earth and through death, co-pilgrims to life hereafter.

All who share a belief in the ultimate Master-Mind should share a concern to know Him and to please Him. What is theology, if not merely a means to get to know the Divine Intelligence? What is religion, if not a response of gratitude to mankind's Landlord and Giver of the food, drink, knowledge, joy and glorythat we cherish?

Just as it once happened to Judaism, the Messiah was being expected to manifest anytime, but when He did appear, the religious leaders were caught unprepared to receive Him!

I fear that something akin to that may once again happen to Christianity, unless we change our tactics. Jesus expressed His concern:

"Nevertheless, when the Son of Man comes... will He find that faith on earth?"

(Lk 18: 8 HCSB)

Refocusing, re-strategizing

Christian leadership is in disarray and with it, the Church. Every general overseer or congregational chief executive officer is king over his partisan group! No one expresses concern that the entire body of Christ may not still be docile to the divine will. Or that the body of Christ might not always be kept perpetually focused on the goal of our Christian faith; that we should periodically (say, once every 50 years) come together to re-evaluate and re-prioritize our goals and strategies to ensure continuous relevance, effectiveness and fidelity; that we have not derailed from the essence – the truth; and that the body of Christ is still together intact.

"But I have other sheep that are not of this fold;
I must bring them also, and they will listen to My voice.
Then there will be **one flock, one shepherd.**" (Jn 10: 16 HCSB)
"I pray for them..."
"Holy Father, protect them...
So that **they may be one as We are one.**" (Jn 17: 11 HCSB)

Fanaticism: Any action that polarizes society in acrimony and rage – tipping one group against another – is of the evil one. Jesus came to the world for ordinary folks like you and me. God does not need the help of powerful men and gorgeous women to make a happy world. Creation is already a perfect beauty.Persons putting on a religious facade to foment trouble are doing their master's (the

Devil's) bidding. (Jn 8: 44). No religious teaching need contradict the golden rule – 'Do to others as you would wish that they do to you' (Matt 7:12). So, why fight and kill your neighbour for a weak and indolent god that cannot fight its own cause?

Let heart speak to heart

An esoteric group whose tenets and practices are shrouded in secrecy and mystery may be into mysticism, voodoo or some other thing.

But Christian religion is all about the truth of our existence. The truth cannot, and should not be different things to different people. Let us all resolve to grasp the truth that we all may walk in the brightness of truth for our common good.

Let us come to dialogue. I challenge the leaders of all the monotheistic religions to a continuing colloquy. Come out and tell the world how your God's stand on the platitudes unveiled in these series differs.

"You will know the truth, and the truth will set you free." (Jn 8: 32 HCSB)

Cultism is the creed that knocks heads against heads. Christianity is the religion that produces peace, love and fraternity.

"A thief comes only to steal and to kill and to destroy. I (Jesus) have come so that they may have life and have it in abundance." (Jn 10: 10 HCSB)

If your religion does not differ in essence from the goals and values disclosed in this book, it means that we are together, witnessing for the same sovereign and gracious God. (I stand to be contradicted that within the book are to be found all the major or significant tenets of the Christian faith).

But if it differs then let the pious reason together. Which religion produces the good of society – the greatest good to the greatest number? That should be the true religion that pays acceptable homage to the good and gracious God.

"Christianity is not a philosophy or a convenient ideology,"[1] but a way of life which the Creator Himself, enjoined on mankind to live. Every human being regardless of race and ethnicity is an equal stakeholder in it.

[1]: Pope Emeritus Benedict XVI: Daily Meditations

So let us walk together in the truth. Let us join hands together, to enthrone peace with justice, truth and godliness among all peoples everywhere. Let us learn from one another.

To this end, the Lord God revealed Himself to humanity through prophets and priests (like Noah, Jacob, Moses, Aaron, Elijah, Isaiah, Daniel, etc.for Christians). The fullness of this revelation comes through Jesus, the Messiah. His mission to earth was to redeem mankind and plant justice on earth.(Isa Chapters 42, 50, 53)

Impunity voids justice; consequently, Jesus, who is to judge the world, will bring to book all evil doers. He will requite to everyone according to his/her deeds on earth at the resurrection of the dead. For justice is vitiated by sin; and the sinner cannot be admitted into the presence of God or into His kingdom.

Peace! That Russia's War on Ukraine

Why do you look on disinterestedly – you inhabitants of the earth?

As peace is ignored, so too, justice and truth.

Today, it is Ukraine; tomorrow (and for a different reason), it could be India, or Japan or even China!Call off that war immediately; usher in peace.

May both sides agree to try out love – as an alternative strategy!

These books hopefully will, besides bridging the gulf that exists between different sects and different religious adherents, also foster among Christians a deeper understanding and fraternity, thus furthering the attainment of the goal of faith, which is obedience to God and salvation for our souls.

"…Christ Jesus who became God-given wisdom,
for us – our righteousness, sanctification and redemption,…"
(1 Cor 1: 30 HCSB)

This book points the way to Jesus; Jesus, the way to God. And with the continuing help of God's Holy Spirit, Jesus leads the one thirsty for God to God, in all His riches, in love, wisdom, strength and glory.

"Righteousness will go before Him
to prepare the way for His steps." (Ps 85: 13 HCSB)

Yes, indeed, because God is our righteousness (Jer 33: 15)

5-Book project

This book, *God, Our Righteousness*, the first in the series, presents a synopsis of what the Lord Jesus Christ taught – directly or indirectly – during His earthly mission arranged thematically for ease of reference.

Living by this divine guide is going by the way of wisdom that never fails. The individual will be empowered to distinguish between what is right conduct and what is wrong (or inappropriate). He will discover a meaning for his life and be oriented for the afterlife, i.e., the life beyond mortal life. He will know by himself without the risk of being misled, how to live the good life, being in command of those things which are within his power to control and assured that God is fully aware and overseeing the rest.

Now, what is true for the individual is equally true for the society he comes from. I am alluding to harmonious person-to-person relationship. For this reason, we have drawn from the wisdom unravelled in this book to address the anxieties, discontents and disputes that are rife in society, which living together throws up. And we point to these divine injunctions as the right way to go towards resolving them (i.e., book 2: *What makes for peace*).

Relying on the same divine revelations, we present in book 3: *Peace from pieces,* how to handle allegations or perceptions of oppression and marginalization of minorities in a godly manner within a multi-racial or multi-ethnic society. We employ the imbroglio between Nigeria and "Biafra", a dissident group within the Federal Republic of Nigeria, to illustrate.

It became pertinent to delve into the ever-green search for an ideal political arrangement for the governance of God's people. What can be as good as a democracy conscribed by these divine platitudes? Book 4, ***Democracy: demos or demons?*** is the outcome.

The final book in the series, ***Understanding the Bible***, as its title suggests, gives tips, based on the author's personal experience, for reading the Bible in a way to ensure a broad consensus with other readers in understanding and interpretation thereof.

Scripture references

In the first book of these series, frequently entire verses or paragraphs from the sacred books are reproduced to save readers' time and from a broad base of versions for consensus-building. More often, the extracts are abridged. Readers may wish to read the full text by referring to the books quoted or their preferred version thereof.

Syntax. For ungrammatical use of upper-case letters and other editorial interventions, please pardon me. It is all about assistance to the reader to signify an allusion to a member of the Holy Trinity: first letters of relevant nouns and pronouns are rendered in the upper case.

Likewise, to avoid disorienting the reader, spellings in Bible quotations have most reluctantly been anglicized (for the international audience) or Americanized (for the American edition) regardless of the spelling used in the version quoted.

This is a minimum interpretational aid for which I feel obliged to do. My task is to interpret the sacred literature, not to reprint them. Please excuse this unconventionality. To see exactly how these excerpts appear in the original text, references must be made to those versions.

Authors and publishers

The Holman Christian Standard Bible (HCSB) is, by divine providence, this project's official reference Bible; it is the version most frequently cited and, unless otherwise indicated, the default reference.

For some reasons, I have culled texts from other publishers also, such as the North American Bible Revised Edition (NABRE); New King James Version (NKJV); Good News Bible (catholic edition) (GNBDK), etc. This, sometimes, is inevitable when the excerpt is from any of the extracanonical books not found in protestant versions (such as the HCSB and the NKJV).

In all these books no excerpts can be reproduced without the copyright owner's consent. This is true also for other copyright authors and publications excerpted into any of these books. I am taking steps to formally obtain their permission. But for time constraints and on account of inadvertent delays and mistakes, I have anticipated their permission. The process is still on-going, so I crave the indulgence of these esteemed colleagues to forbear with me. Thank you.

God, Our Righteousness (Jer 33:15 NKJV)

CHAPTER 1

The Only One

(Zec.14: 9 NABRE)
"Before the mountains were born,
before You gave birth to the earth and the world,
from eternity to eternity,
You are God. (Ps. 90: 2 HCSB)

The Lord God, Almighty

Holy, holy, holy is the Lord of Hosts!
All the earth is filled with His glory! (Isa 6: 3 NABRE)

Only in the Lord are just deeds and power

I am Yahweh, and there is no other;
there is no God but Me,
I will strengthen you, though you do not know Me.
Woe to the one who argues with his maker,
one clay pot among many.
Does clay say to one forming it,
"What are you making?"
Or does your work say, "He has no hands"?
... was it not I, Yahweh?
There is no other God but Me,
a righteous God and Saviour;
there is no one except Me.
Turn to Me and be saved all the ends of the earth.
For I am God and there is no other.
Every knee shall bow to Me,
every tongue swear allegiance;

it will be said to Me:

righteousness and strength is only in the Lord.

(Isa. 45: 5, 9, 21-22, 23-24 HCSB)

In plain language –

"How great is Your goodness that you have stored up for those who fear You and accomplished in the sight of everyone for those who take refuge in You." (Ps. 31: 19)

Rejoice in the Lord, you righteous ones;

Praise from the upright is beautiful.

For the word of the Lord is right,

and all His work is trustworthy.

He loves righteousness and justice;

The earth is full of the Lord's unfailing love

Let the whole earth tremble before the Lord;

Let all the inhabitants of the world stand in awe of Him.

For He spoke, and it came into being;

he commanded, and it came into existence. (Ps. 33: 1, 4-5, 8-9)

Sing to the Lord, bless His name;

proclaim His salvation day after day.

Tell His glory among the nations;

among all people, His marvellous deeds.

For great is the Lord and highly to be praised,

to be feared above all gods.

For the gods of the nations are idols,

but the Lord made the heavens.

Give to the Lord, you families of nations;

give to the Lord glory and might;

give to the Lord the glory due His name!...

Bring gifts and enter His courts; (Ps. 96: 2-5, 7, 8 NABRE)

For all life is Mine: The life of the parent is like the life of the child, both are Mine. Only the one who sins shall die! (Ezk. 18: 4 NABRE)

For more read 18: 5-32

Fear of God

When FEAR is perfected it gives way to love
and this is what loving God entails – to keep His commands.
Jesus Christ has done that before us, and if we are **born again** in Him, the Spirit of God strengthens us. We no longer consider His commands burdensome,
(1 Jn. 5: 3).
Shout triumphantly to the Lord, all the earth
Serve the Lord with gladness,
Come before Him with joyful songs (Ps. 100: 1-2)
"They multiply their sorrows who court other gods..." (Ps. 16: 4 NABRE)
"The heavens declare **the glory of God;** the firmament proclaims the works of His hands. (Ps. 19: 2 NABRE).

"Lord, who can dwell in Your tent?

Who can live on Your holy mountain?
The one who lives honestly, practises righteousness,
and acknowledges the truth in his heart –
who does not slander with his tongue,
who does not harm his friend or discredit his neighbour,
who despises the one rejected by the Lord,
but honours those who fear the Lord,
who keeps his word whatever the cost,
who does not lend his money at interest
or take a bribe against the innocent –
the one who does these things will never be moved (Ps. 15: 1-6 HCSB).
"Those who **hate the Lord** would pretend submission to Him;.. their doom would last forever." (Ps. 81: 15).
"**The earth** and everything in it,
the world and its inhabitants,
belong to the Lord;

for He laid its foundation on the seas
and established it on the rivers (Ps. 24: 1-2).

Who may ascend the mountain of the Lord?

Who may stand in His holy place?
The one who has clean hands and a pure heart,
who has not set his mind on what is false,
and who has not sworn deceitfully.
He will receive blessing from the Lord,
and righteousness from the God of his salvation. (Ps. 24: 3-5 HCSB).

The Lord is good

"I sought the Lord, and He answered me
and delivered me from all my fears.
The angel of the Lord encamps
around those who fear Him, and rescues them.
Taste and see that the Lord is good.
How happy is the man who takes refuge in Him!
The Lord is near the broken hearted;
He saves those crushed in spirit." (Ps. 34: 4, 7-8, 18 HCSB)
"Commit your way to the Lord;
trust in Him, and He will act,...
The salvation of the righteous is from the Lord,
their refuge in a time of distress." (Ps. 37: 5, 39)

God's Eternal Favourites

No favouritism with God.
"Now I really understand that God doesn't show favouritism but in every nation the person who fears Him and does righteousness is acceptable to Him", (Acts 10: 34-35 HCSB)

Who God is: "...God is light...in Him there is no darkness" (1 Jn. 1: 15)

"God is love" (1 Jn. 4: 8, 16)

Moses asked "...What is His name?"

God replied: "I AM WHO I AM..."

"say to the Israelites, YAHWEH, the God of your fathers, the God of Abraham, the God of Isaac; and the God of Jacob has sent me to you. This is My name forever; this is how I am to be remembered in every generation." (Exo. 3: 13-15).

"... **Submit to God**, but resist the Devil and he will flee"...

Be assured of God's mercy and compassion (Js. 4: 7; 5: 11).

For Christians, the revelation about God is in the Bible. The Bible is, in part historical and in part, a compendium of the sayings and activities of prophets and saints – extraordinary clairvoyant individuals.

If you don't believe in the Bible, then find your creator elsewhere. For more on the Bible – see book 5 of this series.

"**Those who know Your name** trust in You

Because You have not abandoned those who seek You, Yahweh.

The nations have fallen into the pit they made;

their foot is caught in the net they have concealed.

The Lord has revealed Himself; He has executed justice,

striking down the wicked

by the work of their hands.

Higgaion, Selah

The wicked will return to Sheol -

all the nations that forget God." (Ps. 9: 10, 15-17)

"Because of **the Lord's faithful love** we do not perish,

for His mercies never end.

They are new every morning;

great is Your faithfulness!" (Lam. 3: 22-23)

Trust only in the Lord

Do not trust in nobles, in man who cannot save when his breath leaves him, he returns to the ground; on that day his plans die (Ps. 146: 3-4).

The Lord reigns! He is robed in majesty;
the Lord is robed, enveloped in strength.
The world is firmly established;
it cannot be shaken. (Ps. 105: 1 HCSB)

Divine Mercy

"The Lord is gracious and merciful
slow to anger and of great kindness.
The Lord is good to all
and compassionate toward all His works. (Ps. 145: 8, 9)
The Lord is faithful in all His words
and holy in all His works.
The Lord lifts up all who are falling
and raises up all who are bowed down. (Ps. 145: 13-14)
Look at how great a love the Father
has given us that we should be called
God's children. And we are! The reason
the world does not know us is that
it didn't know Him. (1 Jn. 3: 1)

"Holy, holy, holy, Lord God, the Almighty, who was, who is, and who is coming"

"Our Lord and God, You are worthy to receive glory and honour and power, because You have created all things, and because of Your will they exist and were created" (Rev. 4: 8, 11)

IMMANUEL

"See, the virgin will become pregnant and give birth to a son, and they will name Him Immanuel, which is translated "GOD IS WITH US."

(Is 7: 14; Matt 1: 23 HCSB).

GOD ALMIGHTY – The Only One

"Look! **God's dwelling is** with humanity, and He will live with them.

They will be His people, and God Himself will be with them and be their God."

"... Look! I am making everything new..." (Rev. 21: 3, 5)

GOD the Creator

" ... the Lord,

Who spreads out the heavens,

lays the foundation of the earth,

and fashions the human spirit within" (Zec. 12: 1 NABRE)

Holy Name

"Not to us, Yahweh, not to us,

but to Your name give glory

because of Your faithful love,

because of Your truth." (Ps. 115: 1)

Idolatry

"Their idols are silver and gold, made by human hands.

They have mouths but cannot speak, eyes, but cannot see.

They have ears but cannot hear, nose but cannot smell.

They have hands but cannot feel, feet, but cannot walk...

Those who make them are just like them,

as are all who trust in them." (Ps. 115: 4-7, 8).

Idolaters

"No one has the perception or insight to say, I burned half of it in the fire,... baked bread on its coals..." (Isa. 44: 19).

The lure of idolatry

"For your own good be extremely careful... not to act corruptly and make an idol for yourselves in the shape of any figure: a male or female form, or the form of any beast on the earth, any winged creature... When you look to the heavens and see the sun, moon or stars... do not be led astray to bow down and worship them. The Lord your God has provided them for all people everywhere under heaven." (Deut. 4: 15-19)

"Today, recognize and keep in mind that the Lord is God in heaven above and on earth below; there is no other." (Deut. 4: 39).

Divine Mercy

"That you may remember and be ashamed, and never again open your mouth because of your disgrace, when I pardon you for all you have done - oracle of the Lord God." (Ezk. 16: 63 NABRE).

The God o f gods

Yahweh is the God of gods! Yahweh is the God of gods! (Jos 22: 22 HCSB).

Fear God!

"Fear the Lord, your God and keep... all His statutes and commandments.... and thus have long life. Be careful to observe them that you may grow and prosper the more..." (Deut. 6: 2-63 Lect.)

"Blessed are you who fear the Lord, who walk in His ways! ..."
(Ps. 128: 1-4 NABRE)
GOD, almighty

"… Worship God, because the testimony about Jesus is the spirit of prophecy." (Rev. 19: 10)

Longing for God

As a dear longs for streams of waters, so my soul longs for You, God.

Send Your light and Your truth, let them lead me.

Let them bring me to Your holy mountain, to Your dwelling place.

Then I will come to the altar of God...

I will praise You... God, my God. (Ps. 42: 1, 3-4 HCSB)

"How lovely is Your dwelling place, Lord of Hosts,
I long and yearn for the courts of the Lord;
my heart and flesh cry out for the living God.
Even a sparrow finds a home
and a swallow, a nest for herself
where she places her young –
near Your alters, Lord of Hosts,
my King and my God.
How happy are those who reside in Your house,
who praise You continually. Selah
Better a day in Your courts
than a thousand anywhere else.
I would rather be at the door of the house of my God
than to live in the tents of wicked people. (Ps. 84: 1-4, 10).

"Praise the Lord!"

Praise, O servants of the Lord!
Praise the name of the Lord!
Blessed be the name of the Lord
From this time forth and for evermore!
From the rising of the sun to its going down
The Lord's name is to be praised.

The Lord is high above all nations,
His glory above the heavens. (Ps. 113: 1-4 NKJV)

Goodness: Pure, and beyond understanding

"Why do you ask me about what is good?" Jesus answered,
"There is only One who is good." (Matt. 19: 17)

GOD: The Father, our Father!

Jesus revealed to us that God is indeed, our Father:
"Therefore, you should pray like this:
Our Father in heaven, ..." (Matt. 6: 9)
To emphasize this, He said, "Do not call anyone on earth your father, because earth you have one father, who is in heaven." (Matt. 23: 9)
So, the fullness of fatherhood lies in God.
CHILDREN OF GOD
"But to all who did receive Him, He gave them the right to be children of God, to those who believe in His name, who were born, not of blood or of the will of the flesh, or of the will of man, but of God." (Jn. 1: 12-13).

Choose Life!

Moses: "I call heaven and earth as witnesses against you today that I have set before you life and death, blessing and curse. Choose life so that you and your descendants may live". (Deut. 30: 19. HCSB)

God's Children

"Everyone who believes that JESUS is the Messiah has been born of God and everyone who loves the Father also loves the One born of Him"

"... everyone who has been born of God does not sin, ... we are of God, and the whole world is under the sway of the evil one"
(1 Jn. 5: 1; 18 – 19 HCSB).

God's Family

"So then you are no longer strangers and sojourners, but you are fellow citizens and members of the household of God". (Eph. 2: 19).

The Kingdom of God

"Don't be afraid, little flock, because your Father delights to give you the kingdom".

Compare, Jesus saying:

"In my Father's house are many dwelling places; if not, I would have told you. I am going away to prepare a place for you". (Jn. 14: 2 HCSB)

Why man is created

"...So that we ... might bring praise to His glory." (Eph. 1: 12 HCSB)

We are brothers and Sisters!

"Don't all of us have one Father?

Didn't one God create us?

Why then do we act treacherously against one another, profaning the covenant of our fathers?

Didn't the one God make us with a remnant of His life breath? And what does the One seek? A godly offspring. So watch..." (Mal. 2: 10, 15 HCSB)

Man, the Prodigal son

A man had two sons (the elder, and the younger). The younger son collected all his belongings, including his inheritance, and set off to a distant country where he squandered everything he had on a life of dissipation.

Coming to his senses, he got up and went back to his father. His father caught sight of him; filled with compassion, ran to his son, embraced him and kissed him; ordered his servants: "Let us celebrate with a feast!"

Now, the elder son had been out in the field, and on his way back heard the sound of music and dancing.

"Your brother has returned"

He became angry and refused to enter the house. His father came and pleaded with him:

"My son, you are here with me always; everything I have is yours. But now we must celebrate and rejoice, because your brother was dead and has come to life again; he was lost and has been found."

For more insights, read the story in full in Luke 15: 1-3, 11-32.

A trustworthy hope

"But I will look to the Lord;

I will wait for the God of my salvation;

My God will hear me.

Do not rejoice over me, my enemy!

Though I have fallen, I will stand up;

though I sit in darkness,

the Lord will be my light." (Mic. 7: 7-8 HCSB)

The Song of Moses and the Lamb

"Lord God Almighty,

how great and wonderful are Your deeds!

King of the nations,

how right and true are Your ways!

Who will not stand in awe of You, Lord?

Who will refuse to declare Your greatness?

You alone are holy.

All the nations will come and worship You,

because Your just actions are seen by all." (Rev. 15: 3, 4. GNBDK)

Choose to serve the Lord

"Now, therefore, revere the Lord, and serve Him in sincerity and in faithfulness;...

Now if you are unwilling to serve the Lord, choose this day whom you will serve,...but as for me and my household, we will serve the Lord."

(Jos. 24: 15, 16 NRSV-CI).

"I am the Lord, there is no other.

I form the light, and create the darkness, …

let justice descend, you heavens, like dew from above,

like gentle rain let the clouds drop it down.

Let the earth open and salvation bud forth;

let righteousness spring up with them!" (Isa. 45: 6, 7, 8 NABRE)

Fear only the Lord

"I shall show you **whom to fear.** Be afraid of the one who after killing has the power to cast into Gehenna; yes,... be afraid of that One."

(Lk. 12: 5 NABRE).

Fear God!

"And now, Israel,

what does the Lord your God ask of you except to fear the Lord."
"Therefore circumcise your hearts and don't be stiff-necked any longer."

(Deut. 10: 12, 16 HCSB)

ADDITIONAL RESOURCES

Let Us Pray:

"May the peoples praise You, O God
may all the peoples praise You!
May the nations be glad and sing for joy,
because You judge the people with justice
and guide every nation on earth." (Ps 67: 3-4 GNBDK)
The Only God (Jn. 5: 44 HCSB)
"Lord, You have been our dwelling place in all generations. Before the mountains were brought forth,
or ever You had formed the earth and the world,
from everlasting to everlasting You are God. You have set our iniquities before You,
our secret sins in the light of Your countenance."
(Ps. 90:1-2, 8 NRSV-CI – A Prayer of Moses....)
"Holy, holy, holy is the Lord of host!
All the earth is filled with His glory!"
(Isa 6: 3 NABRE)

"The heavens declare the glory of God;
the firmament proclaims the works of His hands." (Ps. 19: 2 NABRE)

God of ALL!

Rom. 10: 12 "For there is no distinction between Jew and Greek; the same Lord is Lord of all...
: 13 For "everyone who calls on the name of the Lord will be saved".
"You shall have but one rule, for alien and native-born alike... (Lev. 24: 22)
"You shall have but one rule for the person who sins inadvertently, whether a native-born Israelite or an alien" (Num. 15: 29 HCSB)
"My house shall be called a house of prayer for all peoples"

See also (Isa. 56: 3-7.)
Foreigners and eunuchs: "shall not be cut-off"
"... I will make them joyful."
Forget God? (Deut. 8: 11)
"Be careful that you don't forget the Lord, your God..."
Not as man sees does God see (1 Sam. 16: 10-7)
Mk.10: 18 Why do you call me good? Jesus asked him.
(HCSB) (No one is good but one – God).

Blessed are You God!

Blessed are You on the throne of Your Kingdom,
praise worthy and exalted above all forever
Blessed are You in the firmament of heaven,
praise worthy and glorious forever.
Let the earth bless the Lord,
praise and exalt Him above all forever.
Give thanks to the Lord, Who is good,
whose mercy endures forever (Dan. 3: 54, 56, 74, 89...)
GOD, OUR RIGHTEOUSNESS
"Oh, the depth of the riches
both of the wisdom and the knowledge of God.
How unsearchable His judgments
and untraceable His ways.
For from Him and through Him and to Him are all things.
To Him be the glory forever, Amen. (Rom. 11: 33, 36 HCSB).

One God, Father of all

"You are to divide this land among yourselves according to the tribes of Israel. You will allot it as an inheritance for yourselves and for the foreigners living among you,... "You will treat them like native-born Israelites;... (Ezk. 47: 21-23 HCSB)

THE UNIVERSAL GOD

Damascus – Aram

Isa. 17: 7 "On that day man shall look to his maker, his eyes turned toward the Holy One of Israel."

17: 10 "For you have forgotten God, your saviour, and remembered not the Rock, your strength."

ETHIOPIA

Isa. 18: 7 "Then will gifts be brought to the Lord of hosts from a people tall and bronzed,... a nation strong and conquering, whose land is washed by rivers to Mount Zion where dwells the name of the Lord of hosts."

EGYPT

Isa. 19: 2 "I will rouse Egypt against Egypt; brother will war against brother, neighbour against neighbour... kingdom against kingdom."

: 22 "Although the Lord shall smite Egypt severely. He shall heal them; they shall turn to the Lord and He shall be won over and heal them."

Every good and perfect gift comes from the Lord (Js 1: 17 NABRE)

"For true and just are His judgements." (Rev 19: 2 NABRE)

"Comfort, comfort My people, says our God." (Isa 40: 1)

Our redemption comes from the Father.

"Sheathe your sword! Am I not to drink the cup the Father has given Me?" (Jn 18: 11)

Sovereign God

All you peoples, clap your hands;

Shout to God with cries of gladness.

For the Lord, the Most High, the awesome,

is the great King over all the earth. (Ps 47: 2-3 Lect)

"The words of the Lord are true

And all His works are dependable.

The Lord loves what is righteous and just;

His constant love fills the earth." (Ps 33: 4-5 GNBDK)

Incomparable God

Isa 40: 18 Who will you compare God with? What likeness will you

HCSB compare Him to?

: 19 To an idol? ...

: 25 "Who will you compare Me to, or who is My equal?

Asks the Holy One."

: 28 "Do you not know? Have you not heard?

Yahweh is the everlasting God, the creator of the whole earth.

He never grows faint or weary; there is no limit to His understanding."

: 29 "He gives strength to the weary and strengthens the powerless.

: 30 Youths may faint and grow weary, and young men stumble and fall,

: 31 but those who trust in the Lord will renew their strength; they will soar on wings like eagles; they will walk and faint."

One God, one Lord.

1 Cor 8: 6 "Yet for us there is ONE GOD, the Father. All things are from Him, and we exist for Him. And there is ONE LORD, Jesus Christ. All things are through Him, and we exist through Him."

God, Our Father

Heb 2: 11 "For the One who sanctifies and those who are sanctified all

HCSB have one Father. That is why Jesus is not ashamed to call them brothers."

NABRE: "He who consecrates and those who are being consecrated all have one origin. Therefore He is not ashamed to call them 'brothers'."

The story of Creation

"In the beginning God created the heavens and the earth.

Now the earth was formless and empty,…

Then God said, 'Let there be light', and there was light…

God saw that the light was good, and God separated the light from the darkness…: The first day.

Then God said, 'Let there be lights in the expanse of the sky to separate the day from the night… God made the two great lights – the greater light to have dominion over the day and the lesser light to have dominion over the night – as well as the stars …: the fourth day.

Then God said, 'Let us make man in our own image, according to our likeness.

They will rule all the earth … So God created man in His own image; He created him in the image of God; He created them male and female. God blessed them, …: the sixth day.

"So the heavens and the earth and everything in them were completed.

By the seventh day God completed His work that He had done, and He rested on the seventh day… God blessed the seventh day and declared it holy,…" (Gen 1: 1, 2, 3, 4, 14, 16, 26, 27, 28; 2: 1-2, 3 HCSB)

The only one

"There is only One who is wise,

and we must stand in awe before His throne." (Sir 1: 10 GNBDK)

The Only God

"See now that I alone am He;

There is no God but Me.

I bring death and give life;

I wound and I heal.

No one can rescue anyone from My hand!" (Deut 32: 39 HCSB)

GOD: As professed by Jesus Christ

- The Giver of life

"Just as the Father raises the dead and gives them life so the Son also gives life to anyone He wants to." (Jn 5: 21 HCSB)

See also Jn 5: 26

- Our Great Provider

"… He gave them bread from heaven to eat" (Jn 6: 31 HCSB)

(I am)… the real bread from heaven.

So the one who feeds on Me will live because of Me." "… The one who eats this bread will live forever." (Jn 6: 32, 57, 58 HCSB)

On anxiety about what to eat, drink or wear (Matt 6: 25-33)

"Your heavenly Father knows that you need them."

(Matt 6: 32 HCSB)

- GOD is the Lord
- "The living Father sent Me …" (Jn 6: 57 HCSB)
- "I do nothing on My own but as the Father taught Me …"
- (Jn 8: 28 HCSB)
- "A slave is not greater than his master, a messenger is not greater than the one who sent him." (Jn 13: 16 HCSB)
- "For I have come from heaven not to do My will but the will of Him who sent Me." (Jn 6: 38 HCSB)
- "Just as the Father commanded Me, so I do." (Jn 14: 31 HCSB)
- The Father is the greater

"… The Father is greater than I." (Jn 14: 28 HCSB)

- The Father is God and Father of all

At Mary Magdalene's second visit to the tomb, Jesus instructed her to tell His disciples:

"I am ascending to My Father and your Father – to My God and Your God." (Jn 20: 17 HCSB)

GOD, Jesus (as witnessed by the Disciples):

- **Holy Servant**. Peter and the other Apostles who had seen everything (His teaching, preaching and healing) from the pinnacle (the transfiguration) to the denouement (the crucifixion) of His Messianic ministry call Jesus "the Holy Servant of God."

"Indeed they gathered in this city against Your Holy Servant, Jesus whom You anointed, …" (Acts 4: 27 NABRE)

see also Acts 4: 30; 3: 13, 26.

- **Man**. They also called Jesus a "man"

"… Jesus the Nazorean was a man commended to you by God with mighty deeds, wonders and signs,…" (Acts 2: 22 NABRE)

See also Acts 2: 23.

Worship God!

"Worship God,

Because the testimony about Jesus

is the Spirit of prophecy." (Rev 19: 10 HCSB)

Jesus, the light of the world

"… It's lamp is the Lamb."

(Rev 21: 23 HCSB) see also Rev 19: 20; 20: 2-3.

Holy God

"Holy, holy, holy is the Lord of Hosts;

All the earth is filled with His glory!"

(Isa 6: 3 NABRE)

No god?

"You forgot the God who gave you birth."

"Since they have provoked Me with their 'no god' and angered Me,

with their vain idols, I will provoke them a 'no – people'…"

(Deut 32: 18-21)

God, Our Great Provider
- Wait on the Lord! (Lk 17: 7-10)
- "Then the Lord God formed the man… and the man became a living being. The Lord God planted a garden in Eden, … there He placed the man He had formed.

The Lord God caused to grow out of the ground every tree pleasing in appearance and good for food …" (Gen 2: 7-9 HCSB)
- " … They will rule the fish of the sea, the birds of the sky, the livestock, all the earth, and the creatures that crawl on the earth."

(Gen 1: 26 HCSB)
- "Get up, go to Zarephath… stay there. Look I have commanded a woman… to provide for you there."

"But she said, '… I don't have anything baked – only a handful of flour… and a bit of oil… just now, I am gathering a couple of sticks in order to go prepare it for myself and my son so we can eat it and die.'"

"So she proceeded to do according to the word of Elijah. Then the woman, Elijah, and her household ate for many days. The flour jar did not become empty, and the oil jug did not run dry, according to the word of the Lord He had spoken through Elijah." (1 Kgs 17: 9, 12, 15-16 HCSB)

Our Great Protector.

The Lord preserves His beloved from evil; He preserved Abimelech, King of Gerar, from touching Sarah, the half-sister/wife of Abraham.

(Gen 20: 3, 6)

Our heavenly Father leads us not into temptation, delivers us from evil (Matt 6: 13)

Omnipotent God

- "The Lord answered Moses, 'is the Lord's power limited? You will see whether or not what I have promised happen to you'"
- (Num 11: 23)
- "… Why did Sarah laugh, saying … Is anything impossible for the Lord?" (Gen 18: 13, 14)
- "For nothing will be impossible with God." (Lk 1: 37 HCSB)
- "But Jesus looked at them and said, 'with man this is impossible but with God, all things are possible.'" (Matt 19: 26)
- Exhortation, meditation and reflection

God our creator

Wisdom is seen by Wisdom is seen by its products, God is discernible through His creation. St Irenaeus (c130-202):

"Life in man is the glory of God, the life of man is the vision of God."

The Lord God created man in love in His image; gave him dominion over all His works on earth, as stated in Genesis 1 and 2, He is, thus, our Great Provider. We have an obligation, accordingly to honour and revere Him.

Blessed are all who fear the Lord and who walk in His ways. (Ps. 128: 1 NABRE)

For more, read Ps.128: 2-4 also.

God's Family. We can understand why in some religions it is considered an anathema or blasphemy to say or think of God as our Father. Yes, our Father indeed, He is; but even more so than our earthly fathers, because He made fathers and mothers available for our consolation, some may consider man as God's slave, but this too is rather unfair; for God detests oppression – a corollary of slavery.

Hear what St. Paul tells the Ephesians:

So then, you are no longer strangers and sojourners, but you are fellow citizens with the holy ones and members of the household of God. Don't be afraid, little flock, because your Father delights to give you the kingdom. (Eph. 2: 19, 32) For more, read Eph. 3: 4.

Everybody who believes is a co-heir, member and co-partner of the promises of Christ. Don't all of us have one Father? Didn't one God create us? Why then do we act treacherously against one another, profaning the covenant of our fathers? Didn't the one God make us with a remnant of His life-breath? And what does the One seek? A godly offspring...

(Mal 2: 10, 15)

I will bring them to My holy mountain and let them rejoice in My house of prayer... for my house will be called a house of prayer for all nations.

(Isa. 56: 7) (see also Mk. 11: 15-17).

Exhortation, meditation and reflection

Life with God Is the pleasure and will of God for all mankind. Obedience fosters such wholesome living; sin separates us from God. Contrition and conversion restore our broken relationship. (Deut. 30: 19; Ezk. 33: 11)

"Do I take any pleasure in the **death of the wicked?**" This is the declaration of the Lord God.

"Instead, don't I take pleasure when he turns from his ways and lives?"

(Ezk. 18: 23)

TRUE RELATIONSHIPS

1. God, our Father

"… call no man father on earth" (Matt. 23: 9)

"I am ascending to My Father and Your Father…" (Jn 20: 17)

2. Jesus, our brother!

"Whoever does the will of God is My brother and sister and mother." (Mk. 3: 35)

3. God is our Great Provider, in His Benevolent Kingdom.

In the parable of the sown seed, Jesus remarked
"A man scatters seed on the ground; he sleeps, he rises – night and day, and the seed sprouts and grows – he doesn't know how. The soil produces a crop by itself – first the blade, then the head, and then the ripe grain... but as soon as the crop is ready, he sends for the sickle, because the harvest has come." (Mk. 4: 26-29).
Elisha multiplied the oil for the prophet's son's widow to provide relief for her and her son (2Kgs 4: 1-7)
Adam and Eve became lord over a garden they did not plant (Gen 2)
We are all being into a family and world that pre-exist us!
Jesus fed 5,000 and 4,000 by multiplying the provision of a few loaves and fish that was available (Mk. 6: 35-43; 8: 1-9)
Exhortation, meditation and reflection

4. The Father

For Jesus, another word for God is "**the Father**"; hear him:
"... the true worshippers will worship the Father in spirit and truth. Yes, the Father wants such people to worship Him."
(Jn. 4: 23, 24).
THE PATIENCE OF GOD
"... My servants the prophets, whom I kept sending you, even though you do not listen to them..." (Jer. 26: 5 NABRE)
When God wants to make use of a person as a prophet. He does not show him everything at once. Rather, He shows him bit by bit, a step at a time; Notice, for example, that Isaiah was instructed to marry a prostitute. Jeremiah's Fine loincloth was required to be

concealed in a crevice and at Isaiah, another time to go to the potter to await the word of God there.

Moses was not told *ab initio*, what leading the people of God out of slavery would entail. He most probably would have balked.

Samuel demurred when he was ordered to go and anoint David in place of Saul God's use of imagery, metaphors and allegories – earthly or cultural nuances –to communicate His message, while good as aid to our understanding; then sometimes leads us to take as literal what Is allegorical, making it even harder for us to perceive His true intent.

So, at any particular point in time, we rarely come across the full picture of what the Lord's plan is. Only submission is required of us and He will work His plan through.

To know God, you must understand His nature. That is why Jesus says we must worship God in spirit and in truth: "But the hour is coming, and is now here, when true worshippers will worship the Father in Spirit and truth; and indeed the Father seeks such people to worship Him. God is Spirit, and those who worship Him must worship in spirit and truth."

(Jn. 4: 23-24 NABRE).

Exhortation, meditation and reflection

Fatherhood of God, Our Great Provider

In addition to the fact that the Lord God created the heavens and the earth with all their array, He blesses us on a daily basis for all our needs for the flesh, the spirit and the soul. A father provides for the needs of his family.

Thus in Matt. 6:11 we pray "Give us today our daily bread."

In the first missionary assignment, the twelve were thus instructed "Don't take along gold, silver, or copper for your money belts. Don't take a travelling bag for the road, … or a walking stick, for the worker is worthy of his food". (Matt. 10: 9-10 HCSB)

Love of God (1 Jn 5: 3)

"For this is what love for God is:

to keep His commandments"; not too burdensome because, being of faith as people who have been born of God we have conquered the world - by our faith.

Meditation: God, Our Father.

GOD, Our Father; the eternal Father of all! From Him all fathers and mothers spring up. Thank you, Lord, my God Father!

Oh, what loving kindness father and mothers are made of!

That Mars Probe (a meditation)

On Thursday Feb. 18, 2021, scientists in California, the behest of the Mars discovery adventure enthused at the successful soft-landing of the Rover Space vehicle, "Perseverance." The elation came seven minutes after the Perseverance had touched down on Mars, the time it took the pictures to travel to earth. It was a landmark achievement. The trans-planetary voyage had taken seven months to get to destination, travelling at mind-bungling speed of 12000 miles an hour, reduced to 4000 mph for the descend manoeuvres. Not 120mph and not 400 mph that may be familiar to passengers in auto and airplane travels, but 12,000 and 4,000! This bespeaks how daunting the adventure had been.

Exhortation, meditation and reflection

Why would man ever get himself attracted to such surrealistic and monstrous infinity? 'For curiosity'? To massage our ego for unravelling mysteries? Oh no! It is for knowledge's sake – to gain deeper understanding of the universe? Or, perhaps, it is 'for speculative purposes' – for opportunity to plunder that celestial body of whatever secret treasures there may be locked up there and ferret them out to earth? On the flip side, have we calculated the risk, the adversity such reckless intrusion may provoke by way of rage, reprisal or retribution? But perhaps it is not for cupidity that this brazen effrontery that broke the primordial peaceful co-existence of the planets was undertaken, but as a tribute or deference to power. Yes power hegemony with, or a dominion over, the powers that control yonder (i.e. Mars or the universe). I am befuddled; what is that gem, not native to earth, which we hope to find in outer space? What has the earth lost – a refuge or a fugitive – that we seek to find on Mars? Or is it that we have gotten so much peace here on earth that it has become boring, so we crave trouble for ourselves? We want to contrive the Armageddon?

My spirit is repugnant to go with any of the foregoing reasons or excuses because Mars is, certainly, not ours; it simply is not our property; not our habitat. My heart is remorseful that we ever did.

How dare man invade it? But, perhaps, the politicians and the scientists have done the needful: propelled by a comprehensive cost-benefit analysis had obtained (say, through prayers) a fiat or permit (like a visa) to go there?

A godless society refuses to acknowledge God. It says,
Sun, moon, stars, water and wind each give birth to itself.
Fish, birds, plant life, wild life – even man –
whose intricate anatomy we are familiar with –
all engineered themselves into existence!
What you see is a mere illusion; nothing is real.
There is no God!
Exhortation, meditation and reflection
I understand that over two billion dollars were spent on the project. What a handsome amount! I wish it were spent on perseveringly seeking God or even on the mundane matter of making our world a better place for all.
"The fool says in his heart, "God does not exist".
They are corrupt, they do vile deeds.
There is no one who does good.

The Lord looks down from heaven on the human race to see if there is one who is wise, one who seeks God" (Ps. 14: 1-2 HCSB)

Can anyone imagine a subject as close to, or near to the human heart as his Creator? Every human society has an inkling about who God is. Wouldn't it have been infinitely more rewarding to deploy such huge resources to seek to know more about God than about Mars – about the Creator, rather than the creature? Mars never intruded our mind, and is imperceptible to the eye, ear or other senses.

Yet, I feel some trepidation within me that I could be grossly wrong. How much do I know about these cosmic matters to be able to make intelligible contribution to such debate? Certainly, not for lack of a desire to know. Well, it is not wholly my fault; perhaps the government and the scientists should have taken society along with them. Many may not know the calculations, the mechanism and the robotics; but society, on behalf of whom they act, ought to have a say on the ethics, the morality and the worthiness or propriety of the venture. Why the opaqueness?

My fear is that this endeavour is prefigured in the eating by Adam and Eve of the forbidden fruit in a wild goose chase for more knowledge. Consequently, they were driven out of the garden, their comfort zone!

There is another parallel in the building of the tower of Babel, without God's consent. It ended abruptly in a fiasco.

Recall what happened after the first lunar landing, more than two decades ago. It incurred wrath of someone and was followed by the epidemic 'appolo' (or conjunctivitis)! Why must we remain obdurate and recalcitrant? Why must we persist in obstinacy?

With the invasion of the Moon, Mars and Jupiter, what really is man going after? With his eyes set on the entire universe – is it to acquire it?

CHAPTER 2

Only God Is Wise

How happy are those whose way is blameless,
who live according to the Lord's instruction!
Happy are those who keep His decrees and
seek Him with all their heart.

I have treasured Your word in my heart
so that I may not sin against You.
I gain understanding from Your precepts;
therefore, I hate every false way.
Your word is a lamp for my feet
and a light on my path. (Ps 119:1-2, 11, 104-105)
The steps of a good man are ordered by the Lord,
and He delights in his way. Though he fall, he shall not be
utterly cast down; for the Lord upholds him with His hand.
(Ps 37:23-24 NKJV).

ONLY GODWISE

"I have dealt with great things that I do not understand; things
too wonderful for me, which I cannot know…" (Job 42:3)

"Therefore, I will again confound these people with wonder
after wonder. The wisdom of their wise men will varnish and the
understanding of the perceptive will be hidden."
(Isa 29: 14 HCSB)
The wicked says,
"Let us oppress the righteous poor;
Let us neither spare the widow nor revere the aged…
But let our strength be our norm of righteousness;

for weakness proves itself useless"
(Wis 2: 10, 11 NABRE)

God, Our Righteousness (Compare Jer 33: 16)
Good and upright is the Lord; Thus, He shows sinners the way.
He guides the humble to justice, and teaches the humble His way.
(Ps 25: 8, 9Lect)

I have called … you ignore Me

"Since I have called and you have refused Me, since I have beckoned and no one has taken notice, since you have ignored all My advice and rejected all my warnings, I, for My part, will laugh at your distress, I will jeer at you when calamity comes, when calamity bears down on you like a storm and your distress like a whirl wind, when disaster and anguish bear down on you." (Prov 1: 24-27, L of H)

"Then they shall call to Me, but I will not answer, they shall seek Me eagerly and shall not find Me.

They despised knowledge, they had no love for the fear of the Lord, they would take no advice from Me, and spurned all My warnings: so, they must eat the fruits of their own courses, and choke themselves with their own scheming. For the errors of the ignorant lead to their death, and the complacency of fools works their own ruin;…
(Prov 1: 23-32, L of H)

Our Great Provider

Matt 10: 10
    a) Do not take a spare tunic…
    b) The Levites don't have a share in ………. the Lord is their portion (Deut 18:1-2)

  c) Lord's Prayer: We pray for only the day's bread. (Matt 6:11)
  d) In the gathering of the manna only a day's need for the family was required.

(Exo 16: 17-26)

Exceptions: Joseph in Egypt had to save for seven years as the bulwark against the expected famine.

Agabus (Acts 11: 29) foretold impending famine and the people had to build up reserves.

The Promise

"Fear the Lord, your God and keep… all His statutes and commandments… and thus have long life.

Be careful to observe them, that you may grow and prosper the more…"

(Deut 6: Lect)

Pretence

"Those who hate the Lord would pretend submission to Him…." (Ps 81:15).

God has no favourites; shows no partiality for He is God of all. In every nation everybody who does His will enjoys the favour of His countenance (Acts 10: 34-35 NABRE)

Obedience confers the grace on us to walk with the Lord

(1 Jn 1: 3, 6-7, 27; 1 Jn 2: 4-6; 1 Jn 3:24)

"…Be holy because I, your God am holy" (Lev 19:2)

"… He leads me in the paths of righteousness

for His name's sake" (Ps 23:3 NKJV)

"Falsehood I hate and abhor; your law I love.

Lovers of your law have much peace;

for them there is no stumbling block." (Ps. 119:163, 165 NABRE)

"The Lord is king; let the earth rejoice;

Let the many isles be glad.

Clouds and darkness are around about Him,

justice and judgement are the foundations of His throne.

All who worship graven things are put to shame,

who glory in the things that are naught;

all gods lie prostrate before Him." (Ps 97: 1-2, 7 Lect)

The gods made by human hands:

"Our God is in heaven and does whatever He pleases.

Their idols are silver and gold, made by human hands.

Those who make them are just like them, as are all who trust in them.

(Ps 115: 3-4, 8)

The Kingdom of God

Jesus said "The kingdom of God is not coming with something observable; no one will say, 'Look here!' or 'there!' For you see, the kingdom of God is among you" (Lk 17:20 – 21)

King Solomon at Gibeon - makes a prayer that pleases God.

"… Give Your servant an understanding heart to judge Your people and to distinguish right from wrong." (1 Kgs 3: 7-9)

"How great is Your goodness, Lord,

stored up for those who fear You;

You display it for those who trust You,

in the sight of the children of Adam.

(Ps 31: 20 NABRE)

Revere God; He giveswisdom, knowledge and understanding.

"If you seek it (wisdom) like silver

and search for it like hidden treasure,

then you will understand the fear of the Lord

and discover the knowledge of God.

For the Lord gives wisdom;

from His mouth come knowledge and understanding.

He stores up success for the upright;

He is a shield for those who live with integrity

so that He may guard the paths of justice

and protect the way of His loyal followers.

Then you will understand righteousness, Justice, and integrity – every good path.

for wisdom will enter your mind,
and knowledge will delight your heart." (Prov 2: 4-10 HCSB)

The Ways of the Lord

"Let whoever is wise understand these things,
and whoever is insightful recognize them.
For the ways of the Lord are right,
and the righteous walk in them,
but the rebellious stumble in them." (Hos 14: 9 HCSB)
"But the wisdom from above is first pure,
then peace-loving, gentle, compliant,
full of mercy and good fruits,
without favouritism and hypocrisy." (Js 3:17)

Love God

"For the love of God is this,
that we keep His commandments." (1 Jn 5:3; 2 Jn 1:6 NABRE)
Obedience
The Lord requires of us a diligent observance of His commandments, ordinances and precepts.

Moses warned the Israelites
"You shall not add to the word which I command you, nor take from it,
that you may keep the commandment of the Lord your God"

The Decalogue

"For this command which I am giving you today is not too wondrous or remote for you. It is not in the heavens… nor is it across the sea, … No, it is something very near to you, in your mouth and in your heart, to do it." (Deut 30: 11-14 NABRE)

THE TEN COMMANDMENTS

> ""Today I set before you
> life and prosperity, death and doom.
> If you obey the commandments
> of the Lord, your God...
> You will live and grow numerous...
> If, however, you turn away your
> hearts and will not listen,...
> You will certainly perish;...'" (Deut 30: 15 Lect)

PROLOGUE:

> "... 'The Lord, the Lord
> A God gracious and merciful,
> Slow to anger and abounding in love and fidelity,
> continuing His love for a thousand generations,
> and forgiving wickedness, rebellion, and sin;
> Yet not declaring the guilty guiltless,
> but bringing punishment for their parent's wickedness on children
> and children's children to the third and fourth generations!'"
> (Exo 34: 6-7 NABRE)

THE DECALOGUE (Deut 5: 6-21 NABRE) (Also in Exo 20: 2-17)

i. I am the Lord your God, who brought you out of the land of Egypt, out of the house of slavery. You shall not have other gods beside Me.

ii. You shall not make for yourself an idol or a likeness of anything in the heavens above or on the earth below or in the waters beneath the earth; you shall not bow down before them or serve them. For I, the Lord, your God, am a jealous God, bringing punishment for their parents' wickedness on the

48

children of those who hate Me, down to the third and fourth generation, but showing love down to the thousandth generation of those who love Me and keep My commandments.

iii. You shall not invoke the name of the Lord, your God, in vain. For the Lord will not leave unpunished anyone who invokes His name in vain.

iv. Observe the Sabbath day – keep it holy, as the Lord, your God commanded you. Six days you may labour and do all your work, but the seventh day is a Sabbath of the Lord your God. You shall not do any work, either you, your son or your daughter, your male or female slave, your ox or donkey or any work animal, or the resident alien within your gates, so that your male and female slave may rest as you do. Remember that you too were once slaves in the land of Egypt, and the Lord, your God, brought you out from there with a strong hand and outstretched arm. That is why the Lord, your God, has commanded you to observe the Sabbath day.

v. Honour your father and your mother, as the Lord, your God, has commanded you, that you may have a long life and that you may prosper in the land the Lord, your God is giving you.

vi. You shall not kill.

vii. You shall not commit adultery.

viii. You shall not steal.

ix. You shall not bear dishonest witness against your neighbour.

x. You shall not covet your neighbour's wife. You shall not desire your neighbour's house or field, his male or female slave, his ox or donkey, or anything that belongs to your neighbour.

Prayer

"Most loving Lord, grant me a steadfast heart, which no unworthy desire may drag downwards; an unconquerable heart which no hardship may wear out; an upright heart which no worth less purpose may ensnare.

Impart to me also, O God, the understanding to know You; the diligence to seek You, a way of life to please You, and a faithfulness that I may embrace You, through Jesus Christ, my Lord. Amen" – St Thomas Acquinas (op) (C1225 – 1274)

EPILOGUE:(Thanksgiving)
Almighty and awesome God! We worship You.
You are good,You are great; faithful and merciful.
What a perfect rule of life You have given us;
whatwisdom, packaged in love, goodness and piety!
What needless woes we put ourselves into;
we stumble when we ignore your commandments.
What joy, what bliss, when we live by them;
we gain understanding.
Forever You alone are God!
We thank You, Lord, our God.

The Fear of the Lord is the peak of wisdom

"All wisdom is from the Lord
and remains with Him forever.
The fear of the Lord drives away sins;
where it abides it turns back all anger." (Sir 1: 1, 21-22 NABRE)

Only One

"There is only one who is wise,
and we must stand in awe before His throne."
"The Lord Himself created wisdom;
He saw her and recognized her value,
and so, He filled everything He made with wisdom."
"There is no excuse for unjustified anger;
it can bring about your downfall." (Sir 1: 8-9, 22 GNBDK)

The fear of the Lord

"To fear the Lord is the first step to wisdom.
Wisdom is given to the faithful in their mothers' wombs."
"To fear the Lord is wisdom at her fullest;
she satisfies us completely with her gifts."
"To fear the Lord is the flower of wisdom
that blossoms with peace and good health."
"To fear the Lord is the root of wisdom;
her branches are long life." (Sir 1: 14, 16, 18, 20 GNBDK)
"I WILL CHANGE MY MIND…"
"At one moment I may declare concerning a nation or a kingdom, that I will pluck up and break down and destroy it, but if that nation, concerning which I have spoken turns from its evil, I will change My mind about the disaster that I intended to bring on it. And at another moment I may declare concerning a nation or a kingdom that I will build and plant it, but if it does evil in My sight, not listening to My voice, then I will change My mind about the good that I had intended to do to it." (Jer18: 7 – 10 NRSV – CI)

Things You Must Do

"… the things you must do:
Speak the truth to one another,
Judge with honesty…
Let none of you plot evil against another in your heart,
norlove a false oath.
For all these things I hate –
oracle of the Lord." (Zec 8: 16, 17 Lect)
DISCIPLINE – rely not on your own understanding
"No discipline seems enjoyable at the time, but painful. Later on, however, it yields the fruit of peace and righteousness to those who have been trained by it." (Heb 12: 11)

"Trust in the Lord with all your heart, and do not rely on your own understanding;

Do not despise the Lord's instruction, my son, and do not loathe His discipline;

For the Lord disciplines the one He loves, just as a father, the son he delights in."

(Prov 3: 5, 11-12)

LOVE fulfils the Law

"…Love one another, for the one who loves another has fulfilled the law.

Love does no wrong to a neighbour. Love, therefore, is the fulfilment of the Law."

(Rom 13; 8, 10 HCSB)

Hannah's song:

"The Lord brings death and gives life;

He sends some to Sheol, and He raises others up.

The Lord brings poverty and gives wealth;

He humbles and He exalts.

He raises the poor from the dust and lifts the needy from the garbage pile.

He seats them with noble men." (1 Sam 2: 6-8 HCSB)

Justice

"The course of your judgements, Lord, we await;

Your name and Your memory are the desire of our souls.

My soul yearns for You at night, yes, my spirit within me seeks You at dawn;

when Your judgement comes upon the earth, the world's inhabitants learn justice."

(Isa 26: 8-9 NABRE)

ALL lives belong to God

"Look, every life belongs toMe. The life of the father is like the life of the son – both belong to Me.

The person who sins is the one who will die." (Ezk 18: 4 HCSB)

For elaboration read Ezk 18: 10, 14

God's Will

Jesus admonished the scribes and Pharisees who were aghast that ablution traditions of the elders were not observed by His disciples.

Quoting Isa 29: 31, "they paid lip service to the observance of God's commandment, substituting their own ingenious interpretation and clever arguments to void the will of God." (Mk 7: 7 - 9Lect)

We are accountable

Many godly people suffer infirmities and persecutions and their persecutors seem to get away with it. Is there any gain, therefore, in serving the Lord – many ask.

(Mal 3: 14; Hab. 1: 3-4, 13)

Of course, the Lord remembers His faithful ones and there is accountability for our neglects and sins of commission. (Dan 7: 18)

The Questions That Puzzle Mortals:

You have said:

'It is useless to serve God...'

'Those who commit wickedness prosper,

they even test God and escape.' (Mal 3: 14, 15)

"Why do You tolerate wrong doing? Oppression and violence.... Strife … and conflicts escalates?"

"… justice never emerges. For the wicked restricts the righteous, therefore, justice comes out perverted"

"Your eyes are too pure tolook on evil, and you cannot tolerate wrong doing. So why do you tolerate those who are treacherous? Why are You silent while one who is wicked swallows up one who is more righteous than himself?" (Heb 1: 3 – 4; 13 HCSB)

Or, as Job might have put it, 'Why do bad things happen to good people?'

(Job 30: 20 – 23; 26)

Or, "But where can wisdom be found,

and where is understanding located?" (Job 28: 12, 20 HCSB)

The Answer:

Why God does not deal impulsively with the sinner -

Firstly – There is recompense for the righteous in the Day of Judgement (Mal 3: 16 – 17)

Secondly, sometimes the judgement comes sooner:

"Since you have plundered many nations, all the peoples who remain will plunder you…" (Heb 2: 8)

God's preferred option: repentance and salvation.

"…the wicked person should turn from his way and live. Repent, repent…"

(Ezk 33: 11)

Mercy on the wicked

"Do I take any pleasure in the death of the wicked?"

This is the declaration of the Lord God. "Instead, don't I take pleasure when he turns from his ways and lives?"

"Tell them: 'As I live' – the declaration of the Lord God – 'I take no pleasure in the death of the wicked, but rather that the wicked person should turn from his way and live. Repent, repent of your evil ways! Why will you die, house of Israel?'"

(Ezk 18: 23; 33: 11 HCSB)

The epitome is Jesus – the spotless Lamb of God offered in expiation of our sins on thecross of Calvary (Jn 3: 14-17)

Seek the Lord!

Seek the Lord while He may be found;
call to Him while He is near.
Let the wicked one abandon his way
and the sinful one his thoughts;
let him return to the Lord,
so He may have compassion on him,
and to our God, for He will freely forgive.
"For My thoughts are not your thoughts,
and your ways are not My ways."
This is the Lord's declaration.
"For as heaven is higher than earth,
so My ways are higher than your ways,
and My thoughts than your thoughts." (Isa 55: 6-9 HCSB)
THE LAW
"The law of the Lord is perfect,
refreshing the soul.
The decree of the Lord is trustworthy,
giving wisdom to the simple.
The precepts of the LORD are right,
rejoicing the heart.
The command of the LORD is clear,
enlightening the eye.
The fear of the Lord is pure,
enduring forever.
The statutes of the Lord are true,
all of them just;
more desirable than gold,
than a horde of purest gold,
sweeter also than honey,
or drippings from the comb.
By them Your servant is warned;
obeying them brings much reward." (Ps 19: 8-12 NABRE)

ADDITIONAL RESOURCES
His Covenant

"… the covenant … 'I will put My teaching within them and write it on their hearts.' I will be their God, and they also will be My people."

(Jer 31: 33 HCSB)

God, the Author of life, speaks to us through

Jesus,

"Who is the refulgence of His glory, the very imprint of His being, and who sustains all things by His mighty word…" (Heb 1: 2, 3 NABRE)

For mankind

He is 'the way, the truth and the life.' (Jn 14: 6 HCSB)

Obey Him – God commends Jesus to us:

"This is My beloved Son. I take delight in Him. Listen to Him!" (Matt 17: 5 HCSB)

1 Sam 15: 8-9, 12, 16, 22-24 HCSB

Obedience, sacrifice, presumption, sin.

"He (Saul) captured Agag King of Amalek alive, but he completely destroyed all the rest of the people with sword: Saul and the troops spared Agag, and the best of the sheep, cattle and choice animals, as well as the young rams and the best of everything else."

"But it was reported to Samuel, 'Saul went to Carmel where he set up a monument for himself…'"

Saul answered, "The troops brought them from the Amalekites and spared the best sheep and cattle in order to offer a sacrifice to the Lord, your God."

"Stop!"…

"Then Samuel said:

Does the Lord take pleasure in burnt offerings and sacrifices as much as in OBEYING the Lord?

Look: to obey is better than sacrifices, to pay attention is better than the fat of rams."

"For rebellion is like the sin of divination, and defiance is like wickedness and idolatry."

Rebellion, Defiance… or Presumption

"But Samuel said,

'Does the Lord so delight in burnt offerings and sacrifices as in OBEDIENCE to the command of the Lord? Obedience is better than sacrifice, and submission than the fat of rams. For a sin like divination is rebellion, and PRESUMPTION is the crime of idolatry.'"

(1 Sam 15: 23 Lect)

Faithful and dependable God

"… The Lord remains faithful forever, executing justice for the exploited and giving food to the hungry. The Lord frees prisoners."

"The Lord opens the eyes of the blind. The Lord raises those who are oppressed. The Lord loves the righteous."

"The Lord protects foreigners and helps the fatherless and the widow, but He frustrates the ways of the wicked." (Ps 146: 6-9 HCSB)

"The Lord helps the afflicted but brings the wicked to the ground."

(Ps 147: 6 HCSB)

ALL SCRIPTURE – inspired by God.

"All scripture is inspired by God and is profitable for teaching, for rebuking, for correcting, for training in righteousness,

so that the man of God may be completed, equipped for every **good work**."

(2 Tim 3: 16-17)

God is Our Righteousness

"… I am He; I am the first, I am also the last."

"My own hand founded the earth,
and My right hand spread out the heavens;..." (Isa 48: 12, 13 HCSB)
"I am Yahweh your God,
who**teaches** you for your benefit,
who**leads** you in the way you should go."
"If only you had paid **attention** to My commands..." (Isa 48: 17-19 HCSB)
"Be **attentive** to Me My people..." (Isa 51: 4)
Rom 16: 27 To the only wise God, through Jesus Christ...

God, Our Righteousness

"He leads me in the path of righteousness
for His name's sake." (Ps 23: 3 NKJV)
"Not everyone who says to me, 'Lord, Lord' will enter the kingdom of heaven, but only the one who does the will of My Father..." (Matt 7: 21)

CHRISTIAN UNITY

"...STOP disputing about words. This serves no useful purpose since it harms those who listen." (2 Tim 2: 14)
KEEP THE COMMANDMENTS!!
"...If you wish to enter into life, keep the commandments." (Matt 20: 17 HCSB)
Learn where prudence is, where strength, where understanding; that you may know also where are length of days and life, where light of the eyes, and peace.
She is the book of the precepts of God, the law that endures forever; all who cling to her will live, but those will die who forsake her.
(Bar 3: 14; 4: 1 NABRE)

THE LAW

"Hear, o Israel, **the commandments of life**;
Listen and know prudence!
You have forsaken the fountain of wisdom!
Had you walked in the way of God,
you would have dwelt in enduring peace". (Bar 3: 9, 12-13 NABRE)

Praise and thanksgiving to God, the king of our hearts!

"…Blessed are You, Lord, God of Israel our Father, from eternity to eternity.

Yours, Lord, are greatness and might, majesty, victory and splendour.

For all in heaven and on earth are Yours;
Yours, Lord, is kingship;
You are exalted as head over all.
Riches and glory are from You,
and You have dominion over all.
In your hand are power and might;
it is Yours to give greatness and strength to all.
Therefore, our God, we give You thanks and we praise the majesty of Your name. (1 Chro 29: 10-13 NABRE)
Exhortation, Meditation and Reflection.

Fellowship with God

It is not an abstruse philosophy to think of having fellowship with the awesome God. The Bible tells us that it was His purpose in creating us (Gen 1 & 2). It was in fulfilment of this desire that He sends His servants, the prophets to us and finally, Jesus, His only begotten son. Apostle/evangelist John made this point in his epistles pointing out the way to attain and sustain fellowship with God – by complete obedience to Him and this is achievable through obedience to Jesus and imitation of Him, because, then the Holy Spirit will give us understanding (1 Jn 1: 3, 6-7, 27; 1 Jn 2: 4-6; 1 Jn 3: 24)

The rule by man – 1

King Nebuchadnezzar of Babylon in 597BC at the surrender of King Jehoiachin of Judah made his uncle Mattaniah, king in place of him, and changed his name to Zedekiah. The Priest Ezekiel, who became a prophet five years later, was one of the deportees. Zedekiah later fell out of favour with Nebuchadnezzar and by way of reprisal he made him captive; killed his sons before his very eyes then took out his two eyes from their sockets.

(2 Kgs 24: 8; 25: 1-6; Jer 39: 6-7)

The rule by man – 2

King Herod, the tetrarch to add to the evil things he had done imprisoned John, the Baptist, and later killed him (Lk 3: 19-20)

Your majesties, your excellences and folks - won't you rather be ruled by God than by man?

TRANSCENDENTAL WISDOM

In times past, many peoples were idolaters and life on earth was brutish. As everyone behaved like the Joneses, who could have discerned the righteousness in the precepts and commands of God?

Some of which are:

- No worldly possessions and appurtenances for priests – "the Lord will be their inheritance."

(Deut 18: 1-2)

- The Lord forbids of divination, augury, sorcery, consulting ghosts, calling up the dead "…these nations are being driven away for these detestable practices…" (Deut 18: 10,11)

But for divine revelation, who could have discerned that such practices were abominations to the Sovereign King of kings and Lord of lords? Rather, many will be enraptured to almost worshipping the practitioners of such evils as being clairvoyant and learned.

Exhortation, Meditation and Reflection.

- The Lord commends special favour on the needy, strangers, servants, the newly wedded, etc.
- He places a ban on kidnapping (many generations became slaves, because their forbears were forcibly kidnapped and sold into slavery or because of some societal malevolence) (Deut 24: 7)
- (Deut 24: 5) "IF a man is newly married he must not go out with the army or be liable for any duty… Let him stay at home… to bring joy to the wife.

: 7 a kidnapper (of a fellow citizen) is to be killed.

- 24: 14-15 "You are not to exploit the hired servant" – whether citizen or stranger - pay his wages each day, not allowing the sun to set before you do…
- 24: 17 you must not pervert justice in dealing with a stranger or an orphan…
- 24: 19 when you harvest your vineyard you must not pick it over a second time. Let anything left be for the stranger, the orphan and the widow.
- 25: 4 do not muzzle an ox while it is treading out the corn."
- Unfathomable mercy! The bestial wisdom of most nations on the other hand, is to oppress the weak and despise and discriminate against foreigners. (in favour of their flesh and blood)

"For as heaven is higher than earth,
so My ways are higher than your ways,
and My thoughts than your thoughts." (Isa 55: 9)
"So My word that comes from My mouth
will not return to Me empty,
but it will accomplish what I please

and will prosper in what I send it to do." (Isa 55: 11)

The Lord is my shepherd

> there is nothing I lack
> He renews my life;
> He leads me along the right paths
> for His name's sake (Ps 23:1, 3)

The Rule by Man – 3

Man is brutish and ruthless. His subjects are like grass under his feet. He didn't create any of these and attaches mean value to their lives. A million souls or two countless to him than losing a finger or two of his, politically correct or sweet talk discounted. So why won't you rather be ruled by God – merciful, just and righteous?

Exhortation, Meditation and Reflection.

- King Solomon wasted no time on ascending the throne to do away with a sibling and the perceived enemies of his father – without trial!
- King Ahab craved Naboth's garden; assisted by his consort; got rid of the subject and confiscated the vineyard.
- King Nebuchadnezzar of Babylon esteemed Daniel and his three companions. Yet, that did not deter him from consigning those companions to roasting in an incinerator; or Daniel, himself, from being fed to lions in their den. Only the inscrutable God saved these men (Dan....)
- Herod the Tetrarch was crowned king of Judea about 4BC. He caused the death of the holy infants because by the story of the Magi he perceived a threat to his throne. (Matt 2: 1, 7, 12, 16)
- His successor, having acquired the wife of his brother Philip, jailed John, the prophet, eventually killing him for fun! (Matt 14: 3-12)

- Herod nodded to the killing of Jesus and many of Jesus' disciples, ordering the execution of all the guards set to watch over Peter on account of the miraculous (to him "perfidious") escape from prison of the Apostle. (Acts 12. 2-12; 17-19)
- Only about seventy-five years ago, Hitler and his cohorts caused the death of over twenty million people worldwide to feed his superiority complex. Starting with those he considered subhuman (untremacine) he later turned to execute his fellow compatriots, his mistress and finally himself!

Lord, "May Your Kingdom come!" (Matt 6: 10)

The Apostles' Legacy (for us):

"We must obey God rather than Men" (Acts 5: 29)

The Word

By the word of God, the heavens and the earth were created (Gen 1&2), His word is given to prophets and it never returns to God void, without accomplishing what it is purposed to do. Generally, it is

"to uproot and tear down,

to destroy and demolish,

to build and plant" (Jer 1:10)

Jesus is the word of God, incarnated in the Virgin Mary (Lk 1: 30-35)

Have a taste or steep yourself in wisdom from on high by mastering the teachings of the Lord Jesus, some of which are reproduced by way of an introduction in this book. The fullness is of course is in the Bible.

Exhortation, Meditation and Reflection.

OBEY!

"… Obey … so that you and your children after you may prosper forever…"

(Deut 12:28)
The Lord is King; let the earth rejoice!
Let the poor, the infirm and the oppressed heave a sigh of relief!
For the oppressor will not go unpunished;
The depraved will regret their malice
And the damned eschew the joy in knavery.
You meek, you just, raise your heads!
Be exultant!
For, on that day, all eyes shall see –
That the Lord our God is King!
The Lord is our law-giver.
He is our judge; we have hoped in Him.
He will judge the peoples with fairness
in equity and in mercy.
Maranatha! Come, Lord Jesus!
(see also Ps 97 and Isa 33)

Fear the Lord – obey!

"Blessed are all who fear the Lord,
and who walk in His ways.
What your hands provide you will enjoy;
you will be blessed and prosper:
your wife will be like a fruitful vine within your home,
your children like young olive plants around your table.
Just so will the man be blessed
who fears the Lord." (Ps 128: 1-4 NABRE)

The essence of our Christian formation is for each of us to have the mind of God – to be transformed in mind, heart, soul, and spirit and become a soul for ever seeking communion with God. (see 1 Cor 2: 16). This is the ultimate and that is why He calls Himself, 'Emmanuel'- God with us.

Sin and the Law:

Before the Decalogue, there was an order from God, which Adam and Eve breached. It was followed with punishment – death and ejection. Soon after Cain killed his brother, Abel; it was similarly followed by divine sanction.

Exhortation, Meditation and Reflection.

The flood that extinguished all life, except those in the Ark, was a punishment for sin. Sodom and Gomorrah were burnt out to wipe out the sinners within those cities.

Father Abraham was singled out for blessing for his righteousness (Gen 17:7; 22: 16). Moses and the entire Israel community enjoyed the covenant promises to Abraham.

During the exodus (before the Law), and thereafter, the Israelites were not spared of the rod of God's anger for their backsliding.

Then came Jesus, the Word Incarnate, into the earth's plane. Does that signal that sin is no longer detestable to God? He Himself lived his life on earth without the reproach of sin.

His earthly mission was heralded by the new Elijah (John, the Baptist). He preached repentance and conversion from sinning (Matt 3:2). So, when the Lord (Jesus) commenced His public ministry (after His marathon fasting) He also began by proclaiming repentance – "Repent, for the kingdom of heaven is at hand." (Matt 4: 17 NABRE)

When Moses midwifed the law, significantly, he spent nine verses (Lev 26: 4-12) to declare the blessings attached to their observance; spewed twenty-four verses

(Lev 26: 16-39) to warn about the dire consequences of disobedience and only one verse (Lev 26: 42) for the reward of repentance. It all sounds like our saying, that 'prevention is better than cure'. Temptation to sin and unforgiveness were among the most deadly sins singled out in the model prayer (chapter 15) as well as in some of the Lord's parables.

Pretenders

Those who hate the lord would pretend submission to Him… (Ps 81:15);

God has no favourites; shows no partially for He is God of all. In every nation, everybody who does His will enjoys the favour of His countenance (Acts 10:34-35)

Obedience confers the grace on us to walk with the Lord (1 Jn 1:3, 6-7, 27; 1 Jn 2:4-6; 1 Jn 3:24)

Concerning the Law, Jesus declared:

"It is easier for heaven and earth to pass away than for the law to become invalid."

(Lk 16: 17)

Observance of the law is the first step towards righteousness, and righteousness is the way of life in the kingdom of God. (Lk 17: 20-21)

Exhortation, Meditation and Reflection.

God's will – The Ten Commandments

'God's intention and purpose are reflected in His commandments. These are subverted by men's traditions and self – serving interpretations'[1].

Moses proleptically warned,

"In your observance of the commandments of the Lord, your God… you shall not add to… nor subtract from it." But "observe them carefully…" (Deut 4: 2, 6 NABRE)

The Word of God: life, power, wisdom…

"Oh the depth of the riches and wisdom and knowledge of God!

How inscrutable are His judgements and how unsearchable His ways!"

"For from Him and through Him and for Him are all things.

To Him be glory forever, Amen." (Rom 11: 33, 36 NABRE)

Only by God

"By the Lord are the steps of a man made firm… for the hand of the Lord sustains him." (Ps 37: 23, 24)

WISDOM

"All wisdom is from the Lord
and remains with Him forever.
Before all other things wisdom was created;
and prudent understanding, from eternity.
There is but One, wise and truly awesome,
seated upon His throne - the Lord.
If you desire wisdom, keep the commandments, and the Lord will bestow her upon you;
for the fear of the Lord is wisdom and discipline;
Faithfulness and humility are His delights." (Sir 1: 1, 4, 8, 26 - 27 NABRE)

1: Don Schwager… op cit.

Exhortation, Meditation and Reflection.
Prayer[2]
"For all generations You have been faithful and just in Your judgement, and wonderful in Your power and majesty. Wisely You have created, and wisely You have kept things in being. All that we see shows Your goodness; to all who trusts in You. You are faithful, kind and merciful. Forgive us our wickednesses and injustices, our sins and our transgressions.

Do not weigh down Your servants with the burden of their sins, but purify us and direct the paths we take so that we go forward in purity and innocence of heart, so that all that we do is good and acceptable to You and to those who lead us."

Judgement: Healing a blind man on the Sabbath (Jn 9: 1-41)

Narrator. As Jesus was passing by, He saw a man blind from birth.

Disciple: Rabbi, who sinned, this man or his parents that he was born blind?

Jesus: Neither; it is so that works of God might be made visible through him. I must do the works of Him who sent Me when it is (still) day… while I am in the world, I am the light of the world.

Narrator: Jesus then spat on the ground, from the clay smeared the man's eyes, saying,

Jesus: Go, wash in the pool of Siloam.

Narrator: So, the blind man left, washed and came back, seeing.

Crowd[1]: Isn't it this the one who used to sit and beg?

Crowd[2]: It is

Crowd[3]: No, he is just a look-alike.

Blind man: I am… I am the one.

Crowd: How were your eyes opened?

Blind man: The man called Jesus made mud, spread it on my eyes and told me, 'Go to

Siloam and wash'. I went, I washed and I see!

Crowd: where is He?

Blind man: I don't know.

Narrator: They brought the former blind man to the Pharisees.

2: Extracted from a letter of Pope St Clement I to the Corinthians.

Exhortation, Meditation and Reflection.

Pharisees: Man, how are you able to see?

Blind man: He put mud on my eyes, I washed and I see.

Pharisees[1]: This Jesus is not from God, how can He be working on the Sabbath?

Pharisees[2]: How can a sinful man perform such a miracle?

Pharisees[1]: Young man, what do you say about Him?

Blind man: He's a prophet.

Narrator: The Jews still doubting that he was the blind man summoned his parents.

Pharisees: Is this your son, who you say was born blind? Explain to us how he now sees.

Parents: Surely, this is our son; we know that he was born blind. As to how he now sees, we don't know. Ask him yourselves, he's of age, he will speak for himself.

Narrator: The parents were wary about what to say since the authorities had already agreed that whoever confessed that Jesus was the Messiah would be expelled from the Synagogue.

Pharisees: Young man, come! Give God the glory. We know that this man is a sinner.

Blind man: Whether He is a sinner or not, I don't know. What I know is that I was blind, but now I can see!

Pharisees: What did He do to you? How did He open your eyes?

Blind man: I already told you, but you wouldn't listen. Why do you want to hear it all again? You don't want to become His disciples too, do you?

Pharisees: Balderdash! You are the man's disciple; we are disciples of Moses; we know that God spoke to Moses but this man, we don't know where He is from.

Blind man: Amazing! You don't know where He is from? Yet, He performed the miracle of opening my Eyes! we know that God does not listen to sinners, but He listens to the one who is God-fearing and who does God's will. It is unheard of that anyone ever opened the eyes of a person born blind. If this man were not from God, He would not be able to do anything.

Pharisees: You were born totally in sin, and are you trying to teach us? Get him out!

Narrator: Jesus later found the man outside, and turning to His disciples He taught

them as follows

Jesus: I came into this world for judgement so that those who do not see, might see, and those who do see might become blind.

Reflection:

1. Who is this Jesus – a sinner or a man of God,
What do you say?
2. Who among the characters are in the right?
3. Why can't they all come to the same verdict?

Exhortation, Meditation and Reflection.

Let us pray (for discernment).

Oh God of truth, who gave the world the light of the day in the sun and the light of life in our saviour, Jesus Christ, we surrender our will to You.

Open our eyes and minds to see and host Your truth. Dispel the darkness of lies, and ignorance; of doubt and unbelief from our hearts. Reveal to us the path of life which truly delights You, so we may walk in it in praise of Your glory. Thank You, Lord. In Jesus name, we pray. Amen.

Meditation

The Way; efficacy of intercession
Read Exo 32: 1, 4, 10, 11-14

i. The way:

(God said) "… they have become depraved. They have soon turned aside from the way I pointed out to them,…" (Exo 32: 7, 8 Lect)

ii. The intercession:

"But Moses implored the LORD, His God, saying,…"

"So, the LORD relented in the punishment He had threatened to inflict on His people." (Exo 32: 11, 14 Lect)

"You have wearied the Lord with your words,… By saying, 'All evil doers are good in the sight of the Lord, and He is pleased with them' or 'Where is the just God?'"

(Mal 2: 17 NABRE)

Abraham Our Father in faith

Of all the inhabitants of the earth it pleased God to reveal Himself to Abram, son of Terah, a righteous man like Noah, and He renamed him Abraham.

Abraham was tested. He was commanded to leave his familiar country to resettle in a foreign land and in this way taught to depend upon divine providence. Until Abraham's wife was 86, she was childless. And then, the only child of the union, Isaac, was requested by God for a holocaust offering to Himself. Abraham acquesed in equanimity until he was estopped by God.

He was richly blessed; first child, Ishmael, was by an Egyptian woman (Hagar). After the death of Sarah, he took another wife and had more children. He gave a tenth of his spoils to Melchizedek, king of Salem, priest of God. (Gen 11: 31 – 18: 15)

He died at the age of 175 years.

Exhortation, Meditation and Reflection.

The Promise (to Abraham):

"I will make you into a great nation,

I will bless you,

I will make your name great,

and you will be a blessing,

I will bless those who bless you,

I will curse those who treat you with contempt,

and all the peoples on earth will be blessed through you"

(Gen 12: 2-3 HCSB)

This promise was affirmed by God in a covenant with Abraham by which he and his male descendants were to be circumcised. The covenant is transmitted through Isaac, who begat Jacob (renamed Israel by God.)

God calls Moses

Moses, a child born in Egypt of Hebrew parentage was called by God to lead his own people, the Israelites, out of the wretchedness of slavery into liberation and unto salvation.

The mission was tortuous but with God's help and the support of his brother, Aaron, the priest, Meiram a prophetess and sister, with Joshua, his personal assistant, the advice of Jethro, his Father-in-law and other people of goodwill such as Caleb, the task was accomplished.

The ministry of the Holy Spirit was unveiled; and was crucial to the success attained.

The promise of God to Abraham, which was repeated in turn to Isaac and to Jacob was fulfilled in Moses and David.

(Gen 35: 10-12; 23-26, 42-43; Exo 2-3).

THOU SHALL NOT KILL! (Deut 5: 17; Exo 20: 13)

Jews plotted to kill Saul (Acts 9: 23, 29)

Jews killed Stephen, the first Christian martyr (Acts 7: 59)

They killed Apostle James, (Acts 12: 2)

Till today, man is still headstrong, engaging in savage killing spree.

No condition is permanent – a reflexion

Consider the fate of Agag, king of the Amalekites in the hands of Saul and Samuel

(1 Sam 15: 8, 32-33)

Exhortation, Meditation and Reflection.

Obey!

That God does not mete out punishment instantaneously each time a sin is committed is because He is God, in honour of His sacred name (Isa 48: 9, 11) and on account of His mercy (Jn 8: 11)

Nevertheless, God ought to be obeyed always:

Jesus said, "Didn't Moses give you the law? Yet none of you keeps the law!"

(Jn 7: 19 HCSB)

Keep the commandments!

Jesus says, "If you want to enter into life, keep the commandments." (Matt 19: 17)

To know the Law and the scripture in general is good, and especially knowledge of God (Hos 6: 6).

But let no one be deceived, the knowledge alone may not avail. Righteousness requires that we believe the truth and practise what we believe.

Jesus and the Law

Matt. 5: 17 & 18: Jesus didn't come "to abolish the law, but to complete them", its purpose (righteousness) must be fulfilled.

5: 19 'Pastors' who preach this "will be considered great in the kingdom of heaven."

Jesus says,

"Do not think that I have come to abolish the law or the prophets. I have come not to abolish but to fulfil. Amen I say to you, until heaven and earth pass away, not the smallest letter or the smallest part of a letter will pass from the law, until all things have taken place. (Matt 5: 17-18 NABRE)

For more see Matt 5: 19-20; 7: 12.

WHY?

"Why do you recite my statutes,
and profess My covenant with your mouth,
though you hate discipline
and cast My words behind you?" (Ps 50: 16-17 Lect)

CALL

"Call to me, and I will answer you; I will tell
you wonderful and marvellous things that you
Know nothing about" (Jer 33: 3 GNBDK)

Exhortation, Meditation and Reflection.

The Law

See how magnificent, succinct and compact these laws are? They are the basic rudimentary laws, upon which the people of God shall build their society.

About two relate to our obligation to God; eight our obligations to ourselves and to one another. The abstruse laws are explained painstakingly and persuasively, the ones that touch the ardent desires of the heart of man require no further elucidation.

Society is right to attempt to make these laws cope with the actual complexities of life in secular laws, ordinances and regulations. But we should have separated Divine laws from these other man-made regulations aimed at appropriating them to go farthest. Those ordinances can be dismantled, amended by man to make them more precise, more equitable and more apposite to the times. But the Divine law may not be tampered with; it is immutable!

For example:

The law says, "You shall not kill"; not "You shall stone to death anyone who kills."

It is not enough to know that someone has breached that commandment; the relatives and friends of the slain will demand justice! Now, society can decide on that and even review its decision at a future date according to the circumstances – accidental, homicidal, manslaughter, first or second degree murder.

Whatever measure of retribution is decided upon, it is still incumbent on society to respect God's commandment, "You shall not kill".

All other laws are like that. For example, the commandment, "You shall not commit adultery", didn't say "You shall not commit adultery but shall stone to death transgressors!"

So from 10, society has vicariously attributed to God an awesome 600-plus (a theologian counted 613) commandments, precepts and ordinances, during Jesus' days; some of these Jesus decried, saying

"Woe to you experts in the law!

You have taken away the key of knowledge!

You didn't go in yourselves, and you hindered those who were going in."

(LK 11: 52 HCSB)

(Compare Matt 23:13 HCSB)

By this, we are not reducing our respect for the first generation leaders. They were herdsmen not urbane city dwellers. To control a million people is never an easy task. Moses could not do that all by himself alone. He had to listen to others. What we are saying is that we can always go back to God. (Jer 33:3)

It's never too late to do a good thing.

Exhortation, Meditation and Reflection.

DEPENDENCE ON GOD

1. Oh, with what vast wisdom the creator has fashioned the earth so variegated are the creatures therein, yet all happily co-existing.

The earth is old and sturdy, yet ever so youthful!

It is poised to endure forever at the Creator's will.

2. May all mankind learn to seek wisdom from its very source.

We acquire knowledge.

A man acquires knowledge through experience and learning.

The Creator gave us brain, topping it with instinct.

He gave us a mind to guide beneficially the exercise of our discretion.

We should use these to acquire the wisdom treasure of the ages.

And realize that God, the Creator, loves us. Yes, indeed, He loves us and would do for us anything (good) we ask of Him.

3. We should teach our children to look to God for how their
    lives are to be lived;

to know how far and in what direction to go each day.

Oh, what loving, wise people we would have been!

4. On the contrary, we leap into the unknown future as if we
    ordained everything in it, like Cyclops rushing in mad rage
    at the windmill.

Then we stumble – in pains and avoidable sorrow.

Our lives become lackluster, short and brittle.

All because we do not heed the Lord, our God.

5. A Christian's daughter, against all odds, ties the nuptial knot
    with a non-Christian. She went like a gazelle to the game,
    not recognizing the burden and the danger she's taking on.

She has to convert her spouse or be converted to his faith.

How little she knew of the value of her faith!

Hell got loose when wickedness or unfaithfulness unleashed its
venom on them.

All was foreboded but she did not take notice, seeing love
instead!

6. This king shuns truthful advisers, preferring to surround
    himself with sycophants, suckers and exploiters who want to
    use the king to feather their own nests.

The worldly wise never undertake the risk of speaking truth to
power.

Suave and always politically correct, they never cease to applaud
everything the boss says or does. Having attained power, he too
plods; detesting truth from below and retracting from truth to the
one above.

The entire system swelters with corruption.

Exhortation, Meditation and Reflection.

7. This teenager is becoming the young man-about-town with
    prospects of a boisterous, beautiful life. Well-honed in every
    respect, except the wisdom to embrace divine guidance.

His fun he finds in wild parties; different sex partners heighten his pleasure.

That way, many hearts he breaks and many lives he ruins.

Yet, he thinks he is rollicking in happiness.

He fathers children he would not accept and slips in the social ladder.

Not a few of those children would be delighted to snuff life out of him.

Death snatched a few of them for lack of care; a few sauntered into drugs and some into crime.

Happiness eludes and mocks him! Of course, he is upwardly mobile.

8. Take this other bride who is married to the beau of her life.

She discovered all too soon he was not her spark. And this beau found his wife's health a drain on his lean resources.

Both decided to untie the wedlock and flee!

The woman landed into a cauldron of unhappiness and exploitation;

the man in a fiesta of pub crawling, power intrigues and cultism.

If only they harkened unto the Lord before they bolted.

Truly, the fear of the Lord is the beginning of wisdom.

If only we realize that perfect wisdom lies only with the Lord; that He loves us and can accomplish through us things too great beyond our understanding, we would wisely submit to Him:

"… I will announce what has been hidden from the foundation of the world"

(Matt 13: 35 Lect)

Alas, this is hidden from many; so we grope and pay no heed.

But the Lord is very patient with us, knowing our weaknesses;

He stoops to carry us along in His eternal plan.

He speaks to the prophets a step at a time till his grandiose plan manifests (for example, He spoke to Jeremiah four times in Jer 13: 1-11 before His intension became comprehended.)

The entire ministry of John, the Baptist, was to prepare the people of God to receive the Messiah which he, himself, did not know (at first).

So, the Lord takes us up to great heights one step at a time.

Were it not so, many of us would remonstrate to go along with God, considering ourselves utterly incapable of the task.

Moses did not know the gigantic task ahead of him
before he started to make excuses – "I am a stammerer..."
Exhortation, Meditation and Reflection.

"Man, you have been told what to do, to walk humbly with the Lord..." (.....)

If only we listen!

If only the Jewish rabbi would listen to Jesus, the Son of God, the prophet would not have admonished them:

"So, also I will allow the pride of Judah to rot, the great pride of Jerusalem." (Jer 13: .....)

"The Lord executes acts of righteousness
and justice for all the oppressed." (Ps 103: 6)

"Let them give thanks to the Lord
for His faithful love
and His wonderful works for all humanity." (Ps 107: 8, 15, 21, 31)

CHAPTER 3

Jesus, the Messiah

In the beginning

was the Word,
and the Word was with God, and the Word was God.
He was in the beginning with God.
All things came to be through Him,
and without Him nothing came to be.
What came to be
through Him was life,
and this life was the light of the human race;
The light shines in the darkness,
and the darkness has not overcome it.
The true light, which enlightens everyone,
was coming into the world.
He was in the world,
and the world came to be through Him,
but the world did not know Him.
He came to what was His own
but His own people did not accept Him.
But to those who did accept Him He gave power to become
children of God,
to those who believe in His name, ….
And the Word became flesh
and made His dwelling among us,
and we saw His glory,
The glory of the Father's only Son,
fullof grace and truth. (Jn 1: 1-5, 9-12, 14 NABRE)
JESUS - by Apostle Paul:

"Who, existing in the form of God, did not consider equality with God something to be used for His own advantage." (Phil 2: 6 HCSB)

"What was from the beginning... we... heard... observed... touched... concerning the word of life that life... we testify and declare to you, the eternal life that was with the father... what we have seen and heard we... declare to you so that you may have fellowship along with us; and... with the Father and with His Son Jesus Christ."

"This is the message... God is light and there is absolutely no darkness in Him."

"But if we walk in the light ..., the blood of Jesus His Son cleanses us from all sin."

(1 Jn 1: 1-3, 5, 7 HCSB)

In wisdom and in love

For the word if the Lord is right,
and all His works is trustworthy.
He loves righteousness and justice;
the earth is full of the Lord's unfailing love.
... Your work, Lord!
In wisdom You have made them all;...
May sinners vanish... the wicked no more; bless the Lord, my soul! Hallelujah!
(Ps 104: 24, 35 NABRE)
The word is right... all His work trustworthy;
Righteousness He loves; earth is full of His unfailing love. (Ps 33: 4, 5 HCSB)

"JESUS" (Aramaic: 'the One who saves.')

"He is the image of the unseen God and the first-born of all creation,..."

Fidelis A. Olafusi, Kss

"Before anything was created He existed, and He holds all things in unity." (Col 1: 15; 2: 3)

Compare 1 Jn 1: 1-2 also Jn 1: 1-4, 10-12, 14.

Coming

"SING and rejoice, o daughter Zion!

For lo, I will come to dwell in your midst……"

"Be silent, all people, before the Lord; for He has roused Himself from His holy dwelling."

(Zec 2: 10, 13 NRSV-CE)

"Exult greatly,… Zion! Shout for joy,… Jerusalem!

Behold your king is coming to you,

a just Saviour is He, humble and riding on a donkey, on a colt…

and He will proclaim peace to the nations.

His dominion will be from sea to sea,

and from the river to the ends of the earth. (Zec 9: 9, 10 NABRE)

The WORD

… the word of life…

the life – eternal life – Jesus Christ was with the Father.

… Have fellowship with us

… we write that your joy may be full

… God is light; no darkness at all in Him.

If … we walk in darkness, we lie…

If we walk in light we have fellowship with one another

and the blood of Jesus Christ cleanses us from allsins. (1 Jn 1: 1-7 NKJV)

Chief witness to the Truth

"… for this I was born and … came into the world to testify to the truth.

Everyone who belongs to the truth listens to My voice" (Jn 18: 37)

His Brothers and Sisters – We are!

"My mother and My brothers are those who hear and do the word of God." (Lk 8: 21)

The WORD

The word has been sown, even in you the reader or hearer; but it produces different outcomes in the hearers – parable of the Sower (Mk 4: 1- …..)

The Word. "The Spirit is the one who gives life. The flesh doesn't help at all. The words that I

have spoken toyou are spirit and are life." (Jn 6: 63 HCSB)

My words, … His mouth

"Your God will raise up for you a prophet (like Moses)… put My words into His mouth and shall tell all I commandHim." (Deut 18: 18)

The Law: "…come not to abolish"

"Do not think that I have come to abolish the law or the prophets. I have come not to abolish but to fulfil…" (Matt 5: 17 NABRE)

"For I assure you: until heaven and earth pass away, not the smallest letter or one stroke of a letter will pass from the law until all things are accomplished." (Matt 5: 18 HCSB)

Obey first: The Gennesarat Catch

"As the crowd was pressing in on Jesus to hear God's word… He saw two boats…

The fishermen had left them and were washing their nets. He got into one of the boats… and was teaching the crowds from the boats.

When He had finished speaking, He said… 'Put out into the deep water and let down your nets for a catch.'

"Master," Simon replied, "We've worked hard all night long and caught nothing! But at your word, I'll let down the nets"

When they did this, they caught a great number of fish, and their net began to tear."

(Lk 5: 1, 2-6 HCSB)

Leaving all to follow Christ

"…they came and filled both boats so full that… Simon Peter… fell at Jesus knees and said, "Go away from me,because I am a sinful man, Lord!"

Then they brought the boats to land, left everything and followed Him."

(Lk 5: 7-8, 11 HCSB)

The Lord's Servant

"He will not break a bruised reed,
and He will not put out a smoldering wick;
He will faithfully bring justice.
He will not grow weak or be discouraged
until He has established justice on earth.
The islands will wait for His instruction."
"I, Yahweh, have called You for a righteous purpose,
And I will hold You by Your hand,
I will keep You and appoint You
To be a covenant for the people
and a light to the nations." (Isa 42; 3-4, 6 HCSB)

I am the good shepherd; I lay down my life for the sheep (Jn 10: 14 HCSB)

"… to seek out and to save the lost" (Lk 19:10)

"And just as the Father raises the dead and gives them life, so the Son also gives life to anyone He wants to."

"The Father, in fact judges no one but has given all judgment to the Son."

(Jn 5: 21-22)

"… He bore our sins in His body… so that…

we might live for righteousness" (1 Pt 2: 24 HCSB)

"… the Lord has punished Him for the iniquity of us all"

"… my righteous Servant will justify many, and He will carry their iniquities."

(Isa 53:6, 11 HCSB)

Jesus: the very imprint of God

"… a Son, … through whom He created the universe, who is the refulgence of His glory, the very imprint of His being, and who sustains all things by His mighty word.

When He has accomplished purification from sins, He took His seat at the right hand of the Majesty on High, as far superior to the angels as the name He has inherited…"

(Heb 1: 2, 3-4 NABRE)

Jesus says,

"If you love Me… keep My commandments"

Who Jesus is by Apostle John

Some theologians believe that the gospel and the epistles bearing the name John are authored or inspired by the beloved Apostle who enjoyed membership of the inner circle (peter, James and John) with Jesus. These are some of the ways Jesus is described in those books:

In the beginning, Jesus was there as the word of God, by which God created everything and He later took on flesh and was born as man.(Jn 1: 1-11; 1 Jn1-4)

He is God's son who makes those who believe in Him to be children of God.

(Jn 1: 12-13)

Jn 14: 7 "If you know Me, you will also know My Father, from now on you do know Him and have seen Him."

Jn 14: 6 "Jesus said to him (Thomas) I am the way and the truth and the life. No one comes to the Father except through Me"

Jn 14: 10,11 "… I am in the Father and the Father is in Me…"

14: 9 "… The one who has seen Me has seen the Father…"

14: 10 "… The words that I speak… I do not speak of My own. The father who lives in Me does His works."

14: 11 "Believe Me that I am in the Father and the Father is in Me…"

14: 28 "… If you loved Me, you would rejoice that I am going to the Father; for the Father is greater than I."

Jn 8: 12 "… I am the light of the world, anyone who follows Me will never walk in darkness but will have the light of life."

Jn 8: 42 "Jesus said to them,

'If God were your Father you would love Me, because I come from God and I am here. For I didn't come on my own, but He sent Me.'"

Jn 6: 46 "not that anyone has seen the Father except the One who is from God. He has seen the Father."

Authority over all flesh

"Jesus spoke these things,…"

'for You gave Him authority over all flesh; so He may give eternal life to all You have given Him'" (Jn 17: 1, 2 NABRE)

Who Jesus is – a reformer (Mal 3: 3)

Like refiner's fire He will purify the sons of Levi…

Healing a father's boy (Mk 9: 17-25)

Someone in the crowd said to Jesus, "Teacher, I have brought to You my son possessed by a mute spirit…"

They brought the boy to Him. The spirit immediately threw the boy into convulsions, fell to the ground, rolling around and foaming at the mouth. It had been like this since his childhood. Jesus rebuked the unclean spirit, 'Mute and deaf spirit, I command you: come out of him and never enter him again!'

That was it; the child was delivered immediately.

HEROD

(Lk 9: 9 HCSB) "I beheaded John,…" the vaunting of a principality or power in the person of Herod, (king of Judea)" I had John's head cut off;…" (GNBDK) No remorse!

Jesus, a man of prayer (e.g. Lk9: 18 HCSB) "while He was praying in private and His disciples were with Him,…"

GOSPEL is truth and truth is persecuted

2 Tm 1: 8 …. Your share of hardship for the gospel…

1: 9 He (Jesus) saved us and called us to a holy life…

JESUS, The Son of God

"…Blessed are those who hear the word of God and observe it." (Lk 11: 28 NABRE)

Prophecies concerning the coming of the Messiah:

- "… No longer will your Teacher hide Himself, but with your own eyes you shall see your Teacher." (Isa 30: 20 NABRE)
- "Look! I am coming quickly, and My reward is with Me to repay each person

according to what he has done. I am the Alpha and Omega,
the First and the Last,
the Beginning and the End." (Rev 22: 12-13)

- "… although He had done no violence and had not spoken deceitfully.

Yet the Lord was pleased to crush Him severely.

When You make Him a restitution offering… and by His hand, the Lord's pleasure will be accomplished.

He will see it out of His anguish,…

My righteous Servant will justify many, and He will carry their iniquities.

Therefore, I will give Him the many as a portion…the mighty as spoil,

because He submitted Himself to death…" (Isa 53: 9, 10-12)

The Son of God was revealed to destroy the works of the Devil (1 Jn 3:)

John, the Baptist Testimony:

"Here is the Lamb of God, who takes away the sin of the world! This is the One I told you about: 'After Me comes a man who has surpassed me, because He existed before me.' … I came baptizing… so He might be revealed to Israel. '… He is the One who baptizes with the Holy Spirit.' I have seen and testified that He is the Son of God!" (Jn 1: 29-31, 33-34).

- **My Servant**: to midwife true justice and salvation on earth:

"This is My Servant; I strengthen Him,
this is My Chosen One; I delight in Him.
I have put My Spirit on Him;
He will bring justice to the nations.
I will also make You a light for the nations,
to bring My salvation to the ends of the earth." (Isa 42: 1; 49: 6)

Jesus the 'Messiah' (Greek: 'Christ')

Jesus revealed Himself first to the Samaritan woman that He is the Messiah (Jn 4: 25-26)

Jesus and the Law

Jesus upholds the law and the prophet but His reform is to give their interpretation a human face. (Matt 5: 19)

Woe to you, scribes and Pharisees, you hypocrites.

You pay tithes… and have neglected

the weightier things of the law:

judgment and mercy and fidelity.

(But) these you should have done,… (Matt 23: 23 NABRE)

"… Christ Jesus, who became God-given wisdom for us – our righteousness, sanctification and redemption…" (1 Cor 1: 30)

Jesus: the miracle Worker

Even the sea and the wind obey Him (Mk 4: 41; Matt 8: 27), maniacs submit to His order as do diseases too! (Matt 9: 35; Mk 5: 6-8) "Then those in the boat worshipped Him…"

(Matt 14: 33)

Read a similar incident in Matt 8: 25-27.

His word carries great power.

At the Gennesaret catch, obedience to the word brought about transformation

(Lk 5: 1-11)

"Nothing like this has ever been seen in Israel!" (Matt 9: 33)

Witnesses "The works that I do IN MY FATHER'S NAME testify about Me.

But you don't believe because you are not My sheep." (Jn 10: 25-26)

Prophecies Concerning Jesus Passion:

- "… dry… is My throat;

My tongue cleaves to My Pilate;

You lay Me in the dust of death.

They have pierced My hands and My feet

Dogs…; a pack of evil doers closes in on Me.

…they stare at Me and gloat;
they divide My garment among them;
for My clothing they cast lots.
The generation to come will be told of the Lord,
that they may proclaim to a people yet unborn
the deliverance You have brought."
(Ps 22: 10, 17-19, 32 NABRE)
▪ "Who has believed what we have heard?...
He was despised and rejected by men,
a man of suffering…
He was despised, and we didn't value Him.
Yet He Himself bore our sicknesses,
and He carried our pains;
but we in turn regarded Him stricken,
struck down by God, and afflicted.
But He was pierced because of our transgressions,
crushed because of our iniquities;
punishment for our peace was on Him,
and we are healed by His wounds.
We all went astray like sheep;
we all have turned to our own way;
and the Lord has punished Him
for the iniquity of us all.
He was taken away because of oppression and judgment; …
For He was cut off from the land of the living;
He was struck because of My people's rebellion." (Isa 53: 1, 3-6,
8)

JESUS: "…To give His life – a ransom for many." (Mk 10: 45)
WITNESSES: "God added His Testimony by signs,
wonders, various acts of power, and distribution of the gifts of
the Holy Spirit…"
(Heb 2: 4 NABRE)

Eternal Life – 1

"This is the One who came through water and blood, Jesus Christ, not by water alone, but by water and blood. The Spirit is the One that testifies, and the Spirit is truth. So there are three that testify, the Spirit, the water, and the blood, and the three are of one accord."

(1 Jn 5: 6-8 NABRE)

Eternal Life – 2

"…God has given us eternal life,

and this life is in His Son.

The one who has the Son has life…

I have written these things to you who believe in the name of the Son of God,

so that you may know that you have life. (1 Jn 5: 11, 12-13)

The way of Truth – to eternal life

"…I am the way, the truth and the life…" (Jn 14: 6 NABRE)

"…I am the resurrection and the life; whoever believes in Me,

even if he dies, will live." (Jn 11: 25 NABRE)

'I am the light of the world. Whoever follows Me…

will have the light of life.' (Jn 8: 12 NABRE)

- "For unto us a Child is born,

Unto us a Son is given;

and the government will be upon His shoulder.

And His name will be called

Wonderful, Counsellor, Mighty God, Everlasting Father, Prince of Peace.

Of the increase of His government and peace

there will be no end,….

To order it and establish it with judgment and justice

from that time forward, even forever.

The zeal of the Lord of hosts will perform This" (Isa 9: 6-7 NKJV)

- "She will give birth to a Son,

and you are to name Him Jesus,

because He will save His people from their sins." (Matt 1: 21)

The covenant with David:

- "Moreover… the Lord will make a house for you:

when your days have been completed and you rest with your ancestors…

Your house and your kingdom are firm before Me; your throne

shall be firmly established forever." (2 Sam 7: 11, 12, 16 NABRE)

Who Jesus Is

The Messiah: "This is what is written:

The Messiah would suffer and rise from the dead

the third day, and repentance for forgiveness

of sins would be proclaimed in His name

to all nations, beginning at Jerusalem." (Lk 24: 46-47)

"…I came from God and I am here… He sent Me."

"…I assure you: Before Abraham was, I am." (Jn 8: 42, 58)

The Son of God: "In times past, God spoke… to our ancestors through

the prophets; in these last days,

He spoke to us through a Son,… through whom He created the universe, who is the refulgence of His glory,

the very imprint of His Being,

and who sustains all things by His mighty word.

When He has accomplished purification from sins,

He took His seat at the right hand

of the Majesty On High,

as far superior to the angels…" (Heb 1: 1-4 NABRE)

The narrow gate

"Enter through the narrow gate.

For the gate is wide and the road is broad

that leads to destruction,… many… go
through it. How narrow is the gate and
difficult the road that leads to life,
and few find it." (Matt 7: 13-14)
"Make every effort to enter through the narrow door, because …
many will try to enter and won't be able" (Lk 13: 24)
Good Works:
"He went about doing good…" (Acts 10: 38)

God has chosen us through Christ

to be holy and without fault before Him (Eph 1: 4)
For by the blood of Jesus Christ we are set
free from our sins, i.e., our sins are forgiven (Eph 1: 7)
Jesus Christ is the word of life – eternal life (1 Jn 1: 1-2 GNBDK)
Walk in the light
"But if we walk in the light as He (God) Himself is in the light,
we have fellowship with one another, and the blood of Jesus,
His Son cleanses us from all sin." (1 Jn 1: 7)
- Zachariah to John, the Baptist: "And you, child,… will go to
   prepare His ways."
(Lk 1: 76)
Demons knew Who Jesus was: (e.g. the maniac, "Legion"):
"…what do you have to do with Me, Jesus, You Son of the Most
High God?..." (Lk 8: 28)?
The CROSS

The Cross of Jesus

"… the cross is foolishness to those who are
perishing, but to us… being saved
… power of God"(1 Cor 1: 18)
The sign of Jonah
"This generation (Jesus' contemporaries) is an evil generation.
It demands

a sign, but no sign will be given to it except the sign of Jonah…
as Jonah became a sign to… Nineveh, so also the
Son of Man will be to this generation…
Nineveh… repented at Jonah's proclamation…" (Lk 11: 29-30, 32)

WHY was Jesus Killed?

- The Seed/Destiny - to take away our sins; redeem mankind as the Lamb of God (Isa 53)

High Priest Caiaphas – propitiation (Jn 18: 14; 19:7)

"By the Living God I place you under oath: tell us if You are the Messiah, the Son of God!"(Matt 26: 63, 65 HCSB) (Mk 14: 60, 63)

"… the Son of Man did not come to be served, but to serve, and to give His life – a ransom for many." (Matt 20: 28)

Time for everything:

"…But this is your hour – and the dominion of darkness" (Lk 22: 53 HCSB)

- Immediate Cause: Jesus was considered an outsider to the priestly and Levitical caste, hence a threat to their established position and honour.

("Tell uswith what authority You do these things") (Matt 21: 23)

- Ultimate (legal) reason:

a) Blasphemy – Governor Pilate: "I find no guilt in Him"

Jews: "we have a law… He made Himself the Son of God." (Jn 19: 6, 7) NABRE

b) Treason

Jews: "If you release Him… Everyone who makes himself a king opposes Caesar"

(Jn 19: 12 NABRE) also (Lk 23: 1)

c) A rebel – Jews/Chief Priests: "… crucify Him!... we have no king but Caesar"

(Jn 19: 15) NABRE/HCSB

The Good News and the Word

"I must proclaim the good news of the kingdom of God,
because for this purpose I have been sent." (Lk4: 43 Lect)
The Word:
Jesus teaching and preaching must produce different outcomes
in the hearers
(Mk 4: 3-20)

The Great Commission

"All authority has been given to Me
in heaven and on earth.
Go, therefore, and make disciples
of all nations,… teaching them
to observe everything I have commanded you." (Matt 28; 18-19)

Our Great High Priest

"Therefore, since we have a great high priest… -
Jesus the Son of God – let us hold fast to the confession.
For we do not have a high priest who is unable to sympathize
with our weaknesses, but One who has been tested in every way
as we are,
yet without sin." (Heb 4: 14-15)
Historical Corroboration, Christianity is not a legend.
"In the 15th year of the reign of Tiberius Caesar, while Pontius
Pilate was governor of Judea, Herod was tetrarch of Galilee, his
brother Philip tetrarch of the region of Ituraea and Trachonitis and
Lysanias tetrarch of Abilene, during the high priesthood of Annas
and Caiaphas, God's word came to John…" (Lk 3: 1-2)
The kingdom of God
"In the days of those Kings,… God…
will set up a kingdom… never (to) be
destroyed… it… will itself endure forever." (Dan 2: 44)

- One like a son of man…
"…was given authority to rule,…
glory… Kingdom;… every people,
nation and language should serve Him…
an everlasting dominion that will not pass away…" (Dan 7: 14)

"Don't cry!"

"…dead man seat up!" (Lk 7: 13, 15) were the comforting words Jesus gave the Nain town mother who had lost her only son to death. But Jesus went beyond that to restore her son back to her - alive! (Lk 7: 13-16)

Jesus is full of compassion. He knew the beginning of the end was in sight for His corporeal ministry. He left home – possibly that Mary may not have to witness the full horrors of His passion. Even as He lay dying strangled on the cross, He held a soft-spot for Mary and His disciples. Taking His thought away from Himself and death, He spoke words of consolation to both.

Jesus and sin

"You know that He was revealed so that
He might take away sins,
and there is no sin in Him.
Everyone who remains in Him
does not sin: everyone who sins
has not seen Him or known Him.
Little children, let no one deceive you!
The one who does what is right is righteous,
just as He is righteous.
The one who commits sin is of the Devil,
for the Devil has sinned from the beginning.
The Son of God was revealed for this purpose:
to destroy the Devil's works." (1 Jn 3: 5-8)
"He is expiation for our sins,

and not for our sins only

but for those of the whole world." (1 Jn 2: 2 NABRE)

Jesus, the Messiah – 'King'

The triumphant entry into Jerusalem (Mk 11: 1-10), a spontaneous event which preceded Jesus passion is just one other fulfilment of prophecy. (Zec 9: 9-10)

The Caring Good Shepherd

1) The disciples voyaged to Bethsaida and they encountered a storm which battered their boat as they rowed. Jesus traversed the dead of night, walking on the sea to rescue His own. (Mk 6: 45-51)

They had to know that He did this, because He cared for them.

2) The Good Shepherd of the Flock

"I am the Good Shepherd. The good shepherd lays down his life for the sheep."

"I am the Good shepherd. I know My own sheep and they know Me.

… I lay down My life for the sheep."(Jn 10: 11, 14-15)

My sheep

"My sheep hear My voice; I know them

and they follow Me.

My Father who has given them to Me, is greater than all.

No one is able to snatch them from the Father's hand." (Jn 10: 27, 29)

For more read Heb 13: 20; Mk 10: 45

One flock, one Shepherd

"But I have other sheep that are not of this fold; I must bring them also,

and they will listen to My voice. Then there will be one flock, one shepherd."

(Jn 10: 16 HCSB)

Not My Sheep

"But you don't believe because you are not My sheep." (Jn 10: 26 HCSB)

For more read Heb 13: 20; Mk 10: 45

Jesus revealed Himself first to the Samaritan woman – not to a Jew – that He is the Messiah

(Jn 4: 25-26)

The Testimony:

The people testified –

"He has done everything well…" (Mk 7: 37)

"… Yet wisdom is vindicated by her deeds." (Matt 11: 19 HCSB)

Personal Affirmation

Questioned by the High Priest, Caiaphas, Jesus admitted that "I AM (the Messiah)"

(Mk 14: 61-62)

His dominion: vast, just, equitable and everlasting.

"His dominion will be vast… on the throne of David…

and sustain it with justice

and righteousness from now on and forever…" (Isa 9: 7 HCSB)

Jesus – Mankind's Mediator with the Father.

"for there is one God,

and one mediator between God and humanity,

Christ Jesus, Himself human,

who gave Himself – a ransom for all,

a testimony at the proper time." (1 Tim 2: 5-6 HCSB)

Mystery of the Messiah

"…He strictly ordered His disciples to tell

no one that He was the Messiah." (Matt 16: 20 NABRE)

The First Resurrection

Jesus was raised from the tomb by the Father the third day. (Mk16: 1-16; Matt28: 1-10)

"The tombs were also opened and many bodies of the saints who had fallen asleep were raised. And they came out of the tombs after His resurrection, entered the holy city, and appeared to many." (Matt27; 52-53)

"But now Christ has been raised from the dead, the first-fruits of those who have fallen asleep."

(I Cor 15: 20) Read also: (I Cor 15: 21-28; 35-44; 51-55)

The Great Call

"All things have been entrusted to Me
by My Father.
No one knows the Son except the Father,
and no one knows the Father except the Son
and anyone to whom the son desires to reveal Him.
Come to Me, all of you who are weary and burdened,
and I will give you rest. All of you,
take up My yoke and learn from Me,
because I am gentle and humble in heart,
and you will find rest for yourselves.
For My yoke is easy and My burden is light." (Matt 11: 27-30)

- "Let the heavens be glad, and let the earth rejoice;
Let the sea roar and all that fills it;
Let the field exult, and everything in it.
Then shall all the trees of the forest sing for joy before the Lord;
For He is coming,
for He is coming to judge the earth.
He will judge the world with righteousness,
and the peoples with His truth." (Ps 96: 11-13 NRSV-CI)
"At the presence of the Lord, for He is coming to judge the earth.
He will judge the world with righteousness." (Ps 98: 9 NRSV-CI)

SECOND COMING:

The Day of the Lord

"Look! I am coming quickly,
And My reward is with Me to repay each person according to what he has done.

I am the Alpha and the Omega,
the First and the Last,
the Beginning and the End." (Rev 22: 12-13)
For further reading, see
Zec 14: 7-9; Joel 3: 14-16; Rev 11: 17-19; 21: 1-5, 22-27
HCSB's version of Zec 14: 7 gives another insight;
"it will be a day known only to Yahweh,
without day or night, but there will be
light at evening." (Zec 14: 7 HCSB)

Parousia: Jesus - the judge of the world

"The Father, in fact, judges no one but has given all judgment to the Son." (Jn 5: 22 HCSB)

Judgment

"I am the light of the world. Anyone who follows Me will never walk in the darkness but will have the light of life."

"The Father, in fact, judges no one but has given all judgment to the Son."

"This, then, is the judgment: The light has come into the world, and people loved darkness rather than the light because their deeds were evil for everyone who practices wicked things hates the light and avoids it, so that his deeds may not be exposed. But anyone who lives by the truth comes to the light, so that his works may be shown to be accomplished by God."

"I assure you: Anyone who hears My word and believes Him who sent Me has eternal life, and will not come under judgment but has passed from death to life."

(Jn 8: 12; 5: 22; Jn 3: 19-21; 5: 24. HCSB)

I am making everything new

Rev 21: 3 "Then I heard a loud voice from the Throne:

Look! God's dwelling is with humanity, and He will live with them. They will be His people, and God Himself will be with them

and be their God."
Rev 21: 5 "Then the One seated on the throne said,
Look! I am making everything new…"
Rev 21: 23 "The city does not need the sun or the moon
to shine on it, because God's glory
illuminates it, and its lamp is the Lamb."

JESUS: His Ministry

"The Spirit of the Lord is on Me,
because He has anointed Me
to preach good news to the poor.
He has sent Me
to proclaim freedom to the captives
and recovery of sight to the blind,
to set free the oppressed,
to proclaim the year of the Lord's favor." (Lk 4: 18-19 HCSB)
"Yet to those who are called, both Jews and Greeks,
Christ is God's power and God's wisdom." (I Cor 1: 24)
The mystery of the passion and death of Jesus

The narration of the horrendous torment and grisly death of Jesus Christ began with His betrayal for (30 pieces of silver – "the magnificent price"at which they valued the Messiah (Zec 11: 13 HCSB), His agony, abandonment or solitude in the Garden where He was arrested; His miserable treatment in the hands of the High Priests and the Sanhedrin, the circus trial by Pontius Pilate and condemnation and immediate execution through crucifixion. (Lk 22: 21-23: 56; Jn 18: 1-19: 42)

This cup: the cross of Jesus

"….Father, if you are willing,
take this cup away from Me – nevertheless
not My will, but Yours, be done." (Lk 22: 42)
The passion of Jesus – glory

So, when he (Judas Iscariot) had gone out
(on the betrayal mission) Jesus said,
"Now, the Son of Man is glorified, and God is
glorified in Him." (Jn 13: 31 NKJV)
From the above prayer of our Lord Jesus Christ
We begin to appreciate the dimension of our own crosses.

"summoning the crowd along with His disciples, He said to them, 'if anyone wants to be My follower, he must deny himself, take up his cross, and follow Me.'" (Mk8: 34 HCSB)

Our cross is when our will is on course for a conflict with the will of God; (about to cross the will of God) and we do the needful: conquer it! Subdue our will to the divine will. Thereafter, every other thing is inconsequential.

That is the lesson from Jesus Geneseretprayer: complete resignation!

Qui sera, sera; (what will be, will be)[2]

The Return to Egypt

History nearly repeated itself – the flight to Egypt – in the days of Archelaus, the ethnarch
(4BC-AD6):
"After they were gone, an angel of the Lord suddenly appeared to Joseph in a dream, saying, 'Get up! Take the child and His mother, flee to Egypt, and stay there until I tell you. For Herod is about to search for the child to destroy Him.'" (Matt 2: 13 HCSB)

2 A Latin-America calypso song
LOVE Christ – obey! (Jn 14: 15)
"The one who has My commands and keeps them is the one who loves Me. And the one who loves Me will be loved by My Father. I also will love him and will reveal Myself to him."
(Jn 14: 21)

Jesus predicts His crucifixion

"Just as Moses lifted up the snake in the wilderness, so the Son of Man must be lifted up, so that everyone who believes in Him will have eternal life." (Jn 3: 14-15 HCSB)

Jesus told His disciples,

1) "... I am going away to prepare a place for you. If I go away and prepare a place for you, I will come back and receive you to Myself, so that where I am you may be also." (Jn 14: 2, 3 HCSB) See also Matt 16:21.

2) "Nevertheless I tell you the truth. It is to your advantage that I go away; for if I do not go away, the helper will not come to you; but if I depart, I will send Him to you."

(Jn 16: 7 NKJV)

Jesus Predicts His imminent death

"While going up to Jerusalem, Jesus took the 12 disciples aside privately and said to them on the way":

"Listen! We are going up to Jerusalem. The Son of Man will be handed over to the chief priests and scribes, and they will condemn Him to death Then they will hand Him over to the Gentiles to be mocked, flogged, and crucified, and He will be resurrected on the third day." (Matt 20: 17-19 HCSB)

Four Witnesses to Jesus:

First John the Baptist, 2nd Jesus' works (teaching, preaching, signs and wonders), thirdly the Father and finally the Holy Scripture. (Jn 5: 31-39)

Who Jesus is: Healing the Capernaum demoniac

- "In the synagogue there was a man with an unclean demonic spirit who cried out with a loud voice, 'Leave us alone! What do you have to do with us, Jesus-Nazarene? Have You come to destroy us? I know who You are-the Holy One of God!'

But Jesus rebuked him and said, 'Be quiet and come out of him!'

And throwing him down before them, the demon came out of him without hurting him at all."(Lk 4: 33-35 HCSB)

- In several exorcisms that the Lord performed, the unclean spirits were vociferous shouting, 'You are the Son of God'

"Also demons were coming out of many, shouting and saying, 'You are the Son of God!'But He rebuked them…" (Lk 4: 41 HCSB)

Jesus: The Word and you

"whoever has ears to hear ought to hear" (Lk 8: 8 Lect)

"… these are the ones who, having heard the word with an honest and good heart, hold on to it and by enduring, bear fruit." (Lk 8:15 HCSB)

The Parable of the Sower: The Word

"When a large crowd gathered… people from one town after another… Jesus … spoke…:

'A sower went out to sow his seed. And as he sowed, some seed fell on the path and was trampled, and the birds of the sky ate it up.

Some seed fell on rocky ground, and when it grew, it withered for lack of moisture.

Some seed fell among thorns, and the thorns grew with it and choked it.

And some seed fell on good soil, and when it grew, it produced fruit a hundred fold.'

'… Then His disciples asked Him what the meaning of this parable might be.

He answered,…

The seed is the word of God.

Those on the path are the one who have heard, but the Devil comes and takes away the word from their hearts that they may not believe and be saved.

Those on rocky ground are the ones who, when they hear, receive the word with joy, but they have no root, they believe only for a time and fall away in time of temptation.

As for the seed that fell among thorns, they are the ones who have heard, but as they go along, they are choked by the anxieties and riches and pleasures of life, and they fail to produce mature fruit.

But as for the seed that fell on rich soil, they are the ones who, when they have heard the word, embrace it with a generous and good heart, and bear fruits through perseverance.'" (Lk 8: 4-15 Lect)

His DIVINITY

"so that all people will honour the Son just as they honour the Father. Anyone who does not honour the Son does not honour the Father who sent Him." (Jn 5: 23 HCSB)

Jesus: Pointers to His divinity

- Prophecy: "The Lord says:
You, Bethlehem-Ephrathah,…
from you shall come forth for Me
One who is to be ruler of Israel;
Whose origin is from Old,
from ancient times." (Mic 5: 1-2 Lect)
- His conception is by the power of the Holy Spirit and not by flesh or blood, and the heavens proclaimed His birth. (Lk 1: 35; 2: 9-14)
- The Sabbath, Jonah, Solomon
Jesus told the Pharisees
"But I tell you something greater than the temple is here!"
"for the Son of Man is Lord of the Sabbath." (Matt 12: 6, 8 HCSB)
"…something greater than Jonah is here!" (Matt 12: 41)
"…Look something greater than Solomon is here!" (Matt 12: 42; Lk 11: 31)
- God commended Him to us as Son. He, in all history, is the only One that God commended to mankind as Son

"This is my beloved Son… Listen to Him." (Matt 17:5)
- He is the One from above, from heaven – He is above all. (Jn 3: 31, 34-35) op cit
- His 'form' or nature is divine

"Make your own attitude that of Christ Jesus, who, existing in the form of God,…"
(Phil 2: 5, 6 HCSB)
- The Scriptures: He is from old; the word incarnate, through Him all things were made.

(Jn 1: 1-4, 9-12, 14) op cit

The Messiah's death foretold

"After those 62 weeks the Messiah will be cut off." (Dan 9: 26)
Yahweh,Our Righteousness.
"The days are coming" –
This is the Lord's declaration –
"when I will raise up a Righteous Branch of David. He will reign wisely as king and minister justice and righteousness in the land."
(Jer 23: 5 HCSB)

The Promise: A Prophet like Moses

Moses spoke: "A prophet like me will the Lord, your God, raise up for you from among your own kindred, that is the One to whom you shall listen." (Deut 18: 15 NABRE)

Jesus, are you the Messiah? (Jews demanded a sign)
Jesus gave them five (Jn 5: 31-47):
  i. John, the Baptizer
  ii. His works (teaching, healing and preaching)
  iii. The Father
  iv. The Scriptures
  v. Moses,"on whom you have set your hope" (Jn 5: 45 HCSB)
  vi. You should be able to find in this chapter evidence in support of all five contentions; have you?

"Even though He had performed so many signs in their presence, they did not believe in Him." (Jn 12: 37 HCSB)

The TRUTH: Jesus is chief witness

"…I was born for this,
and I have come into the world for this:
to testify to the truth. Everyone who is of the
truth listens to My Voice." (Jn 18: 37 HCSB)
Jesus, Son of God –

Not by flesh and blood, but by obedience:

"But no one in heaven or on earth or under the earth was able to open the scroll or to examine it."

"…Do not weep. The Lion of the tribe of Judah, the Root of David, has triumphed, enabling Him to open the scroll with its seven seals."

"They sang a new hymn:
'WORTHY are You to receive the scroll
and to break open its seals,
for You were slain and with Your blood,
You purchased for God those from every tribe and tongue, people and nation!
You made them a kingdom and priests for our God, and they will reign on earth.'"

"…Worthy is the Lamb that was slain to receive power and riches, wisdom and strength, honour and glory and blessing." (Rev 5: 3, 5, 9-10, 12 NABRE)

Jesus' Ministry

"He will be like a refiner and purifier; He will purify the sons of Levi and refine them like gold and silver. Then they will present offerings to the Lord in righteousness." (Mal 3: 3 HCSB)

ADDITIONAL RESOURCES

1 Tim 2: 5 "For there is one God and **one Mediator** between God and humanity, Christ Jesus, Himself human."

1 Jn 5: 19 "We know that we are of God, and the whole world is under the sway of the evil one."

: 18 "We know that everyone who has been born of God does not sin… the One born of God keeps him…"

: 17 "All unrighteousness is sin…"

Jn 14: 28 "… I am going to the Father, because the Father is greater than I."

: 30 "… because the **ruler of the world** is coming. He has no power over Me."

1 Cor 1: 9 "God is faithful; you were called by Him into fellowship with His Son, Jesus Christ…"

1 Jn 5; 20 – The True One

"And we know that the Son of God has come and has given us understanding so that we may know the true One. We are in the true One – that is, in His Son Jesus Christ. **He is the true God and eternal life**."

Jesus is God

Isa 40: 5 And the glory of the Lord will appear, and all humanity together will see it, for the mouth of the Lord has spoken.

: 9 Zion, herald of good news,… Jerusalem, herald of good news, raise your voice loudly… say to the cities of Judah, "Here is your God!"

: 10 See, **the Lord God comes** with strength…

: 11 He protects His flock like a shepherd;…

1 Cor 11: 3 "… know that Christ is the head of everyman,… and **God is the head of Christ**."

Eph 3: 11 This is according to His eternal purpose accomplished in the Messiah, Jesus our Lord.

2 Tim 4: 1 I solemnly charge you before God and Christ Jesus, who is going to judge…

1 Cor 8: 6 …. **There is one God, the Father… and there is one Lord, Jesus Christ**. All things are through Him.

: 15 "I am praying

: 17 "Sanctify them by the truth; Your word is truth."

: 23 "… may they be made COMPLETELY ONE, so the world may know You have sent Me and have loved them as You have loved Me."

: 24 "Father, … then they will see My glory which You have given Me because You have loved Me before the world's foundation."

Phil 2: 11 "And every tongue should confess that Jesus Christ is Lord, to the glory of God the Father."

2 Cor 1: 3 (son) **"Praise the God and Father of our Lord Jesus Christ**, the Father of mercies and the God of all comfort."

Jn 17: 3 This is **eternal life**; that they may know **You, the only true God** and the One You have…

Eph 1: 1 Paul, an apostle of Christ Jesus by God's will: to the …

Col 1: 3 "we always thank God, the Father of our Lord…"

1 Cor 1: 3 "Grace to you and peace from **God our Father** and the Lord Jesus Christ."

: 2 "for You gave Him authority over all flesh

So He may give eternal life to ALL you have given Him."

: 3 "This is ETERNAL LIFE: That they may know **You,**

the only true God, and the One You have sent – Jesus Christ."

: 5 "Now, Father, glorify Me in Your presence with that glory I had with You before the world existed."

: 10 "Everything I have is Yours, and everything You have is Mine, and …

: 11 "… Holy Father, protect them by Your name…

so that they may be one as we are One."

THE LAMB OF GOD

"They sing a new hymn: 'worthy are You… for You were slain and with Your blood You purchased for God those from every tribe and tongue, people and nation.

You made them a kingdom and priests for our God, and they will reign on earth.'"

(Rev 5: 9, 10 NABRE)

The voices of many angels

"… they cried out…

'Worthy is the lamb that was slain to receive power and riches … glory and blessing'" (Rev 5: 11, 12)

He cares for the body also – The "mountain of miracles and multiplication"

(Matt 15: 29-31, 32-38 HCSB)

"Moving on from there, Jesus passed along the Sea of Galilee. He went up on a mountain and sat there, and large crowds came to Him, having with them the lame, the blind, the deformed, those unable to speak and many others. They put them at His feet, and He healed them… the crowd was amazed…

He took the seven loaves and fish and He gave thanks, broke them and kept on giving them to the disciples, and the disciples gave them to the crowds. They all ate and were filled. Then they collected the leftover pieces – seven large baskets full. Now those who ate were 4000 men, besides women and children."

Walking with God

"God is light, and in Him there is no darkness at all.

We cannot have fellowship with Him while we continue

to walk in darkness." (1 Jn 1: 5, 6 NABRE)

Rev 19: 8 NABRE

"She was allowed to wear a bright, clean linen garment.

(The linen represents the righteous deeds of the holy ones.)"

Rev 19: 9

"Then the angel said to me, 'write this: Blessed are those who have been called to the wedding feast of the Lamb… These words are true; they come from God.'"

Spirit of prophecy

Rev 19: 10 NABRE

"… 'worship God.' Witness to Jesus is THE SPIRIT OF PROPHECY."

HCSB

"… Worship God, because the testimony about Jesus is the spirit of prophecy"

The Word of God:

Rev 19: 11, 13 (NABRE)
"The heavens opened and there was a white horse;
Its rider was (called) 'Faithful and True'. He judges
and wages war in righteousness."
"He wore a cloak that had been dipped in blood,
and His name was called THE WORD OF GOD."
JESUS, is the word of life – made visible…
"All things came to be through Him, …
What came to be through Him was life,
and this life was the light of the human race,…
the true light, which enlightens everyone,
was coming into the world.
He was in the world,…" (Jn 1: 1-2, 3, 4, 9-10 NABRE)
GRACE, TRUTH FROM JESUS:
"From His fulness we have all received grace in place of grace,
because while the law was given through Moses,
grace and truth came through Jesus Christ."
(Jn 1: 17 NABRE)
Jesus Christ, our wisdom, righteousness, sanctification, redemption, law giver, judge, king, saviour. (1 Cor 1: 30)

Jesus' Ministry

Salvation: "To seek and to save (what was lost)" Lk 19: 10
His Passion prophesied:
"There's a baptism with which I must be baptized, and how great My anguish until it is accomplished!" (Lk 12: 5)

Isa 7: 14 The SIGN

Isaiah said, 'Listen, house of David!

Therefore… a sign: the virgin will conceive, … (bear) a son …"

Matt 1: 21-23

"She will give birth to a son,

and you are to name him Jesus,

because he will save his people from their sins."

Isa 9: 7 HCSB

"His dominion will be vast,

… on the throne of David…

and sustain it with justice

and righteousness from now and for ever."

Jesus, the Word

Rev 5: 8-14

"Heaven and earth worshipped Him (the lamb)

'Worthy are you to receive the scroll…

for you were slain and with your blood you purchased

for God those from every tribe and tongue,

people and nation. You made them a kingdom

and priests for our God…'"

Dan 7: 18

They will reign on earth

Act 3: 26

"God raised up His servant and…"

Daniel's Account – the son of man

Dan 7: 9 "As I watched, thrones were set up and the Ancient of Days took His throne"

: 10 "The court was convened, and the books were opened"

: 13 "I saw coming with the clouds of heaven ONE LIKE A SON OF MAN"

: 14 "He received dominion, splendour and kingship; all nations, peoples, and tongues will serve Him. His dominion is an everlasting dominion…"

: 18 "… the **holy ones** of the Most High shall receive the kingship, to possess it for ever and ever."

: 21 "As I watched, that horn made war against the holy ones and was victorious."

(Explanation for the prevalence of evil.)?

: 22 "Until the Ancient of Days came and judgement… and the time arrived for the holy ones to possess the kingship."

2 Pt 1: 19 Pay attention, "You will do well to be attentive to it"

Rev 5: 5; 22: 16

"The lion of the tribe of Judah, the root of David"

(see also Gen 49: 9; Isa 11: 1, 10; Matt 1: 1)

Acts 3: 20 Jesus, Messiah

"And that He may send Jesus who has been appointed… Messiah"

Isa 11: 10

"On that day the root of Jesse, set up as a signal for the peoples Him the nations will seek out; His dwelling will be glorious"

Jesus – His Teachings: The Word

Js 1: 21B Lect "The word that… is able to save your souls"

Js 1: 18 Lect REBIRTH: "He willed to give us birth by the word of truth…"

Lk 2: 34 Simeon

"Then Simeon blessed them (Mary and Joseph) and told His mother, Mary: 'indeed this child is destined to cause the fall and rise of many in Israel, and to be a sign that will be opposed."

"A New Teaching?"

"Then they were all amazed, so they began to argue with one another, saying, 'What is this? A new teaching with authority!'

He commands even the unclean spirits, and they obey Him.'"

(Mk 1: 27, 28 HCSB)

Four Testimonies to Jesus ministry:

1. John the Baptist: Matt 11: 10-11

2. His works: Jn 10: 25
3. The Father: Deut 4: 12, 15; 1 Jn 2: 14
4. The Scriptures: Deut 18: 15; Matt 24: 5, 24

Those in the tomb will hear His voice – Jn 5: 28-29; (some to life, some to condemnation)

Jn 5: 22, 27 All judgement given to Son.

Jn 9: 40 (Jesus) came that those blind might see; those seeing become blind!

I am the light of the world Jn 9: 5?

Ps 55: 23 Lect "Cast your care upon the Lord,

and He will support you…"

Examples of

1. Jesus Wisdom & Sagacity

(God and Caesar)

"'well, then,' He told them 'Give back to Caesar the things that are Caesar's and to God the things that are God's'" (Lk 20: 25 HCSB)

2. Jesus Revelation of the eternal mysteries

Life after death (Lk 20: 27-36 HCSB)

"For they cannot die anymore, because they are like angels and are sons of God, since they are sons of the resurrection."

(Lk 20: 36 HCSB)

JESUS, the righteousness of GOD

"After three days they found Him in the temple,

sitting in the midst of the teachers, listening to

them and asking them questions, and all who

heard Him were astounded at his understanding…"

(Lk 2: 46-47? NABRE)

Come! Jesus beckons you!

"COME to me, all of you who are weary and burdened,

and I will give you rest."
"… take My yoke and learn from Me,…
For My yoke is easy and My burden is light."
(Matt 11: 28, 29-30 HCSB)

Abide in Me, bear fruit!

"I am the vine, and My Father is the vineyard keeper
Remain in Me and I in you. Just as a branch is unable to produce fruit by itself unless it remains on the vine, so neither can you unless you remain in Me.

I am the vine, you are the branches. The one who remains in Me and I in him produces much fruit, because you can do nothing without Me.

If You remain in Me and My words remain in you, ask whatever you want and it will be done for you.

As the Father has loved Me, I have loved you. Remain in My love.

If You keep My commands you will remain in My love…

So whatever you ask the Father in My name, He will give you."
(Jn 15: 1, 4-5, 7, 9-10, 16 HCSB)

Testimony:

1 Jn 3: 22 HCSB "… (we) can receive whatever we ask from Him
because we keep His commands…"
Obey the Law…!
"Don't assume that I came to destroy the law or the prophets. I did not come to destroy but to fulfil." (Matt 5: 17 HCSB)

116

"… received dominion, glory and kingship;
all peoples, nations should serve Him. His …
an everlasting dominion…" (Dan 7: 14 HCSB)
King of righteousness
Jn 18: 35 "I'm not a Jew, am I?"
"Your people handed you over to me.
What have you done?"
: 37 "You say that I'm a king, … For this I was born
and for this I came into the world, to testify to the truth.
Everyone who is of the truth listens to My voice."
: 38 "… to the Jews again … 'I find no grounds for charging
Him.'"
THE NEW COVENANT
"I will give you a new heart and put a new spirit within you;
I will place My Spirit within you and cause you to
follow My statuses and carefully observe My ordinances."
(Ezk 36: 26, 27 HCSB)

Jesus admonished the evil and perverse generation for asking for a sign.

"No sign shall be given but the SIGN of JONAH"
"… A sign to the gentiles for the forgiveness of their sins."
"… a sign of the new and everlasting covenant for the forgiveness of sins."
As rainbow presages the coming of rain so Jesus is the sign of the times – the time for redemption and the atonement of sins
Covenant
Jer 31: 31-34 I will make a NEW COVENANT with Israel and Judah … My teachings within them.
Lk 22: 20 took the cup (after supper) said "This cup is the New Covenant, by My blood"
Isa 54: 13 GNBDK "I myself will teach your people… give them prosperity and peace."

Jer 32: 40 I will make an everlasting covenant – one heart, one way to fear Me.

Heb 9: 15 The Messiah is the mediator of a new covenant so that the called may receive (the promise of) eternal inheritance.

Ezk 37: 26 "I will make an everlasting covenant of peace with Israel with my laws in their minds & hearts…"

OBEY:

"You shall obey… keep His commandments…" (Deut 30: 10-14)

Jesus Divinity
"Now, Father, glorify Me in Your presence with
that glory I had with You before the world existed."
(Jn 17: 5 HCSB)

Miracle worker
Healing the blind man of Bethsaida (Mk 8: 22-26)

"… At Bethsaida they brought to Jesus a blind man and begged Him to touch him… Then He laid hands on his eyes a second time and he saw clearly…"

The Deaf at Sidon (Mk 9: 2-10)

Jesus went by way of Sidon to the Sea of Galilee. There they brought him a deaf man who also had a speech impediment. They begged Jesus to cure him. Looking into heaven Jesus sighed deeply, and said "Ephphatha!" (That is, 'be opened'). Immediately his ears were opened and his speech difficulty was removed. He spoke clearly.

Jesus, the law and the prophets – listen to Him!

Jesus took Peter, James and John on a high mountain (traditionally thought of as mount Olives) to be alone by themselves.

Jesus' clothing changed becoming dazzling white as no launderer on earth could whiten them.

Elijah with Moses appeared, talking to Jesus. In a cloud a voice was heard, "This is My beloved Son; listen to Him!"

Startled and looking around the disciples no longer saw anyone except Jesus alone.

(Mk 9: 9-10)

GOD Coming (Visiting)

1st Coming

- See, I am going to send My Messenger, … Then the Lord you seek will suddenly come to His temple, the Messenger of the covenant you desire. See, He is coming says the Lord… (Mal 3: 1)
- See, the Lord God comes with strength, and His power establishes His rule. His reward is with Him, and His gifts accompanying (Isa 40: 5, 10)

JESUS the truth

"So, Jesus said to the Jews who had believed in Him, 'If you continue in My word, you really are My disciples;

You will know the truth, and the truth will set you free.'" (Jn 8: 31, 32 HCSB)

"But now you are trying to kill Me, a man who has told you the truth that I heard from God…"

"Jesus said to them (the Jews), 'If God were your Father, you would love Me, because I came from God and I am here. For I didn't come on My own, but He sent Me.'"

"Yet because I tell the truth, you do not believe Me."

"If I am not doing My Father's works, don't believe Me." (Jn 8: 40, 42, 45; 10: 37 HCSB)

Jesus, on Sin:

- "... 'I assure you: Everyone who commits sin is a slave of sin.
- A slave does not remain in the household for ever;
- but a son does remain forever.'" (Jn 8: 34 HCSB)
- "... Jesus... said to him, 'See, you are well. Do not sin anymore, so that something worse doesn't happen to you.'" (Jn 5: 14 HCSB)
- "'Neither do I condemn you', said Jesus. 'Go, and from now on do not sin anymore.'" (Jn 8: 11)

Jesus Divinity: Before Abraham and Moses, I AM.

"Jesus said to them (Jews), 'I assure you: Before Abraham was, I am.'"

(Jn 8: 58 HCSB)

Healing the paralytic: Power of Jesus to forgive sins

On one of those days while Jesus was teaching with pharisees and teachers of the law in attendance, "some men came carrying on a mat a man who was paralysed... since they could not find a way to bring him in because of the crowd, they went up the roof and lowered him on the mat through the roof tiles... before Jesus."

"Seeing their faith He said, 'Friend, your sins are forgiven you!'"

"... so you may know that the Son of Man has authority on earth to forgive sins..."

The paralytic immediately got up before them, picked up what he had been lying on, and went home glorifying God. Then, everyone was astounded..."

(Lk 5: 17-26)

His Coming:

- A sign of Salvation (in the house of His servant, Jacob)
- My beloved Son (Mk 1: 7; Matt 19: 5; Matt 17: 5 HCSB)
- "Let the fields and everything in them exult.

Then all the trees in the forest will shout for joy before the Lord, for He is coming – for He is coming to judge the earth. He will judge the world with righteousness."

(Ps 96: 12, 13)

Jesus, the bread of life

"… Man must not live on bread alone
but on every word that comes from
the mouth of God." (Matt 4: 4 HCSB)
Jesus, the consecrated One
Can you say that the One whom the Father has consecrated and sent into the world blasphemies because I said, 'I am the Son of God?' (Jn 10: 36 NABRE)

He began to teach in the synagogue and many who heard Him were astonished. They said, 'Where did this man get all this? what kind of wisdom has been given Him? What mighty deeds are wrought by His hands?'

(Mk 6: 2)

Jesus is our life!

- "I have come so that they may have life and have it in abundance."
  (Jn 10: 10)
- "I am the Good Shepherd. The Good Shepherd lays down his life for the sheep."

"I lay down My life for the sheep."
"… the Father loves Me, because I am laying down My life so I may take it up again.
No one takes it from Me,…" (Jn 10: 11, 14, 17, 18 HCSB)
Jesus is from antiquity
In the beginning was the word…
and the word was incarnated of the
virgin Mary and became man (Jn 1: 1, 10, 14)

Jesus says,
"I am the good shepherd. I know My own sheep,
and they know Me." (Jn 10: 14 HCSB)
The light of the world
"As long as I am in the world,
I am the light of the world." (Jn 9: 6 HCSB)
Jesus passion prophesied
"I gave My back to those who beat Me,
My cheeks to those who plucked My beard,
My face I did not shield from buffets and spitting.
The Lord God is My help…" (Isa 50: 6, 8 Lect)
PAROUSIA
"I am coming soon" (Rev 22: 7, 12 and 20)
Marana tha (Aramaic) "come, Lord Jesus!" (Rev 22: 20)
Genealogy of Jesus
"The historical record of Jesus Christ, the Son of David, the Son
of Abraham:
Abraham fathered Isaac, Isaac… Jacob,
Jacob fathered Judah…"
"Boaz fathered Obed by Ruth,
Obed … Jesse, and Jesse fathered King David."
"… Then David fathered Solomon by Uriah's wife,
Solomon… Rehoboam…"
"Ahaz fathered Hezekiah, Hezekiah… Manasseh,
Manasseh… Amon, Amon fathered Josiah"
"… Shealtiel fathered Zerubbabel, Zerubbabel fathered
Abiud,…"
"Manthan fathered Jacob, and Jacob fathered Joseph,
the husband of Mary, who gave birth to Jesus who is called the
Messiah."
(Matt 1: 1-16 HCSB)
"…Jesus, Son of David, have mercy on me!" (Lk 18: 38 HCSB)
A little about David
"The Lord said,

'I have made a covenant with My chosen one;
I have sworn an oath to David My servant.
I will establish your offspring forever
and build up your throne for all generations'" Selah

- "… The Lord has found a man loyal to Him, and the Lord has appointed as ruler over His people,…" (1 Sam 13: 14 HCSB)

"After Jesse presented seven of his sons to him, Samuel told Jesse, 'The Lord hasn't chosen any of these.'

'There is still the youngest,… but right now he's tending the sheep.'

"So Jesse sent for him…"

"Then the Lord said, 'Anoint him, for he is the one.' So Samuel took the horn of oil, anointed him…" (1 Sam 16: 10, 11, 12-13 HCSB)

- David the Psalmist

"'I have seen a son of Jesse of Bethlehem who knows how to play the lyre. He is also a valiant man, a warrior, eloquent, handsome, and the Lord is with him.'" And David became Saul's armour-bearer.

(1 Sam 16: 18, 21-22 HCSB)

- David, the killer of lions, the killer of Goliath.

"David answered Saul: '… wherever a lion or a bear came and carried off a lamb from the flock, I went after it, struck it down and rescued the lamb from its mouth. If it reared up against me, I would grab it by its fur, strike it down and kill it.'"

(1 Sam 17: 34-35 HCSB)

"David said to the Philistine: 'You come against me with a dagger, spear and sword, but I come against you in the name of Yahweh of Hosts,… all the world will know that Israel has a God,…'"

"David… took out a stone, slung it, and hit the Philistine on his forehead… and he fell on his face to the ground. David defeated the Philistine with a sling and a stone."

(1 Sam 17: 45, 49-50 HCSB)

▪ The irreconcilable duo: it was either Saul or David.

The prize at stake was the monarchy – Saul realized this early, though David was loyal to him and unambitious. The Lord willed to terminate the dynasty of Saul and to replace it with the house of David.

> ▪ Merab: yes and no! Michal: yes, but 100 Philistine foreskins for bride price! It was treachery; David actually delivered 200 Philistine foreskins!

(1 Sam 18: 12-27)

"Then David got up and secretly cut off the corner of Saul's robe. Afterward, David's conscience bothered him… He said to his men, ' … I would never do such a thing to my Lord, the Lord's anointed. I will never lift my hand against him…'"

(1 Sam 24: 4, 5, 6 HCSB) (Read also 1 Sam 26: 7-11)

▪ David who killed Goliath fled from King Saul!

"Saul has killed his thousands, but David his tens of thousands."

(1 Sam 18: 7 HCSB)

▪ King David

At long last, David became king over the house of Judah (2 Sam 2: 4)

"All the tribes of Israel came at Hebron and said, ' … The Lord said to you, 'You will shepherd My people Israel and be ruler over Israel.'"

"… and they anointed David king over Israel." (2 Sam 5: 2-3) Thus David re-united Judah with Israel in one kingdom.

The blood of Jesus

"…and the blood of His Son Jesus cleanses us from all sin." (1 Jn 1: 7)

John's testimony concerning Jesus

"… I baptize with water, but there is One among you…

whom you do not recognize,

the One who is coming after me, whose sandal strap

I am not worthy to untie." (Jn 1: 26-27 NABRE)

Jesus, ransom for sin.

"When the fullness of time had come,

God sent His son, born of a woman born under the law,

to ransom those under the law so that we may receive adoption"

(Gal 4: 4, 5 NABRE)

"As PROOF that you are sons (by adoption),

God sent the Spirit-of-His-Son into our hearts,

crying out, 'Abba, Father!'" (Gal 4: 6 NABRE)

Name of Jesus

- KING (by the magi saying), "where is the new born KING of the Jews? We saw His star at its rising and have come to do Him homage."

(Matt 2: 2 NABRE)

Foreigners First to Pay Jesus Homage:

"They prostrated themselves and did Him homage." (Matt 2: 11 NABRE)

- Ruler Chief Priests and Scribes: "... Bethlehem... from you shall come a ruler, who is to shepherd My people Israel." (Lk 1: 26-33 NABRE)

CALL – Blessed are "the Called"

"Then the angel said to me, 'write this: BLESSED ARE THOSE WHO HAVE BEEN CALLED TO THE WEDDING FEAST OF THE LAMB." "These words are true; they come from God."

(Rev 19: 9 NABRE)

Prophecy – the 1st Coming

- Thus says the Lord:

'You, Bethlehem Ephratha...

from you shall come forth

for Me one who is to be

ruler in Israel; whose origin

is from of old, from ancient times.' (Mic 5: 1)

"He shall stand firm and

shepherd his flock by the

strength of the Lord in

the majestic name of the Lord,

his God... he shall be peace..." (Mic 5: 3, 4 LECT)

- The King of Israel, the Lord, is in your midst,...

"The Lord your God, is in your midst

a mighty Saviour..." (Zeph 3: 15, 17 NABRE)

(Compare 1 Chr 17: 3, 4, 6, 11, 13 and 14 NABRE)

- "But that night the Lord spoke to Nathan... 'Go, tell my servant David, thus says the Lord: ... I will make you famous like the great ones of the earth... the Lord also reveals to you that He will establish a house for you... I will raise up your heir after you, sprung from your loins, and I will make his kingdom firm. I will be a Father to him, and He shall be a Son to Me...'"

"... and his throne shall be firmly established forever."

(2 Sam 7: 3, 4, 8, 11, 13, 14)

Authority over the elements

"He got up, rebuked the wind,

and said to the sea,

'Silence! Be still!'

And they were terrified and asked

one another, 'who then is this?

Even the wind and the sea obey Him!'" (Mk 4: 39, 41 HCSB)

Blessed mother of Jesus

- ... the moment the sound of your greeting reached my ears, the infant in my womb

leaped for joy. (Lk 1: 44 NABRE)

- "Then his father Zechariah was filled with the Holy Spirit and prophesied; 'Praise the Lord the God of Israel, because... He has raised up a Horn of Salvation for us in the house of His servant David...'"

"... the Dawn from on high will visit us... to guide our feet into the way of peace."

(Lk 1: 67, 68, 69, 78 HCSB)

"In those days and at that time

I will cause to grow up to David

A branch of righteousness;

He shall execute judgement and righteousness in the earth.

In those days Judah will be saved,

And Jerusalem will dwell safely.

And this is the name by which He will be called:

THE LORD OUR RIGHTEOUSNESS.'" (Jer 33: 15-16 NKJV)

Isa 11: 9

The earth being filled with knowledge of the Lord as water covers the sea.

JESUS

Isa 11: 1 King from stump of Jesse – to rule for ever!

Isa 11: 2 would be fully loaded with fear of the Lord, wisdom, understanding…

The crucifixion:

"… Everything written about Me… must be fulfilled." (Lk 24: 44)

Who Jesus is:

"You are from below," He told them,

"I am from above. You are of this world;

I am not of this world." (Jn 8: 23 HCSB)

"See, I am going to send My messenger,

and he will clear the way before Me.

Then the Lord you seek will suddenly come to His temple,

the Messenger of the covenant you desire – see, He is coming,

says the Lord of Hosts." (Mal 3: 1 HCSB)

"When you lift up the Son of Man,

then you will know that I am He,…"

(Jn 8: 28 HCSB)

The very sign that the Jews demanded, Jesus is

"On that day the root of Jesse will stand as a banner for the peoples. The nations will seek Him." (Isa 11: 10)

I AM SENT

"Whoever welcomes this little child in My name welcomes Me. And whoever welcomes Me welcomes Him who sent Me." (Lk 9: 48 HCSB)

JESUS: Prophecies concerning His passion and death:

O.T: 1 Ps 22: 8-9, 17-20, 23-24.

2 Isa 50: 6 – Gave my back to those who beat Me, My cheeks, My face, to spitting.

N.T: Jesus Mortification Prophesied:

1. Mk 14: 8 At the banquet in house Simon, the leper: "She has done what she could; she has anointed My body in advance for burial."

2. Jn 14: 28 "But after I have been resurrected, I will go ahead of you to Galilee."

3. Jn 14: 25 "I assure you: I will no longer drink of the fruit of the vine until that day when I drink it in a new way in the kingdom of God."

4. Mk 9: 9 "As they were coming down from the mountain, He ordered them to tell no one what they had seen until the Son of Man had risen from the dead."

5. Jn 14: 41 "... 'Are you still sleeping and resting? Enough! The time has come. Look, the Son of Man is being betrayed into the hands of sinners.'"

JESUS – The Crucifixion
A. Trial Before The Trial
by the Elders, High Priests, Scribes
(Mk 14: 53-65)
B. Formal Trial:
1. Sanhendrine (Mk 15: 1)
2. At the Governor's Court (Mk 15: 2-15)

JESUS: Sent by the Father

"… because of the crowd standing here I said this, so they may believe You sent Me."

(Jn 11: 42 HCSB)

The Lord, our shepherd

"The Lord is my shepherd, there is nothing I lack." (Ps 23: 1 NABRE)

"… He went about doing good…" (Acts 10: 38)

Jesus – "Source and perfecter of our faith." (Heb 12: 2 HCSB)

I am in the Father, the Father is in Me

"Don't you believe that I am in the Father and the Father is in Me?

The words I speak to you, I do not speak on My own.

The Father who lives in Me does His works." (Jn 14: 10 HCSB)

"… I have made known to you

everything I have heard from My Father." (Jn 15: 15 HCSB)

God's testimony concerning Jesus

"God added His testimony by signs, wonders, various acts of power, and distribution of the gifts of the Holy Spirit." (Heb 2: 4 NABRE)

Jesus, propitiation for our sins; our Redeemer

1. "The Lord was pleased to crush Him in infirmity.
If He gives His life as an offering for sin…
the will of the Lord shall be accomplished through Him.
Because of His affliction,…
through His suffering My Servant shall justify many,
and their guilt He shall bear." (Isa 53: 10-11 Lect)
2. "He was despised and rejected by men,
a man of suffering… and we didn't value Him.
Yet He Himself bore our sicknesses,
and He carried our pains;
but we in turn regarded Him stricken,

struck down by God and afflicted.
But He was pierced because of our transgressions,
crushed because of our iniquities;
punishment for our peace was on Him,
and we are healed by His wounds.
We all went astray… and the Lord
has punished Him for the iniquity of us all.
He was taken away because of oppression and judgement;
… For He was cut off from the land of the living.
He was struck because of My people's rebellion."
(Isa 53: 3-6, 8 NABRE)

Jesus, atonement for our sins.

"And some of you used to be like this (sinning). But you were washed, you were sanctified, you were justified in the name of the Lord Jesus Christ and by the Spirit of our God." (1 Cor 6: 11 HCSB)

Justice on earth

"… My Servant; I strengthen Him,… I delight in Him… (Isa 42:1 HCSB)

His life, a ransom

"For the Son of Man did not come to be served, but to serve and to give His life as a ransom for many." (Mk 10: 45 Lect)

Jesus' ministry

"… I must proclaim the good news of the Kingdom of God, because for this purpose I have been sent." (Lk 4: 43 NABRE)

The Son of God

"Those in the boat worshipped Him and said,

'Truly, You are the Son of God!'" (Matt 14: 33 HCSB)

Meditation and Exhortation

JESUS our Savior: "We[1] know that by taking a body from the virgin He refashioned our fallen nature. We know that His manhood was of the same clay as our own; if this were not so, He would hardly have been a teacher who could expect to be imitated.

If He were of a different substance from me, He would surely not have ordered me to do as He did, when by my very nature I am so weak. Such a demand could not be reconciled with His goodness and justice."

"No. He wanted us to consider Him as no different from ourselves,…" "… He offered His own manhood as the first-fruits of our race to keep us from losing heart when suffering comes our way, and to make us look forward to receiving the same reward as He did, since we know that we possess the same humanity."

"So, let us not be at enmity with ourselves, but change our way of life without delay. For Christ who is God, exalted above all creation, has taken away man's sin and has re-fashioned our fallen nature."

1: St. Hippolytus

On the "Refutation of all heresies"

Compare Heb 4: 14-15

The Crucifixion:

"… thirty pieces of silver"

"throw it into the treasury – the handsome price at which they valued Me."

"so I … threw them into treasury in the house of the Lord." (Zec 11: 10, 13)

Exo 21: 32 prescribed 30 pieces as the legal indemnity for a gored slave.

That, incidentally, was the exact amount the Jewish authorities paid to Judas Iscariot who played out the script written by Zechariah. (Matt 26: 14-16; 27: 5)

"… the house of David and … inhabitants of Jerusalem…

They look on Him whom they have thrust through,

they will mourn for Him as one mourns for an only child and they will grieve for Him as one grieves over a firstborn."

(zech 12: 10 NABRE)

Compare Jn 19: 37

"On that day a fountain will be opened

for the house of David andthe inhabitants
of Jerusalem to purify from sin and
uncleanliness." (Zech 13: 1) (see Jn 7: 38)
Meditation and Exhortation
Resurrection
After death, the resurrection of our Lord on the third day is recounted in the Scriptures
(in Lk 24: 1-12)
According to Apostle Paul:
"Now if Christ is proclaimed as raised from the dead, how can some of you say, 'There is no resurrection of the dead'…"
"For as in Adam all die, so also in Christ all will be made alive."
"… if the dead are not raised:
'let us eat and drink,
for tomorrow we die'" (1 Cor 15: 12, 22, 32 HCSB)
"come to your senses and stop sinning, for some people are ignorant about God…"
(1 Cor 15: 34 HCSB)
(for more about the future boody of the resurrected soul "the seed"), read 1 Cor 15: 35-49.
"sown a natural body, raised a spiritual body."
His Ascension at Bethany (Lk 24: 50-52)
These events, of which the Apostles were eye-witnesses, transformed their faith and they never ceased to worship Him from thence forward.

Jesus Reveals God.

Humanity has made staggering advancement in science, space and technology. Surprisingly, all our knowledge about God comes almost exclusively by divine revelation! Until now, the orientation of the leaders of faith seem to bar, or at least discourage such deliberate effort to seek God. These revelations contain knowledge of the transcendental order and purpose of God in creation. They are revealed through prophets and disseminated by His priests. This life is lived by pious men and women – the saints. The fullness of these revelations and teachings (for Christians) comes through God's beloved Son, Jesus Christ.

He is the One about whom for over a thousand years before His advent on the earth plain, prophecies announced His impending manifestation into the human arena.

His word: teaching, healing and preaching.

His teachings have been paraphrased and presented thematically in the first book of this 5-book project. Indeed, the remaining chapters of this volume encapsulate Jesus teaching, healing, and preaching.

He held His public ministry over barely three and a half years in and around the small area of Judea, Jerusalem, and the lake of Galilee.

Everybody who cared, listened to Him as He drew them to Himself by the power of His astounding signs and miracles which He wrought in the name of God.

Meditation and Exhortation

He taught about **the Kingdom of God,** i.e., how to live the life that pleases God.

The denouement of His Messianic ministry came when He died, a redemptive death – in propitiation for humanity's sins, (1 Pt 2: 24) by crucifixion at the hands of the authorities of His day, at about age 33. Bewildering, devastating and sorrowful as this outcome was to His disciples and admirers (despite profuse prophecies towards that) it did not put an end to the Christian movement He founded, contrary to the intentions of His persecutors.

Two extraordinary phenomena accounted for this: His faith-building ministry (beginning from His resurrection and climaxed by His accession into heaven and then the ministry of His promised successor, the Holy Spirit). (Holy Spirit Baptism)

The eye-witnesses to His public ministry, who also witnessed His death, resurrection and the events in-between and His accession became the pristine leaders (or "fathers") of the Christian faith. Their witnessing empowered by the Holy Spirit culminated in the books of the New Testament of the Holy Bible.

Since these events took place more than 2,000 years ago, no new theological upheaval event has taken place. We are awaiting the next – His eschatological return. This second coming unlike the first, will astound the world in wonders at the constellation and by angelic pageantry. The Lord comes, He comes to adjudge the conduct of mankind, individually. He comes with recompense – heaven for the righteous and retribution – hell for the ungodly.

Simple, almost naïve, as these explanations may seem to be, it is so possibly that the many may be carried along and be saved. Let no one claim ignorance of these momentous matters, it simply will not avail as an excuse that one was an unbeliever.

The Christian faith unveils the truth behind many of life's hidden mysteries – life, death, good and evil conduct, etc.

It provides a guideline for long life and happy living on earth and offers a deeper insight to life beyond the temporal, the ephemeral time spent here on earth.

Christianity is a way of life – a life-style, a universal human culture, approved by God for God's people. Only those who live that life may rightly be called Jesus' Followers.

(Jn 14: 21, 23-24)

"He Himself bore our sins in His body on the tree, so that, having died to sins, we might live for righteousness; you have been healed by His wounds."

(1 Pt 2: 24 HCSB)

Meditation and Exhortation

By believing, have life!
"Jesus performed many other signs… that
Are not written… But these are written so that
You may believe Jesus is the Messiah, the Son
Of God, and by believing you may have life in
His name." (Jn 20: 30-31)
Jesus: His resurrection
For the details read
Jn 20: 1-18
Lk 23:44 -24: 10; 36-52.
Mk 16: 1-11
Matt 28: 1-10
Jesus: His Accession
For details read Lk 24: 50-53 or Matt 28: 16-20.
JESUS: His Messianic Ministry

Jesus is much more than a prophet – not in the style and context of "my father's estate is bigger than your father's." No; seriously speaking, His ministry is God's response to the wickedness in the world. Despite the existence and message of God's messengers – the prophets – wickedness had not abated on earth, thanks to the machination of the Devil – the deceiver, the master of lies. He prowls the world selling lies and half-truths and misleading people away from God.

Isaiah, who lived about 500 years before Christ, prophesied concerning the Messiah that was to come in these words:
"We all went astray like sheep; …
And the Lord has punished Him
for the iniquity of us all.
… although He had done no violence
and had not spoken deceitfully.
Yet the Lord was pleased to crush Him severely
when you make Him a restitution offering, …
"… My righteous servant will justify many,
and He will carry their iniquities."

(Isa 53: 6, 9, 10, 11 HCSB)

He depicted His death in Isa 53: 1, 3-6, 8.

Prophet/King David prophesied concerning His miseries – His passion in Ps 22: 15-16, 18

Meditation and Exhortation

Jesus, Himself intimated His disciples concerning His impending passion (in Lk 9: 22):

"The Son of man is going to Jerusalem where He would suffer many things and be rejected by the chief priests and elders, killed and on the third day rise up."

"I tell you these things now so that when it occurs, you will remember that I told you."

(Jn 16: 4)

"And just as Moses lifted up the serpent in the desert, so must the Son of Man be lifted up" (Jn 3: 14 NABRE)

The mystery of our salvation through the passion and death of Jesus (prefigured in Abraham's Sacrifice, Gen 22: 8) provides proof of God's inscrutable mercy and exposes the deceit of Satan concerning sin, righteousness and judgment (Jn 16: 8)

Jesus died in the hands of the chief priests, Jewish elders and the governor, Pontius Pilate, in the style and manner foretold. But see, from the apparent powerlessness of the founder came a great upsurge of power that has made the Christian faith unconquerable, indeed, the faith with the largest following in the world today. Asceticism, skepticism, persecution, and worldliness, have not prevailed against it – "the power of the underworld." (Matt 16: 18)

The Beginning: the Early Church

"Those… scattered as a result of the persecution that started…

(with) Stephen made their way as far as Phoenicia, Cyprus and Antioch speaking the message…"

"The report … was heard by the church at Jerusalem and they sent out Barnabas to … Antioch. Then he went to Tarsus to search for Saul and … he found him… brought him to Antioch. For a whole year they met with the church and taught large numbers. The disciples were first called Christians at Antioch" (Acts 11: 19, 22, 25-26 HCSB)

That, by itself, is a miracle testifying to the great faith, and providing a clue for the discerning. Another enigma, the cross, far from becoming the shame of Jesus' followers had become a most potent weapon for fighting the devil and an icon of His Messianic ministry.

If anyone (of faith) is feeling oppressed by temptation to commit evil, let him just pick up a crucifix and command Satan, in the name of Jesus Christ, to flee, because Jesus had conquered sin for the redeemed!

For several centuries, this method was used to perform exorcism. Today it is still as powerful as ever in the hands of penitents.

Besides, the very name of Jesus Christ works wonders for the believer. If invoked in circumstances where there is a spiritual warfare, be assured of victory.

Meditation and Exhortation

It is a name above all names in life or in dreams (demonic attacks and nightmares) at this name all knees shall bend and all tongues proclaim Him 'Lord' to the glory of God, the Father (Phil 2: 11) no wonder there is a pious devotion to His holy name dating back for so long.

"JESUS" – Power on the lips of believers.

"God was performing extraordinary miracles by Paul's hands,…"

"Then came some of the itinerant Jewish exorcists attempted to pronounce the name of the Lord Jesus over those who had evil spirits,… seven sons of Sceva, a Jewish chief priest, were doing this.

The evil spirit answered them, 'I know Jesus, and I recognize Paul – but who are you?'

"Then the man who had evil spirit leaped on them, overpowered them all,… so that they ran out of that house naked and wounded." (Acts 19: 8-9, 11, 13-16 HCSB)

For more you may wish to read (Acts 19: 8-20)

He was pierced because of our transgressions (Isa 53: 5 HCSB)

"… He went about doing good." (Acts 10: 38 HCSB, NABRE)

Meditation and Exhortation **The heart of Jesus** which was pierced with a lance as the lamb of God lay dead on the cross of Calvary had become a symbol of God's redeeming love for mankind – our justification (Jn 3: 16-18). There are flourishing devotions to this heart. For centuries His sacred heart became the object of love, admiration, contemplation and veneration by seers, mystics and the pious who are similarly inspired. The efficacy of a devotion to the Heart to obtain perfection for the devotee has gained credence. The revelations made to a 17th century nun, St Margaret-Mary Alacoquyhas boosted the devotion.

Many devout Christians also practice devotion to the precious blood of Jesus shed on Calvary, and to His head that was crowned with thorns.

In His expansive love, capable of hosting as many people as swarm to the ark of salvation, the Redeemer has offered mankind yet another powerful path to salvation, that makes minimum demands, especially on the afflicted: just believe (genuinely) in Jesus and pray: " Jesus, I trust in You!" Your salvation will be as good as your faith or the faith of the person interceding for you. This is the revelation made to a polish 20th century nun, St Maria Faustina. And those who practise the devotion know how blessed they are. That is how simple it is, and how far the Lord has gone to ensure that everyone is saved.

"It is not the will of your heavenly Father that one of these … be lost." Do you think I take pleasure in the death of the sinners, but that they repent?"

(Matt 18: 14; Ezk 33: 11; 18: 23. NABRE)

Be not deceived: the devil will try; indeed strive to dissuade the sinner from seeking mercy. Trust him to exploit your area of greatest weakness – doubt, pride, self-indulgence, greed, envy – to dissuade you, but resist him. (Js 4: 7)

"for our sake, He made Him to be sin who did not know sin, so that we might become the righteousness of God in Him." (2 Cor 5: 21 NABRE)

Because God's purpose (our salvation) is immutable; and Jesus is the same yesterday, today and tomorrow He has continued to raise up prophets to re-direct society and to interpret the scripture afresh to accentuate its relevance to our age and time.

"For the sake of His sorrowful passion,
have mercy on us, and on the whole world."[1]

Divine Grace, Divine Mercy

Apostle Paul laboured relentlessly to communicate the mystery of the Divine mercy even as early as the first century of Christianity.

It was a laborious effort because there never was a thing like that before in human experience. The Jewish rabbi offered goats, sheep and cattle as sin offering and as fellowship offering. Pagan priests offered all sorts of living creatures including human beings, to their gods. For Paul, the sacrifice of Jesus on the cross is infinitely more salutary and / or more propitious than these. In all his letters to the churches (and especially in Rom 5: 12-6: 13) he laboured again and again to communicate the mystery that was revealed to him.

1 Maria Faustina: Divine mercy in my soul, op cit; A prayer (chapter of Divine Mercy) of members of the Divine Mercy Apostolate (catholic church)

Meditation and Exhortation

Lest we misunderstand him, he would ask, 'are we saying that there is grace so sin can flourish?' "No!" He would supply the guiding answer. Yet, Satan would not give up; he had turned the hearts of many from the truth (2 Pt 3: 16). Many now hold that grace is everything; that with the grace coming from faith in Jesus Christ the believer can no longer sin, and no longer had to worry about judgment or seek mercy. The victim is being lured into forgetting that Jesus, the Righteous One, was Himself tempted (to sin) by the devil and that the devil and his agents (the demons) still lurk around to ensnare the unsuspecting; cause misery and separate man from the love of God, the Father. Don't let him beguile you, but be reconciled to God. This is what Pope St Leo, the Greatcalls "the renunciation of sin."

In His ineffable, inexhaustible love, the Lord, the lover of souls, revealed this mystery afresh to St. Maria Faustina, a polish nun, and expatiated it in a step-by-step detail with a visual aid. Even minds that cannot concentrate for long, if their hearts are thereby turned to God in obedience, can have God's mercy. It is one short, easiest, fastest, and surest way to obtain the salvation of our God.

The Resurrection: First three appearances of the risen Lord
First

Very early in the morning Mary Magdalene with intent to anoint the body went to the tomb, accompanied by Mary the mother of James, and Salome but found it empty. Forlorn, she wept at the tomb. Her persistence paid off as she later saw two angels who spoke to her and alas, she saw the Lord Jesus Himself. (Jn 20: 11-16, Mk 16: 1)

Second encounter

The disciples of Jesus on their way to Emmaus were brooding over the crucifixion. "While they were conversing and debating Jesus Himself drew near and walked with them." At the discovering that it was the Lord, Jesus disappeared but the duo returned that same night to Jerusalem – another 7 – miles trek to recount the details to the Apostles (Lk 24: 13- …..)

Third appearance

The Emmaus travellers arrived and "found muddled together the eleven (i.e. with the exclusion of Judas Iscariot), and those with them" mourning and weeping and they recounted to them what had taken place on the way. But they "did not believe them either." (Mk 16: 13 HCSB)

As they were still talking Jesus appeared in their midst. Seeing that they were startled and terrified thinking they were seeing a ghost, He said, "Peace to you! Look at My hands and feet, that it is Myself. Touch Me and see…! (Lk 24: 36) He then showed them His hands and feet and ate a piece of baked fish given to Him. He opened their minds to understand what the scriptures wrote concerning the Messiah's suffering, death and resurrection saying,

Meditation and Exhortation

"Repentance for the forgiveness of sins… be preached to all nations" – "you are witnesses to these things." (Lk 24: 47, 48 NABRE)

"As the Father sent Me, I also send you." (Jn 20: 21 HCSB)

There were at least three other recorded appearances to the Apostles after the above.

Who Jesus Is

Now, deliverance meant a different thing to the Israelite from what God intended. To Jews it was deliverance from imperialist Caesar and other foreign tutelage but for God it was deliverance from the power of sin and Satan (which led them to captivity) that was implied. When the Magi announced the birth of the Messiah the chief priests and elders were non-challant; only King Herod sensing his dominion threatened did something about it. That lukewarm attitude typified their reception of Jesus ministry which they failed to heed.

His salvific ministry of three years was characterized by much self-giving. Jesus sacrificed His leisure and entertained no pleasure. Even food must wait: "I have another food you do not know…" He spent several nights in isolation praying. He taught the people and healed their sick. His self-mortification began with a marathon fast of 40 days and nights. He had no place for romance, wife, or family:

"My mother, my brothers are those who do the will of God"

"My food is to do the will of God and to finish the work…"

"Jesus was a man commended to you by God…"

He was self-effacing and would not court the friendship of the chief priests, King Herod or the governor. His folks were the ordinary folks:

"I have come to seek the lost sheep of Israel."

At 33 Jesus was crucified a sacrificial death, (even as prophesied in the scripture) (Ps 22) under governor Pontius Pilate. The third day by the power of God He shrugged off death and the vestiges of pain and shame to rise alive from the tomb. About 40 days thereafter, He ascended into heaven from Galilee in a quasi-public event, witnessed by His followers. Since then, He bequeathed to believers a most powerful and priceless gift – the Holy Spirit.

"Therefore, God … highly exalted Him and gave Him the name that is above every name,…"

(Phil2: 9-11 HCSB)

Personal testimony

For this reason it is a prosaic thing for me to declare that I am a Christian today, more than by anything else, because in His name my prayers are answered.

Meditation and Exhortation

A Stone, a foundation in Zion

"Look, I have laid a stone in Zion,

a tested stone, a precious corner stone,
a sure foundation; the one who believes
will be unshakeable." (Isa 28: 16 HCSB)
Jesus disciples' Testimony:
"Now we know that You know everything…
by this we believe that You came from God." (Jn 16: 30 HCSB)
Who Jesus is: Teacher and Model.
"All blessings come to us through our Lord (Jesus Christ).
He will teach us, for in beholding His life
we find that He is the best example."
-St Theresa of Avila 1515-1582.
Commendation at the transfiguration (Matt 17: 1-7)
"This is My beloved Son,
I take delight in Him.
Listen to Him."
Transfiguration phenomenon
An extraordinary moment. For a brief moment,
heaven and earth came together – to proclaim Jesus – the One
who must be obeyed.

The Creator communicates with His creation. (compare Moses
at Sinai Exo 20: 1, 18-19)

In Rom 5: 12-6: 13 St Paul referred to the divine justice whereby
the sin of Adam procures death to all, yet by mercy of God – "grace",
and faith in Jesus, the obedient One, restores life.

On Moses and Jesus
"God gave the law through Moses, but grace and truth
came through Jesus Christ." (Jn 1: 17 GNBDK)

Christianity and its concern for the truth

Talking about truth, St Thomas Aquinas describes Truth as the
"actuation of the intellect to reality." The perception of the truth is
a process that brings man into conformity with being.

Meditation and Exhortation

Pope Emeritus Benedict XVI in his meditations[2] describes Truth as "the medium in which man makes contact, whereas it is the absence of truth which closes them from one another."

"Movement towards the truth implies temperance." According to him, "the truth purifies man from egotism, from the illusion of absolute autonomy, and makes him obedient and gives him the courage to be humble. It teaches him to see impunity, through disability, as a parody of freedom and to unmask undisciplined chatter as a parody of dialogue."

St Paul describes the church of Christ as "God's household, which is the church of the living God, the pillar and foundation of the truth" (1 Tim 3: 15)

Jesus: Chief witness to the Truth: "For this I was born… to testify to the truth."

(Jn 18: 37 HCSB)

Jesus encouraged the Jews that believed in Him (also you and me) to continue in His words so that:

"You will know the truth and the truth will set you free." (Jn 8: 32)

Prophecy: Witness to the truth:

"These are My words… -

that everything written about Me

in the Law of Moses, the prophets and

the Psalms must be fulfilled." (Lk 24: 44)

John's Testimony

"The One who comes from above is above all…

The One who comes from heaven is above all.

For God sent Him, and He speaks God's words…

The Father loves the Son and has given

all things into His hands." (Jn 3: 31, 34-35)

2: Daily Meditation, op cit…

"The Truth is incontrovertible. Malice may attack it, ignorance may deride it, but in the end, there it is."

Sir Wiston Churchill[1]

Jesus Prayed and fasted

Jesus was in constant communion with the Father. That is the attestation of the record of His salvific ministry.

At the very beginning was the marathon fast – of forty days and forty nights ( ). Appallingly, this did not deter Satan from trying to cause Him to stumble.

Then followed the night before the selection of the Twelve, He left society to pray all night.

For several other instances, He went into seclusion and prayed, for example, after the miracle of the multiplication of loaves (feeding of the 5,000) and before His and Peter's eerie walk on the sea.

(Matt 14: 22-23)

What manner of man is Jesus?

Let us take a glimpse at Jesus as He met Nathanael more popularly known as Bartholomew (one of the twelve) for the first time:

"Philip found Nathanael, and told him, 'we have found the One Moses wrote about in the Law' (and so did the prophets): Jesus the Son of Joseph, from Nazareth!

'can anything good come out of Nazareth?' Nathanael asked him. 'come and see,' Philip answered.

Then Jesus saw Nathanael coming toward Him and said about him,

'Here is a true Israelite: no deceit is in him.'"

'How do you know me?' Nathanael asked.

'Before Philip called you, when you were under the fig tree, I saw you,' Jesus answered.

'Rabbi' Nathanael replied, 'You are the Son of God! You are the King of Israel!'

Jesus responded to him, 'Do you believe only because I told you I saw you under the fig tree?

You will see greater things than this…' (Jn 1: 45-50 HCSB)

1: British Prime Minister

Meditation and Exhortation

Witnesses to the Truth (In Christian Faith)

- The 3 – Triumvirate of Peter James and John
- The 12 – Apostles
- The 72 – other Disciples
- Ancient prophets and scripture (Psalms)

"For we did not follow cleverly contrived myths when we made known to you the power and coming of our Lord Jesus Christ; instead, we were eye witnesses of His majesty…

'This is My beloved Son.

I take delight in Him!'

And we heard His voice when it came from heaven while we were with Him on the holy mountain." (2 Pt 1: 16-18)

"So we have the prophetic word strongly confirmed." (2 Pt 1: 19)

- John's Testimony: "This is the lamb of God…"
- God: at the transfiguration.
- Holy Spirit e.g. at the Pentecost

Jesus: His divinity

- Jesus, the Son of Man.

"and I saw One like a son of man

coming with the clouds of heaven.

He approached the Ancient of Days

and was escorted before Him.

He was given authority to rule,

and glory, and a kingdom;

so that those of every people, nation, and language

should serve Him.

His dominion is an everlasting dominion

that will not pass away,

and His kingdom is one
that will not be destroyed." (Dan 7: 13-14 HCSB)

- Jesus Christ is the word of life – the life, the eternal life with the Father. (1 Jn 1: 1-2)
- John's Testimony:

"… He is the Son of God!" (Jn 1: 34)

Meditation and Exhortation

- Jesus revealed Himself to the Samaritan woman

that He is the Messiah (Jn 4:25-26)

- The testimony of water, blood, and the Spirit. (1 Jn 5: 7-8)
- Believers in Jesus have the gift from the Father – eternal life! (1 Jn 5: 11, 12-13) (see also Jn 11: 25 NABRE)
- "For a chil d will be born for us, a Son will be given to us

… He will be named Wonderful Counselor,
Mighty God, Eternal Father, Prince of Peace."
"The zeal of the Lord of hosts as accomplished it." (Isa 8: 6; 9: 7 HCSB)

- God promises to raise up a prophet like Moses… (Deut 18: 18)
- "I came from God and … before Abraham was, I am." (Jn 8: 42, 58 HCSB)
- Jesus is God's "Son … through whom He created the universe." (Heb 1: 1-2 NABRE)
- No one comes to the Father except through Jesus (Jn 14: 6)
- Jesus is the King promised David – the Saviour of the world (Zec 9: 9, 10) See also Dan 2: 44; 7: 14
- "The one who has seen Me has seen the Father…"

"… I am in the Father and the Father is in Me." (Jn 14: 9, 11 HCSB)

- "…for the Father is greater than I" (Jn 14: 28 NABRE)
- Declaration from heaven:

"This is My beloved Son,
I take delight in Him.

Listen to Him." (Matt 17: 5 also Mk 9: 7)

- Jesus admitted to Caiaphas, "I am (the Messiah)" (Mk 14: 61-62)
- Jesus is the image of the unseen God...the firstborn of all creation... Before anything was created He existed (Col 1: 15; 2: 3)
- God (in His Son) coming to dwell with Zion (Zec 2: 10, 13)

Meditation and Exhortation

- "The One who comes from above... from heaven is above all..." (Jn 3: 31, 34-35)
- "The Spirit of the Lord is on Me...

He has anointed Me..." (Lk 4: 18-19)

- Failure to honour the Son is failure to honour the Father. (Jn 5: 23)
- Jesus: Exists "in the form of God." (Phil 2: 6 HCSB, NABRE, NKJV)
- "In the beginning was the word, and the word was with God, and the word was God."

"All things were created through Him..."
"Life was in Him, and that life was the light of men."
"...His glory, the glory as the One and Only Son from the Father." (Jn 1: 1, 3-4, 14 HCSB)

- Jesus is "...the word of life, which... existed from the very beginning... heard it... seen it... touched it. When this life became visible... the eternal life which was with the Father..."

(1 Jn 1: 1-2 GNBDK)

- God's Abode: with the one who keeps Jesus' commands.

"If anyone loves Me, he will keep My word. My Father will love him and make Our home with him." (Jn 14: 23)

- Jesus, the resurrection.

"No one can come to Me unless the Father who sent Me draws him, and I will raise him up..." (Jn 6: 44)

- Jesus alone has seen God.

"Not that anyone has seen the Father except the One who is from God. He has seen the Father." (Jn 6: 46)

- "And just as the Father raises the dead and gives them life, so the Son also gives life to anyone He wants to."

"The Father, in fact, judges no one but has given all judgment to the Son." (Jn 5: 21-22)

- "For You gave Him authority over all flesh; so He may give eternal life to all You have given Him." (Jn 17: 2)
- "BECAUSE I LIVE, you will live too."

"In that day you will know that I am in My Father, you are in Me, and I am in you."
(Jn 14: 19-20 HCSB)
Meditation and Exhortation

Some PROMISES of Christ

The Lord Promises -

- "IF we walk in light... the blood of Jesus Christ cleanses us from all sins." (1 Jn 1: 7 NKJV)
- We are Jesus' brothers and sisters

IF we hear and do the word of God (Lk 8: 21)

- Walk in Jesus, the light of the world and you have the light of life:

"...whoever follows Me... will have the light of life." (Jn 8: 12 NABRE)

- "I assure you; whatever you did for one of the least of these brothers of Mine, you did for Me. ... Whatever you did not do... you did not do for Me either." (Matt 25; 40, 45 HCSB)
- We are healed by His wounds, He bore the burden of our iniquities thus justifying many. (Isa 53: 1, 3-6, 9-12)
- "I am the resurrection and the life; whoever believes in Me, even if he dies, will live." (Jn 11: 25 NABRE)
- Believers in Jesus will know the truth and the truth will set them free (Jn 8: 32)
- "IF you remain in Me and My words remain in you, ask... and it will be done for you" (Jn 15: 7 NABRE)
- "...Without Me, you can do nothing." (Jn 15: 5 NABRE)
- "The one who believes in Me, as the Scriptures have said will have streams of living water flow from deep within him. He said this about the Spirit..." (Jn 7: 38-39 HCSB)
- "Keep asking and it will be given to you..."

"Therefore I tell you, all the things you pray and ask for – believe that you have received them, and you will have them." (Matt 7: 7; Mk 11: 24 HCSB)

- "...Forgive and you will be forgiven. Give and it will be given to you..." (Lk 6: 37-38 HCSB)
- "...The one who believes in Me will also do the works that I do. And he will do even greater works than these..." (Jn 14: 12 HCSB)
- IF you believe, these signs will accompany you:

Meditation and Exhortation

"In My name they will drive out demons... speak in new languages,... lay hands on the sick, and they will get well." (Mk 16: 17-18 HCSB)

The banquet of His body and blood

Introduction:
The food for Eternal Life

Discourse at Capernaum:

"…the food that lasts for eternal life which the Son of Man will give you, because God the Father has set His seal of approval on Him." (Jn 6: 27 HCSB)

The Word: Spirit and food for eternal life

- "…Man must not live on bread alone but on every word that comes from the mouth of God." (Matt 4: 4 HCSB)
- "…I have food to eat that you don't know about" (Jn 4: 32 HCSB)
- "'My food is to do the will of Him who sent Me and to finish His work', Jesus told them." (Jn 4: 34 HCSB)

Jesus: The bread of life, the bread of God.

- "…John saw Jesus coming toward him and said, 'Here is the Lamb of God, who takes away the sin of the world!'" (Jn 1: 29 HCSB)
- "Jesus said to them, '… Moses didn't give you the bread from heaven, but My Father gives you the real bread from heaven. For the bread of God is the One who comes down from heaven and gives life to the world.'" (Jn 6: 32-33 HCSB)
- "For this is the will of My Father: that everyone who sees the Son and believes in Him may have eternal life, and I will raise him up on the last day." (Jn 6: 40 HCSB)
- "I am the living bread that came down from heaven. If anyone eats of this bread he will live forever. The bread that I will give for the life of the world is My flesh." (Jn 6: 51 HCSB)

- "Anyone who eats My flesh and drinks My blood has eternal life, and I will raise him up on the last day" (Jn 6: 54 HCSB)
- "And He took bread, gave thanks, broke it, gave it to them, and said, 'This is My body, which is given for you. Do this in remembrance of Me.'" (Lk 22: 19 HCSB) see also (Matt 26: 26)

Meditation and Exhortation

- "Then He took a cup, and after giving thanks He gave it to them and said, 'Drink from it, all of you. For this is My blood that established the covenant; it is shed for many for the forgiveness of sins." (Matt 26: 27-28 HCSB) see also (Lk 22: 20)
- "For as often as you eat this bread and drink the cup, you proclaim the Lord's death until He comes." (1 Cor 11: 26 HCSB)
- "The one who eats My flesh and drinks My blood lives in Me, and I in Him."

"This is the bread that came down from heaven; it is not like the manna your fathers ate – and they died. The one who eats this bread will live forever." (Jn 6: 56, 58 HCSB)

- "The Spirit is the One who gives life. The flesh doesn't help at all. The words that I have spoken to you are spirit and are life." (Jn 6: 63 HCSB)
- "No one can come to Me unless the Father who sent Me draws him, and I will raise him up on the last day." (Jn 6: 44 HCSB) see also (Jn 6: 65)
- For more on this all-important subject, see book 5 of these series understanding the Bible, section on "the bread of life, the bread of God."

The Way To The Cross: Salvation overcomes sin.
Noah's Ark

"Then the Lord said to Noah, 'enter the ark, you and your entire household, for I have seen that you alone are righteous before Me in this generation. You are to take with you seven pairs, a male and its female, of all the clean animals, and two… and seven pairs, male and female, of the birds… seven days from now I will make it rain on the earth 40 days and 40 nights, and I will wipe off from the face of the earth every living thing I have made.' And Noah did everything that the Lord commanded him." (Gen 7: 1-5 HCSB)

Read more on this in Gen 6: 3, 6-8; 7: 7-23

Restitution Offering: Abraham's offering prefigures the crucifixion

"After these things God tested Abraham and said to him, 'Abraham!'

'Here I am,' he answered.

'Take your son,' He said, 'your only son Isaac, whom you love, go, go to the land of Moriah, and offer him there as a burnt offering…'

So Abraham got up early in the morning,… and took with him… his son Isaac. He split wood for a burnt offering and set out to go to the place God had told him about.

On the third day Abraham looked up and saw the place in the distance.

Meditation and Exhortation

When they arrived at the place… Abraham built the alter there and arranged the wood. He bound his son Isaac and placed him on the alter on top of the wood. Then Abraham reached out and took the knife to slaughter his son." (Gen 22: 1-4, 9-10 HCSB)

For more, read Gen 22: 11-14.

Meditation I (suitable as retreat or novena themes

Nine Most memorable events pertaining to the birth of Jesus:

154

1. Prophecies about His birth

Deut 18: 18; Jer 31: 31-40; 32: 40; Ezk 37: 26; Isa 8: 10; Lk 1: 26-35

2. Mary visits Elizabeth: their prophecies

Lk 1: 39-56

3. Angel Gabriel reveals a mystery to Joseph

Matt 1: 19-23

4. Joseph accepts Mary back

Matt 1: 24-25

5. The birth of John: Zachariah's prophecy

Lk1: 67-69, 76-79

6. The family moves to Bethlehem (for the census)

Lk 2: 1-5; Matt 2: 1

7. The birth of Jesus

Lk 2: 6-7, 34; Matt 1: 18-25

8. The Magi pays homage; innocent infants were killed.

Lk 2: 8-20; Matt 2: 1-12

9. The flight to Egypt and return at the death of Herod

Matt 2: 13-23.

Meditation II

Jesus self-immolation: The Way to Calvary.
Reflect on the following themes of the end of Jesus mortal life:
Themes

1. Hosanna: The triumphant entry into Jerusalem

Mk 11: 1-11; Matt 20: 17-19; 21: 1-11; Lk 19: 28-40
Meditation and Exhortation

2. Jesus at the Temple Complex: The discusses

Matt 21: 23-46; 22: 1-23; 39

3. Jesus at table at Simon's house (the pass over meal)

Mk 14: 3-9; 14: 12-21, 26; Matt 26: 6-13; Lk 22: 7-13

4. Conspiracy to kill Jesus: the trial before the trials

Jn11: 55-57; Matt 26: 1-5; 14-16

5. The Lord's (last) Supper: Institution of the Holy Eucharist

Mk 14: 17-26; Jn 13: 1-35; Matt 26: 1-5, 17-25; Lk 22: 14-20

6. The transfiguration at the Mount of Olives

Matt 17: 1-7; Lk 9: 28-31

7. At Gethsemane: Abandonment, prayer and arrest

Lk 22: 21-23, 56; Matt 26: 31-56

8. The (formal) trials: Sanhedrin and Governor's court

Matt 26: 57-27: 2; 11-31

9. The cross, the crowd and Calvary's Golgotha Hill

Matt 27: 32-66; Mk 15: 21-47; Zech 12: 10; 13: 1
The meaning: necessary that prophecies are fulfilled
Lk 24: 26, 46; Acts 3: 18; 17: 3; 26: 23

Jesus' teachings

Very little of Jesus teachings are to be found in this chapter. They are strewn across all the chapters thematically.

The Old, the New or both (Testaments)?

Jesus did not ignore or abolish the Old Testament but He updates and clarifies our understanding thereof, as well as introducing some new concepts. This entire book is intended to be a collation of the Messiah's teaching on the theme of each chapter.

The Messiah is the highest authority man can hope for, since we cannot bear to hear from God directly (Exo 20: 19). We preferred human voice which we are used to and we have it at the highest level – in the incarnate word of God.

"If I have told you about things that happen on earth and you don't believe, how will you believe if I tell you about things of heaven?" (Jn 3: 12 HCSB)

Meditation and Exhortation

"For You gave Him authority over all flesh;

so, He may give eternal life to all You have given Him." (Jn 17: 2 HCSB)

"I know that His command is eternal life.

So, the things that I speak,

I speak just as the Father has told Me." (Jn 12: 50 HCSB)

"… I was born for this, and I have come into the world for this:

to testify to the truth. Everyone who is of the truth listens to My voice."

(Jn 18: 37 HCSB)

Commandments come before tradition or culture

Isa 29: 31 (Jesus quoting Isaiah's prophecy to the scribes and pharisees)

"This people honours Me with their lips, but their hearts are far from Me, teaching as doctrines human precepts'. You disregard God's commandment but cling to human traditions."

Don Schwager: "They devised clever arguments and ingenious interpretations to thwart God's purpose."

UNITY and the banquet of His flesh and blood.

The Eucharist as oneness[1]:

"The love feast of our Lord's supper signposted by the Eucharist…

"… The people of God can only be one."

"If others are hungry, we cannot be opulent…" "same communion"

Note that –

- Because there is only one Jesus, the bred of life (Jn 6: 35)
- They will live forever (Jn 6: 51, 54)
- it is our communion with Jesus (Jn 6: 56) (also 1 Cor 10: 16)
- SIGN OF SEPERATION

"From that moment many disciples turned back from accompanying Jesus" (Jn 6: 66)

1: Daily Meditation by Pope Benedict XV

Meditation and Exhortation

"We are obliged to obey God's commandments." (Js 2: 10; 1: 22)

"Maimonides, a Jewish Rabbi in the 12th century listed 613 commandments in the Old Testament."

Jesus: The Word, the life

"I assure you: if anyone keeps My word, he will never see death – ever!"

(Jn 8: 51 HCSB)

Jesus, the resurrection

"Jesus said to her (Lazarus' sister), 'I am the resurrection and the life. The one who believes in Me, even if he dies, will live.

Everyone who lives and believes in Me will never die – ever…'"

(Jn 11: 25)

Comment:

Thus, Jesus turns the darkness of death into the dawn of a new life.

The Cross

- (Jesus) delivered up by the set plan and foreknowledge of God, you killed. (Acts 2: 25? Lect)
- But He was pierced for our offences; crushed for our sins, upon Him was the chastisement that made us whole; by His stripes we are healed. (Isa 52: 28-29 Lect)

"Any Jesus without the cross is not the Messiah"[2].

Righteousness of God – Like a River – a river of life!

(Ezk 47: 1, 5, 9, 12 HCSB)

2: Pope Emeritus Benedict XVI. Daily Meditations

Meditation and Exhortation.

"Then he brought me back to the entrance of the temple and there was water flowing from under the threshold of the temple toward the east… The water was coming down from under the south side of the threshold of the temple, south of the alter.

… and a river that I could not cross on foot. For the water has risen; it was deep enough to swim in,…

Every kind of living creature that swarms will live wherever the river flows, and there will be a huge number of fish because this water goes there.

… there will be life everywhere the river goes.

All kinds of trees (graces) providing food will grow along both banks of the river. Their leaves (charisms) will not wither, and their fruit (ministries) will not fail. Each month they will bear fresh fruit because the water (wisdom) comes from the sanctuary. Their fruit will be used for food (material well-being) and their leaves for medicine (spiritual blessings)."

Compare (Rev 22: 1-5 NABRE)

"Then the angel showed me the River of Life-Giving Water sparkling like crystal, flowing from the throne of God and of the lamb."

"On either side of the river grew the tree of life that produces fruit twelve times a year, once each month, the leaves of the trees serve as medicine for the nations."

"Nothing accursed will be found there anymore. The throne of God and of the Lamb will be in it, and His servants will worship Him."

"They will look upon His face, and His name will be on their foreheads."

"Night will be no more, nor will they need light from lamp or sun, for the Lord God shall give them light, and they shall reign forever and ever."

Marvellous Jesus

Come with me and meet this Jesus we worship. He is the Son of God; our great teacher, the light of the world, the way, the truth and the life. He is the resurrection and the life – He is our good shepherd and the eternal High Priest of God.

Jesus and the conversion of Saul: (Acts 9: 1-20)

"… Saul still breathing threats and murder against the disciples of the Lord, went to the High Priest and asked letters from him to the synagogues of Damascus, so that … any who were of the way, whether men or women, he might bring them bound to Jerusalem."

"As he journeyed… near Damascus,… suddenly a light shone around him… Then he fell… and heard a voice, saying to him, 'Saul, Saul why are you persecuting Me?'"

"And he said, 'Who are You, Lord?'

Then the Lord said, 'I am Jesus, whom you are persecuting… Arise and go into the city, and you will be told what you must do.'"

Meditation and Exhortation.

"… the men who journeyed with him stood speechless, hearing a voice but seeing no one."

"Then Saul rose from the ground, and… he saw no one. But they led him by hand and brought him into Damascus."

"Now there was a certain disciple at Damascus named Ananias; and to him the Lord said in a vision, 'Ananias… Arise and go to the street called Straight, and inquire at the house of Judas for one called Saul of Tarsus… in a vision he has seen a man named Ananias coming in and putting his hand on him, so that he might receive his sight.'"

"And Ananias went and entered the house; and laying his hands on him he said, 'Brother Saul, the Lord Jesus who appeared to you on the road as you came, has sent me that you may receive your sight and be filled with the Holy Spirit.'"

"Immediately… he received his sight at once and he rose and was baptized."

"… Then Saul spent some days with the disciples at Damascus. Immediately he preached the Christ in the synagogues, that He is the Son of God."

(Acts 9: 1-5, 6-8, 10-12, 17-20 NKJV).

{That was Saul, re-named Paul, the author of more than half the books of the New Testament.}

Jesus – best example

"All blessings come to us through our Lord (Jesus Christ). He will teach us, for in beholding His life we find that He is the best example."[1]

Only God is wise

Living by God's rule of life, mankind stands to enjoy long and happy life.

There was no recorded death in the Old Testament before that of Abel. Cain probably did not know or believe that humans could die just like the other animals until the death of Abel. But God knows.

Philosophy, morality, culture are all dependent and relative to human experience. All suffer from bias and false assumptions.

They lean toward the accepted values of the society from where they emanate.

1: St Theresa of Avila (1515-1582)

Meditation and Exhortation.

How can anyone know that one must not cheat the blind, or slight the deaf or mock the dumb? Your servant is under your power why must you pay his wages promptly? Only God gives the guidance.

Neither egoism nor altruism can get us there, i.e., lead man to that level of clairvoyance to discern what it is that is good or bad.

You cannot defy God and not be seared, Jesus teaches. There is accountability for our actions and inactions in this world (chapter 6). But, there are besides, restitution, retribution and recompense; propitiation, redemption and divine mercy.

Human intellect may comprehend the wisdom of "an eye for an eye and a tooth for a tooth," but certainly, not mercy which, apparently, is beyond the cognition of man. While some learned men[1] have argued in the past that mercy or forgiveness was a detraction from justice, yet, mercy is an all-round sweetness. It is a consolation to the afflicted; a mirthful graciousness to the donor and an ecstatic pleasure to the on-looker. Punishment, retaliation, retribution all make counter-destruction their objective, but mercy – only mercy – rebuilds. Only the stronger can bestow mercy; the weaker may merely condone or absorb a wrong.

Justice flows, mercy follows after.

This topic is treated in Chapter 9.

Only God is wise. He reveals the true path of life to us in trickles according to our ability to understand. He does this through His angels, His prophets and His priests. The fulness of such revelation comes through Jesus Christ and the continuing presence of His Holy Spirit.

"Why do you call Me good?" Jesus asked him. "No one is good but One – God."

(Mk 10: 18; Lk 18: 19 HCSB)

It is pretty easy to see how these teachings are collated by the themes of the chapters. For example, marriage and human sexuality is in chapter 18; Righteousness (or the kingdom of heaven) in chapter 14; His passion and death in chapter 11.

But sometimes, the titles of these chapters may not avail to impinge on the mind all the themes that may have been subsumed under each chapter. The inquirer may have to check over in two or more chapters with cognate subjects (or the index – for latter editions) for any topic he has in mind.

For example, the theme on discrimination, entitled "flesh and blood," can be found in chapter 14; the theme on humility, a Christian virtue, is placed in chapter 8.

"… Jesus Christ,

who became for us God-given wisdom for us –

our righteousness, sanctification and redemption,…" (1 Cor 1: 30 HCSB)

Meditation and Exhortation.

The Lord, our righteousness.

"Behold, the days are coming," says the Lord,

"That I will raise to David a branch of righteousness;

A king shall reign and prosper,
And execute judgement and righteousness in the earth.
… Now this is His name by which He will be called:
THE LORD OUR RIGHTEOUSNESS."
(Jer 23: 5, 6 NKJV)
Jesus – who He is (a reflection)

For three Kaleidoscopic years a young man, walked the street of Jerusalem, Judea and the towns around the sea of Galilee. He was vocal, being didactic and strangely authoritative on virtually all subjects – from sin to Satan, hell to heaven, death and life, from temple to the Sabbath, the law and the prophets.

He did not identify with the elites of His day – the High priests, the scribes, the pharisees or the Sadducees – rather, he criticised them and they in turn were mad at Him. Though not a priest or a Levite, He was often found in the synagogues and the temple where he taught. His words were irresistible, rooted in wisdom and deep understanding. His words also possessed power – power to bind and unbind, to loose and to unloosen. He performed miracles routinely and with great ease: the blind saw, the lame walked, the dumb spoke, the deaf heard, demon-possessed were delivered; the dead rose. Everybody knew this extraordinary man as a weird phenomenon. Whether He was a prophet or a teacher or the One to come (i.e., the Christ) all stake-holders kept guessing.

The man's name is Jesus.

He was at once about the most powerful and powerless man on earth. The elements obeyed Him – wind, storm, demons, diseases all bowed out before Him. He was displeased with a fig tree for not producing fruit and straight away the fig tree began to wither – and was fully withered the following day! Yet, He would not cut a reef that was bruised or put out a smouldering wick. All His powers He exercised while going about doing good.

They did not resolve the riddle of who He was. Because after His death He continued with His salvific ministry. He eventually departed from His followers in a quiet ceremony witnessed by them as they saw Him ascended into the heavens! But that was not until He had introduced a companion-worker of His, called The Holy Spirit, as He would not leave His followers orphaned.

Meditation and Exhortation.

Till this day the Holy Spirit continues the work Jesus had as Jesus Himself had promised – teaching, guiding, prophesising, sanctifying in an ambient of miracles. Jesus commissioned His disciples to spread His message across the globe, delegating to them power the type He Himself had exercised. The Holy Spirit was sent as a helper to assist them.

Let me reveal one Christian secret to you. This Man's name (Jesus) is the most powerful on earth in every generation until date. How? Find that out yourself. All these did not resolve the mystery of who the man was and is. However, theologians, ecclesiastics and his followers all assure us that He is the Messiah. Rather quaint, isn't it? (There are some down-to-earth evidences to that effect). That some sort of quietens the curiosity but I dare say not until humanity knows God perfectly or at least as much as we know human life, the mystery may never go away, altogether!

But what and who did He call Himself?

Jesus is not just a historical figure or an allegory, He is real and still with us today! His other name is "Emmanuel" (meaning, 'God is with us'). He has ordained that His church will never cease to exist on earth and so it has been (this 2000+ years). His power (of doing good) is still as active across the globe today as it was in those three eventful years (of His public ministry). Then the powers were signs; today they are redeeming grace i.e., deeds to bring justice, mercy and the knowledge of God to the farthest ends of the earth.

"… You are in Christ Jesus, who became God-given wisdom for us – our righteousness, sanctification, and redemption…" (1 Cor 1: 30 HCSB)

Heb 2: 11 HCSB "For the One who sanctifies and those who are sanctified all have one Father. That is why Jesus is not ashamed to call them brothers."

NABRE "He who consecrates and those who are being consecrated all have one origin. Therefore, He is not ashamed to call them 'brothers'"

"sheathe your sword! Am I not to drink the cup the Father has given Me?"

(Jn 18: 11)

"… I have life because of the Father." (Jn 6: 57 NABRE)

CHAPTER 4

The Holy Spirit

In The Church

"For we are God's co-workers. You are God's field, God's building."

"Do you not know that you are THE TEMPLE OF GOD, and that the Spirit of God dwells in you?" (1Cor. 3: 9, 16 HCSB)

The Apostles' Pentecost Exploits

"When the day of Pentecost had arrived,... Suddenly a sound like that of a violent rushing wind came from heaven... And tongues, like flames of fire... rested on each one of them. Then they were all filled with the Holy Spirit and began to speak in different languages, as the Spirit gave them ability for speech."

"There were Jews living in Jerusalem, devout men from every nation... A crowd came together and was confused because each one heard them speaking in his own language. And they were astounded and amazed saying, "...How is it that each of us can hear in our own native language? Parthians, Medes, Elamites, those who live in Mesopotamia, in Judea and Cappadocia, Pontus and Asia, Phrygia and Pamphylia, Egypt and ... Libya... visitors from Rome... Cretans and Arabs – we hear them speaking... in our own languages" "... and that day about 3,000 people were added to them." (Acts 2: 1-11, 41 HCSB)

Acts 5:1–10 Ananias and his wife, Sapphira lied to the Holy Spirit concerning the proceeds of their personal property – they died for it.

Matthias Election: Two chosen – Joseph (also known as Barsabbas and Justus) as well as Matthias. Lot fell on Matthias.

Witnessing by the Holy Spirit – You can't buy the gift of God with money.

Simon, alias the power of God, used to practise magic in Samaria. All were astounded and 'paid attention to him for a long time'.

Philip went down to Samaria and proclaimed the Messiah to them, preaching and baptizing. Simon, himself believed and was baptized and became devoted to Philip when he saw 'the signs and mighty deeds that were occurring'.

Peter and John, who were sent from Jerusalem laid hands on the converts. They received the Holy Spirit.

Commercialising Spiritual Gifts:

"When Simon saw that the Holy Spirit was given through the laying on of the Apostle's hands, he offered them money –" "Give me the power too…" "But Peter told him, 'may your silver be destroyed with you, because you thought the gift of God could be obtained with money'" (Acts 8: 18, 20)

Simon said in reply, 'pray for me to the Lord…'

(For more read this in Acts 8: 8-13, 18-24)

The unforgivable Sin "…I tell you, people will be forgiven every sin and blasphemy, but the **blasphemy against the Spirit** will not be forgiven. Whoever speaks a word against the Son of Man, it will be forgiven him. But whoever speaks against the Holy Spirit, it will not be forgiven him, either in this age or in the one to come". (Matt. 12:31-32 HCSB)

Gifts: Speaking in tongues (usually accompanied with prophesying) –

The Twelve Disciples at Ephesus

"While Apollos was in Corinth, Paul travelled through the interior regions and came to Ephesus. He found some disciples and asked them, 'Did you receive the Holy Spirit when you believed?'

'No,' they told him, 'we haven't even heard that there is a Holy Spirit.'"

"When they heard this, they were baptized in the name of the Lord Jesus. And when Paul had laid his hands on them, the Holy Spirit came on them, and they began to speak in other languages and to prophesy. Now there were about 12 men in all." (Acts 19: 1-2, 5-7 HCSB)

HOLY SPIRIT

Will be poured on all, your old men will have dreams. (Joel 2: 28-29). op cit

Unclean Spirits know who Jesus is as in the healing of the Gerasene demoniac:

"What have You to do with me, Jesus, Son of the Most High God?

I beg You… " (Lk. 8:28 NABRE).

Accomplished by His Spirit

"This is the word of the Lord to Zerubbabel:

'Not by might, and not by power, but by My Spirit, says the Lord of hosts'"

(Zech 4: 6 HCSB)

The sent:

"Who are you, o great mountain? Before Zerubbabel you become a plain…

amid shouts of favour, favour, favour" (Zec. 4: 7 HCSB)

The Spirit gives Life

"The Spirit … gives life. The flesh doesn't … the words that I have spoken to you are Spirit and are Life." (Jn. 6:63)

Ask, get the Holy Spirit

"… If you then, who are evil, know how to give good gifts to your children, how much more will the heavenly Father give the Holy Spirit to those who ask Him?…"
(Lk 11: 13 HCSB)

The Holy Spirit

"I am sending the promise of My Father upon you;
but stay… until clothed with power from on high."
(Lk 24: 49)

Another Advocate – to be with you always

And I will ask the Father, and He will give you another Advocate to be with you always, the spirit of truth,… it remains with you, and will be in you."
(Jn. 14: 16 – 17 NABRE).
Walk by the Spirit
"…walk by the spirit and you will not carry out the desire of the flesh." (Gal 5: 16)

On the contrary, the works of the flesh are "sexual immorality, moral impurity, promiscuity, idolatry, sorcery, hatreds, strife, jealousy, outbursts of anger, selfish ambitions, dissensions, factions, envy, drunkenness, carousing, and anything similar."

"We must not become conceited, provoking one another, envying one another." (Gal 5: 16, 22-23, 19-21, 26)

For more on this theme, you will profit by reading: Eph. 5:9-10; 2Cor. 6:3-10;

1Tim. 4:12, 16; 2Pt. 1:5-7.

Different Gifts, One Giver, One Purpose

"For as the body is one and has many parts ... so we are 'the body of Christ, and individual members of it.'" (1 Cor. 12:12, 27 HCSB)

"Now there are different gifts, but the same spirit. There are different ministries, but the same Lord. And there are different activities, but the same God activates each gift in each person." (1Cor. 12:4-6).

Apostles, prophets – healers, helpers, managers and speakers in tongues.

"... God has put the body together,... **so that there would be no division in the body**, but that the members would have the same concern for each other. So if one member suffers, all the members suffer with it; if one member is honoured, all the members rejoice with it." (1Cor. 12:24-26).

For the full message read 1Cor. 12:1-30.

At the approach of the end time –

"After this

I will pour out My Spirit on all humanity; then your sons and your daughters will prophesy, your old men will have dreams, and your young men will see visions.

I will even pour out My Spirit on the male and female slaves in those days."

(Joel 2:28-29) (Act 2-17)

Test the spirits

"Dear friends, do not believe every spirit, but test the spirits to determine if they are from God, because many false prophets have gone out into the world.

: 2 This is how you know the Spirit of God: Every spirit who confesses that Jesus Christ has come in the flesh is from God.

: 3 But every spirit who does not confess Jesus, is not from God. This is the spirit of the antichrist;..."

"We are from God. Anyone who knows God listens to us; anyone who is not from God does not listen to us. From this we know the Spirit of truth and the spirit of deception." (1 Jn 4: 1-3, 6)

The testimony of three

"Jesus Christ – He is the One who came by water and blood,… And the Spirit is the One who testifies, because the Spirit is the truth. For there are three that testify: the Spirit, the water and the blood – and these three are in agreement."

(1 Jn. 5:6-8)

The Spirit in Man

"Thus says God, the Lord,

Who created the heavens and stretched them out,

Who spread out the earth and its produce,

Who gives breath to its people

and spirit to those who walk on it" (Isa. 42: 5 NABRE)

The Spirit is of Power, not of fear!

"For God has not given us a spirit of fearfulness, but one of power, love, and sound judgement." (2 Tim. 1: 7 HCSB).

The Holy Spirit

"Is the down payment of our inheritance for the redemption of the possession to the praise of His glory." (Eph. 1:14 HCSB)

God shows no favouritism; He pours the Holy Spirit on the person who fears Him and does righteousness including gentiles. (Acts 10: 34 – 35; 44 – 45 HCSB).

The Spirit is power of God

"…I am sending the promise of My Father upon you; but stay in the city until you are clothed with power from on high. (Lk 24:49 NABRE).

The Fruits of the Spirit

The fruit of the Spirit is love, joy, peace, patience, kindness, generosity, faithfulness, gentleness, self-control.

"We must not become conceited, provoking one another, envying one another."

(Gal. 5:22-23, 26)

The thoughts of God

"… Similarly, no one knows what pertains to God except the Spirit of God."

(1 Cor. 2: 11 NABRE)

The Spirit and your call

"…from the beginning God has chosen you for salvation through sanctification by the Spirit and through belief in the truth." (2 Thes. 2: 13 HCSB)

TEST

There is spirit of truth and there is spirit of deception. (1 Jn. 4: 1-3)

The Holy Spirit testified (truthfully) that Jesus is the Son of God (1 Jn. 5: 6)

The Counsellor or Advocate or Helper

"This is the Spirit of truth. The world is unable to receive Him because it doesn't see Him or know Him… He remains with you and will be in you." (Jn. 14: 17).

The Ministry of the Holy Spirit

i. "The Helper, the Holy Spirit, whom the Father will send in My name, will teach you everything and make you remember all that I have told you." (Jn. 14: 26 GNBDK)

ii. "…And when He has come, He will convict the world of sin, and of righteousness, and of judgement". (Jn. 16: 8 NKJV)

Another Version put it this way,

"And when He comes, He would prove the world wrong about sin and righteousness and judgement." (Jn. 16: 8 NRSV –CI).

For more on this topic read (Jn 16: 9-11, 13-15)

Another Helper – The Spirit of Truth

"If you love Me, you will obey My commandments

I will ask the Father, and He will give you another Helper, who will stay with you forever; He is the Spirit who reveals the truth about God…"

(Jn. 14: 15 – 17; 15 GNBDK)

Foreboding

"And now I am on my way to Jerusalem, bound in My Spirit, not knowing what I will encounter there, except that in town after town the Holy Spirit testifies to me that chains and afflictions are waiting for me."

"And now I know that none of you will ever see my face again – …."

Paul's farewell address to Ephesus elders (Acts 20: 22-23 HCSB)

Speaking in tongues

i. Strive for love and empowerment to proclaim God's message (prophesy).

"It is love, then, that you should strive for. Set your hearts on spiritual gifts, especially the gift of proclaiming God's message."

ii. "Those who speak in strange tongues do not speak to others but to God, because no one understands them. They are speaking secret truths by the power of the Spirit." (1 Cor. 14: 1, 3 GNBDK)

iii. "Those who speak in strange tongues help only themselves,…" "unless there is someone present who can explain what is said,… (1Cor. 14:4, 5 GNBDK)

iv. "… how will anyone understand what you are talking about if your message is given in strange tongues… Your words will varnish in the air!"

"The person who speaks in strange tongues, then, must pray for the gift to explain what is said…" (1Cor. 14:9, 13 GNBDK)

i. "… If I pray in this way, my spirit prays indeed; but my mind has no part in it."

"…I will (rather) pray with my spirit, but… also with my mind;… sing with my spirit but… also with my mind." (1 Cor. 14: 14 – 15 GNBDK)

"In scripture it was written: '… but even then My people will not listen to Me'. So then,… speaking in strange tongues is proof for unbelievers, while …proclaiming God's message is proof for believers,…" "But if everyone is proclaiming God's message… unbelievers or ordinary people… will be convinced of their sin by what they hear, … bow down and worship God, confessing, 'Truly, God is here among you!'"(1 Cor. 14: 21-22, 24-25 GNBDK)

Miraculous healings by Jesus' Disciples

"… Many wonders and signs were being performed through the Apostles."

(Acts 1:43; 5:12)

Here are some:

i. MAN BORN CRIPPLED full texts: Acts 3: 1 – 10

Peter and John went to the Temple complex at three p.m. to pray. A man lame from birth, who begs for alms at the temple gate, called, 'Beautiful', saw them and begged for help.

"Silver or gold I have not; what I have I give you: In the name of Jesus, the Nazarene, get up and walk!" Peter said.

"…at once his feet and ankles became strong. So he jumped up, stood and started to walk,… entered the Temple… walking, leaping, and praising God."

(Acts 3:6-8 HCSB)

ii. THE HOLY SPIRIT AT THE HOME OF UNCIRCUMCISED CORNELIUS

"Cornelius said, '…three days ago… I was praying in my house at three o'clock in the afternoon.

Suddenly, a man dressed in shinning clothes stood in front of me and said, "Cornelius! … Send someone to Joppa for a man whose full name is Simon Peter. He is a guest in the home of Simon, the tanner of leather who lives by the sea.'"

"While Peter was still speaking, the Holy Spirit came down on all who were listening to his message.""… they heard them speaking in strange tongues and praising God's greatness." (Acts 10: 30-32, 44, 46. GNBDK)

iii. A SORCERER OPPOSED THE MESSAGE

Paul, Barnabas and John Mark came to Paphos. They came across a sorcerer, a Jewish false prophet named Bar-Jesus. He was with the Pro consul, Sergius Paulus... "But Elymas the sorcerer… opposed them and tried to turn the Proconsul away from the faith."

"… Paul ….said … 'Now look! The Lord's hand is against you. You are going to be blind … for a time'. Suddenly…. he went around seeking someone to lead him by the hand." (Acts 13: 6-9)

The Holy Spirit at Jesus Baptism

"And the Holy Spirit descended on Him in a physical appearance like a dove.
And a voice came from heaven:
You are My beloved Son
I take delight in You!" (Lk. 3: 22 HCSB)

My Servant, My Chosen One: My Spirit upon Him

"Here is My Servant whom I uphold.
My Chosen One with whom I am pleased.
Upon Him I have put My Spirit
He shall bring forth justice to the nations." (Isa. 42: 1 NABRE)

Streams of Living Water

- "If anyone is thirsty, he should come to Me and drink! The one who believes in Me, as the scripture has said will have streams of living water flow from deep within him." "He said this about the Spirit…" (Jn. 7: 38, 39 HCSB).
- "With joy you will draw water from the fountain of salvation." (Isa. 12: 3)
- "On that day living water will flow out of Jerusalem…"
- On that day Yahweh will become King over all the earth – Yahweh alone and His name alone." (Zech. 4: 8, 9 HCSB)

ADDITIONAL RESOURCES

HOLY SPIRIT BAPTISM

"Paul said,

'John baptized with a baptism of repentance,

telling the people that they should

believe in the One who would come

after him, that is, in Jesus."

"When they heard this, they were baptized

in the name of the Lord Jesus.

And when Paul had laid his hands on them,

the Holy Spirit came on them,

and they began to speak in other languages

and to prophesy."

Now there were about 12 men in all

(Acts 19: 4-7 HCSB)

The Messiah gave gifts

"For the training of the saints in the work of ministry, to build up the body of Christ

until we all reach unity in the faith and in the knowledge of God's Son…"

(Eph 4: 12-13 HCSB)

The Counsellor's Ministry – Witnessing:

"When the Counsellor comes the One I will send to you from the Father – the Spirit of Truth who proceeds from the Father – He will testify about Me." (Jn 15: 26 HCSB)

"When He comes, He will *convict* the world about sin, righteousness and judgement." (Jn 16: 8)

　*Convict: *"prove to the word that they are wrong" (GNBDK)*

　*Judgement: *"condemnation" (NABRE)*

"About sin, because they do not believe in Me;

About righteousness, because I am going to the Father and, you will no longer see Me; and about judgement, because the ruler of this world has been judged" (Jn 16: 9-11 HCSB)

"Now is the time of judgement on this world; now the ruler of this world will be driven out." (Jn 12: 31)

See also (Rev: 9, 11)
Exhortation, meditation and reflection

Spirit of Light; spirit of darkness

God gave His Word incarnated in the Blessed Virgin Mary to go and experience the world, cleave the darkness of falsehood, revealing the truth as darkness gives way before light. He is to sanctify the world with His own precious blood (thus sparing us of condemnation) and reconciling us back to the Father, the fountain of the Divinity. The Holy Spirit assists in this mission.

"But the counsellor, the Holy Spirit – the Father will send Him in My name – will teach you all things and remind you of everything I have told you."

(Jn. 14: 26).

"But you will receive power when the Holy Spirit has come on you, and you will be My witnesses in Jerusalem, in all Judea and Samaria, and to the end of the earth. (Acts 1:8).

What the Holy Spirit does – Don Schwager[1]

"The Holy Spirit makes faith come alive within us"

"Those who are humble and hungry for God receive His Spirit"

"The Holy Spirit is God's gift to us to enable us to know and experience the indwelling presence of God and the power of His Kingdom"

"The Holy Spirit is the way in which God reigns within each of us."

The Ministry of the Holy Spirit

Eldad and Medad: selected and appointed; approved and anointed.

70 elders were selected and appointed to assist Moses.

Two, Eldad and Medad, failed to attend the Tent of Meeting. The elders who attended became prophets. At the same time, these two also began prophesying, even in the camp! (Num 11: 26-30)

What does that tell us? That God loves to work in collaboration with man? That He is cognizant of due protocol, understanding our weaknesses?

These seem to be the understanding of the early fathers of our faith when they selected a replacement for fallen Apostle Judas Iscariot and the tradition persists by electing successors to the Rock, Simon Peter; appointing priests and bishops by the invocation of the Holy Spirit and laying of hands by these leaders.

1: Don Schwager, Aug.15, 2018. Website: DailyScripture:Servants of The Word.org © 2018.

Consider also all the 70 or 72 that Jesus sent out on the second missionary campaign; they all performed the function of prophets in their respective missions.

"THE HOLY SPIRIT"

"The spirit is the source of holiness, a spiritual light, and He offers His own light to every mind

to help it in its search for truth… the power of the Spirit fills the whole universe, but He gives himself only to those who are worthy, acting in each according to the measure of his faith."

"Simple in Himself, the Spirit is manifold in His mighty works. The whole of His being is present everywhere. Though shared in by many, He remains unchanged; His self-giving is no loss to Himself. Like the sunshine, which permeates all the atmosphere, spreading over land and sea, and yet is enjoyed by each person as though it were for him alone, so the Spirit pours forth His grace in full measure, sufficient for all, and yet is present as though exclusively to everyone who can receive Him. To all creatures that share in Him He gives a delight limited only by their own nature, not by His ability to give."

"The Spirit raises our hearts to heaven, guides the steps of the weak, and brings to perfection those who are making progress. He enlightens those who have been cleansed from every stain of sins and makes them spiritual by communion with Himself.

As clean, transparent substances become very bright when sunlight falls on them and shine with a new radiance, so also souls in whom the Spirit shines become spiritual themselves and a source of grace for others.

From the Spirit comes fore-knowledge of the future, understanding of the mysteries of faith, insight into the hidden meaning of scripture and other special gifts. Through the Spirit we become citizens of heaven, we enter into eternal happiness, and abide in God. Through the Spirit we acquire likeness to God."

Above is a perspective of the Holy Spirit by St Basil, the great, bishop.

http://www.CatholicSaints|Saint/Basil.com

CHAPTER 5

Mary, Joseph and Jesus' Disciples

ARE YOU CALLED?
"IF you love Me, you will keep My commandments." (Jn 14: 15)
"This is how all will know that you are My disciples,
if you have love for one another." (Jn 13: 35 NABRE)
We are Jesus' brothers and sisters IF
we do the will of God – (Lk 8: 21)
'On that day many will say to Me,
'Lord, Lord! Didn't we prophesy in Your name,
drive out demons in Your name, and do many
miracles in Your name?"
The Lord will respond,
'I never knew you; depart from Me,
you evildoers.' (Matt 7: 22-23)
"Not everyone… will enter the kingdom of heaven, but only the
one who does the will of My Father…" (Matt 7: 21)
FLEE!
"When they persecute you in one town
Flee to another." (Matt 10: 23 NABRE)
They jeered even at Jesus!
"The Pharisees, who were lovers of money,
were listening to all these things and scoffing at Him." (Lk 16:
14 HCSB)
"…the Lord ordered that those who preach the gospel should
live by the gospel." (1 Cor 9: 14)
FELLOWSHIP
▪   Our fellowship is with God through His Son.
His anointing gives us knowledge; therefore,

OBEY Him and walk as He walked (1 Jn 1: 3, 6-7, 27; 2: 4-6; 3: 24)

- Many invited, few chosen.

"For many are invited, but few are chosen." (Matt 22: 14)

The rich official Lk 18: 18-23, had the invitation extended to him, but…

Zacchaeus, the chief tax collector, was ready to answer the call, though no-one suspected it! (Lk 19: 1-10)

CHRISTIAN MINISTRY: "That repentance, for the forgiveness of sins would be preached in His name to all nations." (Lk 24: 47)

Jesus says: "IF you continue in My word, you really are My disciples.

You will know the truth, and the truth will set you free." (Jn 8: 31-32)

Authority to preach the gospel

"Go into the world and preach the gospel to the whole creation…."

(Mk 16: 15-16)

Worldliness – Be detached!

"Do not love the world or the things that belong to the world…" (1 Jn 2: 15-17)

Christian fellowship

Seeking justice from an unjust system?

"IF any of you has a legal dispute against another, do you dare go to court before the unrighteous, and not before the saints?

"I say this to your shame! Can it be that there is not one wise person among you who is able to arbitrate between his brothers?

"Instead, believer goes to court against believer, and that before unbelievers!

Therefore to have legal disputes against one another is already a moral failure for you. Why not rather put up with injustice? Why not rather be cheated?"

(1 Cor 6: 1, 5-7 HCSB)

For more, read 1 Cor 6: 1-11

Warning against presumption – 1 Cor 10: 1-13

"Therefore whoever thinks he is standing

secure should take care not to fall." (1 Cor 10: 12)

The Truth and freedom from Fear, anxiety, moral turpitude, etc.

"You will know the truth, and the truth will set you free" (Jn 8: 31)

CLING TO JESUS, the vine

Jesus says:

"I am the vine and My Father is the vine grower. He takes away every branch in Me that does not bear fruit, and everyone that does He prunes so that it bears more fruit. You are already pruned because of the word that I spoke to you. Remain in Me, as I remain in you. Just as a branch cannot bear fruit on its own unless it remains on the vine, so neither can you unless you remain in Me. I am the vine, you are the branches. Whoever remains in Me and I in him will bear much fruit, because without Me you can do nothing." (Jn 15: 1-5 NABRE)

Read the entire discuss, Jn 15: 16-17.

My flesh, … My blood (the communion)

"The one who eats My flesh and drinks My blood lives in Me, and I in him."

(Jn 6: 56)

Not everybody can bear this:

"This teaching is hard! Who can accept it?" (Jn 6: 60, 66 HCSB)

Eating the flesh and drinking the blood: The metaphor explained.

"As they were eating, He took the bread… gave it to them, and said, 'Take it; this is My body.'

Then He took a cup,… He gave it to them and so they all drank from it. He said to them,

'This is My blood… it is shed for many.'" (Mk 14: 22-24 HCSB)

"Your life should be free from the love of money.

Be satisfied with what you have, for He Himself has said, I will never leave you or forsake you." (Heb 13: 5)

Likewise read Evangelist Matthew's account of same in Matt 26: 26-28.

The word

"Do not hold back a word.

Perhaps they will listen and return – each

from his evil way of life." (Jer 26: 2, 3 HCSB)

"IF you remain in Me and My word remain in you,

ask… and it will be done for you." (Jn 15: 7 NABRE)

The one who has is given more

"…Because knowledge of the mysteries of the kingdom of heaven has been granted to you,…To anyone who has, more will be given and he will grow rich; from anyone who has not, even what he has will be taken away."

(Matt 13: 11-12 NABRE)

Service: the greatest.

"…the rulers of the Gentiles dominate them, and the men of high position exercise power over them. It must not be like that among you. On the contrary, whoever wants to become great among you must be your servant, and whoever wants to be first… must be your slave; just as the Son of Man did not come to be served, but to serve and …." (Matt 20: 25-28)

In the kingdom of God, it is SERVICE, not servitude.

1 Pt 5:5 "Be servants of each other."

Ministry of Reconciliation

Everything is from God, who reconciled us to Himself through Christ… That is, in Christ, God was reconciling the world to Himself, not counting their trespasses against them, and He has committed the message of reconciliation to us. Therefore… we plead on Christ behalf, "Be reconciled to God." He made the one who did not know sin to be sin for us, so that we might become the righteousness of God in Him."

(2 Cor 5: 18-21)

The pillar and foundation of the truth

"…God's household, which is the church of the living God, (is) the pillar and foundation of the truth"

(1 Tm 3: 15)

A vocation of service

"So if I, your Lord and Teacher, have washed your feet, you also ought to wash one another's feet. For I have given you an example that you also should do just as I have done for you." (Jn 13: 14-15)

Light and Darkness:

i.   Jesus: The Light of the World
"I am the light of the world. Anyone who follows Me will never walk in the darkness but will have
the light of life." (Jn 8: 12)

ii. For this purpose, disciples of Jesus are to be the salt of the earth and the lamp of the world (Matt 5: 13-16)

iii. "This, then, is the judgement: the light has come into the world, and people loved darkness rather than the light because their deeds were evil. For everyone who practises wicked things hates the light and avoids it, so that his deeds may not be exposed. But anyone who lives by the truth comes to the light, so that his works may be shown to be accomplished by God." (Jn 3: 19-21)

How to resolve disputes between brothers

"If your brother sins against you, go and rebuke him in private. If he listens to you, you have won your brother. But if he won't listen, take one or two more with you so that... every fact may be established. If he pays no attention to them, tell the church..."

"I assure you: whatever you bind on earth is bound in heaven, and whatever you loose on earth is already loosed in heaven." (Matt 18: 15-18)

Be perfect!

This is how –

"IF you want to be perfect,... go, sell your belongings and give it to the poor, and YOU WILL HAVE TREASURE IN HEAVEN. Then come, FOLLOW ME."

(Matt 19: 21) (*Capitals mine*)

Read also Matt 5: 44-45.

Be mindful to practise what you preach

"They tie up heavy loads that are hard to carry and put them on people's shoulders, but they themselves aren't willing to lift a finger to move them."

(Matt 23: 4)

For more of the expectations from you as a disciple read Matt 23: 1-36

Do Nothing... but think the same way, have the same goal

"Fulfil My joy by thinking the same way, having the same love, sharing the same feelings, focusing on one goal. Do nothing out of rivalry or conceit, but in humility consider others as more important than yourselves. Everyone should look out not only for his own interests, but also for the interests of others."

(Phil 2: 2-4)

Bear Fruit

Parable of the Vine and the branches: you had better bear fruit and your grace will be abundant.

Parable of talents: use it else you lose it!You are going to account for what you do with it. (Matt 25: 14-30; Lk 19: 12-27)

Like Master, like servant

"Can the blind guide the blind?

Won't they both fall into a pit?

A disciple is not above his teacher, but everyone who is fully trained will be like his teacher." (Lk 6: 39-40 HCSB)

Temperance

"…When we are reviled, we bless; when we are persecuted, we endure it; when we are slandered, we respond graciously. Even now, we are like the world's garbage, like the dirt everyone scrapes off their sandals." (1 Cor 4: 11, 12 HCSB)

My Father's glory is shown by your bearing much fruit; And in this way you become My disciples.

If you obey My commands, you will remain in My love, just as I have obeyed My Father's commands and remain in His love…" (Jn 15: 8, 10 GNBDK)

The Promise
i. Eternal life

"I assure you: Anyone who hears My word and believes Him-who-sent-Me has eternal life and will not come under judgement…"

(Jn 5: 24, *special punctuation ours*)

ii. The Holy Spirit

"But the Counsellor, the Holy Spirit – the Father will send Him in My name – will teach you all

things and remind you of everything I have told you." (Jn 14: 26)

iii. Love Jesus.

"Jesus answered,
'If anyone loves Me, he will keep My word.
My Father will love him, and we will come to him and
make Our home with him.'" (Jn 14: 23)
The Investiture
Jesus declared,

iv. Greater works

"I assure you: The one who believes in Me will also do
the works that I do. And he will do even greater works than these,
because I am going to the Father." (Jn 14: 12)

v. Asking in My name

"whatever you ask in My name, I will do it so that
the Father may be glorified in the Son. If you ask Me
anything in My name, I will do it." (Jn 14: 13-14)
The 30 and the 50,000 pieces of silver
In Matt 27: 3, 5, the people (Jews) valued the Lord for 30 pieces
of silver, the amount at which they valued the truth. But in Ephesus,
the cost of falsehood and deception was valued at 50,000 silver
pieces:

"…many of those who had practised magic collected their books
and burned them in front of everyone. So they calculated their value
and found it to be 50,000 pieces of silver." (Acts 19; 19 HCSB)

The communion

"(Take), My body" "…My blood" This is the main menu of this
banquet of His love.
(Jn 10: 18)

Under the typology or appearance of bread and wine (Matt 26: 26, 28; 1 Cor 11: 29) This is an allusion to the sacrificial death of Jesus, the Lamb of God.

(Jn 1: 29, 36)

Healing at Lystra

"In Lystra a man… lame from birth… Paul said… 'Stand upright!…' And he jumped up and started to walk around." (Acts 14: 8-11)

"And a man's enemies will be

the members of his household." (Matt 10: 36 HCSB)

Peter's Deliverance from Prison

"On the night before Herod was to bring him out for execution, Peter, bound with two chains was sleeping between two soldiers…" suddenly an angel of the Lord appeared,… and said "Quick, get up!"

"Get dressed… and follow me" so he went out and followed, and he did not know that what took place… was real, but thought he was seeing a vision."

They passed the first and second guard posts, they came to the Iron Gate… which opened to them by itself. They went outside… and immediately the angel left him."

Then Peter… went to the house of Mary, the mother of John Mark where many had gathered and were praying." (Acts 12: 6-10, 11, 12)

"Herod searched and did not find him (Peter), he interrogated the guards and ordered their execution." (Acts 12: 19)

DISCIPLESHIP

- Membership of God's family

"So then, you are no longer strangers and sojourners, but you are fellow citizens with the holy ones and members of the household of God."

(Eph 2: 19)

- Be warned against presumptive prophesy

"But the prophet who dares to speak a message in My name that I have not commanded him to speak, or … - that prophet must die"

(Deut 18:20 HCSB)

Humility: Be not called 'rabbi'!

"But as for you, do not be called 'Rabbi'…"

"The greatest among you will be your servant."

"Whoever exalts himself will be humbled,

And whoever humbles himself will be exalted."

(Matt 23: 8, 11-12 HCSB)

The Great Commission:

Go, witness for Me!

- "Go into the whole world and proclaim the gospel to every creature.

Whoever believes and is baptized will be saved; whoever does not believe will be condemned…"

(Mk 16: 15-16 NABRE)

All nations

- "…All power in heaven and on earth has been given to Me.

Go, therefore, and make disciples of all nations, baptizing them…

teaching them to observe all that I have commanded you. And behold I am with you always until the end of the age." (Matt 28: 18-20 NABRE)

"Jesus answered, 'If anyone loves Me, He will keep My word. My Father will love him, and …make Our home with him. The one who doesn't love Me will not keep My words…'" (Jn 14: 23, 24)

Disciples are the salt and the light

"You are the salt of the earth. But if the salt should lose its taste,…it's no longer good for anything but to be thrown out and trampled on by men.

You are the light of the world. A city situated on a hill cannot be hidden.

…a lamp…gives light for all…in the same way, let your light shine before men,… see your good works and give glory to your Father in heaven." (Matt 5: 13-16 HCSB)

Cost of discipleship: renounce family, self and possessions

Lk 14: 25 Once great crowds were going along with Jesus – He turned and told HCSB them:

Lk 14: 26 … anyone following Me who does not hate his own father, mother, HCSB wife, and children – he cannot be My disciple!

Lk 14: 27 "Whoever does not bear his own cross and come after Me cannot HCSB be My disciple."

Lk 14: 33 "In the same way, none of you can be My disciple unless you give up GNBDK everything you have."

Divine Gifts

No one can have anything… (Jn 3: 27 GNBDK)

"John responded,

'No one can receive a single thing unless it's given to him from heaven.'"

(Jn 3: 27 HCSB)

Virgin Mary, the Blessed Mother of Jesus (Lk 1: 26-28, 42)

"The Word became flesh and took up residence among us…full of grace and truth." (Jn 1: 1, 4, 14)

Jesus:

The Word – 1

"What was from the beginning…concerning the word of life –
…the eternal life that was with the Father and was revealed to us –
…we also declare to you…" (1 Jn 1: 1, 2, 3)

Jesus:

The Word – 2

In the beginning was the Word,
and the Word was with God,
and the Word was God.
Life was in Him
and that life was the light of men. (Jn 1:1, 4 HCSB)

Jesus:

An angel reveals to some shepherds in Judea:

"Don't be afraid, for look, I proclaim to you good news of great joy... for all the people...Today a Saviour, who is Messiah the Lord, was born for you In the city of David." (Lk 2: 10-11)

Mary:

Righteous and devout Simeon's prophecy: "...My eyes have seen Your salvation.

A light for revelation to the gentiles and glory to Your people Israel.

Then Simon blessed them and told His mother Mary: ' ... - and a sword will pierce your own soul – that the thoughts of many hearts may be revealed.'"

(Lk 2:30, 32, 34, 35 HCSB)

ADDITIONAL RESOURCES

5. Mary, Joseph and Jesus' Disciples

Whoever is not against us, is for us.

Matt 9: 38 "'John said… Teacher we saw a man who was driving out demons in Your name, and we told him to stop, because he doesn't belong to our group'"

Matt 9: 39 "'Do not try to stop him, …'"

Matt 9: 40 "'FOR WHOEVER IS NOT AGAINST US, IS FOR US'"

"Follow Me!"

Lk 5: 27 NABRE "…He (Jesus) went out and saw a tax collector named Levi sitting at the customs post.

He said to him, 'follow Me.'

Lk 5: 28 And leaving everything behind, he got up and followed Him."

The Holy Spirit

Acts 8: 18 "When Simon saw that the Holy Spirit was given through the laying on of the Apostle's hands, he offered them money"

Acts 8: 20 "But Peter told him, 'may your silver be destroyed with you, because you thought the gift of God could be obtained with money.'"

Christian Unity

Acts 2: 44-45 "All who believed were together and had all things in common; they would sell their property and possessions and divide them among ALL according to each one's need."

See also (Acts 4: 32; 34-35 NABRE)

Don't be cause to sin Mk 12: 38-40 "Beware of the scribes, who… go around in long robes, and who HCSB want greetings in the market places, the front seats in the synagogues, and the places of honour at banquets.

They devour widow's houses and say long prayers just for show.

These will receive harsher punishment."

Insulted for Christ?

1 Pt 4: 14 If you are insulted for the name of Christ, blessed are you!

Power to All Apostles

Matt 18: 18 "whatever you bind on earth (re. recalcitrant brother)… is bound in (NABRE) heaven…"

Serve Christ, clothed with Him

Gal 3: 27 Being Clothed with Christ – no Jews, infidels etc. YOU ARE ALL ONE IN CHRIST!

Jn 12: 21 "… if anyone serves Me, the Father will honour him."

Upon this rock I will build My church

Matt 16: 16 Peter: "You are the Messiah, the Son of the Living God"

Matt 16: 18 "You are Peter and upon this rock I will build My church and the gate of …"

Matt 16: 19 "I will give you the keys to the kingdom of heaven, whatever you bind on earth shall be bound in heaven; and whatever you loose

on earth shall be loosed in heaven." (c/f Matt 18: 18)

(Comment: Jesus' church means the community that Jesus will gather with Peter as chief witness thereof) Read also Matt 16: 24-27: Condition for Discipleship: self-denial, bear own cross (NABRE)

Not thinking as God does?

Matt 16: 23 "…an obstacle… You are thinking not as God does but as human beings do."

The ELEVEN (i.e., without Judas Iscariot):

"…Peter, John, James, Andrew, Philip, Thomas, Bartholomew, Matthew, James son of Alphaeus, Simon the Zealot, and Judas the son of James"

(Acts 1: 13 HCSB)

"- the number of people who were together was about 120 - …"

(Acts 1: 15 HCSB)

JESUS, MARY, JOSEPH (HOLY FAMILY)

Jesus

"Praise the Lord, the God of Israel, because He has visited and provided redemption for His people ... a horn of salvation ... in the house of His servant David" (Lk 1:68, 69) HCSB

"Because of our God's merciful compassion, the Dawn from on high will visit us: to shine on those who live in darkness ... to guide our feet in the way of peace." (Lk 1:78, 79) HCSB

Devil tests Him, angels serve Him.

"Then the Devil left Him, and immediately angels came and began to serve Him." (Matt 4:11) HCSB

"Then an angel from heaven appeared to Him, strengthening Him."

(Lk 22:43) HCSB

Virgin Mother Mary

"... the angel Gabriel was sent from God ... to a virgin betrothed to a man named Joseph, of the house of David, and the virgin's name was Mary."

(Lk 1:26-27) NABRE

"Rejoice ...! The Lord is with you.

Do not be afraid, Mary, for you have found favour with God. ... You will conceive and give birth to a son ... Jesus. He will be great and ... called the Son of the Most High, and ... God will give Him the throne of his father David. He will reign ... forever, and His kingdom will have no end." (Lk 1:28, 30, 31-33, HCSB)

"Elizabeth was filled with the Holy Spirit. Then she exclaimed ... 'you are the most blessed of women, and your child will be blessed! How could this happen to me, that the mother of my Lord should come to me?'" (Lk 1:41-43) HCSB

(Mary responded): "...Surely from now on all generations will call me blessed, ..." (Lk 1:48, HCSB)

The womb that bore Jesus

As Jesus was speaking to the crowd "a woman from the crowd raised her voice and said to Him,

'The womb that bore You and the one who nursed You are blessed!'

He said, 'Even more, those who hear the word of God and keep it are blessed.'" (Lk 11: 27-28 HCSB)

Mary

"…Elizabeth was filled with the Holy Spirit. Then she spoke out with a loud voice and said,

'Blessed are you among women, and blessed is the fruit of your womb!'" (Lk 1: 41, 42 NKJV)

Mary

then He said to the disciple, "Behold your mother!" (Jn 19:27 NKJV)

MARY – A SIGN

"To that Isaiah replied,

'Listen now, descendants of King David…

Well then, the Lord Himself will give you a sign:

a young woman who is pregnant will have a son

and will name Him 'Emmanuel'.'" (Isa 7: 13, 14 GNBDK)

Joseph, the husband of Mary (Lk 1: 26-27)

- "We found the One Moses wrote about in the Law (and so did the prophets): Jesus the Son of Joseph, from Nazareth!" (Jn 1: 45)

Genealogy:

- "Eliud fathered Eleazer, Eleazer fathered Matthan, Matthan fathered Jacob,

and Jacob fathered Joseph the husband of Mary, who gave birth to Jesus who is called the Messiah." (Matt 1: 15-16)

The angel in Joseph's dream said to him,

- "Joseph, Son of David, don't be afraid to take Mary as your wife, because what has been conceived in her is by the Holy Spirit. She will give birth to a Son, and you are to name Him Jesus…" (Matt 1: 20, 21)
- "When Joseph got up from sleeping, he did as the Lord's angel had commanded him. He married her." (Matt 1: 24)

The Caesar Augustus nativity registration

- "And Joseph went up from the town of Nazareth in Galilee, to Judea, to the city of David, which is called Bethlehem, because he was of the house and family line of David, to be registered along with Mary, who was engaged to him and was pregnant." (Lk 2: 4-5) To Egypt, Flee; Return!
- "…an angel of the Lord suddenly appeared to Joseph in a dream, saying, 'Get up! Take the child and His mother, flee to Egypt, and stay there until I tell you…'

So, he got up, took the child and His mother during the night, and escaped to Egypt."

- "After Herod died, an angel of the Lord suddenly appeared in a dream to Joseph in Egypt, saying, 'Get up! Take the child and His mother and go to the land of Israel, because those who sought the child's life are dead.' So, he got up, took the child and His mother, and entered the land of Israel."

"And being warned in a dream, he withdrew to the region of Galilee."
(Matt 2: 13-14; 19-21, 22)

Joseph

- "… when Joseph got up from sleeping, … he married her."
- "… flee to Egypt … So he got up … during the night, and escaped to Egypt."
- "So he got up took the child and his mother and entered … Israel." (Matt 1:24; 2:13, 14; 21 HCSB)

Parental anxieties over the missing child Jesus (Lk 2: 41-50)

Every year Joseph and Mary with the child Jesus, would travel to Jerusalem for the Passover festival.

The pilgrimage when Jesus was twelve years old was remarkable as "the boy Jesus stayed behind in Jerusalem, but His parents did not know it."

They returned to Jerusalem and for 3 days searched for Him. When they eventually found Him out, it was in the temple and this drama played out:

Jesus:

"Your father", "My Father"

Mary: "Son, why have you treated us like this? Your father and I have been anxiously searching for You."

Jesus: "Why were you searching for Me?

Didn't you know that I had to be in My Father's house?" (Lk 2:48-49 HCSB)

Intercession

"All the people witnessed the thunder and lightning, the sound of the trumpet, and the mountain surrounded by smoke …

'You speak to us, and we will listen', they said to Moses, 'but don't let God speak to us or we will die'.

Moses responded … 'God has come to test you, so that you will fear Him and will not sin.'"

(Exo 20:18, 19, 20) HCSB

"Who among you fears the Lord,

Listening to the voice of His Servant? Who among you walks in darkness; and has no light?

Let him trust in the name of Yahweh; let him lean on his God." (Isa 50:10) HCSB

The goal of our faith – discipleship

"(May) the God of our Lord Jesus Christ, the father of glory, … give you a spirit of wisdom and revelation resulting in knowledge of Him.

May the eyes of (your) hearts be enlightened, that you may know what is the hope that belongs to His call, what are the riches of glory in His inheritance … and what is the surpassing greatness of His power for us who believe, in accord with … His great might, … in Christ, … far above every principality, authority, power and dominion, and every name …" (Eph 1:17-21) NABRE

Call to evangelize – the promise:

"And I say to you, anyone who acknowledges Me before men, the Son of Man will also acknowledge him before the angels of God." (Lk 12:8) HCSB

Forgive sins, and heaven will forgive them!

Jesus endowed His disciples with power to forgive sins, saying. "Receive the Holy Spirit. If you forgive the sins of any, they are forgiven them; if you retain the sins of any, they are retained."
(Jn 20:22, 23) HCSB

God is our Father!

"See what love the father bestowed on us that we may be called, the children of God. Yet so we are. What we should be has not been revealed … we do know we shall be like Him."
Lk 14:11 HCSB Humility
"For everyone who exalts himself will be humbled, but the one who humbles himself will be exalted."

Desirous of wealth?

"But those who want to be rich fall into temptation, a trap, and many foolish and harmful desires, which plunge people into ruin and destruction.

For the love of money is a root of all kinds of evil, and by craving it, some have wandered away from the faith …" (1 Jn 6:9-10, HCSB)

Our circumcision/Christian initiation "You were also circumcised in Him with a circumcision not done with hands, … in the circumcision of the messiah." (Col 2:11, HCSB)

Even Moses had admonished the people:

"Therefore, circumcise your hearts and don't be stiff-necked any longer"

(Deut 10:16 HCSB)

God's People

Coming, coming … the Lord has come!

"Daughter Zion, shout for joy and be glad, for I am coming to dwell among you" – this is the Lord's declaration

"Many nations will join themselves to the Lord on that day and become My people. I will dwell among you, and you will know that the Lord of Hosts has sent Me to you.

Let all people be silent before the Lord, for He is coming from His holy dwelling." (Zec 2:10-11, 13, HCSB) (c/fZec 2:14-15, 17 NABRE)

The prophet's disciple, Elisha.

Note that Elijah did not specifically allow Elisha to go and bid good bye to his parents (1 Kgs 19:19-21)

Jesus command to all disciples (i.e., Christians): "Love!"

My Command: "Love one another …" Jesus told His disciples.

"…Remain in My love. If you keep My commands you will remain in my love, …

This is my command: Love one another as I have loved you."

Jesus Friends: "You are My friends if you do what I command you."

"This is what I command you: love one another." (Jn 15: 9-10, 12, 14, 17, HCSB)

The Kingdom Secrets

"…The secrets of the kingdom of heaven have been given for you to know, but it has not been given to them (non-disciples)" (Matt 13:10, HCSB)

Jesus' Ministry, our obligation.

"I must proclaim the good news of the kingdom of God, because for this purpose I have been sent." (Lk 4:43, lect.)

Disciples' reward – heaven is the goal!

"Nevertheless, … but rejoice because your names are written in heaven."
(Lk 10:20, NABRE)
(See also Exo 32:32)
Listening to Jesus
"Whoever listens to you, listens to Me.
Whoever receives you receives Me and whoever receives Me, receives the One who sent Me."
(Lk 10:16; Matt 10:40, NABRE)
Mary's Precept
"Do whatever He (Jesus) tells you to do!" (Jn 2:5)

Saul, persecutor of Christians becomes a Christ's Witness! (For full insight read Acts 22: 3-16; 9:1-22, 28)

"I answered, 'Who are You, Lord?' He said to me, "I am Jesus the Nazarene …"

"Someone named Ananias, a devout man … having a good reputation with all the Jews residing there, came and stood by me and said, 'Brother Saul, regain your sight.' 'For you will be a witness for Him to all people … be baptized, and wash away your sins by calling on His name.'"

"The following night, the Lord stood by him (Saul) and said, 'Have courage! For as you have testified about Me in Jerusalem, so you must also testify in Rome,'" (Acts 22:8, 12-13, 15-16; 23:11, HCSB)

The Church

"… God's household, which is the church of the living God, the pillar and foundation of the truth" (1 Tm 3:15, HCSB)
We Are God's Children

"We are God's children now, and what we will be has not yet been revealed. We know that when He appears, we will be like Him, because we will see Him..."

(1 Jn 3:2)

The Church (The New Jerusalem)

Then one of the seven angels spoke to me:

Rev 21:9 'Come, I will show you the bride, the wife of the Lamb.' He carried me away in the Spirit ... and showed me the holy city, Jerusalem, coming down out of heaven from God, arrayed with God's glory".

: 12 The city had a massive high wall with 12 gates ... the names of the 12 tribes of Israel's sons were inscribed on the gates."

: 14 "The city wall had 12 foundations, and the 12 names of the Lamb's 12 apostles were on the foundations ..."

: 18 "The building material of its wall was jasper and the city was pure gold ..."

: 19 "The foundations of the city wall were adorned with every kind of precious stone ..."

: 22 "I did not see a sanctuary in it, because the Lord God the Almighty and the Lamb are its sanctuary."

: 23 The city does not need the sun or the moon to shine on it, because God's glory illuminates it, and its lamp is the Lamb."

: 27 Nothing profane will ever enter it: no one who does what is vile or false, but only those written in the Lamb's book of life."

22:1 "Then he showed me the river of living water ... The tree of life was on both sides of the river ... and there will no longer be any curse ... and people .., will reign forever and ever." (Rev 21: 9-27; 22:1-5, HCSB)

Ungodly people barred from entry into the New Jerusalem

"... Worship God." Look! I am coming quickly, and My reward is with Me to repay each person according to what he has done. I am the Alpha and the Omega, the First and the Last, the Beginning and the End."

"Blessed are those who ... may have the right to ... enter the city ... Outside are the dogs, the sorcerers, the sexually immoral, the murderers, the idolaters and everyone who loves and practices lying."

(Rev. 22:9, 12-15, HCSB)

Exhortations, meditation and reflection.

MEDITATION: **Call to be God's people** – total submission to God

When we obey Christ, always and everywhere we seem to give up something very precious to us – our self-will!

In reality, we have given up nothing at all! We have only exchanged something of little or no merit for something of great value – our unrighteousness for the righteousness of God; our foolishness for the knowledge and wisdom that created the universe and made it to endure. We are certainly the better off for it. (Jesus is the refulgence of God's glory, Lk 14:28)

Discipleship reward: A hundred fold (Matt 19:29)

Those parting (from following Him) with what are most dear to them "will receive a hundred fold ... and eternal life."

Discipleship: Your Christian Identity

Your Christian initiation begins usually with the baptism of water for the renunciation of sins. It is usually preceded with catechesis – a process by which the candidate is informed about the significance of the process he is about to undergo.

Usually, after some further time had elapsed, the new convert receives the Holy Spirit baptism.

"We haven't even heard that there is a Holy Spirit." (Acts 19:2, HCSB)

With this the convert is a mature member of the body of Christ. But this does not mean that he is perfect.

"Be perfect as Your Father in heaven is perfect." (Matt 5:48)

Perfection comes through persistent practice of the faith being handed down through participation with others, studying of the scriptures and living the life:

"Therefore, as you have received Christ Jesus the Lord, walk in Him, rooted and built up in Him and established in the faith, just as you were taught, overflowing with gratitude." (Col 2:7 HCSB)

Exhortations, meditation and reflection.

Read also what Paul had to say further on this topic in Colossians chapter 3, especially Col 3:5-9; 12-16. This is the spiritual circumcision to which Christ has called us.

All these processes are geared toward one purpose – to make the converts disciples of the Lord Jesus.

Do you know, or can you imagine, what it is like to be a member of the household of God? Some may think this is simply preposterous; not a few may think it is blasphemous or outright contemptuous of God! But wait; here is – an invitation (to be a member of the household of God, the Most High):

"Then His mother and brothers came to Him, but they could not meet with Him because of the crowd. He was told, 'Your mother and Your brothers are standing outside, wanting to see you.' But He replied to them, 'My mother and My brothers are those who hear and do the word of God.'"

(Lk 8:19-21, HCSB)

What an exciting invitation to be members of the household of God by simply listening to and doing the word of God! The invitation is authentic, it comes from Jesus Christ, the Son of God

Compare Rev 12:17; Lk 11:28

"Even more, those who hear the word of God and keep it are blessed!"

"So then you are no longer strangers and sojourners, but you are fellow citizens with the holy ones and members of the household of God." (Eph 2:19)

JUSTIFICATION: sons of Abraham, sons of God!

Comments

I. "... Scripture makes no exceptions ... sin is master everywhere. In this way the promises (to Abraham and his descendants) ... can only be given to those who have this faith (in Jesus Christ).

"Merely by belonging to Christ (i.e., being baptized in Christ) you are the posterity of Abraham, the heirs he was promised."

Exhortations, meditation and reflection.

"The proof that you are (adopted) sons is that God has sent the Spirit of the Son, into our hearts: the spirit that cries, 'Abba, Father,' and it is this that makes you a son, ... and if God has made you son, then He has made you heir."

II. "The person who puts to death by the Spirit the deeds of our sinful nature will live, says the Apostle (Paul). This is not surprising since one who has the Spirit of God becomes a child of God ... so much so that the Holy Spirit bears witness to our Spirit that we are sons of God."

(Gal 3:15-4:7)

Idolatry: relationship (or possession) above God

"What do the twin parables of the tower builder and a ruler on a war campaign have in common (Lk 14: 28-32)? Both the tower builder and the ruler risked serious loss if they did not carefully plan ahead to make sure they could finish what they had begun."

"Paul, the Apostle reminds us, 'we are not our own. We were bought with a price' (1 Cor 6:19, 20). We were once slaves to sin... but we have now been purchased with the precious blood of Jesus Christ... so we could enter His kingdom of light and truth."

"To place any relationship or any possession above God is a form of idolatry – worshipping the creature in place of the creator..."Don Schwager

Lk 10: 27 Disciples must love God with all our hearts, minds, soul and strength.

Call to Special Ministries – Have you discerned your call?

Moses was to liberate the Israelites from enslavement and cruel labour in Egypt.

Jonah was sent to the Ninevites to liberate them from oppressive sin;

Cyrus to re-build Zion and its temple; Jehu to be king; Elisha to be prophet.

(1 Kgs 19: 16)

Gideon was sent to break the yoke of the Philistines' oppression;

St Patrick, to evangelize Ireland; St Martin de Porres, Mother Theresa of Calcutta, to bring succour to the hopeless and helpless in society; nurse Mary Slezzor – for Christian enlightenment in Calabar, Nigeria.

So you, too, must use your God-given resources, time, talent and treasure to address a Christian need that the Lord has inspired you to do.

"Based on the gift each one has received, use it to serve others as good managers of the varied grace of God." (1 Pt 4: 10)

Exhortations, meditation and reflection.

"We know that all things work together for the good of those who love God: those who are called according to His purpose." (Rom 8: 28)

A majority of the prophets are called for just one purpose – one mission: Elisha, to complete the work of Elijah; John the Baptist, to prepare the way for the Christ, and give witness to Him. What about you, have you discerned your call?

The Law:

Observe, the law and the prophets (Matt 7: 12) but besides, 'be perfect!'

Be Perfect!

"Be perfect, therefore, as Your heavenly Father is perfect." (Matt 5: 48)

Here is the perspective of St John of the Cross on this: 1 St John of the Cross – 1542 – 1591; Carmelite order

"IF you do not learn to deny yourself you can make no

progress in perfection. In detachment, the spirit finds quiet
and repose for coveting nothing.

Nothing wearies it by elation and nothing oppresses
it by dejection, because it stands in the center of its own
humility.

Live in the world as if only God and your soul were in it; then,
your heart will never be made captive by any earthly thing."

1.   Who is the greatest?

The disciples approached Jesus and asked, 'Who is the greatest
in the kingdom of heaven?'

For all so concerned, hear the Lord's response: be "converted
and become like children" if you would enter at all.

"Therefore, whoever humbles himself like this child… is the
greatest in the kingdom of heaven."

(Matt 18: 1-5)

1 St John of the Cross – 1542 – 1591; Carmelite order
Exhortations, meditation and reflection.

2.The First, the last?

Remember: In the parable of the labourers for the vineyard, they
were hired at, and worked for various hours. It pleased the master to
pay each of them the same amount – the usual daily wage.

(Matt 20: 1-15, 16)

No disciple is above his teacher,

No slave above his master.

It is enough for the disciple

that he become like his teacher,

for the slave that he become like his master… (Matt 10; 24, 25
NABRE)

Love of money

Money is good and necessary, but God is the Great Provider. He
knows what we need; He opens His hand and supplies all creatures
what they need.

You can't serve two masters – mammon and God. (Lk 16: 13)

Love of money is the root of all evil (1 Tm 6:10)

FREE!

"You have received free of charge; give free of charge.

…For the worker is worthy of his food." (Matt 10: 8, 10)

You will be hypocritical like the Pharisees, if you make money your god; for they, too, are misled by their love of money (Lk 16: 14) and position.

In the parable of the ten gold coins (Lk 19: 11-22, 23-26) – the stewards were empowered 'to each according to ability.'

Showing that our availability is more important than our ability. The Lord does not call the qualified but qualifies the called.

Meditation: Who is a disciple of the Lord Jesus?

All Christians are disciples each to the extent he or she keeps faith with the commandments of the Lord.

"By their fruits you shall know them" (Matt 7: 16, 20)

Exhortations, meditation and reflection.

Discipleship – a vocation.

Jesus preached the word at great personal sacrifice; large crowds converge on Him all the time and He never turned them away; rather, He would teach them. He and His disciples hardly had a private time. "They did not even have time to eat" (Mk 6: 31)

Thus is the service-oriented vocation of Christianity as exemplified by the Lord, Himself.

But it goes beyond belief or philosophy; it is a way of life – "the kingdom of heaven."

ORTHODOXY: Are you sure that you are standing right?

How are you sure you have not been swindled into false beliefs?

From earliest days – both Paul and the other Apostles – put down this rule of thumb: Any teaching different from those of the Apostles and others who have not gone away from them, is false and are to be avoided. From this grew the Apostolic Tradition.

The Lord has an inner caucus in Peter, James and John to whom many mysteries were exclusively revealed.

Finally the Lord established their collective leadership responsibility when He commissioned them.

"All authority has been given to Me in heaven and on earth. Go, therefore, and make disciples of all nations,…" (Matt 28: 18-20)

Before then, Peter's position was re-entrenched as the leader of the disciples

(Jn 21: 15-17)

For more see chapter 19, entitled "Be One"

To God be the glory:

"So whether you eat or drink or whatever… DO EVERYTHING FOR THE GLORY OF GOD." (1 Cor 10: 31 NABRE)

EXTRAORDINARY POWER

As a Christian or disciple of our Lord Jesus Christ, many are endowed with extraordinary gifts (for the ministry) – love, patience, piety, prophecy, healing, preaching and many others. How beautiful there gifts are when placed at the benefit of the body of Christ, and the entire society in which we live!

Exhortations, meditation and reflection.

If you do not see yourself as stewards for these gifts one could easily fall by the wayside and become arrogant. Learn from a master:

"Now we have this treasure in clay jars, so that this extraordinary power may be from God and not from us." (2 Cor 4: 7)

"God gave, that we may give."[2]

Cost of discipleship: Leave all!

"….first seat down and calculate the cost." (Lk 14: 28, 31)

But Lord, Who knows the future, other than the Lord God?

How could Moses, a fugitive, have accurately calculated what doing the work of God would entail compared with going blindfold into the future as shepherd of the flock of his father-in-law?

When Elisha received Elijah's mantle unexpectedly, how could he have compared his new calling with what he was then doing? "Leaving certainty for uncertainty," as they say?

Anybody who receives the call, should only consider the crown (i.e. the joy and fulfilment that we are serving God!) and never hesitate to make all he has available for the assignment plus prayer. Yes, because God empowers the called; those called must be prayerful. The statement of our Lord in Lk 14: 28 is to dampen the enthusiasm of the many, the throng who want the crown but shun the cross.

Which fun seeker or pleasure hunter would not be dismayed if called to be a 'Jesus', seeing the utterly self-less life the Lord lived? Or similar self-less life lived by Apostle Paul after his call? Like Simon and his brother Andrew, like James and his brother John, who left all – if you receive the call today, leave everything else and embrace it.

Know this, however, to succeed you will need to give up all other interests – family, friends, business, titles, etc.

May we not be possessed by our possessions. Amen.

Possessions

"…every one of you who does not renounce
all his possessions cannot be My disciple." (Lk 14: 33 NABRE)

2: Pope Benedict XVI – Daily meditations.

Exhortations, meditation and reflection.

Can you say with Peter,

'Look, we have left what we had
and followed You.'? (Lk 18: 28)

Discipleship entails nothing less.

He called Levi at his duty post, he left everything instantly and followed Him.

(Mk 2: 14)

Zacchaeus, the chief tax collector left all. (Lk 19: 2, 6, 8)

Reflect also on the two parables in Matt 13: 44-45: the prize – the kingdom of heaven – is a hidden treasure, a priceless pearl.

Resilience:

Like the guy constructing a tower or the beleaguered king with a force of 10,000 men confronting another power with 20,000 men each has to be sure his resources are adequate to the need. (Lk 14: 28-32) Thus balance what you seek to gain, the kingdom of heaven, with the cost of striving for it. (Detachment)

Purity – A requisite for discipleship.

"IF you repent, so that I restore you, in My presence you shall stand;

IF you bring forth the precious without the vile,

You shall be My mouthpiece." (Jer 15: 19 Lect)

"Can two walk together without

agreeing to meet?" (Amos 3: 3)

A Disciple Devoid of Piety?

You are a disciple of a religious founder like Moses, Jesus, Mohammed?

Or even of the founder of your local fellowship centre / 'church'?

Good! You give obeisance to this founder, but are you familiar with any deity to whom you give reverence and obedience?

Quite a number of people give adulation to this founder or the priest representing him whom they see and pay scant attention to the deity which is the object of the religion, of whom they rarely or never see.

Exhortations, meditation and reflection.

"The priests and prophets said to the princes and to all the people, 'this man deserves death; he has prophesied against this city…'" (Jer 26: 11 Lect)

The speakers are priests and prophets, the people closest to God whom you would expect to know the things of God better than the lay faithful. They are the ones orchestrating persecution of Jeremiah the Lord's prophet!... What an irony?

"That REPENTANCE for the FORGIVENESS of sins would be preached in His name to all the nations." (Lk 24: 47)

Discipleship Reward

"…'who, then, is the faithful and prudent steward whom the master will put in charge of His servants to distribute food allowance at the proper time? Blessed is that servant whom his master on arrival finds doing so.'" (Lk 12: 42-43)

"YOU are My witnesses…

and My servant whom I have chosen, so that you

may know and believe Me… that I am He.

No god was formed before Me

and there will be none after Me.

I, I Am Yahweh, and there is no other Saviour but Me." (Isa 43: 10-11 HCSB)

Sift and Sideline

"But now I am writing to you not to associate with anyone who claims to be a believer

who is sexually immoral or greedy, an idolater or verbally abusive, a drunkard or a swindler. Do not even eat with such a person."

"…put away the evil person from among yourselves" (1 Cor 5: 11, 13)

In the same context many religious people are so punctilious in the observance of the rites and rules of their faith but they hardly give a thought to the demands of the deity. Jesus chided the Pharisees and Sadducees for several of such practices. In our day, many religious people actually worship their founder, and feel that doing so they have satisfied all obligations! There is no fear of God in them! Such people are themselves – irascible, violent, greedy, arrogant, discriminating, self-centered, lying, etc.

Exhortations, meditation and reflection.

Outside the fellowship centre

Do you reason that different gods created different folks? It may, of course, massage your ego to think that your god is bigger and stronger than their gods; or that he fights for you against all others!

That overlooks the majestic beauty and coordination we find on earth and in the universe – implying a oneness in authority.

Personality worship automatically leads to discrimination, persecution, religious fanaticism and religious killing and killing for religion. Because the worshipper believes only in his religious founder/ leader but ignores the true God who created all of us and everything.

Love is the most poignant attribute of the sovereign God. He is the God of all – a righteous God who, wants mankind to treat each other with kindness. And whoever does what is right, is righteous. God loves the righteous; but hates wickedness, malice and all evils.

Thus, there are two families – the righteous and the ungodly. God's love has no leaning toward flesh and blood or to cult or clan. You can be assured that God loves you, if you are truly righteous.

First Missionary Commission: The Apostles

Summoning His 12 disciples, Jesus gave them authority over unclean spirits to drive them out, and to heal every disease and sickness. These are names of the 12 Apostles:

Simon Peter; his brother Andrew, James and his brother John, both sons of Zabedee Philip and Bartholomew; Thomas, Matthew, the tax collector, James, the son of Alphaeus, Thaddaeus, Simon, the Zealot and Judas Iscariot, the one who betrayed Him. (Matt 10: 1-7)

Jesus subsequently called Saul (also called Paul) to work for Him uniting him with the mainstream through disciple Ananias. (Acts 9: 1-20; 22: 6-15)

After the crucifixion and accession, and the exit of Judas Iscariot, the Eleven chose Mathias by lot and so he was numbered with the 11 apostles. (Acts 1: 26)

Exhortations, meditation and reflection.

2nd Missionary Journey

The Lord chose another 72 men and sent them out two by two, to go ahead of Him to every town and place where He Himself was about to go…

(Lk 10: 1-12, 17 GNBDK)

Power over demons: oh Lord, revive us again!

The Lord in commissioning the second missionary journey instructed:

"Go on your way; behold, I am sending you like lambs among wolves."

Cure the sick in it AND say to them, 'the kingdom of God is at hand for you.'

Whether you are well received or not, "go into the streets and say, 'the kingdom of God is at hand.'"

It was a successful mission and they rejoiced at their return.

Power to disciples

"Jesus said,

I have observed Satan fall like lighting from the sky. Behold I have given you the power to tread upon serpents and scorpions and upon the full force of the enemy and nothing will harm you."

(Lk 10: 3, 9, 11, 19 NABRE)

Many of us have seen these powers exercised by believers in our lifetime and we need no further evidence that the power has really passed down… We need the power as an integral part of our Christian ministry. Let us crave it, ask for it and the Lord will cause a revival of it, because He knows we need it to function effectively in our various missions.

"As you go, announce this:

'The kingdom of heaven has come near.'" (Matt 10: 7)

The mission

"I have now … filled your mouth with My words.

See, I have appointed you today

over nations and kingdoms

to uproot and teardown,

to destroy and demolish,

to build and plant." (Jer 1: 9, 10)

Who is a Christian?

Exhortations, meditation and reflection.

What is Christianity?

I will answer this question vicariously:

First, every disciple of Jesus Christ is a Christian.

But not every 'Christian' is a disciple. The difference is the extent of conformity with the requirements of discipleship or of followership.

Christianity, therefore, is a fraternity – a way of life. It is more than mere philosophy, an ideologue or that sort of thing.

You can't be a Christian in isolation, just as you cease to be a disciple if you live disparate life, cut away from the master or from other disciples.

The prize of our Christian calling is the kingdom of heaven. See how it works in Matt 20: 1-16: Labourers were hired and worked at different lengths of time, but were paid the same amount for their wages. Yet, the community must eschew envy and rancour.

Apostle Paul puts it this way:

"But now you must also put away all the following: anger, wrath, malice, slander, and filthy language from your mouth. And not lie to one another…"

"Therefore, God's chosen ones, holy and loved, put on heartfelt compassion, kindness, humility, gentleness, and patience, accepting one another and forgiving one another if anyone has a complaint against another. Just as the Lord has forgiven you, so you must also forgive. Above all, put on love – the perfect bond of unity." (Col 3: 8-9, 12-14)

We must learn to give to Caesar what belongs to Caesar and to God total submission and reverence

(Mk 12: 17)

"Turn away from evil and do what is good, and dwell there forever. For the Lord loves justice and will not abandon His faithful ones." (Ps 37: 27-28)

A model or a copycat?

How do you see your Christian life? – Do you often want to be like them? Or you expect them to be like you? Yes, to be like you, because you are like Jesus!

Once you realize that your life is a model for others, a mirror by which others judge themselves a whole lot of responsibility devolves on you. You will make greater effort to be the person you are supposed to be. There will be nothing to bother you because you will expect worse treatment than you get.

Exhortations, meditation and reflection.

"It is enough for a slave to be like the master." So don't look to the world for your values – look to Jesus.

For more on this theme, see "the narrow gate"

"ANYONE who eats My flesh and drinks My blood has eternal life, and I will raise him up on the last day, because My flesh is real food and My blood is real drink." (Jn 6: 54-55 HCSB)

Watchmen, Sentinels

As prophets are the watchmen for the people so are priests, being teachers, are sentinels for them also. And by our baptism in Christ Jesus all disciples share this watchman's responsibility: (Ezk 33: 1-6)

"As for you, son of man, I have made you a watchman for the house of Israel. When you hear a word from My mouth, give them a warning from Me."

(Ezk 33: 7 HCSB)

It has accompanying grace as by this banquet, the diner lives in Christ, and Christ lives in him. (Jn 6: 56)

Christian leaders are commanded to undertake this liturgy "in remembrance of Me" (Lk 22: 19; 1 Cor 11: 24, 25)

It is also a proclamation or gospel of the Lord's death (1 Cor 11: 26), the victory of His salvific ministry (Jesus righteousness) i.e. over the power of sin, Satan and eternal damnation. (The ruler of this world has been judged) (Jn 16: 8-11)

The Living Bread (Jn 6: 51, 54-55)

This is a most important liturgy established by the Lord just a few hours before the commencement of His passion.

In a way, the liturgy is like an emblem or a banner, with which Christ's disciples are associated. It comes in form of a banquet on His body and blood as the main menu 'for the life of the world'

Exhortations, meditation and reflection.

Some disciples found "this teaching too hard" to take in and ceased following Him (Jn 6: 42, 60, 66) for that reason, the liturgy signifies a turning point, a point of separation from those who trusted the Lord completely from those with fickle faith – who deserted:

"they went out from us." (1 Jn 2: 19)

It is sacramental as it connotes that partakers in the banquet are the redeemed whose sins are forgiven and who are pilgrims to everlasting life.

(Jn 6: 40, 47, 54-55, 58)

God's approval for this grace of justification comes in terms of the new covenant sealed with the blood of Jesus. (Jn 6: 27)

Jesus parting words –

To Mary: "woman, behold your son." (Jn 19: 26 NABRE) and

to John (and vicariously to all disciples): "behold your mother" (Jn 19: 27 NABRE)

Oh Mother Mary, you have been bequeathed to us, pray for us, be our helper in times of need. Amen.

At Jesus crucifixion:

At the cross her station keeping[1]

stood the mournful mother weeping

close to Jesus to the last.

"Let me share with you His pain

221

Who for all our sins was slain
Who for me in torments died."
Through her heart His sorrow sharing
All His bitter anguish bearing
Now at length the sword had passed.
(Jn 19: 26; Lk 2: 35)

*1: **Stabat Mater**.* A Roman Catholic dirge at pre-Easter Memorial of Jesus' passion.

Exhortations, meditation and reflection.

God calls you!

If someone told you or you find out by yourself that man sprouts out like grass from the earth and by mutation and adaptation he had become what he is today, won't you be concerned about what he would become tomorrow even after death and what he was before sprouting out?

However, Christian religion has a different explanation for the emergence of man on the earth planet, as the passage quoted from Genesis shows. It explains the origin, purpose and destination of man.

The Creator has designated a role for man in relation to other creatures and also in relation to Himself. If we recognize these and conform, it will be well with us but if we digress or rebel, it is ominous that we would be courting trouble.

"For those He foreknew He also predestined,
to be conformed to the image of His Son...
And those He predestined He also called;
and those He called, He also justified and
those He justified, He also glorified." (Rom 8: 29, 30)

We identify these unique obligation or expectations as divine calls. The average man or woman is expected to fulfil two or more of these roles, namely:

Disciples

My CALL, Your Call.
Nothing is by accident, it is not by chance!
Jer 1:5 Lect "… Before I formed you in the womb I knew you, before you were born I dedicated you a prophet to the nations I appointed you."

i. A call to holiness

"Do you not know that you are the temple of God and that the Spirit of God dwells in you?
If anyone destroys God's temple, God will destroy that
person; for the temple of God, which you are, is holy."
(1 Cor 3:16-17 NABRE)
In this context holiness and righteousness are taken to mean the same thing.
Exhortations, meditation and reflection.
"…'Holy, holy, holy is the Lord God almighty,
Who was and who is to come'" (Rev 4: 8 Lect)

- "…be holy in all your conduct for it is written, 'be holy…'" (1 Pt 1: 15)
- Avoid greed and self-indulgence (Matt 23: 25)
- Give, and it shall be given to you

Forgive, and you shall be forgiven; do what is good.
Be merciful as your Father in heaven is merciful (Lk 6: 30, 35, 38)

- Be doers of the word and not hearers only, deluding yourselves (Jas 1: 22 NABRE)
- Yes, these obligations must be met to walk with the Lord. All have sinned and fallen short of the glory of God and not one is free. For the Psalmist says,

"If You kept a record of our sins, who could escape being condemned? But You forgive us, so that we should stand in awe of You." (Ps 130: 3, 4 GNBDK)

- Mercy and forgiveness are proofs of God's holiness (Ezk 36: 2, 4)
- Now the sting of death is sin, (1 Cor 15: 56)

"for the wages of sin is death, but the gift of
God is eternal life in Christ Jesus, our Lord." (Rom 6: 23)
"All unrighteousness is sin,…" (1 Jn 5: 17)
Everyone who commits sin also breaks the law;
Sin is the breaking of law (1 Jn 3: 4)
The core message of Christianity is,
"Repent, for the kingdom of God is at hand" (Mk 1: 15)
"…Look, you were sold for your iniquity and your mother was put away because of your transgressions. (Isa 50: 1)
Exhortations, meditation and reflection.

- Yes, ravaging war, epidemic, pestilence, famine and natural disasters such as flood are some of the rods with which God calls a rebellious people back to order.
- "Repent (seek the Lord) ten times harder (than you have sinned/strayed away from Him) (Bar 4: 28-29)

For He (God, the Father) chose us in Him (Jesus Christ)….. to be holy and blameless in His sight" (Eph 1: 4)

We cannot attain holiness through our individual or intellectual effort alone.

For example, some people who employed their intellect to argue in favour of the state caring for the most vulnerable members of society through welfare schemes were ridiculed by people of another persuasion; they dubbed it as "sharing misery," but when it is a matter of obedience to the Holy God, you will come to realize that the 'foolishness' of God is better than the wisdom of man. (1 Cor 3: 19; 1: 25)

We can attain this personal sanctification by devotion to prayer, reading the scriptures, and meditating on the word of God and doing what we are taught. Living our lives in line with the lives lived by the saints can be a great guide also.

"You must walk and please God…" (1 Thes 4: 1)

In one brief summary, you must live as one "being born again, i.e., believing in Jesus, the light of the world and abandoning wickedness…"

(Jn 3: 3, 5, 18-20; 1 Pt 1: 23; 2 Cor 5: 17)

ii. Called to be in communion (i.e. fellowship) with God

A prophet's call

"If you bring forth the precious without the vile you shall be my mouth piece."

(Jer 15:19, NABRE)

"… if you return, I will restore you; you will stand in My presence. And if you speak noble words, rather than worthless ones, you will be My spokesman."

(Jer 15:19, HCSB)

Exhortations, meditation and reflection.

Mal 2: 10 Have we not all one Father?

Has not one God created us?

Why, then, do we break faith with each other,

Profaning the covenant of our ancestors?

Mal 2: 15 Did He not make them one, with flesh and spirit?

And what does the One require? Godly offspring!

You don't have to go into trance, see visions, perform wonders or speak in tongues to be in communion with God.

You can know that you are in communion with God if you hear, read or share the word of God and the scriptures and meditate on them regularly.

You will have become a citizen of the kingdom of God, no longer tossed around by the waves of ethnic, tribal, class, or racial prejudice but attentive to the needs of others (including strangers) without discrimination, since we all are children of God.

St John gives the formula – love not the world and its distractions and do the will of God (1Jn 2: 15, 17 NABRE)

We can look at this at two levels –

First, at the individual personal level, this is a call to fellowship with God; then at the community or nation level, this is a call to be God's people. We have all been created by God, but like human offspring's, not all of us honour our parents or are dear to them.

Call to fellowship with God "God is faithful; you were called by Him into fellowship with His

Son Jesus Christ our Lord" (2 Cor 1:18 HCSB)

All who fear the Lord and obey His commandments and precepts, are, indeed, children of God! They can call God, *Abba, Father*!

Adam, our pristine father, was in fellowship with God but hid himself from God:

"I was afraid because I was naked, so I hid" (Gen 3: 10)

Exhortations, meditation and reflection.

There is no hiding place for sin and it separates us from the holy God who created us for communion with Himself. Why would anyone forsake (to enjoy) that sacred communion with God?

"so we are all present before God,…" (Acts 10: 33)

The sinner too, is called to communion with God! But he must first walk away from past wickedness and evil. Jesus explains that He has not come to call the righteous but sinners to repentance. (Lk 5:32)

Two such sinners responded – as models for us all:

First, a woman heard about Jesus. The woman, "who was a sinner found out that Jesus was reclining at table" in the house of Simon, a Pharisee. There she demonstrated her repentance. (Lk 7: 36-50) In the second episode Zaccheus, rich but infamous, heard also that Jesus was passing by, but Jesus saw repentance in his heart.

Jesus was unequivocal in stipulating the terms for His followers:

"Whoever wishes to come after Me must deny himself,
Take up his cross and follow Me." (Mk 8: 34)

iii. Call to discipleship

It was Joshua, Moses assistant and successor, who made the declaration:

"for me and my household, we will serve the Lord." (Jos 24: 2, 3) You may have heard about the call of Elisha by Elija (actually Elija acted on God's command) (1 Kgs 19: 16): Lot… by Abraham, Aaron… by Moses; Andrew and Simon, James and his brother John, by Jesus. These are truly ecstatic and dramatic. But look at Nathaniel's call ("come and see!"), it was more subtle, yet solemn.

Discipleship – for succor

Jesus beckons, and promises:

"Come to Me, all of you who are weary and burdened, and I will give you rest … take up My yoke and learn from Me, … and you will find rest for yourselves. For My yoke is easy and My burden is light." (Matt 11:28-30, HCSB)

Exhortations, meditation and reflection.

Faithful and Prudent Servant:

"Stay awake!" (Matt 24:42)

"Be Prepared …" (Matt 24:44)

"…You have the word of eternal life" (Jn 6: 68)

Of course your dedication is not in vain: 'a hundred times' reward (Matt 19: 29)

You must be steadfast in your fellowship - "neither hot nor cold is not acceptable" –

(Rev 3:16) for example, some complained, "This teaching is hard: who can accept it?" (Jn 6: 60)

Some who don't believe …

And the Lord's response: "But there are some among you who don't believe (Jn 6: 64)

Could that be you?

He who perseveres to the end receives the crown (Rev 3:21)

Your call and its purpose is beyond doubt because He has said it:

- "Go, make disciples of all the nations…" (Matt 28: 18, 20) so once you are steady in the saddle as a disciple, you must go forth and make disciples of others not your personal disciple but disciples of the Lord Jesus Christ. "for we are God's co-workers…

I have laid a foundation as a skilled master builder, and another builds on it. For no one can lay any other foundation than what has been laid down.

That foundation is Jesus Christ." (1 Cor 3: 9, 10-11)

Your Gifts – or the graces of God in your life should not lead you into pride:

"Now, there are different gifts, but the same spirit. There are different ministries but the same Lord. And there are different activities, but the same God activates each gift in each person." (1 Cor 12: 4-6)

"Now you are the body of Christ, and individually members of it." (1 Cor 12: 27)

Exhortations, meditation and reflection.

Inadequate to the task? Leave that to the Master. He will convert your availability to capability. Moses complained of his stammering, Samuel dreaded Saul Jeremiah and Gideon complained about their youthfulness; yet they succeeded.

"If you are ridiculed for the name of Christ, you are blessed,…" (1 Pt 4: 14)

"A slave is not greater than the master; the messenger than the one who sent him" (Jn 13:16)

And even "the dead who die in the Lord from now on are blessed" (Rev 14: 13)

No looking back

"But Jesus said to him, 'no one who puts his hand to the plough and looks back is fit for the kingdom of God'" (Lk 9: 62)

There are three levels of witnessing – with your words, with your deeds and sometimes, inevitably with your blood.

iv. Called to bear fruit

"I chose you from the world to go and bear fruit." (Jn 15: 16)

"You did not choose Me, but I chose you. I appointed you that you should go and produce fruit and that your fruit should remain, so that whatever you ask the Father in My name, He will give you." (Jn 15: 16)

- The word of God has been planted in you; it is the seed and you are the soil on which it is planted. The Lord expects a harvest of a hundred fold, sixty fold from the good soil (Matt 13:23).
- Jesus makes it clear that – "not everyone who says to Me, 'Lord, Lord!' will enter the kingdom of heaven" (Matt 7: 21)
- "'The dead who die in the Lord from now on are blessed' 'yes! Says the spirit', 'let them rest from their labours for their works follow them.'" (Rev 14: 13)

Exhortations, meditation and reflection.
- JESUS is "the way, the truth and the life." Whoever wants to be a disciple of His must first desire a fellowship with God. The Lord may then appoint such as a shepherd of some of His flock:

And again:

- "I chose you before I formed you in the womb;
I set you apart before you were born.

I appointed you a prophet to the nations." (Jer 1: 5)
And yet again:

- "…I watch over My word to accomplish it." (Jer 1: 12)
- Jesus is the vine, His Father the vine keeper, you are the branches. The Father prunes the branch that it may bear fruit but the axe is on all branches that do not bear fruit (Jn 15:5). Because cut away from Jesus, you can do nothing!

Each person to mind his own business and hold the fort. Every vocation is important, if well performed.

Jesus says, "what is that to you?" if I want him to be (this) and you to be (that) (Jn 21: 22)

He reminds us of their common denominator – SERVICE to the people of God.

"You know that the leaders of this world lord it on their people; but for you,

it shall not be so. Whoever wants to be great shall be the servant of all;

whoever wants to be first shall be slave." Is that clearly understood and accepted by you?

To really bear much fruit calls for sacrifices –

"If a grain of wheat does not fall and die it cannot bear much fruit"

Suffering teaches oneself endurance, endurance leads to perfection David would not give a gift to God that costs him nothing.

Exhortations, meditation and reflection.

Let your righteousness (your faith as a Christian, Muslim, whatever) beam brilliant rays of its goodness beyond the precincts of your assembly, sanctuary, mosque, church, etc. Go all out and bear fruit!

"The Lord measures our perfection neither by the multitude nor the magnitude of our deeds, but by the manner in which we perform them." St John of the cross.

That explains why of all the patriarchs, prophets and kings up to the time of John the Baptist, not one was greater than he, yet the least in the kingdom of heaven is greater than he. (Matt 11:11; Lk 7:28)

v. Called to feed the flock – As pastors, bishops, general overseers, rulers, etc.

"Simon… feed My lambs,… shepherd My sheep…, feed My sheep" (Jn 21: 15-17).

That is your mandate, a sacred duty – feed with the physical food and spiritually with words of truth and encouragement as the Master Himself did. Remember always the One who gave you the mandate on whose behalf you are serving – who is the chief shepherd – the shepherd of all (Ps 23: 1-5) and be like Him to the flock you pasture.

The leadership of the Christian faith had descended from Simon Peter and the Apostles to you today at this hour, so too, you, the political leader of the people of God – you are now in the seat of Moses! And you have the charismof David to sway your generation. So do it well – for you are serving the Lord!

"Whatever you did not do to the least of My brothers that you did not do to Me" (Matt 25:45)

As the Father sent Me so am I sending you… (Jn 20: 21)

Elisha in his service said, "…Give to the people to eat, they ate and were filled."

(2 Kgs 4: 42) and he blessed the resource that thus ransomed the prophets widow's son from slavery

(2 Kgs 4: 1-)

David ensured that bread was available for his officers and men; Christ, the good shepherd started his ministry by providing wine at Cana, later he fed 5,000 and 4,000; after His resurrection He fed Peter and his colleagues who were about backsliding with grilled fish.

Exhortations, meditation and reflection.

Feeding, of course, is not restricted to physical food but is all embracing, encouragement, and material welfare.

Apostle Peter says "I exhort (you) the elders among you to shepherd God's flock among you, not overseeing out of compulsion but freely according to God's will; not for the money but eagerly." (1 Pt 5: 1, 4)

And Apostle Paul writes

"An overseer… must be above reproach… self-controlled, sensible, respectable, hospitable, an able teacher, not addicted to wine, not a bully but gentle, not quarrelsome, not greedy,…" (1 Tim 3: 2-3) And as a "man of God… fight the good fight for the faith" (1 Tim 6: 11-12).

Then go out there and bear fruit – fruit of repentance, contrition; the fruit of self-less love, compassion and generosity.

What about the fruits of your growth in the spirit – faith, hope, love, endurance, charity, patience, wisdom, understanding, knowledge and fear of God, self-control?

Let the world see your good work so it may give praise to our Father in heaven.

Lead people to Jesus and raise them for the kingdom.

Finally, be guided by what the prophet says,

Do not feed yourselves – rather, feed the flock! Do not feed off the sheep's milk, wear their wool, slaughter their fatlings, but seek and bring back the strayed and the lost; tend and heal the sick. Don't rule with violence and cruelty. The Lord will demand accountability from you! (Ezk 34: 1-10)

And again,

"Woe to the shepherds who destroy and scatter the flocks of My pasture – oracle of the Lord." (Jer 23: 1 NABRE)

Hearken to the command of the Lord, ('Comfort, comfort My people'), says your God" (Isa 40:1 HCSB)

vi. Called to Secular life

As business men and women, military men and women, professionals – academicians, public servants, teachers, engineers, doctors, scientists, technocrats, artisans, leaders of government and legislature, etc.,

Exhortations, meditation and reflection.

"Based on the gift each one has received, use it to serve others as good managers of the varied grace of God." (1 Pt 4: 10)

The Church has been established because of you! You are called to enter the kingdom of God; that the Way you live your life may be a trustworthy witness to the gospel ethos.

You are called to be the conscience of society, hold dear your Christian values – be the lamp to your community – a light that dispels the darkness of error, falsehood and wickedness.

"Your light must shine in the sight of men… so that seeing your good works, they give the praise to your Father in heaven." (Matt 5: 16)

You are the salt of the world (or at least to your generation) but if the salt loses its taste, it is good for nothing.

You serve the yeast of the kingdom – that adds value – righteousness, truth and praise of God to the communal endeavours.

vii. Call to be God's people

"Our soul waits for the Lord, who is our help and our shield, for in Him our hearts rejoice; in His holy name we trust" (Ps 33:30)

"Blessed is the nation whose God is the Lord, the people He has chosen for His own inheritance." (Ps 33: 12)

"This is My beloved Son; listen to Him" (Matt 17: 5; Mk 9: 7)

On three memorable occasions the gospel recorded the release of the voice of God commending Jesus to mankind as our mentor, teacher, and model of perfection (light of the world) (Jn 8: 12)

Political leaders of God's own people have enormous responsibility in this regard. They have to lead the people in "a pilgrim fellowship"[3] in walking this path of Righteousness.

3: Pope Francis: "overcoming indifference and win peace" re. celebration of the 49th World Day of Peace, Jan 1, 2016.

Exhortations, meditation and reflection.

For forty years, Israel sojourned in the desert learning how to walk with the Lord and raising a new generation in righteousness. It was certainly not an easy road to walk but at the end bliss awaited those who persevered.

That was Zion, but today, it is not so reassuring that the people still wished to be or remain 'the people of God'.

The Lord insistently calls us to, "be attentive to Me, My people; for teaching shall go forth from Me, and My judgement, as light to the peoples."

(Isa 51: 4) NABRE

The holy scriptures tell us that:

"Righteousness exalts a nation but sin is a disgrace to any people"

(Prov 14: 34)

Unbridled nationalism (like in Hitler's Reich) and the blindness and the prejudice of tribalism, ethnicism and racism will ultimately lead to unrighteousness (like hatred of foreigners) since such bigots fail to recognize the universal (i.e., divine) brotherhood of man.

Lazy gods

I wish these unrighteous 'gods' were at least as powerful as the sons of men! Then, they would not need ghostly humans to help them fight their human foes! Dogs don't eat dogs; then, man would not have to fight and ruin a fellow-human who could be an innocent neighbour!

We are all created by God, thus all who answer the divine call are God's people. Each nation or people have to make the choice explicitly or deliberately. Such people or nation must put on the whole amour of God; love one another as God (in Christ) loved us. They should not relent to be their brother's keeper – i.e., lend and share with members who are in dire or higher need than themselves. They should not be untouched by what their neighbours are going through, alleviating their pains and ameliorating their condition:

"When I was hungry you fed me… naked, you clothed me… in prison,…sick, you visited and comforted Me."(Matt 25:4:35-36)

Exhortations, meditation and reflection.

The founding fathers of the USA inserted in their banner, "In God, we trust." Then, Uncle Sam, was known as 'God's own country', an epithet to be coveted.

"But you are a chosen race, a royal priesthood, a holy nation, a people for His possession, so that you may proclaim the praises of the One who called you out of darkness into His marvellous light."

"Once you were not a people, but now you are God's people; you had not received mercy, but now you have received mercy." (1 Pt 2: 9, 10)

Stop! Jesus, the light of the world, beckons on peoples and nations at this hour to, "come to Me…" (Matt 11: 28)

CHAPTER 6

Judgement

What the scriptures say:

Recompense for the upright
"For you will be repaid at the resurrection of the righteous." (LK 14:14 NABRE)

In the last days,

The mountain of the Lord's house will be established at the top of the mountains and will be raised above the hills.

All nations will stream to it.

…They will turn their swords into ploughs and their spears into pruning knives. Nations will not take up the sword against other nations, and they will never again train for war. (Isa 2:2, 4 HCSB)

The Deaths

First death is subject to judgment. All mankind is subject to this.

"I also saw the dead…standing before the throne…and the dead were judged according to their works…

Second Death: No consolation, no redemption.

Then the sea gave up its dead, and Death and Hades gave up their dead; all were judged according to their works. And anyone not found written in the book of life was thrown into the lake of fire. This is the second death,…"

"Blessed are those who wash their robes, so that they may have the right to the tree of life and may enter the city by the gates." (Rev 20:12-13, 15; 22:14 HCSB)

HELL

"And I saw the dead, great and small alike, standing before the throne. Books were opened…the dead were judged according to what they had done…then death and the world of the dead were thrown into the lake of fire." (this lake of fire is the second death)

2ⁿᵈ Coming—becoming impatient?

"The Lord does not delay His promise, as some understand it today, but is patient with you, not wanting any to perish but all to come to repentance."

(2 Pt 3: 9, 15 HCSB)

Are you penitent, and indeed converted?

The Resurrection

"For as in Adam all die, so also in Christ all will be made alive. But each in his own order: Christ, the first fruits; afterward, at His coming, those who belong to Christ."

(1 Cor 15:22-23 HCSB)

Some end-time signs

Peter, James, John and Andrew asked Jesus, "Tell us when will these things happen?…"

Jesus replied:

"Watch out that no one deceives you. Many will come in My name, saying 'I am He,' and they will deceive many. When you hear of wars and rumours of wars don't be alarmed; these things must take place; but the end is not yet…

There will be earthquakes in various places, and famines. These are the beginning of birth pains."

(MK 13:4, 5-8 HCSB)

For more, read further, MK 13:14, 19-26.

2ⁿᵈ Coming: Be prudent, anticipate it

Everybody: "You also must be prepared, for at an hour you do not expect, the Son of Man will come."

"If He comes in the middle of the night, or even near dawn, and finds them alert, those slaves are blessed." (LK 12:40, 38 Lect)

Pastors/Leaders:

"Be ready for service and have your lamps lit."

"Who, then, is the faithful and prudent steward whom the master will put in charge of his servants to distribute the food allowance at the proper time?

Blessed is that servant whom the master, on arrival finds him doing so…"

"But if that servant says to himself, 'my master is delayed in coming,' and begins to beat the servants…to eat and drink and get drunk, then, that servant's master will come on an unexpected day and at an unknown hour and will punish the servant severely…"

"…much will be required of the person entrusted with much, and still more will be demanded of the person entrusted with more."

(LK 12:35, 42-43, 45-46, 48 Lect.)

Recompense

"For it is easy for the Lord on the day of death to repay mortals according to their conduct."

(Sir 11:26 GNBDK)

You do not know the hour of the day.

Jesus says, "Amen, I say to you I do not know you. Therefore, stay awake, for you know neither the day nor the hour." (Matt 25:13 Lect)

For further reading, see LK 12:35, 38, 40-48.

No mercy, unless you show mercy.

"Talk and behave like people who are going to be judged. There will be judgement without mercy for those who have not been merciful." (Js 2:13 HCSB)

Jesus: Victim for sin and Saviour.

"Everyone must die once, and after that be judged by God. In the same manner, Christ also was offered in sacrifice once to take away the sins of many. He will appear a second time, not to deal with sin, but to save those who are waiting for Him." (Heb 9:27-28 GNBDK)

Heaven rejoices! (God punished her for killing His servants)

"Praise God!

Salvation, glory, and power belong to our God!

True and just are His judgments!

He has condemned the prostitute who was corrupting the earth with her immorality.

God has punished her because she killed His servants."

"Praise God!

The smoke from the flames that consume the great city goes up forever and ever!"

"Amen! Praise God!" (Rev 19:1, 2, 3, 4 GNBDK)

"They said a second time;

'Allelua! Smoke will rise from her (who corrupted the earth) forever and ever."

Satan is sealed up—the devil is detained.

"He seized the dragon, that ancient serpent—that is the Devil, or Satan—and chained him up for a thousand years. The angel threw him into the abyss, locked it, and sealed it, so that he could not deceive the nations any more until the thousand years were over. After that he must be let loose for a little while."

(Rev 20:2-3 GNBDK)

The soul of Martyrs

"Then I saw thrones…I also saw the souls of those who had been executed because they had proclaimed the truth that Jesus revealed and the word of God. They had not worshipped the beast or its image…They came to life and ruled as kings with Christ for a thousand years. (The rest of the dead did not come to life until the thousand years were over.)"

"This is the first raising from the dead.

Happy and greatly blessed are those who are included in this first raising of the dead.

The second death has no power over them, they shall be priests of God and of Christ, and they will rule with Him for a thousand years." (Rev 20:4, 5-6 GNBDK)

Satan damned forever

After the thousand years are over, Satan will be let loose from his prison, and he will…deceive the nations… Gog and Magog. Satan will bring them all together for battle…., they… surrounded the camp of God's people and the city that He loves. But fire came down from heaven and destroyed them. Then the Devil…was thrown into the lake of fire and sulfur, where the beast and the false prophet had already been thrown, and they will be tormented day and night forever and ever." (Rev 20: 7, 8, 9-10 GNBDK)

And others

Whoever did not have their names written in the book of the living were thrown into the lake of fire." (Rev 20:12,14-15 GNBDK)

The new heavens and the new earth, which I will make … (Isa 66:22)

A new heaven and a new earth.

"Then I saw a new heaven and a new earth…

I heard a loud voice speaking from the throne:

"Now God's home is with human beings! He will live with them, and they shall be His people.

God Himself will be with them, and He will be their God.

He will wipe away all tears from their eyes.

There will be no more death, no more grief or crying or pain.

The old things have disappeared."

Then the One who sits on the throne said,

'And now I make all things new!'"

"Those who win the victory will receive this from Me: I will be their God, and they will be my children. But cowards, traitors, perverts, murderers, the immoral, those who practise magic, those who worship idols, and all liars—the place for them is the lake burning with fire and sulfur, which is the second death." (Rev 21: 1, 3-5, 7-8 GNBDK)

"LISTEN!" says Jesus.

"I am coming soon! Happy are those who obey the prophetic words in this book!" (Rev 22:7 GNBDK)

Maranatha! Come, Lord Jesus!

Better enter the kingdom trim than be barred from entry.

"If your hand causes your downfall…or your foot…cut it off…if your eye causes your downfall, gouge it out. It is better to enter the kingdom of God maimed or lame or blind in one eye than to have one's entire body thrown into hell—the unquenchable fire, where their worm does not die, and the fire is not quenched." (MK 9:43-48 HCSB)

HELL: A warning

Do everything to escape hell – the horrors there have no ending. Jesus warns His disciples to strive not to be a stumbling block that may cause others to sin.

(Mk 9: 42)

"For everyone will be salted with fire." (MK 9:49 HCSB)

Bear with one another, therefore, "and be at peace with one another." (MK 9:50 HCSB)

"For whoever is not against us is for us." (MK 9:40 HCSB)

The place of feast for all people

"… On mount Zion, the Lord Almighty will prepare a banquet for all the nations of the world – a banquet of the richest food and the finest wine." (Isa 25: 6 GNBDK)

The fear of death

Jesus… that through His death He might destroy the one holding the power of death – that is the Devil – and free those who were held in slavery all their lives by the fear of death." (Heb 2: 14-15 HCSB)

On this mountain
He will destroy the burial shroud,
the shroud over all the peoples,
the sheet covering all the nations;
He will destroy death forever. (Isa 25:7, 8 HCSB)

That Day (of visitation)

"For that day will assault everyone…(on) earth" (LK 21:35)
2nd Coming, Resurrection and Judgement
"Then the righteous will shine like the sun in their Father's kingdom. Anyone who has ears should listen." (Matt 13:43)
"Your dead will live, their bodies will rise…" (Isa 26:19)
"…for look, the Lord is coming…to punish… the earth for their iniquity…"
(Isa 26:21)
"Then there will be signs in the sun, moon and stars; and there will be anguish on the earth among nations bewildered by the roaring sea and waves. But when these things begin to take place, stand up and lift up your heads, because your redemption is near!" (LK 21: 25, 28 HCSB)

For more on the signs read, Matt 24: 4, 11, 14, 24, 27, 29-31.
"Oh, worship the Lord in the beauty of holiness!
Tremble before Him, all the earth.
For He is coming, for He is coming to judge the earth.
He shall judge the world with righteousness,
and the peoples with His truth." (Ps 96: 9, 13 Lect)

Jesus is the resurrection and the life

Jesus says, "I am the resurrection and the life.
… The one who believes in Me, even if he dies, will live." (Jn 11: 25 HCSB)

Putting On Heart-felt Compassion: A Judgement Day Requirement

"I assure you: whatever you did for one of the least of these brothers of Mine,

you did for Me." (Matt 25: 40)

Read all of Matt 25:31-46.

Why doesn't retributive justice show up immediately?

You can glean part of the answer in the parable of the wheat and the weed

(Matt 13:24-30)

"No, he said, when you gather up the weeds, you might also uproot the wheat with them. Let both grow together until the harvest…" (Matt 13:29-30; 36-43)

WHEN?

In Rev 9, a third of humanity were killed by the plague unleashed by the 6th angel of destruction, yet

"The rest of the people…did not repent of the works of their hands to stop worshipping demons and idols…and they did not repentof their murders, their sorceries, their sexual immorality or their thefts." (Rev 9:20.21)

"There will no longer be an interval of time, but in the days of the sound of the seventh angel…then God's hidden plan will be completed…" (Rev 10:6-7)

That day

"Now concerning that day or hour no one knows—neither the angels in heaven nor the Son—except the Father." (MK 13:32)

Judgement

"We thank You, Lord God, the Almighty, who is and who was,

because You have taken Your great power and have begun to reign.

The nations were angry,

but Your wrath has come.

For the dead to be judged..."

(Rev 11:17-18)

Proclamation of the angel with the eternal gospel:

"Fear God and give Him glory,

because the hour of His judgement has come. Worship the Maker of heaven and earth..." (Rev 14:7 HCSB)

Finally, "...the earth was harvested." (Rev 14:16)

"Death and Hades were thrown into the lake of fire." As well as "anyone not found written in the book of life." –the second death (Rev 20:14-15)

The Sign of His Coming—

For details of the signs to watch out for look into Matt 24:3-8; 9-14, 23-27; 29-31

Note in particular: "...you will be hated by all nations because of My name."

"Many false prophets will rise up and deceive many."

"This good news...will be proclaimed in all the world

as a testimony to all the nations."

"False messiahs and false prophets will arise and perform great signs and wonders to lead astray..."

"For as the lightning comes from the east and flashes as far as the west, so will be the coming of the Son of Man."

"Then the sign of the Son of Man will appear in the sky, and then all the peoples of the earth...will see the Son of Man coming on the clouds of heaven with power and great glory"

"And He will send out His angels with a loud trumpet, and they will gather His elect..."

(Matt 24:9, 11, 14, 24, 27, and 30-31 HCSB)

Judging the flock

"The Lord God says to you, My flock:

I am going to judge between one sheep and another; between the rams and male goats.

Isn't it enough for you to feed on the good pasture? Must you also trample the rest of the pasture with your feet?

Yet My flock has to feed on what your feet have muddied." (Ezk 34:17-19)

But read also Ezk 34: 15-16, 20-22; 31

Recompense

"The Son of Man will…repay everyone according to his conduct"

(Matt 16:27 NABRE)

"Do not be amazed at this, because a time is coming when all who are in the graves will hear His voice and come out—those who have done good things to the resurrection of life, but those who have done wicked things, the resurrection of judgement." (Jn 5:28-29)

The Narrow Gate

"ENTER through the narrow gate, for the gate is wide and the road is broad that leads to destruction, and there are many who go through it. How narrow is the gate and difficult the road that leads to life, and few find it." (Matt 7:13-14)

The end time – Daniel's prophecy

"At that time…

There will be a time of distress such as never has occurred since nations came into being until that time.

Many of those who sleep in the dust of the earth will awake,

some to eternal life,

and some to shame and eternal contempt.

Those who are wise will shine

like the bright expanse of the heavens,

and those who lead many to righteousness,

like the stars forever and ever."

(Dan 12: 1, 2-3)

Eschatological – Resurrection of the dead.

"Then there will be a time of troubles, the worst since nations first came into existence.

When that time comes, all the people of your nation whose names are written in God's book will be saved. Many of those who have already died will live again: some will enjoy eternal life, and some will suffer eternal disgrace."

(Dan 12: 1, 2 GNBDK)

"… righteousness and justice are the foundation of His throne." (Ps 97: 2 HCSB)

"… let mountains shout together for joy before the Lord, for He is coming to judge the earth.

He will judge the world righteously

and the peoples fairly." (Ps 98: 8, 9 HCSB)

Men's god and judgement.

- Exo 32: 1 "when the people saw that Moses delayed in coming down from the mountain, they gathered around Aaron and said to him,
- "Come, make us a god who will go before us because this Moses… we don't know what has happened to him!"
- 32: 31 So Moses returned to the Lord and said, 'Oh, these people have committed a grave sin…
- 32: 32 Now if You would only forgive their sin. But if not, please erase me from the book You have written.'
- 32: 33 The Lord…: "I will erase whoever has sinned against Me from My book."
- 32: 34 "Now go, …; see, My angel will go before you." But on the day I settle accounts, I will hold them accountable for their sin."
- 32: 35 And the Lord inflicted a plague on the people for what they did with all Aaron had made.

JUDGEMENT

"I assure you: Whatever you did for one of these brothers of Mine, you did for Me.

… whatever you did not do… you did not do for Me either."

(Matt 25: 44-45 HCSB)
Jesus, the resurrection and the life
"I am the resurrection and the life." (Jn 11: 25)

Resurrection

"'I assure you: An hour is coming, and is now here, when the dead will hear the voice of the Son of God, and those who hear will live.'"

"Do not be amazed at this because a time is coming when all who are in the graves will hear His voice and come out... to the resurrection of life, but ... (the) wicked..., to the resurrection of judgement."

(Jn 5: 25, 28 HCSB)

Eschatological – The Lord's Second Coming

"On that day...
There will be ONE CONTINUOUS DAY... – not day and night, for in the evening there will be light.
... fresh water will flow from Jerusalem,...
This will be so in summer and in winter."
The Lord will be king over the whole earth;
on that day the Lord will be the Only One, and the
Lord's name, the Only One. (Zec 14:6,7-9 NABRE)

Be holy take courage!

- Some holy will fall?

"Some of the wise will fall so that they may be refined, purified and cleansed until the time of the end." (Dan 11: 29)

- "This horn waged war against the holy ones and was prevailing over them until... judgement was given in favour of the holy ones of the Most High. For the time has come and the holy ones took possession of the kingdom."

"To them, kingship, power and greatness of the kingdoms under all of heaven will be given to the people, the holy ones of the Most High."
(Dan 7: 21, 27)

The Apocalypse and Gospel witnessing

"And this Good News… will be preached through all the world for a witness to all nations; and then the end will come." (Matt 24: 14 GNBDK)

The judgement

"Anyone who believes in Him (one and only Begotten Son of God) is notcondemned, but anyone who does not believe is already condemned, because he has not believed in the name of the one and only Son of God."

"This, then, is the judgement: the light has come into the world and people loved darkness rather than the light because their deeds were evil." (Jn 3:18-19 HCSB)

On the day of judgement

"Brood of vipers! How can you speak good things when you are evil? For the mouth speaks from the overflow of the heart.

A good man produces good things from his storeroom of good, and an evil man produces evil things from his storeroom of evil.

I tell you that on the day of judgement people will have to account for every careless word they speak." (Matt 12:34-36 HCSB)

God, our righteousness.

"More tortious than all else is the human heart,
beyond remedy, who can understand it?
I, the Lord, alone probe the mind and test the heart,
to reward everyone according to his ways,

according to the merit of his deeds." (Jer 17: 9-10 Lect)
ACCOUNTABILITY
"For the Son of Man will come with His angels in His Father's glory, then He will recompense everyone according to his conduct." (Matt 16:27)

Day of judgement (Matt 11: 22)

"we shall all have to appear before the judgement seat of God" (Rom 14: 10)

after death (Heb 9: 27) and at the end of the world (Matt 25: 31)

each person will be "judged according to his conduct." (Rev 20: 13)

Those who believe in Jesus will be saved (Acts 16: 30-31) (Mk 16: 16)

Those in sin will earn eternal damnation (2 Thes 1: 9; Matt 22: 13)

(Rev 21: 8)

Jesus is the judge (Jn 5: 22)

That Day

Lk 21: 34 "Beware that your hearts do not become drowsy from carousing and GNBDK drunkenness and the anxieties of daily life and that day catch you by surprise."

: 35 "like a trap. For that day will assault everyone who lives on the face of the earth.

Matt 24: 21 "For at that time there will be great tribulation, the kind that hasn't taken place fromthe beginning of the world until now and never will again!"

It will go well for the righteous.

"Tell the righteous that it will go well for them,

for they will eat the fruit of their labour."

"woe to the wicked – it will go badly for them,

for what they have done will be done to them." (Isa 3:10-11)

"So humanity is brought low, and man is humbled."

"Human pride will be humbled, and the loftiness of men will be brought low; the Lord alone will be exalted on that day."

(Isa 2: 9, 11 HCSB)

The Day of the Lord

"Go into the rocks and hide in the dust... for a day belonging to the Lord of Hosts is coming against all that is proud and lofty; against all that is lifted up...against every high tower, against every fortified wall, ... and against every splendid sea vessel. So human pride will be brought low, and the loftiness of men will be humbled; the Lord alone will be exalted on that day."

(Isa 2:10-17 HCSB)

UNIVERSALITY: SALVATION IS FOR ALL

Matt 8: 11 "I tell you that many will come from east and west, and recline at the table with Abraham,Isaac and Jacob in the kingdom of heaven."

ADDITIONAL RESOURCES

Eternal happiness:

Do you know these – that
- Jn. 3:5 "... no one can enter ... unless they are born of water and the spirit"
- Jn. 6:40 "... everyone who looks to the Son and believes in Him shall have eternal life, ..."
- Matt. 13:49-50 "... at the end of the age, the angels will come and separate the wicked from the righteous and throw them into the blazing furnace ..."
- Matt. 13:40-43 "... burned in the fire, so it will be at the end of the age ..."
- Matt 12:36 "... everyone will have to give account on the day of judgement for ..."

John: Preaching in the wilderness of Judea:

"... But the One coming after me is more powerful than I. I am not worthy to remove His sandals ..."

"His winnowing shovel is in His hand, and he will gather His wheat into the barn. But the chaff He will burn up with fire that never goes out." (Matt 3:11, 12 HCSB)

Eternal bliss:

"But as it is written: what eye did not see, and ear did not hear, and what never entered the human mind – God prepared this for those who love Him." (1 Cor 2:9 HCSB)

Jesus' death – for you and me!

But we do see Jesus – made lower than the angels for a short time so that by God's grace He might taste death for everyone – crowned with glory and honour ... Heb 2:9

The kingdom of God has come?

"I assure you: There are some standing here ... will not taste death until they see the Kingdom of God come in power." (Mk 9:1)

WORKS (Perseverance in righteousness and true faith)

" 'The dead who die in the Lord from now on are blessed.'

"Yes", says the Spirit, "let them rest from their labours, for their works follow them!" (Rev 14:13)

Persevere!

"... if anyone worships the beast and his image ... he will also drink the wine of God's wrath ... be tormented with fire and sulphur ... and the smoke ... will go up forever and ever ..." (Rev 14:9-11)

"'This demands the perseverance of **the saints**, who keep God's commands and their faith in Jesus.'"

(Rev 14:12 HCSB)

Apocalypse: Sin pollutes.

"The earth is polluted because of its inhabitants, for they have transgressed laws, violated statutes, broken the ancient covenant." (Isa 24:5 HCSB)

"On that day (PAROUSIA), the redeemed will exult:

'Look, this is our God; we have waited for Him, and He has saved us. This is the Lord, we have waited for Him. Let us rejoice and be glad in His salvation.'" (Isa 25:9)

Judge rightly!

Dt. 1:16 "I (Moses) commanded your judges ... judge rightly between a man and his brother or a foreign resident.

Dt. 1:17 "Do not show partiality when deciding a case; listen to small and great alike. Do not be intimidated by anyone, for judgement belongs to God."

Justice to the slave

"Whoever kidnaps a person must be put to death whether he sells him or the person is found in his possession." (Ex 21:16 HCSB)

"When men get in a fight … if there is an injury then you must give life for life, eye for eye, tooth for tooth, hand for hand, foot for foot." (21: 22-24)

Oracle against a godless people

"Howl, for the day of the Lord is near;
as destruction from the Almighty it comes.
Therefore all hands are helpless,
The bows of the young-men fall from their hands.
Every man's heart melts in terror.
Pangs and sorrows take hold of them,
like a woman in labour they writhe; …" (Isa 13:6-7 HCSB)

An oracle against godless nations

"Lo, the day of the Lord comes,
cruel with wrath and burning anger;
To lay waste the land
and destroy the sinners within it!
The stars and constellations of the heavens
send forth no light;
The sun is dark when it rises,
and the light of the moon does not shine.
Thus I will punish the world for its evil
and the wicked for their guilt.
I will put an end to the pride of the arrogant,
the insolence of tyrants I will humble." (Isa 13:9-11 HCSB)

"In the days after that tribulation, the sun will be darkened, and the moon will not give its light, and the stars will be falling from the sky, and the powers in the heavens will be shaken … and then He will send out the angels and gather His elect from the four winds, …" (Mk 13:24-28 Lect)

Accountability/Judgement

2 Pt 1:3 You ordained a judgement

Judgement…

"Transgressions … 'for I take no pleasure in anyone's death. So repent and live!'" (Ezk 18: 30, 32)

Death, then judgement

"Just as it is appointed that human beings die once, and after this the judgement."
(Heb 9:27)

HELL: (Richman and Lazarus)

"A place … where there will be wailing and grinding of teeth" (Matt 24:5 NABRE)

(God so hated evil He invented the spectre of hell!)

God's testimony

"And this is the testimony: God has given us eternal life, and this life is in His Son." (1 Jn 5:11 HCSB)

Accept the word, possess eternal life.

"Amen, amen, I say to you, whoever hears My word and believes in the One who sent Me has eternal life and will not come to condemnation …" (Jn 5:24 HCSB)

Salvation

"Then he (the jailer) escorted them (Paul and Silas) out and said, 'Sirs, what must I do to be saved?' So they said, 'Believe in the Lord Jesus and you will be saved …'" (Acts 16:30-31 HCSB)

To whom much is given, much will be expected

"Much will be required of the person entrusted with much, and still more will be demanded of the person entrusted with more." (Lk 12:48 Lect.)

Jesus Second Coming

"Look, the Lord comes with thousands of His holy ones to execute judgement on all and to convict them ..." (Jude 1:14 HCSB)

Jesus 2nd Coming

"Then they will see the Son of Man coming ...

Son of Man seated at right hand of power"

Matt 16:64; 16:28; Mk 13:26, 14:62; Lk 21:27

The days of the Son of Man

"Just as it was in the day of Noah so it will be in the days of the Son of Man. People went on eating ... giving in marriage until the day Noah boarded the ark, and the flood came and destroyed them all."

"... as it was in the day of Lot, people went on eating, drinking, buying, selling, planting, building. On the day Lot left Sodom, fire and sulphur ... destroyed them all."

"... A man in the field must not turn back."

"... two will be in one bed, one will be taken and the other ... left; two women ... grinding grain together: one will be taken and the other left."

"Two ... in a field, one ... taken ... the other ... left."

"Where the corpse is there also the vultures will be gathered." (Lk 17:26-37 HCSB)

When?

"For that day will not come unless the apostasy comes first, and the man of lawlessness is revealed, ..." (2 Thes 2:3 HCSB)

Finally, the second death.

"But the cowards, unbelievers, vile, murderers, sexually immoral, sorcerers, idolaters, and all liars, - their share will be in the lake that burns with fire and sulphur, which is the second death," (Rev 21:8)

Parousia, How?

"Then they will see the Son of Man coming in clouds with great power and glory".

(Mk 13:26 NRSV-CE)

The incorruptible (resurrection) body.

"So it is with the resurrection of the dead:

Sown in the corruption, raised in in-corruption;

Sown in dishonour, raised in glory;

Sown in weakness, raised in power;

Sown a natural body, raised a spiritual body.

If there is a natural body, there is also a spiritual body." (1 Cor 15: 42-44 HCSB)

Sons of God: the sons of the Resurrection:

"Those who are counted worthy to take part in that age (end time) …"

"For they cannot die anymore, because they are like angels and are SONS OF GOD, since they are sons of the resurrection" (Lk 20:35-36 HCSB)

Jesus brother and sister

"Whoever does the will of God is my brother and sister and mother." (Mk 3:35 HCSB)

"Whoever believes that Jesus is the Christ has been begotten by God … this is what LOVING GOD is, keeping His commandments." (1 Jn 5:1-2)

Jesus gives life.

"For you gave Him authority over all flesh; so He may give eternal life to all You have given Him."

(Jn 17:2 HCSB)

Eternal life

"This is eternal life: that they may know You, the only true God, and the One You have sent – Jesus Christ." (Jn 17:3 HCSB)

2ND COMING: Be Prepared For It.

Is the Lord delayed in coming?

"Jesus said to His disciples:

'Gird lions and light your lamps and be like servants who await their master's return from a wedding, ready to open immediately when he comes and knocks.

Blessed are those servants …

And should he come in the second or third watch and find them prepared in this way, blessed are those servants.'" (Lk 12:35, 37-38 HCSB)

JESUS – Only Name, Only Saviour!

"Then peter filled with the Holy Spirit, said to them, …

'Let it be known to all of you, and to all the people of Israel, that this man is standing before you in good health by the name of Jesus Christ of Nazareth, whom you crucified, whom God raised from the dead. There is **salvation in no one else**, for there is **no other name** under heaven given among mortals by which we must be saved.'" (Acts 4:8, 10, 12 NRSV-CI)

The fear of death

"Death, where is your victory?

Death, where is your sting?

Now the sting of death is sin …

Therefore … be steadfast … that

… your labour in the Lord is not in vain." (1 Cor 15:55, 58 HCSB)

Exhortations, Meditation & Reflection

Repent! Repent!! Repent, now!!! This witness shall rise again!

In the 42 dreary months (or 1260 days) (of celestial calendar) when the earth turns away from the Lord, where will you be? Will you be in the Lord (in His sanctuary) or in the horde (in the courtyard)? How tough those days will be!

The two witnesses, two olive trees (divine revelation?) and two lamps (human reasoning?) will be untouchable in those days as "fire comes from their mouths and consumes their enemies." Yet, "when they finish their testimony, the beast that comes out of the abyss will … kill them."

But don't gloat, for the celebration of the depraved will be short-lived: "after three and a half days (celestial calendar) the breath of life from God entered them, and they stood on their feet." and "… They went up to heaven in a cloud."

Guess what? "The survivors (of the horde) were terrified and gave glory to the God of heaven," but further disaster was in the offing. (Rev 11:3, 4-14)

At judgement, the touchstone will not be legality – how scrupulously you have kept the Ten Commandments – but on righteousness.

1. Righteousness

Note that what the sheep did (and what the goats failed to do) belong to the realm of righteousness. The issue is no longer the Ten Commandments (or their amplified version – the ordinances or the Torah) or legality; not even the commandments of the church but simply and unequivocally **doing good**. That is, pure righteousness which can only be attained if you "love one another as I have loved you."

Maranatha! Come, Lord Jesus! (Matt 25:31-46)

2. There is Resurrection.

Jesus assures His doubting Sadducees that there is resurrection of the dead

"… they rise from the dead, …" (Mk 12:25)

God is not a God of the dead but of the living (of course, because, Abraham, Isaac and Jacob live!) (Mk 12:27)

Exhortations, Meditation & Reflection

At the valley of dry bones—

"Dry bones, hear the word of the Lord!

This is what the Lord God says to these dry bones:

I will cause breath to enter you,

and you will live." (Ezk 37: 4, 5 HCSB)

The scenery Ezekiel described above (and in full in Ezk 37: 1-14) foreshadows the **resurrection of the dead.**

"Son of man, can these bones live?" (Ezk 37:3)

Can the One who made man and gave him soul, spirit, bone and body not revive him if He so wishes? Certainly, God is able!

Although this chapter is concerning the restoration of hope of those who were saying: "our bones are dried up and our hope has perished, we are cut off." In their despondency they forgot that nothing will be impossible for God to do.

(LK 1:37; Gen 18:14)

God can meet us all at the points of our respective needs, revive our drooping spirits and restore the soul of the dead. In a way, resurrection is about restitution; we need only to place our trust in Him, Praise God, alleluia!

The day of the Son of Man – unpredictable

Unpredictability will hold sway (LK 17:26-37)

People will ignore the warning as they did in the days of Noah and in the days of Lot.

Judgement: No impunity.

God will not permit impunity among the inhabitants of the earth. This revelation Jesus gave in this parable:

"Again, the kingdom of heaven is like a large net thrown into the sea. It collected every kind of fish, and when it was full, they dragged it ashore, sat down, and gathered the good fish into containers, but threw out the worthless ones.

So it will be at the end of the age. The angels will go out, separate the evil people from the righteous, and throw them into the blazing furnace. In that place there will be weeping and gnashing of teeth." (Matt 13:47-50)

Exhortations, Meditation & Reflection

The brave and the best are applauded by their performance; the lazy and wicked are calumniated by their abomination. This and the certainty of accountability, the Lord communicated in two parallel parables.

The parable of the Ten Minas (Lk 19:11-27)

See how very intricately woven is the end-time story and how profound the message. A kaleidoscope of the events of the (yet to occur) end-time judgement was so picturesquely presented. The Old Testament account was supportive, leaving a scintillating and clear vision of this end of the age recompense and condemnation tribunal.

The One who had left had returned with the glory of heaven with Him.

He separates them like a shepherd does, the sheep from the goat.

Let bigots take note—they are all members of the same flock, which elsewhere (Matt 25:40) He refers to as 'My brothers,' avoiding the use of colours or such terms as 'flesh and blood' and 'gentiles', because these are inappropriate.

It is the wish of God that man be saved. The kingdom has been prepared for us from the beginning of creation (Matt 25: 34) Hell is a latter day contraption for the devil, its fallen angels and those whose work is evil.

Restitution & Retribution: No impunity!

In a parallel account of demanding accountability from his subjects/servants, the points are made:

The nobleman is Jesus; He is going to be away for a while "to receive for Himself authority to be king and then return" (LK 19:12)

His people were the Judaists

The Jewish people were those who "hated him and sent a delegation after him, saying, "We don't want this man to rule over us!" (LK 19:14)

Of course, all who reject the kingdom of heaven belong to this category.

The Lord had empowered each servant: "entrusted his property to them; to one he gave five talents, to another two, to another one, to each according to ability." (Matt 25: 14, 15 NRSV-CE)

And in the other parable, equal amount was given (LK 19:13)

His return is certain as is the kingship (LK 19:15, Matt 25:19)

Then follows judgement: recompense or condemnation.

Read both versions of the parable in LK 19:12-27; and Matt 25: 14-30.

Exhortations, Meditation & Reflection

A vision of heaven: The transfiguration

The vision became necessary to be broached because Jesus was about to undergo a confounding level of torment, persecution, contempt, even death – far from the picture of Him that the disciples were used to – the passion and crucifixion.

The vision opened the curtain for the trio – Peter, James and John to behold the resplendent glory of their master in dazzling dress as He conversed with Moses and Elijah (Matt 17: 1-9).

Among other things, it shows that there is life after death and that Jesus, indeed, stood shoulder high with the greatest. It must be a big factor that steeled their faith in the face of the daunting tragedy of the crucifixion (before the resurrection). That was the appropriate time to relate the vision to the brothers.

The main highlight of the vision was the voice from heaven:

"This is My beloved Son in whom I am well pleased;

Listen to Him."

Other glimpses of heaven given by the Lord Jesus include: In the parable of Lazarus and the rich man

(Lk 16: 24). The other is in the description of judgement at Jesus second coming (Matt 25: 31-46)

Isa 2: 22 "Put no more trust in man, who has only the breath in his nostril, what is he really worth?" (i.e. without God, "cut away from Jesus you can do nothing")

Jesus 2nd coming

You are now in the world. Perchance you did not will it to come to earth in the place and time you did. In the same way, whether you like it or not, whether you believe it or not, you may be raised from the dead. But now, however, you have a chance to do something or an option to do nothing about your eternity.

CHAPTER 7

Sin

The way of thinking of the ungodly
"Let us beset the just one, because… he reproaches us for transgressions…" "…if the just one be the son of God, God will defend him and deliver him from the hand of his foes." "with revilement and torture let us put the just one to the test… Let us condemn him to a shameful death,…" (Wis 2: 12, 17-20 Lect)

Sin and Satan

"War broke out in heaven,… the huge dragon,… called the Devil and Satan, who deceived the whole world was thrown down on earth, …" (Rev 12: 9)
"… everyone who has been born of God does not sin
… and the evil one does not touch him."
"… we are of God, and the whole world is under
the sway of the evil one." (1 Jn 5: 18, 19 HCSB)

Walking in the truth – in love.

"Walking in the truth" is "that we love one another"
"And this is love: that we walk according to His commands.
This is the command… : you must walk in love." (2 Jn 1: 5, 6 HCSB)
SIN, the devil, demons
"The wicked are not like this.
Instead, they are like chaff that the wind blows away. Therefore, the wicked shall not survive the judgement, and sinners will not be in the community of the righteous. For the Lord watches over the

way of the righteous, but the way of the wicked leads to ruin" (Ps 1: 5-6)

"Evil brings death to the wicked,
and those who hate the righteous will be punished."
(Ps 34: 21)
"A little while, and the wicked person will be no more;
though you look for him, he will not be there.
The wicked have drawn the sword and strung the bow
to bring down the afflicted and needy
and to slaughter those whose way is upright.
Their swords will enter their own hearts,
and their bows will be broken.
The wicked man borrows and does not repay,
but the righteous one is gracious and giving.
Turn away from evil and do what is good,
and dwell there forever." (Ps 37: 10, 14-15, 21, 27)
Righteousness
"Do not be conquered by evil
but conquer evil with good." (Rom 12: 21 GNBDK)
"Do not repay anyone evil for evil;
be concerned for what is noble
in the sight of all." (Rom 12: 17 GNBDK)
For more read Prov 3: 4; 1 Thes 5: 15; 1 Pt 3: 9
Jesus: "Do not judge, so that you won't be judged.
For with the judgement you use, it will be measured to you.
Why do you look at the spec in your brother's eye but don't
notice the log in your own eye?"
(Matt 7: 1-3 HCSB) For more read Matt 7: 4-6
"Sow righteousness for yourselves, reap faithful love
break up your unploughed ground
It is time to seek the Lord…" (Hos 10: 12)
JESUS TEACHING:

Anxiety/obsession: Life is more than food; body more than clothing. See the ravens and the lilies so well adorned by God, man is much more valued by God than they (Lk 12: 22-26)

Greed: "one's life is not in the abundance of possessions" (Lk 12: 15) for more see parable of the rich fool.

Hypocrisy: "Beware of the yeast of the Pharisees which is hypocrisy; nothing covered that won't be uncovered; hidden, that won't be made known…"

(Lk 12: 54-56)

Lack of Discernment (or faith) is not an excuse:

"…you know how to read the appearance of the sky, but you can't read the signs of the times." (Matt 16: 3)

You can get the things you cherish through prayer:

"Give me discernment, that I may observe Your law and keep it with all my heart."

(Ps 119: 34)

Proverbs: On wickedness

3: 34 Lect "The curse of the Lord is on the house of the wicked,
but the dwelling of the just He blesses;
when dealing with the arrogant,
He is stern,
but to the humble
He shows kindness."

6: 16-19 "The Lord hates six things; in fact, seven are detestable to Him;
arrogant eyes, a lying tongue, hands that shed innocent blood,
a heart that plots wicked schemes, feet eager to run to evil,
a lying witness who gives false testimony,
and one who stirs up trouble among brothers."

Duplicity

"Nothing is concealed that will not be revealed nor secret that will not be known." (Matt 10: NABRE)

Jesus: propitiation for our sins

"For our sake He made Him to be sin
who did not know sin, so that we might
become the righteousness of God in Him."
(2 Cor 5: 21 NABRE)

"He Himself is the propitiation for our sins, …"
(1 Jn 2: 2)

The blood of Jesus – expiation for sin.

"… My blood… the covenant, it is shed for many for the forgiveness of sins."
(Jn 12: 28)

Be born again:

"Everyone who believes that
Jesus is the Messiah has been born of God…
…everyone who has been born of God
does not sin,…
… we are of God,…"
(1 Jn 5: 1, 18)

Resist, conquer the Devil!

"War broke out in heaven,… the huge dragon,
… ⁺they conquered him by the Blood of the Lamb
and ⁺by the word of their testimony.
⁺Love for life did not deter them…" (Rev 12: 9, 11 Lect)

War against the righteous:

"So the dragon was furious with the woman and
left to wage war against the rest of her offspring –
those who keep God's commands and have
the testimony about Jesus." (Rev 12: 17 HCSB)

"…Christ Jesus became for us WISDOM from God,
as well as RIGHTEOUSNESS, SANCTIFICATION
and REDEMPTION." (1 Cor 11: 30)

Sin everywhere

That is the scenario depicted by the prophet Micah – take the Israelites as a typology of the human race:

Mic 3: 11 Her leaders issue rulings for a bribe,

her priests teach for payment,

and her prophets practice divination for money.

Yet they lean on the Lord, saying,

'Isn't the Lord among us? No disaster will overtake us.'

Mic 7: 2 "Godly people have vanished from the lands;

there is no one upright among the people.

All of them wait in ambush to shed blood;

they hunt each other with a net."

Mic 7: 3 "Both hands are good at accomplishing evil:

the official and the judge demand a bribe;

when the powerful man communicates

his evil desire, they plot it together."

The Christian heritage:

"You will know the truth,

and the truth will set you free." (Jn 8: 31)

The word can save us

"… Rather, blessed are those who hear

the word of God and observe it." (Lk 11: 28 NABRE)

Compare "Through it (the gospel) you are also being saved,

IF you hold fast to the word I preached to you,…"

(1 Cor 15: 2 NABRE)

Contrition comes before forgiveness:

"The wicked, when spared, do not learn justice;

in an upright land they act perversely,

and do not see the majesty of the Lord."

(Isa 26: 10 NABRE)

Docility:

"Submit to God, but resist the Devil

and he will flee" (Js 4: 7)

The depraved
"WOE to those who drag wickedness with cords of deceit
and pull sin along with cart ropes,"
(Isa 5: 18 HCSB)

Hate the Lord God?

"Those who hate the Lord
would pretend submission to Him;
their doom would last forever,
those who hate God" (Ps 81: 15)

Woe to the wicked, the depraved.

"Woe to those who plan iniquity,
and work out evil on their couches;
in the morning light they accomplish it
when it lies within their power." (Mic 2: 1)
CAUSE OF SIN
In the parable of the sower (of the Word) Matt 13: 18-23, the
Evil One was pointed at as the one who stole away the word that was
sown in the heart of that hearer who lacked understanding.
Consequently, he had no chance of remembering the word and
ordering his life in accordance therewith.

Light and Darkness

God is light; if you hate your brother, you are in darkness (1 Jn
1: 5, 9-11)

Sinning with the tongue

Bridle your tongue. "Consider how large a forest a small fire
ignites. Your tongue could be like that fire. Harness it only for good
– praising God"

(Js 3: 3-12; 4: 11-12)

Rebellion, Defiance – Divination and Idolatry

"For rebellion is like the sin of divination, and defiance is like
wickedness and idolatry…" (1 Sam 15: 23)

GIVING

"If someone who has worldly means sees a brother in need and refuses him compassion…"

Love must not be "in word or speech but in-deed and truth."

(1 Jn 3: 17, 18 NABRE)

Divine Mercy

"It is I who sweep away your transgressions

for My own sake

and remember your sins no more." (Isa 43: 25)

Separation from Christ Jesus – Only sin can

"Who can separate us from the love of Christ?

Can affliction or anguish or persecution

or famine or nakedness or danger

or sword?" (Rom 8: 35)

The marks

God is mindful of the righteous, placing His mark on them so the avenging angel would spare them of scourges:

- "When the Lord passes through to strike Egypt and sees the blood on the lintel and the two door posts, He will pass over the door and not let the destroyer enter your houses to strike you." (Exo 12: 23)
- Korah, Dathan and Abiram mustered 250 other Israelites in a revolt against the Israelite leader, Moses. Moses intercession curtailed the wrath of God but the rebels were swallowed alive by the earth.

"So they went down alive to the world of the dead, with their possessions. The earth closed over them, and they vanished." (Num 16: 33)

- Terrible and painful sores appeared on those who had the mark of the beast and on those who had worshipped its image. (Rev 16: 2 GNBDK)

Blood did not deter them – matyrs

"I also saw the souls of those who had been executed because they had proclaimed the truth that Jesus revealed and the word of God… They came to life and ruled as kings with Christ for a thousand years." (Rev 20: 4 GNBDK)

STOP ranting!

"WOE to the one who argues with his Maker, one clay pot among many. Does clay say to the one forming it, 'What are you making?' Or does your work say, 'He has no hands'?"

"TURN to Me and be saved all the ends of the earth, for I am God and there is no other." (Isa 45: 9, 22)

Repent!

"Tell them… The declaration of the Lord God –

'I take no pleasure in the death of the wicked, but rather that the wicked

person should turn from his way and live. Repent, repent of your evil ways! Why will you die house of Israel?'" (Ezk 33: 11 HCSB)

Hypocrisy

"…you…clean the outside… but inside you are full of greed and evil."

(Lk 11: 39 HCSB)

Be godly!

Enemies: love him still; don't hate your enemies. (Matt 5: 44; Lk 6: 27, 28, 32-36)

Be holy!

(1 Pt 1: 15, 16; Lev 19: 2; 1 Thes 4: 3; Eph 1: 4; 2 Cor 7: 1)

The Bad

The soul that desires evil

"The soul of the wicked man desires evil,

his neighbour finds no pity in his eyes." (Prov 21: 7)

The Ugly

"Therefore, put to death what belongs to your worldly nature: sexual immorality, impurity, lust, evil desire, and greed, which is idolatry. But now you must also put away the following: anger, wrath, malice, slander and filthy language from your mouth. Do not lie to one another..." (Col 3: 5, 9 HCSB)

The Beautiful

"Therefore, God's chosen ones, holy and loved, put on heartfelt compassion, kindness, humility, gentleness, and patience, accepting one another and forgiving one another,... above all, put on love – the perfect bond of unity." (Col 3: 12)

SIN, the Devil's

"IF you consider that He is righteous, you also know that everyone who acts in righteousness is begotten by Him.

Everyone who commits sin commits lawlessness, for sin is lawlessness.

You know that He was revealed to take away sins, and in Him there is no sin.

No one who remains in Him sins; no one who sins has seen Him or known Him.

Whoever sins belongs to the Devil, because the Devil has sinned from the beginning. Indeed, the Son of God was revealed to destroy the work of the Devil."

(1 Jn 2: 29; 3: 4-6, 8 NABRE)

"All unrighteousness is sin, and there is sin that does not bring death."

"We know that everyone... born of God does not sin, but the One who is born of God keeps him, and the evil one does not touch him."(1 Jn 5: 17-18 HCSB)

Causes of war and wrangling

"For where there is envy and selfish ambition, there will also be disorder and wickedness of every kind." (Js 3: 16 NRSV-CI)

Criticism

"Don't criticize one another, brothers…
There is one lawgiver and judge…
But who are you to judge your neighbour?" (Js 4: 11-12 HCSB)

Turn back one straying from the truth

"…if anyone among you should stray from the truth and someone bring him back, he should know that whoever brings back a sinner from the error of his way will save his soul from death and will cover a multitude of sins." (Js 5: 19-20 NABRE)

Jesus says, "If your brother sins, rebuke him; and if he repents, forgive him"
(Lk 17: 3)

"The fear of God

drives away sin and anger…
apportions long life."
"…godliness is an abomination to the sinner."
(Sir 1: 20-21; 9: 25 NABRE)

Our Advocate

"… I am writing this to you so that you may not commit sin. But if anyone does sin, we have an Advocate with the Father, Jesus Christ, the Righteous One."
"He is expiation for our sins… for those of the whole world."
(1 Jn 2: 1-2 NABRE)
Joy over a repentant sinner

The sinner who repents is like a lost and found sheep – (Lk 15: 5-6) or a lost and found coin (Lk 15: 9) or even like the sober son in the parable of the prodigal son: "But it was only right we should celebrate and rejoice because your brother here was dead and has come to life; he was lost and is found." (Lk 15: 24, 32)

Don't cave in to your bodily cravings

"… the works of the flesh…: immorality, impurity, licentiousness, idolatry, sorcery, hatred, rivalry, jealousy, outbursts of fury, acts of selfishness, dissensions, factions, occasions of envy, drinking bouts, orgies, and the like. I warn you… those who do such things will not inherit the kingdom of God." (Gal 5: 19-21 NABRE)

But rather, live in the spirit

"…the fruit of the Spirit is love, joy, peace, patience, kindness, generosity, faithfulness, gentleness, self-control."
Against such there is no law. (Gal 5: 22-23 NABRE)

Don't love (i.e., covet anything in) the world

"Do not love the world or the things of the world. If anyone loves the world, the love of the Father is not in him. For all that is in the world, sensual lust, enticement for the eyes, and a pretentious life, is not from the Father but from the world." (1 Jn 2: 15-16 NABRE)

Consolation for the Sinner

"Happy are those whose sins are forgiven,
whose wrongs are pardoned.
Happy is the one whom the Lord does not accuse of doing wrong
and who is free from all deceit.
The wicked will have to suffer,
but those who trust in the Lord
are protected by His constant love." (Ps 32: 1-2, 10 GNBDK)

Forsake sin; Turn back!

"The boastful cannot stand in Your presence;
You hate all evildoers.
You destroy those who tell lies;
The Lord abhors a man of bloodshed and treachery."
(Ps 5: 5-6 HCSB)

The one who causes others to sin

"Woe to the world because of things that cause sin! Such things must come, but woe to the one through whom they come!" (Matt 18: 7 NABRE)

The 2 ways:

"The path of the righteous is like the light of dawn, shinning brighter and brighter until midday.

But the way of the wicked is like the darkest gloom; they don't know what makes them stumble." (Prov 4: 18-19)

STOP doing evil.

"Wash yourselves, cleanse yourselves,
Remove your evil deeds from My sight.
Stop doing evil.
Learn to do what is good.
Seek justice.
Correct the oppressor.
Defend the rights of the fatherless.
Plead the widow's cause."
(Isa 1: 16-17 HCSB)

The day of your punishment is coming

Godly people have vanished from the land;
There is no one upright among the people.

The official and the judge demand a bribe;
the powerful man communicates his evil desire,
they plot it together.
The best of them is like a brier;...
the day of your punishment is coming.
(Mic 7: 2-3, 4 HCSB)
"My people are destroyed for lack of knowledge.
The more they multiplied the more they sinned..."
(Hos 4: 6-7)

Justice and righteousness, not poison and wormwood

"But let justice flow like water,
and righteousness, like an unfailing stream.
... Yet you have turned justice into poison
and the fruit of righteousness into wormwood."
(Amos 5: 24; 6: 12 HCSB)
Useless to serve God? (Mal 3: 13)
Answer: "At that time... a book of remembrance was written before Him for those who feared Yahweh and had high regard for His name. they will be mine... on the day I am preparing. I will have compassion on them." (Mal 3: 16-17)

God is not deceived

"But what do you think? A man had two sons. He went to the first and said, 'My son, go, work in the vineyard today.'

He answered, 'I don't want to!' Yet, later, he changed his mind and went. Then the man went to the other and said the same thing.

'I will, sir' he answered. But he didn't go.

Which of the two did his father's will?" (Matt 21: 28-31 HCSB)

God sees all, knows all!

"The Lord is always aware of what people do;
there's no way to hide from Him."

"The Lord is always watching what people do;…"
"None of their sins is hidden from Him;
He is aware of them all!" (Sir 17: 15, 19-20 GNBDK)

Know God, love God!

Let us strive to know the Lord… (Hos 6: 3 HCSB)
"For it is loyalty that I desire, not sacrifice,
and knowledge of God rather than burnt offerings."
(Hos 6: 6 NABRE)

Why the wicked may not be estopped

"… the wisdom of God said, 'I will send them prophets and apostles, and some of them they will kill and persecute', so that this generation may be held responsible …" (Lk 11: 49-50 HCSB)

"TURN AWAY from evil and do what is good,

and dwell there forever.
For the Lord loves justice
and will not abandon His faithful ones.
They are kept safe forever,
but the children of the wicked will be destroyed."
(Ps 37: 27-28 HCSB)

How to stand your ground against the Devil

"For our battle is not against flesh and blood but against the rulers,…
the authorities… the world powers of this darkness,…"
"…to resist in the evil day,…
stand… with truth like a belt around your waist,
righteousness… and …
… the gospel of peace."
"… take the shield of faith,…"

"Take salvation,
and the sword of the Spirit, which is God's word"
"Pray at all times... stay... in this with
all perseverance and intercession
for all the saints." (Eph 6: 12-18 HCSB)

Note that when Adam faced the wiles of the Devil, (Gen 2: 15-17; 3: 6) he collapsed like a pack of cards; but when Jesus, Himself was tested He deployed those strategies and defeated the Devil squarely, forcing him to retreat.

(Matt 4: 1-11)

"A wicked person desires evil;
He has no consideration for his neighbour."

(Prov 21: 10 HCSB)

Jealousy

"For where jealousy and selfish ambition exist, there is disorder and every foul practice." (Js 3: 16)

The things that cause sin

"Woe to the world because of things that cause sin! Such things must come, but woe to the one through whom they come." (Matt 18: 7 NABRE)

Food does not defile!

"Don't you realize that nothing going into a man from the outside can defile him? For it doesn't go into his heart but into the stomach and is eliminated."

(Mk 7: 18-19 HCSB)

Struggle against sin

"In struggling against sin, you have not yet resisted to the point of shedding your blood"

"...My son, do not take the Lord's discipline lightly or faint when you are reproved by Him." (Heb 12: 4, 5 HCSB)

You must not hate discipline

"Why do you recite My statutes,
and profess My covenant with your mouth,
though you hate discipline?
And cast My words behind you." (Ps 50: 16-17 Lect)
The Law and righteousness
"Now, therefore Israel, what does the Lord, your God ask you
but to fear the Lord… Circumcise therefore the foreskins of your
hearts and be stiff-necked no longer." (Deut 10: 12, 16 NABRE)
Leave your way of life, way of thinking;
take refuge under divine mercy!
"… Listen to Me, and do what I say;
and you will enjoy the best food of all.
Listen now, My people, and come to Me;
come to Me, and you will have life!…
Let the wicked leave their way of life
and change their way of thinking.
Let them turn to the Lord, our God;
He is merciful and quick to forgive." (Isa 55: 2-3 GNBDK)
The 2 – ways: the sinner and the Saviour
"You belong to what is below, I belong to what is above. You are
from below… I am from above…" (Jn 8: 23 HCSB)

Seek the Lord

"If then you were raised with Christ,
seek what is above, where Christ is seated…"
(Col 3: 1 NABRE)
"Glory in His holy name;
Let hearts that seek the Lord rejoice!
Seek out the Lord and His might;
Constantly seek His face."
(Ps 105: 3-4 NABRE)
"As a deer long for streams of water,
so, I long for You, God

the Lord will send His faithful love by day
His song will be with me in the night –
a prayer to the God of my life."
(Ps 42: 1, 18 NABRE)
Metanoia: Are you truly born again?
"…everyone who has been born of God does not sin, but the one who is born of God keeps him, and the evil one does not touch him."
"…the Son of God has come and has given us understanding… We are in the true One – that is, in His Son Jesus Christ. He is the true God and eternal life."
(1 Jn 5: 18, 20 HCSB)

Conquest by the begotten

- "Everyone who believes that Jesus is the Christ is begotten of God…"
- "Everyone who loves the Father loves (also) the one He begets; we know we love God's children "when we love God and obey His commandments."
- "For the love of God is this that we keep His commandments."
- "For whoever is begotten by God conquers the world." "…the victory that conquers the world is our faith."
- The victor over the world is "the one who believes that Jesus is the Son of God." (1 Jn 5: 1, 2, 4, 5 NABRE)

Resurrection:

"Many of those who sleep in the dust of the earth will awake, some to eternal life, and some to shame and eternal contempt." (Dan 12: 2 HCSB)
Only the sinner
"All lives are mine"

Not carnality, but Christ

"Set your minds on what is above, not on what is on the earth.
Therefore, put to death what belongs to your worldly nature:
sexual immorality, imparity, lust, evil desire, and greed, which
is idolatry."

"… you must also put away all the following:
anger, wrath, malice, slander,
and filthy language from your mouth." (Col 3: 2, 5, 8 HCSB)

Only the sinner shall die… These (the righteous) shall surely
live. I have no pleasure in the death of sinners. If a man is virtuous,
he shall surely live.

(Ezk 18: 4, 10, 14 Lect)

Only the sinner

"The Lord replied to Moses: 'I will erase whoever has sinned
against Me from
My book'" (Exo 32: 33, HCSB)

Sin Can Cause Sickness

"Have courage man, your sins are forgiven!" (Mk 2: 5, 10)
Gehazi, the prophet's servant, acquired leprosy. (2 Kgs 5: 21-27)

Come, Turn away from sin!

"Come to the Lord and leave your sin behind…
Return to the Most High and turn away from sin.
Have an intense hatred for wickedness." (Sir 17: 25, 26
GNBDK)

Violence in evangelization, proselytization and Jihads

"A thief comes only to steal and to kill and to destroy." (Jn 10:
10 NABRE)

Notice that not even Islam approves of forceful conversion.
The sixth commandment says you shall not commit murder.

War does not foist conviction on people, or resolve an issue; it achieves at best, only temporary (unrighteous) settlement.

ADDITIONAL RESOURCES

Divine Mercy: **sin no more!**

"Neither do I condemn you," said Jesus.

"Go, and from now on DO NOT SIN anymore" (Jn 8: 11 HCSB)

WICKEDNESS

Ps 10: 3 "For the wicked man glories in his greed, and the covetous blasphemes, sets the Lord at naught."

"Woe to you, Scribes and Pharisees, hypocrites! You clean the outside of the cup and dish but inside they are full of greed and self-indulgence!" (Matt 23: 25)

Flee! Flee from sin!

"You brood of vipers, who warned you to flee from the coming wrath?"

(Matt 3: 7)

"We implore you on behalf of Christ,

be reconciled to God." (2 Cor 5: 21 NABRE)

"… so submit yourselves to God. Resist the devil and he will flee from you."

(Js 4: 7 NABRE)

Good people die, and no one understands…

"Yet the just are taken away from the presence of evil, and enter into peace…"

(Isa 57: 1, 2 NABRE)

…give alms don't blow trumpet to win praise.

"…but don't let your left hand know what your right is doing…" (Matt 6: 2-3)

On Adultery:

If your right eye causes you to sin, tear it out; your right hand…cut it off.

(Matt 5: 28, 29)

Jer 30: 12 SIN as a grievous and incurable disaster

Recompense

Jer 30: 14 "For I have struck you as an enemy would,... because of your enormous guilt and your innumerable sins."

Jer 30: 23 Vengeance: "Look, a storm from the Lord! Wrath has gone out, HCSB a churning storm. It will whirl about the heads of the wicked."

Obey!

"... Teach them to obey everything (Jesus) have commanded you." (Matt 28: 20)

Causing the vulnerable to sin

"Whoever causes one of these little ones who believe in Me to sin, it would be better a millstone is hung around his neck and be drowned in the depths of the sea." (Matt 18: 6)

See it also in Lk 17: 1-2.

To the sinner...

"… I will not listen.

Your hands are covered with blood."

"Wash yourselves, cleanse yourselves…" (Isa 1: 15, 16, HCSB)

PRIDE

"Therefore, the Lord God of Hosts … will kindle a burning fire under its glory."

(Isa 10: 16 HCSB)

"What is pride?[1] It is the inordinate love of oneself at the expense of others and the exaggerated estimation of one's own learning and importance"

"God opposes the proud, but gives grace to the humble" (Prov 3: 34; Js 4: 6)

IDOLATRY

Jerusalem with origin in Canaan land, born unwashed and naked, clothed, embroidered; … your beauty was made "perfect through My splendour" became prostitute wife to the extent of sacrificing her sons and daughters… (Ezk 16: 1-34)

Recompense for sin

"…the person who sins is the one who will die."
The righteous shall live
The ungodly "will not live!"
"The person who sins is the one who will die." (Ezk 18: 3, 9, 10-13, 20, 21)
Peace eludes the wicked
"There is no peace for the wicked, says my God" (Isa 57: 21)
1: Don Schwager (@Dailyscripture.Servants Of The Word.org) C2018.
Call to sinners – repent!
"Jesus said to them in reply,
'Those who are healthy do not need a physician, but the sick do. I have not come to call the righteous to repentance but sinners.'"
(Lk 5: 31, 32 NABRE)

The eternal sin

One very grievous sin – The eternal sin, the sin against the Holy Spirit. There is no forgiveness for this. (Mk 3: 29 NABRE)
Sinner – own worst enemy.
"But those who commit sin and do evil are their own worst enemies"
(Tob 12: 10 NABRE)

Evil desire

"… The desire of the wicked
man will come to nothing." (Ps 112: 10)
Recompense for the wicked
"You also know what Joab son of Zeruiah did to me and what he did to the two commanders of Israel's army,
Abner son of Ner, and Amasa son of Jether.

He murdered them in a time of peace to avenge bloodshed in war…"

(1 Kgs 2: 5 HCSB)

But don't be presumptive

"Neither this man nor his parents sinned…" (Jn 9: 3 HCSB)

RESIST SIN, if necessary to the extent of shedding your blood!

"For consider Him who endured such hostility from sinners against Himself, so that YOU WON'T GROW WEARY AND LOSE HEART" (Heb 12: 3-4, 7)

The thoughts of the wicked

"For, not thinking rightly, they said among themselves…"

"Let us oppress the righteous poor;

let us neither spare the widow nor revere the aged…"

"But let our strength be our norm of righteousness;

for weakness proves itself useless."

"These were their thoughts, but they erred; for

their wickedness blinded them…" (Wis 2: 1, 10-11, 21 NABRE)

Harden not your hearts

"Today, if you hear His voice:

Do not harden your hearts as at Meribah,…" (Ps 95: 7, 8 HCSB)

Matt 3: 2 NABRE

'**Repent** for the kingdom of heaven is at hand' (Also Matt 4: 17)

1 Tim 1: 15-16

Mission of the Redeemer:

… Jesus came… to save sinners

Gal 3: 22

Sin!

… scripture imprisoned everything under sin…

Jer 30: 12

Sin = grievous and incurable disaster

Js 1: 22

"**Be doers** of the word..."
Mk 7: 21-23
From within the man, from his heart come evil thoughts...
Ezk 18: 23, 21, 24
Don't repay evil for evil; be concerned with what is noble.
Sow righteousness, time to seek the Lord.
1 Jn 5: 18, 19
We are of God... whole world under sway of the evil one.
1 Jn 5: 18
Everyone born of God does not sin
Isa 26: 10
The wicked when spared don't learn justice
Lk 17: 3
If your brother sins, rebuke him
Gal 5: 22
The fruit of the spirit is love,...
Sir 27: 30; 28: 2
Wrath and anger... hateful yet sinner hugs them
Ps 37: 27-28
Turn from evil, do good, dwell there forever
Ezk 18: 3, 9, 10, 13
The one who sins is the one to die
Isa 57: 21
No peace for the wicked...
Deut 10: 12, 16
Israel, fear the Lord... circumcise... your hearts; be stiff-necked
no more
Repent! Rev 21: 8 HCSB
John announced "Repent for the kingdom of heaven is at hand."
(Matt 3: 2 NABRE)
See also Lk 10: 9; Mk 1: 15
Jesus too, proclaimed,
"Repent, because the kingdom of heaven has come near." (Matt
4: 17 HCSB)

Mercy for the repentant soul

"This saying is trustworthy and deserving of full acceptance: 'Christ Jesus came into the world to save sinners' – and I (apostle Paul) am the worst of them. But I received mercy for this reason, so that in me, the worst of them, Christ Jesus might demonstrate His extraordinary patience as an example to those who would believe in Him for eternal life." (1 Tim 1: 15-16 HCSB)

Your traditions – Jesus admonishes,

"Disregarding the command of God, you keep the tradition of men."

"You revoke God's word by your tradition that you have handed down."

(Mk 7: 8, 13 HCSB)

The depraved

"Woe to those who call evil good and good evil, who substitute darkness for light and light for darkness, who substitute bitter for sweet and sweet for bitter

(who are) wise in their own opinion and

clever in their own sight...

who acquit the guilty for a bribe and

deprive the innocent of justice." (Isa 5: 20-21, 23 HCSB)

Woe!

"... Woe to him who amasses what is not his – ..." (Hbk 2: 6 HCSB)

SLAVES

"I assure you: Everyone who commits sin is a slave of sin."

"Therefore, if the Son sets you free, you really will be free." (Jn 8: 34, 36 HCSB)

Persevere!

"Let us rid ourselves of every burden and sin that clings to us and persevere in running the race that lies before us." (Heb 12: 1 NABRE)

Stop!

"... 'See, ... stop sinning or something worse ... may happen...'" (Jn 5: 14)

If Jesus had not come...

"If I had not come and spoken to them, they would not have sin. Now they have no excuse for their sin.

If I had not done the works among them that no one else has done, they would not have sin. Now they have seen and hated both Me and My Father."

(Jn 15: 22, 24 NABRE)

The wicked

"But the wicked are like the storm-tossed sea,
for it cannot be still,
and its waters churn up mire and muck.
'There is no peace for the wicked,'
Says my God." (Isa 57: 20-21 HCSB)
The Wicked
"... Why does the way of the wicked prosper?
Why do all the treacherous live at ease?" (Jer 12: 1)
The Lord's response:
"Many shepherds have destroyed My vineyard;
... All the land is desolate,
but no one takes it to heart." (Jer 12: 10, 11)
Ps 34: 21
Evil done brings death to the wicked
"Those who are evil will not survive, but those who are righteous will live because they are faithful to God." (Hbk 2: 4 GNBDK)

"Do I take any pleasure in the death of the wicked?"

This is the declaration of the Lord GOD: "Instead, don't I take pleasure when he turns from his ways and lives?

Now if the wicked person turns from all the sins he has committed,... he will certainly live,...

But when a righteous person, turns from his righteousness and practises iniquity,...

He will die..." (Ezk 18: 23, 21, 24 HCSB)

Exhortation, meditation and reflection

HATRED

If God is your Father and the Father of the other person, why then do you hate that brother of yours?

Are you not playing the card of Cain?

He hated Abel, his brother, and killed him (Gen 4: 1-8)

The sons of Jacob, hated their brother Joseph so much they planned to kill him but instead actually kidnapped and sold him to slave merchants

(Gen 37: 18-28; 36; 45: 28, 46: 7)

Dislike does not hang on for long with a person unless it is tenderly cultivated and given choice accommodation or nurtured with gloating, then, it grows into hatred.

Why will a people of God not think of justice, and if that would not avail, shouldn't they remember mercy?

What then differentials them from the sons of the Devil?

Vengeance

When hatred is sown on a well ploughed ground (of self-pity) and painstakingly nurtured with water (with rhetoric) and fertilizer of lies, it sprouts resentment and the resentment blossoms into venomous fruits of violence – an ogre of killing, maiming, arson and suicide, even genocide.

Violence unleashes further violence through retaliation and resentment until an incendiary circle of vengeance and retaliation subsist which hatred cannot put out.

The hater spends his precious time planning sour evil, instead of a future of goodness for himself. When Satan has taken full possession of him, he begins to derive pleasure in the misfortune of others – his victims. But it is his very own malevolence that will ultimately see the end of him – a wasted, worthless life!

Your grudges find expression in discrimination.

It really does not matter what name you call this discrimination – racism, tribalism, ethnicism, religious bigotry, sexual chauvinism, class struggle – whatever. They are all siblings; ignorance gave birth to them all. For even the one born blind or lame shouldn't take blame for his condition. Much less so, the fact that your victim's culture, sex, or skin colour is different from yours.

Exhortation, meditation and reflection

Why despise that slave whom God can transform into a Joseph, because he was sold into slavery? Retributive justice overtook his abductors and caused all of Israel to become slaves! This can always happen again.

Sow righteousness, reap faithful love (Hos 10: 12)

But sow the seed of righteousness and you will harvest healing and reconciliation.

How? Give (i.e., be kind) and forgive!

Forgive, not only because they cannot fully pay back but also "because they do not know what they are doing." Besides, we also sin and hope for forgiveness (Matt 6: 12, 14-15)

All these would pave the way for healing of the frail nerves and bring about understanding and mutual respect and reconciliation.

On the stake (of the cross) Jesus pleaded with the Father,

"Father, forgive them, because they do not
know what they are doing." (Lk 23: 34)

"The violence of the wicked sweeps them away because they refuse to act justly." (Prov 21: 7 HCSB)

No consolation that Jesus is so much bigger than us. Hear what a fellow disciple, Stephen prayed for as he was being lynched:

"Lord, do not charge them with this sin!" (Acts 7: 60)

So, if I can't do that, and you can't do that either, where then is our Christianity? Where is our righteousness?

"It's not an easy road[1]

we are travelling to heaven…"

"WRATH and anger are hateful things

yet the sinner hugs them tight.

Forgive your neighbour's injustices,

then when you pray your own sins will be forgiven."

(Sir 27: 30; 28: 2 Lect)

1 = Old Christian song. (See Chapter 15)

Exhortation, meditation and reflection

An eye for an eye?

Jesus teaches,

"You have heard…An eye for an eye and a tooth for a tooth. But I tell you, don't resist an evildoer…As for the one who wants to… take away your shirt, let him have your coat as well.

…if anyone forces you to go one mile, go with him two." (Matt 5: 38-41 HCSB)

"Tough," you say? Indeed not natural with most cultures. Just try to comply and you will afterwards discern the wisdom therein.

That is the difference – that is the stuff Christianity is made of – and our Father-in-heaven has not disappointed those who obey Him.

Flee (from violence)!

"At times the best strategy is not to fight but to flee." Often, it is the most effective deterrent from igniting a blaze you cannot control, or creating an atmosphere for evil to foster.

Condemning Others

Retract those accusing fingers on others – the 'they'; you have not yet sanctioned the 'I' and the 'we' sufficiently to bring yourself beyond reproach. Do that first.

Repentance: **Let us pray: A prayer of the penitent**:
"We beg You, Lord, to be our help and our support."
"For all generations You have been faithful
and just in Your judgements, and wonderful
in Your power and majesty. Wisely You have
created and wisely You have kept things in being.
All that we see shows Your goodness;
To all who trust in You, You are faithful,
kind and merciful. Forgive us our wickednesses
and injustices, our sins and our transgressions"
"Come, Lord, let Your face shine upon us so
that we may peacefully enjoy all good things."
"Free us, Lord, from those who hate us without cause.
Give peace and harmony to us and to all the
inhabitants of the earth."
– Excerpts from Pope Clement 1: A letter to the Corinthians

Exhortation, meditation and reflection

Worst Enemy
Sin is the worst enemy of man. It stripes man of the favour, and hence glory, of God. No enemy is more ferocious.
See also Tobit 12: 10
"Now the sting of death is sin,
and the power of sin is the law."
Thanks to God who has given us victory
over sin through our Lord Jesus Christ!

(1 Cor 15: 56, 57)

Idolatry?

"God is Spirit and those who worship Him must worship in Spirit and truth." (Jn 4: 24)

Why do you think the prophet says a thing like this,

"…in those days,… no one will say any longer,

'The Ark of the Lord's covenant'

It will never come to mind, and no one will

remember or miss it. It will never again be made."

(Jer 3: 16 HCSB)

Why is man so over-dependent on the senses? Many a time, the senses take us away from the true God. Our senses and passions can lead us astray.

Man, beware of idolatry.

SIN! DEATH!!

Do you realize that it is more than an encouragement –

It is really a sin not to love? It is indeed, death!

"Whoever does not love remains in death.

Everyone who hates his brother is a murderer,…"

(1 Jn 3: 14, 15 NABRE)

Exhortation, meditation and reflection

HOPE for the Sinner

The hope for the sinner is in repentance; repentance attracts the mercy of God.

The Lord is the master of might. Power attends the Lord whenever He wishes but the Lord delights in clemency (Wis 12: 18 NABRE)

Jesus teaches in the parable of the lost sheep as well as in the parable of the lost coin how the mercy of God embraces a repentant sinner.

"There is joy in heaven over one sinner who repents…"

"There is rejoicing among the angels of God over one sinner who repents…"

(Lk 15: 7, 10)

The parable of the prodigal son (Lk 15: 11-32) further demonstrates the efficacy of repentance. First, the son **confesses** his short-coming,

"Father, I have sinned against heaven and against you…" (Lk 15: 21)

Next, he was **contrite** and finally he turned over a new leaf – he was **converted** to a righteous way of living. All three '**C**'s are implicit in the word "repent".

"**REPENT**" reverberates in the New Testament: Lk 5: 32; 10: 13; 11: 32; 13: 1-5; 15: 7-10; 16: 30; 17: 3-4; 24: 47…

Repent or perish!

One might almost think that God's only reason for making Himself known to man is to proclaim the message,

'Repent!'

'Return to your God!'

'Turn back from your evil ways!'

'I am a holy God; and I can't put up with iniquity.'

All the prophets in the Old Testament proclaim this message.

In the New Testament, John, the Baptist, and later, the disciples of Jesus never ceased to urge people to re-trace their steps from evil doing.

Evil doing comes naturally with man! Adam and Eve, the first man and woman started it all – with their disobedience of God. Their son, Cain, killed his brother, Abel. Till this day, infidelity, betrayal, rape and other sexual perversions, stealing and robbery, idolatry, sorcery, calumny, unforgiveness, etc. still rule many lives. It is as if there is nothing to learn from the story of the flood which wiped out the entire world except the family of Noah, a righteous man.

Exhortation, meditation and reflection

The story of Sodom and Gomorrah and Tyre and Sidon seem to offer only music to our ears – deadly music!

Below are a few of Jesus sayings on the theme:

- "I have not come to call the righteous but sinners to repentance" (Lk 5: 32)
- "Woe… Chorazin! Woe… Bethsaida" (Lk 10: 13)
- "the men of Nineveh … repented", but not His own generation, Jesus admonished (Lk 11: 32)
- "… unless you repent, you will perish…" (Lk 13: 5 HCSB)
- "… unless you repent you will perish as well." (Lk 13: 4)
- "if your brother sins, rebuke him, and if he repents, forgive him"
- "and if he sins against you seven times in a day and… you must forgive him." (Lk 17: 3, 4)

Repentance produces joy in heaven

- "… there will be more joy in heaven over one sinner who repents than over 99 righteous people who don't need repentance" (Lk 15: 7, 10)
- In the parable of the prodigal son note the confession of the prodigal son, "Father, I have sinned against heaven and in your sight…" (Lk 16: 21) and the joy of the alienated father: "this brother of yours was dead and is alive again; …lost and is found." (Lk 16: 32)
- "…Come!

Do not be like a horse or a mule without understanding, that must be controlled with bit and bridle or else it will not come near you."(Ps 32: 8, 9)

"PERHAPS they will listen and return –
each from his evil way of life…" (Jer 26: 3 HCSB)

Exhortation, meditation and reflection

Christianity is a ministry of repentance and divine mercy.

On behalf of Christ, we are appealing to the world to be reconciled to God.

(2 Cor 5: 18-20)

The Patience of the Merciful God

"… My servants the prophets, whom I kept sending to you, even though you do not listen to them…" (Jer 26: 5 NABRE)

"Or do you despise the riches of His kindness, restraint, and patience, not recognizing that God's kindness is intended to lead you to repentance?"

(Rom 2: 4 HCSB)

See how patient the Almighty God is:

Mankind are His audience but He chooses among them One of their kind – very specially chosen with attributes to make them succeed. Then, He painstakingly teaches them through the prophet and at their level of understanding – using symbols, images, parables etc. to aid their understanding and as aide memoire. Knowing our limitations, He leads the prophet a very little step at a time. When the whole mission is accomplished, even the prophet is amazed at what the Lord had accomplished through his frail and unworthy self.

For example, Jeremiah recounts how the Lord spoke to him four times to etch in the prophet's psyche the imagery of the failed linen loincloth.

Jer 13: 1-11)

The message: "so also I will allow the pride of Judah to rot, the great pride of Jerusalem." (Jer 13: 9 NABRE)

Similarly, the Lord captures the panic and pain of a people in flight to exile dramatically to warn a rebellious nation of His impending retribution – "I am a sign for you… they will go into exile, into captivity." (Ezk 12: 1-16)

Depraved nations, see!

Covid 19 (coronavirus), HIV-Aids, Cancer, etc.

"…In all this, His anger is not removed and His hand is still raised to strike."

(Isa 5: 25 HCSB)

Exhortation, meditation and reflection

Sin provokes God's wrath

"…come, you scourges of the city!

Pass through the city after him and strike!"

(Ezk 9: 1, 5 NABRE)

"…put a mark on the foreheads of the men

who sigh and groan over all the detestable

practices committed in it."

"but do not come near anyone

who has the mark."

(Ezk 9: 4, 6)

Mission of the Redeemer

"Here is a saying that you can rely on and nobody should doubt: that Christ Jesus came into the world to save sinners."

The sinner is lost and dead spiritually but the Good Shepherd seeks him out and revives his spirit (lost sheep, prodigal son – parables).

That is the goodwill of God, our Father.

Don't obtain power from the Devil

- Satan tempted even the Lord Jesus:

"Then he took Him up and showed Him all the kingdoms of the world in a single instant. The Devil said to Him, 'I shall give to you all this power and their glory; for it has been handed over to me, and I may give it to whomever I wish. All this will be yours, if you worship me.'"

(Lk 4: 5-7 NABRE)
- "I will not talk with you much longer, because the ruler of the world is coming. He has no power over Me." (Jn 14: 30 HCSB)

The ruler of the world is real, but he is the deceiver!
- "We know that... the whole world is under the power of the evil one."

(1 Jn 5: 19 NABRE)

Excessive self-love

Ensnares one into self-indulgence, results in self-absorption, self-centeredness, greed, fractionalization, lewdness.

Exhortation, meditation and reflection

All sin! Repent!
"...from the least to the greatest,
everyone is making profit dishonestly.
From prophet to priest,
everyone deals falsely." (Jer 8: 10 HCSB)
TRUTH, Unpretentious love
"... There is no truth, no faithful love,
and no knowledge of God in the land!
Cursing, lying, murder, stealing,
and adultery are rampant;
one act of bloodshed follows another.
For this reason the land mourns,
and everyone who lives in it languishes,..." (Hos 4: 1, 2-3 HCSB)
God so hate evil that He invented the spectre of hell
Sin and sickness
"Sin no more" (Jn 5: 14 Lect)
"Your sins, are forgiven you" (Lk 7: 48; Mk 2: 5)

From the above, the Word teaches us that there may be a linkage between sin and sickness, even death, but not invariably so.

Jesus teaches – sin defiles

"For from within, out of people's hearts, come evil thoughts, sexual immoralities, thefts, murders, adulteries, greed, evil actions, deceit, promiscuity,... stinginess, blasphemy, pride and foolishness." "All these evil things come from within and defile a person." (Mk 7: 20-23 HCSB)

Speaking, on the same topic, Fr Al leur[1] warns: 'Guard your heart!'

1: Fr Al leur...

Exhortation, meditation and reflection

Sin – the cause of the fall of man.

Satan lied, sowed the seed of doubt to cause the fall of man. Gen 3: 1-6, 14-19

"… You are dust, and to dust

you shall return." Gen 3: 19 NRSV-CI

Always beware of satanic manipulations and half-truths.

SIN TAILGATES MAN

I **Before the Law**

Adam and Eve were the first man and woman created. They resided in the

Garden of Eden (central Europe). Their two eldest children they named Cain

and Abel.

The Fall of Man

- Adam and Eve transgressed the command of God and God expelled them from the well-watered garden and handed them a life of pain and toil. (Gen 3: 23)

- Cain soon killed his brother Abel, because Abel was in good standing with God. Cain became accursed of God. (Gen 4: 7-8)

- Old world destroyed. The people of the world, the descendants of Adam and Eve continued to sin irrepressibly.

Noah was an exception. To end this generation of sinners and their wickedness God sent a cascade of rainfall for 40 days and 40 nights and flooded the earth. The deluge lasted for 150 days (Gen 7: 24). Only Noah, his wife, their sons and daughters-in-law and the living creatures they took with them into the Ark (boat) escaped annihilation.

The New Earth
Among the descendants of Noah were Abram and Sarai.

Abram was a pious man who found favour with God, who changed his name and that of his wife to Abraham and Sarah, respectively. God promised his descendants would inherit Canaan land and through them the world would be blessed by God, "because you (Abraham) have obeyed My command"
(Gen 22: 18).

Exhortation, meditation and reflection

Sin tailgates man
SLAVERY PROPHESIED
- Abraham wanted an assurance that indeed God would give Canaan to him for good. At this, the Lord said to him that his descendants would be sojourners in a foreign land for 400 years, be slaves there before God would deliver them. (Gen 15: 13-16)

The World Still Immersed In Sin

Sodom and Gomorrah
- Abraham camped in Bethel (Canaan). Lot his nephew whom he had taken along with him, camped near Sodom (Jordan valley). God revealed to Abraham His decision to mete out punishment on Sodom and Gomorrah because the outcry against their wicked deeds was immense. Abraham interceded for them, because of the righteous that may be in

the cities but not as many as five righteous people were in both cities!

They were all lost in debauchery so much so that their men demanded to have sex with the angel visitor of Lot sent by God to destroy the cities! The men thought that the angel was an ordinary man and insisted on having sex with him rather than accepting Lot's counter offer of his two virgin daughters, to spare his visitor.

The two cities were destroyed by a rain of sulphur and brimstone which burnt both cities to ashes.

Enmity Between Brothers

- Isaac begat a pair of twins, Esau and Jacob. Jacob, as a youth, traded a pot of potage for his big brother's (first child) birthright. He also deceitfully obtained at a latter date, their dying father's ultimate blessing meant for Esau, with the connivance of their mother! These put a wedge in the relation between the brothers which forced Jacob to flee. His name was changed by God to Israel.

"… all the nations of the earth will be blessed by your offspring, because Abraham has listened to My voice and kept My mandate, My command, My statuses and My instructions." (Gen 26:4-5)

Exhortation, meditation and reflection

Sin tailgates man
The Exile

- Jacob in Egypt. Jacob's sons conspired to kill their brother, Joseph, because he was a favourite of their father. By fate he was sold to merchants who in turn sold him as a slave in Egypt. Some years afterward there was a severe famine in Canaan. Israel (by his children) sought food to buy in Egypt. Meanwhile, Israel's son, Joseph had become second only to

Pharaoh (the king) in Egypt. The family re-united, settling there.

Moses: the return to Canaan land
- Several years later a king who did not know Joseph ascended the throne in Egypt. Playing the flesh and blood card, the king and his people turned against the Israelites, converting them to slave labour. Their sons they killed at infancy, lest they grew to adulthood and revolt against the Egyptians.

Led by the servant of God, Moses, the Israelites escaped via the Red Sea miracle. (Exo 14: 9-28; Num 33: 11) And "Your God dried up the waters of the Jordan before you …" (Jos 4: 23 HCSB)

II The Law

God made a covenant with the people: they were to be His people and He, their God. He gave them the Ten Commandments ("the Law") etched on stone tablets from above. They were to observe them scrupulously from generation unto generation. (Exo 20: 1-17; Deut 5: 6-21)

Seraph Serpents
"…we have sinned in complaining against the Lord and you."
(Num 21: 7 Lect)
Fear God; "Do not sin."
"Moses answered the people, 'Do not be afraid, for God has come only to test you and put the fear of Him upon you so you do not sin.'"

Exhortation, meditation and reflection

Sin tailgates man
40 days lengthened to 40 years

- The people led by Moses apostatized as Moses communed with God on Mount Sinai. Often times they grumbled against Moses and against God.

When it was time for them to enter the promised-land, they became squeamish and dithered. They would not enter and possess the land, having been intimidated by the giant-like physique of the native people. By such lack of trust in God, they were given over to wandering and meandering in the desert for four decades. Eventually, Moses berthed them at the thresh hold of the promised-land; but it was Joshua who led the people to cross the Jordan and take possession. By their transgression the journey of 40 days was accomplished in 40 years.
(Exo 16: 35; Num 14: 34; Jos 5: 6)

The era of the judges

- The Israelites fought the natives – the Amekalites, the Hitites, the Amokites, Jebusites, etc. Joshua, Aaron, Eleazar, the clan heads (the judges), prophets (like Samson, Deborah, Elijah and Samuel) led the people. There was much corruption and oppression. For example, Abimelech, son to Gideon (Jerubbaal) by slave concubine, playing the flesh and blood card, conspired and slaughtered all but one – Jotham – of his 71 brothers to claim the throne of their father. The people rejected this rule by elders (and prophets like Samuel); thus, rejecting the divine rule, they would rather be like their neighbours and be ruled by kings.

The Kingdom

- Leadership transmuted from the judges, prophets and priests to kings Saul, David, Solomon, Ahab, etc. David was the great grandson of Boaz by Ruth, Moabite daughter-in-law of Naomi (Matt 1: 5-6).

Solomon and many of his successors misled the people to sin who even offered their children in sacrifice to pagan idols.

"Must women eat their own offspring…?" (Lam 3: 20 NABRE)

Exhortation, meditation and reflection

Sin tailgates man

The Messianic Era

- The Lord God sent Jesus, the Nazarene covenant-descendant of David to redeem the people and salvage the Law. Both John, the prophet fore-runner of Jesus and Jesus, the Christ, with numerous numbers of His disciples were murdered for calling the people to righteousness.

III The Waiting Era

- All now seem set for Jesus' Second Coming as He Himself foretold. It would appear that we are already in some early phase thereof. Every evil that ever surfaced in history has been re-enacted in this era. Internecine warfare, desecration of everything that was sacred, martyrdom of the faithful, culminating (thus far) in the large-scale destruction of lives of the first and second world wars. Sexual abominations are rife and no longer elicit societal condemnation. All scriptural restraints on sexual lust and bestiality have been thrown to the wind. Morality has taken a walk away from divine injunctions. So, we are left under the tutelage of libertines who say evil is good and good is evil. The Ten Commandments have become an anachronism which, like everything that has to do with religion, must not be mentioned as a moral compass. Hordes deny God; many pay Him only lip service, while many others are simply indifferent to God.

This matter of sin is strange, because no one has yet claimed to have created himself or any living being.

"The Lord founded the earth by wisdom and established the heavens by understanding." (Prov 3: 19 HCSB)

"The fear of the Lord is the beginning of wisdom, and the knowledge of the Holy One is understanding." (Prov 9: 10 HCSB)

The issue of the day is, shall we give up the struggle against sin or shall the struggle continue until salvation comes?

To be a fun-lover and a pleasure-seeker and be self-indulgent is to capitulate to sin. Examine Jesus' life – He was none of these. We can't succeed without self-control and self-restraint.

Exhortation, meditation and reflection

Sin tailgates man

Yours is to desire holiness, the Holy Spirit will accomplish it in you.

"It is only by enduring himself, by freeing himself through suffering from the tyranny of egoism that man finds himself... his joy, his happiness."[3]

"... we would like to flee from it; ... people mislead us into thinking that one can be human without overcoming oneself; without the suffering, without renunciation of the hardship of self-control."[4]

"There is, in fact, no other way in which one can be saved than by the cross. All offers that promise a less costly way, would flounder, would prove to be false."[5]

On Revenge, violence.

Jesus says
- Whoever slaps you on one cheek, **turn him the other cheek**; the one who is forcing you to go a mile, go two with him! Etc.
- Violence is the tool of the devil, don't play his game with him (Matt 5: 39 HCSB)

Evil for evil? Not right!

"Do not repay anyone evil for evil; be concerned for what is noble…

Do not be conquered by evil but conquer evil with good."
(Rom 12: 17, 21 HCSB)
See also Prov 3: 4; 1 Thes 5: 15; 1 Pt 3: 9

Adultery: "Sweet surrender?" It is a hoax!
Lessons from Jael and Judith (Jgs 5: 24-26; Jdt 13: 13-17)

Divorce: the two have become one flesh (Mk 10: 5-12)
Therefore, what God has joined together, … (Mk 10: 9; Matt 19: 6, NABRE)

The Cross as a Sin Effigy

And at the same time, an emblem of the infinite goodness of God. If, in furtherance of divine justice, God did not spare His only begotten Son, subjecting Him to the pain and vilification of the cross – for the sins of the world though Jesus, Himself was without sin. Then sinner, you better beware of sin with its attendant condemnation.

3, 4, 5: Pope Emeritus Benedict XVI, Daily Meditations (Feb/26/2020)

CHAPTER 8

Leadership

Let us pray
"GOD, be merciful to us and bless us;
Look on us with kindness,
so that the whole world may know Your will;
so that all nations may know Your salvation."
(Ps 67: 1-2 GNBDK)

True Leadership:

(temporal & spiritual – the Church, priests and prophets, kings.)
Give unto the Lord, o you mighty ones,
give unto the Lord glory and strength.
Give unto the Lord the glory due to His name;
worship the Lord in the beauty of holiness. (Ps 29: 1 NKJV)
Why do the nations rebel… plot in vain?
The kings … and the rulers conspire …
against the Lord and His Anointed One.
I have consecrated My king on Zion,
My holy mountain
so now kings be wise,
receive instruction,…
Judges,… serve the Lord…
Pay homage to the Son or …
you will perish in your rebellion…" (Ps 2: 1-2, 6, 10-12)
"May all kings bow before Him,
all nations serve Him.
For He rescues the poor when they cry out;
the oppressed who have no one to help.

He shows pity to the needy and the poor
and saves the lives of the poor.
From extortion and violence He redeems them;
for precious is their blood in His sight." (Ps 72: 11-14 NABRE)

Leadership: **What it is all about**

- "…Christ Jesus… became for us wisdom from God, as well as righteousness, sanctification, and redemption." (1 Cor 1: 30 NABRE)
- King Josiah of Judah

"When the king heard the words of the book of the Law, he tore his garments." (2 Kgs 22: 11 NABRE)

Why would a king burst into mourning on hearing the Laws of the Lord? King Josiah, who ferreted out the Book of the Law, did this on realizing the loftiness and excellence of the laws "which our ancestors did not obey…" (2 Kgs 22: 13 NABRE)

"Next, the king… made a covenant in the presence of the Lord to follow the Lord and to keep His commands, His decrees, and His statutes with all his mind and with all his heart,… all the people agreed to the covenant." (2 Kgs 23: 3)

The difference between a righteous leader and a recalcitrant one is clear.

"Before him there had been no king who turned to the Lord as he did, with his whole heart, his whole being, and his whole strength, in accord with the entire Law of Moses; nor did any king like him arise after him." (2 Kgs 23: 25 NABRE)

King Hezekiah's Dependence on God.

"Hezekiah took the letter from the hand of the messengers, read it, then went up to the Lord's temple, and spread it out before the Lord. Then Hezekiah prayed before the Lord: …" (2 Kgs 19: 14-15 HCSB)

That was the beginning of Sennacherib's defeat and death.

The King of Nineveh: a model of piety

"When word reached the King of Nineveh, he got up from his throne, took off his royal robe, put on sack cloth and sat in ashes. Then he issued a decree… everyone must call out earnestly to God. Each must turn from his evil ways and from the violence he is doing…" (Jon 3: 6-8)

God, almighty!

"But though You are master of might, You judge with clemency;
and with much lenience You govern us;
for power, wherever You will, attends You.
And You taught Your people, by these deeds,
that those who are righteous must be kind;…"
(Wis 12: 18, 19 NABRE)

Fear of God.

They stumble, leaders who have no fear of God in them. Thus, the scripture (Matt 14: 1-12 NABRE) tells us that Herod Tetrarch

I. "Wanted to kill" John, the Baptist; he didn't quite do so because Herod "feared the people for they regarded him as a prophet."

"For even the Son of Man did not come
to be served, but to serve; and to
give His life – a ransom for many." (Mk 10: 45)

II. In spite of that, he had to kill John, all the same "because of his oaths and the guests who were present". When he made a reckless commitment to meet a little girl's request!

How differently the matter would have been if Herod had had the fear of God in him?

Worship the Lord.

O sing to the Lord a new song;
sing to the Lord all the earth.

Declare His glory among the nations,
His marvellous works among all the peoples.
For great is the Lord, and greatly to be praised;
He is to be revered above all gods.
Ascribe to the Lord, O families of the peoples,
ascribe to the Lord glory and strength.
Ascribe to the Lord the glory due His name;
bring an offering, and come into His courts.
Worship the Lord in holy splendour;
tremble before Him, all the earth.
Say among the nations, "the Lord is King!
The world is firmly established; it shall never be moved.
He will judge the peoples with equity."
Let the heavens be glad, and let the earth rejoice;
let the sea roar, and all that fills it;
before the Lord; for He is coming,
for He is coming to judge the earth.
He will judge the world with righteousness,
and the peoples with His truth. (Ps 96: 1, 3-4, 7-11, 13 NRSV-CE)

Be Ready For Service:

"Be ready for service and have your lamps lit.
You must be like people waiting for their master to return…
so that when he comes and knocks,
they can open the door for him at once." (Lk 12: 35-36 HCSB)

Reward for the diligent servant

"That slave… working will be rewarded" (Lk 12: 43)
"Love and truth will meet; justice and peace will kiss.
Truth will spring from the earth; justice will look down from heaven.

Justice will march before Him, and make a way for His footsteps."
(Ps 85: 11-12, 14 NABRE)

Justice:

"Love justice, you rulers of the world. Set your minds sincerely on the Lord, and look for Him with all honesty.

Wisdom is a spirit that is friendly to people, but she will not forgive anyone who speaks against God, for God knows our feelings and thoughts, and hears our every word. Since the Lord's Spirit fills the entire world, and holds everything in it together, she knows every word that people say."
(Wis 1: 1, 6-7 GNBDK)

There is God!

"All the ends of the earth
will remember and turn to the Lord;
All the families of nations
will bow low before Him.
For Kingship belongs to the Lord,
the ruler over the nations.
All who sleep in the earth
will bow low before God;
All who have gone down into the dust
will kneel in homage." (Ps 22: 28-30 NABRE)

The path of the righteous

BLESSED are those whose way is blameless,
Who walk by the law of the Lord.
Blessed those who keep His testimonies,
Who seek Him with all their heart,
Lovers of your law have much peace;
For them there is no stumbling block.

(Ps 119: 1-2, 165 NABRE)
They never do wrong;
they walk in the Lord's ways.
How can young people keep their lives pure?
By obeying Your commands.
Your word is a lamp to guide me
and a light for my path. (Ps 119: 3, 9, 105 GNBDK)
"He judges the world with righteousness,
He executes judgement on the nations with fairness."
"The wicked will return to Sheol –
all the nations that forget God." (Ps 9: 8, 17 HCSB)

Commandment to be righteous:

"…stop doing evil.
Learn to do what is good
seek justice…" (Isa 1: 16, 17)

Judge justly!

"Thus says the Lord of hosts:
Judge with true justice, and
show kindness and compassion
toward each other.
Do not oppress the widow or the orphan,
the resident alien or the poor;
do not plot evil against one another in your hearts."
(Zech 7: 9-10 NABRE)

Divine Verdict

"Since you have plundered many nations,
all the peoples who remain will plunder you,
– because of human bloodshed
and violence against lands, cities,
and all who live in them."

"You have planned shame for your house
by wiping out many peoples
and sinning against your own self.
'Woe to him who builds a city with bloodshed
and founds a town with injustice!'
'For the earth will be filled
with the knowledge of the Lord's glory,
as the waters cover the sea.'"
(Hab 2: 8, 10, 12, 14)

Gird your tongues!

"Not many should become teachers, my brothers, knowing that we will receive a stricter judgement, for we all stumble in many ways. If anyone does not stumble in what he says, he is a mature man who is also able to control his whole body." (Js 3: 1-2 HCSB)

Receive a Priest or a Prophet and you receive Jesus!

"I assure you: whoever receives anyone I send receives Me,
and the one who receives Me receives Him who sent Me."
(Jn 13: 20)
For more on this topic read Matt 10: 40-42.

Speak up!

"Speak up for those who have no voice,
for the justice of all who are dispossessed.
Speak up, judge righteously, and defend
the cause of the oppressed and needy." (Prov 31: 8-9)

Judgement on the shepherds and the sheep

1. Shepherds

"This is what the Lord God says to the shepherds:
Woe to the shepherds… who have been feeding themselves! Shouldn't
the shepherds feed the flock? You eat the fat, wear the wool, and
butcher the fattened animals, but you do not tend the flock. You
have not strengthened the weak, healed the sick, bandaged the
injured, brought back the strays, or sought the lost. Instead you have
ruled them with violence and cruelty."

2. Flock

"The Lord God says to you, My flock: I am going to judge
between one sheep and another, between the rams and male goats.
Isn't it enough for you to feed on the pasture? Must you also trample
the rest of the pasture with your feet? Or isn't it enough that you
drink the clear water? Must you also muddy the rest with your feet?
I will save My flock, and they will no longer be prey for you. I
will judge between one sheep and another." (Ezk 34: 2-4; 17-18, 22)
To the righteous God (Prayer)
"Let my cry for help reach You, Lord!
Give me understanding, as You have promised.
How I long for Your saving help, O Lord!
I find happiness in Your law.
I wander about like a lost sheep;
so come and look for me, Your servant,
because I have not neglected Your laws."
(Ps 119: 169, 174, 176 GNBDK)

Integrity is with the Lord

"Love justice, you rulers of the world.

Set your minds sincerely on the Lord,
and look for Him with all honesty.
Those who do not try to test Him will find Him;
He will show Himself to those who trust Him.
Dishonest thoughts separate people from God,
and if we are foolish enough to test Him,
His power will put us to shame.
Wisdom will never be at home with anyone
who is deceitful or who is a slave of sin.
Everyone who is holy has learnt to stay away
from deceitful people.
He will not stay around when foolish thoughts are being expressed;
He will not feel comfortable when injustice is done."
(Wis 1: 1-5 GNBDK)

The State, the Church and believers

The Lord, our strength.
The words of the Lord are true
and all His works are dependable.
The Lord loves what is righteous and just;
His constant love fills the earth.
Worship the Lord all the earth!
Honour Him, all peoples of the world!
When He spoke, the world was created;
at His command everything appeared.
The Lord frustrates the purposes of the nations;
He keeps them from carrying out their plans.
But His plans endure forever;
His purposes last eternally.
Happy is the nation whose God is the Lord;
happy are the people He has chosen for His own!
A king does not win because of his powerful army;

a soldier does not triumph because of his strength.
War horses are useless for victory;
their great strength cannot save.
The Lord watches over those who obey Him,
those who trust in His constant love.
May Your constant love be with us, Lord,
as we put our hope in You."
(Ps 33: 4-5, 8-12, 16-18, 22 GNBDK)

Freedom from oppression

"Because of the oppression of the afflicted
and the groaning of the poor, I will now rise up,"
says the Lord. "I will put the one who longs
for it in a safe place." (Ps 12: 5 HCSB)

The people of God

"An elder must be blameless;… have only one wife and his children must be believers…

For… a church leader… should be blameless.

… not be arrogant or quick-tempered, or a drunkard or violent or greedy for money.

He must be hospitable and love what is good…
be self-controlled, upright, holy and disciplined."

"In all things you yourself must be an example of good behaviour…"

"For God has revealed His grace for the salvation of the whole human race.

That grace instructs us to give up ungodly living and worldly passions, and to live self-controlled, upright, and godly lives…"

"Remind your people to submit to **rulers and authorities**, to obey them, and to be ready to do good in every way…not to speak evil of anyone, but to be peaceful and friendly and always to show a gentle attitude towards everyone."

"This is a true saying… so that those who believe in God may be concerned with giving their time to doing good deeds, which are good and useful for everyone."
(Tit 1: 6-8; 2: 7, 11-12; 3: 1-2, 8 GNBDK)

The First, the last

Jesus said to the 12 Apostles:
"… IF anyone wants to be first, he must be last of all
and servant of all." (Mk 9: 35 HCSB)
See also Mk 10: 31, 43-45.

Duly constituted Authorities

Jesus admonished Governor Pontius Pilate:
"'You would have no authority over Me at all',
Jesus answered him, 'if it hadn't been given
you from above…'" (Jn 19: 11 HCSB)
"Everyone must submit to the governing authorities,
for there is no authority except from God,
and those that exist are instituted by God." (Rom 13: 1 HCSB)
David:
"He said to his men, 'I swear before the Lord:
I would never do such a thing to my Lord,
the Lord's anointed. I will never lift my hand against him,
since he is the Lord's anointed.'" (1 Sam 24: 6 HCSB)

The whole armour of God

"Finally, build up your strength in union with the Lord and by means of His mighty power."
Spiritual warfare:
"For we are not fighting against human beings but against the wicked spiritual forces in the heavenly world, the rulers, authorities, and cosmic powers of this dark age."
The armour:

"So stand ready, with truth as a belt tight round your waist, with righteousness as your breastplate, and as your shoes the readiness to announce the Good

News of peace. At all times carry faith as a shield; for with it you will be able to put out all the burning arrows shot by the Evil One. And accept salvation as a helmet, and the word of God as the sword which the Spirit gives you. Do all this in prayer, asking for God's help. Pray on every occasion…"

(Eph 6: 10, 12, 14-18 GNBDK)

One Father/Creator.

"Don't all of us have one Father? Didn't one God create us? Why then do we act treacherously against one another, profaning the covenant of our Father's?" (Mal 2: 10 HCSB)

David's Last Words: **rule with justice**

"These are the last words of David:…

The Spirit of the Lord spoke through me,…

'The one who rules the people with justice,

who rules in the fear of God,

is like the morning light when the sun rises

on a cloudless morning,

the glisten of rain on sprouting grass.'" (2 Sam 23: 1, 2, 3-4 HCSB)

Judgement for the exalted

"Hear, therefore, kings and understand; Learn, you magistrates of the earth's expanse!

Terribly and swiftly He shall come against you, because severe judgement awaits the exalted."

(Wis 6: 1, 5 NABRE)

"Your rulers are rebels,

friends of thieves, they all love graft and chase after bribes." (Isa 1: 23) compare Jer 8: 5-7

They who have rejected the instruction of the Lord of Hosts

"Woe to those who drag wickedness with cords of deceit
and pull sin along with cart ropes,"
"Woe to those who call evil good and good evil,
who substitute darkness for light and light for darkness…"
(Isa 5: 18, 20 HCSB)

Prophet and Priest too?

"Small and great alike, all are greedy for gain. Prophet and priest, all practise fraud." (Jer 8: 10 NABRE)

Administer Justice and Righteousness:

"Thus says the Lord:
Do what is right and just.
Rescue the victims from the hand of their oppressors.
Do not wrong or oppress the resident alien,
the orphan or the widow, and do not shed
innocent blood in this place." (Jer 22: 3 NABRE)

Tithes, Judgement, Mercy and Fidelity.

Jesus teaches,
"Woe to you, Scribes and Pharisees, you hypocrites.
You pay tithes… and have neglected the weightier things of the Law:
Judgement and mercy and fidelity (but) these you should have done,…"
(Matt 23: 23 NABRE)

Rulers who destroy and scatter the people

"How terrible will be the Lord's judgement on those rulers who destroy and scatter His people!"

"… You have not taken care of people; you have scattered them and driven them away. Now I am going to punish you for the evil you have done."
(Jer 23: 1-2 GNBDK)
Jesus says,
"…. I chose you. I appointed you… produce fruit …"
(Jn 15:16 HCSB)

Knowledge of God

"My people are destroyed for lack of knowledge.
Because you have rejected knowledge,
I will reject you from serving as My priest.
Since you have forgotten the law of your God,
I will also forget your sons."
"For I desire loyalty and not sacrifice,
the knowledge of God rather than burnt offerings" (Hos 4: 6; 6: 6 HCSB)
"… People without discernment are doomed." (Hos 4: 4, 14 HCSB)

The prophet and the inspired man are fools, for you!

"The days of punishment have come;
the days of retribution have come.
Let Israel recognize it!
The prophet is a fool,
and the inspired man is insane,
because of the magnitude
of your guilt and hostility." (Hos 9: 7 HCSB)

Sealed the treasury of knowledge?

"Woe to you…! You have taken away the key of knowledge!
You didn't go in yourselves, and you hindered those who were going in."

(Lk 11: 52 HCSB)
The Divine Will

The death of the holy infants (Matt 2: 16-18)

Consider divine justice, or rather, God's preferred approach to justice – based upon His omnipotence. He did not avert Herod's perfidy or thwart his slaughter of the innocent infants. Some think He should have done so; but then, Herod would have had no guilt! Other sinners could thus say that God permitted or approved of their wicked acts simply because He had not obstructed them?

Think about this

Rabbi, rabbi! Pastor, pastor!
- "why are you persecuting Me?"
- "who are you, sir?"
- "I am Jesus, whom you are persecuting…"
(Acts 9: 4-5 NABRE)

Obey your leaders, defer to them

"Obey your leaders and submit to them, for they keep watch over your souls as those who will give an account, so that they can do this with joy and not with grief for that would be unprofitable for you." (Heb 13: 17 HCSB)

Practise what you teach (Matt 23: 3)

Lord, You have accomplished all we have done.

"The way of the just is smooth;

the path of the just You make level.

The course of Your judgements, Lord, we await;

Your name and Your memory are the desire of our souls.

My soul yearns for You at night,

yes, my spirit within me seeks You at dawn;
when Your judgement comes upon the earth,
the world's inhabitants learn justice."
"Lord, You will decree peace for us,
for You have accomplished all we have done."
(Isa 26: 7-9, 12 NABRE)
Ahab's terrible fate – obey the Lord!
"when the letter came to them, they took the King's sons and slaughtered all 70, put their heads in baskets, and sent them to Jehu at Jezreel."

(2 Kgs 10: 7 HCSB)

ADDITIONAL RESOURCES

A warning to Rulers (Ps 2: 1, 2, 11, 12)
Ps 2: 1 "why do the nations protest and
the people conspire in vain?
: 2 Kings on earth… and princes
plot together against the Lord
and against His anointed one."
: 10 "And now, kings give heed;
take warning, you rulers of the earth.
Serve the Lord with fear and rejoice before Him,
with trembling rejoice! Accept correction…"
"CRY OUT LOUDLY, don't hold back!
Raise your voice like a trumpet.
Tell My people their transgression
and the house of Jacob their sins." (Isa 58: 1 HCSB)
MAMMON AND PIETY
"… 'Render to Caesar the things that are Caesar's,
and to God the things that are God's'" (Mk 12: 17 NKJV)
RULER'S mandate
"…the Lord has made you king
to carry out judgement and justice." (1 Kgs 10: 7)

Burnt Offerings

"This is the word that came to Jeremiah from the Lord…
This is what the Lord of Hosts the God of Israel says:
'Add your burnt offerings to your other sacrifices, and eat the meat yourselves,
for when I brought your ancestors out of the land of Egypt, I did not speak with them or command them concerning burnt offering and sacrifice.'"

Yet they didn't listen or pay attention but followed their own… stubborn, evil heart… they did more evil than their ancestors."

"… This is the nation that would not listen to the voice of the Lord their God and would not accept discipline. Truth has perished

– it has disappeared from their mouths." (Jer 7: 1, 21-24, 26, 28 HCSB)

Obey, accept discipline: (God's people!)

"However, I did give them this command:

Obey Me, and then I will be your God, and you will be My people.

You must follow every way I command you so that it may go well with you.

(Jer 7: 23 HCSB)

Human sacrifice is detestable

"For the Judeans have done what is evil in My sight."

"… They have set up their detestable things in the house that is called by My name and defiled it.

They have built the High places of Topheth in the valley of Hinnom in order to burn their sons and daughters in the fire, a thing I did not command; I never entertained the thought." (Jer 7: 30-31 HCSB)

Jesus, Our Redeemer

Rev 1: 4 "John: To the seven churches in Asia.

HCSB Grace and peace to you from the One who is, who was, and who is coming; from the seven spirits before His throne

: 5 Jesus Christ the faithful witness, the first born from the dead, and the ruler of the kings of the earth."

: 6 "To Him who loves us and has set us free from our sins by His blood, and made us a kingdom, priests to His God and Father – be glory and dominion are His forever and ever, Amen."

: 8 "I am the Alpha and the Omega," says the Lord God,

"the One who is, who was, and who is coming, the Almighty."

Precious in God's sight.

Matt 18: 10 "… Do not despise one of these little ones,…

… it is not the will of your heavenly Father that one of these little ones be lost."

(1 Cor 3: 9) "For we are God's servants working together."

Humble Peter counsels 'fellow presbyters':

"I exhort the presbyters among you,
as a fellow presbyter and witness…
tend the flock of God in your midst,
overseeing not by constraint but willingly,…
not for shameful profit but eagerly.
… be examples to the flock." (1 Pt 5: 1 Lect)
Peter: the rock and the kingdom
"And so I tell you, Peter:
you are a rock, and on this rock
foundation I will build My church, and
not even death will ever be able to overcome it.
I will give you the keys of the kingdom of heaven…"
(Matt 16: 18-19 GNBDK)

The Church: life giving water from the Sanctuary

"…there was water flowing from under the threshold
of the temple toward the east,…"
"… and it was a river that I could not cross on foot…"
"Every kind of living creature… will live wherever the river flows,
…because this water goes there."
"All kinds of trees providing food will grow along both banks of the river.
Each month they will bear fresh fruit because the water comes from the sanctuary. Their fruit will be used for food and their leaves for medicine." (Ezk 47: 1, 5, 8, 9, 12)
"Do not trust in nobles in man, who cannot save. When his breath leaves him, he returns to the ground; on that day his plans die." (Ps 146: 3-4 HCSB)

Jesus: On leadership, humility and service:

The washing of feet liturgy.

"… You also ought to wash one another's feet"

"For I have given you an example that you also should do just as I have done for you." (Jn 13:14, 15 HCSB)

You may wish to read further to Jn 13: 16-20.

The Great Commission

1) **Mk 16: 15** "Go into all the world and preach the gospel to the whole creation…"

: 17 "And these signs will accompany those who believe:

In My name they will drive out demons, they will speak in new languages… they will lay hands on the sick, and they will get well."

2) **Mk 28: 18** "All authority has been given to Me in heaven and on earth.

: 19 Go, therefore, and make disciples of all nations, baptizing them …

: 20 teaching them to observe everything I have commanded you…"

Judges and leaders: a reprimand:

"How long will you judge unjustly and favour the cause of the wicked? Selah. Defend the lowly and fatherless;

render justice to the afflicted and needy.

Rescue the lowly and poor;

deliver them from the hand of the wicked.

Arise, o God, judge the earth,

for Yours are all the nations."

(Ps 82: 2-4, 8 NABRE)

"Get these things out of here!

Stop turning My Father's house into a market place!" (Jn 2: 16 HCSB)

HUMILITY.

Be humble (before the Lord)!

"Remember that the Lord your God led you… these 40 years in the wilderness, so that He might humble you…" (Deut 8:2 HCSB)

"The humble will eat and be satisfied; those who seek the Lord will praise Him…" (Ps 22:26 _ _ _)

"Though the Lord is exalted, He takes note of the humble; but He knows the haughty from a distance." (Ps 138:6)

"Humble yourselves before the Lord, and He will exalt you." (Js 4:10)

"The fear of the Lord is what wisdom teaches, and humility comes before honour." (Prov 15:33)

"Do nothing out of rivalry or conceit, but in humility consider others as more important than yourselves." (Phil 2:3 HCSB)

"Therefore, whoever humbles himself like this child – this one is the greatest in the kingdom of heaven." (Matt 18:4 HCSB)

"Whoever exalts himself will be humbled, and whoever humbles himself will be exalted." (Matt 23:12) (above in Lk 14:11 and 18:14)

What is humility?

"… that none of you will be inflated with pride…"

What do you have that you didn't receive?

If, in fact, you did receive it, why do you boast as if you hadn't received it?

"We labour working with our own hands.

When we are reviled, we bless; when we are persecuted, we endure it;

When we are slandered, we respond graciously." (1 Cor 4:6-7, 12-13 HCSB)

"…. I will look favourably on this kind of person: one who is humble, submissive in spirit, and trembles at My word." (Isa 66:2)

"Moses was a very humble man, more so than any man on the surface of the earth." (Num 12:3 HCSB)

"Be in agreement with one another. Do not be proud; instead, associate with the humble. Do not be wise in your own estimation." (Rom 12:16)

"… With all humility and gentleness, with patience, accepting one another in love, …" (Eph 4:12)

What do you stand to gain or lose?

"When the Lord saw that they had humbled themselves, the Lord's message came to shemaiah: 'They have humbled themselves; I will not destroy them but will grant them a little deliverance…'" (2 Chr 12:7 HCSB)

"When Rehaboam humbled himself, the Lord's anger turned away from him, …" (2 CHR 12:12 HCSB)

"The sacrifice pleasing to God is a broken spirit. God, You will not despise a broken and humbled heart." (Ps 51:17 HCSB)

"He mocks those who mock, but gives grace to the humble." (Prov 3:34)

"A person's pride will humble him, but a humble spirit will gain honour."

(Prov 29:23)

"When pride comes, disgrace follows, but with humility comes wisdom."

(Prov 11:2 HCSB)

"Human pride will be humbled, and the loftiness of men will be brought low; the Lord alone will be exalted on that day." (Isa 2:11)

"The humble will have joy after joy in the Lord, and the poor people will rejoice in the Holy One of Israel." (Isa 29:19)

A testimony

"Now I, Nebuchadnezzar, praise, exalt and glorify the king of heaven because … He is able to humble those who walk in pride." (Dan 4:37)

Aggressors and all complicit with them.

"I will bring disaster on the world, and their own iniquity, on the wicked. I will put an end to the pride of the arrogant and humiliate the insolence of tyrants." (Isa 13:11)

Legislators and judges – beware!

"Woe to those enacting crooked statutes and writing oppressive laws to keep the poor from getting a fair trial and to deprive the afflicted among My people of justice, …

What will you do on the day of punishment …?

Who will you run to for help?" (Isa 10:1-2, 3 HCSB)

Bad Shepherds

"Woe to the shepherds who destroy and scatter the flock of My pasture," oracle of the Lord. (Jer 23:1 NABRE)

How? It is the Lord's doing!

"How could one man pursue a thousand, or two put ten thousand to flight, unless their Rock had sold them, unless the LORD had given them up?" (Deut 32:30 HCSB)

We need the Church

We need the church of the living God, "the pillar and bulwark of truth"

(1 Tm 3:15 NABRE)

"Fidelity to our identity"

DON'T BE AFRAID OF MEN, ONLY FEAR GOD.

"Yes, I have sinned." Saul replied.

'I disobeyed the Lord's command and your instructions. I was afraid of my men and did what they wanted.' (1 Sam 15:24 GNBDK)

Jesus, the Light of the World:

"Be attentive to Me My people; … for teaching shall go forth from Me, and My judgement, as light to the peoples." (Isa 51:4 NABRE)

Church's Mission: Servants working together

"For we are God's co-workers. You are **God's field, God's building**."

The foundation of our faith "… I have laid a foundation as a skilled master builder, and another builds on it. **But each one must be careful how he builds on it."**

"For no one can lay any other foundation than what has been laid down. **That foundation is Jesus Christ**." (1 Cor 3:9, 10 -11 HCSB)

God's temple

"Do you not know that you are **the temple of God**, and that the Spirit of God dwells in you?"

"If anyone destroys God's temple, God will destroy that person; for the temple of God, which you are is holy." (1 Cor 3:16-17 NABRE)

Desecration of the place of worship:

"… Passover was near …"

"In the temple complex He found people selling oxen, sheep … and the money changers …"

"After making a whip out of cords, He drove everyone out of the temple complex with their sheep and oxen. He also poured out the money changers' coins and overturned the tables."

(To those who were selling doves he said):

"**Get these things out of here! Stop turning My Father's house into a market-place!**" (Jn 2:13-16, HCSB)

Lust: Loss of self-control

"That year, two elders were appointed judges, of whom the Lord said,

'Lawlessness has come out of Babylon, that is, from the elders who were to govern the people as judges.'"

"When the elders saw her enter … they began to lust for her. They perverted their thinking; they would not allow their eyes to look to heaven, and did not keep in mind just judgement." (Dan 13:5, 8-9 NABRE)

Corrupt judges, leaders.

'How you have grown evil with age! Now have your past sins come to term: passing unjust sentences, condemning the innocent, and freeing the guilty, …" (Dan 13:8-9, 52-53 NABRE)

The Victor

"The victor I will give him the right to sit with Me on My throne, just as I also won the victory and sat down with My Father on His throne."

(Rev. 3:21 HCSB)

Service in the Kingdom of heaven

"… and You have made them equal to us …" (Matt 20:12 HCSB)

Egalitarianism – all are equal before God!

Pious Leaders are distinguished by service:

Pagan leaders and the great among sinners "lord it over them … and make their authority over them felt. But it shall not be so among you. Rather, whoever wishes to be great among you shall be your servant. Whoever wishes to be first among you shall be your slave." (Matt 21:26-27 HCSB)

Be reconciled to God!

Therefore, anyone in Christ is a new creation. Old things have passed away. God reconciled us to Himself through Christ and gave us the ministry of reconciliation. God reconciling the world to Himself not counting their trespasses against them and has committed the message of reconciliation to us. We are ambassadors for Christ, … (bidding you to) – "Be reconciled to God" (2 Cor 5:17-20)

GOD, Our Righteousness

"Come to your senses and stop sinning, for some people are ignorant about God." (1 Cor 15:34 HCSB)

Exhortation and Meditation

TRUE LEADERSHIP

No god at all or at best a powerless god?

In the book of wisdom, is spelt out the thinking of the godless. It expresses the thinking of men of power – kings, presidents and other principalities and powers as they seek to ridicule the pious and their Lord by putting such men through harrowing experience of torture, disgrace and humiliation. The ink has not dried up in the long list of martyrs.

These potentiates seem more powerful than the people of God. Jeremiah and Amos cried; Elijah fled, and Jesus was crucified. A majority of the Apostles of Jesus suffered martyrdom. Till this day, pious men and women still lose their lives on account of their faith. Is it not true that God's help avails for the just? (Ps 146: 5-8)

- King Darius asked Daniel, if his God was able to deliver him (Dan 6: 20)

Is it deceptive to trust in the might or willingness of God to save the just, those who trust in Him?

Investigate the matter thoroughly and ground your faith on your findings.

Just to give a little assistance – the benefit of my own faith which I would like to share with you.

- First, that for every man, a time is appointed to be born and to die. A Nigerian song, put this succinctly:

"Today, today – tomorrow no more!

If I die today, I shall die no more!"

Kings die, presidents and emperors are dethroned and die miserable death (example: King Zedekiah) Sometimes their entire household are annihilated! Ordinary folks also die under similar vicissitudes. Nobody knows tomorrow, but the righteous can hope in the Lord.

Some holy will fall

"Some of the wise will fall so that they may be refined, purified and cleansed until the time of the end." (Dan 11: 29)

The Messiah's death

The Messiah dies to accomplish God's transcendental ethereal purposes:
"After those 62 weeks the Messiah will be cut off."
(Dan 9: 26 HCSB)
Exhortation and Meditation

The holy versus the wicked

"This horn waged war against the holy ones and was prevailing over them until… judgement was given in favour of the holy ones of the Most High, for the time had come and the holy ones took possession of the kingdom."
"Then… kingship, power, and greatness of the kingdoms under all of heaven will be given to the people, the holy ones of the Most High."
(Dan 7: 18, 27)

Noble cause:

Isn't it better to die for a noble cause than to persevere in inhuman existence under an obnoxious and godless regime?

The death of the holy infants (Matt 2: 16-18)

If Herod's perfidy were averted by God shielding all those children from massacre how could Herod be held accountable for the same atrocity – for a crime he never committed?

Or how could Rachel's lamentation (Jer 31: 15) over the children taken into exile (Assyrian invasion of Judah C. BC 723 – 722) be understood as a prefigurement of the killing of the innocent infants?

All these sentiments have been expressed all through the Old and the New Testaments, especially the wisdom books.

Pray For Leaders

Was it man or the Lord Himself who appointed Moses, Joshua, Saul and David for the Israelites?

If we submit to the Lord and ask, He is responsive to our yearnings and capable, He will appoint for us shepherds that will take us to the next level. Our duty is to be supportive and pray always for those leaders, following the example of David to King Saul.

"I will give you shepherds who are loyal to Me, and they will shepherd you with knowledge and skill." (Jer 3: 15)

FALSE PROPHETS, DOCTRINES AND BELIEFS.

What should be the correct attitude of societal leadership to religion? Aloofness? Partisanship or utter disdain? What other options?

False doctrine is synonymous to false religion and is postulated by fake prophets and agents of the powers of the world of darkness. It is bad, just as fake medicine is to health therapy, or misinformation is to education.

Exhortation and Meditation

It is costly to ignore or to be indifferent to it as a leader of the people. You can't ignore truth when falsehood is being peddled, it is like ignoring a flare burning the roof of one's home!

It is like being permissive to unfounded rumours, blackmail and slander and sedition or treason, or at the minimum, a public policy which promotes anarchy in society.

The proper attitude is to seek the truth; fund objective research into the truth, etc. Religion is incendiary if you are seen to be partisan, then you are in trouble. "… the truth will set you free"

It's only the truth that liberates people from prejudice, from ignorance as well as from the power of Satan and sin; from wastefulness and inefficiencies as well as from disharmony and discord.

The clear duty of the leaders is to promote consensus on the truth and to open the door permanently until everybody recognises the truth. This is true of science and technology, of economics and commerce as it is true of religion.

For more read chapter 19, "Let them be one!"

Leadership

Leadership is a responsibility, it is not a right.
And to whom much is given, much is expected.
Don't allow yourself to be carried away by the adulation and homage people pay to you.
They really belong to the Lord.
And if anyone withholds it, don't be ruffled!
Lest it makes you to act unjustly.
Remember always, that there is One to whom you are accountable – God!
"For the grace of God has appeared,
saving all and training us to reject
godless ways and worldly desires and to live
temperately, justly and devoutly in this age."
(Tit 2: 11-12 NABRE)

The Proverbial Wisdom of Solomon

The renown of King Solomon for wisdom is not for nothing.
Read 1 Kgs 4: 29 – 10: 29 for some of his exploits.
Now, the supplication of youthful King Solomon is very unusual; it is so insightful and pious not one to be expected from a young potentate but from a mature man at his forties.
Exhortation and Meditation
But when one remembers whose son Solomon was, scion of pious King David and his wonderful consort Bathsheba, you will

begin to understand the influence of such personalities on their beloved son.

So, Solomon was already wise before asking for wisdom. "The fear of the Lord is the beginning of wisdom." And the Lord says whoever has will be given even more; whoever has not, even the little he has will be taken away from him (Talents parable)

In accordance therewith Solomon received

"… what you have asked.

… a wise and understanding heart,

... In addition, I will give you what you did not ask for:

both riches and honour,…" (1 Kgs 3: 12, 13 HCSB)

We have seen in the life of King Solomon, unfortunately, that wisdom and knowledge and riches alone may not avail against lasciviousness and a disavowal of discipline through self-restraint which brings on the affluent and powerful the humility to obey God.

The leadership we deserve

We often get the leadership we deserve, when all else has failed the patience of God then He sends us the leadership that we deserve. A community of the hateful, cheats, trabalists and racists gets a partisan leader (they long for!)

There are leaders or shepherds for the flock to be slaughtered

(Zec 11:4-7) and there are shepherds for the flock to be ransomed (e.g. Moses, Israelites from the Egyptians)

This counsels us to always look beyond the action of the leadership because the Almighty can always get things to go His own way. We should incline unto Him and avoid futile ranting. The followership should embrace righteousness.

For example distraught Elijah, the prophet was instructed to anoint two kings – Hazael for Aram, Jehu for Israel and Elisha a prophet to succeed him.

"Then Jehu will put to death whoever escapes the sword of Hazael, and Elisha will put to death whoever escapes the sword of Jehu."

(1 Kgs 19: 17 HCSB)

That Man May Know The True God.

Who is afraid that mankind may discover the true and only God – the One who created and has been sustaining our planet?

Exhortation and Meditation Look back – idol priests (worshippers) before the advent of Christianity are so jealous for their respective gods (or is it for themselves?). They would do anything to ensure that there is respect for their gods. If their gods lose credibility, then, they themselves are out of business.

Today, there is little difference in the behaviour of the leaders/adherents of the different faiths. The unwritten code seem to be – don't intrude into my zone of influence and I will let you rule in yours! Nobody is concerned about the truth – the real God!

Come to think of it, the world would be the wiser if we can agree on who the Lord God is as we have come to agree about what and where the moon is for example. Therefore, we have made progress in lunar and other space exploration.

Consider what difference it would make if all believers in One God – monotheists – listen to one another with a view to learning from one another.

It may turn out to be for good – for I taking from you a few things I am persuaded you are right upon, and you doing the same from me! In the end each of us would go out from there more enlightened, more insightful – a more knowledgeable person than he had been. We may even decide to coalesce, put our resources together to promote the ultimate truth. Isn't the truth what we are after?

Do you see a role for the secular leaders in this?

The Lord says,

"This is why I am sending you prophets, sages, and scribes. Some of them you will kill and crucify, and some of them you will flog in your synagogues and hound from town to town." (Matt 23: 34 HCSB)

"Give it to the people to eat!" (2 Kgs 4: 43 HCSB)

In the first two missionary commissions, the Apostles and the 72 disciples were respectively charged:

"Take nothing for the road,…"

"Don't carry a money bag, travelling bag or sandals;…" (Lk 9: 3; 10: 4 HCSB)

And also they were invested with power to heal the sick and drive away demons:

"So they went out… proclaiming the good news and healing everywhere."

(Lk 9: 6 HCSB)

"Heal the sick,…"

"… Lord, even the demons submit to us in Your name."

Curiously, the same Lord on the eve of His departure deliberately gave a contrary directive:

Exhortation and Meditation

"But now, whoever has a money bag should take it, and also a travelling bag… a sword, should sell his robe and buy one." (Lk 22: 26) The ecology[1] has changed and so the implements!

The Great Commission (Mk 16: 15, 17; Matt 28: 18-20) is an embodiment of these earlier mandates. I hold that it is not fortuitous that the Lord omitted to talk about mundane provision in this great commission. Earlier on, He had stated that:

"For the worker is worthy of his food" (Matt 10: 10 HCSB)

"Remain in the same house, eating and drinking what they offer, for the worker is worthy of his wages." (Lk 10: 7 HCSB)

Taking all these together, it is clear that the ministers of the gospel are assured of their basic needs by the One who sent them, even though men are to provide these. It is equally necessary for the rank and file to support; even the people ministered to, in as much as they are able to.

Finally, and this is the bottom-line, the ministers themselves, representing the church, are obligated to administer healing and deliverance services alongside the gospel. No one is excused from this obligation. According to Fr. Al Leur[1], the ecology of the mission may be different and so must be the ammunition or strategy to apply. If spiritual healing is lacking, now that the churches are opulent, they should not hoard, but deploy the resources to offer food to the hungry and care to the needy. "Give it to the people to eat;" and hope in the miracle of multiplication for sufficiency.

Separate religion from state (bureaucracy)?

Piety is as good as strength is for a nation.

Separate religion from state? No! Rather, detach state from governmental imposition of "official"/ "approved" religion. Make faith a private personal choice of believers and spare the bloodshed. The Christian church is witness to truth, freedom, peace and justice. But let the creatures pick their choice; they have a greater stake in the preservation of their souls. God gave man free discretion; states must regulate generally – with neither malice nor favour to any. But just as in physics and chemistry, states approval has been unnecessary, so too in faiths professed by citizens, states interference is superfluous.

1 Fr Al Leur: Daily Bread, Presentation Ministries op. cit. Exhortation and Meditation

How Can We Trust The Church?

- Let us look back at the Judaism congregation. The people moving to possess the Promised Land mistrusted the judgement of God; when led to the border refused to enter and take possession. They were being prudent? But human wisdom is foolishness in the sight of God.

(1 Cor 3: 19) This is even more so, since the Lord had revealed the strength of His arm with which He rescued them from their oppressors.

- Okay, they eventually settled in Canaan Land. The Lord made a covenant with them and gave them the Ten Commandments – the Law, which they were to observe scrupulously, not adding to or deleting anything from it. They zealously set out to interpret or extrapolate the law to embrace every facet of the community life. By the time the Rabbi were done, (by Jesus time) the Ten Commandments had elongated to some 613 rabbinic laws and precepts of the Toria according to some observers.

One of the commandment says, do not murder; but a way has been found round it, so murders can be committed lawfully (by judicial process)!

- The Messiah's ministry became ineluctable and God sent Jesus to bring light to the world and cleanse the sons of Levi. The people were brought into the knowledge of this through numerous prophecies and the miracles that attended Jesus ministration. His arrival on the earth platform was announced by angels and prophets alike. King Herod learnt about it and quickly did something to safeguard his throne but the high priests and the rabbi scarcely acknowledged these things and certainly claimed that Jesus was *incognito* to them. They therefore set out to eliminate Him ("strike the shepherd and scatter the flock"). They drove out His followers from their religious assemblies, imprisoned some and killed others. They never allowed His teachings to reform the sons of Levi!

Let us be sure we know who to blame for this:

In their religious assemblies, the vast majority were lay people, then there were the officials – the high priest and priests, the Levites and the elites – Pharisees, Sadducees and Scribes.

In this context, 'the church' refers to both groups of worshippers; for the people without the rabbi is like a flock without a shepherd; and the rabbi without the lay faithful is like a teacher, with a class empty of pupils.

Exhortation and Meditation
- It is now over two millennia since these events took place, but stranger than fiction, both Judaism and Christianity have not been able to solve their differences! Perhaps only one side alone didn't care, for it takes two to tango. Why wouldn't they care? The signs and omens of the past two thousand years, bewildering as they may be to the less discerning, ought to at least call for a review of the Rabbi's position and make them uncomfortable until a reconciliation of their differing view-points are made.

Isn't "the church" letting us down?
- Thanks to the Breach, the Christian church expanded far and wide beyond the cradle of Christianity with the re-discovery of its missionary zeal. Then came Protestantism and the church (*ecclesia*) broke into atomistic entities, each calling itself 'church' (*ecclesiola*?). The fractionalisation is accompanied with ugly bickering:

'no infant baptism'; 'infant baptism is okay';

'justification means the redeemed can't sin again'; 'no, good works are still necessary'.

'There is real presence in the Lord's supper'; 'no, it's mere representation.'

Priestly celibacy, obedience and (material) poverty are good'; 'no, they come from the devil'.

'Women ordination as priests are not liturgical'; 'oh no, they are!'

'Unity of command or orthodoxy is necessary'; 'no, the understanding of everybody who can read the bible is valid!', etc., etc.

Besides, members of these amorphous groups share no commonality of virtues or other attributes to distinguish them from the heathen or the rest of society. Worldliness, rivalry, antipathy, double-talking is as pervasive in their midst as elsewhere! The issue of identity recurs. What is salvation – from earthly necessities and vicissitudes (some say); others say for the soul in Parousia. Satan, the ruler of this world seems to have cornered a large chunk of the body of Christ for itself and appears to be winning.

Exhortation and Meditation

- Now this great growth in ecclesiolae and auto-cephalous groups has posed a grave danger to soul winning. A soul has to believe the truth and act upon that faith to be saved. But then, which is the authentic Christian faith; which church professes the truth? Who, indeed, is a 'Christian'?

Why the deafening calmness; why are we not seeing the exploits of the Holy Spirit? The more we are oppressed by bureaucracy, the less we are guided by the Spirit. Suddenly, the church has become senile! Perhaps many are no longer attentive to the promptings of the Holy Spirit. After all, this is the era of the Holy Spirit

Support for persecuted brethren world-wide has taken the back seat; dynamic evangelisation for souls in jeopardy, a retreat.

How can we trust the church?

- All hope is not lost. The Lord asked if He could find "**that faith**" when He comes back? This was a warning for the redeemed to be alert. A great work needs to be done, and there is no person better qualified to do it than the church.

Fortunately, the Lord has assured that the power of darkness shall not prevail over His church. Jesus victory upon the cross means victory for us to cast out the ruler of this world. The power is in the Holy Spirit; let us listen to Him and the church will be rejuvenated.

Let us come together for deeper knowledge and understanding of our faith. The church is really a sacrament of salvation. It cannot fail; it will not fail. Our life depends upon it. Let us strengthen its magisterium by orthodoxy. She holds the key to eternal life through righteous living and knowledge of God. But knowledge of God comes before reverence for God, while reverence for God brings salvation through righteous living.

God did not intend our pilgrimage to Him to be undertaken as solo effort of individuals. From the beginning, Abraham's blessings were to extend to his descendant and the entire world. This implies walking together in faith. For love, for solidarity and progress; for strength and effectiveness, everybody has a duty, a role. We are definitely stronger[2] (when walking) together.

2: Hilary Clinton (Mrs), 2016 US Presidential Campaign Slogan

Exhortation and Meditation

The role of the leadership is pivotal in this new re-awakening; prayerful and spirit-led and egged on by the followership. What the leadership does or does not do is crucial. Let them tear themselves off self-centredness and greed as they welcome the new ardour of the Spirit. Consider this: most of the decisions taken by the church over the centuries might have been the same prompted by the Holy Spirit, but without the acrimony. With a renewed vigour for orthodoxy, and we all praying together, victory is ours. "Let them be one."

Martyrdom – a noble cause

Martyrs die for noble cause; they are not foolish to lay down their lives because they have the faith that the One who gave them the life has the ability to protect it, and choosing not to do so, has the power to restore it – as He has promised – into eternal life (Dan 12: 2)

Thus, it is better to die for a noble cause than to persevere in inhuman existence under an obnoxious and godless regime. The renegade have an ignoble fate awaiting them here on earth and in the after-life, because it is in the interest of justice that the rash and ruthless one suffer reprisals. These sentiments went through the pages of the Old and New Testaments, and especially the wisdom books (of the Old Testament).

Foul Cause

Some take pleasure to repress, inflict havoc and horror on others; along the way they may lose their lives. It is also possible that they suffer eternal damnation. Satan lives in them – they are "possessed"! But God lives in the just and compassionate, for God is merciful.

- Thus, the America civil war (1861-1865) became inevitable due to the conflict of those two forces of light and darkness; of good and evil. Abraham Lincoln had made the civil rights proclamation, giving liberty to the slave. The Southern (confederate) states would not have it; so they waged war on the Federalists. But still, they had it! The slaves fought on the side of their liberators, though two to four states were against nine, but God was with them. So, they won and freedom went to the slaves, a righteous and greater nation emerged for all. (God's own country)
- Pharaoh also killed the innocent male infants of the Hebrew for fear that if allowed to grow up they might rebel against their oppressors yet, this did not stop Moses, a Hebrew son,

from surviving and liberating his people – **because God wanted it so**.

- Of all the attempts King Saul made to eliminate David and oust him from the kingship, it came to naught! David still emerged king of Israel! (**Because God wanted it so**)

Exhortation and Meditation
The Psalmist says,
"The Lord brings to naught the plans of the nations;
He foils the designs of peoples.
But the plan of the Lord stands forever;
the design of His heart through all generations."
(Ps 33: 10-11 Lect)

- Similarly, Hitler planned to subdue the world to himself and to Germany (World War II). But he ended up annihilating his family and generals and himself (by suicide) and his Germany pushed into capitulation. But because the victors recognised the hand of God in their victory they chose to treat the people with mercy; not all could agree on that, hence, the country was divided into West and East Germany. By the grace of God, they have re-united and the wall of malice broken down. See how hospitable the nation (Merkel's Germany) was to the refuges fleeing from hunger and death in the 21st century. The Germans seem to have learnt their lesson – "contrite".

It is better to die – if one must – for a good cause rather than for an evil end.

The 2 – ways

- The atrocities of the Boars in South Africa can only be matched in reverse direction by the graciousness of the people under Nelson Mandela.

The Boars not only forcefully annexed the land of the Bantu, they set out to subjugate them, restricting the indigenous land-owners to involuntary settlements. And for voicing opposition, sent Nelson Mandela to prison for 22 years. By the will of God and the cooperation of people of God worldwide, Mandela became South Africa president. He realized it was by the finger of God and he was very gracious even to the erstwhile exploiters.

God always wins!

- The mighty and powerful noble class in Russia partnered with soldiers to oppress the landless proletariat but then the soldiers had cause to snap their relationship with the nobility and joined forces with the trade unions to overthrow that evil hegemony, and victory became that of the powerless Soviets, **because it was the will of God**. The Lord is always on the side of the oppressed, the marginalised and the dispossessed if only man will learn from history, and be righteous.

Exhortation and Meditation
Reformation: a necessary but ticklish enterprise.
A very cautious move, a willingness to endure persecution and certainty of call for such a ministry are necessary preconditions for success. For, remember, Jesus was a reformer (Mal 3: 3)

Then … you shall be My people

Jer 7: 23 "Thus says the Lord:
Lect This is what I commanded My people:
Listen to My voice;
then I will be your God and you shall be My people.
Walk in the ways that I command you,
so that you may prosper.
But they obeyed not, nor did they pay heed…"

Listen! The Lord, our God speaks this to the generation before us; does it not also apply to our generation?

Prayer of the church

"Lord, bless your church; guide it with your unfailing love; protect us from what would harm us, and lead us to what will save us. Help us always for without You we are bound to fail. Grant this through Christ, our Lord, Amen." From: Catholic mass liturgy

The Mission of the church:

- Pope Benedict XVI: "The church has to make Him (God) more widely known. She has to bring men to Christ and Christ to men so as to bring God to them and them to God."

"The great and central task of the church today is… to show people this path and to offer a pilgrim fellowship in walking it."

- The church is a life-giving fountain: (Ezk 47: 9, 12)
- The church is the river of life-giving water (Rev 22: 1-3)

St Pope Leo, the great: "be servants of the grace that invites all men to find Christ."

Exhortation and Meditation

Guide the people

Guide us Lord, Great Redeemer[1],
pilgrims through this barren land;
we are weak, but You are mighty,
Hold us with Your powerful hand.
Songs of praises, songs of praises
We will ever give to you
twice

This king spends a huge sum of public funds on science and technology research and his dominion is reputed to have made the most advanced progress in space technology and military weaponry.

But why would he not guide his people to the true God – humanity's landlord and Great Provider – if he really believes there is such a God, in much the same way as he believes in the usefulness of science and technology?

Humanity's Great Puzzle

This is the great question for all humanity. If we suspect that there is a God who is our creator (or has any man claimed to be the one who designed the software and hardware for human procreation?) and who is still relevant in our affairs on earth, why do we neglect to acquire as much knowledge of Him as is possible? Why make it a personal matter for the individual?

- Why can't the state cooperate with private individuals and institutions in seeking to advance knowledge of God – for the good of everybody?
- Is it out of true humanism for leaders to allow society to wallow in ignorance and in incoherence concerning God while the state neglects to verify the truth – if indeed, this matter is considered of any importance?

Jesus says,
"You will know the truth and the truth will set you free." (Jn 8:32 HCSB)
1: An old church hymn (modified)
Exhortation and Meditation
And God says (through His prophet):
"… My people are destroyed for lack of knowledge." (Hos 4:6 HCSB)
God also admonishes us to –
"Seek the Lord while He may be found; call to Him while He is near."
(Isa 55:6 HCSB)
Apostle Paul reflects

"But everything that was a gain to me, I have considered to be a loss because of Christ. More than that, I also consider everything to be a loss in view of the surpassing value of knowing Christ Jesus, …" (Phil 3: 7-8 HCSB)

Jesus the light of the world puts the matter allegorically this way:

"The kingdom of heaven is like treasure, buried in a field, that a man found and reburied. Then in his joy he …. sells everything he has and buys that field.

(Matt 13: 44)

"The kingdom of heaven is like a merchant in search of fine pearls. When he found one priceless pearl, he went and sold everything he had, and bought it." (Matt 13:45-46 HCSB)

Ignorance

But how can anyone obey the Lord that is unknown; if he acts out of mere zealousness he might be deceived to obey someone else, out of ignorance!

"I will cut off … those who turn back from following the Lord, who do not seek the Lord or inquire of Him." (Zeph 1:4, 6 HCSB)

Let us be on our guard who think we are standing lest we fall; we should do self-examination – are we paying "tithes of mint, dill and cumin" while neglecting the weightier issues … of "judgement and mercy and fidelity"? Are we straining out "the gnat" only to "swallow the camel"? God forbid, others have done so before us and they were righteous in their own eyes!

(Matt 23:23)

Aren't we unduly concerned with the cleansing of "the outside of cup and dish but inside" (we condone) "plunder and self-indulgence"? (Matt 23:25)

The fool says there is no God:

"The fool says in his heart, 'God does not exist,'
They are corrupt, and they do vile deeds.

Exhortation and Meditation

There is no one who does good,

God looks down from heaven on the human race to see if there is one who is wise, one who seeks God.

All have turned away, all alike have become corrupt.

There is no one who does good, not even one." (Ps 53:1-3 HCSB)

Put in a different perspective, the wise king says,

"My people, I have seen that many of you are without food and without clothing, but go home, the Lord will supply your needs."

But as many of his subjects are heathen, they ask the king,

"Your majesty, show us the Lord so we can hasten to him to satiate our needs."

And the king replied,

"He is God, the Lord that you serve!"

Reflection:

Has this king any faith himself; any compassion or love for his people? Is he really wise?

An Apostle and leader of the Christian faith asks,

"If a brother or sister is without clothes and lacks daily food and one of you says to them, 'Go in peace, keep warm and eat well,' but you don't give them what the body needs, what good is it? "In the same way faith, if it doesn't have works, is dead by itself." (Js 2:15-16, 17 HCSB)

Princes and rulers, I make no plea for a state religion, any more than for a state chemistry or a state physics. It is a plea for education of the citizenry on an issue the world hypocritically says is of utmost importance.

Moses commanded his people, Israel, to:

"Obey the Lord your God and to follow His commands and statutes …"

(Deut 27:10; 11:27; 10:12 HCSB)

He gave them those commands and statutes.
Exhortation and Meditation
SIN
"My little children, I am writing these things so that you may not sin.

But if anyone does sin, we have an advocate with the Father – Jesus Christ, the Righteous One. He, Himself is the propitiation for our sins, and not only for ours but also for those of the whole world.

And this is the promise that He Himself made to us: eternal life."
(1 Jn 2:1-2, 25 HCSB)

CHAPTER 9

Repentance and mercy

What the scriptures are saying:

I. Obey

- "For God so loved the world that He gave His only son, so that everyone who believes in Him might not perish but might have eternal life. Whoever believes in Him will not be condemned but whoever does not believe has already been condemned…" (Jn 3:16, 18 NABRE)
- Little children, let no one deceive you! The one who does what is right is righteous, just as He is righteous (1 Jn 3:1-3, 7, HCSB)
- "This is how God's children—and the Devil's children—are made evident. Whoever does not do what is right is not of God, especially the one who does not love his brother." (1 Jn 3:1-3, 10 HCSB)

Our love for God

- "For this is what love for God is: to keep His commands. Now His commands are not a burden, because whatever has been born of God conquers the world. This is the victory that has conquered the world: our faith." (1 Jn 5:3-4, HCSB)

Love, or Fear of God?

- *The fear of God…is the beginning of all wisdom…*Actually; it is the beginning of our relationship with God; when love of God leads to reverence, then the fear gives way in the face of perfect love.

- "There is no fear in love; instead, perfect love drives out fear, because fear involves punishment. So, the one who fears has not reached perfection in love." (1 Jn 4:18)

Love of Christ
- Jn 14:15 "If you love Me, you will keep My commands."
- "And I will ask the father and He will give you another counsellor to be with you forever.

He is the Spirit of truth…"

The penitent

Are you willing to learn the ways of the Lord and to walk in the path chosen for you? Are you remorseful for your evil behaviours?

LISTEN, Do What God Says.

"Come, everyone who is thirsty, come to the waters; and you without money, come, buy and eat!

Come, buy wine and milk without money and without cost!

Listen carefully to Me and eat what is good, pay attention and come to Me.

Listen, so that you will live…

Seek the Lord while He may be found; call to Him while He is near.

Let the wicked one abandon his way and the sinful one his thoughts; let him return to the Lord, so He may have compassion on him, and to our God, for He will freely forgive." (Isa 55: 1-3, 6-7 HCSB)

- "The Lord says, 'I will teach you the way you should go; I will instruct you and advise you. Don't be stupid like a horse or a mule which must be controlled with a bit and bridle to make it submit.'" (Ps 32: 8-9 GNBDK)

ii. Repent! Repent!! Repent!!!

1) John's Preaching in Judea: Repent because the Kingdom of heaven has come near.

Preaching in the wilderness of Judea:

"In those days, John the Baptist came preaching... saying, 'Repent...' Then people from Jerusalem, all Judea, and all the vicinity of the Jordan were flocking to him, and they were baptized by him... as they confessed their sins." (Matt 3: 1, 5-6 HCSB)

"...produce fruit consistent with repentance." (Lk 3: 8 HCSB)

2) Jesus Preaching in Galilee—Repent!

"The time is fulfilled, and the kingdom of God has come near. Repent and believe in the good news!" (MK 1:15 HCSB)

3) The Mission of the Twelve (the church)

"As you go, announce this:
'The kingdom of heaven has come near.'" (Matt 10:7)

Repentance – the mission of the Church.

"So they went out and preached that people should repent." (Mk 6: 12 HCSB)

4) Mission of the 72 Disciples

"Heal the sick in that town, and say to the people there, 'The Kingdom of God has come near you.'" (Lk 10: 9 GNBDK)

5) The seven bowls of God's wrath on the earth (Rev 16:1 HCSB)

These seven plagues or disasters all occurred on earth simply because of the earth's wickedness and their refusal to repent. Rather, the scripture says:

"the angel of the waters says: '... they deserve it!'" (Rev 16:6) "they blasphemed the name of God, who had the power over these plagues, and they did not repent and give Him glory." (Rev 16:9)

"...yet they did not repent of their actions." (Rev 16:11)

"...and they blasphemed God for the plague of hail because that plague was extremely severe." (Rev 16:21 HCSB)

Mankind, how long will it take you to be contrite? Admit your faults, turn to God, the Holy God with contrite hearts and pray for mercy. The omnipotent God can solve all your problems if only you will agree to walk only in His ways.

Wars, leprosy, cancer, HIV-Aids, global warming, COVID-19, etc. are like reprimands. Forsake your evil ways; turn to God!

Return to Me!

"Yet even now—oracle of the Lord—
Return to Me with your whole heart,
with fasting, weeping, and mourning.
Rend your hearts, not your garments,
and return to the Lord, your God,
for He is gracious and merciful,
slow to anger, abounding in steadfast love,
and relenting in punishment.
Perhaps He will again relent
and leave behind a blessing,..." (Joel 2:12-13, 14 NABRE)
"...for the Lord is very compassionate and merciful" (Js 5:11)

The Two Ways: recalcitrance and penitence

Penitence: Sodom, Gomorrah and Nineveh as typologies – We have seen how, in spite of Father Abraham's intercession and that of Lot, Sodom and Gomorrah remained steeped in sin and were destroyed.

But the case is different for Nineveh, another city of shame. "Jonah set out on the first day of his walk in the city and proclaimed, 'in 40 days Nineveh will be demolished.' The men of Nineveh believed... proclaimed a fast... from the greatest... to the least.

When the word reached the king of Nineveh, he... took off his royal robe... and sat in ashes... issued a decree... 'No man or beast... is to taste anything... eat or drink water;... (each) must call out earnestly to God... turn from his evil ways... who knows? God may turn and relent... from His burning anger...'"

"Then God saw... they had turned from their evil ways... and He did not (destroy the city)." (Jon 3: 4-10 HCSB)

Thank God, their grain of faith paid off, alleluia!

Love of God

"This is what love for God is: to keep His commands." "Not burdensome because..." (1 Jn 5: 3-4 HCSB)

Repent

Sir 17: 24 "To the penitent God provides a way back...

Lect 17: 25 Return to Him and give up sin...

Dwell no longer in the error of the ungodly..."

Repentance: "There will be more joy in heaven over one sinner who repents than over 99 righteous people who have no need of repentance."

"There will be rejoicing among the angels of God over a sinner who repents."

(Lk 15: 10)

(Lk 13: 1-3) Galileans who suffered "– By no means! If you do not repent you will all perish as they did"

Repentance gives life. (Acts 11: 18)

HCSB: "Then they glorified God saying, 'So God has granted repentance resulting in life even to the Gentiles'"

NABRE: "... they stopped objecting and glorified God, saying, 'God has then granted life-giving repentance to the Gentiles too'"

The Redeemer says proclaim repentance!

"… These are My words that I spoke to you while I was still with you – that everything written about Me in the Law of Moses, the Prophets, and the Psalms must be fulfilled."

"… This is what is written:

The Messiah would suffer and rise from the dead the third day, and repentance for forgiveness of sins would be proclaimed in His name to all the nations, beginning at Jerusalem." (Lk 24: 44, 46-47 HCSB)

iii. Divine Mercy

Jesus depicted the unsurpassable, inscrutable and unfathomable mercy of God in the parable of the Tenant Farmers (LK 20: 9-18). Many of us distance ourselves from such magnanimous patience with which the unfaithful and rebellious tenants were treated which were not promptly aborted to pre-empt the tragic killing of the Landlord's son and heir. (LK 20:14, 15)

Divine Mercy

Another demonstration of the unfathomable mercy of God is in the rescuing from being stoned to death of the woman "caught in the very act" of adultery.

"Let the one without sin…be the first to throw a stone…" was the precept (Jn 8:7 NABRE)

- And for the woman: "neither do I condemn you…go and from now on, do not sin anymore' (Jn 8:11)

Compassion for one another

- Jesus says: Be merciful even as your Father in heaven is merciful (LK 6:36)

"Son, your sins are forgiven" (MK 2:5) were the words of healing Jesus spoke to a paralytic

Apostle James writes: for judgment is without mercy to the one who do not show mercy. (Js 2:13)

Divine mercy avails only to those who show mercy to others.

Rom 5: 6 "for Christ while we are still helpless, Jesus died for us…"

"Do not sin anymore!" (Jn 5: 14 HCSB)

Divine mercy offers unconditional succour.

At Bethesda, the sinner was healed both of his infirmity and (forgiven) his sins. Should he go on sinning? So Jesus admonished him to sin no more, "so that something worse doesn't happen to you." (Jn 5: 14)

Blessed are the merciful for they shall obtain mercy Matt 5: 7

Jesus told the paralytic 'your sins are forgiven you!' This man surely can now start on a clean slate; should he now pile up fresh sins on it?

The same thing applies to all of us justified by Jesus on the cross of Calvary. That spectre of horror (the crucifixion) does it suggest a condonation of sins? Then, why must you go on sinning?

The Parable of the Prodigal Son (LK 15: 11-32)

His father responded with clemency for this prodigal son of his. In just the same manner, God's mercy avails for the penitent. Hence mercy is not condonation.

The Lord is slow to anger, rich in love.(Num 14: 18)

Excess baggage – Jesus puts it this way:

"And if your right hand causes you to sin, cut it off…"

"If your right eye causes you to sin, gouge it out…" (Matt 5:29, 30)

"Happy are those whose sins are forgiven, whose wrongs are pardoned.

Happy is the one whom the Lord does not accuse of doing wrong and who is free from all deceit." (Ps 32: 1-2 GNBDK)

"Because of the Lord's faithful love we do not perish, for His mercies never end.

They are new every morning;

great is Your faithfulness!" (Lam 3:22-23 HCSB)

Divine mercy: David's three options

2 Sam 24: 9-13 – He trusts in God's mercy (2 Sam 24: 14)

David's conscience troubled him, he confessed to God in
contrition –

2 Sam 24: 10

Universal God:

MOAB: A Throne of Mercy

"Let the outcasts of Moab live with you, be their shelter from the
destroyer when the struggle is ended, the ruin complete…"

"A throne shall be set up in mercy,
and on it shall sit in fidelity (in David's tent)
A judge upholding right
and prompt to do justice." (Isa 16: 4, 5 HCSB)

"Behold what manner of love the Father has bestowed on us,
that we should be called Children of God." (1 Jn 3: 1 NKJV)

Divine Mercy (God is circumcising hearts) (Deut 30: 6)

Counterparty obligation

- Concern for others:

"When I was hungry, you did not give Me to eat; thirsty…to
drink; when I was naked, you did not offer Me your dress…"

"Whatever you did not do for one of the least of these, you did
not do for Me either." (Matt 25: 45, 46)

Two parables brought home the message —

First the parable of the Good Samaritan (LK 10: 30-35)

Secondly, the parable of the Rich man and Lazarus (LK 16: 19-
31)

- Divine Justice

"…remember…during your life time you received your good
things…"

"…make friends…by means of the unrighteous money…" (LK
16: 25, 9)

Compassion for one another

- Jesus: "Be merciful even as your Father in heaven is merciful."(LK 6: 36)

Apostle James: "… For judgement is without mercy to the One who hasn't shown mercy; mercy triumphs over judgement." (Js 2: 13)

Divine Justice

Jesus: "Do not judge and you will not be judged; do not condemn, and you will not be condemned. Forgive…it will be forgiven you."(LK 6: 37)

Model prayer: "And forgive us our debts as we also have forgiven our debtors."

Jesus: "For if you forgive people their wrongdoing your heavenly Father will

forgive you as well. But if you don't forgive people, your Father will not forgive your wrongdoing." (Matt 6: 12, 14.)

"So will My heavenly Father do to you unless each of you forgives your

brother from your heart." (Matt 18: 35 NABRE)

"As I have loved you, so you must love one another." (Jn 13: 34)

The 70 times 7 Rule

"Then Peter came to Him and said, 'Lord, how many times could my brother sin against me and I forgive him? As many as seven times?'

'I tell you, not as many as seven', Jesus said to him, 'but 70 times seven.'"

(Matt 18: 21-22 HCSB)

"The Lord is gracious and compassionate,

slow to anger and rich in faithful love.

The Lord is good to everyone;

His compassion rests on all He has made.

Your kingdom is an everlasting kingdom;
Your rule is for all generations.
The Lord is faithful in all His words
and gracious in all His actions.
The Lord helps all who fall;
He raises up all who are oppressed.
All eyes look to You,
and You give them their food at the proper time.
You open Your hand
and satisfy the desire of every living thing.
The Lord is righteous in all His ways,
and gracious in all His acts.
The Lord is near all who call out to Him,
all who call out to Him with integrity." (Ps 145: 8-9, 13-18 HCSB)

iv. Salvation

Courage! Hold the fort! This is what is going to happen:
"Praise God!
Salvation, glory, and power belong to our God!
True and just are His judgments!
He has condemned the prostitute who was corrupting the earth with her immorality.
God has punished her because she killed His servants."
"Praise God!
The smoke from the flames that consume the great city goes up forever and ever!"
"Amen! Praise God!" (Rev 19:1, 2, 3, 4 GNBDK)

The glory of Martyrs

"Then I saw thrones…I also saw the souls of those who had been executed because they had proclaimed the truth that Jesus revealed and the word of God. They had not worshipped the beast or its image…They came to life and ruled as kings with Christ for a thousand years. (The rest of the dead did not come to life until the thousand years were over.)

This is the first raising from the dead.

Happy and greatly blessed are those who are included in this first raising of the dead.

The second death has no power over them, they shall be priests of God and of Christ, and they will rule with Him for a thousand years. (Rev 20:4, 5-6 GNBDK)

A new heaven and a new earth – salvation of our God!

"Then I saw a new heaven and a new earth…

I heard a loud voice speaking from the throne:

"Now God's home is with human beings! He will live with them, and they shall be His people. God Himself will be with them, and He will be their God.

He will wipe away all tears from their eyes. There will be no more death, no more grief or crying or pain. The old things have disappeared."

"Then the One who sits on the throne said, 'And now I make all things new!?

Those who win the victory will receive this from Me: I will be their God, and they will be my children. But cowards, traitors, perverts, murderers, the immoral, those who practise magic, those who worship idols, and all liars —the place for them is the lake burning with fire and sulphur, which is the second death.'" (Rev 21: 1, 3-5, 7-8 GNBDK)

On this mountain

He will destroy the burial shroud, the shroud over all the peoples,

the sheet covering all the nations;

He will destroy death forever. (Is 25: 7, 8 HCSB)

For more on 2nd Coming, Resurrection, & Judgment see Isa 58: 7; Ezk18: 7-12; (Ezk 34: 17; Dan 12: 2)

"Then the righteous will shine like the sun in their Father's kingdom. Anyone who has ears should listen." (Matt 13: 43)

Call to be fruitful – repent!

"When he (John, the Baptist) saw many of the Pharisees and Sadducees… he said to them, 'Brood of vipers! Who warned you to flee from the coming wrath? Therefore, produce fruit consistent with repentance. Even now the axe is ready to strike the root of the trees! Therefore, every tree that doesn't produce good fruit will be cut down and thrown into the fire.'"

(Matt 3: 7, 10 HCSB)

How Apostle Peter sees conversion – A new birth in Jesus

"Praise… God… (for) His great mercy,

He has given us a new birth into a living hope through the resurrection…

Into an inheritance… kept in heaven." (1 Pt 1: 3-4 HCSB)

"And repentance for the forgiveness of sins

will be preached in His name to all nations…" (Lk 24: 47)

Jesus (still saying until now) –

- "Repent, the kingdom of heaven is at hand." (Matt 4: 17)
- "But unless you repent you too will all perish" (Lk 13: 3, 5)
- "…observe the commandments: You shall not commit adultery; you shall not murder…" (Lk 18: 20)
- King Saul did not repent – (1 Sam 15: 24, 26-28)

Ask to be forgiven:

`"Forgive us our sins…" (Lk 11: 4)

Mercy

"That is in Christ, God was reconciling the world to Himself, not counting their trespasses against them…" (2 Cor 5: 19 HCSB)

We – the righteousness of God

"He made the One who did not know sin to be sin for us, so that we might become the righteousness of God in Him." (2 Cor 5: 21 HCSB)

GOD'S Love for us:

"… the love of God made visible in Christ Jesus, our Lord." (….8: 39……)

Merciful God

The Lord is merciful and gracious,
Slow to anger, and abounding in mercy.
He has not dealt with us according to our sins,
Nor punished us according to our iniquities.
For as the heavens are high above the earth,
So great is His mercy toward those who fear Him;
As far as the east is from the west,
So far has He removed our transgressions from us.
As a father has compassion on his children,
so the Lord has compassion on those who fear Him.
(Ps 103: 8, 10-13 HCSB)

ADDITIONAL RESOURCES

FORGIVENESS

Divine mercy

"For I will forgive their wrong doing and never again remember their sin" (Jer 31: 34 HCSB)

- "Now if the wicked person turns from all the sins he has committed, keeps all My statuses, and does what is just and right, he will certainly live; he will not die."

"None of the transgressions he has committed will be held against him" (Ezk 18: 21-22)

- "Yahwch, if You considered sins, Lord, who could stand? But with You there is forgiveness…" (Ps 130: 3, 4 HCSB)

Authority to forgive sins

"As the Father sent Me, so am I sending you; … For those whose sins you forgive, they are forgiven…" (Jn 20: 21, 22?)

Compare: "You are Peter and on this rock I will build My church, and … I will give you the keys of the kingdom of heaven and whatever you bind… is already bound in heaven, and whatever you loose… is already loosed in heaven." (Matt 16: 18, 19)

Eternal life for all

(The testimony of the beloved son of God!)

"For God loved the world so much that He gave His only Son, so that everyone who believes in Him may not die but have eternal life. For God did not send His Son into the world to be its judge, but to be its Saviour."

(Jn 3: 16-17 GNBDK)

Paul the Apostle's testimony: mercy for the repentant.

"I give thanks to Christ Jesus… I thank Him for considering me worthy and appointing me to serve Him, even though in the past I spoke evil of Him and persecuted and insulted Him. But God was merciful to me because I did not yet have faith and so did not know what I was doing."

(1 Tim 1: 12, 13 GNBDK)

Repent, be reconciled to God!

Apostle Paul preached it:

"I testified to both Jews and Greeks about repentance towards God and faith in our Lord Jesus." (Acts 20: 21 HCSB)

"…God, who… gave us the ministry of reconciliation." (2 Cor 5: 18 HCSB)

Exhortation, meditation and reflection

Repent: The 3 C's

The 3 elements of a true Repentance are:
Contrition
Confession and
Conversion

CONTRITION

The parable of the prodigal son gives a clear appreciation of what contrition is like.

"When he came to his sense, he said…I'll get up, go to my father, and say to him, Father, I have sinned…I'm no longer worthy to be called your son…"

(LK 15:17, 18, 19)

This is similar to the reaction of men (Jon 2:16, 3:5) and King of Nineveh (Jon 3:6-8) at Jonah's preaching.

Contrition: Without convincing yourself that what you did was evil or blameworthy, there is no remorse or contrition; and without contrition there can be no conversion or rebirth, without conversion there is simply no repentance. You will surely go back to your vomit.

Hear Paul's testimony:

"Therefore, since we have this ministry… we have renounced shameful secret things, not walking in deceit or distorting God's

message, but commending ourselves to every person's conscience…
by an open display of truth."

(2 Cor 4: 1-2)

Contrition:

"Help us, God our saviour,
on account of the glory of your name.
Deliver us, pardon our sins,
for Your names sake." (Ps 79: 9 NABRE)
Job is contrite and admits his wrongdoing:
"I have dealt with great things that I do not understand; things
too wonderful for me, which I cannot know… Therefore, I disown
what I have said, and repent in dust and ashes." (Job 42:3, 6)

Both King David (2 Sam 12:13-14) and King Ahab (1 KGS
21:27-29) repented after the prophet confronted each with his
wrongdoing. And each got a lighter sentence.

Exhortation, meditation and reflection

Come, return to the Lord!

"Come to the Lord and leave your sin behind…
Return to the Most High and turn away from sin.
Have an intense hatred for wickedness." (Sir 17:25, 26 GNBDK)

Contrition

At Simon's, the Pharisee's house:
"And a woman… who was a sinner stood behind Him at His feet
weeping and..." (Lk 7: 37-38 HCSB)

Prayer of the Contrite: Lord, call us back!

Oh Lord our God, our Perfect Good!

We hear You from the voice of Your prophets, saying, 'Repent! Repent! Come to Me!' Father, here we are, heal us, pardon our guilt.

Lord God, King of mercy and compassion!

Nothing is hidden from You: our sins, our weaknesses. We have no excuses only to plead the blood of Jesus Christ. Let this expiate our sins before You, Oh Lord.

Sin, Oh Lord, often drives us away from Your presence. The voice of Your priests and prophets becomes faint. We are deaf, blind and lost. The dangers of death lurks. Call us back, Lord. Oh Lord, our God, call us back that we may be saved. Amen.

CONFESSION

The example of the prodigal son is telling:

"The son said to him, 'Father, I have sinned against heaven and in your sight. I'm no longer worthy to be called your son." (LK 15:21)

CONFESS your sins to one another…if we confess…forgiveness is given.

(1 Jn 1: 9; see also Ps 25, 32, 38, 39, 51 …)

Confession: Further guide from scripture

"Therefore, confess your sins to one another and pray for one another, so that you may be healed. The urgent request of a righteous is very powerful in its effect." (Js 5:16)

Confession: There are basically two ways to confess one's culpability—one's wrongdoing.

Exhortation, meditation and reflection

First, by telling God or the person offended or sinned against (where possible), what wrong-doing we committed and expressing remorse, requesting for forgiveness (and in many cases have a commitment toward reparation, where possible.)

The second method is simply to admit our wrongdoing to ourselves and to the person wronged with a measure of self-chastisement or regret and express a desire to be forgiven so that trust can be restored.

Confession:

"Both we and our fathers have sinned;

we have done wrong and have acted wickedly." (Ps 106: 6)

"Only acknowledge your guilt –

you have rebelled against the Lord your God,

… and have not obeyed My voice." (Jer 3: 13 HCSB)

"Father, I have sinned against heaven and against you…" (Lk 15: 21)

"If we confess our sins, He (God) is faithful and righteous to forgive us our sins and to cleanse us from all unrighteousness." (1 Jn 1:9)

Both Moses (Num 20: 12, 24-28) and King Saul (1 Sam 15: 20-28) did not show sufficient remorse when God confronted them with their wrongdoing; each gave excuses.

For Catholics, the priest hearing confession in the parish is the equivalent of Elijah or Samuel or Nathan—the prophets of God. They exercise powers given to the church.

For those who do not know, confessing one's sins trains the penitent and sensitizes his conscience, strengthening it against future temptations.

It is not easy for the unrighteous to confess; rather there are other persons, circumstances and chance events that are contributory to the wrong-doing, we play down our culpability by pointing accusing fingers at those persons and situations. This was what Saul did hence the retort: "obedience is better than sacrifice…"

CONFESS your sins to one another…if we
confess…forgiveness is given
(Js 5:16; 1 Jn 1:9)
Exhortation, meditation and reflection
"Therefore, confess your sins to one another and
pray for one another, so that you may be healed.
The urgent request of a righteous person is very
powerful in its effect." (Js 5:16 HCSB)

Confession

When Simon Peter said, 'Go away from me, Lord, because I'm
a sinful man' (Lk 5: 8 HCSB) that was a confession coming from a
contrite heart.

"I'll get up, go to my Father and say to him, Father, I have
sinned…"
(Lk 15: 18 HCSB)
"The son said to him, 'Father, I have sinned against heaven and
in your sight…'" (Lk 15: 21)
"God, turn Your wrath from me – a sinner!" (Lk 18: 13 HCSB)
"Then Jesus said to him, 'If you can?' Everything is possible to
the one who believes."
"Immediately the father of the boy cried out, 'I do believe! Help
my unbelieve.'" (Mk 9: 23-24 HCSB)
Those are the words of a born again former doubter!
CONFESSION (Ps 51: 2, 3 GNBDK)
"I recognize my faults;
For I acknowledge my offense,
and my sin is before me always…"

CONVERSION

This prodigal son of the Lord's illustration actually acted on his
resolution. He has become a new person, no longer a recalcitrant

fugitive in a foreign land but a repentant child who returns to his father for compassion:

"So he got up and went to his father" (LK 15: 20)

In the Nineveh case, "Each must turn from his evil ways and from the violence he is doing…" (Jon 3: 8)

Exhortation, meditation and reflection

Conversion: The totality of the Christian vocation is all about conversion – '**being born again**' a new person in Jesus. This conversion comes through renunciation of sin and Satan. One word for it is Repentance

"…repentance for forgiveness of sins would be proclaimed in His name to all the nations, beginning at Jerusalem."

(Lk 24: 47)

"… RETURN to Me… and I will return to you

Turn from your evil ways

and from your wicked deeds." (Zech 1: 3, 4 Lect)

Walk by the spirit and not by the flesh

For "the works of the flesh are obvious: sexual immorality, moral impurity, promiscuity, idolatry, sorcery, hatreds, strife, jealousy, outbursts of anger, selfish ambitions, dissensions, factions, drunkenness, carousing and anything similar." (Gal 5: 16, 19-21)

True Repentance leads to conversion

Witness this in the conduct of the sinner woman who came to the house of Simon, the Pharisee (LK 7: 36-38)

"And a woman in the town who was a sinner found out that Jesus was reclining at the table in the Pharisee's house. She bought an alabaster jar of fragrant oil and stood behind Him at His feet weeping, and began to wash His feet with her tears. She wiped His feet with the hair of her head, kissing them and anointing them with the fragrant oil." (LK 7: 36-38 HCSB)

Conversion

"But Zacchaeus stood there and said to the Lord, 'Look, I'll give half of my possessions to the poor, Lord! And if I have extorted anything from anyone, I'll pay back four times as much!'" (Lk 19: 8 HCSB)

Thomas' unbelieve gave way – he became a believer proclaiming, "My Lord and my God!" (Jn 20: 28 HCSB)

LOVE has no joy at wrongdoing, not conceited.

(1 Cor 13: 1-6 HCSB)

Exhortation, meditation and reflection

Love of, or reverence for God

For fear gives way when love is perfected.

Conversion: guarantees mercy.

While humanity was still immersed in sin, the Redeemer was given to mankind by God! It is that man may live and not perish. This is a second chance. We must make a good use of it to remain emancipated.

Saul (Apostle Paul) justified the mercy he received, why not you?

Let us pray!

"Be merciful to me, O God,

because of Your constant love.

Because of Your great mercy

wipe away my sins!

I recognize my faults:

I am always conscious of my sins.

Close Your eyes to my sins

and wipe out all my evil.

Give me again the joy that comes from Your salvation,

and make me willing to obey You.

Then I will teach sinners Your commands,

and they will turn back to You.

My sacrifice is a humble spirit, O God;

You will not reject a humble and repentant heart."

(Ps 51: 1, 3, 9, 12-13, 17 GNBDK)

Divine Mercy

It will appear that St Paul's analogy of sin and grace, condemnation and redemption (Rom 5:1-6:13) is pointing to divine mercy:

- The sin of Adam provoked condemnation, and hence death.
- Grace (or divine mercy or clemency or pardon) came — a free gift of God—to set aside judgement, condemnation and death through faith in the One God sent—Jesus Christ;

Redemption comes by His blood (i.e. His death).

Thus in Rom 5:1 St. Paul writes, that "we have been declared righteous (or "justified") by faith in Jesus Christ."

Exhortation, meditation and reflection

And in Rom 5:9, "we have been declared righteous ("justified") by His blood" thus saving us from wrath or condemnation and hence into life! (Parentheses are author's)

Therefore,

Rom 6: urges us to "consider yourselves (Christians) irrepressible by sin but attentive to God through Christ Jesus"

Rom 6:12: He urges us to extirpate sin by refusing to yield to our bodily cravings; and in 6:13, we are not to permit any organ of our body to sin, rather deploy them towards righteousness.

Divine Mercy

God is king of justice but He also knows the therapeutic value of mercy, he thus countenances, as it were, the extenuating and countervailing circumstances that ought to be taken into consideration for true justice to be enacted. In the vineyard of righteousness are two trees, Justice and Charity. The trunk of Charity is mercy; its branches, compassion and empathy. These sprout flowers known as forgiveness (or pardon), and their flowers yield fruits of peace, trust and cooperation.

What Divine Mercy does to the Sinner

Mercy is superfluous to the holy man or woman. But for the sinner it is worth the world! The conditions precedent must be satisfied to be eligible for God's mercy – contrition, confession, conversion – and forgiveness.

"… as we forgive those who sinned against us."

Divine mercy is

"Go, and from now on do not sin anymore."

It is an unconditional pardon.

(Jn 8: 11 HCSB)

Mercy Revealed by God

Who wouldn't rather be ruled by God than by man? A man may commit a very grievous offence, if he repents, he may receive mercy and not lose his life for it. Thus Adam and Eve both committed insubordination; Cain, Moses, Aaron, Meiram and David all sinned at one time or the other, yet none suffered the loss of his/her life in consequence thereof.

Exhortation, meditation and reflection

Now consider a human monarch: defy him on one occasion and the felon is as good as dead. It does not matter your past dedication, competence or loyalty. Your remorse or contrition will not avail; and there is no reprieve for repentance. The life of a powerless subject is never worth more than that of a mere chattel!

That was the fate of David in the hands of King Saul; Abel in the hands of his elder brother Cain; Shedrack, Mischack and Abednego, even Daniel, in the hands of King Nebuchadnezzar. John the Baptist lost his life for the fun of a tipsy King Herod, who also ordered the execution of the prison guards under whose watch Peter was miraculously delivered from the prison. The atrocities of Hitler's Reich still stinks to high heavens. It will never stop appalling the mind.

Human beings may have compassion on their children and parents, but they are incapable of mercy. God discovered mercy and showed us the way. Cain as stated above, murdered his brother, but obtained propitiation and was left off the hook by God. So it was understandable that the 6th commandment simply stated, 'you shall not murder' and not something like "anyone who murders must be killed". Yet, man kills and kills and kills mindlessly. God's servants were martyred; even Jesus, God's Son – was not spared!

Mercy of God and Purgatory.[1]
A. Jesus says:

1. It is the wish of God, the Father that whoever believes in the Son may not perish. Thus, Jesus promises to raise such on the last day.
2. (Jn 6: 37-40)
3. To all who believes in Jesus as the Son of God, Jesus will give eternal life. (Jn 6: 47-48, 51)
4. To the Jews (some) who would not believe in Him, He admonished that they would die in their sins because they failed to believe in the One sent by God. (Jn 8: 24)
5. Some who believe in Jesus will go to hell, even when they plead, 'Lord, Lord, we cast devils in Your name'. The Lord will reply 'Get away from Me, you evil doers!' (Matt 7: 21-23; Lk 13: 25-30.)
6. Whatever you did or did not do for any of the least of these My brothers you do or did not do for Me. (Matt 25: 44-45)
7. Do unto others as you would want them to do to you – this is the Law and the Prophets. (Matt 7: 12, 21)
8. Exhortation, meditation and reflection
9. OBEY! Belief in Jesus is measured by obedience to the word of God, not by lip service. You must be doers of the word. (Lk 6: 46-49; 18: 18-22)

From the above, the old question about faith without works and faith shown by works comes alive.

But, in addition, what happens to people who could not be blamed for their lack of faith in Jesus Christ? Purgatory?

B. Heaven and Non-Christians

Some of those people are
- i. Those who died before Jesus was born;
- ii. Others are those who never heard the word preached to them for any reason.
- iii. The third category we want to consider are those misled by their mentors, the 'pastors' who preached Jesus to them but emphasised the wrong things and whom they believed in.

1: Here is what the Catholic Church says about Purgatory:
Purgatory

1. Catholic Glossary:

"The state or condition in which those who have died in the state of grace, but some attachment to sin, suffer for a time as they are being purified before they are admitted to the glory and happiness of heaven."

2. Catechism of the Catholic Church (2nd edition), 1997:

CCC #1031 "The church gives the name Purgatory to this final purification of the elect, which is entirely different from the punishment of the damned.

The church formulated her doctrine of faith on Purgatory especially at the Councils of Florence and Trent..."

CCC #1032 "This teaching is also based on the practice of the prayer for the dead,... "(Judas Maccabeus) made atonement for the dead that they might be delivered from their sin." From the beginning the church has honoured the memory of the dead and offered prayers in suffrage for them."

Exhortation, meditation and reflection

We know that God is just and merciful. The sinner must get some punishment so that the labour of those who persevered in righteousness may not be in vain. To me, Purgatory, is a perfect answer (for sinners in categories A and B). These get punished alright, but not eternally (at least for those who take advantage of God's Second Chance to purify themselves while in there). Most of humanity will require the mercy of God in the circumstances described under A4 to A7 to make heaven.

Forgive!

No Retaliation
- "Do not be conquered by evil but conquer evil with good.

Do not repay anyone evil for evil; be concerned for what is noble in the sight of all." (Rom 12: 21, 17)

For more see 1 Thes 5: 15; 1 Pt 3: 9

Forgive!
- "Forgive us our trespasses as we forgive those who sinned against us" (Matt 6:12)

Forgive means to let go; it does not require that justice be set aside; rather, after establishing what a just and fair relationship should have been, and deviation there from noted, forgiveness is offered as the balm of reconciliation in place of vengeance to facilitate healing. The injured should be compensated, whenever possible; this can come from third parties. But the purpose of such compensation is not to retaliate but to alleviate the suffering; ameliorate relations, lessen the hurt and promote healing, hence the usefulness of the third party aid. (The parable of the good Samaritan). Contrast that with a situation in which the third party allies with the victim to punish the offender (vengeance) they are sharing grief and pains primarily, rather than promoting goodwill and healing.

For public office holders, who are Christians, the public office is your calling, your ministry, the opportunity or outlet through which you can practise your Christian vocation.

- Charity is the first love of our Christian ministry: "that repentance, for the forgiveness of sins would be preached in His (Jesus) name to all the nations (LK 24:47)
- "…He has anointed Me to preach good news to the poor…to proclaim freedom to the captives…to set free the oppressed, to proclaim the year of the Lord's favour." (LK 4: 18-19 HCSB)

Exhortation, meditation and reflection

Be caring.

Don't allow yourself to benumbed by the cascade of news of horror, wickedness and inhumanity that daily assail us from the print, electronic and social media and thereby become inured and unconcerned.

In the parables of the Good Samaritan, Lazarus and the Richman, as well as in the parable of the unforgiving servant, the Lord insists that we care for what our neighbours are going through.

Mercy is overlooking the injury caused to you by another, in order to move on. It facilitates permanent healing.

Ps 109: 16 "For he did not remember to show mercy but he hounded the wretched poor, and brought death to the broken-hearted."

: 17 "He loved cursing may it come upon him; he hated blessing may none come to him."

"Forgiveness as the Restoration of Truth."

"A Jesus who agrees with everyone and everything – a Jesus without His holy anger, without the hardiness of truth and genuine love is not the real Jesus as He is depicted in the scriptures but… a pitiable caricature."

"The concept of a gospel that fails to convey the reality of God's anger has nothing to do with the gospel of the Bible. True forgiveness is something quite different from weak indulgence."

"Forgiveness is demanding and requires both parties – the one who forgives and the one who is forgiven to do so with all their minds and hearts."

"A Jesus who sanctions everything is a Jesus without the cross; for such a Jesus would not need the torment of the cross to save mankind."

"The cross is being increasingly banished from theology and being re-interpreted as just a vexatious mischance or purely a political event. Only when a relationship between truth and love is rightly comprehended can the cross be comprehensible in the true theological depth. Forgiveness has to do with truth. That is why it requires the sane cross of our conversion. Forgiveness is in fact, the restoration of the truth, the renewing of being and the vanquishment of the lie that lurks in every sin."

"Sin is by nature a departure from the truth of one's own nature and by consequence, the truth of the Creator, God."

Pope Emeritus Benedict XVI: Daily Meditations

Exhortation, meditation and reflection

Forgive!

The Lord commands us:

In a revelation to St. Maria Faustina[2], the Lord enjoined her (and impliedly, all of us) to engage in works of mercy:

"I demand from you deeds of mercy, which are to arise out of love for Me. You are to show mercy to your neighbours always and everywhere. You must not shrink from this or try to excuse yourself. Even the strongest faith is of no avail without works."

So, what are these **works of mercy**? You can figure them out yourself, but the Catholic Church has pointed out to seven "corporal" and seven "spiritual" works of mercy. The former includes giving food to the hungry, clothing the naked, shelter to the homeless/oppressed, etc.

The latter requires us to admonish sinners; instruct the uninformed, forgive offences, be patient with those in errors, pray for the living and the dead, etc.

Forgiveness and mercy

For further meditation read Lk 15: 1-3, 4-31.

Divine Mercy (a meditation):

God in mercy reverses Himself –

1. On the Ninevites, (Jonah was dismayed) (Jon 3: 4, 10)
2. To David, (and Nathan delivered both the curse and the forgiveness) (2 Sam 12: 7-14)
3. On Ahab, king of Israel (reign in Samaria) on Naboth's murder by Jezebel (Elijah gave the sentence and its suspension) (1 Kgs 21: 17-29)
4. Hezekiah's terminal illness: (the Lord pronounces death and proclaims life!) (Isa 38: 1-5)
5. On Israel's idolatry (Isaiah, Jeremiah and Ezekiel declared condemnation and subsequently remission and forgiveness; forsakenness and betrothal! (Jer 31: 34; etc.)
6. In providing Jesus, the acceptable spotless Lamb whose blood is atonement for our sins, the sinner was let go and the one without sin bore the punishment for our transgressions. (Js 1: 10)

2: Maria Faustina (1935 - ?): Divine Mercy in my soul #742.
MERCY

- Is the flip side of Justice – in mercy you don't get the raw deal you deserve, but you get a reprieve you do not merit (under justice)

To the vanquished it is graciousness;

to the victor – it is agape love!

- Through justice you get what you deserve;

Through mercy you obtain a remission of the punishment due to your unrighteousness.

CHAPTER 10

Kindness – Love, Give And Forgive

Love (or fear) of God

"So now I urge you… that we love one another. **And this is love: that we walk according to His commands. This is the command as you have heard it from the beginning, you must walk in love.**"

(2 Jn 1: 5-6 HCSB)

Love of one another

"… Love one another. Just as I have loved you, you must also love one another."

(Jn 13: 34 HCSB)

See it also in Jn 15: 12; 15: 17 HCSB

It's insightful to read all through the entire chapter.

Love of brother

"And we have the command from Him:

the one who loves God must also love his brother." (1 Jn 4: 21 HCSB)

Sincerely prefer good to evil

"Do not let your love be a pretence, but sincerely prefer good to evil. Love each other as much as brothers should and have a profound respect for each other." (Rom 12: 9, 10)

Love your neighbour, even your enemy

"LOVE your enemies… and lend, expecting nothing in return…" (Lk 6: 35)

"…It is more blessed to give than to receive kindness" (Acts 20:35 HCSB)

Making a living by the gospel

"In the same way, the Lord has commanded that those who preach the gospel should earn their living by the gospel" (1 Cor 9:14)

Giving for His sake

"And whoever gives just a cup of cold water to one of these little ones because he is a disciple—I assure you: He will never lose his reward." (Matt 10:42)

"LOVE!" – The Most Important Commandment (Mk12:28-34)

"This is the most important," Jesus answered:

"…the Lord is one. Love the Lord your God with all your heart,…soul,…mind, and…strength. The second is: Love your neighbour as yourself. There is no other command greater than those." (MK 12:29-31 HCSB)

Love Fulfils the Law

"The commandments:

Do not commit adultery;

Do not murder; do not steal;

Do not covet, and whatever other commandment – all are summed up by this: Love your neighbour as yourself." (Rom 13:9 HCSB)

God's love for us:

"Look at how great a love the Father has given us that we should be called God's children. And we are! The reason the world does not know us is that it didn't know Him. Dear friends, we are God's children now, and what we will be has not yet been revealed. We know that when He appears, we will be like Him because we will see Him as He is. And everyone who has this hope in Him purifies himself just as He is pure.

Little children, let no one deceive you! The one who does what is right is righteous, just as He is righteous (1 Jn 3: 1-3, 7 HCSB)

Give!

What do you possess that you have not received? (1 Cor 4:7 Lect)

Believe, or be damned!

"For God so loved the world that He gave His only son, so that everyone who believes in Him might not perish but might have eternal life. Whoever believes in Him will not be condemned but whoever does not believe has already been condemned..." (Jn 3: 16, 18 NABRE)

"This is how God's children—and the Devil's children—are made evident. Whoever does not do what is right is not of God, especially the one who does not love his brother." (1 Jn 3:1-3, 10 HCSB)

Our love for God

"For this is what love for God is: to keep His commands. Now His commands are not a burden, because whatever has been born of God conquers the world. This is the victory, that has conquered the world: our faith." (1 Jn 5:3-4, HCSB)

Love? Or Fear of God?

*The fear of God...is the beginning of all wisdom...*Actually, it is also the beginning of our relationship with God; when love of God leads to reverence, the fear gives way in the face of perfect love.

"There is no fear in love; instead, perfect love drives out fear, because fear involves punishment. So, the one who fears has not reached perfection in love."

(1 Jn 4:18)

Love of brother

"We know that we have passed from death to life because we love our brothers. The one who does not love remains in death. Everyone who hates his brother is a murderer, and you know that no murderer has eternal life residing in Him."

(1 Jn 3:14-15)

Love of Neighbour

"For this is the message we have heard from the beginning: We should love one another."

"Dear friends, let us love one another, because love is from God, and everyone who loves has been born of God and knows God.

The one who does not love does not know God, because God is love. God's love was revealed among us in this way: God sent his One and Only Son into the world so that we might live through Him. Love consists in this: not that we loved God, but that He loved us and sent His Son to be the propitiation for our sins. Dear friends, if God loved us in this way, we also must love one another. No one has ever seen God. If we love one another, God remains in us and His love is perfected in us. And we have this command from Him: The one who loves God must also love his brother." (1 Jn 3:11; 4: 7-12, 21 HCSB)

It is easier to love the brother that we see, so we can love God that we do not see

(1 Jn 4:20)

New Commandment: Love, an ensign of discipleship

"I give you a new commandment: love one another as I have loved you, so you also should love one another. This is how all will know that you are My disciples, if you have love for one another." (Jn 13:34-35 NABRE)

Love is of God; God is love.

"We have come to know and to believe in the love God has for us. God is love, and whoever remains in love remains in God and God in him." (1 Jn 4: 16 NABRE)

Christians – love Christ!

"If you love Me, you will keep My commands."

"And I will ask the Father and He will give you another counsellor to be with you forever.

He is the Spirit of truth…" (Jn 14: 15-16, 17 HCSB)

Power of Love

"Above all, maintain an intensive love for each other, since love covers a multitude of sins."

(1 Pt 4:8 HCSB)

SHARING – You did well!

"Still, you did well by sharing with me in my hardship." (Phil 4:14 HCSB)

Christian meaning of **Love**

I. "Love is patient, love is kind.

It is not jealous, it is not pompous,
It is not inflated, it is not rude,
It does not seek its own interests,
It is not quick-tempered, it does not brood over injury,
It does not rejoice over wrong-doing
but rejoices with the truth.
It bears all things, believes all things,
hopes all things, endures all things."
(1 Cor 13: 4-7 Lect)

II. "Love never fails…"

"So, faith, hope, love remain these three:
but the greatest of these is love."
(1 Cor 13: 8, 13 Lect)

ADDITIONAL RESOURCES

"And whoever gives you a cup of water to drink, because of My name, since you belong to the Messiah – I assure you:
He will never lose his reward." (Mk 9: 41 HCSB)

Support for the Mission

Dear friend Gaius,
"Since they set out for the sake of the Name,
… Therefore, we ought to support such
men so that we can be co-workers with the truth."
(3 Jn 1: 7-8 HCSB)

Almsgiving

Sir 3: 30 "As water quenches a flaming fire
so almsgiving atones for sins."
Sir 30: 31 "The kindness people have done crosses
their paths later on; should they stumble,
they will find support."
Ps 41: 1 "Happy is the one who cares for the poor,
HCSB the Lord will save him in the day of adversity."
Ps 41: 2 "The Lord will keep him and preserve him;
HCSB he will be blessed in the land."

Exhaustible treasure.

Jesus said, "sell your possessions and give to the poor.
Make … for yourselves … an inexhaustible treasure in heaven…"
(Lk 12: 33 HCSB)

Love!

Lk 6: 32 "If you love those who love you, what credit…
Even sinners love those who love them."
: 33 "If you do what is good to those who are good to you,
what credit… Even sinners do that."

: 37 "Do not judge… Do not condemn…
Forgive and you will be forgiven."
"Well for the man who is gracious and lends,
who conducts his affairs with justice;
lavishly he gives to the poor,
his generosity shall endure forever." (Ps 112: 5, 9 Lect)

On tithes and offerings

"Honour the Lord with your possessions and with the first fruits of all your increases so your barns will be filled with plenty…" (Prov. 3: 9 & 10)

Forgive!

"If your brother sins, rebuke him; and if he repents, forgive him" even seven times in a day, forgive him. (Lk 17: 3, 4 NABRE)

Sincerely forgive.

Jesus said, "So will My heavenly Father do to you unless each of you forgives your brother from your heart" (Matt 18: 35 NABRE)
Offer to God from what is precious to you. (2 Sam 24: 16, 18-25 HCSB)
2 Sam 24: 22 "Araunah said to David, 'My Lord… take whatever oxen
: 23 … Araunah gives everything here to the king.'"
: 24 "The king answered Araunah, No, …for I will not offer to the Lord My God burnt offerings that cost me nothing…'"
Repent and turn to God
Matt 21: 28-32
The parable of the two sons – "… you did not repent and believe Him"
When not to engage in holy work (work of mercy)

On the accusation by the Jews that Jesus worked (healing) on the Sabbath, He replied, "My Father is at work until now, so I am at work" (Jn 5: 17 NABRE)

Prayer (for the giver)

"And God, who supplies seed to sow and bread to eat, will also supply you with all the seed you need and will make it grow and produce a rich harvest from your generosity. He will always make you rich enough to be generous at all times…"

(2 Cor 9: 10-11 GNBDK)

SHARE!

Abigail Nabal by sharing saved Nabal's life and became David's wife.

(1 Sam 25: 2-42)

The poor and the needy (preaching of John)

"And the crowds asked him, 'what then should we do?'

He said to them in reply, 'Whoever has two tunics should share with the person who has none. And whoever has food should do likewise.'" (Lk 3: 10-11 NABRE)

Your giving is like a seed sown

Sowing sparingly or bountifully (2 Cor 9: 6-10)

Your motive is important

"And if I donate all my goods to feed the poor, and if I give my body … but do not have love, I gain nothing." (1 Cor 13: 3 HCSB)

The widow who gave from her want

Jesus said, "This poor widow has put in more than all of them…" (Lk 21: 1-4; also Mk 12: 41-44)

On Revenge: heaping fiery coals on the enemy's head

"Do not be conquered by evil but conquer evil with good."

"Do not repay anyone evil for evil; be concerned for what is noble in the sight of all." (Rom 12: 20, 21, 17)

For more see Deut 3: 4, 1 Thes 5:15; 1 Pt 3: 9.
Exhortation, meditation and reflection

Charity

WHY would Mother Theresa of Calcutta lavish her life on charities the way she did?

Why would St. Antony of Padua dissipate his inheritance on the poor?

Could it be their response to Jesus' bidding: "I assure you: whatever you did for one of the least of these brothers of Mine, you did for Me" (Matt 25: 40, 45)

Isn't this what is meant by "speaking, preaching and praying with hands and deeds"?

St. Peter Claver in this account gave a description of how he first spoke with his actions before preaching the gospel:

"Yesterday, 30th May 1627, on the feast of the Most Holy Trinity, numerous blacks, brought from the rivers of Africa, disembarked from a large ship. Carrying two baskets of oranges, lemons, sweet biscuits, and I know not what else, we hurried toward them. We had to force our way through the crowd until we reached the sick. Large numbers of the sick were lying on the wet ground or rather in puddles of mud."

"…They were naked, without any clothing to protect them. We laid aside our cloaks…to build a platform. In that way we covered a space to which we at last transferred the sick by forcing a passage through bands of slaves. This was how we spoke to them, not with words but with our hands and our actions. And in fact, convinced as they were that they had been brought here to be eaten, any other language would have proved utterly useless."[1]

See! Can you glimpse how beautiful Jesus is in the life of His disciples?

1: From a letter by St. Peter Claver (1581-1654): Jesuit, priest, Missionary to Columbia

Exhortation, meditation and reflection

Forgive!

"Forgive us our sins, for we forgive everyone who does us wrong…"
(Lk 11: 4 GNBDK)

Forgive means to let go; it does not require that justice be set aside, rather, after establishing what a just and fair relationship should be, and deviation there from noted, forgiveness is offered at the altar of reconciliation in place of revenge or vengeance to facilitate healing. The injured should be compensated, wherever possible, assistance towards this can come from third parties. The gesture is a palliative and an affirmation that impunity or wickedness is reprehensible. But the purpose of such compensation is not to retaliate but to promote healing, hence the usefulness of a third-party aid. Contrast that with a situation in which the third party aligns with the victim to punish the offender (retribution). They are retaliating grievances and pains instead of promoting goodwill and healing.

For public office holders, who are Christians, the public office is your calling, your ministry, the outlet through which you can practise your Christian vocation.

Charity is the first love of our Christian ministry: "that repentance, for the forgiveness of sins would be preached in His (Jesus) name to all nations."
(Lk 24: 47)

"… He has anointed Me to preach good news to the poor… to proclaim freedom to the captives… to set free the oppressed, to proclaim the year of the Lord's favour." (Lk 4: 18-19 HCSB)

Give, Forgive!

A preacher[1] encapsulated the Christian faith in these words — "We give and we forgive." Surely, that is what the tenet of our faith requires of us — to give (and not expect to receive back) and to forgive because God demands this of us.

So, whether it is your time or your talent or your treasure, just give!

"Some go to the missions by going, some go to missions by giving."[2]

You have been given so you may give. In the miracle of multiplication, the five loaves and two fish fed the thousands.

Ghandi[3] says, the world has enough for everybody's need, but not for everybody's greed.

1: Adekunle Ajala, Pastor KCCC, Denver.

2: Motto: (Nigeria) National Missionary Society of St. Paul (MSP)

3: Mahatma Ghandi, Former India Prime Minister

Exhortation, meditation and reflection

Franklin Delano Roosevelt (32nd president of the USA) says,

"The test of our progress is not whether we add more to the abundance of those who have much, it is whether we provide enough for those who have too little."

Sir Winston Churchill (UK PM: 1940-45; 1951-55) says,

"We make a living by what we get, but we make a life by what we give."

Love, the Good Samaritan Way

Compassion and care for our neighbour actually imply empathy for anyone who may need our helping hand. That is what the parable of the Good Samaritan seems to say. (Lk 10: 30-35)

Read also Lazarus parable (Lk 16: 19-31)

The rich man's fault is a mere (?) lack of empathy and goodness to a fellow son of Abraham!

"Love God!" – is the First Commandment in the Decalogue (see chapter 2)

"**Speak the truth** to your neighbour, even if it hurts" (Eph 5: 21)

Nothing stops you from reneging the statements later on conviction that you were wrong.

Love your enemy; pray for his conversion and accept the changed person. Love is all-powerful. God is love; love overcomes all things (1 Cor 13: 1-2, 4-7)

Read entire chapter (1 Cor 13:1-13)

Pope Emeritus Benedict XVI reflects:

"…man is constructed from within in the image of God to love and to be loved."

"…man is in God's image and thereby is a being whose innermost dynamic is likewise directed toward the receiving and giving of love."[1]

1 Cor 13: "LOVE is sufficient of itself; it gives pleasure by itself and because of itself. It is its own merit, its own reward. Love looks for no cause outside of itself, no effect beyond itself. Its profit lies in the practice. Of all the movements, sensations and feelings of the soul, love is the only one in which the creature can respond to the Creator and make some sort of similar return, however unequal, though it be." St Bernard of Clairvaux (1090-1153). Abbot and Doctor of the Church (from a sermon)

1: Pope Emeritus Benedict XVI Daily Meditations op cit.

Exhortation, meditation and reflection

How to love God – St. Peter Claver

- "To love God as He ought to be loved, we must be detached from all temporal love. We must love nothing but Him, or if we love anything else, we must love it only for His sake."
- "To do the will of God, man must despise his own; the more he dies to himself, the more he will live to God."
- "We know that all things work together for the good of those who love God: those who are called according to His purpose." (Rom 8: 28 HCSB)

What Christians do (Reflection):
In love, we give and we forgive

What is charity?

Return your enemy stray oxen or donkey; care for your enemy's animals lying helpless you must care for it (Exo 23: 5, 6)

Be prepared to lay your lives down for your brothers and care for their needs.

"This is how we have come to know love: He laid down His life for us. We should also lay down our lives for our brothers and care for their needs. If anyone has this world's goods and sees his brother in need but closes his eyes to his need – how can God's love reside in him?

Little children, we must not love with word or speech, but with truth and action." (1 Jn 3: 16-18)

Forgive

"Forgive your neighbour the wrong done to you, then when you pray, your own sins will be forgiven." (Sir 28: 2 NABRE)

Help!

"The Lord has commanded us to help the poor; don't refuse them the help they need." (Sir 29: 9 GNBDK)

CHAPTER 11

Thecross

I lay down my life for the sheep (Jn 10:14 HCSB)
"I gave My back to those who beat Me,

and My cheeks to those who tore out My beard.

I did not hide My face from scorn and spitting." (Isa 50: 6 HCSB)

"...although he had done no violence and had not spoken deceitfully. Yet the Lord was pleased to crush Him severely, when You make Him a restitution offering,… and by His hand, the Lords pleasure will be accomplished.

He will see it out of His anguish,… My righteous Servant will justify many, and He will carry their iniquities.

Therefore, I will give Him the many as a portion… because He submitted Himself to death…"(Isa 53:9-12 HCSB)

THE PASSION OF THE MESSIAH

"But He was pierced because of our transgressions, crushed because of our iniquities; punishment for our peace was on Him, and we are healed by His wounds. We all went astray… and the Lord has punished Him for the iniquity of us all."

"He was taken away because of oppression and judgment;… for He was cut off from the land of the living; He was struck because of My peoples rebellion."

(Isa 53:5-6, 8 HCSB)

JESUS: The Cross

Heb 12:2 GNBDK "Let us keep our eyes fixed on Jesus, on whom our faith depends from beginning to end. He did not give up because of the cross! On the contrary …" (He said) "…But that is why I came to this hour." (Jn 12: 27 HCSB)

"But no one in heaven or earth or under the earth was able to open the scroll"

"One of the (4) elders said to me, 'do not weep, the lion of the tribe of Judah, the root of David has triumphed, enabling Him to open the scroll'"

"…a lamb that seemed to have been slain"

"He came and received the scroll…" (Rev 5: 3, 5, 6, 7)

"…the message of the cross is foolishness to those who are perishing, but it is God's power to us who are being saved." (1 Cor 1: 18 HCSB)

Life: a ransom

"For even the son of man did not come to be served, but to serve; and to give His life- a ransom for many." (MK 10:45 HCSB)

Jesus predicts his death and resurrection. Saying to his Disciples:

"The son of man must suffer greatly and be rejected… be killed and on the third day be raised."(LK 9:22 Lect)

HIS LAST WEEK

Jesus said: "You know that the Passover takes place after two days and the Son of Man will be handed over to be crucified."(Matt 26:2)

Judgement, Salvation

"Now the ruler of this world will be cast out"(Jn 12:31 HCSB)

"...If I am lifted up from the earth, I will draw all people to Myself."

(Jn 12:32 HCSB)

"Get Behind Me, Satan!"

Peter has just debunked the popular notion of the Jews concerning who Jesus was and Jesus had in turn invested him with the leadership of his church then he proceeded to deepen the disciples, knowledge and expectation concerning the Messiah by predicting His (the Messiah's) imminent passion and death. "Peter took him aside... 'oh no, Lord! This will never happen to you!'"

To that Jesus retorted,

"get behind Me, Satan! You are an offense to Me because you're not thinking about God's concerns, but man's."(Matt 16:22, 23 HCSB)

"He ... bore our sins in his body ... so that ... we might live for righteousness"

(1 Pt 2:24 HCSB)

"Blessed to the peacemakers;

they shall be called sons of God"(Matt5:9)

CHRISTFOR ALL (Eph 2:13, 17Lect) "... you who were once far off have become near by the blood of Christ."

"...He who made both one and broke down the dividing wall of enmity ...abolishing the law with its commandments and legal claims, that He might create In Himself one new person in place of the two, thus establishing peace, and might reconcile both with God ,... through the cross..."

REDEMPTION TROUGH THE CROSS OF JESUS

"...know that you were redeemed from your empty way of life inherited from the fathers... with the precious blood of Christ,..."
(1 Pt 1: 18-19)

Trials &Troubles

"...though now for a short time you have had to struggle in various trials so that the genuineness of your faith - more valuable than gold ... may result in praise, glory, and honour at the revelation of Jesus Christ."

(1 Pt 1: 6-7 HCSB)

Fear of persecution

"But even if you should suffer for righteousness, you are blessed. Do not fear what they fear or be disturbed" (1 Pt3:14 HCSB)

Endure suffering, discipline

"For the Lord disciplines the one He loves ...

Endure suffering as discipline: God is dealing with you as sons...

No discipline seemed enjoyable at the time, but painful. Later on, however, it yields the fruit of peace and righteousness to those who have been trained by it."

(Heb 12: 6-7, 11 HCSB)

Dying to Flourish - I

"Jesus answered them,...

'I am telling you the truth: a grain of wheat remains no more than a single grain unless it is dropped into the ground and dies. If it does die, then it produces many grains.'"(Jn 12: 23 – 24 GNBDK)

PRAISE THE LORD OUR COMFORTER

"I will always thank the Lord;
I will never stop praising him.
I will praise him for what he has done;
May all who are oppressed listen and be glad!
Proclaim with me the Lord's greatness;
Let us praise his name together!
The oppressed look to him and are glad;
they will never be disappointed.
The helpless call to him, and he answers;
He saves them from all their troubles.

Find out for yourself how good the Lord is.
Happy are those who find safety with Him.
Honor the Lord, all his People;
those who obey Him have all they need.
Even lions go hungry for lack of food,
but those who obey the Lord lack nothing good.
The righteous call to the Lord and He listens;
He rescues them from all their troubles.
The Lord is near to those who are discouraged;
He saves those who have lost all hope.
Good people suffer many troubles,
but the Lord saves them from them all;
evil will kill the wicked;
those who hate the righteous will be punished."
(Ps 34: 1 -3, 5-6, 8-10, 17-19,21 GNBDK)

ADDITIONAL RESOURCES

Suffering

Acts 9: 16 "… how much he (Saul) must suffer for My name!"

Purification

Gold is purified by fire, faith through suffering:
"Therefore, we ourselves boast… about your endurance and faith in all the persecutions and afflictions you endure."
"… that you will be counted worthy of God's kingdom, for which you also are suffering."
(2 Thes 1: 4, 5)

Tests & Trials

- 1 Pt 4: 12 "… don't be surprised when the fiery ordeal comes among you to test you…"
- 1 Kgs 19: 4 "… Elijah prayed for death, saying: 'This is enough, O Lord take my life, for I am no better than my fathers.'"
- Js 1: 3, 4 Be joyful in trials.

"Knowing that the testing of your faith produces endurance…
… so that you may be mature and complete, lacking nothing."

- Js 1: 12, 14 "A man who endures trials is blessed… he will receive the crown of life that God has promised to those who love Him."

"Each person is tempted when… drawn away and enticed by his own evil desires."

- Heb 2: 10-11 According to St Paul, the taking of flesh by the One from God (I call this abasement) and His subsequent bitter passion even unto death by crucifixion (St Paul calls this "suffering") qualified Jesus – enhanced his eligibility – to mediate between humanity (His "brothers") and God (as

God's high priest (a dominant figure in Jewish worship). By his death, he destroys the one who holds the "power of death" (Heb 2:15)

Take your cross, follow Jesus.

"Whoever wants to be My disciple must take up his cross everyday and follow Me." (Mk 8:34; Lk 9:23; Matt 16:24)

Mercy overwhelms Justice

"For I will re-establish My covenant with you,…
That you may remember and be ashamed,
and never again open your mouth because of your disgrace,
when I pardon you for all you have done – oracle of the Lord."
(Ezk 16: 62, 63 NABRE)

Obey!

- "No one has greater love than this, that someone would lay down his life for his friends.

You are My friends if you do what I command you." (Jn 15: 13-14 HCSB)
  - A grain that dies (sowing of martyrdom)

"I assure you: …whoever loves his life will lose it and the one who hates his life in this world will keep it for eternal life." (Jn 12: 24, 25 HCSB)
  - "But now I am going away to Him who sent Me, and not one of you asks Me, 'Where are You going?'" (Jn 16: 5 HCSB)

Prophecy concerning Christ?

"Let my faith not put to shame those who trust In You, Lord, Lord of hosts"

"Let them not be dismayed on my account those who seek You, God of Israel.

For it is for your sake that I am taunted and covered in confusion…"

"because zeal for your house is consuming me, and the taunts of those who hate you fall upon my head."

"They gave me bitterness to eat; when I was thirsty, they gave Me vinegar to drink." (Ps 69: 6)

Presbyters, overseers, pastors – watch over yourselves and the flock

At Miletus, Paul spoke to the presbyters of the Church of Ephesus:

"Keep watch over yourselves and over the whole flock of which the Holy Spirit has appointed you overseers, in which you tend the Church of God that He acquired with His own blood."

"I have never wanted anyone's silver or gold or clothing… In every way I might have shown you that by hard work of that sort, we must help the weak, and keep in mind the words of the Lord Jesus who Himself said,

'It is more blessed to give than to receive.'" (Acts 20: 28, 33-35 NABRE)

"… I am going to the Father, because the Father is greater than I."

"… because the **ruler of the world** is coming.

He has no power over me." (Jn 14: 28, 30)

Jesus predicts His passion.

Jesus responded to His disciples:

"Look: An hour is coming, and has come, when each of you will be scattered to his own home, and you will leave Me alone. Yet I am not alone, because the Father is with Me."(Jn 16: 32 HCSB)

She has done what she could; she has anointed My body in advance for burial." (Mk 14: 8 HCSB)

Jesus passion – ineluctable

"Now My soul is troubled. What should I say – Father save Me from this hour? But that is why I came to this hour." (Jn 12: 27 HCSB)

Enemies of the cross

"… many live as enemies of the cross of Christ."

"Their end is destruction; their god is their stomach; their glory is in their shame.

They are focused on earthly things." (Phil 3: 18, 19 HCSB)

The Church Triumphant

"… I had a vision of a great multitude, which no one could count,

from every nation, race, people and tongue.

… wearing white robes and holding palm branches"

"These are the ones who have survived the time of great distress; they have washed their robes in the Blood of the Lamb." (Rev 7: 9, 14 NABRE)

Power of God

"… the cross is foolishness to those who are perishing, but to us… being saved… power of God." (1 Cor 1: 18)

Martyrdom, crucifixion: The Stone That the Builders Rejected…

Jesus answered them (the chief priests and the elders of the people),

"Listen to another parable: … a landowner planted a vineyard, put a fence around it, dug a winepress in it,… He leased it to tenant farmers… when the grapes harvest drew near, he sent his slaves… to collect his fruit. But the farmers took his slaves, beat one, killed another and stoned a third. Again he sent other slaves,… and they did the same to them.

Finally, he sent his son to them, 'They will respect my son', he said. But … they seized him, … and killed him. Jesus said… 'The stone that the builders rejected has become the cornerstone... Therefore, I tell you, the kingdom of God will be taken away from you and given to a nation producing its fruit. Whoever falls on this stone will be broken to pieces; but on whoever it falls, it will grind him to powder.'" (Matt 21: 23, 24; 33-37; 39, 42-44 HCSB)

(Compare this text with Isa 5: 1-7)

Jesus – endured the cross, despised the shame

"... Jesus, the source and perfecter of our faith, who for the joy that lay before Him, endured a cross and despised the shame and has sat down at the right hand of God's throne."

(Heb 12: 2 HCSB)

God's unfathomable, transcendental purposes:

"After those 62 weeks the Messiah will be cut off and will have nothing. The people of the coming prince will destroy the city and the sanctuary ... until the end there will be war; desolation are decreed." (Dan 9: 26 HCSB)

Jesus' sign – Jonah!

"... 'He drives out demons by Beelzebul,' ...

And others, as a test, were demanding of Him a sign from heaven."

"He began saying: '... but no sign will be given to it except the sign of Jonah...'"

(Lk 11: 15-16; 29) HCSB

Redemption through the blood

"We have redemption in Him (Jesus Christ) through His blood, the forgiveness of our trespasses, according to the richness of His (God's) grace."

(Eph 1: 7 HCSB)

Tested, yet without sin

"... we have a great high priest...

– Jesus the Son of God –

For we do not have a high priest who is unable to sympathize with our weaknesses but One who has been tested in every way as we are, yet without sin." (Heb 4: 14, 15 HCSB)

Meditation, Exhortation and Reflection.

THE CROSS OF JESUS – I

Jesus suffered rejection as prophesized: a near revolt (LK 4:29), attempted mob assault in his home town of Nazareth, where he was brought up (MK 6: 3-4) and crucifixion at the instance of His own people, by flesh and blood. Jesus said, "for I tell you, what is written must be fulfilled in Me: and he was counted among the outlaws. Yes, what is written about Me is coming to its fulfilment."

(LK 22:37 HCSB)

"Summoning the crowd along with His disciples, He said to them, 'if anyone wants to be My follower, he must deny himself, take up his cross and follow Me.'"

(MK 8: 34 HCSB) (see also Lk 14: 27)

THE CROSS OF JESUS – II

A wooden cross was what the Romans used to execute by crucifixion those condemned…… two other convicted men were executed alongside Jesus on Golgotha hill on that Friday preceding the feast of Passover.

In the typology of Abraham offering Isaac, his son in sacrifice to God, the lamb that redeemed Isaac was offered by God Himself. Similarly, God provided His only begotten Son as the spotless lamb for our redemption, though the people played their part:

"They took the 30 pieces of silver, the price of Him whose price was set by the Israelites." (Matt 27: 9 HCSB)

Ladder to heaven

"Apart from the cross there is no other ladder by which we may get to heaven" "we cannot obtain grace unless we suffer affliction"

"…to attain a deep participation in the divine nature, the glory of the sons of God and perfect happiness of souls"– St Rose of Lima
Meditation, Exhortation and Reflection.

When my will crosses God's will

"What is the 'way of the cross' for you and me? It means that when my will crosses with God's will, then His must be done."– Don Schwager

Societal cross: Mass suffering, slavery and blood shedding.

Jesus died because of the unrighteousness of His people. The cross thenceforth epitomizes man's inhumanity to man. The cross is the effigy of sin. Too manyhowever, thinkthat the cross is for the sinner. But in Jesus cross we know better.

"He went about doing good." In the same manner of thinking, the slave, the minority, the poor, the infirm don't deserve our compassion! "They are the architects of their own misfortune!" We rarely consider how narrowly, we ourselves missed being drawn into the misfortune of such state. What is more, in a wicked world, there is scarcely anything anybody can do to ensure that his offspring is spared of such vicissitude!

In Egypt, with fewer materials slaves were made to produce more bricks (Exo 5:7:8) the situation in Hitler's Gestapo camps is better imagined than recounted. What is certain is that there is always sin before the cross as fire exists before a smoke. If it is not the sin of the victim, or the people he represents, it will be the sin of his oppressors, as in the case of kidnappers and the slave sellers and buyers. Holy God reluctantly abandons a recalcitrant people to their knavery so they can bear the brunt of their own wickedness and repent and return to Him. But the carrier of the cross may just be merely the sacrificial lamb.

The suffering of the many is symptomatic of a people's intractableness, and the immediate symbol of suffering - the flood, the several plagues of Egypt, Elijah type drought and other natural disasters, leprosy, cancer, HIV – aids, covid-19, etc. – are recompense for man's obstinacy in persisting in ungodliness. If accepted for what they are - a call to repentance - the respective communities would again savour peace. If ignored, the misfortunes continue in circles.

God relents and comes to the help of the victims of yesteryears. They are emancipated by His grace. God knows that the direct victims are not necessarily the worst sinners:

> "No I tell you, but unless you repent, you will all perish as well.
> Or those 18 that the towers of Siloam fell on and killed –
> do you think they were more sinful than all the people
> who lived in Jerusalem? NO, I tell you, but unless you repent,
> you will all perish as well."(LK 13: 3-5 HCSB)

Consider also those bitten by the seraph serpents at the time of Moses, they were not necessarily the greatest of sinners

Meditation, Exhortation and Reflection.

Man should follow the example of God and be gracious to those victims and bring succour to them. All the resources of the earth God gives to man. They are more than sufficient for the earth's needs save for the greed and insensitivity of many.

The cross of the disciples – I

Jesus foretold His disciples:

"…you will have suffering in this world. Be courageous! I have conquered the world." (Jn 16:33 HCSB)

The cross of the disciples – II

Jesus had forewarned (the crowd and his disciples): "if anyone wants to be my follower, he must deny himself, take up the cross and follow Me" (MK 8:34)

Persecution of the servants of God had been from before Christ.

After the death of Jehoiada, the priest, Judah's king Joash and the people forsook the Lord. "And began to serve the sacred poles and their idols" although prophets were sent to them to convert them to the Lord the people heed not their warnings. By the spirit of God Zechariah, Jehoiada's son, delivered the word of God. He was stoned to death at the court of the temple. (2 Chr 24:17-25)

You may wish to read also: 1 Pt 4:12-14, 19.

Dying to oneself to flourish - II

St Peter Claver[1] ministered physically and spiritually to slaves when they arrived in Cartagena, Columbia. He reportedly converted some 300,000 of them. He gave this advice:

"To do the will of God, man must despise his own; the more he dies to himself, the more he will live to God."

Your cross

"Then Jesus said to His disciples,

'If anyone wants to come with Me, he must deny himself, take up his cross and follow Me. For whoever wants to save his life will lose it…'" (Matt 16: 24-28)

1: Https. Catholic Saints, Saint Peter Claver

Meditation, Exhortation and Reflection.

Sometimes your cross is alluded to in terms of tests, troubles and trials - all implying a nerve-wracking experience. You just have to pass through it to be the person you are destined to be. When in the bowel of the storm you may not understand: "why me?" Just as many of us may never get ourselves to understand why Jesus had to pass through the enormity of pain and shame of the cross – our odious sins notwithstanding.

They are issues of deep spiritual dimension. But when it is all over, you will begin to understand; you rejoice and are triumphant, that you went through it.

The Cross of Calvary

Our human perception and thinking ordinarily is that the cross is incongruous with God, indeed a sacrilege to think of – a profanation of the omnipotent majesty of God.

No one dare point an accusing finger at a king in the majestic splendour of his court unless he is first pulled down from power and the sceptre taken off him.

But the scripture tells us that in the very beginning was the WORD and the WORD was with GOD and the WORD was GOD...

"the word became flesh..." (incarnated of the Virgin Mary)

(Jn 1: 1, 3, 10, 14 HCSB)

Thus, there must exist some exigencies which have made the crucifixion ineluctable:

"My Father! If it is possible, let this cup pass from Me. Yet not as I will, but as You will." (Matt 26: 39 HCSB)

St Mark, the earliest of the gospels, puts it this way:

"... Abba Father! All things are possible for You. Take this cup away from Me. Nevertheless, not what I will, but what You will." (Mk 14: 36 HCSB)

St Rose of Lima (1586-1617):

"Apart from the cross, there is no other ladder by which we may get to heaven."

St Francis of Assisi:

"By Your Holy Cross You have redeemed the world."

The Cross: a testimony

The most intriguing thing about Jesus is the cross – that is His cross at Calvary – the wooden cross upon which he was crucified.

Meditation, Exhortation and Reflection.

That a part of God – His Word – came down to earth and took on flesh to become one like us sounds outrageous. Yet, it is easier to explain and to believe that than to believe his execution – His death – irreverent and harrowing death on the cross!

Such odious humiliation, pain and disgrace and for what gain? Yes, redemption of fallen man!

Simon Peter, the Rock was of such reasoning. He remonstrated saying, "God forbid! No such thing shall ever happen to you."

(Mk 8: 31-32; Matt 16: 21-22)

But Jesus broke Himself away from Peter and tongue-lashed him, for "not thinking as God does." (Matt 16: 23)

Even with Isaiah's prophecies concerning the suffering Messiah, humanity still cannot reconcile itself with an omnipotent Deity, who calmly surrenders Himself to insults and to endure brutality – even up to the point of death! This is rare!!

Having witnessed this, which man-of-the-world can believe the later stories of His resurrection and accession into heaven? Perhaps only those who love fairly tales!

But, indeed it was the same Jesus, the miracle worker. He was killed! He was raised up! So many overwhelming evidences to that effect exist. But for this author, the most significant of all is His name, the name, "Jesus"! With that, a believer can bring down thrones and principalities, rouse signs and wonders to the glory of God.

A personal testimony

It is a name-above-all-names – in heaven, on earth and under the earth. (Phil 2: 8-11) This is not a prophetic or futuristic statement. Oh no, it is happening! All the miracles recorded for Jesus' disciples in the New Testament attested to the truth of that saying. But it is still happening to this day, as a cursory inquiry into the lives of the saints will confirm. For me, it is the only raison d'être for praying. If prayers are not answered, why waste your time and pleasure praying? Of course, prayers ... to Him or in the name of Jesus are answered. Jesus is, indeed, the Son of God.

Reflection:

Without sin, there would be no cross of Calvary: Jesus would not need to be incarnate and suffer crucifixion. Our sins – the sins of the world caused it. Yes, the wages of sin is death.

Meditation, Exhortation and Reflection.

"Yet it was our pain that he bore,
Our sufferings he endured,
We thought of Him as stricken,
Struck down by God and afflicted."
"But He was pierced for our sins,
crushed for our iniquity.
He bore the punishment that makes us whole,
by His wounds we were healed."
"We had all gone astray like sheep,
all following our own way;
but the Lord laid upon Him
the guilt of us all." (Isa 53: 4-6 NABRE)
(Compare Ps 2; 9, 16-19, 28, 32)
The exaltation of the cross
▪ Jesus replied to them,

"The hour has come for the Son of Man to be glorified. I assure you: Unless a grain of wheat falls to the ground and dies, it remains by itself. But if it dies it produces a large crop." (Jn 12: 23-24 HCSB)

- "Father, glorify Your name! Then a voice came ..."
- "Now, Father, glorify Me ..."
- "... 'Father, the hour has come. Glorify your Son ...'"

(Jn 12: 28; 17:5, 1) HCSB.

Surpassing love

The cross, for many, reminds us of divine mercy – the endless mercy of God and His treasury of inexhaustible compassion. He made a covenant, not to destroy the world again.

It is not strange therefore, that conservative Christians have exalted the cross almost to an instrument in aid of worship as it reminds the worshipper of his/her duty to quit sin, and humanity's eternal indebtedness to God for unmerited love and mercy.

"For God so loved the world that He gave His only Son, so that everyone who believes in Him might not perish but might have eternal life."

(Jn 3: 16 NABRE)

Meditation, Exhortation and Reflection.

Prayer[1]

Holy Father, keep us in Your name,
the name You gave to our Lord Jesus,
that we may be one, just as You and
our Lord are one.
Protect us; guard us in Your name so that
none of us may be lost.

So that the Lord's joy may be completed in us and we ourselves may share in the Lord's joy completely.

Holy Father, keep us from the Evil one and consecrate Your Church in the truth,

Your word is truth.

The Lord Jesus has consecrated Himself to His church;

Bless us then, heavenly Father, that we also may be consecrated in the truth.

Righteous Father, hear our prayer also for those who have come to believe through the witnessing of Your church: may they all be one with the church as You, Father, are in the Son and the Son is in You. May we all be one in You. May we be made completely one.

We make this prayer in accordance with the will, and in the name of our Lord Jesus Christ, amen.

1: Based on Jn 17: 11-19 (Jesus prayer: lifting up His eyes to heaven, Jesus prayed)

Meditation, Exhortation and Reflection.

"Close to the cross"[1]

Close to the cross

O Lord I stand

Asking for grace divine,

Lovingly Jesus take my heart,

Let me claim Thee mine.

Chorus:

Close to the cross, Close to the cross,

Jesus my refuge be;

Close to the cross,

Close to the cross,

Savior who died for me.

Close to the cross

Lest I should stray,

May my heart ever be;

Shield me, O Lord, from sin, I pray,

Let me live for Thee.

Hymn: (an old church elegy):

CHAPTER 12

Temptations, Tests, And Troubles

Blessed are
They who mourn –
For they will be comforted
You when they insult and persecute you
and utter every kind of evil against you
(falsely) because of Me –
Rejoice and be glad for your reward
will be great in heaven. Thus they
persecuted the prophets who were
before you. (Matt 5: 4, 11-12 NABRE)

Are you scared of humiliation?

If you are a Christian, why should you? Jesus, the Master endured crucifixion!

"My child, when you come to serve the Lord prepare yourself for trials."

"Accept whatever happens to you in periods of humiliation, be patient."

"For in fire gold is tested, and the chosen, in the crucible of humiliation."

(Sir 2: 1, 4-5 NABRE)

"…Be on your guard!

…you will be flogged… arrest you… brother will betray brother to death… and you will be hated by everyone because of my name."

Nevertheless, "the good news must first be proclaimed to all nations."

(MK 13: 9, 11-13, 10)

You need self-restraint

"... do not be conformed to the desires of your former ignorance."

"But ... be holy in all your conduct." (1 Pt 1: 14, 15)

Endurance, too!

"You need endurance to do the will of God and receive what He has promised." (Heb 10: 36 NABRE)

Trials are joyful!

"Consider it a great joy, my brothers, whenever you experience various trials, knowing that the testing of your faith produces endurance. But endurance must do its complete work, so that you may be mature and complete..." (Heb 13: 2-4 HCSB).

Be courageous

Jesus says, "I have told you this so that you might have peace in Me. In the world you will have trouble, but take courage, I have conquered the world."

(Jn 16: 33 NABRE)

"For to me life is Christ and death is gain." (Phil 1: 21 NABRE)

Compassionate God: "The God Who Sees"

Hagar was pregnant for Abram and Sarai mistreated her so unbearably that Hagar fled from home into the wilderness. But God was not unaware of her predicament. There, His angel located Hagar, sent her back to her mistress and promised her some goodness.

"So, she called the Lord who spoke to her: ***The God Who Sees***, for she said, 'In this place, have I actually seen the One who sees me?'" (Gen 16: 13 HCSB)

"Get up, go and pick him up and comfort him." (Gen 21: 18 GNBDK)

But Hagar's troubles were not ended yet. After her mistress had her own baby, she this time sent her packing with her son Ishmael. But the mercy of God, once more located her.

"When the water was all gone, she left the child under a bush and sat down about a hundred meters away. She said to herself, 'I can't bear to see my child die.' While she was sitting there, she began to cry. God heard the boy crying, and from heaven the angel of God spoke to Hagar…" (providing succour to her and her son) (Gen 21: 15-17 GNBDK)

Tough times don't last, tough people do!

"A time of affliction brings forgetfulness of past delights; at the end of life, one's deeds are revealed." (Sir 11: 27 GNBDK)

ANTAGONISM

"If the World hates you, just remember that it has hated Me first. If you belong to the world, then the world would love you as its own…"

(Jn 15: 18-19 GNBDK)

I have told you…

Jesus says, "I have told you these things to keep you from stumbling."

(Jn 16: 1 HCSB)

Tests, Trails, and Trouble

Obey, hope and trust in divine deliverance: "…It was not by your sword or bow."(Jos. 24: 12 H

Right and wrong conduct

Peter and John: "Whether it is right in the sight of God for us to obey you rather than God, you be the judges." (Acts 4: 19 LECT)

'LIFE' LOVING versus 'HEAVEN' LOVING.

Jn 12: 25 "The one who loves his life will lose it, and the one who hates his life in this world will keep it for eternal life."

Jn 12: 26 "If anyone serves Me, he must follow Me. Where I am, there My servant also will be."

Sowing Seed

"I assure you: unless a grain of wheat falls to the ground and dies, it remains by itself. But if it dies, it produces a large crop." (Jn 12: 24)

"**Come to Me** all of you
who are weary and burdened,
and I will give you rest.
All of you, take up My yoke
and learn from Me,
because I am gentle and humble in heart,
and you will find rest for yourselves.
For My yoke is easy and My burden is light."
(Matt. 11: 28-30)

Tests and Tribulation

"And I say to you, My friend, don't fear those who kill the body, and after that can do nothing more.

But ...fear Him who has authority to throw people into hell after death…"
(Lk 12: 4-5 HCSB)

Be Hopeful, Your Reward Is Certain:

"Those who sow in tears
will reap with shouts of joy.
Though one goes along weeping,
carrying the bag of seed,
he will surely come back with shouts of joy,
carrying his sheaves." (Ps 126: 5-6)
The Travails of the Apostles (1 Cor 4: 9-13 HCSB)

"For I think, God has displayed us, the Apostle, in the last place, like men condemned to die... a spectacle to the world and to angels and to men.

We are fools for Christ, but you are wise in Christ!

We are weak, but you are strong! You are distinguished, but we are dis-honoured! Up to the present hour we are both hungry and thirsty; we are poorly clothed, roughly treated, homeless; we labour, working with our own hands.

When we are reviled, we bless; when we are persecuted, we endure it; when we are slandered, we respond graciously. Even now, we are like the world's garbage, like the dirt everyone scrapes off their sandals. (1 Cor 4: 9-13 HCSB)

The dead will rise!

"Your dead will live; their bodies will rise: Awake and sing, you who dwell in the dust! For you will be covered with the morning dew and the earth will bring out the departed spirits." (Isa 26: 19)

Martyrdom

"The dead who die in the Lord are blessed...." (Rev 14: 13, 20: 4-6)

Bearing your cross

- Herod vaunts He killed John a man he knew to be pious (Mk 6: 16, 20) no fear of God was in him as are for many men in power:

John's offence "...not lawful for you to have your brother Philip's wife."

(Mk 6: 18)

- "Behold I am sending you like sheep in the midst of wolves; so be shrewd as serpents and simple as doves. But beware of people, for they will hand you over to courts and scourge you in their synagogues... brother will hand over brother to death, and the father his child;..." (Matt 10: 16-17, 21 NABRE)

FLEE!

- "When they persecute you in one town, flee to another."
(Matt 10: 23 NABRE)
"Don't fear those who kill the body
but are not able to kill the soul;
rather, fear Him who is able
to destroy both soul and body in hell." (Matt 10: 28)
"Anyone finding his life will lose it, and anyone losing his life because of Me will find it." (Matt 10: 39) For more read (Matt 10: 29-33)

The thinking of the ungodly

"Let us beset the just one, because … he reproaches us for transgressions… if the just one be the son of God, God will defend him and deliver him from the hand of his foes.

With revilement and torture let us put the just one to the test … let us condemn him to a shameful death…" (Wis 2: 12, 17-20 LECT)

WITHDRAW!

'Discretion', our elders say, 'is better than valour.'

"But the Pharisees went out and took counsel against Jesus to put Him to death. When Jesus realized this, He withdrew from that place."

(Matt 12: 14-15 NABRE)

God, our refuge

"The Lord is a refuge for the oppressed,
a refuge in times of trouble.
For the One who seeks an accounting
for bloodshed remembers them;
He does not forget the cry of the afflicted." (Ps 9: 9, 12)
Jesus predicted the ordeal believers would go through.

"They will ban you from the synagogues. In fact, a time is coming when anyone who kills you will think he is offering service to God." (Jn 16: 2)

"I assure you: You will weep and wail, but the world will rejoice.

You will become sorrowful, but your sorrow will turn to joy." (Jn 16: 20)

Read also Mk 13: 9, 12-13 about these persecutions which are to come on believers before the end time.

The Mystery: 'Lose your life, gain it!'

Jesus says, "The one who loves his life will lose it, and the one who hates his life in this world will keep it for eternal life." (Jn 12: 25)

"I also saw the souls of those who had been executed because they had proclaimed the truth that Jesus revealed and the word of God... They came to life and ruled as kings with Christ for a thousand years."

"This is the first raising of the dead. Happy and greatly blessed are those who are included in this first raising of the dead. The second death has no power over them..." (Rev 20: 4, 5-6 GNBDK)

"... In the seventh month, on the tenth day of the month you are to practise self-denial..." (Lev 16: 29 HCSB)

"Some of the wise will fall so that they may be refined, purified and cleansed until the time of the end." (Dan 11: 29)

Some die because of God's transcendental esoteric purposes –

"After those 62 weeks the Messiah will be cut off." (Dan 9: 26)

"This horn waged war against the holy ones and was prevailing over them until... judgement was given in favour of the holy ones of the Most High, for the time had come and the holy ones took possession of the kingdom."

"Then, kingship, power and greatness of the kingdoms under all of heaven will be given to the people, the holy ones of the Most High."

(Dan 7: 21-22, 27 LECT)

ADDITIONAL RESOURCES

"… by a sudden blow I am taking away from you the delight of your eyes, but do not mourn or weep or shed any tears, groan in silence…"

"That evening my wife died."

"I will now desecrate my sanctuary …"

"Ezekiel shall be a sign for you…" (Ezk 24: 15)

"… you shall not mourn or weep but shall pine away because of your sins and groan one to another" (Ezk 24: 23)

"Endure suffering as discipline: God is dealing with you as sons. For what son is there that a father does not discipline?" (Prov 12: 9)

"Everyone will be purified by fire as a sacrifice is purified by salt" (Mk 9: 42-43, 49, GNBDK)

SUFFERING

"You therefore must endure hardship as a good soldier of Jesus Christ."

(2 Tim 2: 3 NKJV)

Martyrdom

"This saying is trustworthy: for if we have died with Him, We will also live with Him; if we endure, we will also reign with Him; if we deny Him, He will also deny us,…." (2 Tim 3: 11 HCSB)

"In fact, all those who want to live a godly life in Christ Jesus will be persecuted."(2Tim 3: 12 HCSB)

To die for God:

- Latin: "Dulce et decorum est pro patria mori" (English: "sweet and fitting to die for one's country"). Rather, we should say, it is sweet and fitting to die for our Creator. He gives life and He has promised to restore it if anyone loses it for His sake.

The paradox of life

- (a) "He who loves his life will lose it, and the one who hates his life in this world will keep it for eternal life."(Jn 12: 25 HCSB)

- (b) "For whoever desires to save his life will lose it, but whoever loses his life for My sake will find it" (Matt 16: 25 NKJV, compare Mk 8: 35 HCSB)
- "I assure you: unless a grain of wheat falls to the ground and dies, it remains by itself. But if it dies, it produces a large crop." (Jn 12: 24 HCSB)

Condemnation

"Anyone who believes in Him (One and only Begotten Son of God) is not condemned, but anyone who does not believe is already condemned, because he has not believed in the name of the One and only Son of God."

"This, then, is the judgement: the light has come into the world and people loved darkness rather than the light because their deeds were evil."

(Jn 3: 18, 19 HCSB)

On the day of Judgement

"Brood of vipers! How can you speak good things when you are evil? For the mouth speaks from the overflow of the heart.

A good man produces good things from his storeroom of good, and an evil man produces evil things from his storeroom of evil.

I tell you that on the day of judgement people will have to account for every careless word they speak." (Matt 12: 34-36 HCSB)

Motive or intention

"More tortuous than all else is the human heart,
beyond remedy, who can understand it?
I, the Lord, alone probe the mind and test the heart,
to reward everyone according to his ways, according to the
merit of his deeds." (Jer 17: 9-10 Lect)
ACCOUNTABILITY

"For the Son of Man will come with His angels in His Father's glory, then He will recompense everyone according to his conduct." (Matt 16: 27)

"Thus says the Lord: 'This shall not stand, it shall not be!'" (Isa 7: 8 Lect)

"Unless your faith is firm you shall not be firm!"

"The Son of Man... will repay everyone according to his conduct."

(Matt 16: 27 NABRE)

Sinners will go down to the underworld, and all nations that forget God. (Ps 9: 17 Lect)

Judgement Day

"Beware that your hearts do not become drowsy from carousing and drunkenness and the anxieties of daily life, and that day catch you by surprise"

"like a trap. For that day will assault everyone who live in the face of the earth." (Lk 21: 34-35 GNBDK)

See also: Matt 24: 29-31; Mk 13: 24-27; Wis 5: 22; Isa 13: 10; Ezk 32: 7;

Joel 2: 10; 3: 3, 4; 4: 15; Rev 6: 12, 14; 11: 12; Hag 2: 6, 21; Rev 1: 7;

Dan 7: 13-14; Matt 26: 64; Lk 12: 45-46; Mk 13: 33

Matt 24: 21 "For at that time there will be great tribulation, the kind that hasn't taken place from the beginning of the world until now and never will again!"

"**Woe to the wicked** – it will go badly for them,

for what they have done will be done to them." (Isa 3: 10, 11)

Reward of the righteous

"Tell the righteous that it will go well for them, for they will eat the fruit of their labour."

Isa 2: 10-17 The Day of the Lord

"Go into the rocks and hide in the dust... for a day belonging to the Lord of Hosts is coming

against all that is proud and lofty; against all that is lifted up...

against every high tower, against every fortified wall, … and
against every splendid sea vessel. So human pride will be
brought low, and the loftiness of men will be humbled; the Lord
alone will be exalted on that day."
(Isa 2: 22)

UNIVERSALITY: SALVATION IS FOR ALL.

I say to you, many will come from the east and the west, and will
recline with Abraham, Isaac and Jacob at the banquet in the
kingdom of heaven.
(Matt 8: 11)
But the sons of kingdom will be thrown into the outer darkness.
In that place there will be weeping and gnashing of teeth." (Matt 8:
12)

Jesus second coming

You are now in the world. Perchance you did not will it to come
to earth in the place and time you did.

In the same way, whether you like it or not, whether you believe
it or not, you may be raised from the dead. But now, however, you
have a choice to do something or NOTHING about your eternity.

You fool, there are different bodies for … (1 Cor 15: 36, 40)

Endure, persevere!

"My son, do not take the Lord's discipline lightly or faint when
you are reproved by Him, for the Lord disciplines the one He loves
and punishes every son He receives" (acknowledges).

"Endure suffering as discipline: God is dealing with you as sons.

No discipline seems enjoyable at the time, but painful. Later on,
however, it yields the fruit of peace and righteousness to those who
have been trained by it." (Heb 12: 5-6, 7, 11 HCSB)

Sharing in suffering for Jesus

"Share in suffering as a good soldier of Christ Jesus."

"For if we have died with Him,

We will also live with Him;

If we endure, we will also reign with Him…"

(2 Tim 2: 3, 11, 12 HCSB)

"In fact, all those who want to live a godly life in Christ Jesus will be persecuted." (2 Tim 3: 12 HCSB)

Why do some holy fall?

- "Some of the wise will fall so that they may be refined, purified and cleansed until the time of the end." (Dan 11: 29 HCSB)
- God's transcendental eternal purposes.
- "This horn waged war against the holy ones and was prevailing over them until… judgement was given in favour of the holy ones of the Most High, for the time had comes and the holy ones took possession…"

(Dan 7: 21 HCSB)

- Personal accountability

The death of holy infants. (Matt 2: 16-18)

If God had averted Herod's perfidy by shielding all those innocent children from massacre, how could Herod be held accountable for the same crime (which he never committed?)

- Remember, there always will be a time to die!

"For everything there is a season, and a time for every matter under heaven: a time to be born, and a time to die…" (Eccl 3: 1-2 NRSV-CI)

"The Lord is a refuge for the oppressed, a refuge in times of trouble.

Rise up, Lord! Do not let man prevail;

Let the nations be judged in Your presence.

Put terror in them, Lord;

Let the nations know they are only men. Selah." (Ps 9: 9, 19 HCSB)

"The Lord is my strength and my shield;

My heart trusts in Him and I am helped.

Therefore, my heart rejoices

and I praise Him with my song.
The Lord is the strength of His people;
He is a stronghold of salvation for His anointed." (Ps 28: 7-8 HCSB)
"Happy is the one whose help is the God of Jacob,
Whose hope is in the Lord his God." (Ps 146: 5 HCSB)
"**I can do all things** in Him
who strengthens me." (Phil 4: 13 Lect)
The Lamb that seemed to have been slain.
"WHO is worthy to open the scroll and break its seals?"
"But no one in heaven or on earth or under the earth was able to open the scroll..."
"Do not weep. The Lion of the tribe of Judah, the Root of David has triumphed, enabling Him to open the scroll with its seven seals.'"
(Isa 11: 1, 10)
"Then I saw... a lamb that seemed to have been slain. He came and received the scroll."
"'They (worshipped before the throne of God) singing a new hymn:
'Worthy are You to receive the scroll and to break open its seals, for You were slain and with Your blood You purchased for God those from every tribe and tongue, people and nations.'" (Rev 5: 2-3, 5-6, 9 NABRE)
Endure!
"You need endurance to do the will of God and receive what He has promised." (Heb 10: 36 NABRE)

Sent out like sheep among wolves

Thus says the Lord:
"I have come to bring not peace but the sword." (Matt 10: 34 Lect)

"Look, I'm sending you out like sheep among wolves. Therefore be as shrewd as serpents and as harmless as doves."

"Anyone finding his life will lose it,
and anyone losing his life because of Me will find it."

"But the one who endures to the end will be delivered."
(Matt 10: 16, 39, 22 HCSB)
Tests and trials
Raphael (one of the seven angels... of the Lord):
"I will tell you the whole truth
I will conceal nothing at all from you,
... I was sent to put you to the test."
(Tob 12: 11, 14 Lect)

"When you act according to what you feel like doing, rather than what you know and understand God says you should do... We encounter the ruthless reality of the difference between happiness and pleasure."
– R.C. Sproul "knowing scripture" P. 29
Exhortation, meditation and reflection

In the inhumanity of man to man, God is the solace.

In the monstrous inhumanity of society, divine love comes in trickles with the visage of Peter Clavier, Mother Theresa, etc.

Cartagena Columbia 30th May 1627:[1] "...numerous blacks... disembarked from a large ship. ...we hurried toward them. We had to force our way through the crowd until we reached the sick. Large numbers of the sick were lying on the wet ground or rather in puddles of mud. ...they were naked, without any clothing to protect them. We laid aside our cloaks... to build a platform... covered a space to which we at last we transferred the sick (for care)."

Job: There is God; He is awesome

The book of Job is one of the wisdom books of the Bible. Job suffered devastating losses of property, lives and even his personal health for reasons obscure to him and not of his own making. Friends and family deserted him, foes mocked him. Yet in all these, his faith in God was not rocked.

Honour the Lord, your God!

Obedience to God delivers obeisance to man. Never lose your guard; defile not yourself by ignoring self-control.

Cover up your soft belly with self-restraint. Obey the Lord; it confers wisdom, honour and long life; even goodness and contentment. So, why choose to be foolish and be a laughing stock, when the 'Ten Commandments' are all you need to be a sage?

"The Lord says, 'I will teach you the way you should go, I will instruct you and advise you, don't be stupid like a horse or a mule which must be controlled with a bit and bridle to make it submit.'" (Ps 32: 8-9 GNBDK)

Death is a debt; its sting is reserved for all!

There is a Yoruba saying, "Death is a debt." Nobody is spared from it. Say it loud to tyrants and demagogues: no one is immune from it. The joy of it – it comes only but once! This popular Nigerian song captures it all:

"Today, today – tomorrow no more!

if I die today, I shall die no more!"

1: Letter by St. Peter Clavier 1581-1654

Https://catholicsaints.info/saint-peter-claver/

Exhortation, meditation and reflection

That we may not fail.

In the parable of the Sower of the word (Matt 13: 18-23), the Lord bares to us the cost of discipleship. It is not going to be a fun ride all through. We need continual self-examination and resolute commitment to see us through ("a generous and good heart, and bear fruit through perseverance") in the second and third fields, tribulation following the word (satanic machination and agents of the powers of darkness) and worldly cares, especially the lure of riches respectively, were the undoing to the hearers. You have been warned.

FLEE!!

When someone is so powerful as to have no rival – as the Lord God – He chooses when to fight.

Satan and his fellow rebel angels have been cast out of heaven – not so as to turn earth into a continuation battle field. So quite often children of God have to employ the potent weapon of love, not destructive violence to overcome. Flee, rather than fight. Jesus as an infant was fled to Egypt at Archelaus, the ethnarch's prowling. (Matt 2: 13).

This is food for thought for some religious fanatics whose favourite weapon is violence. They are employing the trade mark weapon of Satan. Is it to help a powerless 'god'? Read (Jn 13: 35)

Consider this: sin!

Only sin can separate us from the love of God: "who can separate us from the love of Christ? Can affliction or anguish or persecution or famine or nakedness or danger or sword?" (Rom. 8: 35)

On concupiscence and Christian unity What persecution failed to achieve, will we allow money to accomplish – disunity and disharmony among Christians?

Satan, the arch-enemy of our salvation had tried falsehood, panic and pain – crucifixion, beheading, feeding alive to beasts, roasting alive, etc – yet the church has not been silenced neither the word of life restrained.

Today, many church groups are so opulent that it has threatened the very foundation of our faith – the word of truth. As splinter groups become prosperous, other break always occur not to strengthen evangelism but for the mundane gain of their proprietors. The word is the victim – that is the truth. The gospel message becomes tendentious – sewn to attract the pockets of the listeners, not to pinch their conscience. Fear becomes a handy tool and falsehood an accomplice.

Exhortation, meditation and reflection

What should be the appropriate attitude of a disciple: look elsewhere, or be unperturbed? Jesus, was concerned, so were the fathers of the faith – the apostles.

We should be able to agree on what we believe in, what the faith is all about.

So, where do we go from here? Our enemies mock at us. Shall we allow materialism and concupiscence to destroy the faith where torment and torture have failed?

"… Nevertheless, when the son of man comes,

will He find that faith on earth?" (Lk 18: 8)

For more, see chapter 19 Let Them Be One.

Troubles

Remember the priest, Zechariah, of the Abijah's division, husband of Elizabeth later mother of John the Baptists? "Both were righteous in God's sight, living without blame according to all the commands and requirements of the Lord. But they had no children, because Elizabeth could not conceive, and both of them were far advanced in years" (Lk 1: 6-7)

Does that remind you of Abram and Sarai? For both couples, they had the vicissitude of being childless till old age despite not being sinful. Unlike for Job, where the accuser orchestrated that righteous man's travails, no such clue was available to explain off these couples' tribulation. What do these teach you?

Mary, the mother of Jesus Christ

Had her only child contemptuously treated agonized/traumatized and publicly executed by crucifixion (alongside two evil doers).

Legend has it that Joseph, her husband, had died even before that time. No wonder many call her, 'Mother of Sorrows'.

Till today, the Devil is still after her offspring – those who keep God's commands… (Rev 12:17).

How do we explain her travails?

Certainly, God is not irrational neither does He take delight in bringing sorrows to men.

Surely, there are mysteries yet to be understood by man. One is the eternal plan of God re. our salvation, which explains the woes of the New Eve and the New Adam (Jesus Christ).

Exhortation, meditation and reflection

Still, many of us are not comfortable that such righteous ones should suffer, though with gratitude to God, for the resulting benefit to mankind. We know, by faith that the recompense is enormous. (Rev 20: 4-6)

The feeding of the 5,000

A huge crowd converged on Jesus. "He asked Philip, 'Where will we buy bread so these people can eat?' He asked this to test him, for He Himself, knew what He was going to do."(Jn 6: 5, 6) 'Test' above, impliedly connotes teasing, to teach him.

Many disciples face real trouble in consequence of their faith.

The Crucifixion

Men's heart is pleased when the righteous are vindicated and exalted. Such were the stories of the four Jewish exiles in Babylon – Daniel, Meshrach, Shedrack and Abednego. Three went through a blazing fire and came out unscorched.

Daniel was fed to lions, yet, he came out without harm. But with Jesus, no such comfort comes. He went about doing good, yet within 24 hours He was arrested, maliciously tried, sentenced, and crucified!

Think Job! (Job 42: 2-3, 12, 16) Job seems to prefigure the suffering and recompense of Jesus, the Christ.

"Happy are they who remain faithful under
trials because when they succeed in
passing such a test, they will receive
as their reward the life which God has

438

promised to those who love Him." (Js 1: 12)

"For you know that when your faith succeeds in facing such trials, the result is the ability to endure." (Js 1: 3)

"Test of faith results in praise, glory and honour at Jesus revelation." (1 Pt 1: 7)

Salvation: The old and the new approach

"The law and the prophet lasted until John; but from then on the kingdom of God is proclaimed, and everyone who enters does so with violence." (persecution/martyrdom) (Lk 16: 16)

Exhortation, meditation and reflection

Going back to Egypt?

"Let's appoint a leader and go-back-to-Egypt." (Num 14: 4)

Guard your faith as preciously as life. Set time to think to count your blessings. This enormously, orderly and wondrous life could not have come about out of nothing or by itself. So, when you undergo some trouble and tribulation – remember to bolster your spirit through your faith. See how much it costs the Messiah and the martyrs!

"Whoever loves discipline loves knowledge, but one who hates correction is stupid." (Prov 12: 1)

Several times our predecessors in faith, the Israelites backslid under severe stress. In spite of the pillar of cloud and fire that guide them by day and by night, forgetting the marvellous deeds of the Lord in Egypt including crossing the Red Sea by foot! They caved in, resorting into such utterances of despair as above and even idolatry, this is a sin of rebellion or defiance. It worsens their predicament by provoking the Lord's wrath on themselves.

We ought to learn from them and always remember to pray – praises and supplications.

Moses, their leader interceded propitiously several times for the people – we are of the Lord – the God that answers prayers.

Suffering and struggling

▪ "In struggling against sin, you have not yet resisted to the point of shedding your blood.

Endure suffering as discipline: God is dealing with you as sons. For what son is there that a father does not discipline?" (Heb 12: 4, 7)

- "Don't consider yourself to be wise; fear the Lord and turn away from evil." (Prov 3: 7)
- "…rejoice in our afflictions, because… affliction produces endurance, endurance produces proven character, and proven character produces hope (Rom 5:3, 45 HCSB)

Kings die; presidents and emperors no less. They are dethroned and sometimes together with their entire household are annihilated.

Folks suffer such vicissitudes also in the hands of their oppressors. The difference, the fear that no condition is permanent consumes the mighty more.

"Cowards die many times before their death but the valiant never taste of death but once." – William Shakespeare.

Exhortation, meditation and reflection

Noble Cause.

Is it not better to die for a noble cause than to persevere in inhuman existence under an obnoxious and godless regime?

The renegade have an ignoble fate awaiting them here and in the life hereafter. Because it is in the interest of justice that the rash and the ruthless be punished.

The Death of the Holy Infants (Matt 2:16-18)

If Herod's perfidy was averted by God shielding all those children from massacre how could Herod have been convicted and held accountable (for a crime he never committed?) or how could it be understood that Rachael's lamentations (Jer. 31: 15) over her children taken into exile (Assyrian invasion of Judea: BC 722- 721) is a prefigurement of Herod's atrocity?

Happy are they who remain faithful under trials because when they succeed in passing such a test, they will receive as their reward the life which God has promised to those who love Him. (Js 1:12)

Judgement: Day of judgement (Matt 11: 22)
- "We shall all have to appear before the judgement seat of God" (Rom 14: 10)
- After death (Heb 9: 27) and at the end of the world (Matt 25: 31)
- Each person will be "judged according to his conduct." (Rev 20: 13)
- Those who believe in Jesus will be saved (Acts 16: 30-31) (Mk 16: 16)
- Those in sin will earn eternal damnation (2 Thes 1: 9; Matt 22: 13) (Rev 21: 8) Jesus is the Judge (Jn 5: 22)

The New Jerusalem is going to be here – on earth!
Isa 2: 2-4 "In the LAST DAYS the mountain of the Lord's house will be established at the top of the mountains"
- The place of the gathering of armies for the final battle before the end of the world Armageddon
- The battle involving these armies (Rev 16: 16) Exhortation, meditation and reflection
- The final battle at the end of the world between forces of good and evil: God against the kings of earth
- A catastrophic and extremely destructive conflict (like World War ll)

Isa 2: 9 "So humanity is brought low and man is humbled.
: 11 Human pride will be humbled and the loftiness of men will be brought low, the Lord alone will be exalted on that day."

Anxieties are unnecessary burden.

Don't worry!
"... You are worth more than many sparrows." (Matt 10: 28-31 HCSB)
See also Matt 6: 25-34; Lk 12: 4-7

In his message on a cognate subject, Bishop Ayo-Maria Atoyebi (op)[1] puts it this way:

"Worry not concerning

- The past – because the Lord will take care (of it) by His mercy;
- Tomorrow – leave to His grace;
- To-day – leave to His providence."
- The Psalmist says it all:

"In God, whose word I praise,
in God I trust; I will not fear.
What can man do to me?"
"... this I know God is for me."
(Ps 56: 4, 9 HCSB)

HEAVEN

Poverty, infirmity, persecution are some of the flights to take one into heaven – Abraham's bosom.

"Apart from the cross there is no other ladder by which we may get to heaven." – St Rose of Lima 1586-1617.

1: Rt. Rev. Msgr. Ayo-Maria Atoyebi (op), Bishop of Ilorin diocese in a retreat at Ibadan (Nigeria) C.2007

Exhortation, meditation and reflection

Carry your cross; no cross, no crown!

"It's not an easy road[2]
We're travelling to heaven
For many are the thorns on the way;
It's not an easy road,
But the Saviour is with us,
His presence gives us joy every day"
Chorus: "No, no it's not an easy road (2ice)
But Jesus walks beside me and
brightens the journey,

and lifts my heavy burden this day."
2: (A Catholic hymn)

A little bit of dissembling doesn't matter?

Eleazar, 90: A model or a stumbling block?

"Those in charge... took the man aside, because of their long acquaintance with him, and privately urged him to bring his own provision that he could legitimately eat, and only to pretend to eat the sacrificial meat prescribed by the king.

'At our age it would be unbecoming to make such a pretence; many of the young would think the 90 year old Eleazar had gone over to an alien religion.'

'If I dissemble to gain a brief moment of life, they would be led astray by me,...'" (2 Macc 6: 18, 21, 24 NABRE)

Imprisonment – great good!

"... his majesty has done me such great good with respect to spiritual profit that I trust that among all the great benefits he has heaped so abundantly upon me I count my imprisonment the very greatest."

– St Thomas More (Letter from prison to his daughter, Margaret.)

TRUE HAPPINESS

"Happiness is to rejoice in You
and for You
and because of You.
This is true happiness
and there is no other."

– St Augustine of Hippo, op cit

Exhortation, meditation and reflection

Author's comment:

We may not understand for certainty why God permits the shedding of the blood of the innocent in witnessing, but we know for sure that things can hardly be different, since some powers and principalities are bent on exploiting the dread of death and the anguish that goes with pain to coerce, mislead and dissuade the convert.

Another certainty is that there is a more than commensurate reward for those who endure it to the end. As the Lord that raised Jesus from the dead and gave Him a name above all names in heaven, on earth and under the earth (Phil 2: 14?) Is more than able and willing to give appropriate consolation for martyrdom – which He indeed, has promised:

'Anyone who loses his life for My sake or for the sake of the good news – will gain it'.

"The Lord executes acts of righteousness and justice for all the oppressed,"

(Ps 103: 6 HCSB)

"He raises the poor from dust and lifts the needy from the garbage pile."

(Ps 113: 7 HCSB)

"He guards the footsteps of His faithful ones, but..." (1 Sam 2: 1-10)

Don't lose heart

"So then I ask you not to be discouraged over my afflictions on your behalf, for they are your glory." (Eph 3: 13 HCSB)

Self-donation

1.2 St Paul: The Life of Matyrs.

"Through faith women received their dead relatives raised back to life. Others, refusing to accept freedom, died under torture in order to be raised to a better life. Some were mocked and whipped, and others were put in chains and taken off to prison."(Heb 11: 35-36 GNBDK)

"They were stoned, they were sawed in two, they died by the sword, they wandered about... destitute, afflicted, and mistreated." (Heb 11: 37 HCSB)

"In your struggle against sin you have not yet resisted to the point of shedding blood."(Heb 12: 4 NABRE)

Exhortation, meditation and reflection

"Endure your trials as 'discipline', God treats you as sons. For what son is there whom his father does not discipline?" (Heb 12: 7 NABRE)

"The discipline of the Lord, my son, do not spurn; do not disdain His reproof; for whom the Lord loves He reproves; as a father the son he favours."

(Prov 3: 12 NABRE)

Dismissing demonic seductions

When evil thoughts – sinful suggestions – come probing your mind, dismiss them immediately with the powerful weapon – the name of Jesus. A simple ejaculatory prayer like this may be all that is required:

Jesus, have mercy on me,

Virgin Mary, help me.

St. Joseph – help; I want to obey God as you do!

If the sinful insinuation keeps popping up, as if it won't go, demolish it with a refrain like this:

"Get away from me, Evil! (2ice)

I am the servant of Jesus, the sun of righteousness

Why do you come to me?

Get away from me, Evil, in Jesus name!

Keep singing joyfully, knowing who you are, and you will drive away murderous, suicidal, lecherous and other sinful thoughts from invading your peace.

Moses: "please kill me right now…" (Num 11: 14 HCSB)

Elijah: "… I have had enough! Lord, take my life, for I'm no better than my fathers." (1 Kgs 19: 4 HCSB)

Beware of Taberah and Kibroth-Hatavah (the wilderness of sin) (Num 11: 3-34; Exo 16: 11)

Temptations can be severe and frustrating, still persevere!

CHAPTER 13

Faith

Hear the word of the Lord at the healing of the woman suffering from haemorrhage: "Daughter… your faith has made you well.
Go in peace." (Lk8: 48)
And to the synagogue leader
"Don't be afraid. Only believe, …" (Lk 8: 50)
And in the parable of the rich man and Lazarus:
"If they will not listen to Moses and the
prophets, neither will they be persuaded
if someone should rise from the dead." (Lk 16: 31)
FLESH AND BLOOD
"You are not in the flesh.
On the contrary, you are in the spirit…
you are not debtors to the flesh,
to live according to the flesh
for, if you live according to the flesh
you will die,…
but if by the spirit… you will live." (Rom 8: 9, 13)

Kingdom of Heaven

"Behold, the kingdom of God is among you …" (Lk. 17: 20-21)
"Brothers, I tell you this: flesh and blood cannot inherit the kingdom of God, …" (1 Cor 15: 50)
And a man's enemies will be the members of his household (Matt 10: 36)
Only the wise? No, perhaps even never; you must accept the kingdom of God with child-like trust:
"Amen, I say to you, whoever does not accept

the kingdom of God like a child will not enter it." (Lk 18: 17 NABRE)

"Rather, God chose the foolish of the world
to shame the wise, and God chose the weak
of the world to shame the strong, and God
has chosen what is insignificant and
despised … what is viewed as nothing – to
bring to nothing what is … something." (1 Cor 11: 27-28)
Eternal life
Jesus is the life; His blood cleanses us. He is propitiation for our sins. Eternal life is in Him. (1 Jn 3: 5-11; 2 Cor 5: 21; 1 Jn 1: 7; 5: 11-13)

"The kingdom of heaven is at hand." (Matt 10: 7 NABRE)

The mystery

"I give praise to You, Father,
Lord of heaven and earth, for
although You have hidden these things
from the wise and the learned
You have revealed them to the childlike.
Yes, Father, such has been Your gracious will." (Matt 11: 25-26 NABRE)
Justification
"A man is justified by works and not by faith alone;…"
"For just as the body without the spirit is dead,
so also faith without work is dead.
Foolish man! Are you willing to learn
that faith without works is useless?
… show me your faith without works,
and I will show you faith from my works." (Js 2: 24, 26; 20;18)

FAITH

The Lord is my strength and my shield;

my heart trusts in Him, and I am helped.
Therefore, my heart rejoices,
and I praise Him with my song. (Ps 28: 7)
A MUST DO for salvation
Then the jailer escorted Paul and Silas out of the prison and said,
"Sirs, what must I do to be saved?"
"Believe in the Lord Jesus, you will be saved…" (Acts 16: 30-31)
Witnessing:
Peter and John witnessing to Annas, indeed, the Sanhedrin:
"There is salvation IN NO ONE ELSE,
for there is no other name under
heaven given to people and we must
be saved by it." (Acts 4: 12).

Keep eyes fixed on Jesus:

"Keeping our eyes on Jesus,
the source and perfecter of our faith,…" (Heb 12: 2)
"Therefore, since we have a great high priest
… Jesus the son of God –
let us hold fast to the confession.
For we do not have a high priest
who is unable to sympathize
with our weaknesses, but One who has
been tested in every way as we are,
yet without sin." (Heb 4: 14-15)

Kingdom of heaven: Many called, few chosen,

Jesus uses the imagery of the fishing net cast to sea
which caught all kinds of aquatics – some good, some bad!
to explain why not everyone on earth
will enter into the kingdom of heaven. (Matt 13: 47-51)
On faith and the absence of syncretism.

Jesus teaches:

"Can a blind person guide a blind person?

Will not both fall into a pit?"

"A good tree does not bear rotten fruit,

nor does a rotten tree bear good fruit.

For every tree is known by its own fruit..." (Lk 6: 39, 43-44 NABRE).

Please read also Lk 6:45

"How Are the Dead Raised?"

We are the seed of the resurrection and "what you sow does not come to life unless it dies" (1 Cor 15: 36) for more on this theme, read 1 Cor 15: 35-44; and

for deeper insight 1 Cor 15: 45-58.

Jesus, the Lord Himself says,

"Very truly, I tell you,

unless a grain of wheat falls into the earth

and dies, it remains just a single grain;

but if it dies, it bears much fruit." (Jn12: 24 NRSVCE).

Be childlike

"Jesus, however, invited them: 'let the little children come to me, and don't stop them, because the kingdom of God belongs to such as these. I assure you: whoever does not welcome the kingdom of God like a little child will never enter it." (Lk 18: 16-17)

Some would not believe.

"But there are some among you who don't believe. (For Jesus knew from the beginning those who would not believe...)" (Jn 6: 64)

Jesus: on Faith:

Healing the Capernaum centurion's servant, Jesus remarked: "... not even in Israel have I found such faith." (Lk 7: 9 NABRE)

The following put their faith to action and the actions were duly rewarded:

- The Greek Syrophoenician woman: (Mk 7: 24-30) "for saying this … the demon has gone out of your daughter."
- Woman with 12 years haemorrhage
- "Daughter your faith saved …." (Lk8: 43-48) "If I can just touch His robes I will be made well." (Mk 5: 28)
- Healing of the convulsing only child which the disciples could not heal

(Lk 9: 38-43) – His father's persistency helped.

Put your faith into action

Jesus' disciples were overawed by a storm that threatened to capsize their boat, so they woke Him up from the rear … after calming the storm, the Lord admonished them, "where is your faith?" (Lk 8: 22-25).

WHY Doubt?

In our earthly endeavour to enter the kingdom of heaven, doubts would not avail.

Because our creator demands that we exercise prudence and due diligence to find the truth and go by it. That is the kernel of the parable of the foolish virgins (Matt 25: 2-4; 12-13)

"For the Son of Man
has come to save the lost" (Matt 16: 11)
It is not the will of God
that anyone be lost (Matt 18: 14)

Your Faith: Use it or else you lose it!

This much is decanted from the parable of the talents
(Matt 25: 14-30; Lk 19: 12-27)

Don't be a barren fig tree, if your faith produces no fruit then, examine yourself – you probably are! (Mk 11: 12-14)

What faith can do

"Then the disciples approached Jesus privately and said, 'why couldn't we drive it out?'"

"Because of your little faith, He told them. For I assure you: if you have faith the size of a mustard seed, you will tell this mountain, 'move from here to there' and it will move, nothing will be impossible for you." (Matt 17: 19-20)

Being born again – conversion

"At that time the disciples came to Jesus and said,

'who is the greatest in the kingdom of God?'"

Then, Jesus called a child over, placed him in their midst and admonished then saying:

"I assure you … unless you are converted and become like children, you will never enter the Kingdom of Heaven" (talk less of being greater than anyone there). (Matt 18: 1-5, 7).

Similarly, the Lord unveiled to Nicodemus that one must be born again of water and from above, by the spirit to be able to see the kingdom of God

(Jn 3: 3-13).

"Amen, amen, I say to you,

no one can enter the kingdom of God

without being born of water and spirit.

What is born of flesh is flesh and what is

born of spirit is spirit. Do not be amazed

that I told you, 'you must be born from above.'" (Jn3: 5-7 NABRE).

"How can you believe? While accepting

glory from one another, you don't seek

the glory that comes from the only God." (Jn 5: 44)

Seek the Lord while He may be found;

call to Him while He is near.

Let the wicked one abandon his way

and the sinful one his thoughts; let him return to the Lord,

so He may have compassion on him,

and to our God, for He will freely forgive. (Isa 55: 6-7)

"O woman, great is your faith!" (Matt 15:28 NABRE)

Jesus said this to a Canaanite woman, who got what she supplicated for.

Find out how she demonstrated her faith (Matt 15: 22-28)

Unfailing faith"...He will swiftly grant them justice. Nevertheless, when the Son of Man comes will He find **that faith** on earth?" (Lk 18: 8)

How you listen

"Therefore, take care how you listen.

For whoever has, more will be given to him,

and whoever does not have,

even what he thinks he has will be

taken away from him." (Lk 8: 18)

You cannot afford to believe everything people tell you else you will go to hell! Do you realize that?

Take a cue from the scriptures: an old prophet from Bethel deceived the man of God from Judah on the strength that what he told the man of God was a prophetic message. The docile man of God did not suspect foul play; he was thus led to disobey God with disastrous consequences for him.

(1 Kgs 13: 14-20).

JESUS: Saviour of the world

"For while we were still helpless, at the appointed moment, Christ died for the ungodly." (Rom 5: 6)

God's household: the Christian faith

"Built on the foundation of the apostles and prophets, with Christ Jesus Himself as the cornerstone. The whole building ... grows into a holy sanctuary... for God's dwelling in the Spirit." (Eph 2: 20-22 HCSB)

A chosen race

"But you are a chosen race, a royal priesthood, a holy nation, a people for His possession,

so that you may proclaim the praises of the One who called you out of darkness into His marvellous light." (1 Pt 2: 9 HCSB)

"… WITHOUT FAITH it is impossible to please God, for the one who draws near to Him must believe that He exists and rewards those who seek Him."

(Heb. 11: 6 HCSB)

The one who Fears the Lord

"Hallelujah!
Happy is the man who fears the Lord,
taking great delight in His commands.
His descendants will be powerful in the land;
the generation of the upright will be blessed.
Wealth and riches are in his house,
and his righteousness endures forever.
Light shines in the darkness for the upright.
He is gracious, compassionate and righteous." (Ps 112: 1-4 HCSB)

Your call: Be holy!

"Instead, be holy in all that you do,
just as God who called you is holy.
The scripture (Lev 19:2) says, 'Be Holy because
I am holy'" (1 Pt 1:15-16 GNBDK).

"… God wants you to be holy and completely free from sexual immorality." (1Thes 4: 3 GNBDK)

"All these promises are made to us, my dear friends. So then, let us purify ourselves from everything that makes body or soul unclean, and let us be completely holy by living in awe of God." (2 Cor 7: 1GNBDK)

"Even before the world was made, God had already chosen us to be His through our union with Christ, so that we would be holy and without fault before Him because of His love." (Eph 1: 4 GNBDK)

The foundation of our faith

"The city wall had twelve foundations, and the twelve names of the Lamb's twelve apostles were on the foundations." (Rev 21:14 HCSB)

"Built on the foundation of the apostles and prophets, with Christ Jesus Himself as the cornerstone." (Eph 2: 20 HCSB)

Faith: what it is:

"But if you can do anything have compassion on us and help us", a distraught father wailed. In response Jesus said

"'If you can'? Everything is possible to the one who believes" (Mk 9: 22-23)

How apt, candidate Obama's campaign slogan, "Yes we can!"

Signs and wonders, not sufficient:

"If they will not listen to Moses and the prophets, neither will they be persuaded if someone should rise from the dead." (Lk 16: 19-25, 27-35)

How insightful! Jesus resurrected, Judaists will still not believe Him!

Sons of Abraham

"…understand that those who have faith are Abraham's **sons** so those who have faith, are blessed with Abraham who had faith …" (Gal 3: 7, 9)

Sons of God

"For you are all sons of God through faith in Christ Jesus." (Gal 3: 26)

Call to righteousness – to fellowship with God.

"You are a people sacred to the Lord, your God;

He has chosen you from all the nations on

the face of the earth

to be a people peculiarly His own.

Understand, then, that the Lord your God,
is God indeed,
the faithful God who keeps His merciful covenant
down to the thousandth generation
toward those who love Him and keep
His commandments,…
You shall therefore carefully observe
the commandments,
the statutes and the decrees
that I enjoin on you today." (Deut 7: 6, 9, 11 LECT)
The Goal of faith
"…you believe in Him and rejoice… because you are receiving the goal of your
faith, the salvation of your souls." (1 Pt 1: 8, 9)
Rejoice, heaven is the prize!
Jesus told the seventy-two missionaries,
"Nevertheless, do not rejoice because the spirits are subject to you, but rejoice because your names are written in Heaven." (Lk 10: 20 NABRE)

"IF – you have faith, and do not doubt"

Jesus could have ordered His disciples to cut down a fruitless fig tree, rather He chose to speak to it:

"May no fruit ever come from you again!"

"At once the fig tree withered." Amazed at this, Jesus told His disciples "…If you have faith and do not doubt, you will not only do what was done to the fig tree, but even if you tell this mountain. 'Be lifted up and thrown into the sea,' it will be done. And if you believe, you will receive whatever you ask for in prayer." (Matt 21: 21-22 HCSB)

Confession of faith in Jesus

i. Paul: The gospel I preach to you:

"Now brothers, I want to clarify to you the gospel I proclaimed to you; …"

"… I passed on to you as most important… That Christ died for our sins according to the scriptures, and that He appeared to Cephas, then the twelve.

Then He appeared to James, then to all the apostles, last of all … He also appeared to me." (1Cor 15: 1-8 HCSB)

ii. Peter: Jesus, the Messiah is glorified.

"Men of Israel … The God of Abraham, Isaac and Jacob, the God of our fathers, has glorified His Servant Jesus, whom you handed over and denied in the presence of Pilate, … But you denied the Holy and Righteous One and asked to have a murderer given to you. You killed the source of life, whom God raised from the dead; we are witnesses of this. By faith in His name, His name has made this man strong, whom you see and know …" (Act 3: 12,13-16 HCSB)

iii. Peter: Jesus, our salvation.

"Rulers of the people and elders…

Let it be known to all of you and to all the people of Israel, that by the name of Jesus Christ the Nazarene – whom you crucified and whom God raised up from the dead – by Him this man is standing here before you healthy. This Jesus is the stone rejected by you builders, which has become the cornerstone.

There is salvation in no one else, for there is no other name under heaven given to people, and we must be saved by it."

(Acts 4: 8-12 HCSB)

iv. Peter and the apostles: propitiation for our sins.

"We must obey God rather than men. The God of our fathers raised up Jesus, whom you had murdered by hanging Him on a tree. God exalted this man to His right hand as ruler and saviour to grant repentance to Israel and forgiveness of sins. We are witnesses of these things, and so is the Holy Spirit whom God has given to those who obey Him."

(Acts 5:29-32 HCSB)

v. Peter: To the household of Cornelius: (Act 10:34-43)

"Now I really understand that God doesn't show favouritism, but in every nation the person who fears Him and does righteousness is acceptable to Him."

"God anointed Jesus of Nazareth with the Holy Spirit and with power, and how He went about doing good and healing… we ourselves are witnesses of everything He did…, yet they killed Him… God raised up this Man on the third day and permitted Him to be seen… by us, witnesses appointed before hand by God…

… He is the One appointed by God to be the judge of the living and the dead."

"**FAITH** is the reality of what is hoped for, the proof of what is not seen."

(Heb 11: 1 HCSB)

"For our exhortation didn't come from error or impurity or an intent to deceive. Instead, just as we have been appointed by God to be entrusted with the gospel, so we speak not to please men, but rather God, who examines our heart." (1 Thes 2:3-4)

Faith: A Revelation to the childlike.

"… Father, Lord of heaven and earth…
You have hidden these things from the wise and the learned you have revealed them to the childlike." (Lk 10: 21 LECT)

Jesus says, fear not!

"There is nothing concealed that will not be revealed, nor secret that will not be known.

I tell you My friends, do not be afraid of those who kill the body but after that can do no more." (Lk 12: 2, 4 NABRE)

Apostle Paul writes,

"For God has not given us a spirit of fearfulness, but one of power, love and sound judgement." (2 Tim 1: 7HCSB)

Obedience

"DO whatever He tells you to do,…" (Jn2: 5 HCSB)

PARADISE: Go for it!

The ultimate sublimit of life – paradise – is the promise our faith holds for us:

"What no eye has seen, no ear has heard, nor the heart of man conceived, what God has prepared for those who love Him." (Is 64: 4; 65: 17)

"Many of those who sleep in the dust of the earth will awake, some to eternal life, and some to shame and eternal contempt."

"Those who are wise will shine… and those who lead many to righteousness like the stars forever and ever." (Dan 12: 2, 3 HCSB)

Believe and be saved "Then he (the jailer) escorted them out (Paul and Silas) and said, 'Sirs, what must I do to be save?'So they said, 'Believe on the Lord Jesus, and you will be saved.'" (Acts 16: 30-31 HCSB)

JESUS: Light For All!

- "The people walking in darkness
- have seen a great light;…" (Isa 9: 2 HCSB)
- "…I am the light of the world" (Jn 9: 5 HCSB)
- "I came into this world… in order that those who do not see will see and those who do see will become blind." (Jn9: 39 HCSB)

Purpose of Christian evangelism (Rom 1: 5 GNBDK)

"Through Him God gave me the privilege of being an apostle for the sake of Christ, in order to lead people of all nations to believe and obey."

HCSB (Rom 1: 5)

"We have received grace and apostleship through Him to bring out the obedience of faith among all the nations on behalf of His name."

Trusting man or trusting God?

"Thus, says the Lord:
'Cursed is the man who trusts in human beings,
who makes flesh his strength,
whose heart turns away from the Lord.
He is like a barren bush in the wasteland,
that enjoys no change of season,
but stands in lava beds in the wilderness,
a land, salty and uninhabited.'" (Jer 17: 5-6 NABRE)
"Blessed are those who trust in the Lord;
The Lord will be their trust.
They are like a tree planted beside the waters
that stretches out its roots to the streams:
it does not fear heat when it comes,
its leaves stay green;
in the year of drought, it shows no distress,
but produces fruits." (Jer 17: 7-8 NABRE)

JESUS:

i. The Light

"... I am the light of the world, anyone who follows Me will never walk in the darkness, but will have the light of life." (Jn 8: 12, HCSB)

ii. The truth

"... I am the way, the truth and the life, no one comes to the Father except through Me." (Jn14: 6 HCSB)

iii. The Resurrection

"… I am the resurrection and the life. The one who believes in Me, even if he dies, will live." (Jn11: 25 HCSB)

iv. The life

"Amen, amen, I say to you whoever hears My word and believes in the One who sent Me has eternal life and will not come to condemnation…"

(Jn5: 24)

Apostle Paul on Faith:

"Now faith is the reality of what is hoped for, the proof of what is not seen."

"By faith we understand that the universe was created by God's command,…" (Heb 11: 1, 3 HCSB)

"Now without faith it is impossible to please God, .."

"These all (Abraham, Sarah) died in faith without having received the promises, but they saw them from a distance…"

"All these (Gideon, Barak, Samson, Jephthah, David, Samuel and the prophets) were approved through their faith, but they did not receive what was promised." (Heb 11: 6, 13 and 39 HCSB)

"You judge by human standards.

I judge no one" (Jn8: 15 HCSB)

Signs and faith

"Have you come to believe because you have seen Me? Blessed are those who have not seen and have believed." (Jn 20: 29)

"Jesus performed many other signs in the presence of His disciples that are not written in this book. But these are written so that you may believe Jesus is the Messiah, the Son of God, and by believing you may have life in His name."

(Jn 20: 30-31)

Jesus gives life

"And just as the Father raises the dead and

gives them life, so the Son also gives life

to anyone He wants to." (Jn 5: 21)

The goal of our faith

"…you believe in Him and rejoice… because you are receiving the goal of your faith, the salvation of your souls." (1 Pt 1: 8-9 HCSB)

Eternal life

"This is eternal life; that they may know You, the only true God …and the One You have sent – Jesus Christ." (Jn 17: 3)

Faith, not enough

"His divine power has given us everything required for life and godliness through the knowledge of Him who called us by His own glory and goodness."

"For this very reason, make every effort to supplement your **faith** with **goodness**, goodness with **knowledge**, knowledge with **self-control**, self-control with **endurance**, endurance with **godliness**, godliness with **brotherly affection**, brotherly affection with **love**." (2Pt 1: 3, 5-7 HCSB)

Slavery and the truth

"You will know the truth, and the truth will set you free."

"…everyone who commits sin is a slave of sin" (Jn 8: 32, 34)

Advancement in rocket science and robotics, yet no discernment?

"When you see a cloud rising in the west… a storm… and so it does … and when the south wind is blowing … a scorcher … hypocrites! You know how to interpret … the earth and the sky, but why don't you… this time?"

"…you know how to read the appearance of the sky, but you can't read the signs of the times. An evil and adulterous generation demands a sign, but no sign will be given to it except the sign of Jonah…"

(Lk 12: 54-56; Matt 16: 3-4 HCSB)

Faith: God is faithful

Hence God says:

"My house shall be called a house of prayer for all peoples."

(Isa 56: 7 HCSB)

Jesus decries faithlessness

"You unbelieving generation! How long… how long must I put up with you?"

(Mk 9: 19 HCSB)

Believers (in Jesus) and unbelievers

"The one who is from God listens to God's words…"

"You are of your father the Devil, and you want to carry out your father's desires. He was a murderer from the beginning and has not stood in the truth, because there is no truth in him. When he tells a lie, he speaks from his own nature, because he is a liar and the father of liars." (Jn 8: 44)

Not all can believe

Jesus answered them, "stop complaining among yourselves. No one can come to Me unless the Father, who sent Me draws him, and I will raise him up…"

(Jn 6:43-44 NABRE)

ADDITIONAL RESOURCES

Jesus Himself prays

"And after dismissing the crowd Jesus went up the mountain by Himself to pray." (Matt 14: 15, 2)

Peter seeing how strong the wind, became frightened and began to sink, cried out, 'Lord, save me!' (14: 24) (Matt 14: 13-14, 24)

The meaning of His miracles – They were SIGNS to instil faith.

Matt 14: 31 "O you of little faith, why did you doubt?"

:34 "Those in the boat did Him homage, saying, 'Truly, you are the Son

of God.'"

Our goal (as believers):

1. Salvation. (Isa 33: 22 above) God will save us.

2. Rev 22: 4, 5 "The Lord God shall be our light and we shall reign forever."

(c/f Isa 60: 20)

1 Pt 5: 7 "Cast all your care on Him…, because He cares about you."

5: 8 "Be sober and vigilant! Your adversary, the devil is prowling around like a roaring lion, looking for anyone he can devour"

5: 9 "Resist him and be firm in the faith…"

5: 1 "Presbyters are witnesses to the suffering of Christ."

5: 4 "And when the CHIEF SHEPHERD is revealed, you will receive the

Unfading crown of glory."

ONE FAITH! (Spearheads of denominations – be warned.)

"There is ONE body and one spirit … ONE hope at your calling –" "one Lord, one faith, one baptism."

"One God and Father of all, who is above all and through all and in all."

(Eph 4: 4-6)

Come to the Lord: CALL TO HOLINESS

"Pay attention and come to Me; listen so that you will live.

I will make an everlasting covenant with you,
the promises assured to David." (Isa 55: 3 HCSB)
FAITH AND THE WORD
"For one believes with the heart and so is justified,
and one confesses with the mouth and so is saved."
"But how can they call on Him in whom they have not believed?
And how can they believe in Him of whom they have not heard?
And how can they hear without someone to preach?
And how can people preach unless they are sent? (Rom 10: 10; 12-15 NABRE)
"Thus faith comes from what is heard, and what is heard comes through the word of Christ." (Rom 10: 17)
"I charge you... **proclaim the word**; be persistent ...convince, reprimand, encourage through all patience and teaching." (2 Tim 4: 1-8)
Knowledge of God.
Mk 12: 24 HCSB "... 'Are you not deceived because you don't know the scriptures or the power of God?'
: 27 He is not God of the dead but of the living. You are only deceived."

Believe!

(Jn 20: 27 HCSB) "Don't be an unbeliever, but a believer."

The MESSIAH: For all people

Lk 2: 10 "Don't be afraid, for look, I proclaim to you good news of great joy that will be FOR ALL THE PEOPLE."
Lk 2: 11 "Today a Saviour, who is Messiah the Lord was born for you in the city of David."
Ministry of reconciliation

1 Kgs 18: 37 As in the case of Elijah, Jesus' ministry came about "so that this people may know that You, Lord are God, and are winning back their hearts."

1 Kgs 18: 39 "We should resound individually and collectively as they did, 'the Lord is God; the Lord is God'" or that Exo 24: 3 "We would do all that the Lord had commanded us."

FAITH ISSUES

Matt 21: 21 (The cursed fig tree) "If you have faith and do not waiver, not only will you ... but ... (mountain will move in obedience to you)"

LK 17: 5 The apostles asked Jesus: 'Increase our faith!'

Lk 17: 6 If you have faith the size of a mustard seed, you'll can say to this mulberry tree... and it will obey you.

Matt 11: 23 Jesus reproaches Chorazin and Bethsaida for failure to produce fruit of repentance in spite of "the mighty deeds done in" their midst.

Matt 17: 20 "Because of your little faith,... for I assure you
: 18 if you have faith the size of mustard seed..."

Omnipotent God –

Lk 1: 37 Angel Gabriel's revelation:
"For with God all things are possible."

Gen 18: 14 "Is anything too marvellous for the Lord to do?"

"...about this time next year Sarah will have a son."

Jer 32: 17 Jeremiah "... nothing is too difficult for You."

Jer 32: 27 "I am the Lord, the Lord of all the living! Is there anything too difficult for Me?"

Job 42: 2 Job answered the Lord; "I know You can do ALL THINGS, and that no purpose of Yours can be hindered."

Rom 4: 20 "He (Abraham) did not doubt God's promise in unbelief, rather he was empowered by FAITH and gave glory to God."

Rom 4: 18 Faith in God is righteousness, "...he (Abraham) believed, hoping against hope."

Pray in faith.

Joshua defeated the Amelekites with the unceasing prayer of Moses.

(Exo 17: 13)

Paul revived the boy, Eutychus, who fell down from the storey building.

(Acts 20: 9)

Matt 11: 19 "...disciples...said, 'why couldn't we drive it out?'"

Jesus said this type (exorcism) can only be done through prayer and fasting.

(Lk 11: 20

Ask, cast out doubts

Js 1: 6 "But let him ask in faith without doubting..."

: 7 "That person (doubter) should not expect to receive anything from the

Lord."

Faith – we have all it takes.

2 Pt 1: 3 HCSB "His (Jesus) divine power has given us everything required for

life."

But add to faith:

2 Pt 1: 5 "For this reason, make every effort to supplement your FAITH with goodness ..."

Js 2: 14 "what good ... he has faith but does not have works?..."

: 18 "... 'show me your faith without works, and I will show you FAITH from

My works...'"

: 20 "Foolish man!... learn that faith without works is useless."

: 22 "...by works (Abraham's) faith was perfected."

Js 2 :26 "For just as the body without the spirit is dead, so also faith without works is dead."

Compare Eph 4: 21 HCSB

"Therefore, ridding yourselves of all moral filth and evil, humbly receive the implanted word, which is able to save you."

Add obedience – A new covenant:

"The time is coming when I will make a new covenant with the people of Israel ... and Judah.""...not be like the old covenant...""...they did not keep that covenant."

"The new covenant... will be this: I will put My law within them and write it on their hearts..."

"... teach his fellow citizens to know the Lord, because all will know Me from the least to the greatest." (Jer 31: 31-34 GNBDK)

SEPARATISTS AND SCHISMATICS

Unity in faith: Be one!

Eph 4: 11 "And he personally gave some to be Apostles; some prophets, some evangelists, some pastors and teachers"

: 12 "for the training, ... in the work of ministry, to build the body of Christ."

: 14 "Then we will no longer be little children tossed by the waves and blown around by every wind of teaching by human cunning with cleverness in techniques of deceit."

1 Tim 4: 1 "Now the Spirit explicitly says that in later times some will depart from the faith, paying attention to deceitful spirits and the teachings of demons;

: 2 through the hypocrisy of liars whose consciences are seared"

: 3 "By FAITH we understand that the universe was created by God's command..."

The law and our faith

Gal 3: 24 "The law, then, was our guardian until Christ, so that we could be justified by faith.

Faith saves
Lk 7: 50 "Jesus said…, your faith has saved you; …"

Conversion is obedience to the truth

"But I ask, is it true that they (unbelievers) did not hear the message?

Of course, they did – for as the scripture (Ps 19: 4) says:

'The sound of their voice went out to all the world; their words reached the ends of the earth.'"

(Rom 10: 18 GNBDK)

Faith

"Faith is the reality of what is hoped for, the proof of what is not seen." (Heb 11: 1 HCSB)

"… Faith comes from what is heard and what is heard comes through the message about Christ." (Rom 10: 17 HCSB)

See also Jn 17: 20 – Jesus prays for all believers of the message.

Righteousness through faith

'The word is near you, in your mouth and in your heart…'
(Deut 30: 13, 12; 9, 4; Ps 107: 26; 1 Pt 3: 19)

The Word: the One in you

"… because the One who is in you is greater than the one who is in the world. They are from the world. Therefore, what they say is from the world, and the world listens to them." (1 Jn 4: 4, 5 HCSB)

Do you believe?

"… Father, Lord of heaven and earth… You have hidden these things from the wise and the learned; you have revealed them to the child like."

(Lk 10: 21 Lect)

The fool and the corrupt

"The fool says in his heart, 'God does not exist.'
They are corrupt; they do vile deeds."
"God looks down from heaven on the human race
to see if there is one who is wise,
one who seeks God."
"All have turned away;
all alike have become corrupt.
There is no one who does good, not even one."
(Ps 14: 1; 53: 2-3 HCSB)
You believe in God? Believe in Jesus also.
"You believe in God, believe in Me also." (Jn 14: 1 HCSB)
If only you listen!

You do not believe because you do not listen

"… I came from God and now I am here.
I did not come on My own authority, but He sent Me.
Why do you not understand what I say?
It is because you cannot bear to listen to My message.
You are the children of your father, the Devil,
and you want to follow your father's desires…"
"He who comes from God listens to God's words.
You, however, are not from God,
and that is why you will not listen." (Jn 8: 42, 43-44, 47 GNBDK)
The truth
"… God our Saviour, who wants everyone
to be saved and to come to the knowledge of the truth."
"… There is one God… one mediator
between God and humanity, Christ Jesus…"
(1 Tim 2: 3, 4-5 HCSB)
Purpose of faith
Faith impacts in us –
 1. Obedience to God (Rom 1: 5)
 2. Salvation for our souls (1 Pt 1: 9)

"The one who is righteous by faith will live…" (Rom 1: 17 NABRE)

The truth and Jesus

1. "Jesus is the way, the truth and the life…" (Jn 14: 6)
2. "Yes, for this… I have come to bear witness to the truth." (Jn 18: 37 NKJV)
3. The Holy Spirit is the spirit of truth (Jn 15: 26)
4. Speak the truth…

"For there is nothing hidden that will not become visible; nothing secret that will not be known." (Lk 12: 2)

Persistency in prayer is a sign of faith:

"Then he (Elijah) cried out to the Lord and said 'My Lord God, have You also brought tragedy on the widow I am staying with by killing her son?' Then he stretched himself out over the boy three times. He cried out to the Lord and said, 'My Lord God, please let this boy's life return to him!' So the Lord listened to Elijah's voice, and the boy's life returned to him, and he lived."

(1 Kgs 17: 20-22 HCSB)

IF…

"If you have faith the size of a mustard seed, you would say to this mulberry tree,

'be uprooted and planted in the sea,' and it would obey you." (Lk 17: 6)

FAITH OR TRUST IN THE LORD: (It is not by might)

"A king is not saved by a large army; a warrior will not be delivered by great strength.

The horse is a false hope for safety; it provides no escape by its great power."

(Ps 33: 16)

Have faith

Lot's two sons-in-law to be (of his two daughters) were warned of the impending destruction of Sodom and Gomorrah but for their unbelief, they ignored the warning to get out of the city and they perished. (Gen 19: 14)

Disobedience

"But Lot's wife looked back, and she was turned into a pillar of salt."

(Gen 19: 17, 26)

Everything ... (by faith)

Jesus reprimands the "unbelieving generation" as He was given the account by a man who brought his possessed son to Jesus' disciples for deliverance but it turned out they were unable to heal him. (Mk 9: 17-19)

"Then Jesus said to him, 'If you can'? Everything is possible to the one who believes" (Mk 9: 23)

The World and You

To bear everlasting fruit, who you are matters as well as how you listen; do you reflect on the scripture? In the parable of the Sower (Lk 8: 14-15) Jesus says it is important you do.

"Therefore, take care how you listen. For whoever has, more will be given to him; and whoever does not have, even what he thinks he has will be taken away from him." (Lk 8: 18 HCSB)

JUSTIFICATION

"… and now we hold that faith in Christ rather than fidelity to the Law is what justifies us, and that no-one can be justified by keeping the Law. Now if we were to admit that the result of looking to Christ to justify us is to make us sinners like the rest, it would follow that Christ had induced us to sin, which would be absurd."

"… I cannot bring myself to give up God's gift; if the Law can justify us, there is no point in the death of Christ."

"Are you people in Galatia mad? … Let me ask you one question: was it because you practised the Law that you received the Spirit, or because you believed what was preached to you?"

"… Does God give you the Spirit so freely and work miracles among you because you practised Law, or because you believed what was preached to you?" (Gal 2: 16-17, 21; 3: 1-2, 5 Lect)

PERSEVERANCE

1. Jn 5: 3, 5-9: Only the 38-year old ailment (out of many sick) was cured by Jesus
2. 1 Kgs 18: 44 It took the 7th going back and forth, watching the sky before the servant of Elijah perceived a tiny cloud, the herald of rainfall!
3. Lk 11: 5-8: The host of the night visitor begging for loaves only his persistence availed.

PRAISE GOD!

"… Praise from the upright is beautiful."

"For the word of the Lord is right, and all His work is trustworthy."

"He loves righteousness and justice; the earth is full of the Lord's unfailing love." (Ps 33: 1, 5)

HUMILITY: Syrophoenician Woman Stoops to Conquer

Jesus arrived in the region of Tyre and Sidon, entered a house and wanted no one to know it, but He could not escape notice. Soon, a Syrophoenician woman heard about Him. She came and fell at His feet… begged Him to drive away the demon out of her daughter. (Mk 7: 24-30)

Faith leads one to perseverance

"… The Canaanite woman called out,

C/woman: "Have pity on me, Lord, Son of David! My daughter is tormented by a demon."

Jesus: (no answer)

Disciples: "send her away, for she keeps calling out after us."

Jesus (to the woman): "I was sent only to the lost sheep of the house of Israel."

C/Woman: (kneeling) "Lord, help me."

Jesus: "It is not right to take the food of children and throw it to the dogs."

C/Woman: "Please Lord for even the dogs eat the scraps that fall from the table of their masters."

Jesus: "O woman, great is your faith! Let it be done for you as you wish."

Narrator: Her daughter was healed from that hour.

(Mk 7: 24-30) (Matt 15: 22-28 NABRE)

… JUST HAVE FAITH!

In the New Testament an official of the synagogue, Jairus, had enough faith in Jesus to realize that a desperate situation like a teenage daughter dying could be saved by Jesus' intervention and he went to seek His help. Now, like what happens in such cases, though he had access to Jesus (may be on account of his position in society) but he could not get Jesus to respond to him instantly. Message came to him that it was all over – the 12-year-old had died. Let the master alone! "Disregarding the message that was reported, Jesus told Jairus, 'Do not be afraid, just have faith.'" (Mk 5: 30 - 43) Of course, the daughter was brought to life again.

In another episode a woman with haemorrhage for 12 years believed that "If I could but touch His (Jesus') cloths, I shall be cured." She did and was instantly cured. (Mk 5: 21)

Not all such mountains get removed by the wish of ordinary folks (like the disciples of Jesus (Christians), that is why you have always to pray and fast).

COMPLETE SURRENDER AND DOCILITY:

"A man convinced against his will
is of the same opinion still." – Alexander Pope

"Don't be an unbeliever, but a believer." (Jn 20:27 HCSB)

"Stop your doubting and believe!" (Jn 20:27 GNBDK)

This is the commandment from on high for all of us.

According to a venerable evangelist, Fr Al Leur 1[1], (of blessed memory):

"why dwell in unbelief?"

"But from there, you will search for the Lord
your God, and you will find Him
when you seek Him with
all your heart and all your soul." (Deut 4: 29)
WHY dwell in unbelief? In heresy?

"The great thing about Thomas (Didymus) was that he didn't stay as a doubter."

"… now, you shouldn't dwell on these things. But to dwell on doubts – and especially to do nothing about doubts, especially to build your life around doubt – that is a big problem – a big, big problem."

"I think most people have let some sort of doubts drive their spiritual cars. They let doubt be their steering wheel instead of faith being their steering wheel."

"…A protestant minister, Staghorn, preached, 'make faith your steering wheel and not your spare tyre'"

"A lot of people have made doubt their steering wheel – passive agnosticism! You can doubt if you have a passion for seeking the truth; but a passive agnosticism – building your life around doubt – that is sickening."

(Rev 3:16)

"So, because you are lukewarm, and neither hot or cold, I am going to vomit you out of my mouth." (Rev. 3:16)

1: Of Presentation ministries.com (… redacted from audio podcast)

Exhortation, meditation and reflection

"You don't see long-term agnostics who have a passion for the truth; they found out – not dissenters' opinion – people praying (to) God to show them the truth – a passionate seeker of the truth."

"Move from doubt into commitment!
'If you seek Me, you will find Me' (Deut 4:29)
put your hand on the plough, don't look back."

Apostle Thomas, better known for his scruples on this issue did not dwell forever in unbelief.

"My Lord, and My God!" was the acclamation/affirmation which clearly flushed out his scruples. He proceeded to live his entire life as an apostle, evangelist and missionary to Persia, in India, laying his life down for the faith (in Mylapur, India c.72)

Do you know most of the Apostles could not accept the first visitation of the resurrected Jesus? It was too much for their psyche to take it in but their doubts do us good for now we know they are not an overly credulous bunch. The second appearance in the upper room with doors securely shut and the events afterward convinced them.

"The disbelief of Thomas has done more for our faith than the faith of the other disciples." Pope St. Gregory the Great (homily)

"Do you believe because you see me? How happy are those who believe without seeing Me!" (Jn 20:29 GNBDK)

WITHOUT FAITH you can't ride a bicycle!

Faith is everything in life. For without faith, no one can know his mother or his father; much less know the Lord God whom he has neither seen nor heard His voice. Faith is the passport; righteousness the visa to the kingdom of heaven.

Why is it that not everyone believes in one and the same God (monotheists) and those who do cannot come under a single umbrella of faith in the divinity? Who is fooling who?

First, the truth: the essence of faith is in the truth. A true believer upholds the truth. Jesus is "the way, the truth and the life..." (Jn14:6)

He is the **chief witness** to the truth.

Exhortation, meditation and reflection

A lot of people are entrenched in their ways of thinking and doing things, they are not after the truth but to maintain their aversion to change.

The Devil is the avowed enemy of God and is here on earth as the master of deceit. His strongest weapon is in half truths. His prangs make it harder for anyone to discern the truth. But help in terms of the grace of God, avails.

Brand rivalry. There is the familiar "my father's estate is bigger than your father's" proprietary pride and arrogance. It's all falacy; but no one is interested in the truth – just 'what you have, you hold!' Therefore, forever there will be no consensus on earth about who the true God is, and how to worship Him. Very sad, indeed, because the righteous God will not accept doubt or the lack of faith as plea to exonerate the one who failed to live the life commended to us by the Creator.

More discussion on this all-important subject is continued in chapter nineteen, 'let them be one' and in the companion book, 'understanding the Bible'.

Man is endued with faith. Just as they say anyone who can reflect will know to give thanks. In the same way, revelations apart, anyone who reflects on the world around him will fall into prayers and praising. He will attain some kind of clairvoyance such at least to believe that there is a Master-Mind-coordinator of the various phenomena we come across in nature which exist without and beyond him in such an amazing unity, which defy their vast array – animals and plant life as well as their non-living neighbours. Mother earth amazingly holds all together.

Everybody needs faith!

Oh you agnostics, you atheists – curry faith that you may have the confidence of conviction as to who your mother and your father are, then, you will surely know God!

For me as a person, the overwhelming evidence that my prayers are answered is the bulwark of my faith of the nearness to or presence with us, of the just and benevolent God.

"They will do these things because they haven't

known the Father or Me," (Jn16:3)
"Sanctify them by the truth;
Your word is truth." (Jn 17:17)

Exhortation, meditation and reflection

Are you called? Into what?

Each person should prove himself as he answers these questions. But note, the circumstances of our call are not the same.

Simon and Andrew were at work when they were called.

At a crusade two were called, one offered to follow Jesus (but was told he could not make it.) (Lk 9:57-62)

Philip invited Nathaniel to come and see the Lord (Jn 1:45 Ibid: Jesus p.21); the Gerasene's maniac's call was at the point he received the mercy of God

(Mk 5:8-20); similar thing happened to Mary Magdalene (Mk 16:9)

Blind Bartimaeus of Jericho likewise started following Jesus immediately he met the mercy of God. (Mk 10:46-52)

So, once again, are you called? Into what? If so, do something about your call.

Grace of Faith

The difference between believers and unbelievers is in their respective response to the gift – some zealously, others casually or not all.

You have to open your hands to receive; but salvation is for all.

"For My house shall be called
a house of prayer for all peoples." (Isa 56:7 HCSB)

The earth is the boarding school where saints are formed or the tenets, of the kingdom of God are imbibed. The lesson learnt and the habit formed here will stand us in good stead in heaven.

Notice that the gentiles (the magi) were the first to believe in Jesus (Matt 2:11)

"Whoever does not welcome the kingdom of God like a little child will never enter it!" (Mk 10:15)

"So then, FAITH comes from hearing the message…" (Rom 10: 17 GNBDK)

A person with faith

Our faith confers confidence borne out of knowing the truth:

- Ignorance of the gospel makes the one to suffer the worst poverty (Pope John Paul II)
- Suffers the worst type of problem – suicide, murder inclusive.

Exhortation, meditation and reflection

"Where is your faith?" (Lk 8:25)

Can Jesus be asking you the same question today; read more about the storm His disciples were going through (Lk 8:22). They were to admit their lack of faith when in bewilderment, they said to one another 'who then is this, who

commands even the winds and the sea, and they obey Him?'" (Lk 8:25 NABRE)

So, who is Jesus to you?

But not only the wind and the waves alone that obeyed His Voice, even demons like the Gerasene (Lk 8:26-39) bow out before Him; death (Nain son; Jairus daughter) loses its hold at His command; so also sicknesses (the paralytic, its Simon's mother-in-law) become powerless and even sinners are reformed by nearness to Him.

Pray for gift of faith

Prayer: "Grant me, o Lord a mind to know You, a heart to seek You, wisdom to find You, conduct pleasing to You, faithful perseverance in waiting for You, and a hope of finally embracing You." – St. Thomas Aquinas (cit op)

Faith is a real stuff

A father[1] in the faith speaks on the realism of faith as challenging us to comprehend faith beyond "the sentimentality of mere feelings."

Faith is obedience to the truth.

The realism of faith – Pope Benedict XVI[1]

"Unfortunately, it is all too true that for many people religion has been transmuted into sentiment which has no reality to support it.

Yet, in many respects, another attitude is perhaps more dangerous: the attitude of those who regard themselves as religious, but limit religion to the realm of feeling and allow it no contact with the sober reality of rational daily life as they seek personal gain in communicating the unparallel realism of the divine love."

St Thomas Aquinas on faith

"Believing is an act of the intellect assenting to the divine truth by command of the will moved by God through grace."

1: Pope Emeritus Benedict XVI; Daily Meditations…

Exhortation, meditation and reflection

FAITH: It is faith –

- that makes you to ride on a two-wheel bicycle or motor-cycle (with practice) and you are confident you won't fall off;
- that prompts a father or a mother to bring their children or ward to Jesus in search of divine help (Mk 5:25-34; 7:24-30; 9:17-29)
- that makes you – even you – turn to God, if you will, seek knowledge of God.
- that makes you know your father or your mother – if you do! "…but not everyone can believe" Also (Jn 6:43)

Faith tells the truth

"The hope of Christianity, the outlook of faith –ultimately rests … on the fact that faith tells the truth."

Pope Emeritus Benedict XVI, Daily Meditation 2/26/20

What is faith? Is there God?

The truth: Faith is concerned about the truth – what is true and what is false concerning the origin and end of human life on earth.

Besides human life, the earth swarms with all sorts of living creatures – animals, plant, amphibian and aquatic life, birds and worms! Then there are the invisible living beings, germs, viruses, etc. all co-existing beautifully. But creation also has an enormous junk of non-living objects.

So is there God? Who is He? What should our relationship with Him be? In **view of the sheer monstrosity of these things do** God care for man? How? Isn't He too remote to notice poor tiny me?

And if there is no God, how do we explain these visible and invisible, living and non-living objects? Are angels and demons real or old wives' tales? What about heaven, hell, judgement, visions, mercy? Why is there so much wickedness and impunity on earth? How was the beginning and how would the end (of the earth) be? These are some of the many questions that have puzzled the hearts of men from of old. Religion seeks to answer these and Christian faith is part of religion.

Time there was, when the sun, the moon and stars posed similar unending bewilderment. But such puzzles have since been considerably contained. Man has landed on the moon.

Exhortation, meditation and reflection

But why is much progress not made in religion as is made in science? No major breakthrough in 3,000 years of religion. We still live entirely by 'belief' rather than by the certainty of 'knowledge'. For answers to the enquiries posed earlier, could it be that our modus operandi, are what was wrong? Are we putting the cart before the horse; the answer before the question?

What faith is not.

All great men of God and most theologians agree that faith is not a form of superstition over a non-existent deity. Some objective observers however think otherwise; they say it is the opium of the naïve, a sort of entertainment for jaded nerves.

A government that dares to ban attendance at dramer theatres, cinema houses, and seeks to divert the resources employed therein into other "productive" sectors, would be pulled down in no time; could that explain why religion is also being tolerated?

There is a reality in religion, a truth, which out-weighs such levity. Something real is there in Christian faith that is even more real than you and me or the things we see or hear or touch. Life is more important than bread and our fixation with pride, possession, pleasure and power. No government of the people ought ever treat the subject with indifference, or worse still, with hostility. Governments should invest resources to further knowledge of God.

Faith – St Thomas Aquinas

"Believing is an act of the intellect assenting to the divine truth by command of the will moved by God through grace.

The miracle of the subsistence/survival of the Christian faith.

Normally there could be no conflagration after the flame had been put out completely by water. After the execution of a sect leader, his followers usually are dismayed and dispersed. Not so, with the disciples of the crucified Jesus. Though the shepherd had been killed, the flock would not scamper or scatter. That is the miracle of the subsistence of Christianity, which 2000 years after has not only survived but is thriving as never before.

Jesus was viciously persecuted, unjustly tried by his accusers, scourged by soldiers and ignominiously crucified publicly. No person could expect such rare miracle worker, that compares favourably with the greatest -with Moses and Elijah – to suffer such public humiliation, pain and conquest.

Exhortation, meditation and reflection

Heaven did not fall! No angel defended his innocence and right-standing with God or avenged his cruel murder. He died as everyone else dies – helplessly! The time and talent he put into His ministry, His life and comfort sacrificed, appeared misplaced and expended in vain.

After these things, who would believe the resurrection story or the surrealistic ascension? The Yoruba says "an old man is incinerated, and you are enquiring about his beard?"

So, how did this scenario change? The Pentecost did it all. (Lk 24:49) Between the resurrection and the ascension, the promise had been made by the Master to His disciples to await The Paraclete "in not many days from now". They obeyed. Fifty days afterwards on Pentecost day, Jerusalem was agape with the manifestation of the Holy Spirit in the disciples. They witnessed for Jesus and everybody in Jerusalem – Jews and pilgrims alike – all comprehend/understood them as if they spoke in each listener's mother tongue! Indeed, Babel was reversed on that day!

On that day alone, about 3,000 new converts were added to the rank of the disciples, despite aversion by the religious leaders. Every day the expansion of the followership continued.

The faith seemed to have resurrected with Jesus; it took it those few days to mature and has since been flourishing. It gives life to the world; life of holiness and love; life of kindness and compassion. Mercy has triumphed over judgement (Js 2:14)

That was only the beginning of a phenomenon that has changed and is still changing the world. The resurrection now comes alive. The mystery of the empty tomb hardly lauded the persecutors and the missing body has not been found till today, thus validating the alternative resurrection and ascension explanation.

Christianity was seen as a threat to Judaism, the religion that made the Jews – the only very special people on earth. Its leaders were bent on putting an end to Christianity.

Just as this was going on, a man born crippled, who begged within the temple complex had his infirmity taken away at the name of Jesus, pronounced on him by the apostles Peter and John. This fits the Yoruba adage, "the one whose arms are being chopped off is putting on a ring on his finger!" So, this got Peter and John into prison. (Acts)

Exhortation, meditation and reflection

The powers were intent on killing both Peter and John and ordered their arrest and incarceration to bare their fangs on other disciples. Their witnessing still had not flagged. The prison was secured maximally; court (the Sanhedrin) convened and the prisoners ordered to be brought to trial.

The prison was locked and guards were on the watch all night, but the cell, was empty of its occupier. Bemused and perplexed, even exasperated, they were to learn that the prisoners they were looking for had not vamoosed, after all; they were in the same temple complex preaching the same Jesus, the reason for which they were incarcerated.

Some other forces have now intervened. Undaunted, the powers wanted to get the men killed, but feared the unknown (mob reaction), and had to let them go (after flogging them). But the Apostles went back to the same beat (witnessing for Jesus) with miraculous healing and signs. (Acts 5:12-16)

To suppress these restless and intrepid disciples their enemies instigated a mob and lynched one of them at his witnessing. But dying Stephen prayed (in mercy) for the forgiveness of his tormentors. ( )

James, one of the twelve they killed; then, the authorities laid their hands on the other leader of the group, Peter, to kill him.

Still, the zeal of the disciples did not abate or run out. Rather, a radical co-prosecutor of the disciples, Saul (also known as Paul) suddenly changed tack and became a disciple himself! ( )

Infidelity kills Ananias and Sapphira.

This couple had sold their property and delivered the proceeds at the feet of the Apostles, hiding a little thereof for themselves. But they lied (needlessly) that it was the entire proceeds that they submitted. They dropped dead as they lied, creating panic among the folks. A new standard of ethics and moral behaviour was thus demanded within the new movement. (Acts 5:1-11)

Finally, the name above all names – Jesus.

The disciples, intoxicated as it were, by the Holy Spirit and filled with Jesus, gave relentless witness for Christ in every clime and to every generation; persecution became catalytic to missionary activities. Their enemies, obviously weaponised by Satan (Eph 6:12) and with violence its favoured weapon, pursued till this day the disciples of Jesus, killing, maiming burning and feeding

some to wild animals. In spite of this, the witnessing goes on unstoppable. Christianity has survived (the persecution).

Exhortation, meditation and reflection

It has survived; it's witnessing has never been more robust and vibrant than it is today. The religion is not new to any part of the world. (Matt 24:14)

The world of darkness has added faking to their armoury. By raising up fake preachers and evangelists, they hoped to either dilute or pollute the message, thus making it harder for a soul to know the truth and be saved.

"And this Good News… will be preached through all the world for a witness to all nations; and then the end will come." (Matt 24:14 GNBDK)

In an attempt to grow and wax stronger Christianity suffered a split between Christians in the West of the Roman Empire and those in the East. And just as the momentum was being regained, then came Protestantism, which threatened its very fabric – universality ("Catholicism"). Nevertheless, the momentum may be paused, but evangelism continued to spread like wild fire. (Matt 24:14, supra) has been fulfilled!

Jesus, the eternal High Priest of God has given His word, "the power of darkness shall not overcome the church" (Matt. 16:18)

"Oh, my comrades, see the signal waving in the sky! Onward comes our great Commander, cheer my comrades cheer!

"Hold the fort for I am coming" Jesus signals yet still; wave the answer back to heaven, (An old Christian hymn). "By the grace we will"

Jesus Disciples exalted:

"Now **we know that You know** everything … by this we believe that You came from God." (Jn 16:30 HCSB)

Jesus, more than anyone else in the sacred literature drew attention again and again on **Faith**; see the quotes below:

1. What is Faith?

   i.   The opposite of doubt (Rom 4:20)

   ii.   Working miracles, gift of knowledge of mysteries (1 Cor 13:2)

   iii.   Believe in the One who raised Jesus … from the dead (Rom 4:24)

   iv.   Faith or belief in God's righteousness (Rom 4:18)

Exhortation, meditation and reflection

   i.   Faith is confidence and hope in the sacred truth as revealed to us through the prophets, the Lord Jesus Christ and by the inspiration of the Holy Spirit.

   ii.   Faith comes by hearing (Rom 10:17) the Word, meditating on it and endeavouring to practise what you understand, especially through prayers, fasting, penances and charitable works. (Matt 25:)

iii.   Faith is prayerfulness, since there is a promise that we will be granted anything we ask for prayerfully; we know that God can do everything, so if we trust Him for strength and for help, what can be impossible for us to accomplish?

(Heb 11:1 NKJV) "Now FAITH is the substance of things hoped for, the evidence of things not seen."

2. Can FAITH be acquired, how?

The apostles expressed the perplexity and yearnings in all hearts when they requested plainly from Jesus, "Increase our faith." (Lk 17:5), this rather innocuous demand was met with an intriguing response from our Lord – no commitment. (Lk 17:6 –)

Yet, this request was very similar to other prayers asked by His followers (and others) which instantly were granted; for example – "Lord, teach us now to pray", (Lk 11:1/Mk 9: 14) resulting in the Lord's (model) prayer

"Lord, who sinned, this man or his parent?"

"Why do your disciples not fast?" (Mk 9: 28-29) etc.

Why was this silent response to the apostles' petition, even though Jesus never lost an opportunity to teach them on the importance of faith. In the context in which the petition was made, the Apostles' prayer can be recast thus, "Lord, open the door of power to us!" In this light, Jesus' response becomes more revealing. You don't open a door that is already opened; if anyone still doubts that the door is open then he needs much more than words to cure him of his unbelief. Such were the apostles: they already had the Lord as the Master; He taught them other aspects of faith – prayer, forgiveness of sins and the example of His own life was extremely impressive. So, to realize that the seed was already planted in them which seed required nourishment through their individual prayer, faith then with time they will do so.

To confirm this view, notice how the Lord answered similar questions to put Him before or even after the above request.

Exhortation, meditation and reflection

So the question, can faith be acquired, is answered in Rom 10: 17 "Thus, FAITH comes from what is heard, and what is heard come through the word of Christ." (Rom 10: 17 NABRE)

And in Rom 10:6-8 St Paul further tells us that "The righteousness that comes from faith, says ... 'the word is near you, in your mouth and in your heart (that is, the word of faith that we preach.)"

GOD upholds orderliness, due process and respect for protocol; how are these intrinsic qualities found in FAITH?

Faith clinic (or retreat) themes:

Understanding faith

Game: 1. Individuals allot as many scripture references to each of these themes as you can; discuss at group session.

2. Group: Evaluate those answers; accept or reject working on consensus basis.

1. What is faith?
   Answer – it is
   i.   Working miracles, gift of knowledge of mysteries
   ii. Rom 4: 24 "... believe in the One who raised Jesus... from the dead."(God)
   iii. (others):

2. Can faith be acquired, how?
3. Who and what are to be blamed if a believer's faith is low?
   According to St Paul (Rom 4: 18, 21 NABRE)
   FAITH or belief in God is righteousness

Faith is, therefore, prayerfulness, since with prayer God is our strength and all things are possible. (Lk 1: 37 NABRE)

4. Prophets (and miracle workers): Do they work by Faith or by obedience?

Moses' mission and miracles were all mostly by divine order, few through prayer (like the healing of Miriam and Aaron)

When Peter walked on the sea, for example, it was by obedience.

5. What is the relationship between faith and revelation and miracles?

Through the word the seed of faith grows and heart and mind opens. Yes, because the SEED of faith is already planted in each of us.

Other:

Exhortation, meditation and reflection

6. Can FAITH displace or suspend natural laws?

Yes, for RESTORATION; Yes and No: Yes, defy death (for a while), no, may not permanently defy natural laws. (I.e. divine establishment or order).

Other:

7. What distinguishes FAITH from superstition and gullibility?

The absence of prayer and/or the word (and fasting?);

One is an act of hope in God, and the other an act of fear and ignorance; one exalts God's glory, the other is self-serving. One endures and is restorative and purposive, while the other is both transient and delusory.

8. What is the relationship between faith and prayer; faith and fasting?

"This type can only be done through prayer and fasting."

Prayer and fasting are the nutrients of faith, or if you like, the sword and the shield of faith.

Prayer when it has the element of listening to the word, opens the heart, the mind and the ears of the soul, making way for revelations and faith to be transmitted.

9. GOD is orderliness, due process and respects protocol; how are these intrinsic qualities to be found in FAITH? (i.e., in the person rich in faith)?

Answer:

10. Abraham, and Noah were 'God fearing', before they were drawn into communion with God; Samuel's parents trusted in God and dedicated him to God from infancy, Saul (later, Apostle Paul) has always been zealous for God. These men were drawn into communion with God. So, what is the relationship between "God-fearing" and faith?

11. Moses was a child of circumstance; raised in the courts of Pharaoh, yet himself, a Hebrew offspring – slaves in Egypt. He aligned with the downtrodden Jews rather than with Egyptian overlords. So, he was from that background an ideal material to use to liberate the Hebrews. Cornelius, loved the Jews, himself not a Jew, and was fascinated more to their forms of worship rather than to the worship of pagan gods of Rome. Both Moses and Cornelius became visionaries. What is the relationship between love of God and faith?
Answer: 1 Cor 13: 2-7 HCSB – LOVE perfects faith and godliness.

Other:
Exhortation, meditation and reflection

12. James and John had close relationship with the Lord Jesus. They trusted Him absolutely; so was Simon Peter. These men were exposed to deep mysteries not made available to the remaining 9 (apostles). Such mysteries further entrenched their faith or trust in the Lord to withstand the strongest storms. After the

death of Jesus, they were the instruments used to establish the church. What is the role of faith in all this?

13. How much of faith is a gift and how much a matter of personal responsibility? See also question 2 (above). Miracles are signs to lead people to trust in the divine power of God. Unfortunately, not all who come to knowledge of such signs engage their hearts in trust of God. The Sadducees and the Scribes would not believe, saying by the power of Beelzebub Jesus performed his miracles. So, even miracles do not always lead to faith.

Explain this: in Nazareth, though astounded by the superior wisdom displayed by Jesus, they had no faith in Him; and in spite of the various miracles performed by Jesus, the Scribes and the Pharisees demanded for more signs from Him!

God says (and it was so) that in spite of the great miracles to be enacted by Moses, Pharaoh and his court would resist him.

1. What are the examples today of this phenomenon by people of other faiths and also by followers of other denominations refusal to uphold the truth of faith, despite the evidence available?

2. Am I archetype of them?

Faith is not philosophy.

"We did not follow cleverly devised myths when we make known to you the power and coming of our Lord Jesus Christ, we are witnesses." (2 Pt 1:16)

St. Augustine: "I believe, in order to understand, and I understand, the better to believe."

Exhortation, meditation and reflection

The Gospel speaks to culture also.

"The gospel[1] does not speak only to the individual but to the culture itself. Evangelization is not simply adaptation to the culture either, nor is it a dressing up of the gospel with elements of the culture along the lines of the superficial notion of enculturation…"

"It is adaptation and maturation."

"The Christian faith is open to all that is great, true and pure in world culture. Anyone who evangelises today would start at looking at our culture for those features in it that are open to the gospel the seeds of the word, so to speak, and must strive to develop them further."

Faith does not seek to offer man some sort of psychotherapy. Its psychotherapy is the truth. This is what makes it universal – by nature, missionary.

Understanding and rational engagement of prior given word is a constituted principle of the Christian faith which of necessity spans theology. This trait, moreover, distinguishes the Christian faith from all other religions, even from a purely historical point of view. Theology is a specifically Christian phenomenon, which follows from the structure of this faith."

Trust God

Until man is able to create his own god, there will always be **the factor of the unknown**, the unpredictable in our dealing with our God. Because unless we know as much as He knows we can never be able to adjudicate correctly on some issues, especially those not previously dealt with or revealed to us by God.

Pope Benedict XVI D.M.: "We know God not simply with our understanding but also with our will and with our heart. Therefore, the knowledge of God – the knowledge of Christ – is a path that demands the involvement of the whole of our being."

Faith is no indoctrination

Indoctrination and psychotherapy both involve subjecting the victim into a series of beliefs or statements which, however absurd, are repeated and acted upon as if true.

Advertisers use the same trick to implant their make belief in the sub-consciousness of their listeners. Someone said that lies said over and over again are soon taken for truth!

Faith has no cause to bathe in such deception, for faith is real and works off miracles are not magical acts at all.

(1: Pope Emeritus Benedict XVI, Daily Meditations, op.cit)

Exhortation, meditation and reflection

Therefore, if faith is no science or a form of philosophy, should we accept it as a form of nature study, first revealed by God, Himself? Let's follow the trail diligently then.

"Faith[1] is not a convenient ideology; obedience to the church is its concreteness. The church is our contemporaneity with Christ,…"

You are called (to believe), but do you believe? If so, where is your faith?

Read the parable of a king's banquet Matt 22: 1-14 (See chapter 14 for details)

Grace to believe

Believing is a responsibility of the hearer Like the ball in a football match, only the goal keeper grabs the ball; other players kick it out. Only the hearer who embraces the word can have faith, all who oppose/contradict the word cannot be a believer. therein lies personal responsibility.

Faith is like the gift of language or the eye, no community or person is denied the grace

"My house shall be called a house of prayer for all peoples."
(Isa 56: 7 HCSB)

You don't believe?

494

You are squeamish about accepting Jesus and His teachings? Congratulations! You are not alone in this; for the Scriptures reported that "For not even his brothers believed in Him."

(Jn 7: 5 HCSB)

But be prudent; ensure you are on the right side. Here is something greater than the temple; "the name that is above every name" (Phil 2: 9 HCSB)

Merely lukewarm about God?

"What does it avail to know that there is God, which you not only believe by faith, but also know by reason? What does it avail that you know Him if you think little of Him?"

– St Thomas More Feb 2, 1478 – July 6, 1535

1: - Pope Emeritus Benedict XVI, Daily meditations.

Exhortation, meditation and reflection

Faith's goal is the truth

"Faith[1] has to do with truth;…

Faith does not aim to offer man some sort of psychotherapy, its psychotherapy is the truth. This is what makes it universal, by nature missionary."

"Faith[2], is intrinsically in search of understanding…"

1: Pope Emeritus Benedict XVI: Daily Meditations, Re. 'Faith and our goal.'

2: Daily Meditations, Re. Happiness & the passion of being human

"Faith", by St Thomas Aquinas (1225-1274):

"Believing is an act of the intellect assenting to the divine truth by command of the will moved by God through grace."

FAITH IS –

1. "Affirmation of the basic purpose and meaning of the Old Testament as proclamation of divine promise. And …

2. The gift of the Holy Spirit and denotes acceptance of salvation as God's righteousness, that is, God's gift of a renewed relationship in forgiveness and power for a new life." (Rome 1: 2; 4: 13)

3. "Response to God's total claim on people and their destiny."[1]

FAITH and FEAR

Faith and fear are two sides of the same coin, different ends of the pole.

If you have faith or confidence in God as the One in charge of the affairs of men and in His graciousness and omnipotence you would have no cause to fear. You need only to obey Him.

In the worst case scenario, what will be will be, fear will not stop it.

William Shakespeare says, "of all things most wonderful it seems to me most strange that men should fear, seeing that death, a necessary end, will come when it will…" You can't but agree with the acoustic which defined fear as:

"Fall expectation.

"Appearing Real"

'Appearing real,' indeed!

1: NABRE Editors' notes Re. Righteousness of God from faith to faith. (Rom 1: 17)

Exhortation, meditation and reflection

"Fear not!"

Someone says these words appear in the Bible 613 times!

"For God has not given us a spirit of fearfulness, but one of power, love and sound judgement." (2 Tim 1:7 HCSB)

See also Rom 8: 15.

Faith is trusting and hoping in God

Abraham's faith (Gen 21:8-14; 22:1-18)

Abraham was tested for our sake to reveal to us what faith does, the complete submission or what faith accomplishes of us –
OBEDIENCE to God!

Episode I

Abraham had it tough begetting an offspring, finding favour with God, he had gotten two. At his 100th year the mother of the younger child demanded that he threw out his elder child and his mother!
(Gen 21:8-14).

As Abraham was upset by this, God's voice came demanding that he accedes to his wife's request promising him some consolation! The scripture told us that Abraham promptly complied, "early the next morning!"

Episode II

Abraham was now left with only one son, Isaac. As if his former ordeal was not agonising enough the voice of God came to Abraham acknowledged his love for Isaac, yet demanded that he butcher this only remaining son and turn him into a holocaust offering! (Gen 22:1-10)

The scriptures again testifies that "early the next morning" (as before) Abraham set out to comply with the Lord's behest. Before then, he had made all the necessary preparation taking along with him the wood, the .....? the knife and the son, Isaac .... and slaves for transportation because the journey could be long. He exercised discretion not to broach the subject before any person – the mother of the child, the child, or the servants.

Exhortation, meditation and reflection

Reward.

God blessed Abraham for his obedience. "Because you have done this thing and have not withheld your only son I will indeed bless you ..." "... because you have obeyed my command" (Gen 22:16-18 HCSB)

Agnostics, Animists and Monotheists:
Faith is not giving up hope

Episode III:

Consider the woman with the malaise/issue of blood (Mk 5:24-34)

For 12 years she had suffered this menace which no health expert had been able to alleviate.

Yet, she was still hoping for a cure, she heard about Jesus and believed He could cure her; she turned to Jesus. It paid off for she was cured!

Episode IV:

Jairus faith. (Mt 9: 18-19; 23-26)

This synagogue official, unlike many of his colleagues, the rabbi, saw something in Jesus which made him believe it was right to approach Him for the life of his dead daughter. If he had not approached Jesus. It would have been the end of the road for the daughter. But he did and the daughter regained her life breath!

Personal faith levels

The Catholic Church, to the best of my understanding already recognises what I call personal faith levels. Members with claims or even proven of special gifts are not compelled to drop the exercise of such gifts in what we may call informal liturgical gatherings/settings. Such gifts include – clairvoyance/seeing visions, healing excorcism, precipitate speaking in tongues, etc. oh, how I treasure such freedom! It saves the church from taking free tetous in matters in which clarity is only about to emerge. No doubt orthodoxy benefits all – members and the faith alike. In this manner, our faith, like any other organism, can grow to maturity. Of course, the hierarchy can, indeed as a duty, to warn devotees of excesses. Hard lines on doctrines polarizes the church.

The leadership of the Christian faith has a divine duty to guide believers on the way of truth.

Exhortation, meditation and reflection

Such guidance may take various forms: formal statements of information and explanation; doctrines/doctrinaire, dogmas or decrees. Such decrees should aim to carry along (without any compulsion) the leadership of no less than 90% of the body of Christ. The process is syncrefic and many be found helpful in every cffort/thrust to keep the body of Christ together as one.

For clarity, take for example, some of the different approaches to the Lord's Supper – the banquet of His love. The words of the Lord are unequivocal; "this is My body ..." "... this is My blood." But it is different thing entirely to say that we should give the same reverence to the meal consisting of the flesh and blood as we give to the entire personality of the Lord. Of course in (figure of speech) a part can stand for the whole. Those dithering to accept the real presence and worship food attract our sympathy. If they do this to avoid the greater pitfall of idolatry. The church as taught that God is omnipresent so is it rather delusory to give additional or "special reverence to an image or icon of God, the Father; or God, the son or God the Holy Spirit? Certainly, the two views deserves our respect and could be harmonized or reconciled to sustain unity in our faith/belief as the body of Christ. After all, disunity on fundamental issues of faith benefits only one person – Satan, the enemy of our souls.

CHAPTER 14

Righteousness

Blessed are

- The poor in spirit – for theirs is the kingdom of heaven
- They who hunger and thirst for righteousness –for they will be satisfied.
- The peacemakers – for they will be calledthe children of God
- They who are persecuted for the sake of righteousness–for theirs isthe kingdom of heaven. (Matt 5: 3, 6, 9-10 NABRE)

Be upright

"Do not be agitated by evil doers;
do not envy those who do wrong.
For they wither quickly like grass
and wilt like tender green plants.
Be silent before the Lord and wait expectantly for Him;
do not be agitated by one who prospers in his way,
by the man who carries out evil plans.
Refrain from anger and give up your rage;
do not be agitated – it can only bring harm.
Watch the blameless and observe the upright,
for the man of peace will have a future."
(Ps 37: 1-2, 7-8, 37)
"… Stop doing evil.
Learn to do what is good.
Seek justice.
Correct the oppressor;
defend the rights of the fatherless.

Plead the widow's cause." (Isa 1: 16, 17)

FORGIVE!

You must forgive; that you may be forgiven! (Matt 6: 12, 14; 18: 35)

"Then Peter came to Him and said,

'Lord, how many times could my brother sin against me and I forgive him?

As many as seven times?'"

Forgiveness: The 70x7 Rule.

The Lord replied him:

"I tell you, not as many as seven,... but seventy times seven." (Matt 18: 21, 22)

Thus, in the parable to demonstrate the wisdom of this divine injunction, the parable of the unforgiving servant, Jesus concluded, saying:

"So My heavenly Father will also do to you if each of you does not forgive his brother from his heart." (Matt 18: 35)

Possessions

Jesus says,

"Don't collect for yourselves treasures on earth... But collect for yourselves treasures in heaven,..." (Matt 6: 19-20)

Jesus has said, "Let your light shine before men,

so that they may see your good works

and giveglory to your Father in heaven." (Matt 5: 16 HCSB)

SEEK GOD!

"The Lord looks down from heaven on the human race,

to seeif there is one who is wise,

one who seeks God.

All alike have become corrupt.

There is no one who does good,

not even one." (Ps 14: 2-3)

"Seek the Lord, all you humble of the earth,

who carry out what He commands.
Seek righteousness, seek humility;
perhaps you will be concealed on the day
of the Lord's anger." (Zeph 2: 3)
"… Rejoice, o hearts that seek the Lord!
Look to the Lord in His strength;
seek to serve Him constantly." (Ps 105: 3-4 Lect)
Flee from violence.
"… **the fruit of righteousness** is sown in peace by those who cultivate peace."(Js 3: 18)
Admonish Sinners
"Whoever turns a sinner from the error of his way will save his life from death and cover a multitude of sins."(Js 5:19: 20)
Jesus: Our wisdom
"Blessed are those who are persecuted for righteousness' sake,
for theirs is the kingdom of heaven." (Matt 5: 10 NRSV-CE)
"… Jesus Christ… became for us wisdom from God, as well as righteousness, sanctification, and redemption." (1 Cor 1: 30)
Called According to His Purpose
"We know that all things work together for the good of those who love God: those who are called according to His purpose. For those He foreknew He also predestined to be conformed to the image of His Son. So that He would be the firstborn among many brothers. And those He predestined, He also called; and those He called, He also justified; and those He justified, He also glorified."
(Rom 8: 28-30)
Sing the Lord's praises
"Sing a new song to the Lord;
sing His praise from the ends of the earth…" (Isa 42: 10)
Persecution:
"You will even be brought before governors and kings because of Me, to bear witness to them and to the nations. You will be hated by everyone because of My name. But the one who endures to the end will be delivered."

(Matt 10: 18, 22)

Fear not… (Matt 10: 26-31)

The Law And The Prophets

"Do to others whatever you would have them do to you. This is the law and the prophets." (Matt 7: 12 NABRE)

The Word

"… My mother and my brothers are those who hear the word of God and act on it." (Lk 8: 21 NABRE)

Be gracious to your neighbour as you would to Jesus!

In the gathering of all the nations for recompense and condemnation –

The Lord, the presiding judge would say –

Matt 25: 31-46 when I was hungry, thirsty, naked, homeless, sick, imprisoned… if you did nothing, you are condemned; if you showed care, you get recompensed.

The 'I' above is 'Jesus', because what you do to the least brother/neighbour is deemed done to Him.

Be reconciled first You bring an offering to the alter, but you remember a brother has something against you – reconcile first with that person, so your offering may be acceptable (Matt 5: 23)

Obey God!

"… We must obey God rather than men." (Acts 5: 29)

The righteous – I

"How happy is the man

who does not follow the advice of the wicked

or take the path of sinners

or join a group of mockers!

Instead, his delights is in the Lord's instruction,

and he meditates on it day and night.

He is like a tree planted beside streams of water

that bears its fruit in season

and whose leaf does not wither.

Whatever he does prospers." (Ps 1: 1-3)

The righteous - II

"The eyes of the Lord are on the righteous,
and His ears are open to their cry for help.
The Lord is near the broken hearted;
He saves those crushed in spirit.
Many adversities come to the one who is righteous,
but the Lord delivers him from them all." (Ps 34: 15, 18, 19)
Docility
If only, today, you would listen to His voice:
"Do not harden your hearts…" (Ps 95: 8 L of H)
"Indeed, like clay in the hand of the potter, so are you in My hand, house of Israel." (Jer 18: 6)

Some of us are so hardened of heart, we interpret instructions always in consistency with our preconceptions no matter how disparate. Be docile.

Submit to God, but resist the Devil and he will flee. (Js 4: 7)

United beyond race, language or ethnicity

"For as many of you as have been baptized into Christ have put on Christ like a garment. There is no Jew or Greek, slave or free, male or female, for you are all one in Christ Jesus." (Gal 3: 27-28)

The Rash and the Righteous

1. "Look, his ego is inflated;
he is without integrity.
But the righteous one will live
by his faith." (Heb 2: 4 HCSB)
2. "And this is the message:
'Those who are evil will not survive,
but those who are righteous will live
because they are faithful to God." (Heb 2: 4 GNBDK)
3. "See, the rash have no integrity;
but the just one who is righteous
because of faith shall live." (Heb 2: 4 NABRE)
The righteous will shine.

"Then the righteous will shine like the sun in their Father's kingdom.

Anyone who has ears should listen!" (Matt 13: 43 HCSB)

"**The fear of the Lord** rejoices the heart,

giving gladness, joy, and long life.

The beginning of wisdom is to fear the Lord;

The fear of the Lord drives away sins;

where it abides it turns back all anger." (Sir 1: 12, 14, 21 NABRE)

WHO may ascend the mountain of the Lord?

Who may stand in His holy place?

The one who has clean hands and a pure heart, who has not set his mind on what is false,

and who has not sworn deceitfully. (Ps 24: 3-4)

The Do's and Don'ts of righteousness:

1. **Do's** – St Paul's summary to the Ephesians –**the whole armour of God...**

"Put on the full armour of God so that you can stand against the tactics of the Devil. Stand, therefore, with truth like a belt around your waist, righteousness like armour on your chest, and your feet sandaled with readiness for the gospel of peace.In every situation take the shield of faith, and with it you will be able to extinguish all the flaming arrows of the evil one.

Take the helmet of salvation,

and the sword of the Spirit,

which is God's word

pray at all times... and stay alert in this with all perseverance and intercession for all the saints". (Eph 6: 11, 14-18)

"The light of the righteous shines brightly,

but the lamp of the wicked is put out." (Prov 13: 9 HCSB)

2. **Don'ts** – putting away falsehood, speak the truth.

"Therefore, putting away falsehood, speak the truth, each one to his neighbour, for we are members one of another.

Be angry but do not sin; do not let the sun set on your anger, and do not leave room for the Devil.

The thief must no longer steal, but rather labour, doing honest work with his (own) hands, so that he may have something to share with one inneed.

No foul language should come out of your mouths, but only such as is good for needed edification, that it may impart grace to those who hear.

And do not grieve the Holy Spirit of God, with which you were sealed for the day of redemption. All bitterness, fury, anger, shouting, and reviling must be removed from you, along with all malice.

(And) be kind to one another, compassionate, forgiving one another as God has forgiven you in Christ." (Eph 4: 25-32 HCSB)

Intercede for one another "Therefore, confess your sins to one another and pray for one another, so that you may be healed. The urgent request of a righteous person is very powerful in its effect." (Js 5: 16)

Love

"... Whoever does not do what is right is not of God, especially the one who does not love his brother."

"... We must not love with word or speech,
but with truth and action." (1 Jn 3: 10, 18)

Right standing with God:

- Brother sinning against you (Matt 18: 15-20)

"If your brother sins against you, go and rebuke him in private. If he listens to you, you have won your brother..."

- You sinning against brother (Matt 5: 22-24)

"Leave your gift there at the altar, go first and be reconciled with your brother,…" (Matt 5: 24 NABRE)

The Fear of God

"WHOEVER lives with integrity fears the Lord,

but the one who is devious in his ways despises Him." (Prov 14: 2)

Light shines in the darkness for the upright.

He is gracious, compassionate, and righteous.

He will not fear bad news;

his heart is confident, trusting in the Lord. (Ps 112: 4, 7)

Everyone is welcome to the Kingdom

Jesus reveals: "It is not the will of God that anyone be lost." (Matt 18: 14 Lect)

"… The gentiles are co-heirs, members of the same body and partners of the promise in Christ Jesus…" (Eph 3: 4 HCSB)

"The eyes of the Lord are on the righteous,

and His ears are open to their cry for help.

The Lord is near the broken-hearted;

He saves those crushed in spirit." (Ps 34: 15, 18)

God: Our Great Provider

Young lions lack food and go hungry, but

those who seek the Lord will not lack any good thing.

(Ps 34: 10)

Warning against presumption (1 Cor 10: 1-13)

"Therefore, whoever thinks he is standing secure should

take care not to fall." (1 Cor 10: 12 NABRE)

Avoid Ostentation.

"Take care not to perform righteous deeds in order that people may see them; otherwise, you will have no recompense from your heavenly Father."

(Matt 6: 1 NABRE)

God's goodness

"How great is Your goodness that You have stored

up for those who fear You

and accomplished in the sight of everyone
for those who take refuge in You." (Ps 31: 19)
Adversities and hate of the righteous
"Many adversities come to the one who is righteous,
but the Lord delivers him from them all.
Evil brings death to the wicked
and those who hate the righteous will be punished." (Ps 34: 19, 21)

Righteousness – I

Love! (Even your enemy)
"But to you who hear I say,
Love your enemies, do good to those
who hate you, bless those who curse you,
pray for those who mistreat you.
Do to others as you would have them do to you."
(Lk 6: 27-28, 31)

- Your call to be righteous is a call to be kindly toward all who comes your way.(Lk 6: 27-45)

Righteousness – II

"Practise honesty and integrity. Rescue the man who has been wronged from the hands of his oppressors. Do not exploit the stranger, the orphan or the widow; do no violence, shed no innocent blood in this place."

"Do good and share; share what you have."
(Jer 22: 3; Heb 13: 16 Lect)

In imitation of Christ.

"Do not love the world or the things that belong to the world. If anyone loves the world, love for the Father is not in him. For everything that belongs to the world – the lust of flesh, the lust of the eyes, and the pride in one's lifestyle – is not from the Father, but is from the world." (1 Jn 2: 15-16)

The Narrow Gate – to the kingdom of God.

"Enter through the narrow gate. For the gate is wide and the road is broad that leads to destruction, and there are many who go through it." (Matt 7: 13)

"'Lord', someone asked Him, 'Are there few being saved?'

He said to them,

'Make every effort to enter through the narrow door, because I tell you, many will try to enter and won't be able. But He will say, 'I tell you, I don't know you or where you're from. Get away from Me, all you workers of unrighteousness!'

They will come from east and west, from north and south, and recline at the table in the Kingdom of God.'" (Lk 13: 23-24, 27, 29 HCSB)

Deny yourself, take up your cross.

"Then Jesus said to His disciples,

'If anyone wants to come with Me, he must deny himself, take up his cross and follow Me. For whoever wants to save his life will lose it, but whoever loses his life because of Me will find it. What will it benefit a man if he gains the whole world yet loses his life? Or what will a man give in exchange for his life?'" (Matt 16: 24-26)

For further discussion on this theme, see Chap. 5 (Discipleship)

▪ Your call: Truth and sanctification

"…From the beginning God has chosen you for salvation through sanctification, by the spirit and through belief in the truth." (2 Thes 2: 13 HCSB)

Discipline

Accept discipline (Heb 12: 6), better still, be self-disciplined.

Be voice to the voiceless

"SPEAK UP for those who have no voice, for the justice of all who are dispossessed." (Prov 31: 8 HCSB)

Your Kingdom Come, Your will be done… (Matt 6: 10)
- "The Lord foils the plan of nations,
frustrates the designs of peoples.
But the plan of the Lord stands forever,
the designs of His heart through all generations."
(Ps 33: 10-11 NABRE)
- Ask: "And we have this confidence in Him,
that if we ask anything according to His will,
He hears us." (1 Jn 5: 14 NABRE)
GOD, OUR RIGHTEOUSNESS
"I have treasured Your word in my heart
so that I may not sin against You.
I gain understanding from Your precepts;
Therefore I hate every false way,
Your word is a lamp for my feet,
and a light on my path." (Ps 119: 11, 104-105 HCSB)
FLESH AND BLOOD
- "And a man's enemies will be
the members of his household." (Matt 10: 36 HCSB)

Not by flesh and blood:

- "And Jesus responded,
'Simon son of Jonah, you are blessed
because flesh and blood did not reveal
this to you, but My Father in heaven.'" (Matt 16: 17 HCSB)
- Notice that the gentiles (the Magi) were the first to pay homage to Jesus (Matt 2: 11)
- "A man's enemies are the men of his own household." (Mic 7: 6 HSCB)

Hope in the Lord

"Do not trust in nobles,
in man who cannot save.
When his breath leaves him,
he returns to the ground;
on that day his plans die." (Ps 146: 3-4 HCSB)
Keep the word (Jn 5: 3 HCSB)
Jesus said,
"Even more, those who hear the word of God
and keep it are blessed!" (Lk 11: 28)
A curse, a blessing
"For the devious are detestable to the Lord,
but He is a friend to the upright.
The Lord's curse is on the household of the wicked,
but He blesses the home of the righteous." (Prov 3: 32-33 HCSB)
Serve God
"Do not lack diligence; be fervent in spirit;
serve the Lord." (Rom 12: 11)
Be like Apollos (Acts 18: 25)
The Righteous Reward
"God's blessing is the lot of the righteous,
and in due time their hope bears fruit." (Sir 11: 22 NABRE)
Eternal life
"And this is the testimony: God has given us eternal life, and this life is in His Son." (1 Jn 5: 11 HCSB)
Jesus is the Messiah
"Everyone who believes that Jesus is the Messiah has been born of God…" "because whatever has been born of God conquers the world…"
(1 Jn 5: 1, 4 HCSB)
- Your call
To be holy (1 Cor 1: 2)

All Christians are called to be holy. It means that whether in clerical or secular life you are to allow the gospel ethos to permeate your work.

Call to fellowship with the Lord Jesus (1 Cor 1: 9)

Call to be an apostle (to witness for Christ) (1 Cor 1: 1)

Praises and almsgiving.

"Therefore, through Him let us continually
offer up to God a sacrifice of praise,
that is, the fruit of our lips that confess His name.
Don't neglect to do what is good and to share,
for God is pleased with such sacrifices." (Heb 13: 15-16 HCSB)

Both Prophet and Priest are watchmen

Just as Ezekiel was appointed watchman for the house of Israel (Ezk 33: 7)

Be prepared always!

"… The righteousness of the righteous person will not save him on the day of his transgression; neither will the wickedness of the wicked person cause him to stumble on the day he turns from his wickedness. The righteous person won't be able to survive by his righteousness on the day he sins."

(Ezk 33: 12 HCSB)

The Kingdom of Heaven

In the last days,
The mountain of the Lord's house will be established
at the top of the mountains
and will be raised above the hills.
All nations will stream to it,…
For instruction will go out of Zion
and the word of the Lord from Jerusalem…
Nations will not take up the sword against other nations,
and they will never again train for war.
(Isa 2: 2, 3, 4)

Be perfect!
"Be perfect, therefore, as your
Heavenly Father is." (Matt 5: 48 HCSB)
Acceptable sacrifices
"Don't neglect…
to share, for God is pleased
with such sacrifices." (Heb 13: 16 HCSB)

Look, that poor man is your brother!

"Is there a poor man among you… in any town of yours… Do not harden your heart or close your hand against that poor brother of yours, but be open-handed with him and lend him." (Deut 15: 7-8 Lect)

Be prosperous!

"Be careful to obey all these things I command you, so that you and your children after you may prosper forever, because you will be doing what is good and right in the sight of the Lord your God." (Deut 12: 28 HCSB)

"GIVE, and it will be given to you;…

For with the measure you use

it will bemeasured back to you." (Lk 6: 38 HCSB)

Signs of faith

"These signs will accompany those who believe:

In My name they will drive out demons; they will speak in new languages;… they will lay hands on the sick, and they will get well."

(Mk 16: 17-18 HCSB)

Sin and the devil

"… everyone who has been born of God does not sin, …"

"… we are of God, and the whole world is under the sway of the evil one."

"Everyone who believes that Jesus is the Messiah has been born of God, and everyone who loves the Father also loves the One born of Him."

(1 Jn 5: 18, 19, 1 HCSB)

- Called to be holy…

"For He chose us in Him, before the foundation of the world, to be holy, and blameless in His sight in love." (Eph 1: 4 HCSB)

"… God has already chosen us to be His through our union with Christ, so that we would be holy and without fault before Him."

"Send Your light and Your truth; let them lead me.

Let them bring me to Your holy mountain, to Your dwelling place." (Ps 43: 3 HCSB)

"For by the blood of Christ, we are set free, that is, our sins are forgiven…" (Eph 1: 4, 7 GNBDK)

- **Call to be children of God** (Lk 8: 19-21)

Compare Lk 11: 28 HCSB; Rev 12: 17 NABRE

Discerning the call of God.

Have you recognised how God speaks to you?

He spoke to Peter in a noon day short nap or vision – the kill and eat vision – (Acts 10: 10-20)

The Call of Saul (Apostle Paul)

Consider also the call of Saul, the apostle (Acts 9: 1-22 or 22: 3-16.)

- Call to be one in the truth (all disciples) Jn 17: 17

HCSB: "Sanctify them by the truth; Your word is truth."

NABRE: "Consecrate them in the truth. Your word is truth."

GNBDK: "Dedicate them to Yourself by means of the truth; Your word is truth."

NKJV: "Sanctify them by Your truth. Your word is truth."

Compare above with 1 Pt 1: 22.

Visa to heaven

Do you have what it takes?

"… Go, sell all you have and give to the poor, and you will have treasure in heaven. Then come, follow Me." (Mk 10: 21)

Recompense

- "WHAT no eyes have seen, nor ear heard, nor the heart of man conceived, what God has prepared for those who love Him." (Js 64: 4; 65: 17)
- "Those who are wise will shine… and those who lead many to righteousness like the stars forever and ever." (Dan 12: 3 HCSB)
- "The house of the wicked will be destroyed…"
- "…curse on the household of the wicked." (Prov 14: 11; 3: 33 HCSB)

"The violence of the wicked sweeps them away because they refuse to act justly." (Prov 21: 7 HCSB)

MUST DO to enter Eternal Life – "Love!"

"There was a scholar of the Law who stood up to test Him and said 'Teacher, what must I do to inherit eternal life?'

Jesus said to him, 'What is written in the law? How do you read it?'

He said in reply, 'You shall love the Lord, your God, with all your heart, with all your being, with all your strength, and with all your mind, and your neighbour as yourself.'"

Jesus replied him,

"You have answered correctly; do this and you will live."

(Lk 10: 25-27, 28 HCSB)

The Christian Mantra: Repent!

- "John, (the) Baptist appeared in the desert proclaiming a baptism of repentance for the forgiveness of sins." (Mk 1: 4 NABRE)
- "After John was arrested, Jesus went to Galilee, preaching the good news of God:

'The time is fulfilled, and the kingdom of God has come near. Repent and believe in the good news!'" (Mk 1: 14-15 HCSB)

- The mission of the Twelve

"So they went out and preached that people should repent."
(Mk 6: 12 HCSB)

- The mission of the 70

"… go out into the streets and say, '… Yet know this the kingdom of God is at hand.'" (Lk 10: 10-11 HCSB)

Why alive?

NABRE: "so that we might exist for the praise of His glory, we who first hoped in Christ." (Eph 1: 12)

HCSB: "so that we who had already put our hope in the Messiah might bring praise to His glory." (Eph 1: 12)

Prayer

"God, create a clean heart for me,
and renew a steadfast spirit within me.
Do not banish me from Your presence,
or take Your Holy Spirit from me." Amen. (Ps 51: 10-11)

True righteousness

I gain understanding from Your precepts;
therefore, I hate every false way.
Your word is a lamp for my feet
and a light on my path. (Ps 119: 104-105 HCSB)

"I have treasured Your word in my heart
so that I may not sin against You." (Ps 119: 11 HCSB)

Works of God:

Crowd: "What can we do to perform the works of God?"

Jesus: "This is the work of God – that you believe in the One He has sent."

(Jn 6: 28-29 HCSB)

Live by faith.

"For yet in a very little while,

516

the Coming One will come…
But My righteous one will live by faith;
and if he draws back, I have no pleasure in him."
(Heb 10: 37-38 HCSB)
By your word
"When a sieve is shaken, the husks appear;
so do people's faults when they speak"
"The fruit of a tree shows the care it has had;
so speech discloses the bent of a person's heart."
(Sir 27: 4, 6 NABRE)

SEEK THE LORD – ASPIRE!

"If then you were raised with Christ,
seek what is above, where Christ is seated
at the right hand of God." (Col 3: 1 NABRE)

"Glory in His holy name;

Let hearts that seek the Lord rejoice!
Seek out the Lord and His might;
Constantly seek His face." (Ps 105: 3-4 NABRE)

Thirst for God.

"As a deer longs for streams of water,
so I long for You, God.
I thirst for God, the living God.
When can I come and appear before God?"
"The Lord will send His faithful love by day;
His song will be with me in the night –
a prayer to the God of my life."
(Ps 42: 1-2, 18 HCSB)

You need endurance

"You need endurance to do the will of God
and receive what He has promised."
(Heb 10: 36 NABRE)
The Law
Jesus says, **"Observe the commandments"** (Matt 19: 16-22)

Be perfect

At the onset of our journey in holiness; it was:
"…a tooth for a tooth.
But I say to you, offer no resistance to one who is evil.
So be perfect, just as your heavenly Father is perfect."
(Matt 5: 38)

TRUE RELIGION

"Religion that is pure and un-defiled before God and the Father is this: to care for the orphans and widows in their affliction and to keep oneself unstained by the world." (Js 1: 27 Lect)

JEWS AND GENTILES – ONE GOD, FATHER OF ALL

Lk 14: 15 One at table with Christ exclaimed, 'blessed the one who will feast at the kingdom of heaven'.

: 16 Then Jesus told (him) this parable: A man gave a large banquet, invited many.

: 18 But without exception they all made excuses.

: 21 Then in anger the master instructed his servants to invite all in the town and still there were room left.

: 23 He instructed the servant to go beyond there "into the highways and lanes" to invite people to it.

ADDITIONAL RESOURCES

For God's glory

- "Mankind… act justly, love faithfulness and walk humbly with your God." (Mic 6: 8, HCSB)
- Make fair decisions, show love and compassion… no oppression… (Zec 7: 9-10)

- "… Do everything for God's glory" (1 Cor 10: 31 HCSB)
- "Therefore, whether you eat or drink, or whatever you do, DO EVERYTHING FOR GOD'S GLORY"

"Kept from sinning" – grace for the upright.

"I have also kept you from sinning against Me." (Gen 20: 6 HCSB)

Don't depart from godliness! Sinners repent!

"… The justice of the just will not save them on the day they sin; the wickedness of the wicked will not bring about their downfall on the day they turn from their wickedness. No, the just cannot save their lives on the day they sin." (Ezk 33: 12 NABRE)

Duty to speak truthfully

"But a man named Ananias with his wife Sapphira, sold a piece of property." "However, he kept back part of the proceeds with his wife's knowledge,…" "Then Peter said, … why … keep back part of the proceeds from the field?" "… You have not lied to men but to God!" "… Ananias dropped dead,…" "Instantly she (Sapphira) dropped dead…"

(Acts 5: 1-2, 3, 4-5, 10 HCSB)

"The one who is from God listens to God's words.

This is why you don't listen, because you are not from God."

(Jn 8: 47 HCSB)

Come in; but measure up!

Jesus once more spoke to them (the chief priests and elders of the people) in parables.

The kingdom of heaven may be compared to a king…

He sent out his slaves to summon those invited to the banquet,… 'come to the wedding banquet.'

But they paid no attention and went away… the others seized his slaves,… killed them.

The king was enraged... destroyed those murderers, and ... Then he told his slaves **'The banquet is ready, but those... invited were unworthy**.' Therefore, go to where the roads exit the city and invite everyone you find... The wedding banquet was filled with guests. ... the king ... saw a man there who was not dressed for a wedding. So he said to him, 'Friend, how did you get in here without wedding clothes?'

... 'Tie him up hand and foot, and throw him into the outer darkness, where there will be weeping and gnashing of teeth.'

"For many are invited, but few are chosen."

(Matt 21: 23; 22: 1-14 HCSB)

The sinner has no share in the kingdom.

"Do not be deceived: No sexually immoral people, idolaters, adulterers, or anyone practising homosexuality, no thieves,... will inherit God's kingdom."

(1 Cor 9: 10 HCSB)

Divine guidance

"By the Lord are the steps of a man-made firm... for the hand of the Lord sustains him." (Ps 37: 23, 24 NABRE)

Seek the Kingdom first

"But seek first the kingdom of God and His righteousness, and all these things will be given you besides." (Matt 6: 33 NABRE)

If God be the King of the nation

"... I will appoint peace your governor, and justice your ruler." (Isa 60: 17 NABRE)

Justice and peace

"See, a king will reign justly

and princes will rule rightly."

"No more will the fool be called noble,

nor the trickster be considered honourable." (Isa 32: 1, 5 HCSB)

Think about this –	
It is not an easy road! "The law and the prophets lasted until John; but from then on the Kingdom of God is proclaimed, and everyone who enters does so with violence." (Lk 16: 16 NABRF)	"From the days of John the Baptist until now, the Kingdom of heaven has been suffering violence, and the violent have been seizing it by force." (Matt 11: 12 HCSB)

Justice will bring about peace and security.

"For the fool speak foolishly,
planning evil in his heart:
How to do wickedness,
to speak perversely against the Lord,
to let the hungry go empty
and the thirsty be without drink.
And the trickster uses wicked trickery,
planning crimes:
How to ruin the poor with lies,
and the needy when they plead their case.
Justice will bring about peace;
right will produce calm and security." (Isa 32: 6, 7, 17 HCSB)
Not talk but power "For the Kingdom of God is not a matter of talk but of power."
(1 Cor 4: 20 NABRE)

The 2-ways: the righteous, the wicked

"The path of the righteousness is like the light of dawn, shinning brighter and brighter until mid-day.

But the way of the wicked is like the darkest gloom; they don't know what makes them stumble." (Prov 4: 18, 19)

Not food but righteousness

"The Kingdom of God is not a matter of food and drink, but of righteousness, peace and joy in the Holy Spirit." (Rom 14: 17 NABRE)

Life for everyone

God desires life for everyone: that we embrace righteousness rather than sin.

(Ezk 18: 23; 33: 11; Deut 30: 19)

The kingdom parables: The kingdom of God is –

- Like yeast Which leavened a whole batch of dough (Lk 13: 20-21)
- Like a king who gave a wedding banquet for his son, the invited guests failed to come; others were invited… "For many are invited, but few are chosen." (Matt 22: 2-14)
- Like mustard seed One of the smallest of seeds. When it was fully grown became a large tree. (Mk 4: 30-32, Matt 13: 31-32; Lk 13: 18-19)
- Like a man scattering seed on the land The seed sprouted and grew automatically without any further effort of the man. He harvested it when ripe. (Mk 4: 26-29; Matt)
- Like a sower As he sowed, some seeds fell on the path-way (eaten up by birds), some on rocky ground (became scorched); some fell among thorns (which choked them) and some fell on rich soil, producing fruit – some thirty, some sixty and some a hundred-fold.

"Whoever has ears to hear ought to hear." (Mk 4: 2-20; Matt 13: 1-9)

- Like the man in the parable of the wheat and the weeds. He sowed good seed but his enemy sowed weeds among the wheat and left. "Let both grow together until the harvest." (Matt 13: 24-30)
- Like the treasure buried in a field that a man found and reburied; sold everything he had and bought that field. (Matt 13: 44)
- Like the merchant of fine pearls, which he found, sold all he had and bought. (Matt 13: 45)
- Like a fishing net thrown into the sea, collecting every kind of fish, some good, some bad… (Matt 13: 47-)

- Like a king settling accounts with his slaves. One who owed 10,000 talents was forgiven, but that same slavewould not forgive his fellow slave who owed just 100 denarii. "So my heavenly Father will also do to you" unless each of you forgive his brother… (Matt 18: 23-35)
- Like a landowner who hired workers for his vineyard at various hours from morning to evening and at close of day he paid them an equal wage, the amount contracted with the earliest."So the last shall be first, and the first last." (Matt 20: 1-16)
- Like 10 virgins with lamps – 5 wise, 5 foolish. The groom was delayed. On arrival the fuel is burnt out in the lanterns of the foolish. "Therefore be alert, because you don't know the day or the hour." (Matt 25: 1-13)

Compare (for rewards/recompense) the parable of the minas – the nobleman was departing to a far country, to return later with "the authority to be king". One man made additional 10 for the mina he was given, another 5 and another no gain at all. The master made the one who gained 10, ruler over 10 towns; the one who made 5, ruler over 5 towns, scolded the one with no gain.

"…'To everyone who has, more will be given; and from the one who does not have, even what he does have will be taken away.'"

"'But bring… these enemies who did not want me to rule over them,… slaughter them…'" (Lk 19: 11-27)

- Like a business-man who empowered his assistants with capital of 1, 2, and 5 talents respectively according to their ability. "For to everyone who has, more will be given, and he will have more than enough…" (Matt 25: 14-30)

Aspiring to be Jesus disciple (Christian)? It comes with a cost.

- Which of you commencing to build a tower would not first check his finances that he could complete it before starting? Because… if he could not complete the building for lack of funds… (Lk 14: 24-30)
- Which king facing an aggressor, would not consider the options – whether he had enough resources to overcome the invader or whether to sue for peace. "In the same way… everyone… who does not say goodbye to all his possessions cannot be My disciple." (Lk 14: 31-33)

Humility

"… whoever humbles himself like this child – this one is the greatest in the kingdom of heaven." (Matt 18: 4 HCSB)

The Kingdom of God: at the fulness of time

"The seventh angel blew his trumpet, and there were loud voices in heaven saying: The kingdom of the world has become the Kingdom of our Lord and of His Messiah, and He will reign forever and ever!" (Rev 11: 15 HCSB)

Jesus says,

"**Not everyone** who says to Me,
'Lord, Lord', will enter the kingdom of heaven,
but only the one who does the will of My Father in heaven.
Therefore, everyone who hears these words of Mine
and acts on them will be like a sensible man who built his house on a rock…
But everyone who hears those words of Mine and doesn't
act on them will be like a foolish man who built his own on the sand."
(Matt 7: 21, 24, 26 HCSB)

"We are prophets, we are miracle workers…"

"… didn't we prophesy in Your name, drive out demons in Your name, and do many miracles in Your name?" (Matt 7: 22 HCSB)

The Lord God is calling us now –

"Wash yourselves. Cleanse yourselves.
Remove your evil deeds from My sight.
Stop doing evil.
Learn to do what is good.
Seek justice.
Correct the oppressor.
Defend the rights of the fatherless.
Plead the widow's cause." (Isa 1: 16-17 HCSB)
The Righteous are the chosen race!
"But you are a chosen race, a royal priesthood, a holy nation, a people for His possession, so that you may proclaim the praises of the One who called you out of darkness into His Marvelous light." (1 Pt 2: 9 HCSB)

Give!

- "Happy is the one who cares for the poor…" (Ps 41: 1, 2, 3)
- "Give and it will be given to you; for with the measure you use, it will be measured back to you." (Lk 6: 38 HCSB)

"Make Your ways known to me, Lord;
teach me Your paths." (Ps 25: 4 HCSB) See also 27: 11
Faith, righteousness, grace and sin
The position of Apostle Paul– See also Divine Mercy in Chapter 9– faith in the blood and obedience to the Law of Moses.
Apostle Paul avers that –
1. "… the knowledge of sin comes through the Law." Rom 3:20 HCSB
2. "… God's righteousness has been revealed – attested on the Law and the Prophets – that is … through faith in Jesus Christ, to all who believe…" (Rom 3:21-22 HCSB)

GNBDK puts it thus:

"God's way of putting people right with Himself has been revealed … the law of Moses and the prophets gave their witnesses to it. God puts people right through their faith in Jesus Christ, …" (Rom 3: 21-22 GNBDK)

1. "For all have sinned and fallen short of the glory of God. They are justified freely by His grace through the redemption that is in Christ Jesus." (Rom 3: 23-24 HCSB)
2. "God presented Him as a propitiation through faith in His blood, to demonstrate His righteousness, because in His restraint God passed over the sins previously committed (Rom 3:25 HCSB)

"God offered Him, so that by His blood He should become the means by which peoples' sins are forgiven through their faith in Him. God did this … to demonstrate that He is righteous." (Rom 3:25 GNBDK)

1. Other Readings

Rom 4:3 "For what does the Scripture say?

NABRE 'Abraham believed God, and it was credited to him as righteousness.'" (c/f Gal 3: 6; Rom 4:13)

: 6 "So also David declares the blessedness of the person to whom God credits righteousness apart from works:

: 7 'Blessed are they whose iniquities are forgiven and whose sins are covered.'"

Gal 3: 2 "Tell me this one thing: did you receive God's Spirit by doing

GNBDK what the Law requires or by hearing the gospel and believing it?"

: 11 "Now, it is clear that no one is put right with God by means of the Law, because the Scripture says, 'Only the person who is put right with God through faith shall live.'"

(c/f Hbk 2: 4)

Paul's summary (Rom 3: 28, 31 HCSB)

: 28 "For we conclude that a man is justified by FAITH apart from the works of the law"

: 31 "Do we then cancel the Law through faith? Absolutely not! On the contrary, we uphold the Law."

For further insight, please see reflections section.

To be holy: "… you must walk and please God …" 1 Thes 4: 1

Those who are called

"We know that all Things work together for the good of those who love God:

those who are called according to His purpose.

For those He fore knew He also pre-destined to be conformed to the image of His Son …

And those He predestined He also called, and those He called, He also justified, and those justified, He also glorified." (Rom 8: 28-30)

Prayer

"Let the evil of the wicked come to an end, but establish the righteous."

(Ps 7: 9 HCSB)

Grace to do good work.

God is able to make every grace overflow … so that, having everything you need, you may excel in every good work (*2 Cor 9: 8*)

God knows our weakness

Ps 103: 14 HCSB "For He knows what we are made of, … dust."

The poor, the afflicted.

"Let all kings bow down to Him, all nations serve Him.

For He will rescue the poor who cry out and the afflicted who have no helper

He will have pity on the poor and helpless and save the lives of the poor.

He will redeem them from oppression and violence, for their lives are precious in His sight." (Ps 72:11-14, HCSB)

Being "born-again" (Jn 3: 3, 5, 18-20)

"That is believing in Jesus, the light of the world, and abandoning wickedness…" See also 1 Pt 1: 23; 2 Cor 5: 17.

Kingdom of heaven: Come in, or stay out!

"For I tell you none of those … invited will taste My dinner." (Lk 14: 24)

THE GOOD NEWS!

"The kingdom of God is at hand. Repent and believe **the Good News**."

(Mk 1: 15)

Man's sagacity

"For the children of this world are more prudent in dealing with their own generation than(are) the children of light." (Lk 16:8)

The fear of the Lord:

"Blessed the man who fears the Lord,

who greatly delights in His commands,

his posterity shall be mighty upon the earth,

the upright generation shall be blessed."

(Ps 112: 1-2Lect)

The virtues impacted by righteousness

"And if anyone loves righteousness,

her labours are virtues;

for she teaches self-control and prudence,

justice and courage;

nothing in life is more profitable for mortals than these."

(Wis 8: 7 NRSV-CI)

Exhortation and Meditation.

The Kingdom of heaven.

What should our attitude to the Kingdom of heaven be?

Usually it demands that we give up some things for it.

- "Like the treasure, buried in a field, that a man found and reburied. Then in his joy he goes and sells everything he has and buys that field." (Matt 13: 44)
- "Again, the Kingdom of heaven is like a merchant in search of fine pearls. When he found one priceless pearl, he went and sold everything he had, and bought it." (Matt 13: 45-46)
- The word purifies and amplifies, bringing about long life, sufficiency, even prosperity just like a mustard seed planted; the smallest of seeds though it was, but when full grown became the largest – and accommodating bird's nests in its branches. (Lk 13: 19, Matt 13: 31)
- Or the yeast, a small bit put into some dough, getting all leavened (Matt 13: 31-33; Gal 5: 9)

"Blessed are they whose way is blameless,
who walk in the law of the Lord." (Ps 119: 1)
Whoever does not do what is right isn't righteous

WHAT then, is righteousness?

RIGHTEOUSNESS is a[1] "pure, and simple goodness or godliness."

Read Ezk 18: 5-9

Note, for example,

"He doesn't oppress anyone… does not commit robbery, but gives his bread to the hungry and covers the naked… keeps his hand from wrong-doing… follows My statutes and keeps My ordinances, acting faithfully."

"'…such a person is righteous…' This is the declaration of the Lord God."

(Ezk 18: 9)

1: Don Schwager

Exhortation and Meditation.

You need to be born again – a complete transformation.
Exchange your old self for the new man in Christ;
your old culture and worldly wisdom for the brotherhood
culture of the kingdom.
The Kingdom of heaven
The kingdom of heaven which Jesus came to plant gives succour
to all mankind – comparable to the mustard seed which a man
plants – the smallest of all seeds but when it grows, its umbrage gives
solace. (Mk 4: 30-32)

This is so as it has to do with the formation of the righteous man.
Aristotle is reported as saying that

"Educating the mind without
educating the heart is no
education at all."

The culture and norms of the nations

Do you know that the norms and mores of nations differ a lot? They are not necessarily all grounded in righteousness, but as closer to righteousness as each may be, so much the fewer will be persecution and unrighteousness among the people.

Be vigilant, be zealous, stay awake!

In our pilgrimage to God we must always remember we would pass through judgement. Distractions, moment of dangerous frolics that make us lose our attentiveness to the word or lose our guard against sinning could be catastrophic. This is the dire warning the Lord communicates to us via **the parable of the Ten Virgins**. (Matt 25: 1-13):

Five took their duty with due seriousness, filling their lanterns with fuel, and just in case making provision for extra fuel. The other set of five forgot all that. When the reality dawned upon them that they needed extra fuel, they pursued the easiest escape – begging to share with their more prudent colleagues. These would not take such chances. They went out to buy but returned too late!

"Therefore, be alert, because you do not know either the day or the hour." (Matt 25: 13)

Again in **the parable of the talent** (Matt 25: 14-30), we are admonished not to behave like the one-talent man:

"But his master replied to him, 'You evil, lazy slave!...'" (Matt 25: 26)

Prudent and diligence required, be prepared; never lose focus. (Matt 25: 13)

Exhortation and Meditation.

"So, because you are lukewarm and neither hot nor cold, I am going to vomit you out of My mouth." (Rev 3: 16)

St Paul – On Sin, the Law, Grace and Righteousness

(Being an executive summary of Rom 5: 12-6: 13)

i. Jesus Has Put Us Right With God

SIN becomes cognizant to man through Adam, and death follows; thence all men die because all men sin.

The truth is that sin has been in our world (as also punishment) before Moses and the Law, but no indictment then, because no law could be cited as being infringed. However, death ravaged the world from Adam to Moses even over those who did not sin, in terms of Adam's disobedience; Adam is a prototype of the One-to-come.

ii. Grace and life through Christ

5: 15 The power of grace far out-weighs sin's dominance; by one man's sin many died but behold, by the grace of one man, Jesus Christ, a much more abundance or overreaching grace is availed to many.

5: 16 The gift (of grace) differs from sin in as much as one man's sin brought judgement and condemnation, here many sins procured grace "resulting in justification" (i.e, forgiveness of sin or pardon or mercy)

5: 17 Now, with one man's sin death took over, consider then how by the gift of grace, righteousness which came "through the one man, Jesus Christ", many have pervasively become overcomers in life.

5: 18 The issue is, one sin provoked condemnation for all mankind in just the same way, one righteous act attracted life-giving justification for all.

6: 11 So, you are to make yourself insuppressible by sin, but attentive to God in Christ Jesus.

6: 12 Therefore, extirpate sin by refusing to yield to your bodily cravings.

6: 13 And permit not any organ of your body to sin, but rather turn them over to be instruments of righteousness.

All these foreshadow divine mercy as revealed to Maria Faustina[2].

2: Maria Faustina, polish nun, visionary.

Exhortation and Meditation.

Compare

Jn 3: 16 and Jn 1: 17

"For God loved the world in this way: He gave His One and Only Son, so that everyone who believes in Him will not perish but have eternal life."

(Jn 3: 16)

"For the Law was given through Moses, grace and truth came through Jesus Christ." (Jn 1: 17)

Résumé

Grace: I think we can agree that St Paul uses the word 'grace' to imply the freely given, unmerited favour and love of God. And also the influence or Spirit of God operating in humans to regenerate or strengthen them – in common parlance – mercy, clemency, pardon.

Righteousness

The state of being righteous is characterised by uprightness or moral rectitude or virtue.

Rivalry

Rivalry is not of God. Did you choose to be born a man or a woman; into Africa or Europe; into royal/presidential family or a peasant/proletariat one?

Yet, many of us are not content to dwell on the divine will. Just do what is in your power to do for the good of others – that is true greatness.

"… Whoever wants to become great among you must be your servant, and whoever wants to be first among you must be a slave to all."

(Mk 10: 43, 44 HCSB)

- Your call

Consider the call of the Twelve:

"During those days He went out to the mountain to pray and spent all night in prayer to God. When daylight came, He summoned His disciples, and He chose 12 of them – He also named them apostles."

(Lk 6: 12-13 HCSB)

- Your call to be a believer in the Son of God (or for any special vocation in the church) is not a fortuitous action of yours. It is in accordance with the foreknowledge and plan of the Almighty.

It is a sacred call to be taken up with a due sense of responsibility.

The jailer of Paul and Silas saw the wonders of nature – an earthquake and got converted:

Exhortation and Meditation.

"Then he (the jailer) escorted them (Paul and Silas) out and said, 'sirs, what must I do to be saved?' So they said, 'Believe on the Lord Jesus, and you will be saved…'" (Acts 16: 30-31 HCSB)

Jesus – our model.

Kingdom of heaven: Jesus, a trustworthy Guide – the light in the midst of darkness.

Jesus words are superior illumination than can be obtained from a Global Positioning System (GPS).

Jesus is the light of the world.

"I am the light of the world;

anyone who follows Me will

never walk in the darkness…" (Jn 8: 12 HCSB)

Jesus, the Good Shepherd of the flock.

He leads His people, pilgrims to the kingdom.

He is not the one who says, 'do as I say', but

He says, 'do as I do!'

(Read: Jn 10: 11, 14-16, 27, 29)

He is the Vine,

We could be His branches, if we choose to be righteous

Read more about this in Jn 15: 5

Welcoming the Kingdom like a little child would

Is it scripture, presumption or pride that makes us think that there can be nobody on earth in all ages that can be like Father Abraham, or Moses or Elijah?

We must be teachable else we might poise to teach God!

(Mk 10: 15; Lk 18: 17)

It would appear commendable the punctilious zeal of the Scribes and Pharisees for observance of the Lord's commandments:

"The Scribes and Pharisees were watching Him closely, to see if He would heal on the Sabbath…" (Lk 6: 7 HCSB)

Certainly, it is good to know impostors from the genuine. Perhaps human ingenuity will not take us far enough. We need divine guidance – discernment by His Spirit.

Exhortation and Meditation.

By foreknowledge and wisdom of God

All righteous are welcome into the Kingdom; but the first may be the last!

Like a little child

"I assure you" Jesus says, "whoever does not welcome the Kingdom of God like a little child will never enter it." (Mk 10: 15)

The Mind of God

The essence of our Christian formation is to have understanding of the mind of God. It requires that we be transformed in mind, heart, soul and spirit become a soul forever seeking communion with God:

"For who has known the Lord's mind, that he may instruct Him? But we have the mind of Christ." (1 Cor 2: 16 HCSB)

Why are despots, religious extremists, racists, tribalists and sinners Christians?

There is a kingdom of heaven and there is a kingdom of darkness. Certainly, the kingdom of heaven does not accommodate saints and sinners alike; only the world does.

………. Let your good works shine… (Matt 5: 16)

So, why are operators in the world of the dark – people who cannot own up that they are what they practise – still want to associate with the light?

Adulterers, robbers, thieves, murderers, deceivers, cultists, etc. – why do they want to be seen as believers in Jesus Christ?

Many of them don't understand what Christianity is all about. If they do, they should have moved to other religions that can accommodate them if they are merely seeking solidarity.

Fact is, you can't be any of these things, mentioned above and remain righteous. You just have to come out of them and dissociate yourself from all such ungodliness. Be born again.

If that man, that boy, that girl or that woman from different continents from yours are all God's creatures – and that God is the Father in heaven to us all, how dare you treat any of them unjustly?

If you accept that creed, you are born again – transformed from your old prejudice, or old beliefs and culture – you have attained metanoia.

Exhortation and Meditation.

Fr Al Leur[1] disclosed how some years back he dared to preach on racism, seven stations (in the U.S.) pulled off his podcasts; the first one did so within an hour of their tell-cast!

Let us renounce old habits, old attitudes and old way of life that are incompatible with Christianity. We are called to drop them or drop out!

"...now I am writing you not to associate with anyone who claims to be a believer who is sexually immoral or greedy or idolater or verbally abusive, a drunkard or a swindler. Do not even eat with such a person."

(1 Cor 5: 8, 11 HCSB)

Many, but few

"For many are invited,
but few are chosen." (Matt 22: 14 HCSB)

The Kingdom of God

What it is

This chapter is devoted exclusively to the Kingdom of God. St Matthew calls this in his gospel, the kingdom of heaven. For interpretational purposes we call it in this chapter, 'righteousness'. For the kingdom of God is a kingdom of righteousness. All our Christian formation is about doing good.

When Jesus healed the woman that was bent over for over 18 years on a sabbath and in a synagogue (Lk 13: 10-17) everybody recognised it was an act of kindness but some doubted the propriety of doing so on a sabbath.

"I desire mercy not sacrifice" (Hos 6: 65; Matt 12: 7; 9: 13 HCSB)

The disciples were passing by a grain field on sabbath, hungry, they picked and ate some heads of grain. It is goodness to feed the hungry (Matt 25: 35) or at least allow the hungry to be fed. This is the verdict of the One who is greater than the sabbath.

The sabbath was made for man and not man for the sabbath." (Mk 2: 27 HCSB) Hence, the Son of Man is Lord of the sabbath.

1: Fr Al Leur: Presentation Ministries Ohio, cit op Exhortation and Meditation.

Some doubt to believe those words of Jesus, but were perplexed, asking: "How does He know the scriptures, since He hasn't been trained?"

(Jn 7: 15 HCSB)

Stop judging according to outward appearances (Jn 7: 24HCSB)

It was the same tenet at the feast of the Tabernacle (festival of shelter). Jesus had made a man entirely well on the sabbath (Jn 7: 23; Matt 12: 13). Some advocates of the law found fault with that. The Lord was obliged to admonish us all, "stop judging according to outward appearances; rather judge according to righteous judgement."

Of course, it is there all along – Isaiah's prophecy concerning the Messiah –

"He will not judge by what He sees…" (Isa 11: 3 HCSB)

Knowing the mind of God

If we had said that our entire Christian formation is about doing good, we can put that differently and say that the essence of Christian formation is to train Christians to have the mind of God – to be transformed in mind, heart, soul and spirit and become souls forever seeking communion with God.

(1 Cor 2: 16)

The earth is the boarding school where saints are formed. The lessons learnt and the habit formed here will stand us in good stead in life on earth and in eternal life.

For more, see the section entitled, 'the kingdom parables' and meditate on them.

Who?

(i.e., for whom is the kingdom prepared?)

"Lord, someone asked Him, "Are there few being saved?"

Answer: "make every effort to enter through the narrow door…"
"Get away from Me, all you workers of unrighteousness!"

"There will be weeping and gnashing of teeth… when you see Abraham, Isaac, Jacob, and all the prophets in the kingdom of God, but yourselves thrown out. They will come from east and west, from north and south, and recline at the table." (Lk 13: 23, 28-29 HCSB)

All mankind, it sounds to me. (Isa 56: 7)

Wherein comes forth the anti-semitism sentiments we see from time to time? Jews are only the first fruits and yet must meet the pre-qualification of righteousness.

Exhortation and Meditation.

Where is this kingdom?

It is here, now and hereafter.

"He answered them, 'the kingdom of God is not coming with something observable; no one will say, 'Look here!' or 'There!' for you see the kingdom of God is among you'" (Lk 17: 20-21 HCSB)

Mercy There is divine mercy, but don't be presumptuous about it!

Consider –

- Forgiveness: "Then, He said to her, 'Your sins are forgiven…'" Lk 7: 48
- "See, you are well. Don't sin anymore that something worse may not befall you (Jn 5:14)
- Healing: "Your faith has made you well" Lk 17:19

In all of the above the recipients of mercy and forgiveness have done NOTHING to expiate their sins, yet they received mercy,

But don't be presumptuous still as the Master Himself has said,

- "Many will say to Me, 'Lord, Lord, didn't we prophesy… drive out demons in Your name!...'" (Matt 7: 22)
- "Only those who do the will of My father …" (Matt 7:21)

- "Observe the commandments…" (Mk 10: 19; Lk 18: 20)
- "Teach them to observe everything that I have commanded you…" (Matt 28:20)
- "Why do you call me, Lord, Lord and do not the things I say? (Lk 6: 46)
- "I have not come to abolish the Law but…" (Matt 5: 17)

Reflection: Grace and Salvation

Belief in God confers righteousness;

Obedience to God makes a person holy.

Repentance opens one to God's mercy;

Prayerfulness opens the door of sufficiency,

it is the key to the riches of God in glory and mercy.

Thanksgiving and praises make God's gifts to endure or be protected.

JOB: A model of righteousness

Reading the first few paragraphs of the book of Job one cannot escape being struck intensely of Job as a paragon of excellence in docility to God.

First – God's testimony concerning Job:

"… My servant Job

Exhortation and Meditation.

… there is no one on earth like him, blameless and upright, fearing God and avoiding evil." (Job 1: 8 Lect)

Secondly – Job was put to severe testing –

    i. By God – who did not disclose to Job that he was to be tested by the Devil, so Job was ill-prepared to receive the calamities that befell him.

   ii. By Satan, who brought a cascade of disasters on Job destroying all his material possessions and took away the lives of all Job's children in one fell swoop.

"And so one day, a messenger came to Job and said,

"The oxen … and the asses … the Sabeanscarried them off in a raid, they put the herdsmen to the sword, …"

"While he was yet speaking, another messenger came and said, 'lightning struck the sheep and their shepherds and consumed them, …'"

"While he was yet speaking, another messenger came and said, The Chaldeans … seized the camels, carried them off, (killing) those tending them, …"

"While he was yet speaking, another came and said, 'your sons and daughters were (feasting) … when suddenly a great wind came … and smote … the house … and they are dead …'" (Job 1: 13-19 Lect)

Thirdly, Job is a paradynof complete submission to God. In reaction to the first salvo of woes that befell him. Job taught us complete submission to God as he fell into deep mourning, worshipped God and quipped:

"Naked I came forth … and naked shall I go back again.

The Lord gave and the Lord has taken away;

blessed be the name of the Lord!" (Job1: 20, 21 Lect)

Throughout the other tests that Job was afflicted with (as recounted in the other chapters of the book of Job), Job proved himself worthy of God's earlier commendation as he admonished himself where he stumbled and emptied himself of every grain of pride or arrogance or irreverence. Every Christian should aspire to behave like Job.

Prayer:

We pray that God will not put us to a severe test; we also pray that in every situation or condition in life that He will adorn us with sufficient grace and fortitude to always bear credible and outstanding witness to His name, His glory and honour. May we always be sustained by the goodness of the Lord! Amen.

CHAPTER 15

Prayer

Prayer, Fasting and Thanksgiving

Prayer of faith

Jesus taught, "… If anyone says to this mountain, 'Be lifted up and thrown into the sea' and does not doubt in his heart, but believes… it will be done for him. Therefore, I tell you, all the things you pray and ask for – believe that you have received them, and you will have them." (Mk 11: 23-24)

Community Prayer (or consensus supplication).

"Again, I assure you: If two of you on earth agree about any matter that you pray for, it will be done for you by My Father in heaven. For where two or three are gathered together in My name, I am there among them."

(Matt 18: 19-20 HCSB)

Wining and dining when there should be fasting.

"On that day the Lord, the God of hosts, called for weeping and mourning,… But look! Instead, there was celebration and joy,… Eating meat and drinking wine:

'Eat and drink, for tomorrow we die!'

This message was revealed… from the Lord of Hosts: this iniquity will not be forgiven you until you die, says the Lord, the God of hosts."

(Isa 22: 12-14 NABRE)

Ask, I will do it

"And whatever you ask in My name, I will do, so that the Father may be glorified in the Son."

"If you ask anything in My name I will do it." (Jn 14: 13; 15: 16 NABRE)

When to fast

I. At the commencement

- As Jesus was about to begin His public ministry He fasted. First, He went to John at the Jordan and was baptized. Immediately afterwards He began a 40-days retreat – prayer and fasting.

"Then Jesus returned from the Jordan, full of the Holy Spirit, and was led by the Spirit in the wilderness for 40 days to be tempted by the Devil. He ate nothing during those days,…" (Lk 4: 1-2)

"Immediately, the Spirit drove Him into the wilderness. He was in the

wilderness 40 days,…" (Mk 1: 12-13)

"Then Jesus was led up by the Spirit into the wilderness… After He had fasted 40 days and 40 nights, He was hungry." (Matt 4: 1-2)

- Before selecting the twelve and the Sermon on the Mount:

"During those days, He went out to the mountain to pray and spent all night in prayer to God. When daylight came, He summoned His disciples, and He chose 12 of them – He also named them apostles."

(Lk 6: 12-13)

II. Other times

"Then they said to Him, 'John's disciples fast often and say prayers and those of the Pharisees do the same, but yours eat and drink'

Jesus said to them,

'You can't make the wedding guests fast while the groom is with them, can you? But the time will come when the groom will be taken away from them – then they will fast in those days.'" (Lk 5: 33-35)

How to pray

"…pray in secret; do not babble…" (Matt 6: 5-8 NABRE)

The Model Prayer[1]

Now Jesus was praying in a certain place, when He ceased one of His disciples said to Him, "Lord, teach us to pray,…"

"So, He said to them, 'when you pray, say:

Our Father in heaven,

Hallowed be Your name.

Your kingdom come.

Your will be done

On earth as it is in heaven.

Give us day by day our daily bread

And forgive us our sins,

For we also forgive everyone

Who is indebted to us.

And do not lead us into temptation

But deliver us from the evil one.'" (Lk 11: 2-4 NKJV)

1: For comment thereon see chapter 15:reflections.

See it also in Matt 6: 9-13

For Jesus other teachings on prayer refer to Lk 11: 5-13; Matt 6: 14; 7: 7-11.

Why pray? Jesus teaches:

"Ask and you will receive;

seek and you will find;

knock and the door will be opened to you." (Lk 11: 9 NABRE)

HOW?

1. "Pray always without becoming weary." (Lk 18: 1 NABRE)

"The Lord said,

'Pay attention to what the dishonest judge says.

Will not God then secure the rights of His chosen ones

who call out to Him day and night?

Will He be slow to answer them?
I tell you He will see to it that justice
is done for them speedily.'"

2. We should be importunate and persistent in prayer as the widow in the parable of the unjust judge in Lk 18: 1-8 or in the parable of the neighbour who received a late night guest. (Lk 11: 5-13)

For further reading see Lk 18: 9-14; 35-43; Matt 6: 5-8; 16-18.
What to pray for –
"Seek first the kingdom of God and His righteousness…" (Matt 6: 33)

Forgiveness comes with retribution and recompense in prayer. For details see Matt 6: 12, 14-15.

"For if you forgive people their wrong doing, your heavenly Father will forgive you as well." (Matt 6: 14 HCSB)

- Prayer of the self-righteous who despise others – in parable of the Pharisees and tax collector (Lk 18: 9-14)

Vaunting: "I fast, I pay tithes…"

Humility helps in prayer as it is depicted in the parable of the Pharisee and the tax collector at prayer (Lk 18: 9-14)

"…because everyone who exalts himself will be humbled, but the one who humbles himself will be exalted." (Lk 18: 14 HCSB)

- See, how faith works for Bartimaeus (Mk 10: 46-52):

The healing of the blind beggar on the approach to Jericho (also in Lk 18: 35-43) This fellow refused to be hindered or distracted by the mob who "told him to be quiet, but he was crying out all the more, 'Son of David, have mercy on me, Son of David!'"

"Jesus told him, 'your faith has healed you.'"

- Jesus decries ostentation or display of one's religiosity in prayer (Matt 6: 5-8)
- In fasting – Be discreet. Let it be an affair between you and your God; wear no facade. (Matt 6: 16-18)

Efficacy in Prayer – keep His commands

With faith and a clear conscience we "receive whatever we ask from Him because we keep His commands and do what is pleasing in His sight."

(1 Jn 3: 21-22)

Jesus teaches

At the healing of a man's convulsing only child (with a mute and deaf spirit) which the disciples could not heal:

"This kind can only come out through prayer and fasting."

(Mk 9: 29 HCSB)

Jesus Prays:

Jesus offers the example of his personal prayer life for us all:

"During the day, He was teaching in the temple complex, but in the evening He would go out and spend the night on… the Mount of Olives."

(Lk 21: 37 HCSB)

Contrition, Confession, and Conversion: the 3 elements of repentance

The merciful God wants repentance rather than the death of a sinner.

Both kings David (2 Sam 12: 13-14) and Ahab repented; both got a partial reprieve from God, an abatement of their punishment. (1 Kgs 21: 27-28)

Prayer persuades God

- The Lord also defeated the Assyrian forces, His angel killing 185,000 of Sennacherib's army in one night.

"…Because you prayed to Me about Sennacherib…" (Isa 37: 21)

- King Hezekiah was to die, he sobbed and prayed; he found favour with God who added fifteen years to his life span. (Isa 38: 2-3, 5)

- The Ninevites seemed to understand the value of prayer and their faith saved them in spite of Prophet Jonah's prophecy of sure destruction of the city in 40 days!
- Elisha asked for double the power of Elijah and got it (he met the condition) (2 Kgs 2: 1, 6-14)

Intercession works

- Moses interceded for the idolaters and God's anger was assuaged "The Lord answered Moses, 'I will do this very thing you have asked, for you have found favour in My sight...'" (Exo 33: 17 HCSB)
- Simon Peter got deliverance on the night before Herod was to bring him out for execution... in answer to the fervent prayer of the church (Acts 12: 7, 11-12)

FASTING "Isn't the fast I chose:

To break the chains of wickedness,

to untie the ropes of the yoke,

to set the oppressed free,

and to tear off every yoke?"

"Is it not to share your bread with the hungry,

to bring the poor and homeless into your house,

to clothe the naked when you see him,

and not to ignore your own flesh and blood?" (Isa 58: 6, 7 HCSB)

The full precept is in Isa 58: 3-10 HCSB.

The Lord, My strength

"The Lord is my strength and my shield;

my heart trusts in Him and I am helped.

Therefore, my heart rejoices,

and I praise Him with my song.

The Lord is the strength of His people;

He is a stronghold of salvation for His anointed.

Save Your people, bless your possession

Shepherd them, and carry them forever."
(Ps 28: 7-9 HCSB)
Thanksgiving: The day of the Lord!
It is better to take refuge in the Lord
than to trust in man.
It is better to take refuge in the Lord
than to trust in nobles.
"This is the day the Lord has made;
Let us rejoice and be glad in it.
Lord, save us! Lord please grant us success!
Give thanks to the Lord, for He is good;
His faithful love endures forever."
(Ps 118: 8-9, 24-25, 29 HCSB)
Thanksgiving
"I will always thank the Lord;
I will never stop praising Him.
I will praise Him for what He has done;
may all who are oppressed listen and be glad!"
"Proclaim with me the Lord's greatness;
Let us praise His name together."
"Find out for yourself how good the Lord is.
Happy are those who find safety with Him."
"Honour the Lord all His people;
those who obey Him have all they need.
Even lions go hungry for lack of food,
but those who obey the Lord lack nothing good.
The Lord is near to those who are discouraged;
He saves those who have lost all hope.
Good people suffer many troubles,
but the Lord saves them from them all;"
(Ps 34: 1-3; 8-10, 18-19 GNBDK)

Rescue me, Lord!

"In You, Lord, I take refuge;
let me never be put to shame.
In Your righteousness deliver me;
incline Your ear to me; make haste to rescue me!
Be my rock of refuge, a stronghold to save me.
Into Your hands I commend my spirit;
You will redeem me, Lord, God of truth.
How great is Your goodness, Lord,
stored up for those who fear You;
You display it for those who trust You,
in the sight of the children of Adam.
You hide them in the shelter of Your presence,
safe from scheming enemies.
You conceal them in Your tent,
away from the strife of tongues."
(Ps 31: 1-2,6, 20-21 NABRE)
Adoration
▪ "O sing to the Lord a new song;
Sing to the Lord, all the earth.
For great is the Lord, and greatly to be praised;
He is to be revered above all gods.
Worship the Lord in holy splendour;
tremble before Him, all the earth."(Ps 96: 1, 4, 9 NRSV-CI)
▪ "The Lord reigns! Let the earth rejoice;
let the many coasts and islands be glad.
For You, Lord,
are the Most High over all the earth;
You are exalted above all the gods." (Ps 97: 1, 9 HCSB)
▪ "Sing a new song to the Lord,
for He has performed wonders;
His right hand and holy arm
have won Him victory." (Ps 98: 1 HCSB)

- "Blessed the Lord, my soul;
all my being bless His holy name!
Bless the Lord, my soul;
and do not forget all His gifts,
Who pardons all your sins,
and heals all your ills,
Merciful and gracious is the Lord,
slow to anger, abounding in mercy.
He will not always accuse,
and nurses no lasting anger;
for as the heavens tower over the earth,
so, His mercy towers over those who fear Him.
As far as the East is from the West,
so far as He removed our sins from us.

15. Prayer, Fasting and Thanksgiving

As a father has compassion on his children,
So, the Lord has compassion on those who fear Him."
(Ps 103: 1-3, 8-9, 11-13 NABRE)
Divine Blessing
"May the Lord bless you and take care of you;
May the Lord be kind and gracious to you;
May the Lord look on you with favour and give you peace."
(Num 6: 25-27 GNBDK)

When the Lord is not with you

"Woe to the rebellious children!
… they carry out plan, but not Mine; …
One thousand will flee at the threat of one,
at the threat of five you will flee…" (Isa 30: 1, 17 HCSB)
Our Praise of God
"Therefore, through Him let us continually offer up to God a sacrifice of praise, that is, the fruit of our lips that confess His name.

Don't neglect to do what is good and share, for God is pleased with such sacrifices." (Heb 13: 15-16 HCSB)

The Lord – for all peoples

"For My house shall be called a house of prayer for all peoples,"
(Isa 56: 7 HCSB)
Give thanks to the Lord
"Sing praise to the Lord, all His faithful people!
Remember what the Holy One has done,
and give Him thanks!
His anger lasts only a moment,
His goodness for a lifetime.
Tears may flow in the night
but joy comes in the morning."
(Ps 30: 4-5 GNBDK)

Righteousness of God

The Lord God remains faithful forever,
executing justice for the exploited
and giving food to the hungry.
The Lord frees prisoners.
The Lord opens the eye of the blind.
The Lord raises up those who are oppressed;
The Lord loves the righteous
The Lord protects foreigners
and helps the fatherless and the widow,
but He frustrates the ways of the wicked. (Ps 146: 6-9 HCSB)

Prayer: Rescue me

"Heal me, Lord, that I may be healed;
save me, that I may be saved,
for You are my praise."
"Let my persecutors be confounded – not me!

Let them be terrified – not me!" (Jer 17: 14, 18 NABRE)

Praises: IF the Lord had not been with us…

"If the Lord had not been with us
when men rose up against us,
they might have skinned us alive,
such was their anger.
The waters could have drowned us,
the torrent poured over us,
the foaming waters poured over us.
Blessed be the Lord who saved us from
being torn to pieces by their teeth.
We have escaped, like a bird
from the snare of the fowler.
The snare was broken and we escaped.
Our help is in the name of the Lord
who made heaven and earth." (Ps 124: 2-7 NABRE)
The call of the righteous
The righteous call to the Lord, and He listens;
He rescues them from all their troubles. (Ps 34: 17 NABRE)

The Creator

"My soul praise Yahweh!
Lord my God, You are very great.
You are clothed with majesty and splendour
How countless are Your works, Lord!
In wisdom You have made them all;
The earth is full of Your creatures."
(Ps 104: 1, 24 HCSB)
I love You, Lord, my strength.
"I love You, Lord, my strength!
The Lord is my rock, my fortress, and my deliverer,
My God, my mountain where I seek refuge,

my shield, and the horn of my salvation, my stronghold.
I called to the Lord, who is worthy of praise,
and I was saved from my enemies.
They confronted me in the day of my distress,
but the Lord was my support.
With the faithful You prove Yourself faithful;
with the blameless man You prove Yourself blameless;
with the pure You prove Yourself pure,
but with the crooked You prove Yourself shrewd
for You rescue an afflicted people,
but You humbled those with haughty eyes.
Lord You light my lamp;
my God illuminates my darkness."
(Ps 18: 1-3, 18, 25-28 HCSB)
Sons of God
"For whoever does the will of My heavenly Father
is My brother, and sister, and mother" (Matt 12: 50 Lect)
"The will of the Father – believe in the Son,
have internal life and be raised up" (Jn 6: 40)
Ps 118 (L of H)**Lord, my help**
: 1 "Give thanks to the Lord for He is good,
and His kindness is forever."
: 6 "The Lord is with me, I will fear
nothing that man can do."
: 7 "The Lord, my help, is with me,
and I shall look down upon my enemies."
: 14 "The Lord is my strength and my rejoicing:
He has become my saviour."
: 17 "I shall not die, but live,
and tell of the works of the Lord."
: 19 "open the gates of righteousness:
I will go in and thank the Lord."
: 20 This is the gate of the Lord;
it is the upright who enter here.

: 22 "The stone that the builders rejected
has become the corner-stone."
: 23 It was the Lord who did this –
it is marvellous to behold
: 26 Blessed is he who comes in the name of the Lord.
We bless you from the house of the Lord.
: 27 The Lord is God, He shines upon us!
(Ps 118: 1, 6,7,14,17,19,20,22-23, 26-27) L of H
Ps 150 (L of H) Praise the Lord
: 1 "Praise the Lord in His sanctuary,
praise Him in His mighty firmament.
: 2 Praise Him for His mighty deeds,
praise Him for all His greatness."
: 6 "All that breathes, praise the Lord!
"God does not exist"?
"In all his scheming, the wicked arrogantly thinks:
'There is no accountability, since God does not exist.'
His ways are always secure;
Your lofty judgements are beyond his sight;
he scoffs at all his adversaries.
Cursing, deceit, and violence fill his mouth;
trouble and malice under his tongue." (Ps 10: 4-5, 7 HCSB)
Man's infidelity to man
"Help, Lord, for no faithful one remains;
the loyal has disappeared from the human race."
"They lie to one another;
they speak with flattering lips and deceptive hearts."
(Ps 12: 1-2 HCSB)
God to the rescue
: 6 "on account of the sufferings of the poor,
the groans of the weak, I will rise up," says the Lord.
"I will bring to safety the one whom men despise."
: 9 "…the wicked walk round outside,
where the vilest are most honoured of the children of men."

(Ps 12: 6, 9 L of H)
Ps 36: 2-4, 5 (L of H) the unrepentant sinner
"Evil whispers to the sinner in the depths of his heart:
the fear of God does not stand before his eyes.
Evil flattering light disguises his wickedness, so that he does not hate it.
His words are false and deceitful, he no longer considers how to do good…
He follows the wrong path; he does not hate malice."

Peace, all nations!

Judith 16: 2 "You are the God who crushes battle-lines,…"
(the Lord is great and glorious, He is wonderfully strong.)
Ps 47: 5, 9, 10 God rules over the nations
"God is king over the whole earth!
Sing to Him with all your skill!
God reigns over the nations;
God sits on His holy throne.
… For to God belong the armies of the earth,…"
Adoration
Worship the Lord, all the earth!
Honour Him, all peoples of the world!
When He spoke, the world was created,
at His command, everything appeared.
The Lord watches over those who obey Him,
those who trust in His constant love.
He saves them from death;
He keeps them alive in times of famine."
(Ps 33: 8-9, 18-19 GNBDK)

The Lord, a refuge for the oppressed

The Lord is a refuge for the oppressed,
a place of safety in times of trouble.

(Ps 9: 9 GNBDK)
GOD, Our Righteousness
EJACULATIONS:
Ps 18: 28 Lord, You light my lamp
My God illuminates my darkness.
: 32 GOD – He clothes me with strength
and makes my way perfect.
: 46 The Lord lives – may my Rock be praised!
The GOD of my salvation is exalted.
(Ps 18: 28, 32, 46 HCSB)
Ps 7: 9 (LORD), Let the evil of the wicked come to an end,
HCSB but establish the righteous.
Ps 31: 25 Be strong and take heart,
NABRE all who hope in the LORD.

God is our succour

Ps 34: 5 The oppressed look to Him and are glad;
GNBDK they will never be disappointed.
: 6 The helpless call Him, and He answers;
He saves them from all their troubles.
: 8 Find out for yourself how good the LORD is.
Happy are those who find safety with Him.
: 9 Honour the LORD, all His people;
those who obey Him have all they need.
: 10 Even lions go hungry for lack of food,
but those who obey the LORD lack nothing good.
: 17 The righteous call to the Lord, and He listens;
He rescues them from all their troubles.
: 18 The LORD is near to those who are discouraged;
He saves those who have lost all hope.
: 21 Evil will kill the wicked;
those who hate the righteous will be punished.

Be Docile:

Ps 32: 8 The LORD says, 'I will teach you the way you should go;
HCSB I will instruct you and advise you.
: 9 Don't be stupid like a horse or a mule,
which must be controlled with a bit and bridle
to make it submit.
Trust in the Lord
Lord, be gracious to us
We wait for You.
Be our strength every morning and
our salvation in times of trouble.
For the LORD is our judge;
the LORD is our law-giver,
the LORD is our king
He will save us. (Isa 33: 2, 22 HCSB)
Additional Resources

PRAYER

Matt 14: 13, 23Praying in solitude – He went by Himself to pray
Obedience and Prayer
1 Jn 3: 22 "we receive from Him whatever we ask,
NABRE because we keep His commandments
and do what pleases Him."
Ps 112: **The upright**
: 1 "Hallelujah!
Happy is the man who fears the Lord,
taking great delight in His commands.
: 4 Light shines in the darkness for the upright
He is gracious, compassionate, and righteous.
: 7 He will not fear bad news;
his heart is confident, trusting in the Lord.
: 9 He distributes freely to the poor;…

Lavishly he gives to the poor;

: 10 The desire of the wicked man will come to nothing."

(Ps 112: 1, 4, 7, 9, 10 HCSB)

Ps 9: 17 "The wicked will return to Sheol – all the nations that forget God"

HCSB

9: 19-20 "Rise up, Lord! Do not let man prevail;

Let the nations be judged in Your presence…

… Let the nations know they are only men. Selah."

God does not exist, think the wicked

Ps 10: 2 "In arrogance the wicked relentlessly pursue theafflicted;…"

HCSB

: 4 "In all his scheming, the wicked arrogantlythinks:

'There is no accountability, since God does not exist'"

: 12, 14; "Rise up, Lord God! Lift up Your hand. Do not forget theafflicted." "… The helpless entrusts himself to You;

You are a helper of the fatherless."

Help the upright, Lord!

Ps 12: 1 "Help, Lord, for no faithful one remains; the loyal hasdisappeared

HCSB from the human race."

: 2 "They lie to one another; they speak with flattering lips and deceptive hearts."

Save Us, O Lord!Restore us!

"Listen, Shepherd of Israel –

… Rally Your power and come to save us.

Restore us, God; look on us with favour, and we will be saved."

Lord, God of Hosts, how long will You be angry with Your peoples'prayers?....

"Restore us, God of Hosts; look on us with favour, and we will be saved."

"Return, God of Hosts, look down from heaven and see;
take care of this vine, the root Your right hand has planted,
the shoot that You made strong for Yourself."
"Then, we will not turn away from You; revive us,
and we will call on Your name."
"…look on us with favour, and we will be saved."
(Ps 80: 1, 2, 3-4, 7, 14, 18, 19 HCSB)
Admonish sinners
Isa 58:1 "CRY OUT LOUDLY, don't hold back!
Raise your voice like a trumpet
Tell My people their transgression
and the house of Jacob their sins.
:3 …'Look, you do as you please on the day of your fast,
and oppress all your workers.'
:4 You fast with contention and strife
to strike viciously with your fist…
: 13 "… if you call the Sabbath a delight,
and the holy day of the Lord honourable;
if you honour it, not going your own ways,
seeking your own pleasure, or talking too much;"
(Isa 58: 1, 3-4, 13 HCSB)

SEEK (don't defy) GOD!

"When I summon him (Jacob) he shall approach Me;
how else should one take the deadly risk of approaching Me?"
says the Lord. (Jer 31: 22)

The fear of the LORD

Gives long life and the good of the earth (Ps 34: 11-12)
"Keep your tongue from evil, and your lips from deceitful speech.
Turn away from evil and do what is good; seek peace and pursue it."

(Ps 34: 13-14 HCSB)
REWARD:
"… Those who fear Him lack nothing…" (Ps 34: 9, 10 HCSB)

ETERNAL GOD:

"Long ago, You (My God) established the earth and the heavens are the work of Your hands. They will perish, but You will endure;…"
(Ps 102: 25-26 HCSB)
Prayer: Three promises by the Lord:

i. "Whatever you ask in My name, I will do it

so that the Father may be glorified in the Son,
if you ask Me anything in My name, I will do it." (Jn 14: 13-14 HCSB)

ii. Remain in Christ, bear much fruit.

"If you remain in Me and My words remain in you,
ask whatever you want and it will be done for you.
My Father is glorified by this: that you produce much
fruit AND PROVE TO BE MY DISCIPLES." (Jn 15: 7-8 HCSB)

iii. Ask the Father – in My name.

"In that day you will not ask Me anything.
I assure you: Anything you ask the Father in My name,
He will give you." (Jn 16: 23 HCSB)
"… Ask and you will receive, so that your joy may be complete."
(Jn 16:24 HCSB)

"The LORD is near all who call out to Him,

all who call out to Him with integrity.
He fulfils the desires of those who fear Him;
He hears their cry for help and saves them.
The Lord guards all those who love Him,
but He destroys all the wicked." (Ps 145: 18-20)
Importunacy in prayer.
Lot urged the two angels "so strong" that they agreed to accept Lot's hospitality. (Gen 19: 3)

Learn perseverance from the man ill for 38years.

In a pool called Bethesda lay a large number of ill, blind, lame and crippled.

One man was there who had been ill for thirty-eight years… Jesus… knew that he had been ill for a long time. Jesus said to him, 'Rise, take up your mat and walk!' "Immediately the man became well… and walked." (Jn 5: 2-9 NABRE)

Learn importunacy from blind Bartimaeus

As Jesus drew near Jericho a blind man was sitting by the road begging. Hearing… he inquired… 'Jesus, the Nazarene is passing by,' they told him.

So he called out, 'Jesus, Son of David, have mercy on me!' Then those in front told him to keep quiet, but he kept crying out all the more, '… have mercy on me!'

Jesus stopped… 'Receive your sight!' Jesus told him. 'Your faith has healed you.' Instantly, he could see,… (Lk 18: 38-43)

You can read this also in Matt 20: 29-34; Mk 10: 46-52

Faith and efficacy in prayer: the parable of the widow and the unjust judge Jesus told his disciples a parable to teach them that they should **always pray andnever become discouraged.**

The Judge Mused

"I will see to it that she gets her rights. If I don't, she will keep on coming and finally wear me out."

Then the Lord said,

"Listen to what the unjust judge says.

Will not God grant justice to His elect who cry out to Him day and night? ... I tell you that He will swiftly grant them justice."

"Nevertheless, when the Son of Man comes, will He find that faith on earth?" (Lk 18: 1-8)

Good, gracious God.

"Now to Him who is able to do above and beyond all that we ask or think... – to Him be glory... forever and ever. Amen." (Eph 3: 20, 21 HCSB)

"I pray to You, o Lord, for a time of Your favour." (Ps 6:)

JESUS – the image of God!

"Christ Jesus is the image of the invisible God, the First-born of all creation... all things were created through Him and for Him... and in Him all things hold together." (Col 1: 15-16)

God, Our Righteousness

Give thanks to the Lord, acclaim His name;
among the nations make known His deeds,
proclaim how exalted is His name.
Sing praise to the Lord for His glorious achievement;
let this be known throughout all the earth.
(Isa 12: 4-5 HCSB)
The Law – Love!

"You shall love the Lord your God with all your heart, and with all your soul, and with all your strength, and with all your mind; and your neighbour as yourself." (Lk 10: 27-28)

Acceptable Sacrifices

- A contrite heart

"For You do not desire sacrifice or I would give it;
a burnt offering you would not accept.
My sacrifice, o God, is a contrite spirit;
a contrite, humbled heart, o God
You will not scorn." (Ps 51: 18, 19 NABRE)

- Praise.

"Therefore, through Him let us continually offer up to God a sacrifice of praise." (Heb 13: 15 HCSB)

- Do good and share!

"Don't neglect to do what is good and to share." (Heb 13: 16 HCSB)

- Fasting

Fasting Is a demonstration of faith and hope; feasting when fasting and mourning are called for is a demonstration of despondency and it is a sin.

Fasting is an overt act of humbling oneself before the Lord whom the petitioner trusts. Read Isa 22: 12-14.

Mortification versus righteousness

"Rather, train yourself in godliness, for the training of the body has a limited benefit, but godliness is beneficial in every way, since it holds promise for the present life and also for the life to come." (1 Tim 4: 7, 8 HCSB)

Defective Prayer:

"… Because you don't ask; …you ask
you don't get because…" (Js 4: 1, 2)

Praise The Lord!

"Sing to the Lord and celebrate His name!
Make a road for Him who rides upon the clouds –
'The Lord' is His name."
"May the Lord be praised!
Day after day He bears our burdens;

God is our salvation. Selah"

"Kingdoms of the earth sing to God; celebrate the Lord

Sing to God who rides on the highest heavens, at the origin of all things."

(Ps 68: 4, 19, 32-33 HCSB)

Prayer – **God, our Great Provider.**

Listen, Lord, and answer me, for I am poor and needy.

Protect my life, for I am faithful. You are my God;

save Your servant who trusts in You.

Be gracious to me, Lord, for I call to You all day long.

Bring joy to Your servant's life, because I turn to You, Lord. (Ps 86: 1-4,)

The arrogance of power in mortal men!

"The Lord of hosts has planned it, to disgrace all pride of majesty to degrade all the earth's honoured men." (Isa 23: 9 Lect)

God answers prayers

"…He will not refuse anything He can give." (Rom 8: 32)

Archangel Raphael: On prayer

"Thank God! Give Him praise and glory

Before all the living.

Acknowledge the many good things He has done for you,

by blessing and extolling His name in song.

Honour and proclaim God's deeds,

and do not be slack in praising Him.

A King's secret it is prudent to keep,

but the works of God are to be declared and made known.

Praise them with due honour." (Tob 12: 6-7; 8-9 Lect)

Righteous God

"For upright is the word of the Lord,

and all His works are trustworthy.

He loves justice and right;

of the kindness of the Lord the earth is full." (Ps 33: 4-5)

"For me, prayer is a surge of the heart; it is a simple look turned toward heaven,

it is a cry of recognition and of love, embracing both trial and joy."

St Therese of the child Jesus (1873-1897)

https://catholicsaintsinfo/saint-Therese-of-Lisie

God's will – divine purpose

Asking in accordance with divine will is a sure winner. Young king Solomon demonstrated his love of God by making bounteous sacrifice at Hebron. He dreamt that night of meeting the good pleasure of God who was disposed to bless him in whatever area Solomon desired.

His request was that he might have "understanding heart to judge Your people and to distinguish right from wrong." (1 Kgs 3: 4) No wonder Solomon had in his days, world-wide reputation for sagacity and wisdom.

THANKSGIVING:

Of what good is thanksgiving?

1. To the one who gave thanks –

- He voices out his gratitude and feels good; having shared his joy with the one person he was sure really cared for him.
- He fulfils a societal obligation or expectation that the recipient of a kind act should demonstrate appreciation by acknowledging the other person's good deed. He is thus ethical.
- He attracts honour and good will on himself, as the community, somehow, assumes that he deserves the help he got. Both they and his benefactor are thereby encouraged to do even more for him.

- He is fulfilled, as he too has given back (what was within his reach); the one who withholds such thanksgiving to God is really an idolater.

2. To the One thanked:

- He gets satisfaction that His help is appreciated for what it is – a kind act. It is like a cashier giving a receipt for a remittance received.
- Where the thanksgiving takes place in the full purview of the public, the benefactor receives the acclaim of the entire community, not that of the beneficiary alone.

3. To the society –

- The society is educated as to the class requiring assistance, as well as who to look up to for such help.

Exhortation, Meditation and Reflection.

How they showed their gratitude to God:

Father Abraham
- Abram rescued his nephew, Lot and brought back the women and loot of Sodom taken away by the Chedorlaomer and other three invader kings. Melchizedek, king of Salem and priest to God Most High, blessed Abram; in return, "Abram gave him a tenth of everything." (Gen 14: 8-20 HCSB)

King Solomon

- Solomon occupied the stool of his father David; built the temple and brought back the Ark of the Covenant from Zion, the city of David.

1 Kgs 4: 29 "God gave Solomon wisdom, very great insight, and understanding as vast as the sand of the seashore."

8: 1 At the temples dedication, "Solomon assembled the elders of Israel, all the tribal heads and the ancestral leaders of the Israelites before him at Jerusalem in order to bring the ark of the Lord's covenant...

: 2 So all the men of Israel were assembled in the presence of king Solomon...

: 5 King Solomon and the entire congregation of Israel, who had gathered around him... were sacrificing sheep and cattle that could not be counted or numbered, because there were so many.

: 6 The priests brought the ark of the Lord's covenant to its place...

:10 When the priests came out of the holy place, the cloud filled the Lord's temple, and because of the cloud, the priests were not able to continue ministering, for the glory of the Lord filled the temple." (1 Kgs 4: 29; 8: 1-2, 5-6, 10 HCSB)

Solomon knelt and prayed to God and blessed the people.

8: 63 "Solomon offered a sacrifice of fellowship offerings to the Lord:

22, 000 cattle and 120,000 sheep. In this manner, the king and all the Israelites dedicated the Lord's temple." (1 Kgs 8: 63 HCSB)

The celebration lasted for 14 days and the people were dismissed on the 15th day.

Exhortation, Meditation and Reflection.

A Samaritan town welcomes the Messiah

- The Samaritan town of Sychar received Jesus warmly "because of what the woman said... Therefore,... they asked Him to stay with them and He stayed there two days" (Jn 4: 39-40 HCSB)

A leper thanked his healer

- "But one of them, seeing that he was healed, returned and, with a loud voice, gave glory to God. He fell facedown at His feet, thanking Him. And he was a Samaritan."

"Then Jesus said, 'Were not 10 cleansed? Where are the nine? Didn't any return to give glory to God except this foreigner?'"
(Lk 17: 15-18 HCSB)

Zacchaeus' humility pays off.

- One rich tax collector in Jericho learnt that Jesus was passing bye. "He was trying to see who Jesus was, but he was not able because of the crowd, since he was a short man. So, running ahead, he climbed up a sycamore tree to see Jesus since He was about to pass that way. When Jesus came to the place, He looked up and said to him,

'Zacchaeus, hurry and come down because today I must stay at your house.'

So, he quickly came down and welcomed Him joyfully.

…Zacchaeus… said to the Lord,

'Look, I'll give half of my possessions to the poor, Lord! And if I have extorted anything from anyone, I'll pay back four times as much!'

'Today salvation has come to this house,' Jesus told him, 'because he too is a son of Abraham. For the Son of Man has come to seek and to save the lost.'" (Lk 19: 3-6, 8-10 HCSB)

"Prayer purifies us, reading instructs us."

"All spiritual growth comes from reading and reflection."

St Isidore: Book of Maxims

A DREADFUL DIALOGUE

Hear what the Lord says:

God: "Arise, present your plea before the mountains
and let the hills hear your voice!

… pay attention, o foundations of the earth!

For the Lord has a plea against His people,..." (Mic 6: 1-4)
Exhortation, Meditation and Reflection.
Why do you recite My statuses, and profess My covenant
with your mouth, though you hate discipline
and cast My words behind you?" (Ps 50: 16-17 Lect)
Man: "With what shall I come before the Lord,...
... with burnt offerings,... with thousands of rams,
with myriad streams of oil?
Shall I give my first-born for my crime, the fruit
of my body for the sin of my soul?"
God: "You have been told, o man, what is good,
and what the Lord requires of you: only to do the right
and to love goodness and to walk humbly with your God."
(Mic 6: 6-8 Lect)
"He that offers praise as a sacrifice glorifies Me;
and to him that goes the right way I will show the salvation of
God."
(Ps 50: 23 Lect)
Man: "Who is there like You, the God who removes guilt
and pardons sin...?
Who does not persist in anger forever,
but delights in clemency,...?" (Mic 7: 18)
God: Prodigal Son, return! (Lk 15: 11-32)
Man: "Restore us, o God our Saviour,
and abandon Your displeasure against us" (Ps 85: 5 Lect)
"Show us, o Lord, your kindness
and grant us Your salvation." (Ps 85: 8 Lect)
The Cross: A sign "to the evil and adulterous generation" (Matt
12: 38-40 Lect)

- The Cross effigy – is a reminder that accountability and condemnation await the depraved.
- The Crucifixion – Signifies Divine Justice – the wages of sin is death; He bore our sins.

- The Tomb (i.e., buried) – Hades, the alternative to heaven means eternal eclipse from the face or favour of God.

Exhortation, Meditation and Reflection.
- The Resurrection and Ascension: Evidence (i.e., proof conclusive) of the veracity of these forebodings of the prevalence of mercy over grim justice for those who act now embracing or seeking it, when it is available – as the door will close at the tomb.

(Richman and Lazarus Lk 16: 22-24, 31 HCSB)
Lack of belief is no excuse: faith alone will not avail.
(Matt 12: 6, 41-42)

Prayer for Leaders

Lord, Our God!
Give us leaders
Whose hearts and minds are fastened unto You.
Strengthen them with Your Spirit
that they may always be intent at doing Your will;
that their words and actions may advance Your kingdom on earth.
May these be to our good and
to the praise and glory of Your name.
Amen.
God is love 1 Jn 4: 8, 16
"In prayer we should particularly combat our predominant passion or evil inclination. We should devote continual attention to it, because when it is once conquered we will easily obtain the victory over all our other faults."
St. Vincent de Paul.
St. Ephraem⁺ON PRAYER
"Virtues are formed by prayer.

Prayer preserves temperance.

Prayer suppresses anger.

Prayer prevents emotions of pride and envy.

Prayer draws into the soul, the Holy Spirit, and raises man to Heaven."

⁺ Also knowns as Ephrem of Edessa

The Model (or our Lord's) **Prayer** (Matt 6: 9-13)

This exquisite prayer, extraordinary in many ways, is simple but all-embracing; it is concise and reverential.

Exhortation, Meditation and Reflection.

We impliedly confess our sins therein and forgive others who sinned against us, an acknowledgement of our duty to be gracious to our neighbour in compliance with the will of God, and a powerful inducement to attract divine mercy.

The Lord is great and glorious, He is wonderful and gracious.

Hallelujah – Praise the Lord

PRAYER

Lord, teach us the way to pray most efficaciously!

Minimum requirement:

1. Faith: You will not go to a church or ask for help from God, unless you believe it is worthwhile or prudent to do!
2. Ask!

The church facilitates congregational prayers to opportune members to pray often. But be mindful to make entreaty for your specific need.

"Ask…!" Mere attendance at these prayer sessions, good as it is to build up your faith, is not sufficient to ensure efficacy in your specific earnest desire. Supplicate for it.

1. Persevere!

God is nobody's errand boy who is instructed, and promptly carries out that order! He is not an automatic machine either; He is the Lord! God is love; He will do what is good for you, but you must be patient. Ask perseveringly; don't relent and be guided.

2. How often?

Pray always (and hopefully)!

3. Where?

Anywhere, everywhere!

4. What to pray for:

It is important to have a particular need – a behest – in mind, so that when your petition is granted your faith would grow. Pray for your ardent personal needs, that of the community and intercede for others – friends, family and foes!

5. Be in the Lord's presence, i.e., walk with the Lord (in righteousness). Your prayers cannot then go un-noticed: the Lord is merciful and gracious.

Exhortation, Meditation and Reflection.

Lord, teach us how to make ever efficacious prayers!

Ancillary issues

- Supplementary ingredients of prayer

You may ask, "what then, are the usefulness of such things like fasting, use of incense, candles, unguents, special raiment, laying hands on, prayers lifted from scriptural texts (like //the Lord's prayer and psalms), invocation of saints, intercession by the pastor/prophet/fellow faithful, and many more?"

I share my perspective on the matter:

For attires, they traditionally indicate mood: torn dresses with ashes represent mourning or sorrow; white garment and regal robes denote a victorious or joyful celebration the same way as do weeping and dancing during prayer respectively. Use of unguents (olive oil) water, etc. are useful as symbols for the sacred, as opposed to prosaic or mundane activities.

Laying hands on more accurately define the specific object or person upon whom intervention is supplicated for.

Fasting indicates earnestness or the level of confidence or hope of the supplicant in God's mercy.

Similar remarks can be said about other processes or liturgies undertaken by Christians during prayer, like pilgrimages, prayers-in-situ, etc. They are good and may indicate earnestness but may not by themselves directly enhance the efficacy of the supplicant's prayer. Only trust in God's mercy does.

- ▪ SENT

Compliance with divine injunctions automatically results in miracles. The Lord has already decided on what He would do; He uses man only to announce or explain to fellow humans the meaning of what they are about to observe.

Thus, when Moses was sent, there were extraordinary happenings manifesting the power of God. When Elijah was sent to anoint Elisha, Jehu and Eliazer God has already perfected His intervention at that stage, and the spectacular happenings later were exploits revealing the power of God.

Lord, teach us the way to make ever – efficacious prayers!

CHAPTER 16

Riches and Poverty

"Giving to the poor can make up for sin,
just as water can put out a blazing fire".
(Sir 3: 30 GNBDK)

Riches

"Your life should be free from the love of money. Be satisfied with what you have, for He Himself has said, I will never leave you or forsake you." (Heb 13: 5 HCSB)

The poor, infirm and the needy
"Who is like the Lord our God,
who dwells on high,
who humbles Himself to behold
the things that are in the heavens and in the earth?
He raises the poor out of the dust,
and lifts the needy out of the ash heap,
that he may seat him with princes –
with the princes of His people.
He grants the barren woman a home,
like a joyful mother of children.
Praise the Lord! (Ps 113:5-9 NKJV)

Sell what you have and give alms. Provide yourselves bags which wax not old, a treasure in heavens that failed not, where no thief approaches, neither moth corrupted. (Lk 12: 33)

Giving: A Hundred-fold plus
"Everyone who has given up houses or brothers… or lands for the sake of My name will receive a hundred times more and will inherit eternal life."

(Matt 19: 29)

"The Lord is near the broken-hearted. He saves those crushed in spirit" (Ps 34: 18)

No favouritism

"But if you show favouritism, you commit sin and are… transgressors." (Js 2: 9)

Affluence – Be detached!

"Do not love the world or the things that belong to the world… For everything that belongs to the world – the lust of the flesh, the lust of the eyes, and the pride in one's lifestyle – is not from the Father, but is from the world." (1 Jn 2: 15-16)

"When we give the poor, the Lord considers it as
precious as a valuable ring.
Human kindness is as precious
to Him as life itself." (Sir 17:22 GNBDK)

Riches: Jesus says, "I assure you: it will be hard for a rich person to enter the kingdom of heaven!" "… But with God all things are possible." (Matt 19:23, 26)

Also Lk 18: 24, 27; Mk 10: 23, 28.

Riches: an excess baggage?

If it causes you to stumble, cut it off and throw it away.

(Matt 18: 18 NRSV-C) Read also Lk 12: 33-34, for more on the subject.

"**The oppressed** look to Him and are glad;
they will never be disappointed.
The helpless call to him, and He answers;
He saves them from all their troubles." (Ps 34:5-6 GNBDK)

"The Lord is a refuge for the oppressed, a refuge in time of trouble."
(Ps 9:9 HCSB)

Being Rich

Remember that you don't have to be rich to give. In the bread and fish multiplication miracles, the givers of "the loaves and fish" were not rich.

(Mk 6: 34-44; Matt 15: 32-38)

The rich and the poor

It is enough for a servant to be like his master. (Matt 10: 25; Lk 6: 40)

Jesus the Lord, while in the flesh knew who He was – Son of God, but He chose to live a simple and unpretentious lifestyle. He neither disdained the rich nor endeavoured to flirt with the powerful.

"Foxes have dens and birds of the sky have nests, but the Son of Man has nowhere to rest his head." (Matt 8:20; Lk 9:58)

Prayer: Jesus, meek and humble of heart – Make our hearts like unto Yours![1]

He who has ears ought to listen (Mk 4: 9)

1: A Catholic Prayer (Association of Sacred Heart of Jesus and Immaculate Heart of Mary)

Blessed are the meek – for they will inherit the land (Matt 5:5 NABRE)

The Rich

"Instruct those who are rich…
not to be arrogant or to set their hope on the
uncertainty of wealth, but on God,…
Instruct them to do what is good,
to be rich in good works… generous, willing to share,…"
(1 Tim 6:17-19).

Desire for wealth

"But those who want to be rich fall into temptation, a trap, and many foolish and harmful desires, which plunge people into ruin and destruction. For the love of money is a root of all kinds of evil, and by craving it, some have wandered away from the faith and pierced themselves with many pains". (1 Tim 6:9-10)

"Your life should be free from the love of money. Be satisfied with what you have…" (Heb 13: 5)

The prince of Tyre

The greatest danger with rich people – whether they are rich in power, in possessions or even in learning – is that their wealth induces them to lose a sense of realism. Their success mocks others still struggling and they engage in a delusive self-adulation. Like the prince of Tyre:

"Oh yes, you are wiser than Daniel,
nothing secret is too obscure for you!
By your wisdom and intelligence
You made yourself rich,…
Through your great wisdom in trading you
heaped up riches for yourself –
your heart is haughty because of your riches." (Ezk 28: 3-5 NABRE)

"Pride comes before destruction, and an arrogant spirit before a fall."
(Prov 16: 18 HCSB)

Commerce

"It is hard to remove a peg that is stuck between two stones of a house and it is just as hard to remove dishonesty from buying and selling". (Sir 27: 2 GNBDK)

"The kindness people have done crosses their paths latter on; should they stumble, they will find support."
(Sir 3:30, 31 NABRE)

Lust for wealth

"A person who gets rich without sinfully chasing after money is fortunate. Do you know anyone like that? If so, we will congratulate him for performing a miracle that no one else has ever been able to do." (Sir 31: 8-9 GNBDK)

No condition is permanent or immutable as the Lord forgets no one:

"And raising His eyes toward His disciples He said:

'Blessed are you who are poor, for the kingdom of God is yours.

Blessed are you who are now hungry, for you will be satisfied.

Blessed are you who are now weeping, for you will laugh...

But woe to you who are rich, for you have received your consolation.

But woe to you who are filled now, for you will be hungry.

Woe to you who laugh now, for you will grieve and weep...'"
(LK 6:20-21, 24-25 NABRE)

Insensitivity to the plight of others

"He who shuts his ear to the cry of the poor will himself also call and not be heard" (Prov. 21:13)

"'The Lord decrees no abject poor in society...

'There will be no poor among you, ...

-if only you obey the Lord your God and are careful to follow every one of these commands...'" (Deut.15:4-5 HCSB)

Seek the Lord!

"Seek the Lord, all you humble of the earth, who carry out what he commands. Seek righteousness, seek humility, perhaps you will be concealed on the day of the Lord's anger" (Zeph 2:3)

Jesus said,

"Even more, those who hear the word of God and keep it are blessed"

(Lk 11:28)

"Therefore, through Him let us continually offer up to God a sacrifice of praise, that is, the fruit of our lips that confesses His name.

Don't neglect to do what is good and to share,

for God is pleased with such sacrifices." (Heb 13:15-16 HCSB)

The Boast of the Poor and the Rich

"The brother of humble circumstances should boast in his exaltation, but the one who is rich should boast on his humiliation because he will pass away like a flower of the field." (Js 1:9-10 HCSB)

"Those Christians who are poor must be glad when God lifts them up, and the rich Christians must be glad when God brings them down, for the rich will pass away like flower of a wild plant." (Js 1:9-10 GNBDK)

The charitable receives divine mercy

i. Cornelius –

"God is pleased with your prayers and works of charity, and is ready to answer you" (Acts 10: 4, 31 GNBDK)

ii. Dorcas (also called Tabitha):

"She spent all her time doing good and helping the poor"

(Acts 9:36-42)

Of course, she was raised to life at the behest of the beneficiaries.

Pure religion

"Pure and undefiled religion before our God and Father is this: to look after orphans and widows in their distress and to keep oneself unstained by the world" (Js 1: 27 HCSB)

Favouritism

"You must never treat people in different ways according to their outward appearance"

"God chose the poor people of this world to be rich in faith and to possess the kingdom which He promised to those who love Him but you dishonour the poor! Who are the ones who oppress you and drag you before the judges? The rich!"

(Js 2:1, 5-6 GNBDK)

Vows: "Sacrifice a thank offering to God and pay your vows to the most high. Call on Me in the day of trouble; I will rescue you, and you will honour Me."

(Ps 50: 14-15 HCSB)

Turning your face away

"My child do not mock the life of the poor;
do not keep needy eyes waiting.
Do not grieve the hungry, nor anger the needy.
A beggar's request do not reject; do not turn your face away from the poor."

(Sir 4:1, 2, 4 GNBDK)

The Lord: a stronghold for the needy

"For you have been a stronghold for the poor,
a stronghold for the needy person in his distress,
a refuge from the rain, a shade from the heat.
When the breath of the violent is like rain against a wall.
Like heat in a dry land, You subdue the uproar of barbarians…

He silences the song of the violent." (Isa 25:4,5....)

Almsgiving

Old Testament: "As water quenches a flaming fire, so almsgiving atones for sins."

"Happy is the one who cares for the poor, the Lord will save him in a day of adversity."

"The Lord will keep him and preserve him; he will be blessed in the land You will not give him over to the desire of his enemies"

"The Lord will sustain him on his sickbed; You will heal him on the bed where he lies" (Ps 41:1-3 HCSB)

New Testament
Jesus said,
"Sell your possessions and give to the poor.
Make ...... for yourselves...... an inexhaustible treasure in
heaven ......For where your treasure is, there your heart
will be also." (Lk 12:33-34 HCSB)

"Those who want to be rich are falling into temptation and into a trap and into many foolish and harmful desires, which plunge them into ruin and destruction.

For the love of money is the root of all evils, and some people in their desire for it have strayed from the faith..." (1 Tm 6:9-10 NABRE)

The words of the sage:

Riches

- "A good name is more desirable than great riches, and high esteem, than gold and silver." (Prov. 22:1 NABRE)
- "My son, why increase your anxiety, since whoever is greedy for wealth will not be blameless?
- Even if you chase after it, you will never overtake it; and by fleeing you will not escape." (Sir 11:10 NABRE)

The rich and the poor

- "The rich and the poor have this in common:
The Lord made them both."
"The rich rule over the poor and the borrower is a slave to the lender."
(Prov 22: 2,7 HCSB)
- "Don't rob a poor man because he is poor, and don't crush the oppressed at the gate, for the Lord will take up their case and will plunder those who plunder them." (Prov. 22:22-23 HCSB)

In the encounter with the rich official (LK 18:18-23)

Jesus gave the precept he requested:

Sell all that you have and distribute it to the poor….. (LK 18:22)

Salvation for the rich

"How hard it is for those who have wealth to enter the kingdom of God! For it is easier for a camel to go through the eye of the needle than for a rich person to enter the kingdom of God." (LK 18:22, 24-25)

(Except that grace is available to offer assistance.)

Make friends for yourselves with dishonest wealth, so that when it fails, you will be welcome in the eternal dwellings. (The rich man in the Lazarus and rich man parable (Lk 16: 19-25, 27-31) failed to do this)

"Don't collect for yourselves treasures on earth,…

But collect for yourselves treasure in heaven,

where neither moth nor rust destroys,and where thieves

don't break in and steal,for where your treasure is,

there your heart will be also." (Matt 6:19-21)

"Servant serving two masters

No servant can serve two masters… you cannot serve God and mammon (Lk16:13) The life Jesus lived is the model.

Whose?

In the parable of the rich farmer (Lk12:16-20) the rich farmer thought of saying to himself, "take it easy; eat, drink and enjoy yourself"

"But God said to him, you fool, this very night your life is demanded of you.

And the things you have prepared – whose will they be?"

Your Father Knows That You Need Them

The Lord warns against undue concern for food, clothing, etc., as unbelievers do. "… Your Father knows that you need them. But seek His kingdom, and these things will be provided for you. Sell your possessions and give to the poor…" (Lk 12:30, 31, 33)

Renounce Possessions

"In the same way everyone who does not renounce his possessions cannot be My disciple" (Lk 14:33 Lect)

Detachment, the kingdom and the reward

"When Jesus heard this, he told him, 'You still lack one thing: sell all that you have and distribute to the poor, and you will have treasure in heaven. Then come, follow Me'" (LK 18:22 HCSB)

"Then Peter said, 'Look, we have left what we had and followed you'

'I assure you: There is no one who has left a house, wife or brothers, parents or children because of the kingdom of God who will not receive many times more at this time, and eternal life in the age to come.'" (LK 18:28-30 HCSB)

ADDITIONAL RESOURCES

Loan the lord

"**Kindness** to the poor is a loan to the Lord and
He will give a reward to the lender." (Prov 19:17 HCSB)
God does not take delight in oppression
"... I live in a high and holy place,
and with the oppressed and lowly of spirit,
to revive the spirit of the lowly
and revive the heart of the oppressed." (Isa 57:14 HCSB)

Time ticks

Ps 90:12 "Teach us to number our days carefully so that we may develop wisdom in our heart."

Weep and wail!

"... You rich, weep and wail ... your gold and silver have corroded, ...". "The wages you withheld from the workers ... are crying aloud ..." (JS 5:1-5 NABRE)

Beware of consumerism – living a life of seeking after wanton pleasure:

"Mortals cannot abide in their pomp. They are like the animals that perish." (Ps 49:12 NRSV-Ci)

The afflicted

"You sinners frustrate the plans of the afflicted, but the Lord is his refuge." (Ps 14:6 HCSB)

Extortioners and oppressors:

"Though the Lord is on high yet He regards the lowly; but the proud He knows from afar." (Ps 138:6 NKJV)

Humility is better than gifts

"My child conduct your affairs with humility, and you will be loved more than a giver of gifts.

Humble yourself the more, the greater you are, and you will find favour with God." (Sir 3:17-18 Lect)

Jesus: on almsgiving

Then He said to the host who invited Him, "When you hold a launch or a dinner, do not invite your friends or your brothers or your relatives or your wealthy neighbours, in case they may invite you back and you have repayment.

Rather, when you hold a banquet, invite the poor, the crippled, the lame, the blind; blessed indeed will you be because of their inability to repay you. For you will be repaid at the resurrection of the righteous." (Lk 14:12-14 Lect.)

The iniquity of Sodom

"Now this was the iniquity of your sister Sodom: She and her daughters had pride, plenty of food, and comfortable security, but didn't support the poor and needy. They were haughty and did detestable things before Me, so I removed them …"
(Ezk 16:49-50 HCSB)
Give!
"Give … don't have a stingy heart when you give, and because of these the Lord your God will bless you in all your work and in everything you do"
"For there will never cease to be poor people in the land; …"
(Deut 15:10-11)
Salvation for the rich
"If you wish to be perfect, go and sell what you have and give to the poor then come, follow Me (Matt 19:26 NABRE)

"For human beings this is impossible, but for God all things are possible."

(Matt 19:21 NABRE)

Tobit and Cornelius

Were distinguished in charity in the foreign lands of their sojourn; both were bounteously rewarded.

Tabitha (Dorcas) got her life back for being gracious (Acts 9:36-41)

A secret

The angel Raphael's admonition (to Tobit and Tobiah) Was: "Do good, and evil will not find its way to you. Prayer and fasting are good, but better than either is almsgiving accompanied by righteousness .... It is better to give alms than to store up gold; for almsgiving saves one from death and expiates every sin. Those who regularly give alms shall enjoy a full life; ..." (Tob 12:7, 8, 9 Lect)

Hear this!

"Hear this you who trample upon the needy and destroy the poor of the land: ..."

"I will turn your feasts into mourning and all your songs into lamentations." (Amos 8:4, 10; Tob 2:6 NABRE)

Profiteering and wealth seeking

- "For the sake of profit many sin, and the struggle for wealth blinds the eyes." (Sir 27:1 NABRE)

Hasty to get rich?

- "...But if you are in a hurry to get rich, you are going to be punished."

(Prov 28:20 GNBDK)

What can make a man poor?

- "If you make gifts to rich people or oppress the poor to get rich, you will become poor yourself." (Prov 22:16 GNBDK)
- "... Hard for the rich to enter?." (Mt 19:23-24 NABRE)

- "If you love money, you will never be satisfied; if you long to be rich, you will never get all you want. It is useless." (Eccl 5:10 GNBDK)
- "Give ... He will always make you rich enough to be generous at all times, so that many will thank God for your gifts which they receive ..." (2 Cor 9:11 GNBDK)
- "From whom much is given, much is expected." (Lk 12:48)
- Jesus life depicts how life in the kingdom is to be lived – selflessly in service to others, in obedience to God. The poor widow donated the highest – because she gave ALL ... (though that ALL may be as little as it was) (Mk 12:43)

LOVE OF MONEY

You can be rich, without having an inordinate love of money. Father Abraham was one such fellow. But for the leaders of the church, it is an anathema to love money (1 Tim 3: 4, 8 GNBDK)

Detachment (but not necessarily asceticism) is absolutely a necessary condition for success as a disciple of Jesus.

It was on account of lack of detachment that made that rich ruler unable to follow Jesus (Mk 10: 21). It was his love of money that predicated Judas Iscariot to fall into the trap of hoarding and betrayal of his master.

You cannot serve two masters: mammon and God. (Lk 18: 13)

For more see chapter on discipleship.

Exhortation, Meditation and Reflection.

There are some fine men and women who practised detachment; they were from very affluent families, yet rejected the allures of a life of luxury, power and pleasure; used their money to lift up the wretched of the earth, give hope to the afflicted, thus acquiring treasures in heaven and becoming disciples. Such were: Levi and Zacchaeus, chief tax collectors; St Anthony of Padua, St Catherine of Sweden, St Cajetan of Thiene, (1480 – 1547), to mention just a few.

On Giving (Christian charity, tithes and offerings)

The enemies of our salvation, chief among whom is Satan and his accomplices, have tried out fear, panic and pain – crucifixion, beheading, feeding humans alive to beasts, roasting men alive, etc. to suppress the faith yet the church would not be put to silence by the atrocities of these powers of darkness. In recent times there is relative peace in the church of Christ Jesus. Indeed, many church groups have become so opulent that church unity is threatened by the wealth of splinter church group founders. As our enemies mock us, it is fair to admit that not all founders flounder in this way. Likewise, not all the conservative churches are immune to the wealth virus.

The danger is that the prosperity of these microscopic churches and the great multitude of their congregation, have become the measure of their success!

This is notwithstanding what the Lord has forewarned us about that:

"If the world hates you, understand that it hates Me before it hated you. If you were of the world, the world would love you as its own. However, because you are not of the world…the world hates you". (Jn 15:18-19)

Now, what are we to do to tame the menace of concupiscence and curb its excesses from destroying the very foundation Christ has built so that righteousness and grace may increase among men? We must keep the struggle on, we must not lose our focus.

1. The Scripture

True, the following scripture is a trustworthy guide:

"Whoever sows sparingly will also reap sparingly, and whoever sows bountifully will also reap bountifully, each must do as already determined, without sadness or compulsion, for God loves a cheerful giver.

Exhortation, Meditation and Reflection.

Moreover, God is able to make every grace abundant for you, so that in all things, always having all you need, you may have an abundance for every good work.

"The one who supplies seed to the sower and bread for food will supply and multiply your seed and increase the harvest of your righteousness. You are being enriched in every way for all generosity, which through us produces thanksgiving to God,…"

"Thanks be to God for His indescribable gift." (2 Cor 9:6-8, 10-11, 15 NABRE)

Pay correct tithes; receive blessing without measure.

"Will a man rob God? Yet you are robbing Me! You ask, 'How do we rob You?'"

"By not making the payments of the tenth and the contributions. You are suffering under a curse, yet you – the whole nation – are still robbing Me. Bring the full tenth into the storehouse **so that there may be food in My house**. Test me in this way," says the Lord of Hosts. "See if I will not open the floodgates of heaven and pour out a blessing for you without measure. I will rebuke the devourer for you." (Mal 3:8-11 HCSB)

2. The correct interpretation.

Jesus unobtrusively and discreetly corrected the misapprehension of those verses in the hands of the covetous by telling His disciples that the poor widow who made a low coin offering was the one who sowed the most, because –

"They all gave out of their surplus, but out of her poverty has put in everything she possessed – all she had to live on." (Mk 12:44 HCSB)

'Concern for the meek and the lowly', you would say? These also have to be our concern. Our fathers in the faith accepted the message.

Both in Jerusalem and in Thessalonica, they got from those who had and shared among all, according to their need. "From each according to ability, and to each according to need," became the creed. Unfortunately, some who are averse to socialism and welfarism derogated those words of charity, but they are divine; and are implied in (2 Cor 9:10-11 NABRE) quoted above, "… (God) will supply and multiply your seed and increase the harvest of your righteousness. You are being enriched every day for all generosity…"

Exhortation, Meditation and Reflection.

Let me assure church leaders from my personal experience that without exporting fear and guilt on the lowly members of the congregation who have not much to give, you may, nevertheless, have even more than you get by extortion if the church were encouraged to make voluntary contributions.

Case 1: The laity were proposing a charity visit and societies were encouraged to obtain voluntary contributions from their members. A major society in the parish was not responsive so I spoke privately to its president. To my utter amazement, there and then he made a 'personal donation' that exceeded the combined contribution of about a dozen societies!

Case 2: In another instance, much earlier in time, we, at society level, were planning to raise fund for the church building project. After the meeting a lady (a prospective member) approached me privately and gave an envelope of an amount that was more than the total pledged by all the society members at that meeting.

To come back to our original concern that money can ruin our chances of coming together for the zeal of the gospel as a formidable front – disciples of the same Lord – "one flock, one shepherd", we need to guard against extortion. For more, read the chapter, "Let them be one"

Richman and Lazarus

The parable of the rich man and Lazarus thus aptly codified the precept of the Lord on wealth and penury. The first part of the anecdote (Lk 16: 19-25) shows that God expects compassion and help from the rich to the poor.

"Make friends for yourselves by means of the unrighteous money so that when it fails, they may welcome you into eternal dwellings." (Lk 16: 9)

The dishonest but, shrewd steward (Lk 16:1-8) already has a knack for applying this principle to his advantage.

"Whoever is faithful in very little is also faithful in much, and whoever is unrighteous in very little is also unrighteous in much." (Lk 16:9-10 HCSB)

Exhortation, Meditation and Reflection.

Recompense

Another point made is divine recompense:

"Son, remember that during your life you received your good things, ... but now he is comforted here ...." (Lk 16: 25)

Even in this world stage, we find that some offspring of the poorest, and the least fruitful couple become very rich and very fruitful! This is in spite of the great odds against them.

Listen, and be guided!

In the second part of the parable (Lk 16: 27-35) a third point is made that now is the time to learn and be guided by the law and the prophets (Lk 16: 29, 31).

The Inanities about riches

The stumbling blocks the rich have to surmount are more dangerous than those of the average faithful.

This is because wealth changes the mien of most men – the wealthy become less humble, more haughty. For some, wealth is taken as a proof of wisdom, hence arrogance follows.

For this reason, they make more enemies than (true) friends with their money. They then proceed to spend a fortune on security, yet are not secure.

The more asinine of these insane behaviours is that they make a laughing stock of themselves – buying what they don't need, losing good money to gamblers and swindlers; many refuse to pay correct taxes, duties, wages and professional fees.

Their money is their god and are in the cult of personality worship – being servile to those they look up to (the rich and the powerful) but supercilious to those they look down upon, including peers; pompous in the way they assert their opinions and are self-conceited.

The wealthy are often accorded deference by the many, mostly sycophants. But the truth spoken to them by the few, is often disdained and ignored.

With such booby traps, how can the rich make an acceptable prayer? Like the Pharisee (rich in religiosity) in the parable of the two at prayer, the self-importance and conceit is unhidden – "they have received their reward."

Exhortation, Meditation and Reflection.

The precept is,

"Then repay to Caesar what belongs to Caesar, and to God what belongs to God" (LK 20: 25)

OBAMA[1]: On the poor

i. The poor: from frustration to fury

"I know, I have seen the desperation and disorder of the powerless; how it twists the lives of children on the streets of Jakarta or Nairobi in much the same way as it does the lives of children on Chicago's South Side; how narrow the path is for them between humiliation and untrammeled fury, how easily they slip into violence and despair"

ii. Poverty: racial profiling and the slide to destitution

"You might just be bored or alone. Everybody was welcome to the club of disaffection"

"They were more than satisfied, they were relieved – such a pleasant surprise to find a well-mannered young black man who didn't seem angry all the time"

"That was the problem with booze and drugs, wasn't it? At some point, they couldn't stop that ticking sound, the sound of certain emptiness"

Treasure in heaven

This incident was recounted in the missionary work of Apostle Thomas in India. The missionary reportedly had a palace for an Indian king, Guduphara in India.

"He offered to build a palace for an Indian King that would last forever; the king gave him money, which Thomas promptly gave away to the poor; he explained that the palace he was building was in heaven not on earth" www.catholicsaints//Apostle Thomas.

[1]: Barack Obama (43rd President of the USA): "Dreams from my father Three Rivers Press, N.Y.

Watch out, and be on guard against greed.

Someone from the crowd said to Jesus,
"Teacher, tell my brother to divide the inheritance with me"
Jesus replied, "Friend, who appointed Me a judge or arbitrator over you?"
Exhortation, Meditation and Reflection.
Greed
"He then told them,
'watch out and be on guard against all greed because one's life is not in the abundance of his possessions.'"

Store it in heaven

"Then he told them a parable (of a rich farmer): (LK 12: 13-20HCSB)

"That is how it is with the one who stores up treasure for himself and is not rich toward God." (Lk 12: 21)

Meditation:

"God gives that we may give"[1]

"I was born poor, I lived poor; I wish to die poor" (*Pope St Pius X's will*)

1: Pope Emeritus Benedict XVI: Daily Meditation

Charity: [1]God points us to the way of charity.

"Look back to the beginning of the history of faith – Abraham in the end, does not offer anything he has prepared himself but has offered the lamb that has been offered to him by God. This lamb in the brambles ... the God who gives to us that we may give."

"God gives that we may give."

Good will come to a man who (gives)

... Generous gifts, lends and gives to the poor Re Ps 112:5, 9; 2 Cor 9:6, 7, 10

1: Pope Benedict XVI: Daily Meditations (podcasts) op cit

Exhortation, Meditation and Reflection.

A preacher[1] reminded us that

"The rich help the poor in this life, and the poor help the rich in the world to come."

"You receive without giving; give without receiving, for what goes around comes around."

SHARING does not create, but eliminates poverty and penury

Sharing surplus does not create poverty to those who share, rather their generosity rids the society of existential living, poverty and penury.

Consider

Old Testament –
- Elisha and the widow of the old prophet (2 Kgs 4:1-7)
- "Give it to the people to eat": Elisha and the first fruit (2 Kgs 4:43 NABRE)
- The gathering of the manna: Whatever was gathered sufficed over the period for which it was intended.
- The widow of Zarephath's generosity to Elijah: The flour and the oil never exhausted.

New Testament – Sharing could lead to transformation: Example –
- Water to wine at marriage in Cana (Jn 2:1)
- Further instances of sharing (hunger to full stomach):
- Jesus feeding the 5,000, and Jesus feeding the 4,000
- Note that Cornelius, the centurion and Dorcas did not become poor despite their sharing. (Acts 9:36 - 10:4)

1: Anon: A reflection at Our Lady of Loreto, Centennial, Co (USA) (Sept 18, 2022)

Exhortation, Meditation and Reflection.

PRINCIPLE:
- A well does not dry up because many people are drawing from its water, it keeps being replenished whether few or many draw from it.
- If you close your fist around what you already have so that nothing goes out, nothing will come in too!
- Consider a village community of 24 households, each with an average family size of 5, - a billionaire's + 4. If they share, the community will be affluent and happy. If they refuse to share there will be colossal wastage, poverty and crime. As it is with a micro community, even more true it is with a macro community.

- QE: This plays out in the adoption of American Quantitative Easing policy, by which the state made free loans and grants to employers so they could keep on paying wages during Covid 19 pandemic. Thus the economic catastrophe was contained by the world. In a previous era it would have led to business recession an economic depression and the collapse of many economies.

Detachment[1]

"If you do not learn to deny yourself, you can make no progress in perfection."

"In detachment, the spirit finds quiet and repose for coveting nothing. Nothing wearies it by elation, and nothing oppresses it by dejection because it stands in the centre of its own humility."

"The Lord measures our perfection neither by the multitude nor the magnitude of our deeds, but by the manner in which we perform them."

Prepare to enter the kingdom in detachment and self-donation.

1: St John of the Cross (1542-1591) (Doctor of mystical theology)

Exhortation, Meditation and Reflection.

"... not by exaltation but by humility is man delivered ... loving their enemies, being joyful in suffering, patient in adversity, pardoning injuries and showing comfort and compassion to the hopeless and the helpless."[1]

[1]: Don Schwager: Reflections@Dailyscripture.net

Advert

We need the time and talent of concerned individuals. Join us in furthering the objectives of this ministry **within every congregation and every national boundary**. You may also give of your treasure. Thank you.

For more information visit www.vanguard for integrity, peace and progress Or contact us:

The Director, International Office,
Vanguard for Integrity Peace and Progress,
15600 E. Caley Pl., Centennial,
Co. 80016, USA.
E-mail:

CHAPTER 17

Salvation:Orthodoxy, Heresy, and Apostasy

Chair of Moses:

"The Scribes and the Pharisees are seated in the chair of Moses. Therefore, do whatever they tell you, and observe it. But don't do what they do, because they don't practise what they teach." (Matt 23: 2-3)

Chair of Peter:

"And I also say to you that you are Peter,

and on this rock I will build My church,

and the forces of hades will not overpower it.

I will give you the keys of the kingdom of heaven, ..."

(Matt 16: 18-19 HCSB)

Peter appointed shepherd

"Simon, son of John… feed My lambs…" (Jn 21: 15-17 NABRE)

The Antichrist

"They went out from us, but they did not belong to us; for if they had belonged to us, they would have remained with us. However, they went out so that it might be made clear that none of them belongs to us."

"Who is the liar, if not the one who denies that Jesus is the Messiah?...

I have written these things to you about those who are trying to deceive you."

(1 Jn 2: 19, 22, 26)

"Many deceivers…; they do not confess the coming of Jesus Christ in the flesh. This is the deceiver and the antichrist."

"Anyone who does not remain in Christ's teaching but goes beyond it, does not have God… do not receive him into your home…"

(2 Jn 1: 7, 9-10 HCSB)

Strange teachings lead people astray.

"Don't be led astray by various kinds of strange teachings; for it is good for the heart to be established by grace and not by foods,…" (Heb 13: 9 HCSB)

Presumptive Prophecy:

"WHEN a prophet speaks in the Lord's name and the message does not come true or is not fulfilled, that is a message the Lord has not spoken. The prophet has spoken presumptuously.

Do not be afraid of him." (Deut 18: 22 HCSB)

Paul: On False Apostles

"…those who seek a pretext for being regarded as we are in the mission…" "…such people are false apostles, deceitful workers, who masquerade as apostles of Christ." "… Satan masquerades as an angel of light. So it is not strange that his ministers also masquerade as ministers of righteousness…"

(2 Cor 11: 12-14 NABRE)

Read also Col 2: 2-4 NRSV-CI

Jesus is divine (Col 2: 8-9 HCSB):

"Be careful that no one takes you captive through philosophy and empty deceit… and not based on Christ. For the entire fullness of God's nature dwells bodily in Christ."

"Let no one disqualify you, insisting on ascetic practices and the worship of angels, claiming access to a visionary realm and inflated without cause by his unspiritual mind." (Col 2: 18 HCSB)

FALSE PROPHECIES AND FAKE PROPHETS.

"In the beginning of the reign of Zedekiah, king of Judah, in the 5th month of the 4th year, Hananiah the prophet, son of Azzur,… (Proclaimed):

'Thus says the Lord of hosts,... I have broken the yoke of the king of Babylon. Within two years I will restore... all the vessels... Nebuchadnezzar... carried away to Babylon... Jaconiah son of Jehoiakim... and all the exiles... I will bring back...' Thereupon, Hananiah... took the yoke bar from the neck of Jeremiah... and broke it.

After... the word of the Lord came to Jeremiah:

'by breaking a wooden yoke bar, you make an iron yoke!...

... they shall serve him; even the wild animals I have given him... ...Hananiah! The Lord has not sent you... I am sending you from the face of the earth this very year you shall die...'

Hananiah the prophet died in the 7th month in that year" (i.e. two months after his false prophecy) (Jer 28: 1-17)

A similar prophetic disunity occurred in Bethel when a man of God from Judah came to Bethel when Jeroboam was incensing the alter and prophesied the birth of Josiah who will unleash the wrath of God on the fake priests. This old prophet deceived and misled the man of God by a fake prophesy, and this caused the life of the man of God. (1 Kgs 13: 1-30)

Straying from the truth (Js 5: 19-20)

"... Know that whoever turns a sinner from the error of his way will save his life from death and cover a multitude of sins." (Js 5: 20

One Foundation: Jesus

"... But each one must be
careful how he builds on it. For no one can lay
any other foundation than what has been laid down.
That foundation is Jesus Christ." (1 Cor 3:11 HCSB)
Power to bind and to loosen
"Blessed are you, Simon son of Jonah. For flesh and blood has not revealed this to you,...

And I say to you, you are Peter, and upon this rock I will build My church, and the gates of the nether world shall not prevail against it.

I will give you the keys to the kingdom of heaven. Whatever you bind on earth shall be bound in heaven, and whatever you lose on earth shall be loosed in heaven."

(Matt 16: 17-19 NABRE)

Be One!

The Lord asked the Father: **"… Sanctify them by the truth…"**

"Holy Father, protect them by Your name… so that they may be one as We are one. Sanctify them by the truth; Your word is truth."

"I pray not only for these, but also for those who believe in Me through their message: may they all be one." (Jn 17: 11, 17, 20-21 HCSB)

Another gospel? A curse be on the preacher!

"I am surprised at you! In no time at all you are deserting the one who called you by the grace of Christ, and are accepting another gospel. Actually, there is no "other gospel", but I say this because there are some people who are upsetting you and trying to change the gospel of Christ.

But even if we or an angel from heaven should preach to you a gospel that is different from the one we preached to you, **may he be condemned to hell!"** (Gal 1: 6-8 GNBDK)

"…the gospel that I preach is not of human origin." "…it was Jesus Christ Himself who revealed it to me." (Gal 1: 11, 12 GNBDK)

The gospel – a trammel, not to be cast away:

"Woe to those who call evil good and good evil,
who substitute darkness for light and light for darkness,
who substitute bitter for sweet
and sweet for bitter.
…who are wise in their own opinion

and clever in their own sight
…heroes at drinking wine,
who are fearless at mixing beer,
who acquit the guilty for a bribe
and deprive the innocent of justice." (Isa 5: 20-23 HCSB)

Things that cause sin

"Woe to the world because of things that cause sin! Such things must come, but woe to the one through whom they come!" (Matt 18: 7 NABRE)

The true God and eternal life

"…that the Son of God, has come and has given us understanding so that we may know the True One. We are in the True One – that is, in His Son Jesus Christ. He is the true God and eternal life." (1 Jn 5: 20 HCSB)

THEY WENT OUT FROM US

"They went out from us… not really of our number; if they had been, they would have remained with us. Their desertion shows that **none of them was of our number.**" (1 Jn 2: 19 NABRE)

Pursue Peace!

"Pursue peace with everyone, and holiness without it no one will see the Lord.

Make sure… that no root of bitterness springs up, causing trouble, and by it, defiling many." (Heb 12: 14, 15 HCSB)

"But avoid irreverent, empty speech, for this will produce… even greater godlessness." (2 Tim 2: 16 HCSB)

Some men from Judea (an instance of presumptive teaching)

"Some men came down from Judea and began to teach the brothers, 'unless you are circumcised according to the custom prescribed by Moses, you cannot be saved!" (Acts 15: 1 HCSB)

Apostasy

"During that time there was a major disturbance about the way". Read Acts 19: 23-41 for how Demetrius was able to mobilize some people for a major uproar against the faith.

Paul, to the Ephesians: **Be on the alert!**

"I testified to both Jews and Greeks about repentance toward God and faith in our Lord Jesus…"

"Be on your guard for yourselves and for all the flock that the Holy Spirit has appointed you to as overseers, to shepherd the church of God, which He purchased with His own blood. I know … that savage wolves will come in among you, not sparing the flock. And men will rise up from your own number with deviant doctrines to lure the disciples into following them. Therefore, be on the alert…" (Acts 20: 21, 28-31)

The apostasy of the Jews from Asia

Read about this also in Acts 21: 21-23: 11; 23: 12-24: 27.

Miracles wrought through Paul

"God was performing extraordinary miracles by Paul's hands, so that even facecloths or work aprons that had touched his skin were brought to the sick, and the disease left them and the evil spirits came out of them."

(Acts 19: 11-12 HCSB)

But who are you?

"I know Jesus, and I recognise Paul – but who are you?" (Acts 19: 15 HCSB)

The Earliest Evangelism Message.

The earliest teaching of the Apostles, from the day of Pentecost upwards centred on –

1. The God of Abraham, Isaac and Jacob "glorified His servant Jesus…, the Author of Life" whom "you put to death, but God raised Him from the dead; of this we are witnesses." (Acts 2: 32; 3: 13, 15 NABRE)

2. "Repent, be baptized… receive the gift of the Holy Spirit." (Acts 2: 38 HCSB)

3. Know with certainty that God has made this Jesus … both Lord and Messiah! (Acts 2: 36)

4. "… He (Jesus) is the One appointed by God to be the judge of the living and the dead… through His name everyone who believes in Him will receive forgiveness of sins." (Acts 10: 42-43 HCSB)

Further accounts of the teachings of the Apostles can be found in the books of the New Testament other than the Gospels.

Prophets and pastors doing their own thing.

"The Lord says,

- 'The prophets and the priests are godless; I have caught them doing evil in the temple itself.

The paths they follow will be slippery and dark; I will make them stumble and fall. I am going to bring disaster on them;…'"

"…they help people to do wrong, so that no one stops doing what is evil…" (Jer 23: 11-12, 14 GNBDK)

- "The Lord said, 'I did not send these prophets, but even so they went. I did not give them any message, but still they spoke in My name.'" (Jer 23: 21 GNBDK)

- "I am against those prophets who take each other's words and proclaim them as My message. I am also against those prophets who speak their own words and claim they came from Me." (Jer 23: 30-31 GNBDK)

- **IF** – "But if a prophet presumes to speak a word in My name that I have not commanded, or speaks in the name of other gods, that prophet shall die."

(Deut 18: 20 NABRE)

ADDITIONAL RESOURCES

17. Orthodoxy

Jesus the Master Plan of our faith

1 Cor 3: 10 "…I (Paul) have laid a foundation as a skilled master builder, and another builds on it.

But each one must be careful how he builds on it."

1 Cor 3: 11 "For no one can lay any other foundation than what has been laid down, that foundation is Jesus Christ."

1 Jn 4: 3 **the antichrist**… their teaching belongs to the world; and the world listens to them.

4: 6 we belong to God and anyone who knows God listens to us,

while anyone who does not belong to God refuse to hear us. This is how we know the Spirit of truth and the spirit of deceit.

One Causing Another to Lose Faith: (see also Matt 18: 6-9, Lk 17: 1-2)

Mk 9: 42 "if anyone should cause one of these little ones to lose his GNBDK faith in Me, it would be better for that person to have a large millstone tied round his neck and be thrown into the sea."

: 43 "so if your hand makes you to lose… (the kingdom) cut it off!…"

On true and false doctrine:

Matt 6: 22, 23 "The lamp of the body is the eye. If your eye is sound,

NABRE your whole body will be filled with light; but if your eye is bad, your whole body will be in darkness. And if the light in you is darkness, how great will the darkness be."

THE WORD OF GOD

Isa 55: 10 "For just as rain and snow fall from heaven and do not return there without saturating the earth and making it germinate and sprout, and providing seed to sow and food to eat,

: 11 so My word that comes from My mouth

will not return to Me empty,

but it will accomplish what I please

and will prosper in what I send it to do."
Preserve justice, do what is right!
Isa 56: 1 "Preserve justice and do what is right,
for My salvation is coming soon,
and My righteousness will be revealed."

False Prophecies

Jer 14: 14 HCSB
"But the Lord said to me,
'these prophets are prophesying a lie in My name.
I did not send them, nor did I command them or speak to them.
They are prophesying to you a false vision, worthless divination,
the deceit of their own minds.'"
FALSE PROPHETS
Jer 23: 11 "because both prophet and priest are ungodly,…
HCSB : 12 Therefore… I will bring disaster on them,…"
23: 21 "I did not send these prophets,
yet they ran with a message!
I did not speak to them,
yet they prophesied."
: 25 "I have heard what the prophets who prophesy a lie in My name have said, 'I had a dream! I had a dream!'
: 28 The prophet who has only a dream should recount the dream, but the one who has My word should speak My word truthfully, for what is a straw compared to grain? – this is the Lord's declaration."

Sound doctrine or myths and fables: On which side are you?
2 Tm 4: 3-4, 5 NKJV
: 3 "For the time will come when they will not endure sound doctrine, but according to their own desires,… they will heap up for themselves teachers;…
: 4 turn their ears away from the truth, and be turned aside to fables."

: 5 "But you be watchful… endure afflictions…"

The essence of sound doctrine

"Beloved you must say what is consistent with sound doctrine…" (Tit 2: 1 Lect)

"… teaching what is good,…

… so that the word of God may not be discredited.

… showing yourself as a model of good deeds in every respect

… so that the opponent will be put to shame

without anything bad to say about us." (Tit 2: 1-8 Lect)

"Trust the Lord with all your hearts,

and do not rely on your own understanding."

(Pro 3: 5 HCSB)

True faith, tradition and dogma – a slippery path.

"They also presented false witnesses who said, '…for we heard him say that Jesus, the Nazarene, will destroy this place and change the customs that Moses handed down to us'"

(Acts 6: 13, 14 HCSB)

"Trust in the Lord with all your heart,

on your own intelligence do not rely." (Pro 3: 5 NABRE)

No perfect Knowledge yet.

"For we know partially and we prophesy partially…

At present we see indistinctly, as in a mirror.

But then face to face.

At present I know partially;

then I shall know fully…" (1 Cor 13: 9, 12 Lect)

TRADITION AND SIN

So, the Pharisees and Scribes questioned Him, 'Why do your disciples not follow the tradition of the elders but instead eat a meal with unclean hands?'

(Mk 7: 1-13)

Response:

This people honour Me with their lips,
but their hearts are far from Me;
in vain do they worship Me,
teaching as doctrines human precepts. (Isa 29: 13)

"How well you have set aside the commandment of God in order to uphold human tradition!"

JESUS: On False Teaching

"… Pharisees and Scribes… said … 'your disciples break the tradition of the elders… not wash hands when they eat…'"

Jesus "said to them… you break the commandment of God… Hypocrites, well did Isaiah prophesy about you… '…in vain do they worship me, teaching as doctrine human precepts.'"

Then His disciples… said to Him, 'Do you know the Pharisees took offence (at)… what you said?'

"He said in reply, 'Every plant that My heavenly Father has not planted will be uprooted.'"

"'… they are blind guides…'" (Matt 15: 1-2, 3-9, 12-14 NABRE)

"He also told them a parable: 'can the blind guide the blind? Won't they fall into a pit?'"(Lk 6: 39 HCSB)

FALSE PROPHETS (See also: False Teachings)

Matt 7: 15 Jesus says "Beware of false prophets who came to you in sheep's clothing but inwardly are ravaging wolves."

Matt 7: 16 "You'll recognise them by their fruit…" (ditto for 7: 20)

(Matt 15: 12-14 HCSB)

"'Every plant that My heavenly Father didn't plant will be uprooted.

Leave them alone! They are blind guides. And if the blind guide the blind both will fall into a pit.'"

The Antichrist

Lord, bring light into our darkness.

2 Jn 1: 7 Antichrist against the anointed One;
willmake a pretence of religion…

theantichrist will want to spiritualize Jesus and deny His incarnationagainst the church.

Matt 24: 5 Many will come attempting to impersonate Jesus Christ!

Mk 13: 21 'Look, the Messiah is here …' – do not believe; it will even try the faithof the chosen

Mk 13: 20 The Lord will shorten his days to save mankind

1 Jn 2: 18 Many antichrists have appeared – heretics

1 Jn 2: 20 He is a'Liar', the one denying Christ is the antichrist.

1 Jn 4: 2, 3 _ _ _ _ _ _ _ _ _ _ _ _

2 Thes 2: 3 The lawless one (son of destruction),Law-denying, not…

Remain in Christ's Teaching

"Anyone who does not remain in Christ's teaching but goes beyond it, does not have God. The one who remains in that teaching, …has both the Father and the Son." (2 Jn 1: 9 HCSB)

Don't revel in being a Diotrephes! (3 Jn 1: 9)

Impurity and error

"For our exhortation didn't come from error or impurity or an intent to deceive instead, …we speak not to please men, but rather God, who examines our hearts." (1 Thes 2: 3-4)

Judgement, Mercy and Fidelity

"… you pay tithes of mint, dill and cumin, and have neglected the weightier things of the law: judgement and mercy and fidelity.

But these you should have done without neglecting the others." (Matt 23: 23-24 Lect)

Lk 11: 42/ Matt 23: 23 NABRE

Mightier things.

"You neglected the mightier things of the law: judgement and mercy and fidelity…"

False Teaching

"Now the Spirit explicitly says that in later times some will depart from the faith, paying attention to deceitful spirits and the teachings of demons."

(1 Tim 4: 1 HCSB)

One Lord, one faith, one hope

"Therefore, I… urge you to walk worthy of the calling you have received, with all humility and gentleness, with patience, accepting one another in love, diligently keeping the unity of the Spirit with the peace that binds us."

"There is one body and one Spirit – just as you were called to one hope at your calling – one Lord, one faith, one baptism, one God and Father of all – who is above all and through all and in all." (Eph 4: 1-6 HCSB)

Jesus "in the flesh" – the antichrist.

"Many deceivers have gone out into the world; they do not confess the coming of Jesus Christ in the flesh. This is the deceiver and the antichrist." (2 Jn 1:7 HCSB)

Fanciful Visions!

"Both prophet and priest are godless!

In My very house I find their wickedness –

oracle of the Lord."

"… they speak visions from their own fancy,

not from the mouth of the Lord."

"they say, …to everyone who walks in

hardness of heart, 'no evil shall overtake you.'"

(Jer 23: 11, 16-17 NABRE)

My people perish for lack of knowledge.(Hos 6: 2)

Add not, nor subtract

(Deut 4: 2) In your observance of the commandments… you shall not add to or subtract from it. Observe them CAREFULLY…

Individual interpretations

(Isa 29: 31) They paid lip service to the observance of God's commandments substituting their own ingenious interpretations and clever arguments to void the will of God

The Magisterium: "…do whatever they tell you, and observe it, but…" (Matt 23: 3 HCSB)

(Rev 2: 2) "You have tested those calling themselves apostles and are not,…"

(Mk 12: 28-34) The most important commandment of the law: Love God, love your neighbour as yourself.

Right leadership

Those who are wise will shine… and those who lead many to righteousness, like the stars forever and ever.(Dan 12: 3 HCSB)

Accord; be united!

(1 Cor 1: 10) Now, I urge you… that all of you AGREE in what you say… no divisions… be united with the same understanding and the same conviction.

In the name of Jesus Christ…

"Teacher, we saw someone driving out demons in your name and we tried to prevent him because he does not follow us."

"Don't stop him," said Jesus… (Mk 9: 39 Lect)

Food does not defile.

"… Listen to Me, all of you, and understand:

Nothing that goes into a person from outside can defile him,

but the things that come out of a person are what defile him." (Mk 7: 14-15)

The Fruit: life, or the destruction of lives?

"The fruit of righteousness is a tree of life,

but violence takes lives away." (Prov 11: 30 NRSV-CI)

Guard the truth.

"Be on your guard for yourselves and for all the flock… to shepherd the church of God… I know that… savage wolves will come in among you, not sparing the flock. And men will rise up from your own number with deviant doctrines to lure disciples into following them."
(Acts 20: 28-30 HCSB)

Consulting Mediums and Spiritists

"Do not turn to mediums or consult spiritists, or you will be defiled by them. I am Yahweh your God." (Lev 19: 31)
Spirit of promiscuity
"My people consult their wooden and their divining rods inform them. For a spirit of promiscuity leads them astray; they act promiscuously in disobedience to their God.

My friends, do not believe every spirit, but test the spirits to determine if they are from God, because many false prophets have gone out into the world."
(Tit 2: 13, …)
Exhortation, Meditation and Reflection

On development (of doctrine):

St Vincent of Lepins: "Is there to be development of religion in the church of Christ? Certainly, there is to be development."
"… but it must be development of the faith, not alteration of the faith. Development means that each thing exists to be itself whilst alteration means that a thing is changed from one thing into another…"
The Word: Let it quench your thirst, and not your thirst the word.
Excerpts from A Commentary by St. Ephrem, Deacon:

"Lord, who can comprehend even one of your words? We lose more of it than we grasp,… For God's word offers different facets according to the capacity of the listener, and the Lord has portrayed His message in many colours, so that whoever gazes upon it can see in it what suits him within it. He has buried manifold treasures, so that each of us might grow rich in seeking them out."

"And so whenever anyone discovers some part of the treasure, he should not think that he has exhausted God's word. Instead, he should feel that this is all that he was able to find of the wealth contained in it…"

"Be glad then that you are overwhelmed, and do not be saddened because He has overcome you. A thirsty man is happy when he is drinking, and he is not depressed because he cannot exhaust the spring. So let this spring quench your thirst, and not your thirst the spring…"

"Be thankful then for what you have received, and do not be saddened at all that such an abundance still remains. What you have received and attained is your present share, while what is left will be your heritage. For what you could not take at one time because of your weakness, you will be able to grasp at another if you only persevere. So do not foolishly try to drain in one draught what cannot be consumed all at once, and do not cease out of faint heartedness from what you will be able to absorb as time goes on."

Abstain from heresy

St Ignatius of Antioch[1]: "I strongly urge you,… to be nourished exclusively on Christ's fare, abstaining from the alien food that is heresy."

Heresy according to Fr Al Luer is a spiritual JunkFood causing spiritual Anorexia.

1: St Ignatius of Antioch, Letter to the Trallians
"ANYONE who does not remain
in Christ's teaching but goes beyond it,
does not have God. The one who remains
in that teaching, this one has both the Father and the Son."

615

(2 Jn 1: 9 HCSB)

Blind guides: Brood of vipers. (Matt 23: 15-17 HCSB)

"… You travel over land and sea to make one proselyte, and when he becomes one, you make him twice as fit for hell as you are!"

"Woe to you blind guides who say 'whoever takes an oath by the sanctuary, it means nothing. But whoever takes an oath by the gold of the sanctuary is bound by his oath.' Blind fools! Which is greater, the gold or the sanctuary that sanctified the gold?"

A block cannot resist the storm flood standing alone – a tree does not make a forest – if you are a disciple your strength will be in belonging to the authentic body of disciples. "They went out from us, but they did not belong to us..." And if you are not with us, then you are against us. ( ) certainly, if your fellowship is not with the Apostles and your teaching is not rooted in Christ, It must be in the Devil, meaning that you are an antichrist;

"Snakes! Brood of vipers! How can you escape being condemned to hell?" (Matt 23: 33)

A warning against presumption.

"None is greater than Me!" "My congregation is the biggest." "I know it all!" Remember the gate is wide and the road broad that leads to destruction; many go through it.

Those are symptomatic of the underlying malaise that had continued to drive a wedge between the efforts at arriving at a kerygmatic creed for our faith.

It was not Martin Luther who first started it, only the wound has refused to heal, indeed, it has festered. The Roman Catholic Church was similarly accused by the Eastern (Orthodox) church for the latter's refusal to continue with a united front. But even before these, Moses had been rebuffed, "you have gone too far! Everyone in the entire community is holy…" (Num 16: 3)

Then, God showed the difference; He can do it again!

Thus, as it was, so it may ever be! But that does not provide us an alibi for saying different opposing things about the faith we profess: about the teaching and preaching of Jesus and His Apostles. Who gains by this scenario other than the evil one?

Exhortation, Meditation and Reflection

We should put our differences aside and agree on the authenticity of our faith and who the teacher of last resort is among us; for continual guidance and clarification (orthodoxy) who is that person or institution?

"Therefore, whoever thinks he is standing secure should take care not to fall."

(1 Cor 10: 12)

Apostles and disciples-in-communion.

Presumptive Teaching
Speculative Teaching
Tendentious Teaching
Demonic Teaching

Certainly all these cannot be right! Or what would one then make of the authentic teaching of the Lord Himself and of His duly commissioned, well groomed and anointed Apostles and disciples-in-communion? I mean disciples who shared in the faith and teaching of St Peter, and the other Apostles and disciples of Jesus who are a communion with him, who have not broken faith or trust on the kernels of the faith?

"The Church":

"I assure you: Whatever you bind on earth is already bound in heaven." (Matt 18: 17, 18 HCSB)

Certainly, Jesus did not imply the church of Satan (Rev.) or churches based on tendentious, speculative or presumptive teachings discussed above. He was referring to the church He established Himself (as per Matt 16: 17-19) "built on the foundation of the apostles and prophets, with Christ Jesus Himself as the cornerstone." (Eph 2: 20 HCSB)

The Darkness of Heresy vis-à-vis the light of truth

In Genesis, darkness and bleakness co-existed before light and life. God has delighted in giving mankind day and night, male and female. So long as there is the truth, there must be falsehood for the difference to manifest. Thus, heresy is by no means a wholesale evil; no, it makes us to appreciate and focus more on the marvellous beauty and brightness of the truth of the word.

But the messenger of God should not be hospitable to both. Only those who belong to the devil may peddle lies. It is thus of paramount importance for disciples to dissociate themselves from those who delight in confusing and confounding the little ones as proof of their faithfulness to the Lord.

This is a different matter from witch-hunting, which is alien to Christianity.

Exhortation, Meditation and Reflection.

The Lord says,

"Or how can you say to your brother, 'Brother, let me take out the speck that is in your eye', when you yourself don't see the log in your eye? Hypocrite! First take the log out of your eye, and then you will see clearly to take out the speck in your brother's eye." (Lk 6: 42 HSCB)

Orthodoxy and heresy are not matters for finger-pointing on persons.

Being born again

Everyone who announces the good news ought to be intent always at realizing the goal for our Christian formation. The essence of Christian formation is to have the mind of God, i.e., to be transformed in mind, heart, soul and spirit and be conformed to

God. Each has to become a soul seeking communion with, and submission to God.

Preaching the gospel from extraneous motives

Improper motive leads to undue emphasis and outright distortion and suppression of the true message – a thorn in the flesh it is in this age of misinformation and disinformation.

Preaching from subterranean motives leads to undue emphasis, scant attention to matters of grave concern and outright distortion of facts. The truth is suppressed by disinformation. It is as bad as blasphemy.

"To be sure, some preach Christ out of envy and strife, but others out of goodwill.

What does it matter? Just that in every way, whether out of false motives or true, Christ is proclaimed." (Phil 1: 15, 18 HCSB)

But, brothers and sisters, be watchful; because disinformation from ulterior motives frequently ends up proclaiming not Christ, but the antichrist; not salvation but doom, to its hearers.

"Many deceivers have gone out into the world;…" (2 Jn 1: 7 HCSB)

"Don't be led astray by… strange teachings…" (Heb 13: 9 HCSB)

Our exhortation

For our exhortation didn't come from error or impurity or an intent to deceive. (2 Thes 2: 3-4)

Reform can easily be hijacked by Satan

Whether anyone likes it or not, the devil will try to ensnare people out of the truth and away from obedience to God. (Gen 3: 1-5) Thus, apostasy exists as long as there is orthodoxy.

Exhortation, Meditation and Reflection

Don't take your zeal for the truth as a call for reform. First, establish that you have the sinews – a capacity to endure persecution (from the left or from the right); if you lack the call, you may end up destroying the very edifice you set out to renovate and you would more appropriately be called a destroyer rather than a builder. How could you resist the devil unless you are sent?

Remember, Jesus is a reformer (Mal 3: 3); but it takes two to tango; Judaism would not be reformed yet Jesus succeeded (in Christianity) but without the following of the rabbi!

Just as Jesus and His disciples were going out, "a demon – possessed man who was unable to speak was brought to Him. When the demon had been driven out, the man spoke. And the people were amazed, saying, 'Nothing like this has ever been seen in Israel!'

But the Pharisees said, 'He drives out demons by the ruler of the demons!'" (Matt 9: 32-34 HCSB)

"Cultural Blind spots"[1]

"2 Cor 4: 4: …blinded by the god of the present age."

Cultural blindness are like scales that obscure our vision to the truth of the word.

The Institution of human slavery, infanticide.

Onesimus means 'useful' in English. Philemon was the slave master.

"How can they take three slaves and sell them for six pigs?"

Consider the ethnic cleansing of the Third Reich… the Milad Massacre in Vietnam where thousands of lives were destroyed.

How can slavery be acceptable in its time and not recognised as reprehensible?

In a book on St Peter Claver and his work in 1600 in Colombia by Angel Sanpierra Morale quoted there was a passage in which a papal bull by Pope Nicholas V to the king:

"It is granted to... king of Portugal that he may claim for himself and his descendants any Saracens, kingdoms... any possessions that they may possess ... and subject the aforesaid persons to perpetual slavery"

1: Fr Al-Leur, Daily Bread, op. cit. (redacted from the oral podcast).

Exhortation, Meditation and Reflection.

"John 8: 31 – unless we abide in the word, we may not be able to overcome such cultural blind spots which blind us from seeing as reprehensible such cultural practices of our time such as infanticide, all forms of abortion; euthanasia, etc."

Liberation and Salvation[1]

In his meditation on the above theme, which is really on the essence of truth, his holiness, Pope Emeritus, Benedict XVI has this to say:

"But what can liberate man?

Who liberates him and to what? Put even more simply, what is human freedom? Can man become free without truth – i.e., in falsehood?

Liberation is about the truth. Liberation without the truth will be a lie – will be deception and thus man's enslavement and man's ruin."

If we ever can make progress to grapple with the truth about the godhead – to know God, we must be committed to separating truth from lie; to demystify as many 'mysteries' as possible. In truth, we deal with certainty, which is far superior to uncertainty or assumption. This is how mankind has moved forward in our knowledge of the earth, sun and moon. Knowledge advances our faith, while ignorance our fear!

Reason is indispensable to wisdom and wisdom to discerning the truth. You cannot dispense with record and be wise, for the Scripture says, "thus, while revelations and visions cannot be queried or be subjected to human evaluation, there is a lot we can do before any such claims are accepted! Otherwise, we would be putting the cart before the horse. That is where reason comes handy. Experience has shown that visions or revelations may be misinterpreted; the use of human language to describe heavenly matters may demand a mastery of language far above the ability of the visionary, which the subject may not adequately possess. Such interpretations can be challenged or even proved to be faulty, leading to wrong conclusions. Yet, with a rigorous application of the same reason, fresh vistas or truths that are unassailable may become manifest. Nothing is sacrosanct and unalterable about the truth.

1: Daily Meditation of Pope Benedict XVI

Exhortation, Meditation and Reflection.

We have got to learn to separate the truth from the myth; the message from the messenger. Liberate religion from the captivity of assumption/misinformation and superstition, then the truth will emerge. We know by reason that there is God; God is real, and this is confirmed by revelation. Who is afraid that age old beliefs may be smashed? That is for good, if it will thus unveil the truth, so let it be. The truth will set us free.

Faith will prosper and be fruitful when based on confident truth. Not only faith comes by grace, even reason and every other good gift comes to us (from God) by grace.

We can benefit from scholarship or research into the content, nature and dependability or validity of visions, apparitions, dreams and their limitations, if any. This becomes imperative because of fakes. Besides, we have evidence that these can be induced by use of herbs, meditations (yoga?), fasting or denial of food, mortification (asceticism) practices; prayer and faith. What is the relationship of trance to visions and dreams?

The scripture truculently enjoins us to seek God! We do this by due exercise of industry and diligence. Sometimes revelation comes as a reward for obedience and such diligence.

God's kingdom is the kingdom of light; but there is also another kingdom – the kingdom of darkness. Truth belongs to the kingdom of light; cynicism, doubt and denial to the kingdom of darkness. We have true or valid doctrines but so also are fake; we need reason to reveal the difference. How wonderful it would be if we can make ever efficacious supplications? Only the truth can lead us there. We want to be able to tap into God's wisdom, God's help in tackling human challenges, Jesus is the way, the truth and the life; He invites us 'Come to Me.' If we seek the truth we should be anxious to take advantage of that offer. But are we? Jesus says, 'Be One!' but we stay apart as separate islands, dishing out tendentious or opionated teachings about the truth. Many are comfortable with that also! Come off it. The truth is bitter, and many will rather listen to only what they want to hear.

Intellect in believing
1. "Now we know that You KNOW EVERYTHING and don't need anyone to question You. By this we believe that You came from God." (Jn 16: 30 HCSB)

Exhortation, Meditation and Reflection.
2. "And he went into synagogue and spoke boldly for three months, reasoning and persuading concerning the things of the kingdom of God." (Acts 19: 8 NKJV)

The Truth

"… Every fact must be established by the testimony of two or three witnesses."

"For we are not able to do anything against the truth, but only for the truth."

"Finally, brothers, rejoice. Become mature, be encouraged, be of the same mind, be at peace, and the God of love and peace will be with you."

(2 Cor 13: 1, 8, 11 HCSB)

On who has the final say in interpreting the Scripture

The Need

Secular authorities have long come to terms with the certainty that there will be misapprehension among persons on very important issues that ought to be clarified, for example, on the rights and duties between borrowers and lenders or even between husbands and wives! Thus, laws are promulgated, but there could be issues in the interpretation of such laws – hence the introduction of a supposedly free-from-bias judicial system.

The Arbiter

Who, then, can we trust to clarify to us everything about Christ's life and teaching?

We have, naturally, different schools of thought on the matter. Some say,

1. Individuals.

Your personal understanding (of scripture) should build the bulwark of your faith. "A man convinced against his will is of the same opinion still."[1]

But we are all learners; it is faster and surer to acquire knowledge if someone who is versed on the subject takes us through. Besides, in the case of irreconcilable differences with a fellow adherent of the faith, how do you win him over to you or you to him? It is important, that we remain in communion – isn't it?

2. The Church.

The magisterium of the church comes to our help. This accords with Jesus teaching on dispute resolution mechanism (Matt 18: 16-17).

Exhortation, Meditation and Reflection.

The church pontificates! You know we all – prophets/priests, monks, the religious and the faithful – constitute the body of Christ, the church; our leaders speak for us in one voice, in unanimity. Although some of us may be given to emotions, others to reason, still others to subjectivism, and others go for objective reality, the church is the referral body, the arbiter. Guided by the Holy Spirit, she establishes the fact – for the time being.

Yes, **'for the time being,'** because we gain deeper insight over time, and the church cannot afford to ignore glaring evidence that has become open in the future. Really, isn't that the core of our grouse with Judaism, that it would not accommodate any 'new' facts, even when it comes from God?

But if we must admit the truth, nobody can walk by other people's faith. To bear fruit, you must own the faith yourself! It is little comfort that the church had decreed what the faith should be. If, for now, you are not convinced, then you don't share in it, though you must accept it!

Hence, we the church, should listen to what the people are saying so we can clear some of their concerns and we must also listen to God, who speaks to the church through her members.

My take is this: let us tolerate (within the same body of Christ) persons with dissenting opinions on one or other issue of doctrine that is really not fundamental to the faith; that would not impugn the integrity of the faith or impinge negatively upon the obligations of the individual to God (and to man) and that would not make such individual unrighteous. If doing this enlarges our consensus base, so good! "We are stronger together!"[2]

"If we stand together, we shall rise together!"[2]

1:Alexander Pope

2:Mrs. Hilary Clinton, former US Senator, secretary of State and Presidential candidate (2016 election)

Exhortation, Meditation and Reflection.

On unity in faith and oneness in apostleship.

Apostle Paul, to the Galatians:

"… I want you to know, brothers, that the gospel preached by me is not based on human thought… but it came by a revelation from Jesus Christ."

"But when God who… called me… was pleased to reveal His Son… so that I could preach Him among the Gentiles, I did not immediately consult with anyone. I did not go up to Jerusalem to those who had become apostles before me…"

"Then after three years, I did go to Jerusalem to get to know Cephas… But I didn't see any of the other apostles except James…"

"Then after 14 years, I went up again to Jerusalem with Barnabas… I went up according to a revelation and persecuted? To them the gospel I teach…"

"… **false brothers smuggled in, who came secretly to spy… But we did not give up and submit to these people…**"

"Now from those recognised as important – they added nothing to me. On the contrary, they saw that I had been entrusted with the gospel for the uncircumcised, just as Peter was for the circumcised, since the One at work in Peter… was also at work in me…"

"When James, Cephas and John recognized as pillars, acknowledged the grace that had been given to me, they gave fellowship to me… agreeing that we should go to the Gentiles and they to the circumcised. They asked only that we would remember the poor, which I made every effort to do."

(Gal 1: 11-12, 15-16, 18-19; 2: 1-2, 4-7, 9-10 HCSB)

Let us – all Christians, but especially the leadership – put on our thinking caps. What does the above passage tell us about the necessity for a meeting of the minds on our understanding of our faith and on orthodoxy? What was Jesus' position thereon? Then, why are we acting differently?

Let us also remember the other side of the story as told in the Acts of the Apostles –

    i.   Saul, the persecutor: Acts 8:1
   ii.   The call of Saul (later baptized): Acts 9: 1-7, 15-18

iii. Saul (now Paul) first visit to Jerusalem and the role played by that holy man, Barnabas: Acts 9: 26-28
iv. Finally, the build-up of that enviable Antioch church: Acts 11: 22-24, 25-26.

Exhortation, Meditation and Reflection.
Let us discontinue fellowship with false brothers, but the faithful must first be together in fellowship.

A history of the division in the church

The origin of non-same fellowship sharing Christian bodies.
1. The Split. Disagreement over the addition of the Folioque (See Chapter 19).
2. Martin Luther and the protestant movement

The dispute
Martin, a German Roman Catholic priest disagreed with his colleague, his superiors and the church on the following issues (interalia):

- On power of the Pope to grant indulgences, Luther contradicted Johann Tetzel, a Dominican friar in 1517. He wrote to Tetzel's superior, Archbishop Albert of Mainz, sending alongside a copy of his 95 thesis which he entitled, "Disputation against scholastic theology."

Albert formally requested Rome to commence official proceedings to ascertain the works orthodoxy.

- Fund-raising for building the basilica of St. Peter.

Luther was opposed to it, querying why wouldn't "the pope, whose wealth today is greater than the wealth of the richest Crassus build with his own money rather than…"

- On papal primacy on theological interpretation, Luther contradicted, offering instead, *sola scriptura*, or the doctrine of the primacy of the bible.

On whose biblical interpretations are authoritative and the role of established theologians therewith, and the power of councils (such as the papal consistory of 1520 or the subsequent papal commission raised to examine Luther and which found his teachings heretical), Luther was for self-interpretation by the faithful and has this to say:

"…even general councils such as the council of Constance (1414-18) can be in error when they promulgate opinion on the faith."

Johann Eck, commenting on Luther's position as postulated at the Leipzlg public debate (1519) considered Luther's position to be identical with that of Jan Hus, which the council of Constance had declared heretical.

Exhortation, Meditation and Reflection.

- On the need for priestly celibacy, Luther described it as "the work of the Devil." He, himself got married to Katherine of Borg, a former nun and proselyte on June 13, 1525. The couple had five children.

- Luther disagreed with his co-travellers in the protestant movement he had precipitated at the Marburg Colloquy (Oct 1-4, 1529). For example, with H. Zwingli?on the real presence of the body and blood of Christ in the eucharist. Luther disagreed that Jesus was spiritually?present in the communion host but not physically present. Similarly, by 1523 Luther departed to go for? more radical reforms with other reformers like Thomas Murtzer?, Martin Bucer, Philipp Melanch Cho

- Luther's position on Anabaptists was that "They should be hanged as seditionists"

- On Jews – they "should be expelled and their synagogue burned."

Effort at resolution

Cajetan, head of Dominican order was assigned to examine Luther's teaching at Augsburg. Luther described him as "an evasive, obscure and unintelligible theologian."

Heretical not heretical: A papal consistory was raised in 1520 to examine Luther to give him opportunity to defend or renounce his teaching. This was followed by a papal commission on the same issue. The former found his teaching heretical, while the latter (consisting of important monastic orders) confirmed that Luther's propositions were "scandalous and offensive to pious ears" but that they were not heretical.

Luther showed no remorse. So, on June 15, 1520 Pope Leo issued the bull which formally charged that 41 sentences in Luther's writings were heretical.

Luther was given 60 days to recant and another 60 days to make a report thereof to Rome.

Luther's response was a tract which he entitled "Against the execrable bull of the anti-christ" And on December 10, 1520 Luther made a bonfire of a copy of the bull in the public gaze.

Failure of détente – Luther convicted a heretic.

On January 3, 1521 was published a papal bull – which declared Luther a heretic.

Exhortation, Meditation and Reflection.

Ordinarily, Luther should have been apprehended by the secular government of his residence as a condemned heretic. But Charles V, newly elected German king indicated he was not disposed to act on the conviction of a German without proper hearing. The formal hearing was held at Worms on March 6, 1521. Luther did not recant any of the 41 indictments. So, on May 25, 1521 Charles V signed the edict against Luther and he was placed into protective custody.

A keen observer[1] reflected on this scenario thus, "Luther, a single individual presumed to challenge 1,500 years of Christian theological consensus."

The split within the split.

All these led to a division in the Western Roman Catholic Church, with some supporting the church and others, Luther. In no time, the 'protestants' could not hold together extending into different folds such as Lutheranism, Calvinism, Anglican communion, Anabaptists and anti-trinitarians, etc. Thus, bringing to fulfilment the prophetic words of AlekseiStepanovichKhomiakov (ASK).

Who was Martin Luther?

A German priest, theologian (and reformer?). He celebrated his first mass in May 1507. He was one of two chosen by his colleagues to make a representation to Pope Julius II.

He petitioned the theology faculty of the University of Erfurt to confer him a doctorate in theology. (Granted ultimately on their behalf by the university of Whitten burg in 1512). He later precipitated the protestants' movement that queried or offered an alternative reformation of age-old Christian beliefs and tradition.

After he had been formally declared a heretic and was placed in protective custody, he translated the New Testament into German language.

In 1539 Philip of Hesse (Landgrave) secretly married his wife's lady-in-waiting, with Luther's tacit support. It created a bigamy issue.

1: Dutch humanist Desiderius Erasmus.

Exhortation, Meditation and Reflection.

Before the revolution that Luther's protest ushered in no individual, but only the church, could found new Christian worship centres. Even today, most professional have found it necessary to restrict the practice of their profession to duly certified members. That way, the members of the public are protected from quacks and the reputation of the profession itself is safeguarded.

Christianity in the world today – an anomie.

The break continues till today. It has become the new norm. In many countries many religious people found their own churches in just the same way as secular clubs are formed, but often more frequently. Today, in Nigeria alone, there are more than 3,000 autocephalous Christian worship centres.Someone may ask, so then, what is wrong with that? Everything; nothing is right about it!

Orthodoxy, Protestantism and growth of free churches

"Not everyone should be teachers," lest the less informed among us may "cause others to stumble," even if unintentionally. The situation foists doubt on the flock instead of faith; weakness of the body of Christ, instead of strength. A lack of direction replaces purposiveness in Christian evangelism – i.e., growth by objectives (GBO) – salvation, is replaced with growth by greed (GBG). This shows off by forsaking the true path (the kingdom of God) for earthly glory. Many of these churches are not attentive to the Holy Spirit, but listen to Satan! Righteousness recedes; mass apostasy, prophesied, becomes increasingly unpreventable. As denominations flourish, growth in the knowledge of God stagnates.

Break-away occurs every second from existing mother churches. Is there anything we can do to avert this disaster – this binary fission?

The way forward

First, we can stop focusing on individuals; from henceforth our focus should be on institutions – from heretics to heretical institutions – institutions which do not qualify for the appellation, 'Christian.' That way, we would be separating the grain from the chaff and impeding the precocious growth of the weed among the wheat.

Why should anybody be killed by man (warfare apart)? Remember, "thou shall not kill."

Exhortation, Meditation and Reflection.

Murdering individuals for holding personal views not congruent withsociety's is hardly a valid exception. Besides, such religious killing tends to legitimatize the killing of pious people by demonic regimes. Struggling Christian entities ought to be assisted to stand firm; fakes, should be shown the way out – through denial of fellowship with them.

Like Luther, many of us suffer from some idiosyncrasies. We should learn to tolerate and accommodate one another. Perhaps, John Wesley's Methodists may then have remained an ecclesiola in ecclesia in the Anglican church, strengthening the latter, particularly in the Americas.

Perhaps there are many more lessons to learn from history, if we are so disposed to.

The dividers are divided: The Anglican church succumbs to a split

If Christianity had walked away from Judaism, because the latter would not absorb reform, the splinter groups that emerged from the crack in the Western Roman Catholic Church themselves underwent division atomistically for different causes. Western Catholicism broke into pieces because of the disrespect for duly constituted authority. The splinter groups emerging, like the Anglican Communion, could not hold together because of one or other of the aforementioned reasons.

In the case of John Wesley's[1]methodism, he was a full-time cleric of the Anglican communion until the end of his life. He did not set out to oppose that authority, or to create a new church, but he was zealous for the faith – for Christ. Split eventually occurred because there was no informal channel of communication between the echelons of the Anglican church, between the priests and laity and the higher ecclesiastics. Today, some churches hold synods which meet periodically; through its auspices various members of the church can talk to each other about their concerns on the faith – the priests, the religious and the lay faithful. That way, the church had ceased to be looked at as that of the pastor but as "our church."

1: John Wesley, 17

Exhortation, Meditation and Reflection.

Wesley's charisms

The primitivist motif:

Like in the early Christian community, Wesley's interest was to deepen the faith of believers as part of renewal of that old fervour.

Free (or believers') church:

Denominational allegiance is anti-thetical to that goal. Consequently, it is understandable therefore, that Wesley's goal was "forming a genuine people of God within the Anglican institutional church."

Nevertheless, one does not need to be an Anglican or a Methodist to be admitted into membership: "for their union with us we require no unity in opinion."

Discipline.

Wesley operated on the belief that the church must exercise discipline on a covenant commitment to Christian values as expected of a Christian community – to live and maintain the values of the kingdom of God in an inclement cultural environment "to be a Christian in a deteriorating hedonistic society."

To him, the church needs a structure based on norms of community discipline and mission. Thus, in 1748 Wesley reduced the Bristol society membership from 900 to 730. Some of the reasons for this were irregular attendance, wife-beating, etc.

All members were, of course, accountable to him personally (through their leaders).

He recognised the spiritual dimension of the church beyond that of a secular club; "it is a sacramental community." He postulated that "discipline has the relationship to justification that works have to faith…"

Missionary zeal:

Wesley's first love to build a genuine people of God led him into forming little bands of God seekers. He started from the street – from the Fetter lane society established in 1738, to the Newcastle-upon-Tyne (Sandgatestreet) open air preaching of May 30, 1742. To farther deepen penetration in evangelism he formed his itinerant band of travelling lay preachers. Ultimately, it led to the planting of his Methodist societies and church in America, the then new world. The appointment of local presbyters became insistent to enhance control beyond what he could accomplish from far away England.

Exhortation, Meditation and Reflection.

Who Wesley was

He was an Anglican clergyman and founder of the Methodist church which became about the largest "free church" in the protestant tradition.

For him "church" stands for believers in Christ thus, under-playing or denying the hierarchical structure as an essence. To him 'church unity' is fostered by the Christian Koinonia in the Holy Spirit. Apostolicity meant, "the succession of apostolic doctrine in those… faithful to the Apostolic witness."

His ecclesiology: "In religion, I am for as few innovations as possible," the first century Christian communities were his model.

Prevenient grace: He believed that on their own, human beings could not take the ………. smallest step toward God; but God's grace was prevenient.

Activism: He believed that the struggle for social justice sprang from the Bible – by building a community that was faithful to the scriptures.

CHAPTER 18

Marriage, Divorce and Human Sexuality.

"And whoever marries a divorced woman commits adultery."
(Matt 5: 32 HCSB)

For the Singles –

Jesus' teaching(Matt 19: 10-11 Lect)
"Some are incapable of marriage
because they were born so;
some, because they were made
so by others;
some, because they have
renounced marriage for the
sake of the kingdom of heaven."
Man, leader of the family
"So, the Lord God called out to the man and said to him,
'Where are you?'"
"… Your desire will be for your husband, yet he will rule over
you."
(Gen 3: 9, 16 HCSB)
Do you know that
Anyone who joins himself to a prostitute becomes one body with
her?

- For "the two will become one flesh." (1 Cor 6: 16)
- "Run from sexual immorality!..." (1 Cor 6: 18 HCSB)
- "… Your body is a temple of the Holy Spirit within
  you,therefore glorify God in your body." (1 Cor 6: 19, 20
  NABRE)

636

"… Know that Christ is the head of every man, and a husband the head of his wife, and God the head of Christ." (1 Cor 11: 3 NABRE)

IF marriage were indissoluble (Matt 19: 3-12)

Here is a condensed account of a conversation between a set of Pharisees and Jesus:

Pharisee: For what reason can a man divorce his wife?

Jesus: None; except, perhaps, the wife's unfaithfulness.

Pharisee: Why, then, did our law permit a man to issue his wife a writ of divorce and send her away?

Jesus: It was a concession by Moses; but from the origin of marriage, God instituted it to be lifelong.

Jesus Disciple: Master, if marriage goes the way You have espoused it – what a mirthless life awaits the married man?

The two have become one flesh – no longer two.

"Therefore, what God has joined together

man must not separate." (Matt 19: 6 NABRE)

Jesus: You ignore the grace of God; there is no cause to be despondent.

Jesus implied that divine wisdom makes husband and wifeone flesh, no longer two. And we know that every work of God exudes great wisdom.

RAPE

"The man who raped her must give the young woman's father 50 silver shekels, and she must become his wife because he violated her. He cannot divorce her as long as he lives." (Deut 22: 29)

Marriage and the single life

Marriage is treated in the scripture as a sacred gift to humanity by which man participates in procreation. (Gen 1: 28)

"… Be fruitful; multiply fill the earth…"

The patriarchs were married as well as most of the prophets. Of the twelve or fourteen apostles (counting Matthias and Paul) only

Simon Peter was alluded to as married and throughout his apostolic call, he seemed to have put his marriage at the back stage. Joseph and Mary were married, but Jesus Himself was single and celibate.

Adultery is evil

Always remember, the 6th commandment, "You shall not commit adultery." (Matt 6:27)

Men, especially the lewd, should beware of lechery. Learn the lesson in the pranks of the Jael and the Judith of this world.(Jgs 5: 24-26; Jdt 13: 13-17)

Women, refrain from seducing men or engaging in adultery.

"She anointed her face with fragrant oil; fixed her hair with a diadem, and put on a linen robe to beguile him." (Jdt 16: 7, 8 NABRE)

Divorce

In response to some Pharisees' enquiries on divorceJesus said,

"But from the beginning of creation God made them male and female. For this reason a man will leave his father and mother and be joined to his wife, and the two will become one flesh. So they are no longer two, but one flesh. Therefore, what God has joined together, man must not separate."

(Mk 10: 6-9 HCSB)

"Better to live on the corner of a roof

than to share a house with a nagging wife." (Prov 21: 9 HCSB)

"Whoever divorces his wife and marries another commits adultery against her. Also if she divorces her husband and marries another, she commits adultery." (Mk 10: 11-12 HCSB)

Apostle Paul on Marriage and the single life

- "A man does well not to marry. But because there is so much immorality, every man should have his own wife and every woman her own husband. …each should satisfy the other's needs. A wife is not the master of her own body, but the husband is; in the same way a husband is not the master of his own body, but the wife is. Do not deny yourselves to each other,…" (1 Cor 7: 1, 2-5 GNBDK)

- Unmarried and widows

"… Better for you to continue to live alone… But if you cannot restrain your desires, go ahead and marry – it is better to marry than to burn with passion."

"An unmarried man concerns himself with the Lord's work… to please the Lord. But a married man concerns himself with worldly matters,… to please his wife and so he is pulled in two directions."

(1 Cor 7: 8, 32-34 GNBDK)

Lust and same sex unions

The Missing Tribe of Israel:

Free thinkers and Mob Instincts (Jgs 19: 1-21: 25 HCSB)

"In those days, when there was no king in Israel, a Levite living in… Ephraim acquired a woman in Bethlehem in Judah as his concubine. But she… left him for her father's house… for four months. Then, her husband… went after her.

His father-in-law, the girl's father, detained him… eating and drinking together. On the… fifth day,… the girl's father (attempted persuading the man to stay) but the man was unwilling to spend the night. He arrived (at) Jerusalem… his concubine with him… (at) sun set (and) they stopped to… spend the night at Gibeah… (land of Benjamin). There, an old man (an Emphraimite) residing in Gibeah decided to take care of (them) (and) brought (them) to his house.

While there, enjoying themselves, all of a sudden, perverted men… surrounded the house and beat on the door,

"Bring out the man… so we can have sex with him!"

Old man: "No, don't do this evil… this horrible thing. Here, …my virgin daughter and the man's concubine… use them."

The Marital Mandate

"God blessed them and God said to them,
'Be fruitful, multiply, fill the earth, and subdue it.
Rule the fish… the birds… and every creature
that crawls on the earth." (Gen 1: 28 HCSB)

If you wish to know more about this episode, which almost exterminated one of the twelve tribes (Benjamin), continue the reading in the scripture quoted above.

The message: sexual perversity is not of recent origin, but like robbery and murder has been with man from of old.

See, the sorrows that are harvested when libertines have their way!

What nation is it that would rather not be guided by divine wisdom?

"For the wisdom of this world is foolishness with God…"

And again, "the Lord knows that the reasonings of the wise are meaningless." (1 Cor 3: 19-20 HCSB)

Meditation: Spouses – reflect on this:

"The Lord God said: It is not good for the man to be alone. I will make a helper suited to him…" (Gen 2: 18, NABRE)

"… and they became one flesh." (Gen 2:24 HCSB)

Marriage and the single life.

"Marriage must be respected by all, and the marriage bed kept undefiled, because God will judge immoral people and adulterers." (Heb 13: 4 HCSB)

Lust: the ordeal of Susanna, wife of Joakim

"When the old men saw her enter every day for her walk, they began to lust for her. They suppressed their consciences; they would not allow their eyes to look to heaven, and did not keep in mind just judgements." (Dan 13: 8 Lect)

"… the two old men got up and hurried to her, 'Look', they said, 'the garden doors are shut, and no one can see us; give in to our desire, and lie with us. If you refuse, we will testify against you that you dismissed your maids because a young man was here with you.'" (Dan 13:19-20 Lect)

Of course, Susanna did not yield to these randy elders' demand and they carried out what they threatened. Being judges, they condemned her to death in the presence of her husband and children. Nemesis, of course, caught up with them and they lost their own lives into the bargain, while Susanna was spared.

Read more about it in Daniel (Greek Version) chapter 13: 1-62.

ADDITIONAL RESOURCES

Exhortation and Meditation
Human Sexuality.

The Lord told Adam and Eve to go and multiply and fill the surface of the earth. He certainly understands the heart of men that some of them will have scruples doing this (fruitfulness). Probably for that reason, He made the thrill and excitement of erotic love combined with the joy of watching one's offspring grow to be so irresistible and inexhaustible.

Only this time, the Lord demands of us self-restraint and compliance with His ordained precepts.

We know, too, that there would be many, even in those days, who would feel differently about marriage considering the disgust expressed by the disciple.

Think of a couple like Zachariah and Elizabeth, for example. Eve was certainly the best soul mate and help mate that could be found for Adam.

Here are a few of the more important things that can make a marriage work:

1. **Commitment** on the part of both spouses to follow the plan of God and hold on to their soul mates. In adversity we quickly forget the delights of the past; though tough times don't last.

Both spouses ought to be committed to making their relationship to be at its best, indeed happiest for the other, despite all odds.

2. **Godliness**: Remember you are not alone in the marriage; God created the man and the woman a perfect fix (physiologically) for each other; He also set forth the rules — obey them. I assure you, all will work out well if you do. Leave it all to God. How much of your spouse do you know before marriage: future health prospects and life-span, tragedies, fruitfulness, etc.? Impliedly, you trusted God for these; then stick to God. A prospective spouse may have less

643

than half a chance for attaining the prosperity and happiness together as is obtainable with the present partner. You can't tell.

Bring your best into the marriage.

3. Strive to bring the best of your humanity into the marriage (and indeed into the family), while being persevering to endure what your spouse cannot or will not change! An entire lifetime home deserves such nurturing.

Exhortation and Meditation

Each spouse should personally do away with vices and bad habits as part of being his/her best – lying, nagging, drunkenness, drug addiction, unfaithfulness, slothfulness, intolerance, quick temper, uncouth language. Oh yes, it can be done!

Remember, such continuing effort is worthwhile since this is the strongest panacea for peace in the world – persevering toleration of one another.

Individual freedom.

No one will do your will all of the time. Even humans don't do the will of their Creator – all of the time!

Encourage each other to develop their peculiar God-given talents to the utmost; don't stifle them.

Persuade; avoid hectoring and recalcitrance

4. Set goals and mutually decide on major changes thereof together; be alternative to, anticipate and supply the needs (information and otherwise) of your spouse. Use persuasion (it is your duty) rather than being didactic or peremptory in communicating your preferences.

No nagging, no mockery: assist your spouse to stay out of trouble.

5. Avoid resentment, nagging or mockery or scoffing, being disdainful or petulant; rather, heartily celebrate each other's goodness explicitly at set times (e.g., wedding anniversaries, etc.) and at every opportunity informally. Be generous in complimenting every good act of your spouse (that way, you

are pointing at what you esteem, thereby re-enforcing that behaviour of the spouse to turn it into a habit).

Strive always to empathize with each other as behoves one's best friend on earth. For that is what you should be to your spouse — in spite of who he/she is.

Don't look elsewhere for that friendship; instead of deriding, do your level best to get him/her stay out of trouble.

6. Give and Forgive

If you are in love – to give (love), and to take offence (being jealous) may be more natural than you think. But even where the love has cooled down somewhat every spouse still has the duty to be generous to the other.

Exhortation and Meditation

Don't be self-centred or tight-fisted. Remember, if you won't give in cash, you can give in kind.

Go the extra mile to give (what is in your power to) that which your spouse loves or greatly desires in; the joy in his or her look is more than adequate recompense for you.

Then, never harbour a grudge against your spouse. Don't dwell on differences already resolved in the past. Do everything to disperse any hard feeling soonest. Forgive, if a wrongdoing has been committed against you; talk your displeasure or unhappiness over with your spouse, if the matter would not go away. The goal of either spouse should always be to procure happiness for the other or dissipate any unhappiness as fast as possible. Remember, the two of you are one flesh now!

7. Pray!

Yes, pray with faith together and individually, often and fervently, for everything you desire for yourself, your spouse and your children. God delights to pamper us by acceding to our petitions. Make profuse use of that grace to obtain wisdom, contentment and right-standing with God for yourselves.

For more, see the second book of this 5-piece work entitled:

"What makes for peace".

Holy Matrimony

Reflecting on the union between husband and wife and their children, Pope Emeritus Benedict XVI[1] says thus:

"Man is created with a need for others that he may pass beyond his own limits... He is not made to be alone... but he is made to turn to someone else..."

"Man and woman belong to each other"

"Whenever any two people give themselves in marriage to each other and between them give life to children this touches the holiness – the mystery of human existence which goes beyond the realm of what I can control or dispose off or being involved until further notice or until I find something better. I simply do not belong to myself alone..."

1: Pope Benedict XVI, Daily Meditations (idem)

Exhortation and Meditation

"That is why the association of husband and wife is regarded... within the sphere of the sacred as being answerable before God."

Perversity: Immoral sexual behaviours

Permit not your senses to be numbed through frequent mentioning of the forbidden or the absurd. There are things that are natural just as there are things that are bizarre and abhorrent; things that are sacred as well as things that are profane. That line that separates these things must not be obscured by inadvertence or indecency or impiety, lest we become obtuse.

The Yorubas have a saying, 'ohun to yeni l'oyeni;okunorun ko y'edie.' (English: decorum is about what is fit and proper; a rope on the neck is inappropriate for a hen.) It is glaringly obvious that a woman is made for a man and vice versa. A man and a woman may celebrate their God-given love in the church. But it is a sacrilege for an unmarried man or woman or a celibate priest or nun to exhibit their amorous erotic fondness in the house of God; it is a desecration!

646

Who, but a reprobate, will endorse a sexual relationship between a mother and her son, or between a father and his daughter; or between a human being and an animal? The scripture considers these as vile and bestial. God's commandment on this subject has been vindicated by medical science.

This bestiality may arise out of ignorance (irrepressible curiosity) about proper conduct, or of the impropriety of these relationships; by foolishness (not to exercise self-control), or by demonic manipulation, (abhorrent curiosity), or physiological malformation, or from extraordinary loneliness of a recluse.

Whatever is the origin, anyone who finds himself/herself thus defiled by such debasement should come out of it; be remorseful, repent, be cleansed and be born again. This obscenity is as old as sin. The practice may have grown more widespread in our permissive society, it does not validate it. Persons with physiological malformations ought to seek appropriate medical help, not in gender change as such.

A human heart will initially upbraid its owner and condemn these acts as incest and bestiality. Where the victim ignores such internal revulsion, he or she loses moral restraint and may begin to derive pleasure from such iniquity. To indulge in such unnatural sexual behaviour is a sin, a disobedience to God, and to recruit the naïve into such reprehensible conduct is a sin against society. That is not freedom, any more than drunkenness, lewdness and suicide are.

Exhortation and Meditation

"The freedom of a human being is the freedom of a limited being… We can possess it only as a shared freedom.

Only if we live in the right way with one another and for one another can freedom develop."[1]

A perverse (or libertine) society with a morbid sense of sin may give such practices partial acceptability – 'do, if it pleases you.'

But the scripture says, 'no!'

This is an abomination and it could incur a generational curse on the society, with adverse consequences especially for its misled youth. Such society is complicit by not admonishing and chastising the aberrant and chastising them.

I understand that deviousness is now so rife that a man cohabits with a fellow man. A woman with another woman; that some depraved men sought pleasure in watching a beast (e.g.a dog) mate with a woman! What depravity!

What inexorable fate awaits them and their permissive society! Repent! Repent now!!

These happenings have recorded antecedents for our learning purposes:

- Some fallen angels were known to consummate sexual relationship with human females (Gen 6: 1-2)

These got pregnant and bore hybrid beings known as nephilim.
- Sodom and Gomorrah perished for homo-sexual practices (Gen 19: 4-11)
- Dinah, Jacob's daughter, was raped by Shechem, resulting in a massacre (Gen 34: 1-4, 25-26)
- Israel virtually lost one of its tribes when the perverted insisted on homosexual sexual act, and in lieu of which they gang-raped a man's mistress to death (Jgs 19: 22-26, 27-20: 48)
- Sisera lost his life in the hands of Jael, Hebe's wife (Jgs 4: 17) just as did Holofernes in the hands of Judith in different adulterous escapades. (Jdt 12: 11-13: 8 NABRE)
- King David had affairs with Uraiah's wife, bringing death to Uraiah and to David's house. (2 Sam 12: 10)
- David's son, Amnon raped his half-sister, Tamar – giving the sword a free rein in the house of David. (2 Sam 13: 1-14, 28-18: 33)

Exhortation and Meditation
Resentment, nagging and violence in marriage

Angst should not be cultivated but dissipated at the earliest opportunity because its end leads to resentment, withdrawal, nagging, and ultimately hatred and rejection of the other spouse. The other spouse responds with bewilderment, detachment and sometimes irritability or even violence. This should not be so. Discuss your injury with your partner and both of you should learn to communicate with each other in words, in silence and by gestures.

Nagging is mainly associated with women, withdrawal with men.

An anecdote speaks of an ancient Greek philosopher – Plato – who had a nagging wife. The man lounged unperturbed as she ranted. Her anger did not abate, so she got a bowl of water and poured it over him. His response – 'oh yea, I thought so; that after thunder comes rainfall!'

Nagging has destroyed very many otherwise precious relationships. Avoid it like a plague. And both should avoid violence even more.

Eve – was she a compliment or an accessory to Adam?

Was the first recorded wife an optional accessory or enhancer to Adam's life or a necessary complement thereof for life's journey?

Answer: After the bone had been taken from Adam's ribs, he never became complete by himself anymore. Eve had become the complement – a necessary adjunct, a soul mate or comforter in life's odyssey.

That should be understood by every husband and wife as the role and goal divinely assigned to the partners as they wade through the wilderness of a life of togetherness.

"Then the Lord God said,

'It is not good for the man to be alone.

I will make a helper as his complement.'"

"The man gave names to all the livestock, to the birds… and to every wild animal, but for the man no helper was found as his complement."

"So the Lord God… took one of his ribs and closed the flesh… Then the Lord God made the rib… into a woman and brought her to the man. And the man said:

This one at last, is bone of my bone and flesh of my flesh; this one will be called, 'woman', for she was taken from man." (Gen 2: 18, 21, 22-23 HCSB)

Exhortation and Meditation

Notice the wisdom from on high: He did not make the bone taken from Adam into another man, perhaps less strong. For there could be love lost between them someday, or a rivalry leading to a parting of the way or an enslavement. The Lord God desired and enshrined happiness for both spouses!

Christian Morality – a burden?

"Moral obligation is our dignity."[1]

"Moral obligation is not men's prison from which he must liberate himself in order finally to be able to do what he wants. It is moral obligation that constitutes his dignity and he does not become more free if it is discarded. On the contrary, it is a step backward to the level of a machine – a mere thing."

"If there is no longer any obligation to which he can and must respond in freedom then, there is no realm of freedom at all! The recognition of morality is the real substance of human dignity. Morality is not men's prison, but rather the divine element in him."

Children are the face of God's love for humans

Have you noticed how mothers and fathers pamper their children? They are so indulgent to their offspring almost to the extent of not noticing or acknowledging their faults! Don't look down on such parents – God wanted it that way!

God's love for us is so vast that He could not be satisfied with our neighbours dispensing His love to us (on His behalf). So, the Lord founded families, or rather, parenthood. Parents are endowed with such superfluous and ineffable love,the counterpart ofwhich can only be found in God – i.e., in God's love for man. Isn't that the reason why the holy God is just and at the same time merciful? Mercy is alien to man's psyche; the more powerful a potentiate is, the less mercifully he rules!

We marvel, when we observe the monstrous things that God has done to ensure that parents dispense His unfailing loveto their offsprings unfailingly.

1: Pope Emeritus Benedict XVI, Daily Meditations

Exhortation and Meditation

First, He made man for woman, and woman for man, so the duo can form a partnership for the upbringing of their young. Their lives as individuals may not reach the apex of fulfilment until somehow, they flirt with each other! God made the craving for the opposite sex so irresistible that men and women may always long to be together, usually without considering the consequences of such hibernation, as if being together was by itself the end of the adventure.

It is a trap, as it were, that the Almighty God uses to bring recalcitrant man into always doing His will in that respect, without the need for Him to invoke punishment from time to time or to coerce them into the act. Man and woman cannot stop themselves from savouring that exquisite intimacy with each other; it is pleasurable for its own sake! Never mind that some cultures have attempted to douse that craving by doing something to the female genitals.

The excitement does not end with the first experience. Rather, the experience is addictive. That is all they have to do and a child comes their way!

A child is at the same time, a prodigious gift to a couple, although they may not have realized this at first. So left to themselves alone, they may as well kill the child! The advice of elders who may have experienced that wonderful blessing which children are, may not avail.

So, God did the next great and wonderful thing: He programmed parents to have such a vast and unreasoning love for their offsprings, right from the day they are discovered to be in the womb! They just couldn't stop loving them! I have seen mal-formed infants, their parents love them all the same! I have seen dullards and, in some cases, ugly boys and girls yet, they are the darlings of their parents! If you ever wondered why this is so, know that God made it so. That way, they dispense the unfailing love of God copiously on the young, tender, growing children.oh, what infinite goodness of God, it is goodness beyond our understanding!

That seems to be the goal; but many still do not discern it.

So, God did not stop there either; He gives joy to the parents at every developmental stage of the child – looking, crawling, walking, talking, etc. Even, after the child had become an adult and a parent, their forebears still get delighted and excited at every progress of the child (of yesteryears).

Exhortation and Meditation

Material giftsto the elderly parents from their children only intensify that joy, that fulfilment. They are like icing to the cake.

Because parents love every child, they would not permit the older or the strong to oppress the younger or the weak! That way,God's love is manifested in the family. But parents most important obligation is to inculcate in their offspring the knowledge and fear of God. That is the ultimate. Thus, it is only through marriage that their responsibility can be accomplished, and the kindness and love of God transmitted in the family line, and ultimately in the entire society. Marriage is sacred:

"What God has joined together; man must not separate".

(Mk 10:9; Matt 19:6 HCSB)

PROSTITUTION

The Ten Commandments are a brief and concise commandment of God. Possibly made so that man may have no excuse of forgetting to observe any of them. One of the commandments says you shall not commit adultery. And we know that every sexual engagement not with one's spouse is an adulterous act – whether you call it fornication or whoring or by whatever other names. Prostitution, therefore, falls into this class.

Causes:

- For the individual, it is doubtful if anyone in her right senses would ever deliberately engage in whoring. Distress, anguish, frustration and other circumstances beyond control often lead women to it. But people don't seem to realize this, they seem to blame the whore for her plight. The sacred literature (Christian's and Muslim's) contains references wherein prophets marry widows, loose women or even harlots. This probably is so, because their predicament is not always of their own making. At any rate, the Lord God delights in clemency and compassion.
- But what can a woman do who is fastened to a marriage where the parties are incompatible? What happens to a woman who fled that relationship with no welcoming home to go back to? Or with no independent source of income to keep body and soul together?

Exhortation and Meditation
- A mother with two or more children in the above circumstance may wait for the ideal spouse to emerge, but may fail to get one before her patience runs out.
- Some such women tried avoiding outright prostitution by cohabiting with some men, but those men failed to provide the needs of the women or their children, especially for widows without a tangible source of independent income. They take to whoring as a short-term solution.

- Some marriages are ruined for lack of fruitfulness. If the woman's subsistence is threatened, prostitution offers immediate relief.
- In modern era, and especially in places where the national economy is so wretched and spineless, many girls and house-wives are lured into prostitution and slavery in foreign lands by traffickers who beguile them by untrue account of their intentions. In the foreign land, the traffickers seize their travelling documents and place the women in brothels to engage in commercial sex or to work as house-helps, usually without any rights. The traffickers share the proceeds.

The problem

Harlotry is a big problem. The problem threatens to overwhelm the whore as well as her society.

- This business brings many afflictions to the practitioners: not the least is in contacting and spreading sexually transmitted diseases, including herpes, HIV-AIDS, etc.
- Some women get pregnant in the process and try abortion to mitigate their sorrows. Some are not that fortunate to procure the abortion: the business is slowed down, income falls. Some lose their lives in the process due to inadequate medical care during the pregnancy or at child birth.
- Some bear the children to life, which they embrace but due to inadequate care (single motherhood) they lost the children later.
- Women, whose failed relationships lead to disenchantment with marriage and with life become distraught, and estranged from society.

Exhortation and Meditation

The very poor among them go into Prostitution which makes them to lose the opportunity to find a suitable spouse or even take advantage of career development opportunities. Fulfilment eludes them, they end up in alcoholism, drug addiction, prostitution, homicide and suicide.

Very few of the women are lucky, they found real husband among one of their patrons.

- Lawless men/customers are a pain in the neck; some of these will not settle the price agreed (more prevalent with some security personnel). Others, after the demand and supply even go to the extreme of drugging the women, stealing their money and dumbing them somewhere!

- Nations that use police raids to arrest or intimidate these women complicate a fate that is already miserable. Most of the women have no 'home' to return to. So, after a brief respite or freedom from the officers, they return to the same beat. The misfortunes of the whore are innumerable.

- For the society, miscreants and criminals patronise these women, making the need for a 'home' unnecessary and thereby making it more difficult to locate and apprehend them by security personnel.

- The children of the whore – both those they had before or those they bore in the course of the business, are subject to high mortality rate due to inadequate maternal/parental care. If they survive, many turn to criminality for survival, having lacked vocational or professional training.

- The women in drugs become an economic burden to society.

Dealing with epidemics of sexually transmitted diseases creates a hole in public treasury, just the same way as criminality does.

Overall, the breakdown of morality in society caused by prostitution and other perverse sexual behaviours, such as same sex marriages, constitutes an assault on the institution of marriage and an unquantifiable damage to society.

Way forward

A righteous approach to solving this problem must pay attention to its causes, the plight of the victims and its consequences on the moral health of society.

Exhortation and Meditation

- A good sex-and marriage-education, including a knowledge of the divine injunctions on the subject, would go a long way to guide the inexperienced or naïve, and help them avoid the pitfall.

- Full employment will offer alternative job options for the low-skilled. Vocational training at state expense by the home governmentswould greatly alleviate the distress victims experience, especially those trafficked into prostitution. Such vocational (and professional) training to be balanced, must include elementary concepts of marketing and record-keeping (book-keeping).

- For humanity's sake, the host government should accord full refugee status to the trafficked victims, establish a procedure whereby the women may advance to full citizenship. Traffickers should be severely punished.

- Social security, if efficiently run, can mitigate the role of penury in dragging women to whoring. It may also enable the commercial sex worker to obtain adequate medical assistance – to prevent infections, thwart unwanted pregnancies, and procure safe and lawful abortions where necessary.

- State assistance to rehabilitate victims into normal life is absolutely a societal moral obligation. Afterall, societal imbalances caused the problem in the first instance. Medical help, especially physiotherapy, should be available to these victims at state expense. Prostitutes' patrons can always find alternative and legitimate ways to satisfy their natural urge.

- Children are a heritage both of their parents and of society. For the society, children are also an economic input. If well trained, they raise productivity level in the society. Hence the state must ensure adequate and appropriate education and training for all its citizens, if necessary, on a payback basis (i.e, when the trainees have graduated and have begun to make earnings). The increase in productivity will benefit the nation.
- Whoring, like indolence and addiction to excessive food, drinks and pleasure, are not usually crimes. Society should employ persuasion and incentives to dissuade victims from continuing in the business.

The use of force to arrest victims by security agents lacks the milk of human kindness; it flows from a lack of empathy.

CHAPTER 19

Let Them Be One

HCSB	Jn 17:17	NABRE
Holy Father—		Holy Father—
"Sanctify them by the truth;		"Consecrate them in the truth
Your word is truth."		Your word is truth."

What the scriptures are saying:

"Pay **obedience to the truth,** having purified yourselves for sincere love of the brothers, love one another earnestly from a pure heart." (1 Pt 1:22 HCSB)

"… remain in Ephesus so that you may instruct certain people **NOT to teach different doctrine** or to pay attention to myths and endless genealogies. These promote empty speculations rather than God's plan, which operates by faith." (1 Tim 1: 3 HCSB)

1 Tm 6:3 **"Whoever teaches something different…**

:4 is conceited, understanding nothing…

From these come envy, rivalry, insults, evil suspicions and mutual friction among people with corrupted minds, who are deprived of the truth, supposing religion to be a means of gain."

"…**I am the light of the world.** Whoever follows Me will not walk in darkness, but will have THE LIGHT OF LIFE." (Jn 8:12 NABRE)

IF — "But if we walk in the light as He is in the light, then we have **fellowship with one another,** and the blood of His son Jesus cleanses us from all sin."

(1 Jn 1:7 NABRE)

IF — "But if you have bitter envy and selfish ambition…don't brag and deny the truth.

For where envy or selfish ambition exists, there is disorder and every kind of evil." (Js 3:14, 16)

In unity, nothing will be impossible

"**IF** they…do this as one people, all having the same language, then nothing they plan to do will be impossible for them." (Gen 11:6 HCSB)

I urge you brothers, …agree in what you say and… BE UNITED in the same mind and in the same purpose. (1 Cor 1:10)

See also Phil 2: 2

FACTIONS – Cast them out

It is inevitable that factions will grow up:

"There have to be factions among you in order that those who are approved among you may become known." (1 Cor 11:19)

This is because we cannot all be compliant—for every twelve there is a Judas Iscariot. Isn't it?

Paul's farewell address to the Ephesus Church elders at Miletus:

"**Be vigilant!**" "Keep watch over yourselves and over the whole flock…in which you tend the church of God that He acquired with His own blood. I know that after my departure savage wolves will come among you, and they will not spare the flock. And from your own group, men will come forward perverting the truth to draw the disciples away after them. So be vigilant…"

(Acts 20:28-31 NABRE)

SHARING

"WHAT do you possess that you have not received?…" (1 Cor 4:7)

"The community of believers (in Jerusalem) was of one heart and mind… they had everything in common." (Acts 4: 32 NABRE)

Be One!

Come together in oneness, in faith and...

"It was He who 'gave gifts', He appointed some to be apostles, others to be prophets, others to be evangelists, others to be pastors and teachers. He did this to prepare all God's people for the work of Christian service, in order to build up the body of Christ. And so, we shall all come together to that **oneness in our faith** and in our knowledge of the Son of God..." (Eph 4:11-13 GNBDK)

"Accept anyone who is weak in faith, but don't argue about doubtful issues."

"Therefore, let us no longer criticise one another. Instead decide never to put a stumbling block or pitfall in your brother's way." (Rom 14: 1, 13)

"Now, I urge you, brothers, to watch out for those who cause dissensions and obstacles contrary to the doctrine you have learned. **Avoid them**, for such people do not serve our Lord Christ but their own appetites. They deceive the hearts of the unsuspecting with smooth talk and flattering words."

(Rom 16: 17-18)

"Can two walk together without agreeing to meet?"

(Amos 3: 3 HCSB)

Different gifts, same Giver; different activities — same purpose

"Now, there are different gifts, but the same Spirit. There are different ministries, but the same Lord."

"To one is given a message of wisdom through the Spirit; to another a message of knowledge by the same Spirit; to another, faith;...to another gifts of healing...to another, the performing of miracles, to another prophecy, to another distinguishing between spirits, to another, different kinds of languages, to another, interpretation of languages. But one and the same Spirit is active in all these, distributing to each person as He wills."

(1 Cor 12:4-5, 8-11)

For elaboration read also 1 Cor 12:4-31.

The Messiah gave gifts

"For the training of the saints in the work of ministry, to build up the body of Christ until we all reach unity in the faith and in the knowledge of God's Son... Then we will no longer be little children, tossed by the waves and blown around by every wind of teaching, by human cunning with cleverness in the techniques of deceit." (Eph 4:12-14 HCSB)

For what to do, see Eph 4:25-32

His speck and your log

"Why do you look at the speck in your brother's eye, but don't notice the log in your own eye?"

"...Hypocrite! First take the log out of your eye, and then you will see clearly to take out the speck in your brother's eye" (LK 6:41, 42 HCSB)

A Tree, by its fruit

"A good tree does not bear rotten fruit, nor does a rotten tree bear good fruit. A good person, out of the store of goodness in his heart, produces good."

"...for from the fullness of the heart the month speaks." (LK6:43, 45 NABRE)

THAT THEY MAY BE ONE

"...They are in the world, and I am coming to You. Holy Father, protect them by your name... **so that they may be one as We are one.**"

"**May they all be one,...May they also be one in Us,...**"

"**...May they be one as we are one.**"

"**...May they be made completely one,...**" (Jn 17:11, 20-23 HCSB)

"By this all people will know that you are My disciples,

if you have love for one another." (Jn 13:35 HCSB)

How do you know that you are in the Lord?

The Vine, the branches
"I am the vine; you are the branches. The one who remains in Me and I in him produces much fruit, because you can do nothing without Me."
"Remain in Me, and I in you. Just as a branch is unable to produce fruit by itself unless it remains on the vine, so neither can you unless you remain in Me."
(Jn 15:4-5 HCSB)

Separatists: They went out.

"They went out from us…not really of our number; if they had been, they would have remained with us. Their desertion shows that none of them was of our number." (1 Jn 2: 19 NABRE)

The Eucharist:

Are we truly in communion?
"Because there is one bread, we who are many, are one body, for all of us share that one bread." (1 Cor 10:17)

No need to be pompous – serve!

"Now there are different gifts, but the same spirit. And there are different activities, but the same God activates each gift in each person. So that there would be no division in the body, but that the members would have the same concern for each other." (1 Cor 12: 4, 6, 25)
HUMILITY is service
"Jesus… said to them 'whoever wants to

be first must place himself LAST of all
AND be the SERVANT of all.'" (Mk 9: 35 GNBDK)

Oneness

"There is no Jew or Greek, slave or free, male or female; for you are all one in Christ Jesus.

And if you belong to Christ, then you are Abraham's seed, heirs according to the promise." (Gal 3: 28-29 HCSB)

Walk Worthy of Your Call

"Therefore I, the prisoner of the Lord, urge you to walk worthy of the calling you have received, with all humility and gentleness, with patience, accepting one another in love, diligently keeping the unity of the Spirit with the peace that binds us."

"There is **one body** and **one Spirit**—just as you were called to **one hope** at your calling — **one Lord**, **one faith**, **one baptism**, **one God** and Father of all, Who is above all and through all and in all."
( )

"Now grace was given to each one of us according to the measure of the Messiah's gift." (Eph 4:1-7)

Power to Bind and to Loosen

- "But whoever causes the downfall of one of these little ones who believe in Me —it would be better for him if a heavy millstone were hung around his neck and he were drowned..." (Matt 18:6 HCSB)

Read also Matt: 18:7-11; MK 9:42
- And again Jesus gave us a formula for restoring (Matt 18:15-17) and if necessary, expelling a member:

"And so I tell all of you:

What you prohibit on earth will be prohibited in heaven, and what you permit on earth will be permitted in heaven." (Matt 18:18 GNBDK)

- "… He breathed on them and said,

Receive the Holy Spirit. If you forgive the sins of any, they are forgiven them; if you retain the sins of any, they are retained." (Jn 20: 22-23 HCSB)

Discipleship Mandate:

"…As the father sent Me, I also send you." (Jn 20:21)

"Go, therefore, and make disciples of all nations, baptizing them…"

(Matt 28:19)

And Peter's investiture:

"…you are Peter, and on this rock I will build My church, and the forces of Hades will not overpower it. I will give you the keys of the kingdom of heaven, and whatever you bind on earth is already bound in heaven, and whatever you loose on earth is already loosed in heaven."

(Matt 16: 18-19 HCSB)

Be like-minded.

"Now finally, all of you should be like-minded and be sympathetic, should love believers, and be compassionate and humble." (1 Pt 3:8 HCSB)

Love, serve others.

"Above all, maintain an intense love for each other, since love covers a multitude of sins."

"…Fulfill my joy by thinking the same way, having the same love…consider others as more important than yourselves." (Phil 12:1-3 HCSB)

"Based on the gift each one has received,

use it to serve others, as good managers of the varied grace of God."

(1 Pt 4: 8, 10 HCSB)

Sincerity and truth.

"Therefore, let us observe the feast, not with the old yeast or with the yeast of malice and evil, but with the unleavened bread of sincerity and truth."

(1 Cor 5:8 HCSB)

God Working in You

"For it is God who is working in you, enabling you both to desire and to work out His good purpose. Do everything without grumbling and arguing."

(Phil 2:13-14 HCSB)

Effect of unorthodox (heretical) teachings:

- "You lock up the kingdom of heaven before men. You do not enter yourselves nor do you allow entrance to those trying to enter." (Matt 23:13 Lect.)
- Because strange teachings lead people astray (Heb 13:9)

We are urged to put passion with its dissensions, disorder and foul practice apart. (Js 3:16)

'With Paul'… 'with Apollo': Envy and Strife (1 Cor 3:1-9)

If we are, indeed, God's co-workers—His servants—why should anyone work at cross purposes?

The Apostates' doom

"These are the ones who are like dangerous reefs at your love feasts. They feast with you, nurturing only themselves without fear. They are waterless clouds…fruitless, twice dead, pulled out by the roots…wandering stars for whom the blackness of darkness is reserved forever!"

"These people are discontented grumblers, walking according to their desires; their mouths utter arrogant words, flattering people for their own advantage. These people create divisions and are unbelievers, not having the Spirit."

"Have mercy on those who doubt; save others by snatching them from the fire…" (Jude 1: 12-13, 16, 19, 22-23, HCSB)

Walk by the Spirit

"I say then, walk by the Spirit and you will not carry out the desires of the flesh." (Gal 5: 16 HCSB)

But for more understanding read also Gal 5: 17-26.

Difficult to stick together; persevere, don't break rank

"We must consider how to rouse one another to love and good works. We should not stay away from our assembly, as is the custom of some, but encourage one another." (Heb 10: 24, 25 NABRE)

Be one! Be conciliatory.

"ACCEPT anyone who is weak in faith, but don't argue about doubtful issues."

"One who eats must not look down on one who does not eat…"

"One person considers one day to be above another day. Someone else considers every day to be the same…"

"Therefore, let us no longer criticize one another. Instead decide never to put a stumbling block or pitfall in your brother's way."

"So then, we must pursue what promotes peace and what builds up one another." (Rom 14: 1, 3, 5, 13, 19 HCBS)

Prophecies concerning the churches:

- **Ephesus.** "…you cannot tolerate evil. You have tested those who call themselves apostles and are not, and you have found them to be liars." (Rev 2: 2 HCSB)
- **Sardis.** "… I know your works; you have a reputation for being alive, but you are dead." (Rev 3: 1 HCSB)
- **Laodicea.** "I know your works, that you are neither cold nor hot. I wish that you were cold or hot."

"So,… I am going to vomit you out of My mouth. Because you say, "I'm rich; I have become wealthy and need nothing," and you don't know that you are wretched, pitiful, poor, blind and naked."
(Rev 3: 15-16, 17 HCSB)

Don't do what they do:

"Therefore, do whatever they tell you, and observe it. But don't do what they do, because they don't practise what they teach." (Matt 23: 3, 13, 23, 24)

"Woe to you…hypocrites! You pay tithes of mint, and dill and cumin and have neglected the weightier things of the law: judgement and mercy and fidelity. [But] these you should have done. (Matt 23:23 NABRE)

HCSB translated it thus, "…you neglected the more important matters of law—justice, mercy and faith. These things should have been done without neglecting the other."

"Blind guides! You strain out a gnat, yet gulp down a camel!"
(Matt 23:3, 13, 24 HCSB)

Jesus Unites Jerusalem with Tarsus through Barnabas.

Read: Acts 11: 22-26 for details.

Paul was reunited with the other Apostles by the Lord, who said:

"But get up and go into the city, and you will be told what you must do"

(Act 9:6)

The disciple Ananias finished the job,

"The Lord Jesus…has sent me so that you can regain your sight and be filled with the Holy Spirit. (Acts 9:17)

"Immediately he began proclaiming Jesus in the synagogues: 'He is the Son of God'" (Acts 9:20)

Be one in word, mind and goal

"I urge you, brothers, in the name of our Lord Jesus Christ, that all of you agree in what you say, and that there be no divisions among you, but that you be united in the same mind and in the same purpose." (1 Cor 1: 10 NABRE)

Turning away … to a different gospel!

"I am amazed that you are so quickly
turning away from him who called you
by the grace of Christ and are turning to
a different gospel…"
"… a curse be on him!"
"… I now say it again; if anyone
preaches… a gospel contrary to what
you received, a curse be on him."
(Gal 1: 6-7, 8-9 HCSB)

Preaching another Jesus, a different gospel or receiving a different Spirit.

"… Such people are false apostles, deceitful workers who masquerade as apostles of Christ." (2 Cor 11: 4, 13 NABRE)

Avoid these people:

- "… lovers of self, lovers of money, boastful, proud, blasphemers, disobedient to parents, ungrateful, unholy, unloving, irreconcilable, slanderers, without self-control, brutal, without love for what is good, traitors, reckless, conceited, lovers of pleasure rather than lovers of God, holding to the form of godliness but denying its power. Avoid these people!

For among them are those… led along by a variety of passions, always learning and never able to come to a knowledge of the truth." (2 Tim 3: 2-5, 6, 7 HCSB)

- "… 'in the end time there will be scoffers walking according to their own ungodly desires. These people create divisions and are unbelievers, not having the Spirit.'" (Jude 1: 17 HCSB)

A major Challenge against the emergence of a universal Christian doctrine– ignorance.

What does religion have in common with ignorance? It is an avowal that all that there is to know has been known! Nothing else exists besides what is already known.

This has retarded growth in knowledge; theology does not acquire new knowledge at the speed the physical sciences do, like electronics, for example. But this need not be so. Let us cut off this unedifying umbilical cord with ignorance, and make progress.

Yes, we can; for where knowledge is disdained, ignorance is blissful. Of what value are corpses in a cemetery anyway? Every such foreclosure of enquiry is a shackle on acquiring knowledge of God. It opens up a field day to the frenetic dreamer and the charlatan. Who is afraid of the truth; those fresh discoveries may stultify long-cherished ideas which were thought of as being immutable? That present scholasticism (or even theology) as rather sly.

"The truth will set us free!"

By revelation God gave the lead; let us follow it up through and through.

"Seek the Lord!" when He may be found ( )

"I planted, Apollo watered, but God caused the growth."

"each will receive his own reward according to his own labour. For we are God's workers."

(1 Cor 3: 6, 8-9 HCSB)

Unity of faith

"And He gave some as Apostles, others as Prophets,...

To equip the holy ones for the work of ministry,

for building up the body of Christ..."

"Until WE ALL ATTAIN TO THE UNITY OF FAITH...

so that we may no longer be infants, tossed by waves

and swept along by every wind of teaching arising

from human trickery, from their cunning,

in the interest of deceitful scheming." (Eph 4: 11)

How do we handle blind guides among us?

Turn a blind eye? Here's what Jesus says of them:

Matt 15:12-14; 18:7, 15-17,18, Mk 9:42-43. See chapter 17 for more.

Whoever has ears to hear, ought to listen. (MK 4:9, 23; 7:16)

Be One Miracles Not a Reliable Test of No Evil-Doing "Many will say to Me on that day,

'Lord, Lord, did we not prophesy in Your name?

Did we not drive out demons...

...do mighty deeds in your name?'" (Matt 7: 22 NABRE)

Jesus says, "I have told you these things to keep you from stumbling." (Jn 16:1)

Their god is their stomach (Phil 3: 19)

No servant can serve two masters
"Therefore, my dear brothers, **be steadfast**,
immovable, always excelling in the Lord's work,
knowing that your labour in the Lord is not in vain."
"Be alert, stand firm in the faith,
act like a man, be strong.
Your every action must be done with love."
(1 Cor 15: 58; 16: 13-14 HCSB)
Agree our dear denominations: **Euodia&Syntyche.**
"I urge you Euodia and I urge Syntyche to agree in the Lord."
(Phil 4: 2 HCSB)

Enemies of the cross

"… enemies of the cross of Christ.
Their end is destruction;
their god is their stomach;
their glory is in their shame.
They are focused on earthly things."
(Phil 3: 18, 19 HCSB)
1 Cor 15: 33 **Evil company corrupts character**
"Do not be deceived: 'Bad company corrupts good morals.'"
US President T. Roosevelt: "believe you can, you are half way there"
And again. "Do what you can…"
Matt 6: 24, 33. HCSB
You can't serve God and self (money) "… slaves of God, of money."
Slaves serving two masters – Mammon and God – (seek the kingdom of God and His righteousness…)

ADDITIONAL RESOURCES

Exhortation, Meditation and Reflection.

Let Them Be One!

I have revealed Your name
to the men You gave Me from the world.
They were Yours, You gave them to Me,
and they have kept Your word.
I pray for them.
I am not praying for the world
but for those You have given Me,
because they are Yours. (Jn 17: 6, 9)
Holy Father,
protect them by Your name
that You have given Me,
so that they may be one as We are one. (Jn 17: 11)
I pray not only for these,
but also for those who believe in Me
through their message.
May they all be one,
as You, Father, are in Me and I am in You
may they also be one in Us,
so the world may believe You sent Me. (Jn 17: 20-21)
I have given them the glory You have given Me.
May they be one as We are one.
I am in them and You are in Me.
May they be made completely one,
so the world may know You have sent Me
and have loved them as You have loved Me (Jn 17: 23)

Jesus: A reformer, the model.

Are you a reformer? Behold Jesus – a God-sent Reformer! (Mal 3: 3) What lesson can we learn from His approach and methodology?

- He attempted to enhance the understanding of the divine will in Judaism by working from within. And in doing so, He fulfilled prophecy that He would not put out a lamp that was tapering or cut a reef that was bent.

Note that Jesus could have disdained and distanced Himself from the temple and the synagogues to minister in open air crusades and in His own worship centres. That would have signalled the beginning of the end of Judaism.

- He recognised the leadership – the Chief Priests, Scribes and Pharisees as sitting on the chair of Moses - "therefore, do and observe all things whatsoever they tell you…" (Matt 23: 2-3 NABRE)

Exhortation, Meditation and Reflection.

Jesus vision for His church

From the above scripture can anyone deny their import that it is the plan and wish of the author and finisher of our faith, our Lord Jesus Christ, that His followers should be in communion with one another in togetherness? No statement of the Lord on any other subject appears more lucid, more explicit or to carry as much emphasis and repetition.

Made one by the Holy Spirit

The Lord instructed the Apostles to remain in Jerusalem – they should not disperse – until they had received the Holy Spirit baptism. And when on that first Pentecost day, the promised Counsellor came on them, the most significant outcome was in making them one!

They all began to preach – the same theme – the mission of the Messiah. With so much force and persuasiveness that about 3, 000 converts were made in just one day!

"Then they were all filled with the Holy Spirit and began to speak in different languages…

There were Jews…, devout men from every nation… a crowd came together and was confused because each one heard them speaking in his own language '… Parthians, Medes, Elamites; those who live in Mesopotamia, in Judea and Cappadocia, Pontus and Asia… – we hear them speaking … in our own languages.'" (Acts 2: 4, 5, 9-11 HCSB)

The message: "Repent… and be baptized… in the name of Jesus Christ for the forgiveness of your sins." (Acts 2: 38 HCSB)

It may sometimes be necessary for unity to be loose

It may be necessary for unity to be loose, confederate type in order for it to endure:
"John said to Him,
'Teacher, we saw someone driving out demons in Your name, and we tried to stop him because he wasn't following us.'
'Don't stop him,' said Jesus, 'because there is no one who will perform a miracle in My name who can soon afterward speak evil of Me. For whoever is not against us is for us.'" (Mk 9: 38-40 HCSB)

Remember, Jesus Himself, was rejected by the Jews, among other reasons, because He was considered an outsider – not a priest, and for being a Nazarene! (Mk 11: 28; Lk 20: 1-2)

Exhortation, Meditation and Reflection.

Divisions versus syncretism

'Don't stop him'. What does that precept hold for ecumenism? What does it augur for our methodology?

Be alert, however, as the Lord warns that time would come when "false messiahs and false prophets will rise up and will perform signs and wonders to lead (many) astray" (MK 13:21-23)

HYPOCRISY: The leaven among Christian sects

Heed the admonition of the Lord to His disciples –

"Look out, and beware of the leaven of the Pharisees and Sadducees"

(Matt 16: 6 NABRE)

Of course, the leaven (or yeast) of the Pharisees is hypocrisy. Hypocrisy has driven the wedge among Christian sects to keep us permanently apart!

Ask yourself, could it be the voice of the Lord resonating from the pages of this chapter? Heed Him now! Don't ignore the word. Don't persist in rebellion. Drop your pride.

To some extent, the Lord Himself anticipated some dissent – positive separation – as there could be no compromise between light and darkness, good and evil, truth and falsehood. So indeed, the Lord has said:

"I am not praying for the world but for those You have given Me…" (Jn 17: 9)

Internal dissent

Some measure of dissent from within – a sort of minority view – may be excused, indeed inevitable, if we would be true to ourselves. It is perfectly natural and to a huge extent 'normal' in our world scenario where one must reckon with the antics of the deceiver, at least in the short run. Indeed, elsewhere in this book I advocated for what I call 'personal faith levels'. What is unacceptable is contradiction in the message by the body of Christ itself; the word must be so proclaimed that there would be cohesion, not falling apart; unity, not separation; diversity, not disparity; one communion, not several; in one word, one tenet.

I overheard someone say that "the U.S.A has about 300 different Christian sects unable to come together because they are contemptuous of each other!" Lagos (Nigeria) probably has 1, 000 and each new day witnesses the birth of several more as the fractionalisation is on-going. This must stop.

Exhortation, Meditation and Reflection.

All (who are for Christ) say, 'This must stop!' It is time to separate the men from the boys – and this is not by the vastness of the congregation because lies sell faster than truth; neither is it by the opulence of the proprietor/founder because although 'you say, "I am rich…" you don't know that you are wretched, pitiful, poor, blind and naked.' (Rev 3: 17 HCSB)

The Lord said that 'a house divided against itself falls.' If Christians are divided against themselves how can their house stand? Except that we have this consolation, the power of the underworld shall not prevail against the church.

Our Differences:

Some of us have observed different attitudes to matters of doctrine, puzzling our keen observers and potential proselytes to the chagrin of the disciples among us.

Examples:

   i. The banquet of the body and blood of Jesus, what is it— real presence or metaphysical?

  ii. Forgiveness of sins: what is the relevance, if any, of confession, contrition and conversion to repentance?

 iii. What is the final say of the entire body of Christ on married clergy, celibate priesthood or a mixture of both?

 iv. Sinning: can a redeemed ("born-again") Christian ever sin again—the role of "grace" and 'good works'.

  v. Authoritative & Definitive Scripture

Are generally acceptable Bible texts, books, and translations desirable or achievable?

   i. Ecumenism: Can a leadership be forged among Christians, recognizable as the voice of the Lord (even if acting on general counsel) whom we are all duty bound to accept (even if for the time being) on issues that are potentially divisive? (for example: rites of ordination, baptism, canonization, the creed, schisms, heresies, etc.)

  ii. Can a consensus be reached on the basis of recognizing prophets and prophecies?

  iii. A review of the role of women in the church (of the future): women ordination.

  iv. Methodology — The how, what and when of valid structured ecumenical dialogues.

Exhortation, Meditation and Reflection.
"The gospel addresses culture[1]."
"The gospel does not stand beside culture, it is addressed not only to the individual but to the culture itself.

Christian faith is open to all that is great, true and pure in world culture."

Revelation addresses denominations!

Smyrna

Rev 2: 9 HCSB "… those who say they are Jews and are not but a synagogue of Satan."

Philadelphia

Rev 3: 9 HCSB "Take note! I will make those from the synagogue of Satan,… I will make them come and bow down at your feet…"

Pergamum

Rev 2: 12-13 "… you live – where Satan's throne is! And you are holding on to My name and did not deny your faith on Me,…"

Thyatira

Rev 2: 20 HCSB "… you tolerate the woman Jezebel, who … teaches and deceives…

: 24 "I say to the rest of you in Thyatira,… who haven't known the deep things of Satan… I do not put any other burden on you."

PS: Which is… or where does your assembly or denomination belong to (honestly)?

1: Pope Emeritus Benedict XVI: Daily Meditations, op cit. Exhortation, Meditation and Reflection.

My brothers and sisters –

"wouldn't it be great to have the body of Christ united?"[1] – Fr. Al Leur (Please answer this question, don't dodge it, and don't stop until you have done something about it.)

Capricious kings and emperors in the Dark Ages, swept over territories and peoples lacking strong leadership to form empires and domination of peoples. Surely, there is wisdom in recognising and deferring to duly constituted authorities. Why should Christianity render itself a victim for such assailant?

The path of the reformer is fraught always with ambush and with various potholes and puddles. He must make haste slowly lest he destroys the very edifice he started out to renovate. He must shun invidious posturing and utterances.

Women ordination, married clergy – Let us bear the following in mind

- The first man to be created was Adam; the next – a companion to Adam – Eve, a woman.
- Adam toyed with his leadership when he got Eve to beguile him to disobey God and eat of the forbidden fruit (Gen 2)
- There are different traits between man and woman, which make them more suitable for different types of activities and roles. For example, though we all possess reason and emotion, men delve more into reason, women more into emotion.
- The Lord Jesus, tried to avoid confrontation with established custom as much as possible, and to prioritize His salvific ministry over cultural issues. Thus, He left the Jewish society, being patrilineal, as it was. My guess is that if it were a matrilineal society, He would have done the same. Our

culture, values, must not impede the spread of the Good News.

- Prophets existed in both sexes from beginning of faith – Moses, Aaron, Miriam, Deborah, etc. but males dominated this class. Levitical priests are, of course, all male.

Rev Fr. Al Leurof the Presentation Ministries.
Exhortation, Meditation and Reflection.

- Jesus' ministry was missionary and pioneering. His disciples were sent out as sheep in the midst of wolves. Women could not fit in; but still there were some ministering women. They fulfilled a very useful role – I dare to say, doing catering and perhaps counselling the womenfolk also.
- The universal Church has great powers:

Whatever she binds on earth is bound in heaven. ( ) Let us concede to her the right to make rulings.

- The church is where two or three are gathered in His name. ( ) It implies that Jesus would rather have us together than that we go our separate ways.
- Holy Spirit, our helper. Jesus has not left the church orphaned; the Holy Spirit is available to help us. Do we listen to His counsel? If the Holy Spirit has not given a positive direction on a very sensitive matter, you have no cause to change the *status quo*. The Holy Spirit does not equivocate. He would not say a conflicting thing to the universal church and to you!
- Let's stick to the ruling of the universal church for we are stronger together. United we stand, divided we fall! (Lk 11: 18; Mk 3: 26)

Weren't Moses, Aaron and Miriam prophets? (Num 12: 2)
There are prophets, and there are "prophets"…

Their ministries are not the same and they don't all stand or remain on same step in the same hierarchy.

Some prophets prophesied only but once (Num 11: 25) some prophesied throughout their life time. Some prophets, like Jonah, rebelled and were reluctant to carry out God's command; others outrightly succumbed to demonic manipulation, reneged and became ruined; some prophets prophesied from their own fancy, they delivered not God's message. So, there are prophets and there are prophets.

If we are humble and devout, we shall have no difficulty to know how to work with one another, in carrying out God's command will pose no problem. (Num 12: 4-8) With pride, even priests may not submit to the lawful order of their superiors (despite their vows of obedience)!

Think about this: **winning the race**

"Don't you know that the runners in a stadium all race, but only one receives the prize? Run in such a way to win the prize. Now everyone who competes exercises self-control in everything.

Exhortation, Meditation and Reflection.

However, they do it to receive a crown that will fade away, but we, a crown that will never fade away." (1 Cor 9: 24-25 HCSB)

Authentic Christian Faith = orthodoxy

On orthodoxy, our concern is about purity in adoration and uniformity in thought, word or deed – in doctrine. That in our enthusiasm or lack of suspicion we, or a large portion of our co-believers, are not beguiled into straying away from the truth, from the substance of our faith; that other things, however fascinating, are not being substituted for the real objects of our worship as laid down by the Master Himself. Or that we may not have inadvertently ceased to please the Lord.

Should any of the above happen, it will be a real disaster as we then would be chasing after the shadow while thinking we are pursuing the substance!

How then can we expect to clinch the prize of our faith? In faith we set out on a pilgrimage to return to our place of origin – to our Creator, joyfully. If we get distracted and head elsewhere, we may simply find ourselves where we do not wish or plan to be. There is help, however– the Holy Spirit – but we must first make ourselves docile.

Christian unity

On Christian unity, we are concerned with our identity as a group, as a community – who we are and what people see us to be. Are we faithful to our identity?

We are obliged to engage in evangelism. A successful evangelism has to do with a product – how marketable we present it as a desirable end and people's perception of our group as an effable society of fair-minded, honest and caring bunch. But we are not re-designing the product. The faith has undergone several millennia of defining and imparting its substance to us. Our duty is to be truthful to the faith – a high fidelity of allegiance and loyalty. We are not selling a new or different product, even though we should be open to the Holy Spirit to renew and refresh our practice of the faith – our adoration and our mode of interacting with our neighbours. While all are welcome on board, we are not concerned with numbers *perse*.

Exhortation, Meditation and Reflection.

We may be lured into believing that we don't have to be on our guard to get those things done – they are simple and easy! Nothing can be farther from the truth. We have been warned about the impending end-time large-scale apostasy – how fake prophets/wonder workers and impersonators with the beast, the enemy of our piety will attempt to change religion the content of our faith. We have been fore-warned and we ourselves are seeing some pernicious changes that have already taken place. Why then are we seemingly unconcerned? The purpose we are fore-warned is not for information about the inevitability of that evil. But for action, it is to strengthen our resolve not to permit it just as the Ninevites worked to avert the evil outcome prophesied by Jonah. It worked for them; and it could also work for us if we are as determined to resist the evil and steadfast in our love for God and be vigilant and jealous for His honour and glory. God is merciful, and with God, we shall win the battle.

Pray about Christian unity and fuel your lamps to take action. If we are sincere to make our Christian home base secure, and indeed absorb faiths that are compatible, we need sound doctrine—based on the TRUTH.

Merciful and gracious is God; He would most certainly grant us what is good for our souls if we ask perseveringly.

Now, there can be no compromise between evil and good; between darkness and light. May the Holy Spirit guide us.

Who is leader of Christians on Earth?

In other words, who is the chief spokesman for Christ on earth?

Let Christian leaders put aside dissension and tell their followers—and indeed, the world— who today is successor to Peter? Or that there is a vacuum.

Who among you, selfish arrogance aside, possesses the key of the kingdom?

We are anxiously waiting for answer—because leadership is everything.

"Then Jesus said to them, 'All of you will have your faith shaken, for it is written: 'I will strike the shepherd, and the sheep will be dispersed.'" (MK 14:27 NABRE)

The rebellion of Korah, great grandson of Levi (and others) (Num 16: 1-40, 49)

Those rebels dared Moses:

"You have gone too far!

Everyone in the entire community is holy,…

Why then do you exalt yourself above the Lord's assembly?" (Num 16: 3)

Exhortation, Meditation and Reflection.

Let that not continue in our age; let's give honour to whom honour is due—the voice of Christ in our midst. The cost of Korah's rebellion was 14,700 dead!

What defines the Christian?

1. The Truth:

Jesus is the way, the truth and the life. (Jn 14: 6 HCSB)

Jesus told Governor Pontius Pilate in His self-defense:

"… 'I was born for this, and I have come into this world for this: to testify to the truth.

Everyone who is of the truth listens to My voice.'" (Jn 18:37 HCSB)

2. Witnessing and the baptism of the Holy Spirit
The Holy Spirit: the witness of truth.

"When the counsellor comes, the One I will send to you from the Father—the Spirit of truth, who proceeds from the Father—He will testify about Me."(Jn 15:26)

"But you will receive power when the Holy Spirit has come on you, and you will be My witnesses in Jerusalem, in all Judea and Samaria, and to the ends of the earth." (Acts 1:8 HCSB)

"Go… make disciples of all nations, baptizing them…" (Matt 28:19)

3. Righteousness (or membership of the kingdom of heaven)

"If you consider that He [God] is righteous, you also know that everyone who acts in righteousness is begotten by Him." (1 Jn2: 29 NABRE)

Holiness, love and kindness are the distinguishing attributes of a true Christian.

4. Expectancy of His 2nd Coming and our hope of heaven.

Separatists and Schismatics: "Let Them Be One"

Who are the Christians?

We may have heard the question asked, 'who are these Christians?' Except in purely homogenous Christian enclaves the question keeps popping up – in top government circles, among adherents of other religions, even among fellow Christians. People are bewildered when one considers the utterances and deeds of the leadership of these Christian sects, especially with regard to their relationship to their neighbours. Is there a common thread running through the fabrics of all claiming to be 'Christians', or how else can one distinguish them in their diversity?

Exhortation, Meditation and Reflection.

When they speak of Jesus standpoint on public policies, especially on political issues, their racism or ethnicity speaks louder than the Christian charity in them!

The Church

General de Gaul is reported as saying,

"Letatcestmoi" (= the state is me) with the same penchant, to many general overseers and pastors, "the church is me." I own it – I am the proprietor, the prophet, the priest, even the chief theologian! Should this be so: aren't we talking about the church of Jesus Christ? Whose interest is it that these differences should persist? How do we all get to speak one voice – the voice of truth, the word of the Lord?

"...the believers are of one mind and heart" (Acts 4: 32).

They wore a different culture from those in vogue, and this was recognised as consistent with the teaching of Jesus Christ, hence they gave them the appellation "Christians" (Acts 4: 33)

Which is a Christian Fellowship?

Wouldn't it be a wonderful assistance if someone desirous of knowing more about Christianity could find help by entering into just any Christian assembly? But that cannot be presumed today as the assemblies bear various designations, do different things, profess different tenets, etc.

But should this ideal be realized, it will incentivize different groups and sects to stay on course.

It may even discourage unethical practices, and curb heretical leanings.

Staying on line means greater uniformity or conformity with the goals and practices of evangelism. Such might foster even greater cooperation and mutual respect among worship centres.

With similarity in our messaging, our evangelization thrust would become more effective, our message more persuasive. We should expect to garner a bigger haul of converts into our fishing nets.

Remaining United (Acts 15: 1-6, 22 HCSB)
Dispute Resolution: (in Antioch over circumcision)

i. The Local Church (Antioch)

"Some men came down from Judea and began to teach the brothers: 'Unless you are circumcised... you cannot be saved!'

Exhortation, Meditation and Reflection.

"But after Paul and Barnabas had engaged them in serious argument and debate (NKJV says it thus: "… after no small dissension and dispute") the church arranged for Paul and Barnabas and some others… to go up to the Apostles and elders in Jerusalem concerning this controversy."

ii. The Universal Church: The Jerusalem Council.

"When they arrived at Jerusalem,… they reported… But some of the believers… said, 'It is necessary to circumcise them…'"

"Then the Apostles and elders assembled to consider the matter."

"Then the Apostles and the elders,… decided to select men… and to send them to Antioch with Paul and Barnabas…"

Commenting on the above scripture, Fr Al Leur[1] (in a redacted podcast) asked,

"How can you have unity when there are unresolved issues, and possibly unresolvable issues?"

He proffered, "We need unity in controversy… to submit to authority… a defined leadership, (in order) to bear fruit… bear fruit abundantly."

"When you look at the alternative, it is something like hell on earth."

"Everybody doing 'his own thing' is a recipe for totalitarianism, for abuse, for disorder, for failure."

1: Fr Al Leur, Presentation Ministries, Cincinnati, Ohio, USA. Exhortation, Meditation and Reflection.

According to Fr Al Leur, the Jerusalem council had "no agreement, nevertheless there was unity." (I suppose, by that he meant no unanimity, but in our democratic tradition that hardly poses a problem.)

In his days, there were about 25,000 different Christian groups in the USA. Indeed, these are the outlook of demonization – *"Demoninations".*

I consider Fr Al Leur's comments on the delight experienced by the gentile converts (Antioch) germane to this topic:

"Submission is not capitulation… It requires a denial of oneself, or dying to oneself…"

"It requires tremendous strength to be submissive; only the strong submit."

"Sweet submission is not forcing a change by rebellion, not rebelling for (having) a different opinion, or perception or ways of doing things (moral indignation excepted)."

"In Eph 5: 21, all Christians are expected to be submissive to one another."

"There is a lot of blessing in submission … hope… we have unity, we have order…"

Why can't you read the times…?

Answer: "Spiritual obtuseness, …superficiality, a dim dullness" (Fr Al Leur)

"By what authority?"

"When He entered the temple complex, the chief priests and the elders of the people came up to Him as He was teaching and said, 'By what authority are you doing these things? Who gave you the authority?'" (Matt 21:23 HCSB)

That these were rhetorical questions is indicated by the fact that they gave Jesus no opportunity to answer the first question before asking the second question. They anticipated that no answer Jesus could give would be satisfactory.

What bishop or pastor would today tolerate an unauthorized cleric or individual to mount the podium and teach his congregation or any section thereof?

How do we expect God to announce His prophets? With particular reference to Jesus, the angels spoke to the Shepherds and the Magi spoke to Herod and Herod spoke to the chief priests and scribes (Matt 2: 1-8; Lk2: 8-20) Before then, they knew to expect the Messiah. Herod did something for himself, but the chief priests and scribes did nothing about the revelation. The works of Jesus, full of miracles should have made them insightful, but they were not.

Exhortation, Meditation and Reflection.

Jesus grew up among them and the picture of what happened when He was aged 12 (Lk 2:41-47) was indicative of what He did in other years before the full commencement of His public ministry.

The important question is, how do the authorities recognize the prophets so as to hear the word of God—i.e., new prophecies not in the scriptures or told to a member of the hierarchy? History has a way of repeating itself, but besides that, suppose the Lord, speaks to the church using a righteous humble man like Simeon (Lk 3:25-35) from a less fancied denomination? How do we listen to God and behave differently from the chief priests and scribes?

The hierarchy established by the Lord

Consider Paul's induction and his subordination to the brothers in Jerusalem; consequently, he became recognized as an Apostle, despite the fact that he received no grooming with the Twelve.

God recognized the role of leadership in the affairs of men as an irreplaceable catalyst for progress and growth. This has since been discovered by management science. Thus, when Aaron and Meiran – one a priest and prophet, the other a prophetess – were evincing traits that were supercilious or not entirely deferential to God's servant, Moses, God plastered Meiran with leprosy (Perhaps because of his priestly responsibilities Aaron received only admonition). Alas, not one of them was separated from Moses; both still recognised Moses leadership which made them go back to him and beg. Compare God's mercy with the contrite duo to the fate that befell the co-conspirators of Korah's rebellion (Num 16: 1-40, 49).

Before Moses went the way of mortals, he was commanded to invest Joshua as his successor, which he did.

Jesus took the position to situate the place of leadership or orthodoxy in religion. While empathising with the Jewish people for the harsh interpretation of the law by the Scribes, Sadducees and Pharisees, He nevertheless, reminded the people that these were sitting on the chair of Moses; they should therefore be obeyed, although individuals could aspire to higher levels of personal sanctity.

He subsequently established the chair of Peter, as the rock upon which His church was to be built. He did not stop there, but commissioned the twelve apostles and the 72 other disciples/missionaries, thus 'separating the men from the boys', as we say: All serious disciples knew who these men were. By that step Jesus is saying, 'reformers, good you are zealous, but be guided'.

Exhortation, Meditation and Reflection.

They say, 'united we stand, divided we fall'. This has been proven in that since the end of World War II, 75 years ago, the world has enjoyed some peace, because mankind was united under the United Nations Organisation (UNO). Of course, there could not be two or more UNO's if the world is to secure its peace. A single leadership is called for if Christian evangelism would attain its purpose.

"How good and how pleasant it is,

when brothers dwell together as one!" (Ps 133: 1 NABRE)

Why are Christians divided and remain so?

This is intended to be a diagnostic, rather than a blame-apportioning or judgemental exercise.

Nevertheless, it may utterly be impossible for what we do, not to be misconstrued as finger-pointing. We ask anyone who is hurt to forgive us. Our concern with retrospection is to find out what could have been done but might not have been done. Our goal is the way forward, how to guide the future, since history has a way of repeating itself.

1. Demonic Factor

It is usually soothing to look elsewhere to explain off one's woes, rather than focus on oneself. Let us, therefore, hope on common ground as we blame Satan, an external foe, for the seeming lack of cohesion among Christian bodies. This is consistent with the Revelation story and accords with the Genesis explanation for the fall of Adam (and therefore man, his descendants).

690

On that devilish note, or rather demonic factor, we decant that the goal of the evil one is to keep Christianity from attaining its purpose. By making the Good News erratic; stultify the message, and drive a wedge between the witnesses thereby turning into a mirage the expressed wish of the Author and Finisher of our faith that "they be one."

All the Devil needs do is to recruit agents that will pursue his agenda as against the Lord's (Remember that from of old, there had been such persons at the gathering of children of God Lk 4: 33; Mk 1: 23; Job 1: 6) At great risk are the unsuspecting souls, candidates for salvation, who are led into believing, for example, that there is a delusory easier path to salvation, than through repentance. The Devil is a deceiver, a master of half-truths and those human recruits of his peddle the same trade.

Everyone active in evangelism should continually inquire into themselves who their activities most benefitted – the Lord and His redeemed or Satan and perdition? "By their fruits you shall know them."

Exhortation, Meditation and Reflection.

As Pharaoh's magicians faked Moses miracles so 'prophets' and 'pastors' raised by Satan can be expected to fake authentic prophets and priests of God and then ruin the work of the latter towards salvation: was it not the same guy, Satan, who caused Job his miseries?

Give Satan his due: this guy squared up with the Son of God, Himself – not with-standing that the latter had strengthened Himself through fasting for 40 days and 40 nights. Yes, he failed in his mission to derail His ministry. But it was only for the time being. He took only a break to come back later.

(Lk 4: 1-13)

Who, then, can Satan not accost?

Other factors

From the prospective of history, Christians remain divided for these other major reasons also:

- Pride
- Pleasure
- Passion
- Possession
- Anarchism
- Ignorance
- Misapprehension
- Ignoring God
- Lack of courage

A little is said about each of these challenges further on in this chapter. But for now, let us examine in some detail what the absence of vision does.

2. No vision or goal for unity

Disciples with no focus on unity easily fall prey to the cunning of the Devil as their evangelistic or reformist zeal are ambushed, hijacked and desecrated.

We must be conversant with the goal of the Master Himself:

"Let them be one". Efficiency in achieving the goal of evangelisation demands that we give a thought to the strategy laid down by the Master Himself, to the gain that can accrue from synergising our activities or the loss of effectiveness that comes from dissension and in-fighting. Ultimately, we waste our resources as the trophy eludes us.

Exhortation, Meditation and Reflection.

Our personal goal is to be builders, not destroyers; to be good team players, not to be stars on our own in rivalry with Jesus! Our reformation should be to sanctify and add steam; not desecrate and lose the faith.

At the beginning of this sub-chapter, we reproduced some excerpts from the Holy Scripture wherein is unfolded Christ's vision for His church – "that they may be one…"

Oneness means unity; a monolithic structure either in a pyramid of authority descending from Christ Himself or a uniformity or sameness or unanimity in the content of their message to the world – a distinctly recognisable Christian tenet. When Moses appointed the 72 elders, the Holy Spirit ensured that they evinced the same characteristics – prophesying.

And when Jesus appointed the twelve and the 72 missionaries, He gave them the same charge and the same operational procedure. They left in two's at the appointed time and returned to base with the same success story.

To replace Judas Iscariot, the one ensnared by the Devil, the church appointed Mathias, but Christ seemed to have appointed a replacement in Saul (Paul) – though unknown to them at the material time: Paul was subjected to the church from the onset. All fourteen were Apostles, yet one chose to belong elsewhere. He separated himself from the body of Apostles. The remaining thirteen stood together as one body of Apostles – persecution, distance, could not separate them.

And so, Paul was able to say,

"… I had been entrusted with the gospel for the uncircumcised, just as Peter was for the circumcised. Since the One at work in Peter for an apostleship to the circumcised was also at work in me for the gentiles." (Gal 2: 7-8)

Changes over time are inevitable in life, yet, most of us are uncomfortable with them. The word of God must address the issues of our day – things not necessarily in vogue in Moses' and Christ's days. Such should not create a chasm between true followers of Christ. A central authority on doctrine can be a help.

By a hind view, when Martin Luther would not acquiesce to the dogmatic view of the church, he unwittingly opened the gate for separatists to exist on account of differences of opinion! In all of these, only one end is served – the Devil's! Give the Devil an inch, he will take a mile. From then, and until now, the operative principle has been "disagree, disengage and disaggregate." Jesus foresees this but He gave His word that the power of darkness shall not overwhelm His church.

Exhortation, Meditation and Reflection.

St Paul, concerned about schisms and divisions in the church he co-founded in Corinth wrote these:

"I urge you, brothers,… that all of you agree in what you say, and that there be no divisions among you, …" (1 Cor 1: 10)

"…there is one bread, we who are many are one body for all of us share that one bread." (1 Cor 10: 17)

"So that there would be no division in the body, but that the members would have the same concern for each other. So, if one member suffers, all the members suffer with it; if one member is honoured all the members rejoice with it." (1 Cor 12: 25-26)

To the other churches he harped on the same theme:

"…fulfil my joy by thinking the same way, …focusing on one goal. Do nothing out of rivalry or conceit, but in humility consider others as more important than yourselves."

(Phil 2: 2-3 HCSB)

"Therefore I… urge you to walk worthy of the calling you have received,… accepting one another in love, diligently keeping the unity or the Spirit with the peace that binds us. **There is one body and one Spirit… one Lord, one Faith, one Baptism, one God and Father of all**." (Eph 4: 1-7)

"And so we shall all come together to that oneness in our faith and in our knowledge of the Son of God;…" (Eph 4: 13)

"I am amazed that you are so quickly turning away… to a different gospel …"

But even if we or an angel… should preach… a gospel other than what we have preached… a curse be on him!"

"… I now say again: if anyone preaches… a gospel contrary to what you received, a curse be on him!" (Gal 1: 6, 8-9 HCSB)

We pursue oneness, not just because there is strength in unity (just as a player does not displace a team) but especially because we would be more persuasive if we all teach the same tenets, and enjoin the practice of the same virtues. This goal should not only appeal to, but also galvanize all of us who do not belong to the synagogue of Satan (Rev 2: 8; 3: 9). Do you cut into this vision? The early church to this end, deemed it necessary to require the faithful to profess the essence of their faith in the form of the Apostles (Nicene) creed to remind each of them that the Apostles, the saints (or worthy elders) are not only the pillars of the church of which Christ is the foundation and cornerstone, but that their lives are the beacons to guide us all through to salvation.

Christ Banner. People must be able to distinguish the goats from the sheep; "Those who call themselves apostles and are not." (Rev 2: 2)

Exhortation, Meditation and Reflection.

Nonchalance. Can we afford to be unconcerned about that? We do so at our peril. (Rev 3: 16)

Other Reasons why we are apart.

We explain briefly what we mean by these hereunder:

3. Pride

Top among internal factors frustrating the unity of Christendom is pride. Intellectual arrogance and pomposity, pedantry; I know-it-all syndrome; philosophical and metaphysical radicalisation; absence of meekness to tolerate alternative views or the temerity of the errant ones.

When Martin Luther came up with his 95 theses and 41 sentences, a few of these and his other writings were found to be erroneous (i.e., heretical) by his superiors (the church) and required to recant. At Augsburg and at Leipzig (1519) and at Worms (1521).

He bluntly refused. Assured of the support of some principalities and powers that were with their own secret agenda, he rebuffed unabashedly the stand of established theologians and the saints which determined the tradition of the church for the past 1,500 years. Braggadocio apart, there's no virtue in being a heretic. One eyed man cannot over-rule the reluctance of a score blind men (talk less of two 2-eyed men), unless they part ways!

Thus, it is not a question of who was right but the absence of patience which humility commends in situations such as that.

Hoping that truth will be out someday. After all, the Lord had declared that the power of darkness shall not overcome His church – do we believe He has the power to accomplish this?

4. Pleasure

It is unfortunate but true that some people find pleasure in the pains and misfortune of others. Such people are ready recruits for radicalisation in matters of religion. We have different gifts. Some are gifted inspirational speakers/preachers, others the gift of prophecy, etc. these are to be put into use within the church for the mutual benefit of the body of Christ. Some are not content to do this playing to the gallery, they are bent to exploit those gifts for monetary and other personal gains.

Concupiscence is at the heart of many who feel that their calling cannot find ample scope for fulfilment within the church. If Apostle Paul had behaved that way, surely, he would not have lacked followers, would he? And he would not have succeeded the way he did. But he is, surely, our mentor?

Exhortation, Meditation and Reflection.

5. Possession (or Mammon)

No doubt a lot of people are into ministries in these days of relative peace in Christendom to serve their pockets or mammon. Not that it is wrong to earn a living from doing what is needful and perhaps what you are most talented at doing. My grudge is that their involvement in evangelism should draw them into deeper knowledge of the faith and an active zeal for ecumenism. Everyone active in evangelism should have re-discovered this and not ignore it because the matter is urgent. The problem is that you cannot serve mammon and at the same time serve God. No-one can serve two masters. You are either in the right calling – worshipping God and depending entirely upon His providence (Lk 22: 35) or your goals are elsewhere, like earning great wealth or honour or power! Such are in the wrong vocation.

(Matt 23: 25) Jesus warned leaders to avoid GREED and SELF-INDULGENCE.

6. Passion

You are an adherent of a particular faith about which you know so well (like I do in my faith) but you disdain passionately every other faith (of which you know next-to-nothing about) you are prepared to kill and maim to get others to conform (to your own faith), perhaps in accordance with the perceived tenets of your faith. That is fine. Whatever is worth doing at all, is worth doing well! St Paul was a man of that zeal (for Judaism; as Saul, he was a Pharisee and son of a Pharisee). I had said that was fine; but one could be misguided and in these days that politically we have discovered the benefit of democracy as a system of synthesising ideas, concepts and recognising and reconciling preferences, and choices and satisfying the greatest need of the greatest number, we should always listen to others and bear with them for their choices and preferences. We let the majority to have their way while working assiduously (by persuasion) to sell your views so they could become the predominantly accepted choices, concepts or practice. Extremism or radicalism only destroys, it does not build nor accumulate any good. Actually, it cheats the majority and minorities of their rights!

The matter is complicated when there is a deep-seated anger, resentment, rage or revenge motive in the protagonist. It blinds him and his followers entirely to reason. It is as futile to attempt to resurrect the dead as it is to persuade him to relent or to repent!

"Where do the wars and … the conflicts among you come from? Is it not from your passions that make war within your members? You covet but do not possess. You kill and envy but you cannot obtain; you fight and wage war.

Exhortation, Meditation and Reflection.

You do not possess because you do not ask. You ask but do not receive, because you ask wrongly, to spend it on your passions." (Js 4: 1-3 NABRE)

Rivalry, selfish ambition

"For where jealousy and selfish ambition exist, there is disorder and every foul practice." (Js 3: 16 NABRE)

7. Anarchism

Who is the church? Who are saints – can anyone on earth be so sure that someone else has made heaven? "Why traditions; I am a Bible-believer!" Everybody can understand the Bible, if you are intelligent enough. Why lean on the interpretation of another, even when this is of councils of theologians and high ecclesiastics? These and similar issues are associated with people with anarchist tendencies. They are slow to recognise the importance of duly constituted authority; to admit that wisdom and specialisation, like common sense, are not so diffused, after all! But when their own authority is impugned or brought to questioning, they balk and are exasperated. Whether one likes it or not, leadership is everything for collective success to be attained. Although leadership can be formal or informal but the need for formal authority is a divine wisdom and the success of the emancipation of Jews in Pharaoh's Egypt and exodus to the promised land owed much to the leadership of Moses.

Because Samuel was uncontested as leader, Saul could be crowned king without strife or scorn. Because there were avaricious and capricious kings and emperors in the Dark Ages, these swept over territories and peoples lacking strong leadership to form empires and dominion over them. Surely, there is wisdom in recognising and deferring to duly constituted authorities. Why should Christianity render itself frail for such assailants?

The path of the reformer is fraught always with ambush – various pot holes and puddles. He must make haste slowly lest he destroys the very edifice he started out to renovate. He must shun invidious posturing and utterances. You could just be a despot wreaking your demagoguery on the meek to whom God has given reason and discretion. God never appointed you a policeman or judge and executioner over His people. Honour the commandment – "You shall not murder!"

8. Ignorance

"The church of the living God is the pillar and foundation of the truth."
(1 Tim 3: 15 HCSB)
Exhortation, Meditation and Reflection.
Former British Prime Minister, Sir Winston Churchill[2], says of truth that, "the truth is incontrovertible. Malice may attack it, ignorance may deride it, but in the end, there it is." But it is he, who also observed that "a lie gets half way around the world before the truth has a chance to get its pants on."

Truth, indeed, is sacrosanct; it is immutable. Ignorance of the truth is deadly; how can an action be wise when based on anything other than the truth? To forget the past is to wallow in ignorance. Nobody builds a superstructure without an infrastructure. Whoever discards experience scuttles education.

Someone[1] did say that "your best teacher is your last mistake." You must know the vision of God for the incarnation; it is embodied in Christ's church, and the charge Christ gave the leaders and shepherds of His flock. You overseer or founder – remember Christ is the chief shepherd and you are tending His flock. It is His flock, not yours. This job can hardly be done well by ignoring the wisdom of the ages – how it all began and how the task was being done through the teaching and actions of the leaders. How can one guard against one's own unintentional errors? Surely, **we are stronger together**.

"My brothers and sisters, not many of you should become teachers…"

(Js 3: 1 GNBDK)

All are called to discipleship but not all are called to tend the flock.

9. Misapprehension

Many of us misconstrue the word of God. He is either speaking to a generation, to a person, race or people or to all peoples in all generations. Any hard-line interpretation may bring trouble. When Jonah told the Ninevites, that in 40 days their city would be destroyed, he did not offer to them an option to repent. But they discerned the will of God, confessed their sins and repented with fasting. God saw this and restrained from wreaking the havoc He threatened against them. They were happy and thanked God and held Jonah to be a great prophet.

When desolate Ruth, the Moabite, abandoned her people and country folks to follow Naomi to Israel, what future would such a forlorn young woman see ahead of her to take such action?

1: Anonymous 2: Sir Winston Churchill (1874-1965), British Prime Minister 1940-1945, 1951-1955.

Exhortation, Meditation and Reflection.

It turned out to be a leap of faith – with bounteous blessings for her and of joy inexplicable (Ruth 3: 10-4: 17) she became a sign – one of the earliest that the Messiah belongs to all! Don't people see that we can be at different levels of maturity in our spirituality? It calls for sober reflection, mutual tolerance and forbearance.

We have imperfect knowledge of things that are; not to talk of the things of the future. Our memories fail us; our understanding of things (including the scripture) change with time.

So, why must we go solo or be so sure of our standing and that we cannot err, stumble or fall?

"…Do whatever they tell you…" (Matt 23: 2, 3)

There is some wisdom in orthodoxy. All those rules on interpretation – the exegesis, the hermeneutics – attest to this. Those who keep to Biblical revelations alone, for understanding of Christianity seem to think that God is struck by a paralysis and therefore, no longer active; or that He is on exile, or in a marathon sleep or on a sabbatical since the Bible days. Their very claim to be prophets and seers controvert that view. God is still very active and in control, unveiling new revelations and inspiring deeper understanding.

God is alive and still in charge.

That is why those ecumenical councils such as at Nicaea (325), Ephesus (1431) and Trent (1545-1564) fulfil needed purposes; expectedly and as promised, His Spirit guided them.

10. Ignoring God (not listening to God)

Due to entrenched interests everyone is going his own way and doing his own thing. Religion is now a bourgeoning business and only lip service is paid to God. True piety is hard to find. That is why we ignore His purpose.

"You don't know what you're asking … to sit at My right and left …It belongs to those for whom it has been prepared by My Father."

(Matt 20:22,23 HCSB)

We listen to Him no more! Before the separation of religion from the state, it is understandable that nationalism and power oscillation fuelled schisms. Today, the globe has become ever so compact; every man or woman is a citizen of the world. We, believers in one God, are one huge family.

Exhortation, Meditation and Reflection.

Why can't Christians re-discover their brotherhood? Our failure is adversely impacting on other spheres of life – pogroms in non-Christian nations, destruction of ancient monuments, etc. If things continue this way catastrophic global war may come too soon. If Christians cannot resolve their differences, how can they help others to resolve theirs? "May they all be one in Us."

Reformer's path is ever mired with puddles and potholes. Let us be attentive to God. Since 1948 when the World's Council of Churches was inaugurated and 1961 when Pope John XXIII established the Secretariat for the promotion of Christian unity (60 years past) a lot of water has passed under the bridges but nothing has changed in the template. To some, Christian unity means no more than collaboration across the aisles. It is a deviant trait when so-called Christians profess different interpretations of the word of God for being of different sects.

11. Fear – or the lack of Courage

"… You live where Satan's throne is! But you are holding on to My name, not denying your faith in Me…" (Rev 2: 13)

To be frank, we need courage to challenge the status quo; courage like in the church in Pergamum – to speak the truth to our colleagues and courage to act in accordance with the responsibilities of our office. This century is still young. What agenda for Christian unity will you allow the Lord, the Chief Shepherd of His flock, to inspire in you? Involve your congregation to pray over this and challenge their ingenuity to propose how to go about it. The Holy Spirit possesses other fruits which would be of benefit in this endeavour if we seek them.

"I know your works, that you are neither cold nor hot. I wish that you were cold or hot." (Rev 3: 15 HCSB))

Commitment bears a direct relationship to courage. Once you have made up your mind let your commitment be total. Inspire others with your vision; no vacillation, no prevarication. Unity is easier to accomplish before the zeal runs out, before resources committed to it dry up.

"Continuous effort – not strength or intelligence – is the key to unlocking

our potential." – Sir Winston Churchill.

"It is always time to do the right thing."

US congressman, Rep John Lewis.

Exhortation, Meditation and Reflection.

"Do what you can with what you have,

where you are!"

26th US President, Theodore Roosevelt.

The Way Forward

"The church of the living God is the pillar and foundation of the truth."

(1 Tim 3: 15)

1. Notice, 'the church' not 'the churches.'

The truth cannot be found in the variant opinions of the many; but is beneficial if upheld by the many. The truth is in the purview of the Christian church, and it must be dutifully guarded. We would be deceiving ourselves if we fail to assign this responsibility to a defined person or institution, deluding ourselves that all Christians would do it. That is mere buck passing – a dereliction of duty – and is not going to work. Having a central governing body for Christian doctrine world-wide does not permit of equivocation.

2. The question to resolve is when? What? How and where?

For a starter, let there be convoked meetings of Pentecostals, evangelicals, charismatics and other major groupings to take a pragmatic decision on the need (or otherwise) for Christian unity and what that term entails in terms of doctrine, amalgamation or federation, corporate existence, creed, etc. I believe that the orthodox churches and the Roman Catholic Church were doing something along that line, may they continue. Overall, the achievement has been paltry and the tempo very slow. Like other common folks, I know I can be very naïve in these matters. Yet, we are sounding a note that we are impatient for progress. All who feel that way should push for action. That is one-way momentum can begin from the bottom, for we are all stakeholders, aren't we? We will have a more strident voice in communal, national and world affairs if Christians are truly united under Jesus and the Holy Spirit.

"There is a time to take cover and a time to take over."[1]

This is the time to take over and enter into the glory reserved for the children of God. "Let them be one." All servants of the Lord should say "amen!" and zealously work towards its accomplishment.

1: Pastor Bolaji Goodman.

Exhortation, Meditation and Reflection.

3. With a firm commitment to this objective, start from where you are and reach out to your neighbour so as to win him over (to Christian unity). Then work with others to federate all Christian denominations within your country into broad sub-groups of conservatives, Pentecostals, Evangelicals and *nouveau* Christian churches/groups, leaving the Catholics and the orthodox churches to dialogue together. Let whichever group is first ready to proceed make overtures to the others for regional and world ecumenical dialogues. A journey of a thousand miles begins with the first step. Be the one to take that first step.

1. Agree on earliest and latest dates for the new world Christian unity conference. Taking a cue from there, let the dates for the national, regional and continental conferences fall into place.

2. Discuss the agenda for this first new global Christian unity colloquium at each forum; prioritize the topics on the agenda, and set time frames for their implementation.

3. Remember the raison d'etre for church unity – the truth, i.e., purity of doctrine, disavowal of heresy, zero tolerance for schism; recognising and designating who the ultimate authority on Christian theology is, i.e., the occupier of the chair of Peter.
4. The first (new) world colloquium may be held in Rome or in Jerusalem. Likewise, the momentum may start from the head or from the tail; all Christians are duty bound to sustain the momentum.

Let Them Be One! (a meditation)

What is the norm, the goal we are after?

Answer: "…one flock, one shepherd."

What is disunity?

Its apparent symptom is, many flocks, many shepherds.

That is where we are now, in disarray – completely unacceptable.

Call to win the world for God

Winning the world back to God (WWBG) is the challenge Christians face – both the leadership and the followership; nothing less.

Exhortation, Meditation and Reflection.

What are the challenges we face in this task?

- Finger pointing among the leadership

A growing organism, like the church, must undergo various changes to adapt and be relevant to changing situations. Patience and forbearance is called for on the side of the reformer and the ultra-conservative.

A dynamic church needs to move forward to adapt to the changing environment or else become irrelevant. Yet, many people will say old wines are sweeter than new.

- Nonchalance or apathy towards the attainment of the goal. This springs naturally from inattentiveness to the word –

"be one."

Let us cease to listen to ourselves alone, rather listen to Jesus speak to us from the mouth of another – whose view may differ or challenge ours.

- Differences in opinion. Let us separate facts from fiction, truth from assumption; still there will be differences in opinion, arising from our different background and individual temperament, among others. Should these divide us? Our commission is much more important than all these. It is strange to expect everybody to like the same thing or have the same preferences. Our task is to manage our differences such that they don't escalate into disputes and altercations. We can agree to have camaraderie and love and we need humility and be goal-oriented always.

- Are there other obstacles? Of course, there are many others – inability or unwillingness to forgive, satanic seduction, intellectual arrogance, impious obstinacy, human error, un-trammelled passion (Js 3: 16) and too many subterranean influences and ulterior motives such as the sovereignty factor (manifesting as nationalism and nationalisation);

"some whose god is their stomach", etc., as discussed elsewhere in this chapter. The consolation is we have all it takes to surmount these (2 Pt 1: 3) – the word, the Holy Spirit, our docility and doggedness. We must keep the flag of unity flying once again; every generation deciding how best to do so. We can learn from the politicians how to make compromises.

(Lk 16: 8)

"IF then there is… encouragement in Christ,… consolation of love…fellowship with the Spirit,… affection and mercy, fulfil my joy by thinking the same way, having the same love, sharing the same feelings, focusing on one goal. Do nothing out of rivalry or conceit, but in humility consider others as more important than yourselves." (Phil 2: 1-3 HCSB)

The evil gain

The forces that pull or keep us apart produce only evil:

- Many become lukewarm or bogged down in pursuance of the Great Commission to evangelize the world, contented with retaining those who strayed into their denomination. Many completely ignore authentic Christian formation.
- Many Christians have accepted division among Christian sects as an inexorable fate for which they woefully have resigned to live by. This was the prognosis which prompted the Lord to ask,

"Nevertheless, when the Son of Man comes will He find that faith on earth?" (Lk 18: 8 HCSB)

- "But woe to you…! You lock up the kingdom of heaven from people. For you don't go in, and you don't allow those entering to go in." (Matt 23: 13 HCSB)
- Various kinds of strange teachings lead the flock astray (Heb 13: 9)

Disunity among Christians

The force to pull apart, alluring to many, has always been there; threatening and often times over-reaching the cleavages that make for unity; crushing the will for solidarity and mutual survival.

First, this should be of grave concern to all Christians, since this, in no doubt, is contrary to the will of the Lord, Himself. (Jn 10: 16)

Secondly, the division we witnessed most frequently are of people walking away from their brethren, rarely an outcome of expulsion or excommunication. Why has that become normal, especially keeping the separation permanent? Somebody is being hypocritical; there appears to be no allegiance to the truth. We should be able to agree on the essential message of our faith.

"They went out from us, but they did not belong to us; for if they had belonged to us, they would have remained with us. However, they went out so that it might be made clear that none of them belonged to us."

(1 Jn 2: 19 HCSB)

The Lord had warned us to beware of the leaven of the Pharisees, which is hypocrisy. Are we not being pulled apart today by this leaven?

Exhortation, Meditation and Reflection.

Fuelled by self-seeking, self-centredness, self-absorption, the gospel message has become secondary. It is all hypocrisy – the homage that vice pays to virtue.[2]

Denominations: how it all started, the lessons.

The Split (by AlekseiStepanovich Khomiakov[1] – ASK)

The split of the then universal church into the East Orthodox Church and the West Roman Catholic Church (in 1064) was caused, (according to ASK, a passionate defender of the East, and fierce critic of the West) "by the addition of *folioque* to the creed by the West Roman Catholic Church", that "artificial outward union of a strongly centralized authoritarian system headed by the new and unique official, the Pope."

"This split is a heresy against the dogma of the unity of the church."

It "lay precisely in the arbitrary disregard of the community of all believers in favour of a local opinion."

This action that results in the breach (according to ASK) is a repudiation of *'Sobornost'* – "the true community of life, love, faith and understanding to be found in the church."

By the breach, the Eastern (Greek) autocephalous church, actually became to all intents and purposes, local churches. Without unification Jerusalem, Thessalonica, Antioch, Constantinople (Istanbul) remain the local communes that they were! It was thus a small thing for them to be persecuted with impunity by secular authorities in subsequent ages. On the other hand, it is unimaginable that the Western church could have grown so expansively into the New World and beyond if it has not had a captain (or shepherd).

HOW IT ALL BEGAN

I. the Split: The East Viewpoint

The Filioque clause in the Nicene Creed (that the Holy Spirit proceeded from the Father and from the Son), and inserted there by the Charlemagne court theologians was condemned by Constantinople (between 858 and 886) as heretical.

1: (also called, Aleksey StepanovichKhomyakov (Russia) 1804-1860)

2: Rev. Fr. Shola (OP), Homily @ St. Jude CC, Mafoluku, Lagos.

Exhortation, Meditation and Reflection.

According to the Encyclopedia Britannica –

"The orthodox church is a fellowship of autocephalous churches[3], i.e., economically and administratively independent. The ecumenical patriarch of Constantinople held titular (or honorary) primacy for the Eastern churches."

From the 4th to the 11th century, Constantinople (now Istanbul), the centre of Eastern orthodoxy was also the capital of the Eastern Roman (or Byzantine) Empire, while Rome fell under the Holy Roman Empire.

"Eastern orthodoxy is the large body of Christians who follow the faith and practices that were defined by the first seven ecumenical councils"[4] and it is "one of the three major doctrinal and jurisdictional groups of Christianity."

"Characterised by its continuity with the Apostolic Church…" "Its adherents live mainly in the Balkans, the Middle East and former Soviet countries."

"The word orthodox ("right believing") has traditionally been used in Greek speaking Christian world to designate communities

… who preserved the true faith (as defined by those councils). In English usage the church is referred to as the Eastern (or Greek) Orthodox Church."

The community has some 300million adherents world-wide.

The third major group is the oriental[7] orthodox community.

7: members: Armenian Apostolic Church, the Ethiopian TewaHedo Orthodox Church, the Eritrean TewaHedo Orthodox Church, the Coptic Orthodox Church, the Syriac Orthodox Patriarchate of Antioch and the Malankara Orthodox Church of India.

Exhortation, Meditation and Reflection.

From the time of the council of Chalcedon, 451, to the late 20th century the Oriental Orthodox churches were out of communion with the Roman Catholic Church, and later with the Eastern Orthodox Church "because of a perceived difference in doctrine regarding the divine and human natures of Jesus".

Both the Roman Catholic Church and the Eastern Orthodox Church began dialogue in the 1950s with the Oriental Orthodox Churches resolving "many of the ancient Christological disputes".

In the Western church, there was reform leading to the enforced celibacy of the clergy (initiated by the works of Cluny (France)). Papal delegates came to Constantinople in 1054 on a conciliatory move with the Byzantine patriarch, Michael Cerularius (reigned 1043-58). The effort yielded only mutual ex communications – the 1054 Schism.

The rejection of the primacy of the Bishop of Rome (the Pope) was the principal point dividing the orthodox[3] from Rome Catholics. Conciliar theory held that an ecumenical council[4] was superior to the Pope – Canon 28 (Chalcedon (451).

In the Political upheavals following the fall of the empire of Constantinople (1204) –

- Rome gained the ascendancy, appointing its own patriarchs in Hagia (Sophia) as well as replacing with Latin prelates, the Greek patriarchs of Antioch and Jerusalem and Thomas

Morosini was installed Patriarch of Constantinople, confirmed by Pope Innocent III. It lasted till 1261 when on the recapture of Constantinople orthodox Patriarch once again occupied Sophia (the see of Hagia).

3: In the 21st century autocephalous churches included, (1) Constantinople (Istanbul), (2) The church of Alexandria, (3) Antioch (headquarters in Damascus Syria), (4) Jerusalem, (5) Russia, (6) Ukraine, (7) Georgia, (8) Serbia, (9) Romania, (10) Bulgaria, (11) Greece, (12) Albania, (13) Poland, (14) the Czech, (15) Slovak republics and (16) America.

The first autocephalous churches were headed by "Patriarchs", the others (including the 3 'autonomous' churches of Crete, Finland and Japan) were headed by archbishops – both titles were "strictly honorary."

The Patriarch of Moscow established (in 1970), the autocephalous orthodox church "in America". In October 2018 the Russian orthodox church severed its ties with the ecumenical patriarchate of Constantinople (because the patriarch, Bartholomew I approved the independence of Ukraine church from the Russian; formal recognition to the Ukrainian church was given in January 2019.)

Byzantine Christianity, about 1000CE (i.e., at the beginning of the 2nd millennium of Christian history) was at the peak of its (Constantinople) world influence and power.

The Eastern Church upheld the ideology that there was to be ONLY ONE universal Christian society, the "Oikumene."

The authority of the Patriarch of Constantinople as the ecumenical patriarch was bolstered by canon 28 (of the council of Chalcedon 451) since Constantinople had become the "New Rome", the seat of the emperor and the senate.

Exhortation, Meditation and Reflection.
- The Union of Florence (July 6, 1439) saw the coming together of the Constantinople church with Rome under the

Decree of Union. Filioque and Roman Primacy were conceded.

But the decree of union was subsequently renounced by most of the signatories from the East, by 1472.

Uniates are Eastern Catholics who returned to communion with the Pope.

- The Russian Patriarchate was abolished in 1721 by Tsar, Peter the Great, who transferred the administration of the church into a department of state known as the "Holy Governing Synod"

"Weakened by the Schism of the old believers, the church found no spokesman to defend its rights and passively accepted the reforms" (of Peter the Great), i.e., until 1917[5]

4: The Ecumenical Councils:

1. Nicaea, 325 -; 10. 2 Lateran, 1139 -; 19. Trent, 1545;
2. Constantinople, 381 -; 11. 3 Lateran, 1179 -; 20. 1 Vatican, 1869
3. Ephesus, 431 -; 12. 4 Lateran, 1215 -; 21. 2 Vatican, 1962
4. Chalcedon, 451 -; 13. 1 Lyons 1245 -;
5. 2 Constantinople, 553 -; 14. 2 Lyons, 1274 -;
6. 3 Constantinople, 680 -; 15. Vienne, 1311 -;
7. 2 Nicaea, 787 -; 16. Constance, 1414 -;
8. 4 Constantinople 869 -; 17. Basel and Ferrara – Florence, 1431, 1438.
9. 1 Lateran, 1123 -; 18. 5 Lateran, 1512;

The common purpose of the first 8 councils was to determine whether specific theological novelties were orthodox or heretical. The rest of the councils dealt with church discipline and morals.

"Pope John XXIII underlined one of the principal themes of the 2nd Vatican council the re-union of all Christians with the church of Rome."

"Protestants recognize… the first four councils, but as first expressed by Martin Luther do not regard ecumenical councils and their canons as binding on the conscience."

Exhortation, Meditation and Reflection.

Liturgy: called the Greek rite, was not usually celebrated daily, as in the West, and it was always sung, leavened bread was used in the Eucharist, (Rome: unleavened bread) and communion was given to laymen in both kinds – i.e., bread and wine.

Parish priest might marry prior to ordination; monks and bishops might not marry.

Church Government was by a holy synod, a board of bishops and laymen.

Other Churches

There were many churches apart from those directly under the patriarchs e.g., Mount Sinai (made up of the monastery of St Catherine; its archbishop was the abbot. Also, the Monastic community of Mt. Athos (in Greece)).

Oikumene

Do Christians still want *Oikumene* today? Yes, it will make the church to be STRONGER, PURER AND MORE FRUITFUL AND RESULT ORIENTED.

All along we have emphasized Christian unity. Church unity is different from Christian unity. While you cannot have Christian unity (the goal) without a measure of church unity (the strategy), you can have "church unity" – a periodic gathering of the leaders of world Christian sects (all autocephalous) with pomp and pageantry – without Christian unity; that is to say, without the DNA of unity, which is cohesion.

JOSAPHAT[6] – A hero of church unity

Raised in the orthodox Church, which on November 23, 1595 in the union of Brest, united with the Church of Rome. Became a monk in the Ukrainian order of St Basil ("Basilians") in 1604 at age 20. He was ordained a priest in 1609.

5: After the Bolshevik Revolution priests and bishops were killed, Russian bishops residing abroad in 1920 formed the Russian orthodox church outside Russia, leading to a split (1927) in Russian orthodoxy.

6: https://catholicsaintJosaphatkunseye

Following Russian's seizure of Crimea in 2014, and subsequent encouragement of separatists in E. Ukraine leading to a renewed putsch for the independence of the Ukrainian church, the

Ecumenical patriarch of Constantinople in 2018 reversed the decision of 1686 and formally

recognised (in 2019) the independence of that church, headed by the metropolitan of Kiev.

(It is a merger of 3 or more churches).

Exhortation, Meditation and Reflection.

Josaphat's superior, Samuel, never accepted unity with Rome, and he was against the Uniat. The Archbishop of Kiev removed Samuel, replacing him with Josaphat. He was consecrated Archbishop of Polotsk, Lithuania in 1617.

A dissident group, set up anti-Uniat bishops for each Uniat one, spread accusation that Josaphat had "gone Latin." They placed a usurper on the archbishop's chair (while he was attending the diet of Warsaw in 1620.)

In late 1623 an anti-Uniat priest, Elias, was removed. The removal of the priest led to a mob protest; the mob martyred Josaphat.

II. **The Breach and Martin Luther**[1]**:** to break down or to build up?

Martin Luther precipitated the protestant movement shattering the peace and unity of western Christendom; leaving in its trail, Roman Catholicism, Lutheranism, Calvinism, the Anglican communion, the Anabaptists, the anti-Trinitarians and more.

Before Luther there had been disturbing disquiet in the Western (Roman Catholic) church but Luther was the first that got away with that rebuff with no single hair on his head being singed.

Martin Luther had featured in two previous protests in the decade before 1517. First, with the (Erfurt) faculty, he petitioned it for the award of a degree to him and secondly, he was chosen to represent his course mates in their petition to Pope Julius II on a group interest. Still seething with discontent, he embarked upon the writing of his theses entitled: "Disputation against scholastic theology."

1: Martin Luther, 1483 – 1546.

Exhortation, Meditation and Reflection.

The immediate cause was a preaching in 1517 by a Dominican friar, Johann Tetzel, on indulgence. Luther slammed an alarm in a protest to the friar's superior, Archbishop Albert of Mainz, requesting him to estop Tetzel from preaching such views and forwarded a copy of his 95 theses with the petition, and circulated other copies thereof among his friends. The archbishop was not amused and he forwarded Luther's theses to Rome for formal scrutiny to ascertain their orthodoxy.

Along the way, Cajetan, a very distinguished theologian and head of the Dominican order was asked to examine those writings.

Besides the indulgence issue, Luther faulted the church on the issue of personal responsibility to internalize grace for salvation, citing Rom 1: 17. Salvation is exclusively by grace, appropriated by faith. And in thesis 86, he decried the pope's wealth and opposed collection of contribution from laity for the building of proposed St Peter's Basilica; the pope's wealth could finance it, he asserted.

After a consistory had examined the writings, Luther was on June 15, 1520 required to recant 41 statements in his various writings. He would not budge. Rather, he made a public bon fire of a copy of the papal bull which declared those writings heretical. He called the pope (Pope Leo) in a tract as "an antichrist". Cajetan, he described as "an evasive, obscure and an unintelligible theologian."

715

He regarded priestly celibacy as "the work of the Devil." Zwingli and others, who felt his reforms didn't go far enough, he called names. "Anabaptists should be hanged as seditionists"; "Jews should be expelled and their synagogues burnt."

In doing all these he was under the protégé of newly crowned German monarch, Charles V and Philip of Hesse (Landgrave) who had a bigamy issue.

He got married to Katherine of Bora, a former nun, in 1525 and the couple had five children.

Luther probably thus ignited the embers of German anti-Semitism which became a conflagration during Hitler's World War II.

The Church

Khomiakov derided this development (Protestantism) as the substitution of "private rational judgement for *sobornost.*"

"But this private rational opinion… would not stop with Luther. Indeed, the decomposition of Protestantism was swift, sure and frightful."

Exhortation, Meditation and Reflection.

Afterwards, Luther translated the New Testament into German language. He contributed much to the dogma, ***sola scriptura***, that encouraged individual interpretation of the Bible as the sole source of religious authority.

"Church" to him was a community of the faithful, a priesthood of all believers.

In his assault on the authority of the Western (Roman Catholic) church, one thing seems clear: Luther knew where he was coming from, but never seemed to give a thought to where he was heading to.

III. The Methodist Church and John Wesley[2]

"For in Christ Jesus, neither circumcision nor uncircumcision accomplishes anything; what matters is faith working through love."
(Gal 5: 6 HCSB)

The above scripture, according to John Wesley shaped his notion of "church".

First, the institutional church which is steeped in antiquity – apostolic succession and tradition.

Second, when it suits (or by expediency – as when he had to ordain itinerant lay preachers as priests and appoint presbyters (in the USA), church is "a fellowship of believers who shared both the Apostles experience of God's living presence and a zeal for evangelism … whom the Holy Spirit had endowed with special gifts of prophecy and leadership." (a free church or believers' church, simpliciter!)

"… my two principles: the one, that I dare not separate from the church (of England), that I believe it would be a sin so to do; the other, that I believe it would be a sin not to vary from it in the points above mentioned."

His right to ordain ministers (for USA) he derived specifically "from the Anglican triad of scripture, reason and antiquity." These he fine-tuned and added 'experience' to arrive at the Wesleyan quadrilateral of scripture, reason, tradition and experience.

2: John Wesley, Anglican Clergyman, 1703 – 1791.

Exhortation, Meditation and Reflection.

Methodist Societies

A cleric of the Anglican communion, Wesley experienced the fervour to live early age Christian experience. His contact with Peter Böhler, a missionary in Britain of Count Nicholas von Zinzendorf's the Moravian Brethren, marked a turning point in his Christian vocation. The Fetter Lane society and the Sandgate Str. (London) open air crusades were the precursors of Wesley's open-air revival, especially his adoption of organisational framework of classes, bands and societies. The aim was to build a network of these informal gathering of Christians desirous of deepening their faith throughout the main bodies of the Christian churches without separating from them. Note that both Böhler and Zinzendorf were Lutherans, just as Wesley was Anglican.

Likewise, Wesley's aim was far from creating a separate church, but "a dynamic apostolic community" operating as a church within the churches of the society's members. Of course, they were particularly welcome in the Church of England.

The need for discipline (which is a shade of orthodoxy) was soon recognised, though exercised by Wesley himself. It made the societies to become increasingly more institutional. Cards were issued to members quarterly and delinquents would not have their cards renewed. You need the card to partake in monthly love feasts just as delinquents cannot join the select societies but must remain in 'penitents.'

In 1748, Wesley reduced Bristol societies from 900 to 730. Some of the misdemeanours that attracted his sanction were: cursing, habitual Sabbath breaking, drunkenness, selling liquor, quarrelling, wife beating, etc.

To organise and drive the societies Wesley appointed lay itinerant preachers.

They were taught to "face mobs, brave any weather; subsist without means, to rise at 4 and preach at 5" etc.

"These societies… were much needed means of restoring the *Koinonia*, the Spirit, the message and the sense of mission" of the earliest church communities.

Needless to say, that most of these innovations had given way within Methodism between the 19th and 20th centuries.

The Wesleyan societies could have been lay societies within the Anglican communion, Wesley had no such authority.

Exhortation, Meditation and Reflection.

Perhaps if the Anglican communion had taken more than a cursory look at what Wesley was doing, Methodism might have taken a different course; become an *ecclesiola* within an *ecclesia*, in much the same way the religious orders such as Franciscans, Augustinians, Dominicans and Jesuits are in the Catholic Church. That opportunity was frittered. Methodism expanded faster to America than the Church of England. Stirred initially by renewal or living faith, Wesley's success meant he was in a strong position not to capitulate to the Anglican. So, another church has been born!

"I am fully convinced that our own church (Church of England), with all her blemishes, is nearer the scripture plan than any other in Europe." Declared Wesley.

The story of Methodism and the other two earlier breaches recounted, give us opportunity for introspection and hindsight. Borrowing the words of Howard A. Snyder[3]:

"What is the shape of our life together as the people of God in the world?"

Since the Protestant revolution and especially in the past century Christian churches had grown exponentially. Everyone of such churches was autocephalous. It had rendered as obsolete or a 'nobody's business' such issues like uniformity in faith and doctrine, although the Lord has not changed His charge – "… be one!"

Laodiceans, be warned!

Jesus admonishes the church in Laodicea to be "either hot or cold"; He would dissociate Himself from those who would rather sit on the fence.

Reflecting on this vis-à-vis the subject of Christian unity, it is rather very disturbing to observe that the vast majority of Christians belong to that group, especially with regard to their zeal or eagerness for orthodoxy, the live wire behind a dynamic genuine Christian conversion (evangelism).

3: Howard A. Snyder: Author, Wesley
Exhortation, Meditation and Reflection.

How many of us really care about such matters? And of those who care that the church should be empowered to carry out her mission, how many take any steps what-so-ever toward accomplishing this objective? The good news is that there is still room for repentance.

To the angel of the church in Laodicea

"… I will spit you out of my mouth…"

"Be earnest, then, and repent." (Rev 3: 15-16, 19 NABRE)

Growing slack in zeal? (Rom 12: 11 GNBDK)

Do not; for it is not yet over until it is over. Do not allow this apparently unstoppable slide towards fractionalisation since the split, to oppress you; to make you think that the situation cannot be different – many flocks, many shepherds! No, it can be. This degeneracy started only about 500 years ago. The situation was different in the preceding 1,500 years of Christianity. Our weakness caused it and our strength shall reverse it. We have to have "one flock, one shepherd." The battle has only just begun. Take up the gauntlet and take heart; we are fighting under the banner of Jesus. They are people like you that are needed. Put on the full armour of God. (Eph 6: 11-18)

Let them be one

"Unity is not for the weak but for the strong" to make them even more formidable. It is easier for a strong and united Roman Catholic Church to stretch an olive branch and reach out to its estranged brethren; a strong and united Pentecostal, charismatic or evangelical entity to make overtures to other members within the group than for the weaker – its intention may come under suspicion. Let us cooperate for the triumph of the word of God.

Turn him back!

"… if any among you strays from the truth, and someone turns him back, let him know that whoever turns a sinner from the error of his way will save his life from death and cover a multitude of sins." (Js 5: 19-20 HCSB)

Unifying Forces: The Holy Spirit and Christ.

1. Eldad and Medad

Eldad and Medad were made one with the 70 others by the power of the Holy Spirit. They were appointed elders of the people, but remained in the camp while the 70 others (appointed elders) were in the Assembly. Yet, all 72 were prophesying – the two at the camp, the 70 at the Assembly. (Num 11: 25-29)

Exhortation, Meditation and Reflection.

2. The Jerusalem church and the Missionaries

Just so, too, Saul and the communities in Antioch, Ephesus etc. and the disciples in Jerusalem were brought into unity by the power of Jesus and the Holy Spirit through the instrumentality of Ananias, Barnabas and Paul (Acts 9: 17; 11: 25). Thus, was fulfilled the expressed desire of the Lord that all His flocks should come together as "one flock, one shepherd"

(Jn 10: 16 HCSB)

Truly, Eldad and Medad in the Old Testament, Paul, Ananias and Barnabas in the New Testament stand for endorsement – for orthodoxy and a united discipleship. Why will our generation not oblige the Lord?

Why would three sane men describe an elephant which they had touched and fondled as three entirely different objects, if not that they were blind?

Paul and Barnabas disagree; thank God, the church remains one!

"Both Judas and Silas, who were also prophets themselves…"
There was disagreement between Paul and Barnabas over taking John Mark along with them (Acts 15: 36-39)

"…such a sharp disagreement that they parted company, and Barnabas took Mark with him and sailed off to Cyprus."

"Then Paul chose Silas and departed…" (Acts 15: 40)

Meditation: In retrospect, do you think the same outcome could not have been reached in a more congenial or charitable manner?

'…Let them be one!'

Concern for the body of Christ

Call to tend the flock (Acts 20: 28)

Jesus: Simon, son of Jonah,

do you love Me more than these?

Simon (Peter): Yes Lord; You know that I love You.

Jesus: Feed My lambs! (pause)

Simon, son of Jonah, do you love Me?

Simon (Peter): Yes Lord, You know that I love You.

Jesus: Tend My sheep! (pause)

Simon, son of Jonah, do you love Me?

Simon (Peter): (pause) Lord, You know all things.

You know that I love You.

Jesus: Feed My sheep!… (Jn 21: 15-17)

Exhortation, Meditation and Reflection.

Leaders of Christ's flock, what do you make of above liturgy? A stream that forgets its source dries up; a house that is divided against itself falls.

Our take is that this (liturgy) is in furtherance of the earlier investiture of Peter as the rock upon which Christ's church was to be built, a formal re-instatement.

We can be rest assured that Jesus, the Son of God was not unaware of Simon's love for, and loyalty to Him. The Lord was instilling a recondite message by the repetition – *Simon, love Me and love Me even more than the others do; with that love, feed them, tend them.*

That is the mandate – the task – for the leader of Christendom. It is a profound legacy and the behest is accordingly issued in earnestness, solemnity and sobriety. The message sank into Simon gradually. It made him sober – see with what gentleness and humility he guided the other Apostles and disciples – he considered himself a mere *primus inter pares*, loving, feeding and washing their feet.

A section of the flock understood that this legacy is to be passed on when Simon goes the way of mortals. But the other section still clung to

"I'm with Paul" or "I'm with Apollos" or "I'm with Cephas" (1 Cor 1: 12 HCSB)

For that reason, adequate cognition was not gained of Simon's investiture as head (on earth) of the body of Christ.

Unity of Command: Hierarchical Succession

Jesus commended the order of hierarchical succession to the people of God when He pointed out that the Scribes and Pharisees occupy the seat of Moses and therefore are to be obeyed.

David saw in King Saul, 'the anointed of God', the one occupying Moses' chair in his day; for that reason, he could not be disloyal to him – he would flee from, rather than fight him!

We need Cephas!

We need Cephas – unity of command – don't we?

Don't we need a final arbiter, a co-ordinator, umpire, prefect – a father of last resort in case of differences among us so we do not blow apart? It does not change the fact even if the occupier of this office is under a restriction to be guided by the advice of a consistory or other ecumenical council.

The alternative is that everyone goes his separate ways. That is just not right; not good enough for the flock of the Lord. Everyone with his own disparate interpretation of the word? That would be beguiling and unhelpful; everybody allegedly "hearing the Spirit."

Exhortation, Meditation and Reflection.

Why then, the differences in the message preached, unless they heard from contrary spirits, and not from the same and only Holy Spirit of God – the down payment of the inheritance of the body of Christ, the Spirit of truth?

Evangelization gains

At the first Pentecost, by His power, all in Jerusalem became one; everyone heard the Apostles in their mother tongues. In just one day more than 3,000 new converts were added to the number of believers. That is what the Holy Spirit does; if the result is different, it portends evil.

Of course, lies sell for some time. Besides, every coin has two sides: too much centralization leads to rigidity and hautiness on the part of these who sit at the apex of the pyramid. It makes slower the realization of the long term corporate objective – evangelism and care of the poor. In between there is room to manoeuvre.

Thus every mature organisation tends to become stale and decadent over time. Protestantism by giving a jolt to the older church made the latter more responsive to the needs of the flock than ever before. It gave it a fresh lease of life. A new flame of evangelism, began to burn over the new world, in Africa and Australia and New Zealand. The Eastern orthodox churches were left out.

But Protestantism also accentuated the impact of concupiscence leading to the near utter neglect of the church's twin mission of care of the infirm, the physically challenged and the poor, not to mention the need of prisoners.

People perceived opulence within the cloisters of the church. It had led to plunder of church properties and loss of lives of clerics, especially during revolutions such as in France and the USSR.

"Give it to the poor."

It may not put an end to criminology, but the Church ought to have quit tokenism and fully institutionalize its obligation to those charities.

To bridge the gulf

Today, unless we deceive ourselves, there are so many strands of the body of Christ – not seeing eye to eye and cacophonous in their utterances. They align with the Devil as 'god-sent'; they shun the saints as 'accursed'! They court the one and despise the other. The wedge has been planted in-between us (Christians) and if nothing is done, the gulf can only become wider not narrower, until such a time that there will be no resemblance between us at all!

Exhortation, Meditation and Reflection.

But who is to tell the differences between the two? Who is to guide the faithful? Whose mouth can be trusted to speak the truth? Who is to tell who among us is in error? Jerusalem did in the days of the Apostles. (Acts 15: 22-25) If we do our bit, then we know that the power of darkness will not overcome the church. But how long shall the strife last – 40 days or 40 years? The answer is with us.

The antecedents: –

- **Moses Investiture**: use what you have to get what you want.

"Now, go! I am sending you to Pharaoh to bring My people, the Israelites, out of Egypt."

The Lord said to him: "What is in your hand?"

"A staff," he answered.

"Now go, I will assist you in speaking and teach you what you are to say." (Exo 3: 10; 4: 2, 12 HCSB)

Moses brother: Aaron, the Levite

"He will speak to the people for you: he will be your spokesman and you will be as god to him." (Exo 4: 16 HCSB)

Eliakim's Investiture

"My servant, Eliakim…"

"I will give him complete authority… He will have the keys of office; what he opens, no one will shut, and what he shuts, no one will open."

"I will fasten him firmly in place like a peg,…" (Isa 22: 22, 23 GNBDK)

Jesus, the Stone

"Look, I have laid a Stone in Zion, a tested Stone, a precious Corner-stone, a sure Foundation; the one who believes will be unshakable."

(Isa 28: 16 HCSB)

"Here is My Servant whom I uphold, My Chosen One with whom I am pleased. Upon Him I have put My Spirit; He shall bring forth justice to the nations."

"… He will faithfully bring forth justice."

"…the coastlands will wait for His teaching." (Isa 42: 1, 2-3, 4 NABRE)

Simon Peter, the rock

"… You are Peter, and on this rock I will build My church, …" (Matt 16: 22, 23 HCSB)

The Issue is: Who is that Peter – the rock of our Christian faith in our age and time?

"You will know the truth and the truth will set you free." (Jn 8:32 HCSB)

See how Simon exercised this stewardship

- "Therefore, as a fellow elder and witness… of the Messiah… I exhort the elders,… shepherd God's flock… not overseeing out of compulsion but freely, according to God's will; not for money but eagerly, not lording it over those entrusted to you, but being examples to the flock." (1 Pt 5: 1-3 HCSB)

- "...you younger men, be subject to the elders. And all of you clothe yourselves with humility toward one another... Humble yourselves that God may exalt you." (1 Pt 5: 5-6 HCSB)
- "...all of you should be like-minded and sympathetic, should love believers, and be compassionate and humble." (1 Pt 3: 8)
- "So rid yourselves of all malice, all deceit, hypocrisy, envy, and all slander... desire the pure spiritual milk so that you may grow by it for your salvation." (1 Pt 2: 1-2 HCSB)
- Be on your guard! "...be aware of this: scoffers will come in the last days to scoff, living according to their own desires." (2 Pt 3: 3 HCSB)
- "... The untaught and unstable twist them (Paul's letters) to their own destruction, as they also do with the rest of the Scriptures. Therefore, dear friends, since you know this in advance, be on your guard, so that you are not led away by the error of lawless people..." (2 Pt 3: 16-17 HCSB)
- "Be hospitable to one another without complaining... the gift each has received, use it to serve others, as good managers of the varied grace of God." (1 Pt 4: 9-10 HCSB)

We should listen also to Apostle James:

- "... For we all stumble in many ways. If anyone does not stumble in what he says, he is a mature man who is also able to control his whole body." (Js 3: 2 HCSB)
- "Don't criticize one another, brothers..."
- "Brothers do not complain about one another, so that you may not be judged..."

"My brothers, if any among you strays from the truth,… let him know that whoever turns a sinner from the error of his way will save his life from death and..." (Js 4: 11; 5: 9, 19 HCSB)

Exhortation, Meditation and Reflection.

Why you should have a concern for Christian unity

Let Them Be One

Why you should have concern for Christian Unity and aversion against apathy with which it is treated by many Christian leaders:

First – It is because Jesus Christ Himself broached the subject and gave it such enormous attention as per John's gospel.

Other disciples, notably Apostles Paul and Peter, Jude Thaddeus, felt the same concern.

Secondly – Today there is proliferation, fractionalization and decimation growing, rather than unity among so-called Christian sects. We would have been stronger together.

Worse is that such activities are counter-productive; some are agents of Satan, parading themselves as *Bona fide* Christian leaders!

There is this Urgent need

1. To remove the camouflage and streamline efforts at strengthening evangelism.
2. For the guidance of new converts, the true faith and its adherents should be separated, and be self-manifest.

But I have not seen the leadership of the sects of Christians doing anything along that line.

Only recently, however, the reason became urgent: many of the leaders probably don't know what goes on within other sects – in terms of false and misleading teaching and practices. Why are they comfortable with a stance of 'live and let's live'?

Eucharist separates the authentic from the fake (Jn 6:52-66)

"We, though many, are one body…" (1 Cor 11: 29 HCSB)

FACTIONS – Denominations:

Methodist, Baptist, Catholic, Evangelical, Pentecostal, Lutheran, Anglican…

"For you are all ONE in CHRIST" (Gal 3: 28, 29)

Exhortation, Meditation and Reflection.

JESUS: "Where two or three are gathered together in My name…"

"if two or more of you agree to bind anything on earth, …"

Paul (to the Corinthians): "… I hear that when you meet as a church, there are divisions among you…" (1 Cor 11: 18)

(Last Word) Universality, pro-Catholicism…

Let us come together and "be one."

This book is not denominational; not for East Christians, not for West, but for all – catholicism, universality!

No excellence, no perfection is claimed for it. My plea: "to err is human…"

But let us in togetherness find out the errors and uphold the truth. Let us re-start the conversation from somewhere, from here!

It should be possible for Christians to agree on what is the truth.

May the good Lord bless us as we come together to give concerted witness to the truth of the Good News. Amen.

Christian Unity: an agenda

I. Definitions

1. Primate: Designation for executive head of a worship centre or group of such centres or of a standalone church/corporate entity.
2. (National) Chief Christ Missionary (or Ambassador):

Stands for the executive head or chief spokesperson for all Christians within a national state, say USA, Nigeria, Israel.

3. Regional/Continental: chairman of conference.

If it is desirable to have ecumenical conferences at regional (e.g., West Africa, North America, etc.) levels or even at continental levels (such as Europe, Asia, etc.) the usual nomenclature (chairman, secretary, treasurer, etc.) for offices within a meeting is suggested.

4. This nomenclature (Chairman, secretary, treasurer, etc.) is suggested also for all other ecumenical meetings at city, provincial or other intra-state level.
5. President, World Ecumenical Conference.

Exhortation, Meditation and Reflection.

For the apex dialogue, we leave the leaders to choose suitable appellation for officers at that level and ultimately for the office that is the chief representative of Jesus on earth.

II. Preliminary: accepting the call for unity.

We know that Jesus did not plant any church besides the Jewish temple and synagogues that He met. Of course, He laid the foundation by His doctrinal differences with that group and especially by instituting a distinct sect of disciples and Apostles of which Peter was conferred with its leadership. He did command them to spread the good news across the entire world. The good news has indeed reached the entire world. As we await His second coming, we should at the same time brace up for the antichrist. This chapter proposes a return to a sort of compact unity. What, in the opinion of Christian leaders, is Christ's mind for 'unity' on the global stage? Would He have appointed non-interacting independent leaders for the flocks outside Israel? Or would He have extended Peter's authority over all the continents?

We trust the scriptures would be a guide and so we have highlighted a few in V (below) and pointed out many more in this chapter. From these and guided by the Holy Spirit we enjoin each primate to hold formal and informal meetings on the need or otherwise for Christian unity, beginning from His own flock and extending to other primates around. The objective is to take a position and make a commitment towards actualisation of the position taken at city, state or national level. In short, energise the movement toward understanding and actualization of unity. Some nations may already have an existing platform (like in Nigeria: The Christian Association of Nigeria – CAN) under whose auspices such formal and informal discussion can take place. Every concerned Christian can be involved at the informal level. We can call this a bottom to top approach.

The bishops of the very large denominations can bring out the subject at their dioceses and authorize pastors to sound the matter among themselves and bring up suggestions, which could lead to formal and informal discussion up to the highest council of such bodies. A committed group should be able to reach out to other large denominations informally ever before taking a final commitment of its own. The goal should be to overcome inertia (or abhorrence of change) and to expedite the attainment of the goal at the earliest possible time.

Exhortation, Meditation and Reflection.

A suitable app may be an asset by suggesting alternative procedures and prompting the next action and date due, so all can understand in advance necessary procedures.

It should be the goal to make the two concurrent approaches meet at one point for synergy.

III. Agreement on fundamentals

What should the objective or purpose for Christian unity be?
1. **For identity?** To determine which group can be classified as a "Christian" religious body/worship centre. Wouldn't it serve a good purpose to alert the flock of the existence of wolves in their midst?
2. **Doctrine**: what are the minimal essential beliefs of the Christian faith, a kerygma of Christian beliefs?

3. **Procedure**: what is your group's opinion as to the best way to accomplish this unity?
4. **Unity**. As true Christians what do we sincerely believe
   a) That this new foray for unity is, or is not essential for the good of all not only in time of peace but also in time of persecution?
   b) If essential, that it is or is not achievable?
5. **Secular authorities**: Do we need or should we seek national legislative fiats for effective implementation of decisions taken, considering historical antecedents and to curb the proliferation of dubious or fake groups parading themselves as authentic Christian sects? Alternatively, are laws necessary to protect the free exercise of the faith especially in totalitarian regimes?

A decision on these issues seem necessary as a group commits itself to Christian unity. A resolution on such topics ought to be taken at most ecumenical conferences.

IV. Implementation

Christian unity as is being understood herein is a destination, not an unending process; and as such a path should be charted to get there expeditiously and with cost efficiency in the usage of time and other resources. The procedure is the path, unity the destination. Anyone inspired can start informal consultation with superiors and colleagues; raise the talk informally at church/parish councils, pastors' meetings or other suitable fora or suggest the start of formal talks to appropriate authorities or for horizontal integration of efforts to make a thrust. Formal meetings will gain time and traction if they kick off with the agenda suggested in this piece.

Exhortation, Meditation and Reflection.

Observers and official delegates (between two and six) can represent every participating institution. The number of votes by each institution may be regulated to give more weight to those showing greatest commitment, or in proportion to the population of their congregation.

Decisions taken at these formal conferences may only be considered persuasive yet, rather than mandatory (for compliance) on member institutions until such time that the apex conference may direct otherwise.

No doubt there are other approaches to get to unity, other than the one suggested above. The above is tendered as a default procedure or most embracing and most likely to succeed.

V. The Word

At every step along the way let us be mindful of God's will. The word will lead us on. A brief selection is below, but the body of this chapter contains some considered most apposite.

- A kingdom divided against itself cannot stand; a house divided against itself falls (Mk 3: 24, 25)
- Even Satan knows the Bible and has his own interpretation thereof (Matt 4: 6; Lk 4: 6, 9-10).
- Let them be one as I and the Father are One (Jn 17: 21 NABRE)
- Christian brotherhood: whoever does the will of God is in the brotherhood. (Mk 3: 35)
- Apostle Peter: "Be united" heart and soul (Acts 4: 34-35)
- Shepherd God's flock among you according to God's will…(1 Pt 5: 2; 2 Pt 2: 1-2; 2 Pt 3: 3, 16, 17)
- Apostle Paul: Let them agree heart and mind in what they say; no divisions. (1 Cor 1: 10)
- We, though many, are one body (1 Cor 11: 23-25, 29)
- Anyone doing something different is accursed (1 Jn 4: 5-6)?
- Apostle John: Beware of the antichrist (1 Jn 2: 18, 19; 4: 5-6)
- Satan church – test those who call themselves apostles and are not (Rev 2: 2; 3: 1, 15-17)

733

- Apostle Jude (Thaddeus): Ostracize those peddling different doctrines and hence divisions (Jude 1: 3-5, 6, 11, 16-19)
- Only God

Exhortation, Meditation and Reflection.

"I planted, Apollo watered, but God gave the growth." "…only God who gives the growth." (1 Cor 3: 6-7 HCSB)

- Be humble, respect the elders!

"In the same way, you younger men, be subject to the elders."

"…because God resists the proud but gives grace to the humble."

(1 Pt 5: 5)

CHAPTER 20

Jews, Others.

The HOPE

"But upon Mount Zion shall be deliverance, and there shall be holiness; and the house of Jacob shall possess their possessions." (Oba 1:17)

"When you are in distress…you will return to the Lord your God in later days and obey Him.

He will not leave you, destroy you, or forget the covenant with your fathers…" (Deut 4: 30-31 HCSB)

Listen My people!

"For, as the loincloth clings to a man's loins, so I made the whole house of Israel and the whole house of Judah cling to Me

—oracle of the Lord—to be My people.

My fame, My praise, My glory. But they did not listen." (Jer 13:11 NABRE)

Jesus says,

- "I am the way, the truth, and the life – no one comes to the father except through Me. (Jn 14:6)
- "…Nothing is concealed that will not be revealed no secret that will not be known."
- You will know the truth, and the truth will set you free. (Jn 8:32 HCSB)

Obey!

Your revered prophet warned long ago:

"Obedience is better than sacrifice; to listen better than the fat of rams…"

(I Sam 15:22-23)

Or is that precept true for Saul alone?

Accept the truth

What the leadership (of Jewish faith) have not been able to bear is The Truth!

Jesus is the way, the truth and the life… (Ibid)

He is the holiest man that ever lived—a Jew by flesh and blood. You need to listen to Him:

"…you who hear Me: love your enemies, do good to those who hate you, bless those who curse you, pray for those who ill-treat you. Be merciful just as your Father in heaven is merciful (LK 6:27-28, 36) GNBDK

That is what holiness is about: "Be holy! (Lev 19:2)

A Prophet like Moses

God promised through Moses to send a prophet like Him (Dt 18:18). The word of God is not void—Jesus is the prophet. Jesus is the Promise

He says,

"But now I tell you: love your enemies and pray for those who persecute you so that you may become the children of your Father in heaven, for He makes His sun to shine on bad and good people alike and gives rain to those who do good and to those who do evil." (Matt 5:44-45) GNBDK

Called to be in fellowship

"Even before the world was made, God had already chosen us to be His through our union with Christ, so that we would be holy and without fault before Him because of His love." (Eph 1:4) GNBDK

"Children, let no one deceive you. The person who acts in righteousness is righteous…whoever sins belongs to the Devil…Indeed the Son of God was revealed to destroy the works of the Devil. No one who is begotten by God commits sin, because

God's seed remains in him; in this way, the children of God and the children of the Devil are made plain; no one who fails to act in righteousness belongs to God, nor anyone who does not love his brother.

(1 Jn 3:7-10 NABRE)

So, this is not determined by flesh and blood!

"If you consider that God is righteous, you also know that everyone who acts in righteous is begotten by Him. (1 Jn 2:29 NABRE)

Jesus says,

- "I was sent only to the lost sheep of the house of Israel" (Matt 15:24)

Righteousness is begotten by Him(Jesus) for our sins. Everyone who commits sin, commits lawlessness, for sin is lawlessness. You know that He was revealed to take away sins, and in Him there is no sin." (1 Jn 2:29, 3:4, 5 NABRE)

Not his will!

It is not the will of God for humanity to perish in hell fire, though justice may demand that the sinner should thus suffer:

"…it is not the will of your heavenly Father that one of these little ones be lost." (Matt 18:14 CCSB)

Righteousness is not by flesh and blood.

The righteous are children of Abraham and children of God. Naomi is a Jew by flesh and blood, and Ruth isn't. But she became the great grandmother of David. Begetting Obed, the father of Jesse, the father of David." (Ruth 4:17)

Listen to John the Baptizer's admonition:

"And don't presume to say to yourselves, 'We have Abraham as our father.' For I tell you that God is able to raise up children for Abraham from these stones!" (Matt 3:9)

While the world accepts Jesus Christ, His generation would not (and till date His people would not?) Governor Pontus Pilate had this to say to Jesus,

"…I'm not a Jew, am I?" "Your own nation and the chief priests handed you over to me. What have you done?" (Jn 18:35)

The Lord, Himself said, "My mother and My brothersare those who hear and do the word of God." (LK 8:21)

Not by flesh and blood… Apostle Paul

"Brothers, I tell you this:

Flesh and blood cannot inherit the kingdom of God, and corruption cannot inherit incorruption." (1 Cor 15:50)

The sons of the kingdom

"I tell you that many will come from east and West, and recline at the table with Abraham, Isaac, and Jacob in the kingdom of heaven.

But the sons of the kingdom will be thrown into the outer darkness. In that place there will be weeping and gnashing of teeth."(Matt 8:11-12) That this adversity may not happen is the reason for that scripture.

The Works of God – "believe!"

The scripture further tells us that some people asked Jesus, "What can we do to perform the works of God?"

"Jesus replied, 'this is the work of God—that you believe in the One He has sent.' (Jn 6:28-29)

Saul's (Paul's) Patriotism

"…I glory in my ministry in order to make my race jealous and thus save some of them." (Rom 11:13, 14 NABRE)

Also (Rom 9:2-3) "…Wish I am accursed for my people's sake…" (Rom 9:2-5)

More beatings?

Why do you want more beatings?

Why do you keep on rebelling?

The whole head is hurt,

And the whole heart is sick

Zion will be redeemed by justice,

her repentant ones by righteousness." (Isa 1:5, 27 HCSB)

The Messiah

Jesus went into the region of Caesarea Philippi, and the following conversation took place between Him and His disciples:

Jesus: Who do people say that the Son of Man is?

Disciple 1: Some say you are, John, the Baptizer

Disciple 2: Others say you are Elijah

Disciple 3: Yet others say you are Jeremiah, or one of the prophets.

Jesus: But you—who do you say that I am?

(a little silence, then)

Peter: You are the Christ, the Son of the living God.

Jesus: Blessed are you, Simon, son of Jonah. Flesh and blood have not revealed this to you, but My Father in heaven. And I say to you—you are Peter—and upon this rock I will build My church. The gates of the netherworld shall not prevail against it."… I will give you the keys to the kingdoms of heaven.Whatever you bind on earth shall be bound in heaven; and whatever you loose on earth shall loosed in heaven", and all of you, Listen! Keep that secret to yourselves for now.

(Matt 16:13-20)

Jesus fraternized with Pharisees

LK 14:1 "One Sabbath when He went to eat at the house of one of the leading Pharisees…"

Jn 3:1-2 2. "There was a man from the Pharisees named Nicodemus, a ruler of the Jews. This man came to Him at night…"

Jn 19:40 "…they (Joseph of Arimathea and Nicodemus) took Jesus' body and wrapped it in linen clothes with the aromatic spices…for burial" (Matt 21: 28-32)

Repent now! How long? Turn back to God.

"The chief priests and the elders came to Him and asked, 'What right have you to do these things? Who gave you this right?"

So, Jesus said to them, "I tell you: the tax collectors and the prostitutes are going into the kingdom of God ahead of you. For John the Baptist…" Came to you showing you the right path to take, and you would not believe him; but the tax collectors and the prostitutes believed him. Even when you saw this, you did not later change your minds and believe him." (Matt 21:23, 31-32 GNBDK)

For the parable used by Jesus to anchor His teaching, read it in Matt 21:28-31 (and in this book in chapter 7)

Was Jesus hungry for human honours?

By this claim to be Son of God and Messiah, was Jesuscraving for honour from the Jews?

Of course not! Indeed, He had to shroud His identity for a while, preferring to style himself 'Son of Man'! The people who are zealous for honour or power are to be found in the courts – to cohort with the governors, or in King Herod's court, the chief priests, etc. But Jesus was detached from these people. He recognized the ministry of John, the Baptist, yet would not join His ministry to John's.

The scripture anticipated a faux pas by the Jewish people, hence the Messiah had to suffer. It is a question of "old wines are better than new." In a way, this is commendable; as no serious believer should accept every specious claim (to speak for God). The problem however, is for how long will such fastidiousness stand in the way of salvation?

Jesus

This is He, of whom the prophet prophesied

"The house of David and…inhabitants of Jerusalem"

"…they, look on Him whom they have trust through, they will mourn for Him as one mourns for an only child…" (Zec 12:10)

Yet,"On that day a fountain will be opened for the house of David and the inhabitants of Jerusalem to purify from sin…" (Zec 13:1 HCSB)

"…Yet you did not turn to Me" (Amos 4:6, 8, 9, 10, 11)

Prophet killing by the Jews

Zachariah: 2 Chr 24:17-25

After the death of Jehoiada, the priests, "They forsook the temple of the Lord…and began to serve the sacred poles and other idols. Zachariah, son of Jehoiada, the priest prophesied at the King's order he was stoned to death at the very court of the Lord's temple."

In similar manner, John the Baptist, Jesus, Stephen, and Apostles James, Paul, Peter, etc. were killed by the Jews.

The Jews (and others)

"Therefore go … and invite everyone you find to the banquet." – parable of a king's son wedding (Matt 22:9 HCSB)

"… Now I really understand that God doesn't show favouritism." (Acts 10:34 HCSB)

"There is no favouritism with God." (Rom 2:11 HCSB)

All nations:

"In the last days the mountain of the Lord's house will be established

At the top of the mountains…

All nations will stream to it" (Isa 2:2 HCSB)

The Gentiles and Jews

"Not flesh and blood…"

- "And he was a Samaritan"(Luke 10:33)
- Non-Jews paid the first homage to the Messiah(Matt 2:1)
- Jesus earliest self-revelation was to the Samaritans.(Jn 4:9, 39)
- Jesus began His public ministry from Galilee of the nations (Jn 3:22, Matt 4:12, 17)
- What is Jerusalem? – The birthplace of all nations.( )

- Who is Jesus? – A light to the gentiles and the glory of "your people, Israel" (Lk 2:32)

Jesus is light to gentiles and the glory of Israel.

Jesus Christ, though rejected by the people of His flesh and blood nevertheless, remains the glory of Israel:

"a light for revelation to the gentiles, and glory for your people Israel."

(Lk 2:32 NABRE)

Flesh and Blood are usually invoked or provoked for evil, for conspiracy and for complicity by way of discrimination

For whom then, is the kingdom prepared?

"And there will be wailing and grinding of teeth when you see Abraham, Isaac and Jacob and all the prophets in the kingdom of God and you yourselves cast out

(Lk 13:28 LECT)

"They will come from east and west, from north and south, and recline at the table in the kingdom of God." (Lk 13:29 HCSB)

You have now seen Him (Jesus); accept Him!

"…but your Teacher will not hide Himself any longer. Your eyes will see your Teacher… your ears will hear … 'This is the way. Walk in it.'" (Isa 30:20, 21 HCSB)

Priests, teachers: listen; you have been forewarned!

"For the lips of a priest should guard knowledge, and people should seek instruction from his mouth, because he is the messenger of the Lord of Hosts."

"You, on the other hand, have turned from the way. You have caused many to stumble by your instruction…" (Mal 2:8 HCSB)

Surprised? He has come!

"See… the Lord you seek will suddenly come to His temple, the Messenger of the covenant you desire – see, He is coming," says the Lord of Host

Are you in the number?

"But who can endure the day of His coming? And who will be able to stand when He appears? For He will be like a refiner's fire and like cleansing lye... He will purify the sons of Levi and refine them like gold and silver. Then they will present offerings to the Lord in righteousness (Mal 2:7-8; 3:1-3 HCSB)

The child has been born for us!

... a great light; a light has dawned... for a child will be born for us, ... He will be named Wonderful Counsellor, Mighty God, Eternal Father, Prince of Peace.

"Oh, that today you would hear His voice

Do not harden your hearts as at Meribah..." (Ps 95:7, 8 NABRE)

The Dominion will be vast... to establish and sustain it with justice and righteousness from now and forever..." (Isa 9:2, 6-7 HCSB)

Judgement: the paradox

"Jesus said,

'I came into this world for judgement, in order that those who do not see will see and those who do see will become blind.'" (Jn 9:39 HCSB)

Jesus: The Word incarnate

In days to come,

The mountain of the Lord's house shall be established as the highest mountain and raised above the hills.

All nations shall stream toward it...

For from Zion shall go forth instruction, and the word of the Lord from Jerusalem. (Isa 2:2-3 NABRE)

Jacob and Israel—

"I have swept away your transgressions like a cloud and your sins like a mist.

Return to Me.

For I have redeemed you." (Isa 44:22)

ADDITIONAL RESOURCES

The Patriarchs and the beginning of faith

- Abraham tested (Gen 22: 1-19)

"After these things God tested Abraham…

'Take your son', He said, 'your only son Isaac, whom you love, go to the land of Moriah, and offer him there as a burnt offering on one of the mountains I will tell you about!'

So, Abraham got up early in the morning, saddled his donkey, and took with him… his son Isaac… On the third day Abraham looked up and saw the place in the distance."

"When they arrived at the place… Abraham built the altar there and arrange the wood.

Then Abraham reached out and took the knife to slaughter his son.

But the angel of the Lord called to him from heaven and said, 'Abraham, Abraham…'

'Do not lay a hand on the boy or do anything to him. For now I know that you fear God,…'"

"Abraham looked up and saw a ram… so Abraham … offered it as a burnt offering in place of his son." (Gen 22: 1, 2-3, 4, 9-11, 12, 13 HCSB)

Jacob Becomes Israel

- "God said to Jacob, 'Get up! Go to Bethel and settle there. Build an altar there to the God who appeared to you when you fled from your brother Esau.'

So, Jacob… came to Luz (that is, Bethel) in the land of Canaan… Jacob built an altar there… because it was there that God had revealed Himself to him when he was fleeing from his brother.

God appeared to Jacob again… and He blessed him:

'Your name is Jacob;

You will no longer be named Jacob,

but your name will be Israel.'"

(Gen 35: 1, 6, 9 HCSB)

"There is no magic curse against Jacob and no divination against Israel."

"How beautiful are your tents, Jacob your dwellings, Israel.

Those who bless you will be blessed, and those who curse you will be cursed." (Num 23: 23; 24: 3, 9 HCSB)

"Israel, you are like a young wife deserted by her husband and deeply distressed.

But the Lord calls you back to Him and said,

'… with deep love I will take you back.

… I will show you My love for ever.'"

(Isa 54: 6, 7, 8 GNBDK)

Moses and Israel's emancipation

Moses led Israel to liberation – across the Red Sea
(Ex 12: 29-39; 13: 17; 14: 31)

- "What have we done? We have released Israel from serving us."

(Exo 14: 5 HCSB)

"The Egyptians – all Pharaoh's horses, and chariots, his horsemen and his army – chased after them and caught up with them as they camped by the sea…"

"… Then the Israelites were terrified and cried out to the Lord for help."

"But Moses said to the people, 'Don't be afraid… for the Egyptians you see today, you will never see them again.'

The Lord said to Moses,… 'lift up your staff, stretch out your hand over the sea, and divide it so that the Israelites can go through the sea on dry ground.'"

"The Egyptians set out in pursuit…

… So, Moses stretched out his hand over the sea, and at day break the sea returned to its normal depth. While the Egyptians were trying to escape from it… None of them survived.

That day the Lord saved Israel from the power of the Egyptians…"

Jesus, the Messiah: rejected yet pre-eminent

- It is good that the gospel should first be preached to you (Jews) (Acts 13:46)

"All nations will stream to it,… For instruction will go out of Zion and the word of the Lord from Jerusalem." (Isa 2: 2, 3 HCSB)

"And the good news must first be proclaimed to all nations."

"… Go into all the world and preach the gospel to the whole creation."

(Mk 13: 10; 16: 15 HCSB)

"This good news… will be proclaimed in all the world as a testimony to all nations. And then the end will come." (Matt 24: 14 HCSB)

FOR HIS NAME'S SAKE

"In order that people will praise My name,

I am holding My anger in check;

I am keeping it back and will not destroy you."

"What I do is done for My own sake –

I will not let My name be dishonoured

or let anyone else share the glory

that should be Mine and Mine alone."

(Isa 48: 9, 11 Jews)

"… The Holy God of Israel will save you –

He is the ruler of all the world."

"I turned away angry for only a moment,

but I will show you My love for ever."

"Justice and right will make you strong…"

(Isa 54: 5, 8, 14 GNBDK)

Jerusalem, the peace of justice, the glory of God's worship.

"… wrapped in the mantle of justice

from God; you will be named…
the peace of justice, the glory of God's worship"
"For God is leading Israel in joy…
with the mercy and justice that are His."
(Bar 5: 2, 9 NABRE)

Judaism and Christianity (Mk 2: 18-22 HCSB)
(The issue addressed by Jesus is more than fasting)
Question: "Why do John's disciples and the Pharisees' disciples fast but Your
disciples do not fast?"
Answer:
1. The party is still on: "The wedding guests cannot fast while the groom is with them, can they? But the time will come… and then they will fast."
2. Something new is happening:

"No one sews a patch of unshrunk cloth on an old garment. Otherwise, … a worse tear is made."

"And no one puts new wine into old wineskins. Otherwise, … the wine is lost as well as the skins. But new wine is for fresh wineskins."

What is your case against God?
"My people,
What have I done to you?
Testify against Me!" (Mic 6: 3 HCSB)
"your (Israel's) salvation lay in conversion and tranquillity; your strength in complete trust (of God)…" (Isa 30: 15?)
All are blessed!
"… saying, 'Egypt My people, Assyria My handiwork, Israel My inheritance is blessed.'" (Isa 19: 24 HCSB)
Jews – A beacon for mankind
"By His own choice, He gave us a new birth by the message of truth so that we would be first fruits of His creatures." (Js 1: 18 HCSB)

748

Circumcision:

"We are the circumcision, we who worship through the Spirit of God, … and do not put confidence in flesh." (Phil 3: 3-8)

You Mountains!

"Why gaze with envy, you mountain peaks, at the mountain God desired for His dwelling? The Lord will live there forever!" (Ps 68: 16 HCSB)

Don't discriminate!

Abraham's eldest child, Ishmael, was born to him by a gentile (Egyptian) slave woman.

"Abram was 86 years old when Hagar bore Ishmael to him." Ishmael was circumcised at 13 and lived for 137 years, "Abraham was 100 years old when his son Isaac was born to him." (Gen 16:16; 17:15, 21:5 HCSB)

"I shall count Rahab and Babylon among those who acknowledge Me. The Philistines, Tyrians, Ethiopians – all have their birthplace here. Of Zion it will be said, 'Here is the birthplace of all people: the Most High Himself has set it firm.' The Lord shall write in the book of the nations: 'Here is their birthplace.'"

(Ps 87: 4-6 NABRE)

"Yet my people have exchanged their glory for useless idols" (Jer 2:3, 11 HCSB)

… They have abandoned Me, the fountain of living water, only to dig cisterns for themselves, leaky cisterns that hold no water." (Jer 2: 13)

Meditation and Exhortation

Do You Know Jesus? Do you know God?

"I give praise to you, Father, … for although you have hidden these things from the wise and learned, You have revealed them to the childlike."

No one knows the Son except the Father, and no one knows the Father except the Son and anyone...the Son wishes to reveal Him to" (Matt 11:25, 27)

Answer the call as Jesus beckons –

"Come to Me...take My yoke...and learn from Me..." (Matt 11:28)

The Lord beckons on all to come! The truth assails your assumptions and preconceptions. All mankind suffers from such predilection.

But lo, the Messiah is here!

Look no further, elsewhere!

All prophecies concerning the Messiah have been fulfilled. His throne (in honour of David) lasts forever (Ps 89:4-5, 29-30)

Jerusalem, the high mountain of the Lord is the most coveted hill on earth and everybody goes there in pilgrimage (but not on account of Judaism—but of Christianity and Islam!)

"Why don't you know how to interpret this time?" (LK 12:56 HCSB)

Your hope is your accuser!

Jesus said,

"Do not think that I will accuse you to the father. Your accuser is Moses, on whom you have set your hope. For if you believed Moses, you would believe Me, because he wrote about Me." (Jn 5:45-46)

Misdirected Exuberance or is it Pride?

Why will they not enter—the kingdom of God we are called into, midwifed by Jesus, the son of God? (Mk 10:15 Matt 23:13)

Or is it a matter of:

"A man convinced against his will is of the same opinion still"?

"The scribes and the Pharisees watched Him closely to see if He would cure on the Sabbath, so that they might discover a reason to accuse Him."

Meditation and Exhortation

And after the cure, "…they became enraged and discussed together what they might do to Jesus." (LK 6:7, 11 NABRE)

Improper motive and over confidence make us less docile?

These words seemed to have paraphrased Jesus' teaching on that occasion (LK 6:8-10)

"The time is always right to do good."

The Holy Spirit gives discernment, Jesus' promise of the Holy Spirit has been fulfilled – be one with us; join us and receive the Spirit of discernment.

JEWS AND THE DIVINE COMMANDMENT

"This is My beloved Son

In whom I am well pleased

Listen to Him!" (Matt 17:5)

Those words were pronounced among the Jewish people in the twilight of the down side of Jesus earthly ministry. They are the words from heaven and the speaker was God the Father!

Those words were not promulgated for Jesus; indeed, Jesus ordered the witnesses not to make known the content of the vision until after His resurrection. Because its time was for after the resurrection. Neither was it meant for the three witnesses – Peter, James and John, except to the extent that as chief witnesses for Christ they were to make public the content of the vision, later on. They already believed in Jesus. They had since done that.

To whom then, was the orderintended or given?

To the Jewish Rabbi, of course! The chief priests, the scribes and the pharisees, all who conspired to kill Jesus. Jesus would shortly no longer speak to them in person but His words are in the mouths of His duly commissioned Apostles and disciples.

Empowered in their witnessing by the Holy Spirit these are the ones to remind the leaders of Judaism and the entire people of God what the authentic words of The Redeemer are.

Meditation and Exhortation

As important as this commandment of God is, namely that we all should listen to the Son, the vision itself is no less important.

The interpretation of the vision

Our father Abraham was obliged to offer a sacrifice to God of his son of the covenant, Isaac. Yet, by divine providence a substituted lamb was provided by God Himself and that offering was made without loss to Abraham.

This is a typology of the greatest sacrifice of all time – the lamb of God, Jesus Christ, offered for the forgiveness of sins.

Therefore, in the vision, Moses, the chief steward of God's laws and Elijah, representing all the prophets were in attendance and in accord with Jesus, the Lord of the New Covenant. In that conclave, man, represented by three Jewish persons, Peter, James and John,completed the ensemble.

Moses, Elijah and God are saying loud and clear that Jesus interprets the mind of God – the laws and the prophets with utmost fidelity and to God's approval.

Why then, have the Jews not been listening, orwhat further do they expect God to do to communicate His command to them? When will they now obey God and listen to Jesus?

Of course, there are and always have been exceptions – Jesus believing Jews.

On generalization

Generalization, they say, are odious. Unfortunately, however, it is the easiest and simplest way to identify a group, howbeit not all members behave exactly alike. We dedicate this chapter to Jews, or more accurately to Judaists i.e. Jews who still do not believe in Jesus. But we are not unaware that we have Christians among the Jewish people. In fact, the pristine leaders of the Christian faith were all Jews and Judaists before their conversion. All the prophets and priests of the Old Testament sprung from Abraham, Isaac and Israel.

So, what are we saying? That this chapter is addressed to the section of this people of God who are yet to discern in Jesus, the promised Messiah, i.e, the on-going act of God in the salvation, not only of the Jews, but of all mankind.

Meditation and Exhortation

Jesus decried some behaviour of the Pharisees and scribes – yet some of them believed Him and were His disciples (secretly for their own peace) such were: Nicodemus (Jn 19:39), Joseph of Arimathea (Lk 23:5) and Gamaliel (Acts 5:34).One invited Him to dinner at his house (Lk 11:37) and Jairus besought Him to revive his only daughter (Lk 8:41); a group of them warned Him to flee a place because of Herod's blood thirstiness (Lk 12:31). So, what need we say more? Jerusalem is the birthplace of all nations. (Ps 87:5)

How hardened of heart are the Jews? Repent! Repent!! Repent!!!

Righteousness is traversing the earth without you; you should have been in the forefront. Father Abraham believed and was considered righteous.

Streams of glory flow from Judaism and now rightly belong to Christianity and Islam.

Why, because Judaism refused to be reformed.

The Lord sent to His holy mountain, first, Moses and then Jesus.

The one they ambushed, the other they murdered. Affliction after affliction assailed the people, each followed by a brief respite.

The Lord sent prophet after prophet. Some they killed; few escaped.

But the Lord is faithful, fulfilling His promises to Zion. The promise first made to Abraham and then Jacob. From east and from the west, from north and from the south, the Lord has raised children for Abraham – these are the generation of the righteous (Matt 3:9; LK 3:8)

Zion's gates remain open to pilgrimsseeking the face of the God of Jacob.

It is already happening…

"and many nations will come and say,

'come, let us go up to the mountain of the Lord,

He will teach us about His ways

So, we may walk in His paths.'

For instruction will go out of Zion

And the word of the Lord from Jerusalem." (Mic 4:2)
And again,
"Bethlehem, Ephrathah, …
One will come from you to be ruler
over Israel for Me.
Meditation and Exhortation
His origin is from antiquity, from eternity.
He will stand and shepherd them
In the strength of Yahweh,
In the majestic name of Yahweh His God.
They will live securely, for then His greatness will extend to the
ends of the earth. (Mic 5:2, 4)

From Zion, Light; to Zion, wealth of the nations.

"Arise, shine, for your light has come,
And the glory of the Lord shines over.
Nations will come to your light,
And kings to the brightness of your radiance.
Your gates will always be open;
They will never be shut day or night
So that the wealth of the nations
`May be brought into you,
With their kings being led in procession,
The sons of your oppressors
Will come and bow down to you;
All who reviled you
Will fall facedown at your feet.
They will call you the city of the Lord,
Zion of the Holy One of Israel
…I will appoint peace as your guard
And righteousness as your ruler.
Violence will never again be heard of in your land;
Devastation and destruction

Will be gone from your borders.
But you will name your walls, salvation
And your gates, praise." (Isa 60:1, 3, 11, 14; 17, 18)
Read also Zechariah 9:9-10.
Meditation and Exhortation
It is happening already: The prophecies concerning Jesus have been fulfilled.

Many Jews of his day definitely believed in John the Baptist as a prophet of God. Now, the same angelGabriel, who prophesied the birth of John also prophesied the birth of Jesus. (LK 1:5)

Note that John's father, Zechariah belonged to the hierarchy of the Jewish faith (the priestly division of Abijah) LK 1:5.

Here was what the angel said to Mary of her child yet to be conceived:

"…You will conceive and give birth to a Son, and you will call His name Jesus.

He will be great and will be called the Son of the Most-High,
And the Lord God will give Him
The throne of His father David,
He will reign over the house of Jacob forever,
And His kingdom will have no end." (LK 1:31-33)
Read – 2 Sam 7:12, 13, 16; Dan 7:13-14; 2:44Mic 4:7

Jesus the Nazorean has established a flourishing kingdom of God that has certainly taken over the entire earth. And it looks certain, even to the uninitiated eye, that the kingdom is for eternity.

Foreigners – gentiles – believed in Jesus.

Many foreigners – high and low – contemporaries of Jesus residing among the Jews believed in Jesus and their faith appropriated blessings such as healing and salvation to their entire household.

One of such, a centurion, spoke to the Lord, in these terms:

"Lord, I am not worthy to have you come under my roof. But only say the word, and my servant will be cured…"

To which Jesus responded, "I assure you: I have not found anyone in Israel with so great a faith! Go. As you have believed, let it be done for you." His servant was cured that very moment. (Matt 8:8, 10, 13)

Contrast that with Jairus faith. He was a synagogue official who came to invite Jesus to travel to another community to resuscitate his dead daughter.

Many of the them (Jews) were saying (of Jesus), "He has a demon and He's crazy! Why do you listen to Him?" (Jn 10:20)

Meditation and Exhortation

Gentiles first to pay homage to Christ

"After Jesus was born in Bethlehem… wise men from the east arrived unexpectedly in Jerusalem, saying, 'where is He… born king of the Jews? For we… have come to worship Him. Entering the house, they saw the child with Mary His mother, and … they worshiped Him…and presented Him with gifts.'"

(Matt 2:1-2, 10-11 HCSB)

Is not it time yet for the Israelites to listen to Jesus?

Jews need not allow themselves to be confounded by the gory reality of the cross; Jesus has overcome death – the first fruit of the resurrection. He is now basking in God's unquenchable glory as unveiled in the divine mercy image (Chapter 3). That is the truth.

Heed your prophet's warning:

Samaria: how long will they be incapable of innocence? (Hos 8:5)

Judah: The lies that their ancestors followed have led them astray. Can two walk together, without agreeing to meet?

Israel: return to Yahweh your God, for you have stumbled in your sin (Isa 14:1)

Judaists: Seek Yahweh and live. (Amos 5:6)

John, the Baptist: teaching and testimony

"A brood of vipers! Who warned you to flee from the coming wrath? Therefore, produce fruit consistent with repentance…for I tell you that God is able to raise up children for Abraham from the stones! (LK 3:7-8)

John's witness: I am baptizing you with water for repentance, but the One who is coming after me is mightier than I. I am not worthy to untie His sandals. He will baptize you with the Holy Spirit and fire.

His winnowing fan...will clear His threshing floor and gather His wheat into His barn, but the chaff He will burn with unquenchable fire." (Mt 3:11-12 NABRE)

1. Isaiah prophesized: "When the Lord washes away the filth of...Zion, and purges Jerusalem's blood...with a blast of judgement, a searing blast

(Isa 4:4 NABRE)

So, God's people have to be holy, not by presumption. The people themselves decide: must these cleansings be a recurrent process like a recurring decimal?

Meditation and Exhortation

Need the people of God have multiple religions to approach the same one God? Repent now!

Accept the reforms God sent His Son to accomplish in the faith. God foretold it through His prophets.

Let the survivors, the branch of the Lord embrace Christ from now on and forever, Amen. (Isa 4:2 HCSB)

"Whoever listens to you listens to Me and whoever receives Me, receives the One who sent Me." (LK 10:16 NABRE)

Eternal betrothal

"I will take you to be My wife forever.

I will take you to be My wife in righteousness, justice, love and compassion.

I will take you to be My wife in faithfulness, and you will know Yahweh.

(Hos 2:19-20)

Don't tarry; it is time to seek the Lord. It is time to close the gap between Judaism and Christianity. The prophecy that the knowledge and praise of God would spring from Zion, from Jerusalem has been fulfilled—through Christianity (and Islam)! Enough, of that pride; God loves all His children!

Moses was appointed to bring the people of God out of slavery into the Promised Land.

A journey of forty days became forty years.

Prophets appointed before Christ all pointed the way to righteousness. Through righteousness to God, the Father. How long shall it take for the Jews to respond?

Repent, Chorazin, believe the Lord!

"Woe to you, Chorazin! Woe to you Bethsaida! For if the mighty deeds done in your midst had been done in Tyre and Sidon, they would long ago have repented…it will be more tolerable for Tyre and Sidon on the day of judgement than for you. (Matt 11:21-24 NABRE)

"Whoever will not receive your evangelists or listen to your words…Amen, I say to you, it will be more tolerable for the land, Sodom and Gomorrah on the day of judgment than for that town. (Matt 10:14-15)

Meditation and Exhortation

Stop rebelling

"Listen, heathens, and pay attention, earth,
For the Lord has spoken:
'I have raised children and brought them up,
But they have rebelled against Me.'
The ox knows its owner,
And the donkey its master's feeding trough,
But Israel does not know;
My people do not understand."
"If you are willing and obedient,
You will eat the good things, of the land.
Zion will be redeemed by justice,

Her repentant ones by righteousness.

(Isa 1:2-3, 19 and 17 HCSB)

Is it True?

Is the case still the same today, that the Jews know neither Jesus nor the Father? (Jn 8:19)

Is not it time to change that?

"But since the Pharisees and experts in the law had not been baptized by him (John the Baptist), they rejected the plan of God for themselves." (LK 14:16-24)

Do these events pose a riddle to you?

Clue: Enter like a little child

"'I assure you' Jesus says, 'whoever does not welcome the kingdom of God like a little child will never enter it.'" (Matt 10:15)

Take it that God is appealing to His chosen people that NOW is the time – be reconciled to God (2 Cor 5:20)

Are the leadership of Judaism the tenant farmers in Jesus' parable (MK 12:1-12)

Judaism high priests and others now occupying the chair of Moses must supply an answer to themselves on this question and act prudentially. It is not too late, it is always the right time to do good.

Meditation and Exhortation

Jesus: the wisdom from God

Hear what a former stalwart in Judaism (Rom 9:2-3) and now a father of the Christian confraternity has to say concerning Jesus:

"…Christ Jesus…became for us wisdom from God, as well as righteousness, sanctification and redemption." (1 Cor 1:30)

Isaiah voiced out the Lord's exasperation,

"What more could I have done for My vineyard than I did?"

For the vineyard of the Lord of Hosts is the house of Israel, and the men of Judah (Isa 5:4, 7)

And Jesus clarifies the issue further, in the parable of the Marriage Banquet's invited guests. (Lk 14:15-24)

And then in the parable of the tenant-farmers, MK 12:1-12

The tenant farmers beat one, insulted and beat a second, killed a third and would not spare the son, the heir.

Don't spurn the call!

Take advantage of the patience and mercy of God. The parable of the banquet treated with disdain by the invitees is about your call.(Matt 22:1-14)

Accept it now! It is not too late to do so!

Jesus is the Stone that the builders – the rabbi – had rejected.

Behold, it has become the corner-stone. (MK 12:10)

"See, I am laying a stone in Zion,

Stone that has been tested,

Precious cornerstone as a sure foundation;

Whoever puts faith in it will not waiver." (Isa 28:16 NABRE)

Now Believe and Confess Jesus!

"Even though He had performed so many signs in their presence, they did not believe in Him. Nevertheless, many did believe in Him even among the rulers, but ... they did not confess Him, so they would not be banned from the synagogue." (Jn 12:37, 42 HCSB)

Prophet Jeremiah

"Israel was holy to the Lord, the first fruits of His harvest." (Jer 2:3)

Meditation and Exhortation

"Anyone who has ears should listen!" (Matt 13:9)

"Gross is the heart of this people..." (Matt 12:15 NABRE)

OTHERS

To: God's Own Country, watch out!

A permissive society endangers the souls of future generations by tolerating evil. What legacy would you rather leave behind for your offspring?

Godlessness, intractableness, incorrigibility, or libertarianism, liberalism, or braggadocio?

Aren't you entering a phase in which good and bad have become indistinguishable? Wherein to be good is bad, and to be bad is good? Think about that.

Walking with God.

Foolish people depend so much on the Global Positioning System (GPS) they invented to guide them aright within their very backyard. But care little for guidance through the world they did not create.

Watch out! See the fate of the nations that have forgotten God; the nations that turned away from God. They reaped the fruits of their folly.

Divine law was the bed rock of the nation's laws before they cut their teeth. Then, they sang the anthem, "In God we trust."

"When I am afraid, I will trust in You."

"In God, whose word I praise,
in God I trust; I will not fear.
Meditation and Exhortation
What can man do to Me?"
(Ps 56: 3, 4 HCSB)
God bless America.

To: the rest of the world:

Africa

If you cannot beat them (the pace-setters of the world), join them!

Let God be glorified by your radiance.

Arab-Israeli Imbroglio: remove hate, embrace peace!

Today, as I write this piece (October 2023), marks a month since when Hamas started the latest war with Israel. These destructive forays have become perennial. War beats and calls for ceasefire have become a ding-dong affair; war and peace alternate in the region as a seesaw tragic frolic! Neither side appeared to be war-weary, or to have a vision as to what to do and when, to bring the situation to normalcy.

But God has spoken through His prophets –

"The fruit of righteousness is sown in peace
by those who cultivate peace." (Js 3:18 HCSB)

"Justice and right will make you strong." (Isa 54:14 GNBDK)

Now, both parties claim to be God-fearing. Why then, will they not heed the word of God? He is Father to all!

"Love is the perfect bond of all." (Col 3:14 HCSB)

"Just as you want others to do for you, do the same for them." (Lk 6:31 HCSB)

Whether one-, two- or more states' solution, the earth is only one; and must accommodate all of us.

Meditation and Exhortation

Hatred opens the floodgate to violence to come in; and violence in turn, seduces violent reprisal and hatred!

Let them try something new – embrace righteousness beyond ethnic/state borders.

Once it was written:

"For the vineyard of the Lord of Hosts is the house of Israel,
and the men of Judah, the plant He delighted in.

He looked for justice but saw injustice, for righteousness, but heard cries of wretchedness." (Isa 5:7 HCSB)

Your true flesh and blood – for the one who is righteous – are those who practise righteousness in accordance with the commandment of God, our Creator.

You will secure an enduring peace only when all parties agree to enthrone righteousness and deal with one another with compassion.

"There is life in the path of righteousness, but another path leads to death." (Prov 12:28 HCSB)

My favour (Isa 60:10)

"Then you will see and be radiant, and your heart will tremble and rejoice, because the riches of the sea will become yours and the wealth of the nations will come to you." (Isa 60:5 HCSB)

Wherefore are the anti-Semitism sentiments, the strife and the taboos?

Is it because Jews are special God's people?

Of course, that they are special is obvious, first fruits. That they are God's people is beyond dispute.

Some are last who … and some are first who will be last.

But hear what Jesus told His Jewish audience on the theme, for whom the kingdom is prepared for (LK 13:23):

"Strive to enter through the narrow door, for many…will not be strong enough. After the Master…has arisen and locked the door…He will say to you… 'I do not know where you are from.'

And you will say, 'We ate and drank in Your company and You taught in our streets.'

Meditation and Exhortation

Then He will say to you 'I do not know where you are from. Depart from Me, all you evildoers!' And there will be wailing and grinding of teeth when you see Abraham, Isaac, and Jacob and all the prophets in the kingdom of God and you yourselves cast out. For behold, some are last who will be first, and some are first who will be last." (LK 24-30 NABRE)

Surely, a journey of several miles begins with the first step. Jesus is the ultimate prize promised to Abraham, Isaac, and Israel. His nativity was not in the West or East or North or South, but in Israel! His origin is from antiquity.

That makes the Jewish people very special.

It is sufficient for a pilgrim to be admitted into the kingdom, but note that "some are last who will be first; and some are first who will be last." All righteous are one – the true people of God!

Jews and Gentiles are co-heirs

"… Understand my insight about the mystery of the Messiah. This was not made known to people in other generations as it is now revealed to His holy apostles and prophets by the Spirit: The Gentiles are co-heirs, members of the same body, and partners of the promise in Christ Jesus through the gospel.

(Eph 3:4, 5-6 HCSB)

Come join us, let's do it together!

Jesus says, "every scribe who has been trained for the kingdom of heaven is like the master of a household who brings out of his treasure what is new and what is old." (Matt 13:52 NRSVCE)

Prayer for the Jewish People

LORD, thaw their hearts and open their eyes. Grant repentance to them. Let them come to embrace the light of life and retrieve their heritage—Your covenant with Abraham, Isaac, and Israel. You have exalted Mount Zion, your holy mountain; make Your people forever exultant also.

Have compassion, on Your people, Lord. Let the sons of Abraham know peace—the descendants of Ishmael and Isaac. For they are all Yours! For Your name's sake, oh Lord, remember. Your mercy and Your faithfulness. In Jesus' name we pray, Amen.

God, Our Righteousness(Jer 33:15 NKJV)

CHAPTER 21

Glossary

Bible References - Abbreviations Used

Old Testament		Old Testament	
Gen	Genesis	Nah	Nahum
Ex	Exodus	Hab	Habakkuk
Lev	Leviticus	Zep	Zephaniah
Num	Numbers	Hag	Haggai
Dt	Deuteronomy	Mal	Malachi
Jos	Joshua		
Jdg	Judges		
Rut	Ruth	**New Testament**	
1 Sam`	1 Samuel	Matt or Mt	Matthew
2 Sam	2 Samuel	Mk	Mark
I Kgs	1 Kings	Lk	Luke
2 Kgs	2 Kings	Jn	John
1 Chr	1 Chronicles	Acts	Acts of the Apostles
2 Chr	2 Chronicles	Rom	Romans
Ezr	Ezra	1 Cor	1 Corinthians
Neh	Nehemiah	2 Cor	2 Corinthians
Tob	Tobit	Gal	Galatians
Jdt	Judita	Eph	Ephesians
Est	Esther	Phil	Philippians
1 Mac	1 Maccabees	Col	Colossians
2 Mac	2 Maccabees	1 Thes	1 Thessalonians
Jb	Job	2 Thes	2 Thessalonians
Ps	Psalms	1 Tim	1 Timothy

Prov	Proverbs	2 Tim	2 Timothy
Eccl	Ecclesiastes	Tit	Titus
Song	Songs of Solomon	Phle	Philemon
Wis	Wisdom	Heb	Hebrews
Sir	Sirach (Ben),orEcclesiasticus	Js	James
Isa	Isaiah	1 Pt	1 Peter
Jer	Jeremiah	2 Pt	2 Peter
Lam	Lamentations	1 Jn	1 John
Bar	Baruch	2 Jn	2 John
Ezk	Ezekiel	3 Jn	3 John
Dan	Daniel	Jud	Jude
Hos	Hosea	Rev	Revelation
Jl	Joel		
Am	Amos		
Ob	Obadiah		
Jon	Jonah		
Mic	Micah		

Versions frequently used.

Unless otherwise indicated, the Bible passages quoted in this book are from the Holman Christian Standard Bible (HCSB), Holman Bible Publishers, Nashville, Tennessee © 2009.Other versions frequently cited are:

Good News Bible (Catholic Edition) in Septuagint order (GNBDK);New American Bible Revised Edition (NABRE);Lectionary for Mass in the USA (at other times for mass in UK); New King James Version (NKJV), New Revised Standard Version, Catholic Interconfessional(NRSV-CI) © 1989 (National Council of Churches of Christ in the USA).

Excerpts are also quoted from other versions not mentioned above, but occurless frequently, e.g. from the Liturgy of Hours (L of H), etc.

Made in United States
Troutdale, OR
11/14/2024